תלמוד בבלי

מהדורת נאה

זבחים חלק א

Steinsaltz Center

ירושלים

KOREN

ease note that the number ranges that appear at the bottom of each daf of the Vilna pages
dicate the corresponding pages of the Koren Talmud Bavli translation and commentary.

תלמוד בבלי

KOREN TALMUD BAVLI

THE NOÉ EDITION

זבחים

ZEVAḤIM

Daf 2a through Daf 15b

COMMENTARY BY
Rabbi Adin Even-Israel
Steinsaltz

EDITOR-IN-CHIEF
Rabbi Dr Tzvi Hersh Weinreb

SENIOR CONTENT EDITOR
Rabbi Dr Shalom Z Berger

EXECUTIVE EDITOR
Rabbi Joshua Schreier

STEINSALTZ CENTER
KOREN PUBLISHERS JERUSALEM

Supported by the Matanel Foundation

Koren Talmud Bavli, The Noe Edition
Vol. 29a: Tractate Zevaḥim, Daf 2a through Daf 15b
Paperback, ISBN, 978-965-7767-17-7

First Hebrew/English paperback edition, 2021

Koren Publishers Jerusalem Ltd.
PO Box 4044, Jerusalem 91040, ISRAEL
PO Box 8531, New Milford, CT 06776, USA
www.korenpub.com

Steinsaltz Center

Steinsaltz Center is the parent organization of institutions established by Rabbi Adin Even-Israel Steinsaltz

PO Box 45187, Jerusalem 91450 ISRAEL
Telephone: +972 2 646 0900, Fax +972 2 624 9454
www.steinsaltz-center.org

הִנֵּה יָמִים בָּאִים, נְאֻם אֲדֹנָי יֱהֹוִה, וְהִשְׁלַחְתִּי רָעָב בָּאָרֶץ,
לֹא־רָעָב לַלֶּחֶם וְלֹא־צָמָא לַמַּיִם, כִּי אִם־לִשְׁמֹעַ אֵת דִּבְרֵי יהוה.

Behold, days are coming – says the Lord God – I will send a hunger to the land, not a hunger for bread nor a thirst for water, but to hear the words of the Lord. (AMOS 8:11)

The Noé edition of the Koren Talmud Bavli
with the commentary of Rabbi Adin Even-Israel Steinsaltz
is dedicated to all those who open its covers
to quench their thirst for Jewish Knowledge,
in our generation of Torah renaissance.

This beautiful edition is for the young, the aged,
the novice and the savant alike,
as it unites the depth of Torah knowledge
with the best of academic scholarship.

Within its exquisite and vibrant pages,
words become worlds.

It will claim its place in the library of classics,
in the bookcases of the Beit Midrash,
the classrooms of our schools,
and in the offices of professionals and business people
who carve out precious time to grapple with its timeless wisdom.

For the Student and the Scholar

DEDICATED BY LEO AND SUE NOÉ

Steinsaltz Center

Executive Director, Steinsaltz Center

Rabbi Meni Even-Israel

Managing Editor

Rabbi Jason Rappoport

Senior Content Editor

Rabbi Dr. Shalom Z. Berger

Editors

Rabbi Dr. Joshua Amaru, *Coordinating Editor*
Rabbi Yehoshua Duker, *Senior Editor*
Rabbi Yedidya Naveh, *Content Curator*
Rabbi Avishai Magence, *Content Curator*
Rabbi Yehonatan Eliav, *Hebrew Edition*
Rabbi Gershon Kitsis, *Hebrew Edition*
Menucha Chwat
Rabbi Yonatan Shai Freedman
Rabbi Ayal Geffon
Rabbi Uri Goldstein
Noam Harris
Yisrael Kalker
Rabbi Tzvi Chaim Kaye
Rabbi Yonatan Kohn
Sholom Licht
Catriel Lev
Elisha Loewenstern
Rafi Miller
Rabbi Jonathan Mishkin
Rabbi Eli Ozarowski
Rabbi David Sedley
Rabbi Jonathan Shulman
Rabbi Michael Siev
Avi Steinhart
Rabbi David Strauss

Copy Editors

Aliza Israel, *Coordinator*
Ita Olesker
Debbie Ismailoff
Shira Finson
Ilana Sobel
Deena Nataf
Eliana Kurlantzick Yorav
Erica Hirsch Edvi
Sara Henna Dahan
Oritt Sinclair

Language Consultants

Dr. Stéphanie E. Binder, *Greek & Latin*
Rabbi Yaakov Hoffman, *Arabic*
Dr. Shai Secunda, *Persian*
Shira Shmidman, *Aramaic*

Technical Staff

Tani Bednarsh
Adena Frazer
Yaakov Shmidman
Shaltiel Shmidman
Nava Wieder

KOREN

Design & Typesetting

Dena Landowne Bailey, *Typesetting*
Tani Bayer, *Jacket Design*
Raphaël Freeman, *Design & Typography*

Images

Eliahu Misgav, *Illustration & Image Acquisition*
Daniel Gdalevich, *Illustration & Image Acquisition*

Introduction by the Publisher

The Talmud has sustained and inspired Jews for thousands of years. Throughout Jewish history, an elite cadre of scholars has absorbed its learning and passed it on to succeeding generations. The Talmud has been the fundamental text of our people.

Beginning in the 1960s, Rabbi Adin Even-Israel Steinsaltz שליט״א created a revolution in the history of Talmud study. His translation of the Talmud, first into modern Hebrew and then into other languages, as well the practical learning aids he added to the text, have enabled millions of people around the world to access and master the complexity and context of the world of Talmud.

It is thus a privilege to present the *Koren Talmud Bavli*, an English translation of the talmudic text with the brilliant elucidation of Rabbi Steinsaltz. The depth and breadth of his knowledge are unique in our time. His rootedness in the tradition and his reach into the world beyond it are inspirational.

Working with Rabbi Steinsaltz on this remarkable project has been not only an honor, but a great pleasure. Never shy to express an opinion, with wisdom and humor, Rabbi Steinsaltz sparkles in conversation, demonstrating his knowledge (both sacred and worldly), sharing his wide-ranging interests, and, above all, radiating his passion. I am grateful for the unique opportunity to work closely with him, and I wish him many more years of writing and teaching.

Our intentions in publishing this new edition of the Talmud are threefold. First, we seek to fully clarify the talmudic page to the reader – textually, intellectually, and graphically. Second, we seek to utilize today's most sophisticated technologies, both in print and electronic formats, to provide the reader with a comprehensive set of study tools. And third, we seek to help readers advance in their process of Talmud study.

To achieve these goals, the *Koren Talmud Bavli* is unique in a number of ways:

- The classic *tzurat hadaf* of Vilna, used by scholars since the 1800s, has been reset for great clarity, and opens from the Hebrew "front" of the book. Full *nikkud* has been added to both the talmudic text and Rashi's commentary, allowing for a more fluent reading with the correct pronunciation; the commentaries of *Tosafot* have been punctuated. Upon the advice of many English-speaking teachers of Talmud, we have separated these core pages from the translation, thereby enabling the advanced student to approach the text without the distraction of the translation. This also reduces the number of volumes in the set. At the bottom of each *daf*, there is a reference to the corresponding English pages. In addition, the Vilna edition was read against other manuscripts and older print editions, so that texts which had been removed by non-Jewish censors have been restored to their rightful place.
- The English translation, which starts on the English "front" of the book, reproduces the *menukad* Talmud text alongside the English translation (in bold) and commentary and explanation (in a lighter font). The Hebrew and Aramaic text is presented in logical paragraphs. This allows for a fluent reading of the text for the non-Hebrew or non-Aramaic reader. It also allows for the Hebrew reader to refer easily to the text alongside. Where the original text features dialogue or poetry, the English text is laid out in a manner appropriate to the genre. Each page refers to the relevant *daf*.

- Critical contextual tools surround the text and translation: personality notes, providing short biographies of the Sages; language notes, explaining foreign terms borrowed from Greek, Latin, Persian, or Arabic; and background notes, giving information essential to the understanding of the text, including history, geography, botany, archaeology, zoology, astronomy, and aspects of daily life in the talmudic era.
- Halakhic summaries provide references to the authoritative legal decisions made over the centuries by the rabbis. They explain the reasons behind each halakhic decision as well as the ruling's close connection to the Talmud and its various interpreters.
- Photographs, drawings, and other illustrations have been added throughout the text – in full color in the Standard and Electronic editions, and in black and white in the Daf Yomi edition – to visually elucidate the text.

This is not an exhaustive list of features of this edition, it merely presents an overview for the English-speaking reader who may not be familiar with the "total approach" to Talmud pioneered by Rabbi Steinsaltz.

Several professionals have helped bring this vast collaborative project to fruition. My many colleagues are noted on the Acknowledgments page, and the leadership of this project has been exceptional.

RABBI MENACHEM EVEN-ISRAEL, DIRECTOR OF THE STEINSALTZ CENTER, was the driving force behind this enterprise. With enthusiasm and energy, he formed the happy alliance with Koren and established close relationships among all involved in the work.

RABBI DR. TZVI HERSH WEINREB שליט״א, EDITOR-IN-CHIEF, brought to this project his profound knowledge of Torah, intellectual literacy of Talmud, and erudition of Western literature. It is to him that the text owes its very high standard, both in form and content, and the logical manner in which the beauty of the Talmud is presented.

RABBI JOSHUA SCHREIER, EXECUTIVE EDITOR, assembled an outstanding group of scholars, translators, editors, and proofreaders, whose standards and discipline enabled this project to proceed in a timely and highly professional manner.

RABBI MEIR HANEGBI, EDITOR OF THE HEBREW EDITION OF THE STEINSALTZ TALMUD, lent his invaluable assistance throughout the work process, supervising the reproduction of the Vilna pages.

RAPHAËL FREEMAN, EXECUTIVE EDITOR OF KOREN, created this Talmud's unique typographic design which, true to the Koren approach, is both elegant and user friendly.

It has been an enriching experience for all of us at Koren Publishers Jerusalem to work with the Steinsaltz Center to develop and produce the *Koren Talmud Bavli*. We pray that this publication will be a source of great learning and, ultimately, greater *avodat Hashem* for all Jews.

Matthew Miller, Publisher
Koren Publishers Jerusalem
Jerusalem 5772

Contents

For the vocalized Vilna Shas layout, please open as a Hebrew book.

Introduction to **Zevaḥim**

The sacrificial service in the Temple is one of the fundamental topics of the Torah, and Jewish belief is that it is one of the spiritual pillars upon which the world stands.[1] Although the Temple was destroyed, and the *halakhot* of the Temple service have come to be known as: *Halakha* for the messianic period,[2] they have always been studied thoroughly. A complete order of the Talmud, *Kodashim*,[3] was devoted to these topics.

Plan of the Temple

1. Eastern Gate
2. Women's Courtyard
3. Chamber of the Nazirites
4. Chamber of the Oils
5. Chamber of the Lepers
6. Chamber of the Wood
7. Stairs to Israelite Courtyard
8. Gate of Nicanor
9. Chamber of Pineḥas the Dresser
10. Chamber of the Griddle-Cake Offering
11. Israelite Courtyard
12. Platform
13. Priests' Courtyard
14. Chamber of Hewn Stone
15. Chamber of Parhedrin
16. Chamber of the Exile
17. Chamber of the Salt
18. Chamber of the Parva
19. Chamber of the Rinsers
20. Chamber of the Hearth
21. Gate of Water
22. Chamber of the House of Avtinas
23. Pillars
24. Tables
25. Rings
26. Altar
27. Ramp
28. Basin
29. Between the Entrance Hall and the Altar
30. Stairs between the Entrance Hall and the Altar
31. Opening of the Entrance Hall
32. Entrance Hall
33. Chamber of the Knives
34. Gate of the Sanctuary
35. Sanctuary
36. Golden Altar
37. Table of the Shewbread
38. Candelabrum
39. Curtain
40. Holy of Holies
41. Ark of the Covenant
42. Gate of the Firstborn
43. Gate of Kindling
44. Gate of the Spark
45. Gate of the Offering
46. Gate of the Chamber of the Hearth

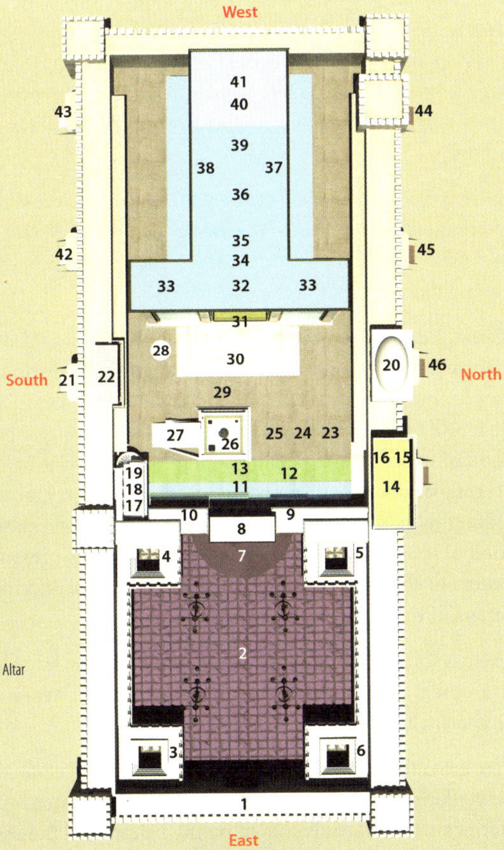

Tractate *Zevaḥim*, referred to in the Talmud as: Slaughter of Offerings,[4] delineates the *halakhot* of animal offerings, and in particular, the *halakhot* of sacrificing them, e.g., the location of their sacrifice, the sacrificial process, and the manner in which animal offerings can be disqualified.[5] The *halakhot* of meal offerings are detailed in tractate *Menaḥot*.

Tractate *Zevaḥim* does not discuss topics such as the species from which each type of offering is brought, when it is brought, and for what purpose. These matters are addressed in other tractates, several of which are not in the order of *Kodashim*.[6] The details of the daily Temple service are described in tractate *Tamid*.

Although the *halakhot* of offerings are described in the Torah at length,[7] they are not organized in categories and according to principles, and many practical details are not explicit. Furthermore, the Torah allocates few verses to cases where the sacrificial process was not performed properly. These gaps are filled by the tradition of the Sages, which is recorded in the Mishna and Talmud in tractate *Zevaḥim*. Accordingly, the purpose of the tractate is to define and classify the *halakhot* of the different types of offerings, and to state the *halakha* in cases of deviation from the proper manner of sacrifice, whether unwittingly or intentionally.

Animal offerings can be categorized in several ways. One categorization is into animal offerings and bird offerings, both of which are discussed extensively in this tractate. The types of animal from which offerings may be brought can also be divided by species, age, and sex. While some offerings can be brought from a wide variety of animals, others must be brought from a narrower range in terms of species, age, and sex.

One may also distinguish between offerings of the most sacred order and offerings of lesser sanctity. Even within the former category, offerings whose blood is presented inside the Sanctuary are considered more sacred than offerings whose blood is presented on the altar in the courtyard.

Offerings differ from each other also with regard to the location in which they are sacrificed. Certain offerings may be slaughtered only in the northern portion of the Temple courtyard, whereas others may be slaughtered anywhere in the courtyard. The blood of some offerings is presented on the upper half of the external altar, the blood of other offerings is presented on the lower half, and the blood of a third category of offerings is presented in the Sanctuary, or even in the Holy of Holies. Within the category of offerings whose blood is presented on the external altar, the blood of some is presented once, that of others is presented twice on two opposite corners of the altar, and the blood of still other offerings is presented on all four corners of the altar.

Whereas some offerings, e.g., communal offerings, must be sacrificed at a designated time, others are brought for atonement whenever necessary, and others are brought voluntarily, as gifts to God.

There are offerings whose meat may not be eaten at all, e.g., inner sin offerings and burnt offerings; there are offerings whose meat is eaten by priests; and there are some offerings whose meat is shared by the priests and the owner of the offering. Some may be eaten only on the day they are sacrificed and on the following night; others may be eaten on the following day as well.

Four sacrificial rites are required for all animal offerings: Slaughtering the animal, collecting its blood in a service vessel, conveying its blood to the altar, and presenting the blood on the altar. Bird offerings require two sacrificial rites: Killing the bird by pinching the nape of its neck, and presenting its blood on the altar. Once these rites have been performed properly, the offering is accepted. Still, the priests are afterward obligated, in the case of burnt offerings, to burn the offering on the altar, or in the case of other animal offerings, to burn specific portions on the altar. Only birds sacrificed as sin offerings do not have any portions that are burned on the altar.

Whether or not lack of precision in the sacrificial process disqualifies an offering depends on the type of offering. Some are disqualified by any deviation from their defined location, time, and sacrificial process, while others are not disqualified so easily.

Offerings can be disqualified not only if the one sacrificing the offering deviates from the correct sacrificial process, but also if he lacks proper intent. There are several levels of improper intent: If one performs one of the main sacrificial rites of an offering with intent that it be burned on the altar or eaten after its designated time, the offering is rendered *piggul*. Not only is *piggul* disqualified as an offering, but one who partakes of its meat is liable to receive the punishment of excision from the World-to-Come [*karet*]. If the intent of the one performing the rite is to burn the offering on the altar or to eat its meat outside the designated area, the offering is disqualified but it is not rendered *piggul*, and one who eats its meat is not liable to receive *karet*. Other intentions, namely, sacrificing an offering of a certain type for the sake of an offering of a different type or for the sake of the wrong person, do not disqualify most offerings, but they do prevent them from satisfying the owner's obligation. In the case of a sin offering or a Paschal offering, such intent disqualifies the offering as well.

The prohibition by Torah law against sacrificing an offering outside the Temple is also addressed in this tractate, as its *halakhot* are parallel to those of sacrifice inside the Temple. The general halakhic topic of mixtures of permitted and forbidden foods is discussed tangentially.

The tractate also cites certain differences between the *halakhot* of offerings and other areas of *halakha* with regard to biblical exegesis. In addition, the halakhic discussions in the tractate are illuminated by several passages of *aggada*.

Tractate *Zevaḥim* consists of fourteen chapters, the first six of which are included in the present volume:

Chapter One focuses on offerings sacrificed with improper intent, either for the wrong person or for the sake of a different offering.

Chapter Two discusses offerings disqualified by improper sacrifice or sacrifice by an unfit individual. It also commences discussion of offerings sacrificed with intent to consume them beyond their designated time or area.

Chapter Three completes the examination of intent to consume an offering beyond its designated time or area, and also mentions inappropriate intentions that do not disqualify an offering.

Chapter Four addresses cases where *piggul* or other disqualifying circumstances are irrelevant.

Chapter Five contains a general description of the different types of animal offerings, their areas of sacrifice and consumption, and the designated times they may be eaten.

Chapter Six mainly deals with the location and manner in which bird offerings are sacrificed.

NOTES

1 *Avot* 1:2.

2 *Zevaḥim* 45a.

3 The order of *Kodashim* exists only in the Babylonian Talmud and not in the Jerusalem Talmud. Some early authorities assert that there was an order of *Kodashim* in the Jerusalem Talmud and it was lost.

4 *Sanhedrin* 51b.

5 With regard to specific types of offerings, other tractates discuss their sacrificial process in greater detail. For example, the sacrificial process of the Paschal offering is delineated in tractate *Pesaḥim*, and the Yom Kippur service is discussed in tractate *Yoma*.

6 For example, the *halakhot* of the Festival peace offering and the burnt offering of appearance in the Temple, brought on the pilgrimage Festivals, appear in tractate *Ḥagiga* in the order of *Moed*; the nazirite's offerings are delineated in tractate *Nazir* in the order of *Nashim*; the offering brought for taking a false oath is discussed in tractate *Shevuot* in the order of *Nezikin*; the offering for an unwitting communal sin is discussed in tractate *Horayot*, also in the order of *Nezikin*; and the *halakhot* of a leper's offering are detailed in tractate *Nega'im* in the order of *Teharot*. Conversely, tractate *Ḥullin*, which discusses the slaughter of non-sacred animals, appears in the order of *Kodashim*.

7 Most of the *halakhot* of offerings are described in Leviticus. The others are stated in Exodus, Numbers, and Deuteronomy.

Introduction to **Perek I**

That which has gone out of your lips you shall observe and do, according to what you have vowed freely to the Lord your God.

(Deuteronomy 23:24)

This is the law of the burnt offering, of the meal offering, and of the sin offering, and of the guilt offering, and of the consecration offering, and of the sacrifice of peace offerings.

(Leviticus 7:37)

And you shall sacrifice the Paschal offering unto the Lord, your God.

(Deuteronomy 16:2)

And you shall say: It is the sacrifice of the Lord's Passover.

(Exodus 12:27)

And the priest shall make atonement for him concerning his sin, and he shall be forgiven.

(Leviticus 4:26)

This chapter discusses the status of offerings that have been sacrificed with improper intent. Two improper intentions are discussed: Intent to sacrifice the offering for the sake of a different type of offering for which it was not consecrated, and intent to sacrifice it for a person other than the one bringing it.

Sacrificing an offering with improper intent is always prohibited, but only in some cases does it disqualify the offering, thereby discontinuing its sacrificial process and rendering its meat prohibited for consumption. The chapter addresses which types of offerings are disqualified due to improper intent, and in cases where the improper intent does not disqualify the offering, whether the sacrifice of the offering satisfies its owner's obligation despite the prohibited intent.

Also examined are the sacrificial rites during which prohibited intent can disqualify an offering or prevent the fulfillment of its owner's obligation. This *halakha* applies to the four rites involving the blood of the offering: Slaughtering the animal, collecting its blood in a service vessel, conveying the blood to the altar, and, lastly, presenting the blood on the altar, which is the final step in propitiating God and effecting atonement for the offering's owner. Although these rites are performed for all animal offerings, there are differences between them: Only slaughter may be performed by a non-priest, and conveying the blood to the altar is sometimes unnecessary, e.g., in a case where the offering is slaughtered next to the altar.

The chapter also addresses the status of the offering in cases where the one sacrificing it had improper intent only during one of the four sacrificial rites, or where he had both the proper and improper intent in succession while performing the same rite.

מתני׳ כָּל הַזְּבָחִים שֶׁנִּזְבְּחוּ שֶׁלֹּא לִשְׁמָן – כְּשֵׁרִים, אֶלָּא שֶׁלֹּא עָלוּ לַבְּעָלִים לְשֵׁם חוֹבָה, חוּץ מִן הַפֶּסַח וְהַחַטָּאת, הַפֶּסַח בִּזְמַנּוֹ, וְהַחַטָּאת בְּכׇל זְמַן;

MISHNA **All slaughtered offerings that were slaughtered not for their own sake,**[H] i.e., during the slaughtering the slaughterer's intent was to sacrifice a different offering, **are fit,**[N] and one may continue their sacrificial rites and partake of their meat where that applies. **But** these offerings **did not satisfy the obligation of the owner,**[N] who is therefore required to bring another offering. This is the *halakha* with regard to all offerings **except for the Paschal offering**[B] **and the sin offering.**[B] In those cases, if the owner sacrificed them not for their own sake, they are unfit. But there is a difference between the two exceptions. **The Paschal offering** is unfit only when sacrificed not for its sake **at its** appointed **time,** on the fourteenth day of Nisan after noon, while **the sin offering** is unfit **any time** that it is sacrificed not for its sake.

רַבִּי אֱלִיעֶזֶר אוֹמֵר: אַף הָאָשָׁם, הַפֶּסַח בִּזְמַנּוֹ, וְהַחַטָּאת וְהָאָשָׁם בְּכׇל זְמַן. אָמַר רַבִּי אֱלִיעֶזֶר: הַחַטָּאת בָּאָה עַל חֵטְא וְהָאָשָׁם בָּא עַל חֵטְא, מָה חַטָּאת פְּסוּלָה שֶׁלֹּא לִשְׁמָהּ, אַף הָאָשָׁם פָּסוּל שֶׁלֹּא לִשְׁמוֹ.

Rabbi Eliezer says: The guilt offering[B] **too** is unfit when sacrificed not for its sake. According to his opinion, the correct reading of the mishna is: **The Paschal offering** is unfit only **at its** appointed **time,** while **the sin offering and the guilt offering** are unfit **at all times. Rabbi Eliezer said** in explanation: **The sin offering is brought for** performance of **a transgression and the guilt offering is brought for** performance of a **transgression. Just as a sin offering is unfit** when sacrificed **not for its sake, so too, the guilt offering is unfit** when sacrificed **not for its sake.**

יוֹסֵי בֶּן חוֹנִי אוֹמֵר: הַנִּשְׁחָטִין לְשֵׁם פֶּסַח וּלְשֵׁם חַטָּאת – פְּסוּלִין;

Yosei ben Ḥoni says: Not only are the Paschal offering and the sin offering unfit when slaughtered not for their sake, but also other offerings **that are slaughtered for the sake of a Paschal offering**[N] **and for the sake of a sin offering are unfit.**

שִׁמְעוֹן אֲחִי עֲזַרְיָה אוֹמֵר: שְׁחָטָן לְשֵׁם גָּבוֹהַּ מֵהֶן – כְּשֵׁרִין, לְשֵׁם נָמוּךְ מֵהֶן – פְּסוּלִין.

Shimon, brother of Azarya,[P] **says** that this is the distinction: With regard to all offerings, if **one slaughtered them for the sake of** an offering whose level of sanctity is **greater than theirs, they are fit;** if one slaughtered them **for the sake of** an offering whose level of sanctity is **less than theirs, they are unfit.**

HALAKHA

That were slaughtered not for their own sake – שֶׁנִּזְבְּחוּ שֶׁלֹּא לִשְׁמָן: All slaughtered offerings, whether individual or communal, that were slaughtered not for their sake are fit, but they do not satisfy the obligation of the owner. The exceptions to the rule are the sin offering and the Paschal offering, which are unfit if they were slaughtered not for their sake (Rambam *Sefer Avoda, Hilkhot Pesulei HaMukdashin* 15:1).

NOTES

All slaughtered offerings that were slaughtered not for their own sake are fit – כָּל הַזְּבָחִים שֶׁנִּזְבְּחוּ שֶׁלֹּא לִשְׁמָן כְּשֵׁרִים: They are fit after the fact; the sacrificial rites must be performed with the proper intent *ab initio*, as the Gemara derives from verses (see 4a). Furthermore, it is derived that any inappropriate intent during the performance of one of the sacrificial rites is prohibited (see 29b).

But did not satisfy the obligation of the owner – אֶלָּא שֶׁלֹּא עָלוּ לַבְּעָלִים לְשֵׁם חוֹבָה: Examples of obligatory offerings include sin offerings, burnt offerings brought on the pilgrimage Festivals, and offerings brought to fulfill an owner's vow (see Rashi).

Rabbeinu Peretz writes that if it is a gift offering of a specific animal, whose owner is not obligated to bring another offering in its place if it is lost, the owner is not obligated to bring another offering when it is slaughtered not for its own sake.

That are slaughtered for the sake of a Paschal offering – הַנִּשְׁחָטִין לְשֵׁם פֶּסַח: Rashi explains that they are unfit only if they are slaughtered at the appointed time for sacrificing the Paschal offering. At any other time, just as a Paschal offering that is sacrificed for the sake of other offerings is still fit, so too, other sacrifices that are slaughtered for the sake of a Paschal offering are still fit (see 11a).

PERSONALITIES

Shimon brother of Azarya – שִׁמְעוֹן אֲחִי עֲזַרְיָה: Shimon, brother of Azarya, was a *tanna* who lived during the destruction of the Temple in the same generation as Rabbi Eliezer and Rabbi Yehoshua, who were disciples of Rabban Yoḥanan ben Zakkai. He is mentioned several times in the Mishna. According to the Rambam, the Azarya mentioned here refers to the father of Rabbi Eliezer ben Azarya. Accordingly, Shimon and Azarya were priests, and descendants of Ezra (see *Berakhot* 27a).

Although Shimon was a greater scholar than his brother Azarya, Shimon is known as the brother of Azarya, since the wealthy Azarya supported him (see *Vayikra Rabba* 25:2).

BACKGROUND

Paschal offering – פֶּסַח: The Torah commands that all adult Jews bring an offering to the Temple on the afternoon of the fourteenth of Nisan to be eaten that evening after nightfall. The offering may be a male lamb or goat in its first year (see Exodus, chapter 12 and Deuteronomy 16:2). The Paschal offering is considered an offering of lesser sanctity. It may be slaughtered anywhere within the Temple courtyard. Its blood is poured above the base of the altar. It can be brought by groups of individuals acting in partnership, and some of its *halakhot* resemble those of communal offerings. For example, it can be sacrificed on Shabbat, or in a state of ritual impurity when the majority of the public has that status.

Sin offering – חַטָּאת: If a Jew unwittingly commits a transgression that is punishable by *karet* if he had performed it intentionally, he is obligated to bring a sin offering. A sin offering brought by an individual is either a female lamb or a female goat in its first year. It must be slaughtered in the northern section of the Temple courtyard. The blood is placed on each of the four corners of the altar. The fats of the sin offering are burned on the altar, and its meat is eaten by the priests. Other sin offerings are brought in certain cases as part of the purification rites at the conclusion of a period of ritual impurity, e.g., that of a woman who has given birth. There are other sin offerings that serve to atone for the public, as well as special sin offerings brought by the leaders of the people to atone for transgression.

Guilt offering – אָשָׁם: A guilt offering is one of the offerings of the most sacred order and may be eaten only by priests on the day it is sacrificed and on the following night. The *halakhot* of its slaughter, the sprinkling of its blood on the altar, and the burning of its fats are like those governing the peace offering. A ram is the only animal used for a guilt offering. The types of guilt offerings described in the Torah (see Leviticus 5:15–26) can be divided into three categories: The guilt offerings of a nazirite and a leper; the provisional guilt offering, brought when there is uncertainty whether or not a transgression warranting a sin offering was performed; and a definite guilt offering, which is the standard guilt offering, so called to underscore the difference between it and the provisional guilt offering. The definite guilt offering is brought, for example, for misuse of sacred property.

כֵּיצַד? קׇדְשֵׁי קֳדָשִׁים שֶׁשְּׁחָטָן לְשֵׁם קׇדָשִׁים קַלִּים – פְּסוּלִין, קׇדָשִׁים קַלִּים שֶׁשְּׁחָטָן לְשֵׁם קׇדְשֵׁי קֳדָשִׁים – כְּשֵׁרִין; הַבְּכוֹר וְהַמַּעֲשֵׂר שֶׁשְּׁחָטָן לְשֵׁם שְׁלָמִים – כְּשֵׁרִין, שְׁלָמִים שֶׁשְּׁחָטָן לְשֵׁם בְּכוֹר וּלְשֵׁם מַעֲשֵׂר – פְּסוּלִין.

How so? Offerings of the most sacred order,[B] e.g., sin offerings and burnt offerings, **that one slaughtered for the sake of offerings of lesser sanctity,**[B] e.g., peace offerings, **are unfit. Offerings of lesser sanctity that one slaughtered for the sake of offerings of the most sacred order are fit.** Likewise, there is a distinction between different offerings of lesser sanctity. **The firstborn** animal **and the** animal **tithe**[N] **that one slaughtered for the sake of a peace offering are fit,** as the sanctity of peace offerings is greater. **Peace offerings that one slaughtered for the sake of a firstborn** animal **or for the sake of** an animal **tithe are unfit.**

גמ׳ לָמָּה לִי לְמִיתְנָא: ״אֶלָּא שֶׁלֹּא עָלוּ״? לִיתְנֵי: ״וְלֹא עָלוּ לַבְּעָלִים לְשֵׁם חוֹבָה״!

GEMARA The mishna teaches: All slaughtered offerings that were slaughtered not for their sake are fit, but they did not satisfy the obligation of the owner. The Gemara asks: **Why do I** need the mishna **to teach** this *halakha* using the language: **But**[N] **they did not** [*ella shelo*] **satisfy** the obligation of the owner? **Let it teach** simply: **And they did not** [*velo*] **satisfy the obligation of the owner.** What does the word: But [*ella*], add?

הָא קָא מַשְׁמַע לָן: לַבְּעָלִים הוּא דְּלֹא עָלוּ לְשֵׁם חוֹבָה, אֲבָל בִּקְדוּשָּׁתַיְיהוּ קַיְימִי וְאָסוּר לְשַׁנּוּיֵי בְּהוּ,

The Gemara responds: By adding **this** word, the mishna **teaches us** that the only deficiency with regard to these offerings **is that they did not satisfy the obligation of the owner, but they retain their sanctity,**[N] **and it is** still **prohibited to deviate** from the protocol **of their** sacrificial process, i.e., the remaining rites must be performed with proper intent.

וְכִדְרָבָא, דְּאָמַר רָבָא: עוֹלָה שֶׁשְּׁחָטָהּ שֶׁלֹּא לִשְׁמָהּ – אָסוּר לִזְרוֹק דָּמָהּ שֶׁלֹּא לִשְׁמָהּ.

And this *halakha* is **in accordance with** the statement **of Rava, as Rava says:** With regard to **a burnt offering that one slaughtered not for its sake,**[H] it is still **prohibited to sprinkle its blood** on the altar **not for its sake.**

אִיבָּעֵית אֵימָא סְבָרָא, אִיבָּעֵית אֵימָא קְרָא. אִיבָּעֵית אֵימָא סְבָרָא: מִשּׁוּם דְּשַׁנֵּי בָּהּ, כֹּל הָנֵי לִישַׁנֵּי בָּהּ וְלֵיזִיל?

The Gemara adds: **If you wish, propose a logical argument** to support this statement, and **if you wish, cite a verse**[N] as proof. The Gemara elaborates: **If you wish, propose a logical argument:** Just **because** one **deviated** from protocol **in its** sacrifice once, i.e., in its slaughter, could it be that **he should continue to deviate** from protocol **in all** the rest of the sacrificial rites? One deviation does not justify additional deviations.

אִיבָּעֵית אֵימָא קְרָא: ״מוֹצָא שְׂפָתֶיךָ תִּשְׁמֹר וְעָשִׂיתָ כַּאֲשֶׁר נָדַרְתָּ לַה׳ אֱלֹהֶיךָ נְדָבָה״ וגו׳, הַאי ״נְדָבָה״?

And **if you wish, cite a verse: "That which has gone out of your lips you shall observe and do; according to what you have vowed** [*nadarta*] **freely** [*nedava*] **to the Lord your God,** even that which you have promised with your mouth" (Deuteronomy 23:24). The Gemara interprets the words *nadarta* and *nedava* exegetically: Can **this** verse be referring to **a gift** offering [*nedava*]?

BACKGROUND

Offerings of the most sacred order – קׇדְשֵׁי קֳדָשִׁים: Burnt offerings, sin offerings, guilt offerings, and communal peace offerings are included in this category. The following regulations apply specifically to these offerings: They are slaughtered only in the northern section of the Temple courtyard. Those offerings that are eaten may be eaten only on the day the animal is sacrificed and on the night following that day. They may be eaten only by male priests and only within the Temple courtyard. The prohibition against misappropriating Temple property, i.e., unlawful use of consecrated property, applies to these offerings as soon as they are consecrated. Once their blood is sprinkled on the altar, the prohibition against misappropriation continues to apply to the portions of the offering consumed on the altar but not to the portions of the offering that are to be eaten.

Offerings of lesser sanctity – קׇדָשִׁים קַלִּים: Included in this category are the various types of individual peace offerings, the thanks offering, the nazirite's ram, the male firstborn of a kosher animal, the animal tithes, and the Paschal offering. These offerings may be slaughtered anywhere in the Temple courtyard. With the exception of the thanks offering, the nazirite's ram, and the Paschal offering, they may be eaten during a period of two days and the intervening night from the time they were sacrificed. They may be eaten by the priests; by the priests' wives, children, and slaves; and, with the exception of the firstborn, by the people bringing the sacrifices and any ritually pure individual that they invite, other than an uncircumcised male. There is no requirement to eat them within the Temple premises, but they must be eaten within the walls of Jerusalem. The prohibition against misuse of consecrated property applies only to those portions of offerings consumed on the altar and only after the blood has been sprinkled on the altar.

HALAKHA

A burnt offering that one slaughtered not for its sake, etc. – עוֹלָה שֶׁשְּׁחָטָהּ שֶׁלֹּא לִשְׁמָהּ וכו׳: It is prohibited to perform any of the sacrificial rites with the wrong intent. Therefore, even if an animal offering was already slaughtered not for its sake, or a handful of a meal offering was removed not for its sake, whether intentionally or unwittingly, the other sacrificial rites must still be performed for the sake of the offering being sacrificed, in accordance with Rava's statement (Rambam *Sefer Avoda*, *Hilkhot Pesulei HaMukdashin* 15:3, and see 18:1).

NOTES

The firstborn animal and the animal tithe – הַבְּכוֹר וְהַמַּעֲשֵׂר: These are considered offerings of lesser sanctity, just like the peace offering. In fact, their sanctity is even less than that of the peace offering, due to several practical distinctions: Their owners are not required to place their hands on the head of the offering, they do not require libations, and their blood is sprinkled only once above the base of the altar, not on each corner. Furthermore, there is no portion of these offerings that is given to the priests. Although the firstborn animal is eaten by priests, that is because they are considered the owners of this offering.

But [*ella*] – אֶלָּא: Rashi explains that the word *ella* is superfluous, since the mishna presumably uses the most concise wording possible. *Tosefot Tukh* explains that the word *ella* indicates that the only deficiency in these offerings is that they do not satisfy the obligation of the owner. Accordingly, it is assumed that the mishna uses this word to suggest an additional element of fitness beyond that which is understood from the phrase: All slaughtered offerings that were slaughtered not for their own sake are fit. Therefore, the Gemara asks what this additional element is.

They retain their sanctity, etc. – בִּקְדוּשָּׁתַיְיהוּ קַיְימִי וכו׳: *Tosefot Tukh* explains that these offerings retain their original designation. For example, a burnt offering that was slaughtered for the sake of sacrificing a peace offering is still a burnt offering. Therefore, it is still prohibited to perform any of its other sacrificial rites not for the sake of a burnt offering (see *Rosh HaMizbe'aḥ*).

If you wish propose a logical argument, if you wish cite a verse – אִיבָּעֵית אֵימָא סְבָרָא אִיבָּעֵית אֵימָא קְרָא: This sentence is used frequently in the Talmud to introduce a suggestion of two proofs for the matter under discussion, one logical and the other from a verse. After this introductory statement, the Gemara repeats this expression and elaborates. Sometimes the logical argument is mentioned first, and sometimes the verse is mentioned first.

Several commentaries ask why it is necessary to bring proof from a verse where there is logical proof, as a logical reason for a *halakha* is considered superior to a derivation from a verse (see *Bava Kamma* 46b). Some answer that both proofs are cited in cases where the logical proof is not irrefutable, meaning that even if the logical proof is refuted, there is also proof from a verse. Others add that in these cases, the logical proof is effective only for the matter to be considered rabbinic law, whereas proof from a verse renders it Torah law.

נֶדֶר הוּא! אֶלָּא, אִם כְּמָה שֶׁנָּדַרְתָּ עָשִׂיתָ – יְהֵא נֶדֶר, וְאִם לָאו – נְדָבָה יְהֵא.

It is already referred to as **a vow** offering [*neder*]. **Rather,** the verse indicates that **if you did what you vowed** to do, i.e., you sacrificed your vow offering properly, **it shall be** a satisfactory **vow** offering; **and if** you did **not** sacrifice it properly, **it shall be** rendered a voluntary **gift** offering[N] unrelated to the vow, and shall not satisfy the obligation of your vow.

וּנְדָבָה מִי שָׁרֵי לְשַׁנּוּיֵי בָּהּ?

The Gemara concludes: **And is it permitted to deviate** from protocol **in** the sacrifice of **a gift** offering *ab initio*? Clearly it is not. Evidently, even if one of the sacrificial rites was performed for the sake of sacrificing a different offering, it is still prohibited to perform any of the other sacrificial rites in the incorrect manner.

אֲמַר לֵיהּ רָבִינָא לְרַב פָּפָּא: לָא הֲוֵית גַּבַּן בְּאוּרְתָּא בִּתְחוּמָא בֵּי חַרְמָךְ, דְּרָמֵי רָבָא מִילֵּי מְעַלְּיָיתָא אַהֲדָדֵי וְשַׁנֵּי לְהוּ.

§ **Ravina said to Rav Pappa:** Since **you were not with us last night within the** Shabbat **limit**[B] **of Bei Ḥarmakh,**[NB] you did not hear **that Rava raises a contradiction between** two **superior** mishnaic **statements**[N] **and teaches their** resolution.

מַאי מִילֵּי מְעַלְּיָיתָא? תְּנַן: כָּל הַזְּבָחִים שֶׁנִּזְבְּחוּ שֶׁלֹּא לִשְׁמָן כּוּ׳; טַעְמָא דְּשֶׁלֹּא לִשְׁמָן, הָא סְתָמָא – עָלוּ נָמֵי לַבְּעָלִים לְשֵׁם חוֹבָה, אַלְמָא סְתָמָא נָמֵי כְּלִשְׁמָן דָּמֵי;

What are these **superior statements? We learned** in the mishna: **All slaughtered offerings that were slaughtered not for their sake** are fit, but they did not satisfy the obligation of the owner. Rava infers: **The reason** they do not satisfy the obligation of the owner is specifically **that** they were slaughtered **not for their sake. But** if offerings were slaughtered **without specification** of intent, **they, as well, satisfied the obligation of the owner.**[H] **Apparently,** if one performs any action **without specification** of intent, it is **also considered as** if he performed it expressly **for its sake.**

וּרְמִינְהִי: כָּל הַגֵּט שֶׁנִּכְתַּב שֶׁלֹּא לְשֵׁם אִשָּׁה – פָּסוּל, וּסְתָמָא נָמֵי פָּסוּל!

And Rava **raises a contradiction** from another mishna (*Gittin* 24a): **Any bill of divorce**[B] **that was written not for the sake of** the **woman**[H] in question is **not valid. And** it is derived from the continuation of that mishna that if a bill of divorce was written **without specification** as to which woman it is referring, it is **also not valid.**

NOTES

A vow offering and a gift offering – נֶדֶר וּנְדָבָה: The difference between a vow offering and a gift offering is that in the case of a vow offering, one accepts upon himself, in general terms, the obligation to bring an offering, whereas in the case of a gift offering, one consecrates a specific animal as an offering. One of the practical ramifications of this difference is that if the animal consecrated as a gift offering is lost or disqualified, the individual is no longer responsible for it. By contrast, in the case of a vow offering, the individual remains responsible to replace the animal if it is lost or disqualified.

Within the Shabbat limit of Bei Ḥarmakh – בִּתְחוּמָא בֵּי חַרְמָךְ: Rava's discourse was on Shabbat night, and Rav Pappa was not able to attend because he was outside the Shabbat limit (Rashi).

Superior statements – מִילֵּי מְעַלְּיָיתָא: This Aramaic expression generally refers to the statements of the Sages that were cited in the study hall. In several places in the Talmud, a Sage is cited as having requested that another Sage tell him the superior statements of a certain Sage, e.g., Rav, Rav Ḥisda, or Rav Yosef, that were mentioned in the study hall. In other places it is stated that a certain Sage requested of his colleagues that certain superior statements be attributed to him. A Sage who was absent from the study hall was liable to miss superior statements that were conveyed at the time.

HALAKHA

Without specification they as well satisfied the obligation of the owner – סְתָמָא עָלוּ נָמֵי לַבְּעָלִים לְשֵׁם חוֹבָה: One who sacrifices an offering must do so for the sake of the offering being sacrificed and for the sake of its owner. One must have this intent while slaughtering the animal, collecting the blood, conveying the blood, and sprinkling the blood on the altar. Nevertheless, even if one performs any of these sacrificial rites without specific intent, the offering is fit, and it satisfies the obligation of its owner; in accordance with the opinion of Rava (Rambam *Sefer Avoda, Hilkhot Ma'aseh HaKorbanot* 4:10).

Any bill of divorce that was written not for the sake of the woman – כָּל הַגֵּט שֶׁנִּכְתַּב שֶׁלֹּא לְשֵׁם אִשָּׁה: Any bill of divorce that was not written for the sake of the man and woman getting divorced is not valid (Rambam *Sefer Nashim, Hilkhot Geirushin* 3:1; *Shulḥan Arukh, Even HaEzer* 131:1).

BACKGROUND

Shabbat limit – תְּחוּמָא: A Shabbat limit is the border of a Jewish settlement or of the temporary residence of one or more Jews, determined at the onset of Shabbat. It is defined as two thousand cubits outside the residence. By rabbinic decree it is not permitted for a person to travel on Shabbat beyond this limit. On Shabbat Sages would leave their cities to deliver lectures and sermons in nearby villages. One's ability to learn Torah on Shabbat was often dependent on his ability to travel to the locale to which the Sage would come without going beyond the Shabbat limit.

Bei Ḥarmakh – בֵּי חַרְמָךְ: This city, also called Ḥarmakh, or according to other readings, Harman or Bei Harman, was located on the Shanvata River. Some propose that the source of the name is the Persian word harman, meaning granary.

Location of Bei Ḥarmakh

Bill of divorce – גֵּט: The basic text of a bill of divorce includes the declaration of the husband that he divorces his wife and that it is permitted for her to marry any other man. The husband is identified by his name and the name of his father, and the wife by her name and the name of her father. The document must contain the date on which it was written and the signatures of two witnesses. In talmudic times a bill of divorce could be written privately by a scribe at the request of the husband. In later generations it became customary for a bill of divorce to be written in a rabbinical court that had expertise in this field, so that no halakhic difficulties would arise that might lead to the invalidation of the document.

NOTES

Ordinary slaughtered offerings stand designated for their own sake, etc. – זְבָחִים בִּסְתָם לִשְׁמָן עוֹמְדִין וכו׳: Both the sacrifice of an offering and the writing of a bill of divorce are valid only if performed with the proper intent. The difference between them is that since an offering is designated for its purpose by its owner from the time of its consecration, its slaughter is automatically for its own sake, without specification by the one who slaughters it. Only if he slaughters it for the sake of sacrificing with the intent to sacrifice a different offering is it disqualified with regard to the obligation of the owner. By contrast, a wife is not designated for divorce unless her husband instructed that a bill of divorce be written for her. Therefore, if a bill of divorce was not written specifically for her, it cannot be used to divorce her.

Since the *tanna* taught, etc. – אַיְּידֵי דִּתְנָא וכו׳: This expression is employed frequently in the Talmud and is used to explain unnecessary or ostensibly inaccurate statements made by the *tanna'im* for the purpose of maintaining uniformity. At times, such an expression is used in one statement so that it conforms to the style of an adjacent statement. This can occur either in the former or the latter of the two statements, including even cases where the two statements were stated by different *tanna'im*.

This method can be employed twice with regard to the same tannaitic source, i.e., once a certain expression is employed due to the style of another expression, a third expression can be used due to that expression. There is one instance where this method is employed three times with regard to the same mishna (see *Yevamot* 3a).

Although this method is used mostly to explain *mishnayot*, it is sometimes used with regard to *baraitot*; see, e.g., *Bava Kamma* 109a. In fact, a *baraita* that explains a mishna can be understood as employing inaccurate wording to conform to the style of that mishna.

וְשַׁנֵּי: זְבָחִים בִּסְתָם לִשְׁמָן עוֹמְדִין, אִשָּׁה בִּסְתָמָא לָאו לְגֵירוּשִׁין עוֹמֶדֶת.

And Rava **resolves** the contradiction: **Ordinary slaughtered offerings stand** designated **for their own sake.**[N] From the time that the offering is consecrated, its presumed end is that it will be slaughtered for the type of offering for which is was consecrated. Therefore, even if the one slaughtering it has no particular intention, it is in effect considered slaughtered for its own sake. By contrast, **an ordinary wife does not stand** designated **for divorce.** Therefore, a bill of divorce is never presumed to be referring to a given woman unless it is specified explicitly.

וּזְבָחִים בִּסְתָמָא כְּשֵׁירִין, מְנָלַן? אִילֵּימָא מֵהָא דִּתְנַן: כָּל הַזְּבָחִים שֶׁנִּזְבְּחוּ שֶׁלֹּא לִשְׁמָן כו׳, וְלָא קָתָנֵי ״שֶׁלֹּא נִזְבְּחוּ לִשְׁמָן״; גַּבֵּי גֵּט נַמִי הָקָתָנֵי: כָּל הַגֵּט שֶׁנִּכְתַּב שֶׁלֹּא לְשֵׁם אִשָּׁה – פָּסוּל, וְלָא קָתָנֵי ״שֶׁלֹּא נִכְתַּב לְשֵׁם אִשָּׁה – פָּסוּל״!

§ The Gemara asks: **And from where do we** derive that **slaughtered offerings are fit** and even satisfy the obligation of the owner if slaughtered **without specification? If we say** it is **from that which we learned** in the mishna: **All slaughtered offerings that were slaughtered not for their sake** are fit, but these offerings did not satisfy the obligation of the owner, **and** it **does not teach** this using the language: All slaughtered offerings **that were not slaughtered for their sake** are fit, but these offerings did not satisfy the obligation of the owner, this cannot be. One cannot infer from this language that slaughter without specification is valid, since the Mishna **also teaches with regard to a bill of divorce: Any bill of divorce that was written not for the sake of the woman is not valid, and it does not teach: That was not written for the sake of the woman is not valid,** and it is a given that a bill of divorce written without specification is not valid.

אֶלָּא מֵהָא, דִּתְנַן: כֵּיצַד לִשְׁמָן וְשֶׁלֹּא לִשְׁמָן – לְשֵׁם פֶּסַח וּלְשֵׁם שְׁלָמִים; טַעְמָא דְּאָמַר לְשֵׁם פֶּסַח וּלְשֵׁם שְׁלָמִים, הָא לְשֵׁם פֶּסַח וּסְתָמָא – כָּשֵׁר, אַלְמָא סְתָמָן כְּלִשְׁמָן דָּמֵי;

Rather, perhaps it is derived **from that which we learned** in a mishna (13a): **How are** offerings slaughtered **for their sake and** then **not for their sake?** For example, one might slaughter the Paschal offering **for the sake of a Paschal offering and** then **for the sake of a peace offering.** The Gemara infers: **The reason** such an offering is unfit is **that he says** that he is slaughtering it **for the sake of a Paschal offering and** then he says that he is slaughtering it **for the sake of a peace offering. But** if he says that he is slaughtering it **for the sake of a Paschal offering, and** then slaughters it **without specification,** it is **fit. Apparently,** slaughtering an offering **without specification is considered as** if one slaughtered it **for its sake.**

דִּילְמָא שָׁאנֵי הָתָם, דְּאָמַר: כָּל הָעוֹשֶׂה – עַל דַּעַת רִאשׁוֹנָה הוּא עוֹשֶׂה!

The Gemara responds: **Perhaps there it is different, as** the mishna **is saying** that **anyone who performs** an action **performs** it **with** his **original intent** in mind. Therefore, since he specified initially that he was slaughtering the offering for the sake of a Paschal offering, there are no grounds to assume that he then changed his mind. Here, by contrast, he pronounced no initial statement of proper intent.

אֶלָּא מִסֵּיפָא: שֶׁלֹּא לִשְׁמָן וְלִשְׁמָן – לְשֵׁם שְׁלָמִים וּלְשֵׁם פֶּסַח; טַעְמָא דְּאָמַר לְשֵׁם שְׁלָמִים וּלְשֵׁם פֶּסַח, הָא סְתָמָא וּלְשֵׁם פֶּסַח – כָּשֵׁר;

Rather, perhaps this *halakha* is derived **from the latter clause** of that mishna: How are offerings slaughtered **not for their sake and** then **for their sake?** For example, one might slaughter the Paschal offering **for the sake of a peace offering and** then **for the sake of a Paschal offering.** The Gemara infers: **The reason** it is unfit **is that he says** he is slaughtering it **for the sake of a peace offering and** then he says he is slaughtering it **for the sake of a Paschal offering. But** if he started slaughtering it **without specification and** then slaughtered it **for the sake of a Paschal offering,** it is **fit.** Apparently, if one slaughters an offering without specification it still satisfies the obligation of the owner.

דִּילְמָא שָׁאנֵי הָתָם, דְּאָמַר: יוֹכִיחַ סוֹפוֹ עַל תְּחִילָּתוֹ!

The Gemara responds: **Perhaps there it is different, as** the mishna **is saying** that **his ultimate** intent **proves** the nature **of his original** intent. Since his ultimate intent was to sacrifice a Paschal offering, that was presumably his original intent as well. Here, by contrast, there is no ultimate expression of proper intent.

אִי נַמִי, אַיְּידֵי דִּתְנָא ״לִשְׁמָן וְשֶׁלֹּא לִשְׁמָן״, תְּנָא נַמִי: ״שֶׁלֹּא לִשְׁמָן וְלִשְׁמָן״!

Alternatively, it can be explained that even if one's ultimate intent is not considered proof of his original intent, the mishna still uses the same term in both clauses to preserve symmetry. **Since** in the former clause the *tanna* **taught**[N] using the language: **For their sake and** then **not for their sake,** teaching that original intent is considered proof of ultimate intent, the *tanna* **also taught** the second clause using the language: **Not for their sake and** then **for their sake.** In any event, there is no proof from that mishna that an offering slaughtered without specification satisfies its owner's obligation.

אֶלָּא מֵהָא, לְשֵׁם שִׁשָּׁה דְּבָרִים הַזֶּבַח נִזְבָּח: לְשֵׁם זֶבַח, לְשֵׁם זוֹבֵחַ, לְשֵׁם שֵׁם, לְשֵׁם אִשִּׁים, לְשֵׁם רֵיחַ, לְשֵׁם נִיחוֹחַ, וְהַחַטָּאת וְאָשָׁם לְשֵׁם חֵטְא.

Rather, perhaps this *halakha* is derived **from that** mishna (46b), which states: **The offering is slaughtered for the sake of six matters:**[H] **For the sake of** the particular **offering; for the sake of the one sacrificing** the offering, i.e., the owner; **for the sake of God; for the sake of** consumption by the **fires**[N] of the altar; **for the sake of** sacrificing it in a manner that gives **an aroma;**[N] and **for the sake of pleasing** God. **And the sin offering and a guilt offering** are slaughtered **for the sake of** atonement for the **sin.**

אָמַר רַבִּי יוֹסֵי: אַף מִי שֶׁלֹּא הָיָה בְּלִבּוֹ לְשֵׁם אַחַת מִכׇּל אֵלּוּ – כָּשֵׁר, שֶׁתְּנַאי בֵּית דִּין הוּא; אַתְנוּ בֵּית דִּין דְּלָא לֵימָא לִשְׁמוֹ, דִּילְמָא אָתֵי לְמֵימַר שֶׁלֹּא לִשְׁמוֹ.

The mishna on 46b continues: **Rabbi Yosei said: Even** in the case **of one who did not have in mind** to slaughter the offering **for the sake of** any **one of these,** the offering **is fit, since** this **is a stipulation of the court.**[B] The Gemara explains Rabbi Yosei's opinion: The **court stipulated that** one **should not say** that he is slaughtering the offering **for its sake, lest he come to say** that he is slaughtering it **not for its sake.** Therefore one should not specify his intent at all.

וְאִי סָלְקָא דַּעְתָּךְ סְתָמָא פָּסוּל, קָיְימִי בֵּית דִּין וּמַתְנוּ מִילְּתָא דְּמִיפְּסִיל בֵּיהּ?

The Gemara infers: **And if it enters your mind** that if one slaughters an offering **without specification** it is **unfit, would the court arise and stipulate a matter that disqualifies** the offering? Clearly, an offering slaughtered without specification is fit and satisfies the obligation of the owner.

וְגַבֵּי גֵט דִּסְתָמָא פָּסוּל מְנָלַן?

§ The Gemara asks: **And with regard to a bill of divorce, from where do we** derive **that** if it is written **without specification** as to which woman it is referring, it is **not valid?**

אִילֵימָא מֵהָא דִּתְנַן: הָיָה עוֹבֵר בַּשּׁוּק וְשָׁמַע סוֹפְרִים מַקְרִין: ״אִישׁ פְּלוֹנִי גֵּירֵשׁ פְּלוֹנִית מִמָּקוֹם פְּלוֹנִי״, וְאָמַר: זֶה שְׁמִי וְזֶה שֵׁם אִשְׁתִּי – פָּסוּל לְגָרֵשׁ בּוֹ;

If we say it is inferred **from that which we learned** in a mishna (*Gittin* 24a): In the case of a man who **was passing through the marketplace, and he heard scribes**[H] who write bills of divorce **dictating** to their students: The **man so-and-so divorces so-and-so from** the **place** of **such and such, and** the man **said: This is my name and that is the name of my wife,** and he desires to use this bill for his divorce, this bill is **unfit to divorce** his wife **with it,** that is not a proof.

דִּילְמָא כִּדְרַב פָּפָּא, דְּאָמַר רַב פָּפָּא: הָכָא בְּסוֹפְרִים הָעֲשׂוּיִין לְהִתְלַמֵּד עָסְקִינַן, וְלָא אִיכְּתוּב לְשׁוּם כְּרִיתוּת כְּלָל!

It can be explained: **Perhaps** the mishna is **in accordance with** the explanation **of Rav Pappa. As Rav Pappa says: Here we are dealing with scribes who are wont to practice**[B] writing bills of divorce; **and** this bill of divorce is a draft and **was not written for the sake of severance,** i.e., divorce, **at all.** But if a bill of divorce is written to be used for divorce, perhaps it is fit even if written without specifying the woman in question.

אֶלָּא מֵהָא:

Rather, derive this *halakha* **from** the subsequent clause in **that** mishna:

NOTES

For the sake of consumption by the fires – לְשֵׁם אִשִּׁים: Rashi explains, based on the Gemara later (46b), that an offering must be slaughtered with the intent that its flesh will be consumed by the fire on the altar, and not merely roasted.

For the sake of an aroma – לְשֵׁם רֵיחַ: Rashi explains, based on the Gemara later (46b), that an offering should be slaughtered with the intent that it will be burned raw on the altar, so that its burning will emit an aroma, and not that it will be roasted first and then burned on the altar. The Rambam explains that it should be slaughtered with the intention of burning it on the altar only for the sake of its aroma.

HALAKHA

For the sake of six matters, etc. – לְשֵׁם שִׁשָּׁה דְּבָרִים וכו׳: One who slaughters a burnt offering must have six intentions in mind: That he is slaughtering it for the sake of the particular offering, that he is slaughtering it for the sake of the owner, that the sacrifice is for the sake of God, that it will be burned and consumed by the fires, that it will be burned only for the sake of its aroma, and that the scent will be pleasing to God. Nevertheless, even if he slaughters it without these intentions, it is valid. One who slaughters a sin offering or a burnt offering must have in mind the specific sin for which it was brought (Rambam *Sefer Avoda, Hilkhot Ma'aseh HaKorbanot* 4:11).

And heard scribes, etc. – וְשָׁמַע סוֹפְרִים וכו׳: If a scribe wrote a bill of divorce for the purpose of practicing his craft, and a man then saw it and discovered that the names written in it were those of him and his wife and his city of residence, and he subsequently used it to divorce his wife, the divorce is not valid. Even a bill of divorce that was written to be used for divorce but not for a specific married couple is not valid (Rambam *Sefer Nashim, Hilkhot Geirushin* 3:1; *Shulḥan Arukh, Even HaEzer* 131:1).

BACKGROUND

Stipulation of the court – תְּנַאי בֵּית דִּין: This refers to a halakhic assumption applicable in many areas, with regard to legal acts, agreements, dedications to the Temple, and the like. The *halakha* assumes that these legal acts have been performed in accordance with a condition stipulated by the court. Even if those who wrote a document or performed the act did not state the condition explicitly, they are regarded as if they had done so, because the court has authorized it. In some cases, these stipulations cannot be waived even by explicit stipulation. Stipulations of the court were instituted either to promote the general welfare of society or to solve specific social problems. Such stipulations are found in almost every area of *halakha*.

Scribes who are wont to practice – סוֹפְרִים הָעֲשׂוּיִין לְהִתְלַמֵּד: Novice scribes would study from the experts the craft of writing documents and the formulations of the different types of documents. Their studies would include practicing writing documents, including bills of divorce. It was possible for a bill of divorce that was written only for practice to incidentally contain the names of a husband and wife who were planning to get divorced, along with the name of their locale and the date upon which they were planning to get divorced.

יָתֵר עַל כֵּן, כָּתַב לְגָרֵשׁ אֶת אִשְׁתּוֹ וְנִמְלַךְ, מְצָאוֹ בֶּן עִירוֹ וְאָמַר לוֹ: "שְׁמִי כִּשְׁמֶךָ וְשֵׁם אִשְׁתִּי כְּשֵׁם אִשְׁתְּךָ" – פָּסוּל לְגָרֵשׁ בּוֹ;

Moreover, if a husband **wrote** a bill of divorce with which **to divorce his wife but** later **reconsidered,**[H] **and a resident of his town found him and said to him: My name is** the same **as your name, and my wife's name is** the same **as your wife's name,** and we reside in the same town; give me the bill of divorce and I will use it, the bill of divorce is **unfit** for the second man **to divorce** his wife **with it.** Evidently, even if the bill of divorce was written to be used for divorce, if it was not written specifically for the given woman it is not valid.

דִּילְמָא שָׁאנֵי הָתָם, דְּאִינְתִּיק לֵיהּ לְשֵׁם גֵּירוּשִׁין דְּהַהוּא!

The Gemara responds: **Perhaps there it is different, as** the bill of divorce **was** specifically **designated** For **the sake of that** man's **divorce,** and therefore it is not valid for the second man's divorce. But a bill of divorce that was written without specification might be valid if written for the sake of divorce.

אֶלָּא מֵהָא: יָתֵר עַל כֵּן, יֵשׁ לוֹ שְׁתֵּי נָשִׁים שֶׁשְּׁמוֹתֵיהֶן שָׁווֹת, כָּתַב לְגָרֵשׁ אֶת הַגְּדוֹלָה – לֹא יְגָרֵשׁ בּוֹ אֶת הַקְּטַנָּה;

Rather, derive it **from** the subsequent clause in **that** mishna: **Moreover, if he has two wives whose names are identical,**[H] and he **wrote** a bill of divorce **to divorce the older** one, and then reconsidered, **he may not divorce the younger** one **with it.** Evidently, a bill of divorce must be written specifically to divorce a specific wife.

דִּילְמָא שָׁאנֵי הָתָם, דְּאִינְתִּיק לֵיהּ לְשֵׁם גֵּירוּשִׁין דְּהַהִיא!

The Gemara responds: **Perhaps there it is different, as** the bill of divorce **was** specifically **designated for the sake of the divorce of that** other wife.

אֶלָּא מֵהָא: יָתֵר עַל כֵּן, אָמַר לַלַּבְלָר: "כְּתוֹב, וּלְאֵיזוֹ שֶׁאֶרְצֶה אֲגָרֵשׁ" – פָּסוּל לְגָרֵשׁ בּוֹ;

Rather, derive it **from** the subsequent clause in **that** mishna: **Moreover, if he said to the scribe** [*lalavlar*]:[L] **Write** a bill of divorce for one of my two wives who have identical names, **and I will** use it to **divorce whichever** one of them **that I want,**[H] this bill of divorce is **unfit to divorce** either wife **with it.** Evidently, it must be written for the divorce of a specific woman.

דִּילְמָא שָׁאנֵי הָתָם, דְּאֵין בְּרֵירָה!

The Gemara responds: **Perhaps there it is different, as there is no** retroactive **designation.**[B] The designation of the bill of divorce cannot be determined retroactively. It cannot be used for either wife because it was possibly written for the sake of the other wife. But a bill of divorce written without specification may be valid.

אֶלָּא מֵהָא: הַכּוֹתֵב טוֹפְסֵי גִיטִּין – צָרִיךְ שֶׁיַּנִּיחַ מְקוֹם הָאִישׁ וּמְקוֹם הָאִשָּׁה וּמְקוֹם הָעֵדִים וּמְקוֹם הַזְּמַן; וְאָמַר רַב יְהוּדָה אָמַר שְׁמוּאֵל: אַף צָרִיךְ שֶׁיַּנִּיחַ מְקוֹם "הֲרֵי אַתְּ מוּתֶּרֶת לְכׇל אָדָם".

Rather, derive it **from that** mishna (*Gittin* 26a): With regard to a scribe **who writes the standard** part of [*tofesei*][L] **bills of divorce**[H] in advance, so that when one requests a bill of divorce, he will have to add only the details unique to the case, **he must leave** empty **the place** of the name **of the man, and the place** of the name **of the woman, and the place** of the names **of the witnesses, and the place of the date. And** in addition, **Rav Yehuda says** that **Shmuel says:** A scribe **must also leave the place of** the essential phrase: **You are hereby permitted to** marry **any man,** since it must be written for the sake of that specific woman. Evidently, a bill of divorce must be written for a specific husband and wife, and if not it is not valid, even if it was written for the sake of divorce.

HALAKHA

If a husband wrote a bill of divorce to divorce his wife but reconsidered – כָּתַב לְגָרֵשׁ אֶת אִשְׁתּוֹ וְנִמְלַךְ: If a man wrote a bill of divorce for his wife but then reconsidered, and then another man from the same town said to him: My name and my wife's name are the same as your name and your wife's name, and he took the bill of divorce and used it to divorce his wife, it is not a valid bill of divorce, despite the fact that it was written for the sake of divorce, as it was not written for the specific husband and wife who eventually used it (Rambam *Sefer Nashim, Hilkhot Geirushin* 3:2; *Shulḥan Arukh, Even HaEzer* 131:2).

Two wives whose names are identical – שְׁתֵּי נָשִׁים שֶׁשְּׁמוֹתֵיהֶן שָׁווֹת: If a man has two wives whose names are identical, and he wrote a bill of divorce for one of them, and then changed his mind and used it to divorce the other one, the bill of divorce is not valid, as it was not written for the sake of the wife whom he gave it to (Rambam *Sefer Nashim, Hilkhot Geirushin* 3:3; *Shulḥan Arukh, Even HaEzer* 131:3).

I will use it to divorce whichever one that I want – לְאֵיזוֹ שֶׁאֶרְצֶה אֲגָרֵשׁ: If a husband has two wives whose names are identical, and he instructed a scribe: Write a bill of divorce for one of my wives and I will divorce whichever one of them I wish with it, and he divorced one of them with it, it is uncertain whether or not this is a valid divorce. The *Kesef Mishne* explains that it is uncertain whether the principle of retroactive designation is accepted with regard to matters that are Torah law. Therefore, the *halakha* reflects the stringent elements of both possibilities (Rambam *Sefer Nashim, Hilkhot Geirushin* 3:4; *Shulḥan Arukh, Even HaEzer* 131:4).

A scribe who writes the standard part of bills of divorce – הַכּוֹתֵב טוֹפְסֵי גִיטִּין: Due to the ordinance for the benefit of the scribes, the Sages rendered it permitted for one to write the standard part of a bill of divorce in advance. When the scribe writes this standard part, he must leave room for the husband's name, the wife's name, the date, and the statement: You are hereby permitted to marry any man. These essential elements must be written for the sake of the specific man and woman (Rambam *Sefer Nashim, Hilkhot Geirushin* 3:7).

LANGUAGE

Scribe [*lavlar*] – לַבְלָר: From the Latin libellarius, meaning based on contracts, or librarius, meaning a scribe, writer, or professional writer of contracts and other documents.

Standard part [*tofes*] – טוֹפֶס: From the Greek τύπος, *tupos*, meaning an engraving, or that which is formed by a stamp. By extension, it means anything that follows the same standard form in many different places. Sometimes the word *matbe'a* is used in place of this word, with a similar meaning. The standard part of a legal document contains the phraseology common to all documents of that kind.

The essential part [*toref*] of a legal document is the part that changes in each transaction, such as people and place-names, special conditions, amounts of money, and the like.

Since a bill of divorce must be written especially for the sake of the woman who is being divorced, the essential part of it that reads: You are hereby permitted to any man, is also a part of the *toref*.

BACKGROUND

Retroactive designation – בְּרֵירָה: This refers to the question whether an item that was not explicitly designated initially for a specific purpose can retroactively be considered as if it were designated for that purpose from the outset. This could apply, for example, in a case where one declares that the tithe from his granary will consist of the last tenth remaining after the rest of the produce has been consumed. If the principle of retroactive designation is accepted, his separation of the tithe is valid, as, although the tithe he designated did not exist as a distinct and separate entity when he made his statement, the tithe is retroactively that remaining tenth. It is considered as if it were so from the outset. There is a dispute among the Sages whether to accept the principle of retroactive designation or not. In practice, the principle is generally accepted with regard to questions of rabbinic law but not concerning matters of Torah law.

תּוּ רָמֵי מִילְּתָא אַחֲרִיתִי. מִי אָמַר רַב יְהוּדָה אָמַר רַב: חַטָּאת שֶׁשְּׁחָטָהּ לְשֵׁם עוֹלָה – פְּסוּלָה, שְׁחָטָהּ לְשֵׁם חוּלִּין – כְּשֵׁירָה; אַלְמָא דְּמִינָהּ מַחֲרִיב בָּהּ, דְּלָאו מִינָהּ לָא מַחֲרִיב בָּהּ?

§ Ravina continued to inform Rav Pappa of Rava's statements: Rava **further raises another contradiction: Did Rav Yehuda say** that **Rav says** that **a sin offering that one slaughtered for the sake of a burnt offering**[B] **is unfit,** whereas if one **slaughtered** the animal **for the sake of** consumption of **non-sacred** meat,[H] it **is fit?**[N] **Apparently,** only improper intent that is **of its type,** i.e., for the sake of another offering, **ruins** the offering and renders **it** unfit, whereas wrong intent that is **not of its type,** i.e., for the sake of consumption of non-sacred meat, is disregarded and **does not ruin it.**

וּרְמִינְהוּ: כָּל הַגֵּט שֶׁנִּכְתַּב שֶׁלֹּא לְשֵׁם אִשָּׁה – פָּסוּל; וַאֲפִילּוּ לְשֵׁם גּוֹיָה נָמֵי פָּסוּל!

And Rava **raises a contradiction** from the aforementioned mishna (*Gittin* 24a): **Any bill of divorce that was written not for the sake of** the **woman** who is being divorced with it **is not valid;** and by inference, **even** if it was written **for the sake of a gentile woman,** it is **not valid.** With regard to the matter of divorce, a gentile woman is not of the same type as a Jewish woman, as the *halakhot* of bills of divorce are irrelevant to her.

וְשַׁנֵּי: גֵּט, דַּל גּוֹיָה מִינֵּיהּ – הָוֵה לֵיהּ סְתָמָא, וּסְתָמָא פָּסוּל. קָדָשִׁים, דַּל חוּלִּין מִינַּיְיהוּ – הָוֵה לֵיהּ סְתָמָא, וּסְתָמָא כְּשֵׁירִים.

And Rava **resolves** the contradiction: If **a bill of divorce** is written for the sake of a gentile woman it is not valid, because if you **remove** the intent for the sake of **a gentile woman from it, it is** considered to be **without specification** of the woman who is divorced with it, **and** a bill of divorce written **without specification is not valid.** But if **sacrificial** animals are slaughtered for the sake of consumption of non-sacred meat, they remain fit, since if you **remove** the **non-sacred** intent **from them, they are** considered to be **without specification, and** offerings slaughtered **without specification are fit.**

וּרְמָא מִילְּתָא אַחֲרִיתִי. מִי אָמַר רַב יְהוּדָה אָמַר רַב: חַטָּאת שֶׁשְּׁחָטָהּ לְשֵׁם עוֹלָה – פְּסוּלָה, שְׁחָטָהּ לְשֵׁם חוּלִּין – כְּשֵׁירָה; אַלְמָא דְּמִינָהּ מַחֲרִיב בָּהּ, דְּלָא מִינָהּ לָא מַחֲרִיב בָּהּ?

§ **And** Rava **raised another contradiction: Did Rav Yehuda say** that **Rav says** that **a sin offering that one slaughtered for the sake of a burnt offering** is **unfit,** whereas if one **slaughtered it for the sake of** consumption of **non-sacred** meat it is **fit? Apparently,** he holds that only improper intent that is **of its type ruins it,** whereas wrong intent that is **not of its type does not ruin it.**

וְהָתַנְיָא: ״תּוֹכוֹ״ – וְלֹא תּוֹךְ תּוֹכוֹ, וַאֲפִילּוּ כְּלִי שֶׁטֶף מַצִּיל!

But isn't it taught in a *baraita*: The Torah states with regard to ritually impure carcasses of creeping animals: "And every earthen vessel into **whose interior** any of them falls, anything that is in its interior shall be impure" (Leviticus 11:33). From the word "interior" it is derived that only food in its interior is rendered impure, **but not** any food that is in **the interior of its interior,**[H] i.e., in another vessel within the earthenware vessel. **And** this is the *halakha* not only if the inner vessel is an earthenware vessel; **even** if it is a metal or wooden **vessel,** which is purified though **rinsing**[N] in a ritual bath and is therefore susceptible to impurity from its exterior, it nevertheless **protects**[N] food that is inside it from being rendered impure. Evidently, even a vessel that is not of the same type serves to nullify the status of the interior of an earthenware vessel.

BACKGROUND

Burnt offering – **עוֹלָה**: A burnt offering is totally consumed on the altar in the Temple. A burnt offering may be brought from male cattle, sheep, goats, pigeons, or doves. Private individuals generally bring this offering as a gift offering. There are times when it is sacrificed to atone for the willful non-fulfillment of a positive mitzva or for immoral or idolatrous thoughts, and there are certain situations where individuals are required to bring a burnt offering together with other offerings. Many of the communal offerings, e.g., the daily offering and many of the additional offerings brought on Shabbat and Festivals, are burnt offerings.

Burnt offerings are considered sacrifices of the most sacred order. They must be slaughtered in the northern portion of the Temple courtyard and their blood is placed on the two opposite corners of the altar, i.e., the northeastern and southwestern corners, so that it touches all four sides. Afterward, the animal's hide is removed and given to the priests, and its limbs are separated. The remainder of the blood is then poured out at the base of the altar and the limbs are sacrificed on the altar.

NOTES

If one slaughtered it for the sake of non-sacred meat it is fit – **שְׁחָטָהּ לְשֵׁם חוּלִּין כְּשֵׁירָה**: The Rambam rules that although a Paschal offering is similar to a sin offering in that both are disqualified if they are slaughtered for the sake of the wrong offering, a Paschal offering that is slaughtered for the sake of consumption of non-sacred meat is disqualified, whereas a sin offering is not. This ruling is derived in the Jerusalem Talmud from the verse: "It is the offering of the Lord's Passover" (Exodus 12:27). The Rambam also writes that in a case where a sin offering was slaughtered for the sake of consumption of non-sacred meat, although the offering is fit, it does not satisfy the obligation of its owner. The Ramban (*Milḥamot HaShem* on tractate *Rosh HaShana*) maintains that it does satisfy the obligation of the owner (see Rambam's Commentary on the Mishna, and *Sefer Avoda*, *Hilkhot Pesulei HaMukdashin* 15:11).

A vessel purified through rinsing – **כְּלִי שֶׁטֶף**: Wood or metal vessels are purified through rinsing, i.e., immersion in a ritual bath. Earthenware vessels cannot be purified without breaking them. The term rinsing is based on the verse: "And every vessel of wood shall be rinsed in water" (Leviticus 15:12), and on the verse: "And if it be cooked in a copper vessel, it shall be scoured, and rinsed in water" (Leviticus 6:21). While a vessel purified through rinsing becomes impure by means of simple contact with a source of ritual impurity, earthenware vessels contract impurity only on the inside, and then only when the source of ritual impurity enters their inner airspace (see Leviticus 11:33). Vessels of both types impart ritual impurity to food and liquids by those means through which they are susceptible to impurity.

And even if it is a vessel purified through rinsing it protects – **וַאֲפִילּוּ כְּלִי שֶׁטֶף מַצִּיל**: One might have thought that only if the inner vessel is earthenware does it prevent the food inside it from contracting impurity from a source of impurity in the outer vessel, because an earthenware vessel is unique in not being susceptible to impurity from its exterior. Therefore, since the inner vessel cannot be rendered impure by the outer vessel, the food inside it also remains pure. By contrast, since a vessel purified through rinsing is susceptible to impurity from its exterior, one might have thought that it cannot prevent food inside it from contracting impurity (Rashi).

HALAKHA

For the sake of consumption of non-sacred meat – **לְשֵׁם חוּלִּין**: If a sin offering was slaughtered for the sake of another type of offering, e.g., a burnt offering, it is unfit. If it was slaughtered for the consumption of non-sacred meat, it is fit, but it does not satisfy the obligation of its owner (Rambam *Sefer Avoda*, *Hilkhot Pesulei HaMukdashin* 15:4).

But not the interior of its interior – **וְלֹא תּוֹךְ תּוֹכוֹ**: If a vessel has an impure item in it, and the vessel was put inside an earthenware vessel so that its brim projects out of the earthenware vessel, the earthenware vessel is pure, even if the impure item is in its airspace. The source for this is the expression in the verse "into whose interior," which excludes the interior of its interior.

Similarly, if an earthenware vessel is impure, and another vessel containing food is inserted inside so that its brim projects out of the former, the food is not rendered impure, even if it is in the airspace of the earthenware vessel; as the verse states: "Anything that is in its interior shall be impure," excluding the interior of its interior (Rambam *Sefer Tahara*, *Hilkhot Kelim* 4:8–9).

HALAKHA

An oven that one divided with boards – תַּנּוּר שֶׁחֲצָצוֹ בִּנְסָרִים: If there is an impure item on one side of an earthenware vessel, and that vessel was divided with a partition from its base to its brim, the entire vessel is impure, including the section of the vessel on the other side of the partition, as a vessel is not normally divided with a partition. Therefore, if an oven was divided with boards and an impure item was found on one side, the entire oven is impure (Rambam *Sefer Tahara, Hilkhot Kelim* 4:7).

A round barrel that is broken and plugged up with straw – כַּוֶּורֶת שֶׁהִיא פְּחוּתָה וּפְקוּקָה בְּקַשׁ: A broken barrel is not considered a vessel and therefore does not prevent the transmission of impurity between its contents and an earthenware vessel in which it is placed, even if the barrel is plugged up with straw; in accordance with the opinion of the Rabbis, who disagree with Rabbi Eliezer (Rambam *Sefer Tahara, Hilkhot Kelim* 4:11).

וְשַׁנֵּי: עֲשׂוּ חוּלִּין אֵצֶל קָדָשִׁים כִּמְחִיצָה אֵצֶל תַּנּוּר, מָה מְחִיצָה אֵצֶל תַּנּוּר לָא מְהַנְיָא לַהּ כְּלָל, אַף חוּלִּין אֵצֶל קָדָשִׁים לָא מְהַנְיָא לֵיהּ כְּלָל.

And Rava **resolves** the contradiction as follows: A vessel purified through rinsing is actually considered of the same type as an earthenware vessel, since they are both vessels. Concerning the *halakhot* of impurity, the equivalent of intent with regard to the consumption of non-sacred meat is an item that is not a vessel at all; the Sages **rendered non-sacred** meat **with regard to sacrificial** animals **like a partition with regard to** an earthenware **oven: Just as a partition in an oven is not effective at all** in preventing the transmission of impurity from one side to the other since it is not a vessel, **so too,** slaughtering an offering for the consumption of **non-sacred** meat **is not effective at all with regard to** rendering **sacrificial** animals unfit.

דִּתְנַן: תַּנּוּר שֶׁחֲצָצוֹ בִּנְסָרִים אוֹ בִּירִיעוֹת, וְנִמְצָא שֶׁרֶץ בְּמָקוֹם אֶחָד – הַכֹּל טָמֵא.

This is **as we learned** in a mishna (*Kelim* 8:1): In the case of **an oven that** one **divided**[B] **with boards**[H] **or with curtains, and** the carcass of **a creeping animal**[B] **was found in one place, all** of the food in the oven, including that on the other side of the partition, is rendered **impure.**

כַּוֶּורֶת שֶׁהִיא פְּחוּתָה וּפְקוּקָה בְּקַשׁ וּמְשׁוּלְשֶׁלֶת לַאֲוִיר הַתַּנּוּר, שֶׁרֶץ בְּתוֹכָהּ – הַתַּנּוּר טָמֵא, שֶׁרֶץ בַּתַּנּוּר – אוֹכָלִין שֶׁבְּתוֹכָהּ טְמֵאִין, וְרַבִּי אֱלִיעֶזֶר מְטַהֵר.

The mishna continues: In the case of **a round barrel**[B] **that is broken and plugged up with straw**[HB] **and lowered into the airspace of the oven,** if the carcass of **a creeping animal is inside** the barrel, **the oven** is rendered **impure.** And if the carcass of **a creeping animal is in the oven,** the **food that is inside** the barrel is rendered **impure.** The broken barrel is not considered a vessel despite its being plugged up with straw, and therefore it does not prevent the transmission of impurity between the creeping animal and the oven. **And Rabbi Eliezer deems** the food in the barrel **pure.**

BACKGROUND

An oven that one divided – תַּנּוּר שֶׁחֲצָצוֹ: When one needed to bake a small item in a large oven, one would divide the oven by inserting in it a hard partition vertically, so that he would not have to heat the entire oven. Furthermore, a large oven was also a convenient storage place for cooked or baked food, due to its size and the fact that it could be sealed. Therefore, a less substantial partition would be used to separate between different food items, e.g., food that belonged to different people.

Replica of clay oven from late antiquity

Creeping animal – שֶׁרֶץ: There are just eight creeping animals, small mammals, and lizards, whose carcasses impart ritual impurity upon contact, or through the airspace of an earthenware vessel (see Leviticus 11:29–30). There is no clear oral tradition with regard to the identity of the animals listed in the Torah; therefore, determining their identity involves educated conjecture. Among the suggestions offered are that *ḥoled* is a rat, *akhbar* is a mouse, *tzav* is a dab lizard, *anaka* is a gecko, *koaḥ* is a monitor lizard, *leta'a* is the common lizard, *ḥomet* is a skink, and *tinshemet* is a chameleon.

Round barrel [*kavveret*] – כַּוֶּורֶת: Round wicker barrels were often used as beehives in antiquity. In modern Hebrew, the word *kavveret* means beehive.

Plugged up with straw – פְּקוּקָה בְּקַשׁ: Straw, i.e., the dry grain stalks that remain after threshing, had a low monetary value but was very useful. It was used as construction material; as a cover for fruit or utensils, either to protect them or to hide them; as a convenient platform upon which to place things; as wrapping material; for roofs; and for other purposes. Straw was also used as fuel; although it burns quickly, it is also ignited easily. It was used for heating, baking, and cooking. One of the uses of straw was to seal cracks, e.g., cracks in the ground, in walls, or in utensils.

Wicker beehive similar to those used during talmudic times

אָמַר רַבִּי אֱלִיעֶזֶר: קַל וָחוֹמֶר, אִם הִצִּיל בְּמֵת הֶחָמוּר, לֹא תַּצִּיל בִּכְלִי חֶרֶס הַקַּל?

The mishna continues: **Rabbi Eliezer said:** My opinion can be inferred ***a fortiori*****:** **If** a barrel or any other partition between some item and a corpse under the same roof **protects** the item **from** becoming impure, even though impurity imparted by **a corpse**[B] is **severe** in that it lasts seven days, **shouldn't** a partition **protect** food **in** the airspace of **an earthenware vessel** from impurity imparted by the carcass of a creeping animal, **which is mild** by comparison?

אָמְרוּ לוֹ: לֹא,

The mishna continues: The Rabbis **said to him:** Your inference is **not** correct.

BACKGROUND

Ritual impurity imparted by a corpse – טוּמְאַת הַמֵּת: Corpses are the ultimate primary source of ritual impurity [*avi avot hatuma*]. A person or item rendered impure by a corpse becomes impure at the level of a primary source of ritual impurity [*av hatuma*], and imparts that impurity to people and garments for a period of seven days. A corpse transfers impurity by contact and by being carried, and also, uniquely, by what is known as impurity imparted in a tent. The latter form of transference takes place if an individual is under the same roof as a human corpse. Ritual impurity is caused not only by a whole corpse but also by parts of it, although there are many complex details with regard to the parts of a body considered significant enough to impart this form of impurity. Many authorities claim that only Jewish corpses impart this impurity. Another unusual feature of impurity caused by corpses is that a metal utensil or vessel that touches a corpse assumes the status of the corpse itself and causes anyone who touches it or comes under the same roof with it to become impure at the level of a primary source of ritual impurity. The *halakhot* of ritual impurity imparted by a corpse appear primarily in tractate *Oholot*.

Perek **I**
Daf **3** Amud **b**

אִם הִצִּיל בְּמֵת חָמוּר – שֶׁכֵּן חֲלוּקָה בְּאוֹהָלִין, תַּצִּיל בִּכְלִי חֶרֶשׂ הַקַּל – שֶׁאֵין חֲלוּקִין בְּאוֹהָלִין?

If a partition **protects** an item **from** impurity imparted by **a corpse,** which is **severe,** this is only **because** such impurity is unique in that it is imparted to that which is in the same tent, i.e., under the same roof, and **tents are divided**[N] by partitions. If so, **should** a partition **protect** food from impurity imparted **in an earthenware vessel, which,** although **mild, is not divided by** partitions, like **tents** are?

הָתֵינַח לְרַבָּנַן, לְרַבִּי אֱלִיעֶזֶר מַאי אִיכָּא לְמֵימַר?

The Gemara notes: The comparison between non-sacred meat vis-à-vis offerings and a partition in an earthenware vessel **works out well according to** the opinion of **the Rabbis,** who hold that a partition does not prevent transmission of impurity inside an earthenware vessel. But **according to** the opinion of **Rabbi Eliezer,** who maintains that a partition is effective in an earthenware oven, **what can be said?**[N] How is this compatible with the principle that an item is not affected by something not of its type?

רַבִּי אֱלִיעֶזֶר קַל וָחוֹמֶר קָאָמַר.

The Gemara responds: **Rabbi Eliezer** agrees with this principle. Yet he **says** that a partition in an earthenware vessel is effective due to his ***a fortiori*** inference, which overrides the principle that an item is not affected by something not of its type.

אִי הָכִי, הָתָם נַמִּי לֵימָא קַל וָחוֹמֶר: קָדָשִׁים מְחַלְּלִין קָדָשִׁים, חוּלִּין לֹא כׇּל שֶׁכֵּן?

The Gemara challenges: **If that is so,** that an *a fortiori* inference overrides this principle, **let us say an *a fortiori*** inference **there as well,** with regard to a sin offering that was slaughtered for the consumption of non-sacred meat: If slaughtering sacrificial animals for the sake of other **sacrificial** animals **desecrates** those **sacrificial** animals, **all the more so** is it **not** clear that slaughtering them for the consumption of **non-sacred** meat desecrates them?

אֶלָּא, טַעְמָא דְּרַב כְּרַבִּי אֶלְעָזָר, דְּאָמַר רַבִּי אֶלְעָזָר: מַאי טַעְמָא דְּרַב? ״וְלֹא יְחַלְּלוּ אֶת קׇדְשֵׁי בְּנֵי יִשְׂרָאֵל אֵת אֲשֶׁר יָרִימוּ לַה׳״ – קָדָשִׁים מְחַלְּלִין קָדָשִׁים, וְאֵין חוּלִּין מְחַלְּלִין קָדָשִׁים.

The Gemara responds: **Rather, the reasoning** behind the statement **of Rav**[N] that a sin offering slaughtered for the consumption of non-sacred meat is fit is not in accordance with this principle at all, but it is **in accordance** with the opinion of **Rabbi Elazar. As Rabbi Elazar says: What is the reasoning** behind the statement **of Rav?** The verse: **"And they shall not desecrate the sacred items of the children of Israel, which they set apart unto the Lord"** (Leviticus 22:15), teaches that only improper intentions for the sake of **sacred items,** i.e., offerings, **desecrate sacred items, but non-sacred** intent **does not desecrate sacred items.**

אַלְמָא, אָתָא קְרָא אַפְּקֵיהּ מִקַּל וָחוֹמֶר, הָכָא נַמִּי: לֵיתֵי ״תּוֹכוֹ״ לְאַפְּקֵיהּ מִקַּל וָחוֹמֶר!

The Gemara notes: **Apparently,** an inference from **a verse** can **come to rule out** a conflicting ***a fortiori*** inference. If so, **here too,** with regard to a partition in an oven, **let** the verse "and every earthen vessel into **whose interior** any of them falls" **come to rule out** Rabbi Eliezer's ***a fortiori*** **inference**[N] that a partition prevents food in an oven from becoming impure.

NOTES

Because tents are divided – שֶׁכֵּן חֲלוּקָה בְּאוֹהָלִין: In other words, since it is common for a tent to be divided into separate rooms with a partition, a partition is recognized with regard to the *halakhot* of impurity imparted by a corpse, since such impurity is uniquely transmitted in a tent, i.e., to that which is under the same roof.

According to Rabbi Eliezer what can be said – לְרַבִּי אֱלִיעֶזֶר מַאי אִיכָּא לְמֵימַר: In other words, Rav's principle is apparently subject to a dispute between *tanna'im* and is not universally accepted (Rashi).

Rather the reasoning of Rav – אֶלָּא טַעְמָא דְּרַב: *Tosefot Tukh* explains that the word: Rather, demonstrates that the Gemara rejects its initial premise that Rav's statement is based on the principle that an item is not affected by something that is not of its type, and cites a verse as an alternative basis for his statement. This interpretation is slightly difficult, as the Gemara continues to discuss the opinion of Rabbi Eliezer, indicating that this answer pertains specifically to his opinion.

To rule out Rabbi Eliezer's *a fortiori* inference – לְפַקֵּיהּ מִקַּל וָחוֹמֶר: In other words, the need to derive from the term "whose interior" that if a vessel is put in an earthenware vessel it separates between the contents of the two vessels indicates that a partition does not separate between the sides of an earthenware vessel. If a partition had been an effective divider despite the fact that it does not have its own interior, certainly a vessel that has its own interior would be an effective divider in the airspace of an earthenware vessel. It would not have been necessary to derive this *halakha* from the verse (see Rashi).

הַאי "תּוֹכוֹ" מִיבָּעֵי לֵיהּ לְאוֹכָלִין שֶׁגִּיבְּלָן בְּטִיט וְהִכְנִיסָן לַאֲוִיר תַּנּוּר; סָלְקָא דַּעְתָּךְ אָמִינָא: הוֹאִיל וּבִנְגִיעָה לֹא מְטַמֵּא, בַּאֲוִירוֹ נַמִי לֹא מְטַמּוּ, [קָא מַשְׁמַע לָן].

The Gemara responds: **This** expression: **"Whose interior,"** does not indicate that a partition is ineffective, as it **is necessary to** teach another *halakha*, namely, that **food that one kneaded with clay,**[B] covering it from all sides, **and put in the airspace of an oven** that had the carcass of a creeping animal in it is impure. Because it might **enter your mind to say** that **since** the food **cannot become impure by touching** an impure item, as the clay serves as an interposition, **it also cannot become impure** by being put **in the airspace of** an impure oven. The phrase "in whose interior any of them falls" **teaches us** that the food does contract impurity.

וְרַבָּנַן: הָנָךְ לָא צְרִיכִי קְרָא.

The Gemara asks: **And** as for **the Rabbis,** who apparently do interpret the verse as teaching that a partition is ineffective in preventing the contracting of impurity in an earthenware vessel, how do they derive that food covered with clay and placed in an impure oven is impure? The Gemara answers: **These** matters **do not need a verse** to teach them. Such food has the same status as any other food in an impure oven, and the *halakha* therefore is self-evident.

רַב יוֹסֵף בַּר אַמִי רָמֵי שִׁינּוּי קוֹדֶשׁ אַשִּׁינּוּי בְּעָלִים, וּמְשַׁנֵּי.

§ **Rav Yosef bar Ami raises a contradiction** between Rav's statement with regard to **deviation** with regard to the type **of offering,** i.e., slaughtering for the sake of a different type of offering, **and** Rav's statement with regard to **deviation** with regard to the **owner,** i.e., slaughtering for the sake of someone other than the offering's owner, **and** he then **resolves** the contradiction.

מִי אָמַר רַב: חַטָּאת שֶׁשְּׁחָטָהּ לְשֵׁם חַטָּאת – כְּשֵׁירָה, לְשֵׁם עוֹלָה – פְּסוּלָה; אַלְמָא דְּלָאו מִינָהּ מַחֲרִיב בָּהּ, דְּמִינָהּ לָא מַחֲרִיב בָּהּ?

The contradiction is as follows: **Did Rav say** that **a sin offering that one slaughtered for the sake of** another **sin offering,** i.e., one that the owner is obligated to bring for a different transgression, is **fit,** but that if one slaughtered it **for the sake of a burnt offering** it is **unfit? Apparently,** slaughtering an offering with an improper intention **not of its type ruins it;** whereas intent that is **of its type does not ruin it.**

וְהָאָמַר רַב: חַטָּאת שֶׁשְּׁחָטָהּ עַל מִי שֶׁמְּחוּיָּיב חַטָּאת – פְּסוּלָה, עַל מִי שֶׁמְּחוּיָּיב עוֹלָה – כְּשֵׁרָה; אַלְמָא דְּבַר מִינָהּ מַחֲרִיב בָּהּ, דְּלָאו מִינָהּ לָא מַחֲרִיב בָּהּ!

But doesn't Rav say that **a sin offering that one slaughtered for** a person who is not its owner but **who** nevertheless **is obligated** to bring **a sin offering** is **unfit,** whereas if one slaughtered it **for** a person **who is obligated** to bring **a burnt offering,** it is **fit?**[N] **Apparently,** an improper intention that is **of its type ruins** the offering, whereas intent **not of its type does not ruin it.**

וּמְשַׁנֵּי: הָתָם "וְשָׁחַט אֹתָהּ לְחַטָּאת" אָמַר רַחֲמָנָא, וַהֲרֵי חַטָּאת לְשֵׁם חַטָּאת נִשְׁחֲטָה;

And he **resolves** the contradiction as follows: **There,** with regard to deviation from the type of offering, **the Merciful One states** in the Torah: **"And slaughter it for a sin offering"** (Leviticus 4:33). **And** here **a sin offering was slaughtered for the sake of a sin offering,** and therefore although it was for the sake of a different sin offering, it remains fit.

הָכָא "וְכִפֶּר עָלָיו" כְּתִיב, עָלָיו – וְלֹא עַל חֲבֵירוֹ, חֲבֵירוֹ דּוּמְיָא דִּידֵיהּ, שֶׁמְּחוּיָּיב כַּפָּרָה כְּמוֹתָהּ.

Here, concerning deviation with regard to the owner, it **is written** in the Torah concerning a sin offering: **"And he shall be forgiven"** (Leviticus 4:26), indicating that specifically **he,** the owner, **but not another** person, shall be forgiven. Therefore, if a sin offering is slaughtered for the sake of another person, it is unfit. **The other** person to whom this is referring is presumably **similar to him,**[N] the owner of the sin offering, in **that he is obligated** to make **atonement similar to** that of the owner. Therefore, if the other person is obligated to bring a burnt offering and not a sin offering, this disqualification does not apply.

רַב חֲבִיבָא רָמֵי שִׁינּוּי בְּעָלִים אַ"תּוֹךְ תּוֹכוֹ", וּמְשַׁנֵּי.

§ **Rav Ḥaviva raises a contradiction** between Rav's statement concerning **deviation** with regard to the **owner and** the aforementioned *baraita* concerning **the interior of its interior,** i.e., a vessel placed in an earthenware vessel, **and resolves** the contradiction.

וּמִי אָמַר רַב: חַטָּאת שֶׁשְּׁחָטָהּ עַל מִי שֶׁמְּחוּיָּיב [חַטָּאת – פְּסוּלָה, עַל מִי שֶׁמְּחוּיָּיב] עוֹלָה – כְּשֵׁירָה; אַלְמָא, דְּמִינָהּ מַחֲרִיב בָּהּ, לָאו מִינָהּ לָא מַחֲרִיב בָּהּ?

The contradiction is as follows: **But did Rav say** that **a sin offering that one slaughtered for** a person other than its owner but **who is** also **obligated** to bring **a sin offering** is **unfit,** whereas if one slaughtered it **for** a person **obligated** to bring **a burnt offering, it is fit? Apparently,** an improper intention that is **of its type ruins it,** whereas intent that is **not of its type does not ruin it.**

BACKGROUND

Food that one kneaded with clay – אוֹכָלִין שֶׁגִּיבְּלָן בְּטִיט: People would sometimes cover food with clay before putting it in the oven, either to prevent it from heating up too quickly, or in order to help the food retain a certain shape. After the food was baked, the clay covering would serve as a container and a means of preserving the food.

NOTES

For a person who is obligated to bring a burnt offering it is fit – עַל מִי שֶׁמְּחוּיָּיב עוֹלָה כְּשֵׁרָה: Since a sin offering cannot be brought voluntarily, as it is brought only by one who is obligated to bring it for committing a sin, intent to sacrifice a sin offering for a person who is not obligated to bring one is meaningless and therefore disregarded.

The other is similar to him – חֲבֵירוֹ דּוּמְיָא דִּידֵיהּ: This presumption is based on the principle that an item is affected only by something that is of its type (Rashi).

וְהָתַנְיָא: ״תּוֹכוֹ״ – וְלֹא תּוֹךְ תּוֹכוֹ, אֲפִילּוּ כְּלִי שֶׁטֶף מַצִּיל!

But isn't it taught in a *baraita* that if the carcass of a creeping animal is found inside an earthenware vessel, the vessel's **interior** is rendered impure **but not the interior of its interior,** and **even a vessel** purified through **rinsing,** if placed in the earthenware vessel, **protects** food inside it from contracting impurity? Evidently, impurity in the airspace of an earthenware vessel can be contained by something not of its type.

וּמְשַׁנֵּי: אַרְבָּעָה ״תּוֹכוֹ״ כְּתִיבִי (תּוֹכוֹ): תּוֹךְ, תּוֹכוֹ, תּוֹךְ, תּוֹכוֹ;

And Rav Ḥaviva **resolves** the contradiction as follows: The expression: **Whose interior** [*tokho*], **is written four** times. In other words, in the verse: "And every earthen vessel into whose interior [*tokho*] any of them falls, anything that is in its interior [*tokho*] shall be impure" (Leviticus 11:33), the word *tokho* is mentioned twice, and each time, the verse could have written: The interior. Since the possessive: Its, is added to each instance, the verse is interpreted exegetically as though the word interior [*tokh*] were mentioned four times: **Interior** [*tokh*], **whose interior** [*tokho*], **interior** [*tokh*], and **its interior** [*tokho*].

חַד – לְגוּפֵיהּ, וְחַד – לִגְזֵירָה שָׁוָה,

One of these is necessary **to** teach the matter **itself,** that an impure earthenware vessel imparts impurity to food in its airspace; **and one** instance is used **for a verbal analogy**[B] between the two instances of the word interior, from which it is derived that an earthenware vessel itself contracts impurity from impure items in its airspace.

חַד – תּוֹכוֹ שֶׁל זֶה וְלֹא תּוֹכוֹ שֶׁל אַחֵר, אִידָּךְ – תּוֹכוֹ וְלֹא תּוֹךְ תּוֹכוֹ, וַאֲפִילּוּ כְּלִי שֶׁטֶף מַצִּיל.

One indicates that **the interior** airspace **of this,** i.e., an earthenware vessel, renders food impure, **but not the interior of another** type of vessel, which imparts impurity only through contact; and **the other** instance indicates that **its interior, but not the interior of its interior,** imparts impurity, **and** that **even a vessel** purified through **rinsing,** if placed in the earthenware vessel, **protects** food inside it from becoming impure. Consequently, it is derived from a verse that inside an earthenware vessel, other vessels not of its type can block the transmission of impurity. Since this halakha is derived from a verse written in that context, there is no reason to assume that a similar *halakha* would apply to slaughter.

BACKGROUND

Verbal analogy – גְּזֵירָה שָׁוָה: The verbal analogy is a fundamental talmudic principle of biblical exegesis, appearing in all the standard lists of hermeneutical principles. If the same word or phrase appears in two places in the Torah, and a certain *halakha* is explicitly stated in one of these places, it is inferred on the basis of verbal analogy that the same *halakha* applies in the other case as well. Certain restrictions were placed on the use of this principle to prevent unfounded conclusions being drawn. Most significantly, one cannot infer a verbal analogy on one's own, i.e., only a verbal analogy based on received tradition is valid.

Perek **I**
Daf **4** Amud **a**

מְנָלַן דִּבְעֵינַן זְבִיחָה לִשְׁמָהּ? דְּאָמַר קְרָא: ״וְאִם זֶבַח שְׁלָמִים קָרְבָּנוֹ״ – שֶׁתְּהֵא זְבִיחָה לְשֵׁם [שְׁלָמִים].

§ The Gemara asks: **From where do we** derive **that we require** that an offering's **slaughter** be performed **for its own sake?** It is derived from a verse, **as the verse states: "And if his offering is a sacrifice** [*zevaḥ*] **of peace offerings"** (Leviticus 3:1), teaching **that slaughter** [*zeviḥa*] **must be** performed **for the sake of a peace offering.**[NB]

וְדִילְמָא הַיְינוּ שְׁמַיְיהוּ!

The Gemara challenges: **But perhaps** when the verse states: "A sacrifice of peace offerings," "a sacrifice of peace offerings" **is** simply **the name of** this type of offering, and is not referring to intent of the one slaughtering it.

מִדִּכְתִיב: ״הַמַּקְרִיב אֶת דַּם הַשְּׁלָמִים״ ״הַזּוֹרֵק אֶת דַּם הַשְּׁלָמִים״, וְלָא כְּתִיב ״זֶבַח״, וְהָכָא כְּתִיב ״זֶבַח״ – שְׁמַע מִינָּהּ: שֶׁתְּהֵא זְבִיחָה לְשֵׁם שְׁלָמִים.

The Gemara answers: **From** the fact **that it is written** in other verses: **"Who offers the blood of the peace offering"** (Leviticus 7:33), and: **"Who sprinkles the blood of the peace offering"** (Leviticus 7:14), **and** the term: **A sacrifice** [*zevaḥ*], **is not written,** whereas **here,** in this verse, the term: **"A sacrifice** [*zevaḥ*] of peace offerings," **is written, learn from it that** the slaughter [*zeviḥa*] **must be** performed **for the sake of a peace offering.**

אַשְׁכְּחַן זְבִיחָה, שְׁאָר עֲבוֹדוֹת מְנָלַן?

The Gemara asks: **We found** a source for the *halakha* that **slaughter** must be performed for the sake of the offering being sacrificed. **From where do we** derive that the **other** sacrificial **rites,** i.e., collecting the blood, conveying it to the altar, and sprinkling it on the altar, must also be performed for the sake of the offering?

NOTES

For the sake of a peace offering – לְשֵׁם שְׁלָמִים: This discussion about the obligation to sacrifice an offering for its own sake and for the sake of the owner is relevant with regard to a peace offering. The Gemara discusses later (4b) the source for these *halakhot* with regard to other offerings.

BACKGROUND

Peace offering – שְׁלָמִים: Male and female cattle or sheep or goats may be sacrificed as peace offerings. As offerings of lesser sanctity they may be slaughtered anywhere within the Temple courtyard. Their blood is sprinkled on the two opposite corners of the altar in such a manner that it will touch each of the altar's four sides. Part of each peace offering is burned on the altar; part, namely, the breast and the right hind leg, is given to the priests; and the rest is eaten anywhere in Jerusalem by the person bringing the offering, either on the day the animal is sacrificed, on the following day, or during the intervening night. Any ritually pure Jew may join the owner in partaking of the peace offering. With the exception of the Festival peace offering and a few other cases, peace offerings are brought voluntarily, i.e., they are gift offerings.

וְכִי תֵּימָא: לֵילַף מִזְּבִיחָה; מַה לִּזְבִיחָה שֶׁכֵּן נִפְסְלָה שֶׁלֹּא לְשֵׁם אוֹכְלִין בְּפֶסַח!

And if you would say: Let us derive from the fact that **slaughter** must be performed for the sake of the offering that the other sacrificial rites must be performed for the sake of the offering as well, this derivation can be refuted, as slaughter has a unique element of stringency: **What** is unique **about slaughter?** It is unique **in that with regard to a Paschal offering,** the offering is **disqualified** if it is slaughtered **not for the sake of those who eat** it.[N] If the Paschal offering is slaughtered for the sake of people who are incapable of eating it, such as one who is too ill to eat, it is disqualified. By contrast, performing other rites with this intent does not disqualify the offering. Therefore, one cannot assume that a *halakha* that applies to slaughter applies to other rites as well.

אֶלָּא אָמַר קְרָא: ״הַמַּקְרִיב אֶת דַּם הַשְּׁלָמִים״ – שֶׁתְּהֵא קַבָּלָה לְשֵׁם שְׁלָמִים.

The Gemara answers: **Rather, the verse states: "Who sacrifices** [*hamakriv*] **the blood of the peace offering"** (Leviticus 7:33),[N] referring to the one who collects the blood of the offering, as the Gemara will explain. This phrase indicates **that** the **collection** of the blood[B] **must be** performed **for the sake of a peace offering.**[N]

וְלִכְתּוֹב רַחֲמָנָא בְּקַבָּלָה, וְלֵילַף שְׁחִיטָה מִינָּהּ!

The Gemara challenges: **And let the Merciful One write** this *halakha* in the Torah only **with regard to** the **collection** of the blood, **and we would derive from it** that **slaughter** must also be performed for the sake of the offering.

מִשּׁוּם דְּאִיכָּא לְמִיפְרַךְ: מַה לְּקַבָּלָה שֶׁכֵּן פְּסוּלָה בְּזָר וְאִשָּׁה.

The Gemara answers: **Because** such a derivation **can be refuted** as follows: **What** is unique **about collection** of the blood? It is unique **in that it is not valid** if performed **by a non-priest or a woman,** whereas slaughter can be performed by any competent Jew. Therefore, one cannot assume that a *halakha* that applies to collection applies to slaughter as well.

אַשְׁכְּחַן שְׁחִיטָה וְקַבָּלָה, זְרִיקָה מְנָלַן?

The Gemara asks: **We found** a source for the *halakha* that **slaughter and collection** of the blood must be performed for the sake of the offering. **From where do we** derive that this *halakha* applies to the **sprinkling** of the blood[B] as well?

וְכִי תֵּימָא לֵילַף מֵהָנֵי – מַה לְּהָנֵי שֶׁכֵּן טְעוּנוֹת צָפוֹן, וְיֶשְׁנָן בַּחַטָּאוֹת הַפְּנִימִיּוֹת!

And if you would say: Let us derive from these rites, i.e., slaughter and collection, that this *halakha* applies to the sprinkling of the blood as well, this derivation can be refuted: **What** is unique **about these** rites? They are unique **in that** for offerings of the most sacred order, it is **required** that they be performed in the **north** of the Temple courtyard. **And** furthermore, these rites **are** performed **in the** sacrifice of **inner sin offerings**[B] as well as standard sin offerings. The sprinkling of the blood on the external altar, by contrast, is performed in all portions of the Temple courtyard, and it is not performed in the sacrifice of inner sin offerings, whose blood is sprinkled only in the Sanctuary.

BACKGROUND

Collection of the blood – קַבָּלָה: These are the four standard sacrificial rites pertaining to offerings: Slaughtering the animal, collecting its blood in a vessel, conveying the blood to the altar, and sprinkling it on the altar. Collecting refers to the act of receiving the blood that spurts from the neck of a sacrificial animal when it is slaughtered. The blood is received in one of the sacred vessels used in the Temple. Collection may be performed only by a priest. Although collection of the blood is not mentioned explicitly in the Torah as an independent rite, it is a necessary stage in the process of sacrificing offerings. Conveying the blood is not an essential rite in practical terms; if the offering is slaughtered close to the altar it is possible to sprinkle the blood immediately without conveying it.

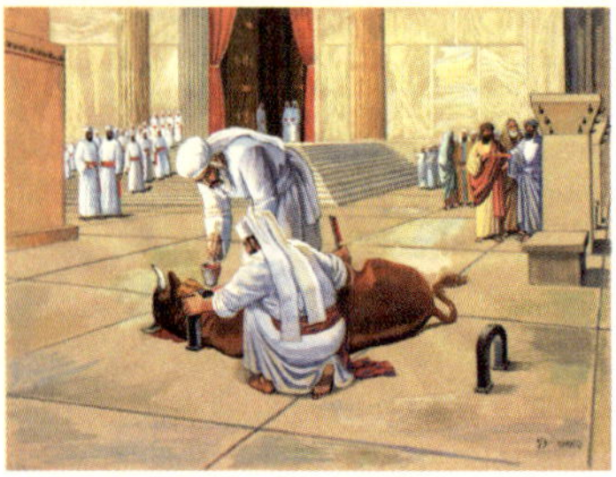

Slaughter of the bull in the Temple courtyard on Yom Kippur

Sprinkling of the blood – זְרִיקָה: This term refers to the presenting of sacrificial blood on the altar. It is one of the four sacrificial rites involved in the sacrifice of every animal offering in the Temple. The manner in which the blood was presented on the altar varies according to the nature of the particular offering. The presenting of blood on the altar is the essential element for an offering to bring about atonement. Accordingly, as soon as the blood is presented as required on the altar, the person who brought the offering has achieved atonement, even if the later sacrificial rites associated with the offering are not completed in the required manner.

Sprinkling the blood on the altar

Inner sin offerings – חַטָּאוֹת פְּנִימִיּוֹת: These are offerings whose blood is sprinkled in the Sanctuary or in the Holy of Holies. This category includes the Yom Kippur bull and the Yom Kippur goat, whose blood is sprinkled between the staves of the Ark, on the curtain, and on the golden altar. Other such offerings are the bull for an unintentional communal sin, the bull of the anointed priest, and the goat of idol worship, whose blood is sprinkled on the curtain and on the golden altar. In all these cases, unlike other offerings, any omission occurring in the ceremony of sprinkling the blood disqualifies them. The remaining blood is poured on the western base of the altar. The flesh of these sacrifices is not eaten, but is burned outside Jerusalem after being cut up into pieces, with all its inner parts and excreta. Ordinary sin offerings are occasionally called outer sin offerings, in contrast to the inner ones, since their blood is sprinkled on the external altar.

NOTES

A Paschal offering is disqualified if slaughtered not for the sake of those who eat it – נִפְסְלָה שֶׁלֹּא לְשֵׁם אוֹכְלִין בְּפֶסַח: A unique aspect of the Paschal offering is that its primary mitzva is not to sacrifice it, but to eat it. If it is slaughtered for one who is incapable of eating it, e.g., for one who is too infirm or too ill to eat the offering, it is disqualified. This is derived from the verse: "According to every man's eating you shall slaughter the lamb" (Exodus 12:4). It is not disqualified if any of the other rites are performed not for the sake of those who eat it.

Who sacrifices the blood of the peace offering – הַמַּקְרִיב אֶת דַּם הַשְּׁלָמִים: This sentence is interpreted in reference to collecting the blood, as the Gemara states explicitly later on, because it is the first rite mentioned in the verse after slaughter (Rashi). It cannot be referring to conveying the blood to the altar, as that rite is dispensable (Rashi on 13a).

That collection of the blood must be performed for the sake of a peace offering – שֶׁתְּהֵא קַבָּלָה לְשֵׁם שְׁלָמִים: This is derived from the superfluous term "of the peace offering." Since the entire passage discusses the peace offering, it would have been sufficient for the verse to state: "Who offers the blood."

אֶלָּא אָמַר קְרָא: ״הַזּוֹרֵק אֶת דַּם הַשְּׁלָמִים״ – שֶׁתְּהֵא זְרִיקָה לְשֵׁם שְׁלָמִים.

The Gemara answers: **Rather, the verse states: "Who sprinkles the blood of the peace offering"** (Leviticus 7:14), indicating **that** the **sprinkling** of the blood **must be** performed **for the sake of a peace offering.**

וְלִכְתּוֹב רַחֲמָנָא בִּזְרִיקָה וְלֵילַף מִינַּהּ!

The Gemara challenges: **And let the Merciful One write** this *halakha* only **with regard to sprinkling, and we would derive from it** that it applies to slaughter and collection as well.

מִשּׁוּם דְּאִיכָּא לְמִיפְרַךְ: מָה לִזְרִיקָה – שֶׁכֵּן חַיָּיב עָלֶיהָ זָר מִיתָה.

The Gemara answers: That would not be sufficient, **because** such a derivation **can be refuted,** as sprinkling has a unique element of stringency. **What** is unique **about sprinkling?** It is unique **in that a non-priest is liable to** be punished with **death** at the hand of Heaven **for** performing **it.**[N]

אַשְׁכְּחַן כּוּלְּהוּ, הוֹלָכָה מְנָלַן?

The Gemara asks: **We found** a source for this *halakha* with regard to **all** four rites save **conveying** the blood to the altar. **From where do we** derive that this latter rite must also be performed for the sake of the offering?

וְכִי תֵּימָא לֵילַף מִכּוּלְּהוּ – מָה לְכוּלְּהוּ שֶׁכֵּן עֲבוֹדָה שֶׁאִי אֶפְשָׁר לְבַטְּלָהּ, תֹּאמַר בְּהוֹלָכָה שֶׁאֶפְשָׁר לְבַטְּלָהּ!

And if you would say: Let us derive from all the other rites that conveying the blood must also be performed for the sake of the offering, this derivation can also be refuted: **What** is unique **about all of** the other rites? They are unique **in that** each of them is **an indispensable rite. Would you say** that any requirement that applies to those rites necessarily applies also **with regard to conveying** the blood, **which is dispensable?** If an offering is slaughtered by the side of the altar, it is unnecessary to convey its blood to the altar.

אֶלָּא אָמַר קְרָא: ״וְהִקְרִיב אֶת הַכֹּל הַמִּזְבֵּחָה״, וְאָמַר מָר: זוֹ הוֹלָכַת אֵבָרִים לַכֶּבֶשׁ; וְתַנְיָא: ״וְהִקְרִיבוּ״ – זוֹ קַבָּלַת הַדָּם; וְאַפֵּיק רַחֲמָנָא בִּלְשׁוֹן הוֹלָכָה, לְמֵימְרָא דְּהוֹלָכָה לָא תִּפְקָה מִכְּלַל קַבָּלָה.

The Gemara answers: **Rather, the verse states: "And** the priest **shall sacrifice** [*vehikriv*] **the whole,** and make it smoke **upon the altar"** (Leviticus 1:13), **and the Master said** that **this** is referring to **conveying** the **limbs** of the offering **to the ramp** of the altar. **And it is taught** in a *baraita* with regard to the verse: **"And** Aaron's sons, the priests, **shall present** [*vehikrivu*] the blood" (Leviticus 1:5), that **this** is referring to the **collection of the blood. And** one can infer that **the Merciful One expresses** collection of the blood **in the** same **language** used for **conveying, to say that you should not exclude conveying from the category of collection** of the blood. Therefore, the *halakhot* of collection apply to conveying.

וְאַשְׁכְּחַן שִׁנּוּי קוֹדֶשׁ, שִׁנּוּי בְּעָלִים מְנָלַן?

The Gemara asks further: **And we found** a source for the *halakha* concerning **deviation** with regard to the type of **offering,** i.e., that an offering may not be slaughtered for the sake of a different type of offering. **From where do we** derive the *halakha* concerning **deviation** with regard to the **owner,** i.e., that an offering may not be slaughtered for the sake of one who is not the owner?

אָמַר רַב פִּנְחָס בְּרֵיהּ דְּרַב אַמִּי, אָמַר קְרָא: ״וּבְשַׂר זֶבַח תּוֹדַת שְׁלָמָיו״ – שֶׁתְּהֵא זְבִיחָה לְשֵׁם תּוֹדָה; אִם אֵינוֹ עִנְיָן לְשִׁינּוּי קוֹדֶשׁ, דִּנְפְקָא לַן מֵהָתָם – תְּנֵהוּ עִנְיָן לְשִׁינּוּי בְּעָלִים.

Rav Pinḥas, son of Rav Ami, says: The verse states with regard to a thanks offering: **"And the meat of the sacrifice** [*zevaḥ*] **of his thanksgiving peace offering** shall be eaten on the day of his offering" (Leviticus 7:15), apparently indicating **that** its **slaughter** [*zeviḥa*] **must be** performed **for the sake of a thanks offering.**[B] And **if** this language **is not** needed **for the matter**[B] **of deviation** with regard to the type of **offering,** and in fact it is not, **as we** already **derived** this *halakha* **from there,** i.e., the verse cited concerning peace offerings, **apply it** to the **matter of deviation** with regard to the **owner.**[H] It is thereby derived that an offering must be slaughtered for the sake of its owner.

NOTES

A non-priest is liable to be punished with death at the hand of Heaven for performing it – חַיָּיב עָלֶיהָ זָר מִיתָה: Although it is prohibited for a non-priest to collect or convey the blood, and doing so is a desecration of the sacrificial rite, a non-priest is liable to receive the punishment of death at the hand of Heaven for performing the four standard sacrificial rites: Sprinkling the blood, burning the portions of the offering that are consumed on the altar, pouring libation wine, and pouring the libation water on *Sukkot*. The element common to all these acts is that they are all considered complete rites, i.e., they do not serve as preparatory rites for other rites.

BACKGROUND

Thanks offering – תּוֹדָה: The thanks offering is specified in the Torah as a unique type of peace offering. The Sages received a tradition, based on Psalms 107, with regard to the circumstances that render one obligated to bring a thanks offering. Along with the animal, typically a sheep or goat, one also brings a meal offering in the form of forty loaves of four varieties, ten of each. The four types of bread are: Leavened loaves called *ḥallot*, loaves of *matza* called *ḥallot matza*, thin cakes called *rekikin*, and *matzot* called *revukha*.

If it is not needed for the matter – אִם אֵינוֹ עִנְיָן: This form of reasoning is one of the thirty-two hermeneutic principles of Rabbi Eliezer, son of Rabbi Yosei. According to most authorities, the conclusions drawn from them are as authoritative as they would be if they were explicitly written in the Torah (see *Yad Malakhi*). This principle is applied when a verse is superfluous in the context in which it is written. At the same time, the verse is never applied to matters totally unrelated to the meaning of the text.

HALAKHA

Slaughter for its sake – זְבִיחָה לִשְׁמָהּ: While sacrificing any type of offering, one must have the type of offering and its owner in mind. This applies to slaughtering the animal, collecting the blood, conveying the blood to the altar, and sprinkling it on the altar. This *halakha* is derived from the verse: "And the meat of the sacrifice of his thanksgiving peace offering," which indicates that the sacrifice must be performed for the sake of a peace offering, or for whichever offering it is (Rambam *Sefer Avoda, Hilkhot Ma'aseh HaKorbanot* 4:10).

LANGUAGE

Abba – אַבָּא: Abba literally means my father. People address their father in this manner out of respect. Similarly, some refer to their father as Abba Mari, meaning: My father, my teacher. Children would normally refer to their grandfather as Abba too.

The name Abba also served as an honorific in the period of the Mishna and Talmud, similar to the name Mar that was used in Babylonia. Scholars who were elderly and commanded respect but were not ordained as rabbis were often referred to as Abba so-and-so. Elijah the prophet was sometimes referred to as Abba Elijah.

The name Abba is also used as a given name. From the mishnaic period to the present day, many people have carried this name, including several distinguished rabbis.

PERSONALITIES

Abba Ḥanin – אַבָּא חָנִין: Abba Ḥanin, also referred to as Abba Ḥanan, lived in the third and fourth generations of *tanna'im*. The appellation Abba was not his given name but an honorific. Abba Ḥanin was a disciple of Rabbi Eliezer, and he taught many of his teacher's statements, both in *halakha* and *aggada*. He was a colleague of Rabbi Shimon Shezuri and had many discussions and disputes with him. Many of Abba Ḥanin's statements are mentioned in the *Mekhilta* and *Sifrei Bamidbar*. In some places he is found to have engaged in disputes with Rabbi Yoshiya and Rabbi Yehoshua, disciples of Rabbi Yishmael. He also transmitted certain statements of Rabbi Yehoshua. There exists one statement of Abba Ḥanin's that is his own statement and not a citation of another *tanna*.

וְהַאי לְהָכִי הוּא דְּאָתָא? הָא מִיבְּעֵי לֵיהּ לְכִדְתַנְיָא: ״וּבְשַׂר זֶבַח תּוֹדַת שְׁלָמָיו״, אַבָּא חָנִין אוֹמֵר מִשּׁוּם רַבִּי אֱלִיעֶזֶר, בָּא לְלַמֵּד: תּוֹדָה שֶׁשְּׁחָטָהּ לְשֵׁם שְׁלָמִים – כְּשֵׁרָה, שְׁלָמִים שֶׁשְּׁחָטָן לְשֵׁם תּוֹדָה – פְּסוּלָה. מָה הֶפְרֵשׁ בֵּין זֶה לָזֶה? תּוֹדָה קְרוּיָה שְׁלָמִים, וְאֵין שְׁלָמִים קְרוּיָה תּוֹדָה!

The Gemara asks: **But does this** verse **come to** teach **this** ***halakha*****? Isn't it necessary for that which is taught** in a *baraita*: Concerning the phrase **"and the meat of the sacrifice of his thanksgiving peace offering," Abba**[L] **Ḥanin**[P] **says in the name of Rabbi Eliezer: It comes to teach** that **a thanks offering that one slaughtered for the sake of a peace offering is fit;** whereas **a peace offering that one slaughtered for the sake of a thanks offering is unfit. What is** the **difference between this** offering **and that**[N] offering? **A thanks offering is called a peace offering** in that verse, **but a peace offering is not called a thanks offering.**

אֲנַן מִ״זֶּבַח״ קָאָמְרִינַן.

The Gemara answers: **We are saying** that it is derived **from** the superfluous term: **"Sacrifice** [*zevaḥ*]," that the slaughter [*zeviḥa*] must be performed for the sake of the owner. The term "peace offering" teaches Abba Ḥanin's ruling.

וְאַכַּתִּי מִיבְּעֵי לֵיהּ: חַטָּאת וְאָשָׁם מִנַּיִן? תַּלְמוּד לוֹמַר: ״זֶבַח״!

The Gemara disputes this: **But** the term "sacrifice [*zevaḥ*]" is **still necessary** to serve as the source for another halakhic midrash: **From where** is it derived that the meat of **a sin offering and a guilt offering** may be eaten only on the day the animal is sacrificed and the following night, like a thanks offering? **The verse states:** "And the meat of the **sacrifice** [*zevaḥ*] of his thanksgiving peace offering shall be eaten on the day of his offering." The phrase teaches that not only thanks offerings, but any slaughtered offering [*zevaḥ*] is subject to this time limit unless the Torah specifies otherwise.

אִם כֵּן, נִכְתּוֹב קְרָא ״וּבְשַׂר תּוֹדַת שְׁלָמָיו [זֶבַח]״, מַאי ״זֶבַח״? שְׁמַע מִינָּהּ תַּרְתֵּי.

The Gemara answers: **If that were so,** i.e., if the term "sacrifice" indicated only that a sin offering and a guilt offering may be eaten only for the period of time for which a thanks offering may be eaten, **let the verse write: And the meat of his thanksgiving peace offering sacrifice. What** is indicated by the mention of the word **sacrifice** before the phrase "his thanksgiving peace offering"? Rather, **conclude two** conclusions **from it.**[N]

אַשְׁכְּחַן זְבִיחָה, שְׁאָר עֲבוֹדוֹת מְנָלַן?

The Gemara asks: **We found** a source for the *halakha* that **slaughter** must be performed for the sake of the owner. **From where do we** derive that the **other** sacrificial **rites** must also be performed for the sake of the owner?

וְכִי תֵּימָא לֵילַף מִזְּבִיחָה; מָה לִזְבִיחָה שֶׁכֵּן פּוֹסֵל שֶׁלֹּא לְשֵׁם אוֹכְלִין בְּפֶסַח!

And if you would say: Let us derive from slaughter that the other rites must be performed for the sake of the owner as well, this derivation can be refuted: **What is unique about slaughter?** It is unique **in that with regard to a Paschal offering,** slaughter **not for the sake of those who eat** it **disqualifies** the offering, whereas performing the other rites not for the sake of the owner does not.

נֶאֶמְרָה זְבִיחָה בְּשִׁינּוּי קוֹדֶשׁ, וְנֶאֶמְרָה זְבִיחָה בְּשִׁינּוּי בְּעָלִים; מָה זְבִיחָה הָאֲמוּרָה בְּשִׁינּוּי קוֹדֶשׁ – לֹא חִלַּקְתָּ בֵּין זְבִיחָה לִשְׁאָר עֲבוֹדוֹת, אַף זְבִיחָה הָאֲמוּרָה בְּשִׁינּוּי בְּעָלִים – לֹא תְּחַלֵּק בָּהֶן בֵּין זְבִיחָה לִשְׁאָר עֲבוֹדוֹת.

The Gemara answers: A term of **slaughter is stated with regard to deviation** from the type of **offering, and** a term of **slaughter is stated with regard to deviation** with regard to the **owner. Just as** concerning the term **slaughter stated with regard to deviation** from the type of **offering, you did not differentiate between slaughter and** the **other** sacrificial **rites,** and all four rites must be performed for the sake of the offering, **so too,** concerning the term **slaughter stated with regard to deviation** in the context of the **owner, you should not differentiate between slaughter and** the **other** sacrificial **rites.**

NOTES

What is the difference between this and that – מָה הֶפְרֵשׁ בֵּין זֶה לָזֶה: A thanks offering is a specific type of peace offering. Therefore, if one intends to sacrifice it for the sake of a peace offering, his intent is essentially correct, although it is not properly specific. By contrast, if one sacrifices a peace offering for the sake of a thanks offering, his intent is incorrect, as a regular peace offering is not a thanks offering.

Conclude two conclusions from it – שְׁמַע מִינָּהּ תַּרְתֵּי: Although it is derived from the word sacrifice that other animal offerings are also included in the time limit for eating them, the location of this word in the verse indicates an additional *halakha*: That the offering must be sacrificed for the sake of a thanks offering.

אִיכָּא לְמִיפְרַךְ: מַה לְּשִׁינּוּי קוֹדֶשׁ, שֶׁכֵּן פְּסוּלָהּ בְּגוּפָהּ, וְיֶשְׁנוֹ בְּאַרְבַּע עֲבוֹדוֹת,	The Gemara counters: This derivation **can be refuted: What** is unique **about deviation** from the type of **offering,** as opposed to deviation with regard to the owner? It is unique with regard to four matters: First, it is unique **in that its disqualification concerns** the essence of the offering **itself. And** second, it is unique in that deviation from the type of **offering applies to** the **four** sacrificial **rites,**[N] whereas performing a rite for the sake of the owner is relevant only to the sprinkling of the blood, which atones for the owner.
וְיֶשְׁנוֹ לְאַחַר מִיתָה, וְיֶשְׁנוֹ בְּצִיבּוּר כְּבְיָחִיד!	**And** third, it is unique in that deviation from the type of offering **applies** even **after** the **death** of the owner, when the owner's heir brings the offering, whereas intent for the sake of the owner is irrelevant after the owner has died. **And** fourth, it is unique in that deviation from the type of offering **applies with regard to communal** offerings[N] **as well as with regard to individual** offerings, whereas employing the term owner is irrelevant with regard to communal offerings, which are owned by the public.

NOTES

And it applies to the four sacrificial rites – וְיֶשְׁנוֹ בְּאַרְבַּע עֲבוֹדוֹת: This statement does not mean that performance for the sake of the owner is not required in all four sacrificial rites, as this requirement is precisely the *halakha* whose source the Gemara is discussing. Rather, this statement means that while the type of offering is relevant to all four rites, the identity of the owner is relevant only to the sprinkling of the blood, since this is the rite that atones for him. This is why the Gemara (10a) states that slaughtering an offering with the wrong owner in mind disqualifies it only if the intent of the one who slaughtered it was that the blood would be sprinkled for the sake of the wrong person. If he slaughtered it for the sake of the wrong person but did not have this intent concerning the sprinkling of the blood, the offering is fit (Rashi; *Tosefot Tukh*).

And it applies with regard to communal offerings, etc. – וְיֶשְׁנוֹ בְּצִיבּוּר וכו׳: Whereas slaughtering a communal offering of one type for the sake of a different type of offering, e.g., a communal sin offering for the sake of a burnt offering, constitutes a change of the type of offering, improper intent vis-à-vis the owner does not apply to communal offerings, as every individual is considered a member of the public and is therefore a co-owner of the offering. In fact, even sacrificing the offering for the sake of a gentile, who is not a member of the community, does not disqualify it, according to the principle stated earlier (3b) that intent for the sake of the wrong owner disqualifies the offering only if he is obligated to provide an atonement similar to the owner's atonement (*Tosafot*).

Perek **I**
Daf **4** Amud **b**

וְאַף עַל גַּב דְּתַרְתֵּי לָאו דַּוְקָא, תַּרְתֵּי מִיהָא דַּוְקָא.	**And although two** of these distinctions **are not precise,** the other **two are in any event precise** distinctions, based upon which a distinction can be drawn.
מַאי שְׁנָא שִׁינּוּי בְּעָלִים דְּלָא הָוֵי פְּסוּלוֹ בְּגוּפוֹ? מַחֲשָׁבָה בְּעָלְמָא; שִׁינּוּי קוֹדֶשׁ נַמִי מַחֲשָׁבָה בְּעָלְמָא הוּא. אֶלָּא, כֵּיוָן דְּאַחְשְׁבָהּ פְּסָלָהּ – הָכָא נַמִי כֵּיוָן דְּאַחְשְׁבָהּ פְּסָלָהּ!	The Gemara explains why two of the distinctions are not precise: **What is different** about **deviation** with regard to the **owner,** such **that its disqualification does not concern** the offering **itself?** It is that this **merely** constitutes a change of **thought. Deviation** from the type of **offering is also merely** a change of **thought;** the offering is not physically affected. **Rather,** this distinction between deviation with regard to the owner and deviation from the type of offering is false; one should claim that if deviation from the type of offering **disqualifies it once** the one who slaughtered it **had** that **intent, here too, once** the one who slaughtered it **had intent** to deviate from its owner, **he disqualified it.**
וּלְרַב פִּנְחָס בְּרֵיהּ דְּרַב מָרִי, דְּאָמַר: יֵשׁ שִׁינּוּי בְּעָלִים לְאַחַר מִיתָה, תַּרְתֵּי מִיהָא אִיכָּא לְמִיפְרַךְ!	The Gemara explains the difficulty with the second distinction, the case where the owner died: **And according to Rav Pineḥas, son of Rav Mari, who says** that disqualification by **deviation** with regard to the **owner applies** even **after** the owner's **death,** there is no distinction in this regard between deviation from the type of offering and deviation with regard to the owner. **In any event, there are two** remaining distinctions based on which the comparison between a deviation from the type of offering and a deviation with regard to the owner **can be refuted.**

אֶלָּא אָמַר רַב אַשִׁי: אָמַר קְרָא ״וְנִרְצָה לוֹ לְכַפֵּר עָלָיו״ – וְלֹא עַל חֲבֵירוֹ.

Rather, Rav Ashi says that the *halakha* that it is prohibited to sprinkle the blood for the sake of one other than the owner is derived from a verse. **The verse states: "And it shall be accepted for him to atone for him"** (Leviticus 1:4), teaching that the sacrificial rite that atones for the owner, namely, the sprinkling of the blood, must be performed specifically for him, **and not for another.**

וְהַאי לְהָכִי הוּא דְּאָתָא? הַאי מִיבָּעֵי לֵיהּ לְכִדְתַנְיָא: ״וְנִרְצָה לוֹ לְכַפֵּר עָלָיו״, רַבִּי שִׁמְעוֹן אוֹמֵר: אֶת שֶׁעָלָיו – חַיָּיב בְּאַחְרָיוּתוֹ, וְאֶת שֶׁאֵינוֹ עָלָיו – אֵינוֹ חַיָּיב בְּאַחְרָיוּתוֹ;

The Gemara asks: **But does this** verse **come to** teach **this** *halakha*? Isn't **it necessary for that which is taught** in a *baraita*: With regard to the verse: **"And it shall be accepted for him to atone for him** [*alav*]**," Rabbi Shimon says:** This indicates that in a case where one consecrated an animal as an offering and it died or was lost, if it was initially incumbent **upon him** [*alav*] to bring an offering, i.e., if he had accepted upon himself a personal obligation to bring an offering, **he bears responsibility for it,**[N] i.e., he is obligated to bring another offering in its stead. **But** if it was **not** incumbent **upon him** [*alav*] to bring an offering, i.e., if he consecrated a specific animal without accepting upon himself any personal obligation, **he does not bear responsibility for it** if it dies or is lost.

וְאָמַר רַב יִצְחָק בַּר אַבְדִּימִי: מַאי טַעְמָא? כֵּיוָן דַּאֲמַר ״עָלַי״ – כְּמַאן דְּטָעוּן לֵיהּ אַכַּתְפֵיהּ דָּמֵי!

And Rav Yitzḥak bar Avdimi[P] **says: What is the reasoning** behind this distinction? **Once** a person **said:** It is incumbent **upon me** to bring an offering, it is considered **as though** the offering is **loaded upon his shoulders.** He does not discharge his obligation until he brings some offering.

רַב אַשִׁי מִ״וְּנִרְצָה לוֹ לְכַפֵּר״ קָאָמַר.

The Gemara answers: **Rav Ashi says** that the *halakha* that it is prohibited to sprinkle the blood for the sake of one other than the owner is derived **from** the phrase **"And it shall be accepted for him,"** not from the term "for him," on which the *baraita* is based.

אַשְׁכְּחַן זְבִיחָה וּזְרִיקָה, קַבָּלָה מְנָלַן?

The Gemara asks: **We found** a source for the *halakha* that **slaughter and the sprinkling**[N] of the blood must be performed for the sake of the owner. **From where do we** derive that the **collection** of the blood must also be performed for the sake of the owner?

וְכִי תֵּימָא לֵילַף מִזְּבִיחָה וּזְרִיקָה – מָה לִזְבִיחָה וּזְרִיקָה שֶׁכֵּן עֲבוֹדָה שֶׁחַיָּיבִין עָלֶיהָ בַּחוּץ!

And if you would say: Let us derive from slaughter and sprinkling that collection must also be performed for the sake of the owner, this derivation can be refuted: **What** is unique **about slaughter and sprinkling?** They are unique **in that** each is **a rite for which one is liable** to be punished with death at the hand of Heaven if he performs it **outside** the Temple.

אֶלָּא אָמַר רַב אַשִׁי: אָתְיָא מֵאֵיל נָזִיר, דִּכְתִיב: ״וְאֶת הָאַיִל יַעֲשֶׂה זֶבַח שְׁלָמִים״ – שֶׁתְּהֵא עֲשִׂיָּיתוֹ לְשֵׁם שְׁלָמִים; וְאִם אֵינוֹ עִנְיָן לְשִׁינּוּי קוֹדֶשׁ, דְּנָפְקָא לֵיהּ מֵהָתָם – תְּנֵהוּ עִנְיָן לְשִׁינּוּי בְּעָלִים.

Rather, Rav Ashi says that the *halakha* that the collection of the blood must also be performed for the sake of the owner **is derived from** the case of **a nazirite's ram.**[B] **As it is written: "And he shall offer the ram for a sacrifice** [*zevaḥ*] **of peace offerings** unto the Lord" (Numbers 6:17), indicating **that its offering should be** performed **for the sake of a peace offering. And if** the verse **is not** necessary for the **matter of deviation** from the type of **offering, as we derived that from there,** i.e., the verses cited earlier (4a), **apply it** to the **matter of deviation** with regard to the **owner.** It is thereby derived that its sacrificial rites must be performed for the sake of its owner.

אֲמַר לֵיהּ רַב אַחָא בַּר אַבָּא לְרָבָא, אֵימָא: ״יַעֲשֶׂה״ – כְּלָל, ״זֶבַח״ – פְּרָט, כְּלָל וּפְרָט – אֵין בַּכְּלָל אֶלָּא מַה שֶּׁבַּפְּרָט, זְבִיחָה אִין, מִידֵּי אַחֲרִינָא לָא!

Rav Aḥa bar Abba said to Rava, in objection to this derivation: Say that the term: **"Shall offer," is a generalization** and: **"A sacrifice** [*zevaḥ*]**," is a detail.** According to the principles of biblical hermeneutics, where there is a **generalization and a detail,**[B] **the generalization includes only that which is** specified **in the detail.** Accordingly, **slaughter** [*zeviḥa*], **yes,** must be performed for the sake of its owner; but **no other** rite must be performed for the sake of its owner in order for the offering to be fit.

NOTES

If it was incumbent upon him [*alav*] he bears responsibility for it – אֶת שֶׁעָלָיו חַיָּיב בְּאַחְרָיוּתוֹ: In other words, the exegetic interpretation of the verse: "And it shall be accepted for him to atone for him [*alav*]," is that in a case of *alav*, i.e., a personal obligation to bring an offering, the fulfillment of his obligation is accepted only once the offering can atone, i.e., once it is sacrificed. By contrast, gift offerings are accepted once they are consecrated (see Commentary of the Ra'avad on *Torat Kohanim* and Rabbeinu Hillel on *Torat Kohanim*).

We found a source for slaughter and sprinkling – אַשְׁכְּחַן זְבִיחָה וּזְרִיקָה: The source for slaughter is the verse "and the meat of the sacrifice of his thanksgiving peace offering," as explained earlier (4a). The source for sprinkling is the verse "And it shall be accepted for him to atone for him."

BACKGROUND

Nazirite's ram – אֵיל נָזִיר: The nazirite's ram is a peace offering included among the sacrifices brought by the nazirite on the day he completes his period as a nazirite. The nazirite's ram differs in certain respects from other peace offerings: A special portion, the cooked foreleg, is given to the priest. Also, the offering may be eaten only on the day it was sacrificed and the following night (see Numbers 6:14–21).

A generalization and a detail – כְּלָל וּפְרָט: When a generalization in the Torah is followed by its detail or details, it is assumed that the generalization refers only to what was specified in the details. For example, the Torah states that burnt offerings may be brought "from animals, from the herd, and from the flock" (Leviticus 1:2). "Animals," a generalization, includes cattle and animals from the flock, but since these were specified separately, after the generalization, it is derived that only cattle and animals from the flock may be sacrificed as burnt offerings, not other animals. The generalization was included in such cases to prevent one from drawing inferences by analogy from the details cited to include additional details.

PERSONALITIES

Rav Yitzḥak bar Avdimi – רַב יִצְחָק בַּר אַבְדִּימִי: Rav Yitzḥak bar Avdimi was a third-generation Babylonian *amora*, not to be confused with Rabbi Yitzḥak bar Avdimi, who was a first-generation *amora* in Eretz Yisrael and was a disciple of Rabbi Yehuda HaNasi. He was famous for his many interpretations of biblical verses, and Rava, his disciple and a fourth-generation Babylonian *amora*, would say that any verse that is not explained by Rav Yitzḥak bar Avdimi is left unexplained. Rav Yitzḥak bar Avdimi brought evidence of, and allusions to, many statements of the Sages in the Bible itself.

אִי כְּתִיב ״יַעֲשֶׂה שְׁלָמִים זֶבַח״ – כִּדְקָאָמְרַתְּ, הַשְׁתָּא דִּכְתִיב: ״יַעֲשֶׂה זֶבַח שְׁלָמִים״ – הֲוָה לֵיהּ כְּלָל שֶׁאֵינוֹ מָלֵא, וְכׇל כְּלָל שֶׁאֵינוֹ מָלֵא – אֵין דָּנִין אוֹתוֹ בִּכְלָל וּפְרָט.

The Gemara answers: **If** it had been **written: Shall offer** the ram **for peace offerings as a sacrifice** [*zevaḥ*], it would be **as you say.** The clause: Shall offer the ram for peace offerings, would be considered a generalization, and: Sacrifice [*zevaḥ*], would be a detail. **Now that it is written: "Shall offer** the ram **for a sacrifice** [*zevaḥ*] **of peace offerings,"** the term "shall offer" is **an incomplete generalization,**[N] as the term "for a sacrifice" interrupts between "shall offer" and "peace offerings." **And one cannot derive** a *halakha* from **any incomplete generalization by** employing the principle of **a generalization and a detail.**

רָבִינָא אָמַר: לְעוֹלָם דָּנִין, וְ״לַה׳״ – חָזַר וְכָלַל.

Ravina says there is a different answer: **Actually, one can derive** a *halakha* from verses with incomplete generalizations using the principle of a generalization and a detail. **And** the reason this *halakha* applies to other rites besides slaughter is that by adding the term **"unto the Lord,"** it **then makes a generalization.**[N]

אֲמַר לֵיהּ רַב אַחָא מִדִּיפְתִּי לְרָבִינָא: וְהָא לָא דָּמֵי כְּלָלָא קַמָּא לִכְלָלָא בַּתְרָא, כְּלָלָא קַמָּא מְרַבֶּה עֲשִׂיּוֹת וְתוּ לָא, כְּלָלָא בַּתְרָא – כֹּל לַה׳, וַאֲפִילּוּ שְׁפִיכַת שִׁירַיִים וְהַקְטָרַת אֵימוּרִין! הָא תָּנָא דְּבֵי רַבִּי יִשְׁמָעֵאל בִּכְלָלֵי וּפְרָטֵי דָּרֵישׁ כִּי הַאי גַּוְונָא.

Before Ravina concluded his interpretation, **Rav Aḥa of Difti said to Ravina: But the former generalization is dissimilar to the latter generalization. The former generalization includes** only the essential sacrificial **actions and nothing more,** whereas **the latter generalization** includes **any** sacrificial duty **unto the Lord, and even pouring** the **remains** of the blood on the base of the altar **and burning** the **sacrificial portions** of the offering on the altar. Ravina responded: **The school of Rabbi Yishmael taught generalizations and details in cases like this.**

כְּלָל וּפְרָט וּכְלָל – אִי אַתָּה דָּן אֶלָּא כְּעֵין הַפְּרָט, מָה הַפְּרָט מְפוֹרָשׁ – עֲבוֹדָה וּבָעֵינַן לִשְׁמָן, אַף כֹּל – עֲבוֹדָה וּבָעֵינַן לִשְׁמָן.

Ravina concludes his explanation: Since the term: "Unto the Lord," is another generalization, the verse is formulated as **a generalization, and a detail, and a generalization,** and **you may deduce** that the verse is referring **only** to items **similar to the detail. Just as the** mentioned **detail,** slaughter, is **defined** as an essential **rite and we require** that it be performed **for the sake of** the owner, **so too, we require** that **every** essential **rite** be performed **for the sake of** the owner.

אִי מָה הַפְּרָט מְפוֹרָשׁ – עֲבוֹדָה וְחַיָּיבִין עָלֶיהָ בַּחוּץ, אַף כׇּל עֲבוֹדָה וְחַיָּיבִין עָלֶיהָ בַּחוּץ; שְׁחִיטָה וּזְרִיקָה אִין, קַבָּלָה וְהוֹלָכָה לָא!

The Gemara asks: **If** the verse is referring only to actions similar to the detail, not all of the essential rites are necessarily included. Perhaps it should be derived that **just as the** mentioned **detail,** slaughter, is **defined** as an essential **rite, and one is liable** to be punished with death at the hand of Heaven **for** performing **it outside** the Temple, **so too, any** essential **rite** for which **one is liable** to be punished with death at the hand of Heaven **for** performing **it outside** the Temple is included in the verse. Accordingly, **slaughter and sprinkling** the blood **are** included, but **collection** of the blood **and conveying** it are **not.**

אִי נָמֵי, מָה הַפְּרָט מְפוֹרָשׁ – דָּבָר הַטָּעוּן צָפוֹן וְיֶשְׁנוֹ בְּחַטָּאוֹת הַפְּנִימִיּוֹת, אַף כׇּל הַטָּעוּן צָפוֹן וְיֶשְׁנוֹ בְּחַטָּאוֹת הַפְּנִימִיּוֹת; שְׁחִיטָה וְקַבָּלָה אִין, זְרִיקָה לָא!

Alternatively, it could be derived that **just as the** item mentioned in the **detail** is clearly **defined** as **an action that requires** performance in the **north** of the Temple courtyard **and is** performed **in the** sacrifice of **inner sin offerings, so too, any** rite **that requires** performance in the **north and is** performed **in the** sacrifice of **inner sin offerings** is included in the *halakha*. Accordingly, **slaughter and collection are** included;[N] **sprinkling** the blood **is not.**

אִיכָּא לְמֵימַר הָכִי, וְאִיכָּא לְמֵימַר הָכִי, שְׁקוּלִין הֵן וְיָבֹאוּ שְׁנֵיהֶן. לִישָּׁנָא אַחֲרִינָא: וְחָדָא חֲדָא תֵּיקוּ בְּמִילְּתָא.

The Gemara answers: Both possibilities are equally valid; **this** derivation **can be said and that** derivation **can be said.** Either collection or sprinkling might be included in the *halakha*. Consequently, **they are equal, and** therefore **both are included.** Or according to **another version** of the Gemara's answer, they are equal, **and** therefore **each one,** i.e., both collection and sprinkling, **shall stand in** its **status.**

אִיבָּעֵית אֵימָא: זְרִיקָה מִדְּרַב אָשֵׁי נָפְקָא.

The Gemara provides an alternative answer: **If you wish, say** instead that **sprinkling is derived from** the verse **that Rav Ashi** cited: "And it shall be accepted for him to atone for him." Therefore, when the verse states: "And he shall offer the ram for a sacrifice of peace offerings unto the Lord," indicating the inclusion of rites similar to slaughter, it is apparently referring not to sprinkling but to collection.

NOTES

An incomplete generalization – **כְּלָל שֶׁאֵינוֹ מָלֵא**: The principle of a generalization and a detail applies only if the generalization is itself a complete statement, and the detail narrows it to a specific case. In this case, the term "shall offer," is not a complete statement, as it does not clarify which type of offering shall be offered. Since the detail interrupts the generalization before it is fully introduced, the principle of a generalization and a detail does not apply.

It then makes a generalization – **חָזַר וְכָלַל**: The principle of a generalization, and a detail, and a generalization, is an extension of the principle of a generalization and a detail. Whereas in the case of a generalization and a detail, the generalization includes only that which is spelled out in the detail, in a case where there is another generalization after the detail, the detail is interpreted as an example of a more general category, which includes matters that are similar to the detail.

Slaughter and collection are included – **שְׁחִיטָה וְקַבָּלָה אִין**: If collection of the blood is included, conveying the blood is also included, as the *halakhot* of the latter are always juxtaposed with those of the former, as derived from a verse (see 4a).

אַשְׁכַּחַן אֵיל נָזִיר, שְׁאָר שְׁלָמִים מְנָלַן?

The Gemara asks: **We found** a source for the *halakha* that **a nazirite's ram** must be sacrificed for the sake of its owner. **From where do we** derive that this *halakha* applies with regard to **other peace offerings** as well?

וְכִי תֵּימָא נֵילַף מֵאֵיל נָזִיר, מַה לְּאֵיל נָזִיר שֶׁכֵּן יֵשׁ עִמָּהֶן דָּמִים אֲחֵרִים!

And if you would say: Let us derive from a nazirite's ram that all peace offerings must be sacrificed for the sake of their owners, this derivation can be refuted: **What** is unique **about a nazirite's ram?** It is unique **in that there is other blood,** i.e., there are other offerings, a sin offering and a burnt offering, that must be brought by a nazirite together **with** his ram.

אִם כֵּן, נִכְתּוֹב "שְׁלָמָיו", מַאי "שְׁלָמִים"? לְרַבּוֹת כָּל שְׁלָמִים.

The Gemara answers: **If that is so,** if this *halakha* is unique to a nazirite's ram, **let the verse write: His peace offerings** [*shelamav*]. **What** is indicated by writing **"peace offerings** [*shelamim*]**"?** It is written **to include all** types of **peace offerings.**

אַשְׁכַּחַן שְׁלָמִים, שְׁאָר כָּל קֳדָשִׁים מְנָלַן?

The Gemara asks: **We found** a source for the *halakha* that **a peace offering** must be sacrificed for its own sake and for the sake of its owner. **From where do we** derive that this *halakha* applies with regard to **all other offerings?**

וְכִי תֵּימָא, נֵילַף מִשְּׁלָמִים – מַה לִּשְׁלָמִים שֶׁכֵּן טְעוּנִין סְמִיכָה וּנְסָכִים וּתְנוּפַת חָזֶה וָשׁוֹק!

And if you would say: Let us derive from a peace offering that all offerings must be sacrificed with these intentions, this derivation can be refuted: **What** is unique **about a peace offering?** It is unique **in that it requires placing hands** on the head of the offering,[B] **and** it is accompanied by **libations,**[B] **and** it requires the **waving**[B] **of** the **breast and** the right **hind leg** by the priest and owner together. No other offering possesses all three of these requirements.

אֶלָּא, אָמַר קְרָא: "זֹאת הַתּוֹרָה לָעֹלָה וְלַמִּנְחָה וְלַחַטָּאת וְלָאָשָׁם וְלַמִּלּוּאִים וּלְזֶבַח הַשְּׁלָמִים", הִקִּישָׁן הַכָּתוּב לִשְׁלָמִים: מַה שְּׁלָמִים – בֵּין שִׁינּוּי קוֹדֶשׁ בֵּין שִׁינּוּי בְּעָלִים בָּעֵינַן לִשְׁמָהּ, אַף כֹּל – בֵּין שִׁינּוּי קוֹדֶשׁ בֵּין שִׁינּוּי בְּעָלִים בָּעֵינַן לִשְׁמָהּ.

The Gemara answers: **Rather, the verse states: "This is the law of the burnt offering, of the meal offering, and of the sin offering, and of the guilt offering, and of the consecration offering, and of the sacrifice of peace offerings"** (Leviticus 7:37). **The verse juxtaposes** all types of offerings **with peace offerings,** indicating that **just as we require** the sacrifice of **a peace offering** to be performed **for its sake, both** concerning **deviation** from the type of **offering and** concerning **deviation** with regard to the **owner, so too, we require** the sacrifice of **every** type of offering to be performed **for its sake, both** concerning **deviation** from the type of **offering and** concerning **deviation** with regard to the **owner.**

אֵימָא: הֵיכָא דְּשַׁחֵיט לְהוּ שֶׁלֹּא לִשְׁמָהּ לִיפַּסְלוּ!

§ Having established the source for the requirement to sacrifice offerings with the rightful owner and the specific type of offering in mind, the Gemara inquires: Why not **say** that in a case **where** one **slaughtered them not for their sake, they are disqualified?** Why, according to the mishna, do they remain fit?

אָמַר קְרָא: "מוֹצָא שְׂפָתֶיךָ תִּשְׁמֹר וְעָשִׂיתָ כַּאֲשֶׁר נָדַרְתָּ" וגו׳, הַאי נְדָבָה? נֶדֶר הוּא! [אֶלָּא], אִם כְּמָה שֶׁנָּדַרְתָּ עָשִׂיתָ – יְהֵא נֶדֶר, וְאִם לָאו – יְהֵא נְדָבָה.

The Gemara answers: **The verse states: "That which has gone out of your lips you shall observe and do; according to what you have vowed** [*nadarta*] freely [*nedava*] to the Lord your God, that which you have promised with your mouth" (Deuteronomy 23:24). The Gemara interprets the words *nadarta* and *nedava* exegetically: How can the offering mentioned in **this** verse be **a gift** offering [*nedava*]? **It is** already referred to as a **vow** offering [*neder*]. **Rather,** the verse indicates that **if you did what you had vowed** to do, i.e., sacrificed your vow offering properly, **it shall be** a satisfactory **vow** offering; **but if** you did **not** sacrifice it properly, **it shall be** rendered a voluntary **gift** offering. Although it does not satisfy the obligation of your vow, it remains a valid offering.

וְאִיצְטְרִיךְ "מוֹצָא שְׂפָתֶיךָ" וְאִיצְטְרִיךְ "זֹאת הַתּוֹרָה"; דְּאִי כְּתַב רַחֲמָנָא "מוֹצָא", הֲוָה אָמִינָא

And it was necessary for the Torah to include the verse: **"That which has gone out of your lips," and it was necessary** to include the verse: **"This is the law."** As, **had the Merciful One written** in the Torah only the verse: **"That which has gone out** of your lips," **I would say**

BACKGROUND

Placing hands on the head of an offering – סְמִיכָה: All offerings brought to the Temple by an individual, with the exceptions of the firstborn of a kosher animal, a Paschal offering, and an animal tithe, require the person bringing the offering to perform the rite of placing hands. This is accomplished by pressing down with all one's strength both of one's hands between the horns on the head of the animal to be sacrificed, before it is slaughtered. No communal offerings require this rite except the bull brought for an unwitting communal sin and the scapegoat on Yom Kippur. When performing this ritual for a sin offering, a guilt offering, or a voluntary burnt offering, the person bringing the offering also recites a confessional prayer. An offering requiring placing of hands is not invalidated if this ceremony is not performed. Women are not obligated to perform the rite of placing hands. According to some opinions, they may perform a ritual approximating it if they so desire.

Libations – נְסָכִים: Wine sacrificed on the altar is referred to as a libation. Wine libations are brought together with burnt offerings of animals and peace offerings, as well as with the leper's sin offering and guilt offering. Different quantities of wine are required, depending on the animal that is sacrificed: One-fourth of a *hin*, i.e., three *log*, where a *log* is between 300 and 600 ml, accompanies any sheep or goat offerings; one-third of a *hin*, or four *log*, is brought in conjunction with a ram; and half a *hin*, or six *log*, is brought with a bullock. Libations of wine can also be brought as independent, voluntary offerings. The wine is brought to the top of the altar where it is poured into a receptacle. From there it flows through a spigot onto the altar and through a hole in the top of the structure.

Waving – תְּנוּפָה: A waving action is performed with peace offerings, the thanks offering, and the nazirite's ram. Following the slaughter of the animal and the sprinkling of its blood on the altar, the animal carcass is skinned; its fats, kidneys, and tail are removed, and the breast and hind leg are separated. These parts are grasped by the individual bringing the offering, and the officiating priest puts his hands beneath those of the offering's owner. Together they wave the sacrificial parts in the four directions of the compass, then up and down. If a thanks offering is being brought, four bread loaves of different types are placed above the pile of animal parts before the waving commences. In two instances, a live animal is waved before it is slaughtered: The *Shavuot* lambs and the leper's guilt offering are both waved by the priest as an initial step in sacrificing these offerings. Apart from these animal offerings, there are several meal offerings that are waved as well. The *omer* meal offering is brought on the sixteenth of Nisan and waved by the priest. The meal offering of a *sota* is waved by the woman suspected of adultery. Following the nazariteship term of a man or a woman, the hind leg of the ram brought as a peace offering is waved by the nazirite, along with a wafer [*rakik*] and a loaf of bread. First fruits brought to the Temple by the farmer are also waved by him and the priest together.

לָא יָדַע בְּמַאי – כְּתַב רַחֲמָנָא: ״זֹאת הַתּוֹרָה״, וְאִי כָּתַב רַחֲמָנָא ״זֹאת הַתּוֹרָה״, הֲוָה אָמִינָא לִיפַּסְלוּ – כְּתַב רַחֲמָנָא: ״מוֹצָא שְׂפָתֶיךָ״.

that we **do not know what** requirement does not disqualify the offering if not fulfilled. Therefore, **the Merciful One writes** the verse: **This is the law,** juxtaposing all offerings with a peace offering, which must be performed for its own sake. **And if the Merciful One had written** only the verse: **This is the law, I would say** that offerings sacrificed not for their sake **should be disqualified.** Therefore, **the Merciful One writes** the verse: **That which is gone out of your lips,** teaching that they are accepted, though they do not satisfy their owners' obligations.

רָמֵי רֵישׁ לָקִישׁ עַל מְעוֹהִי בֵּי מִדְרָשָׁא וּמַקְשֵׁי: אִם כְּשֵׁרִים הֵם – יְרַצּוּ, וְאִם אֵין מְרַצִּין – לָמָּה בָּאִין?

§ **Reish Lakish raised a difficulty while lying on his stomach in the study hall:**[B] **If** offerings that were sacrificed for the sake of the wrong type of offering or someone other than the owner **are fit, let them propitiate** God,[N] i.e., let them satisfy the obligation of their owners; **and if they do not propitiate** God, **why are they brought** as offerings at all?

אָמַר לוֹ רַבִּי (אֱלִיעֶזֶר) [אֶלְעָזָר]: מָצִינוּ בַּבָּאִין לְאַחַר מִיתָה שֶׁהֵן כְּשֵׁרִין וְאֵין מְרַצִּין, דִּתְנַן: הָאִשָּׁה שֶׁהֵבִיאָה חַטָּאתָהּ וּמֵתָה – יָבִיאוּ יוֹרְשִׁין עוֹלָתָהּ, עוֹלָתָהּ וּמֵתָה – לֹא יָבִיאוּ יוֹרְשִׁין חַטָּאתָהּ.

Rabbi Elazar said to him: We have found a precedent for this **in** the case of offerings **brought after** the **death** of their owners, **as they are fit, but they do not propitiate** God, as they do not have owners requiring atonement. This is **as we learned** in a mishna (*Kinnim* 2:5): With regard to **a woman** after childbirth **who brought her sin offering**[B] **and** then **died,**[H] the **heirs shall bring her burnt offering.** If she brought **her burnt offering and** then **died,** the **heirs shall not bring her sin offering.**[N] Evidently, a burnt offering is sacrificed even if it does not satisfy its owner's obligation.

אֲמַר לֵיהּ: מוֹדֵינָא לָךְ בְּעוֹלָה, דְּאָתְיָא לְאַחַר מִיתָה, אָשָׁם דְּלָא אָתֵי לְאַחַר מִיתָה מְנָלַן?

Reish Lakish **said to him: I concede to you with regard to a burnt offering**[N] that it is sacrificed even if it does not satisfy its owner's obligation, **since it is brought** even **after** its owner's **death** in the case of the woman who died after bringing her sin offering. But **from where do we** derive that **a guilt offering, which** is brought for atonement and therefore **not brought after** its owner's **death,**[N] is brought even in a case where it was slaughtered not for its sake and therefore will not satisfy its owner's obligation?

אֲמַר לֵיהּ: הֲרֵי מַחְלוֹקְתְּךָ בְּצִידּוֹ, רַבִּי אֱלִיעֶזֶר אוֹמֵר: אַף הָאָשָׁם.

Rabbi Elazar **said to him: Your** side of the **dispute** is written in the mishna **next to** the opinion that you find difficult.[N] Following the opinion in the mishna (2a) that only a sin offering and a Paschal offering are disqualified if they are slaughtered for the sake of the wrong type of offering, the mishna teaches that **Rabbi Eliezer says: The guilt offering too** is unfit when sacrificed not for its sake.

אָמַר: זֶהוּ שֶׁאוֹמְרִין עָלָיו אָדָם גָּדוֹל הוּא? קָאָמִינָא אֲנָא מִשְׁנָה שְׁלֵימָה, וְאַתְּ אָמְרַתְּ לִי רַבִּי אֱלִיעֶזֶר!

Reish Lakish **said** in reference to Rabbi Elazar: **Is he** the one **of whom people say** that **he is a great man?**[N] **I am referring to the entire mishna,** specifically to the opinion of the first *tanna*, which is the accepted *halakha*. **And you say to me** that the opinion of **Rabbi Eliezer** resolves my difficulty?

BACKGROUND

Reish Lakish raised a difficulty while lying on his stomach in the study hall – רָמֵי רֵישׁ לָקִישׁ עַל מְעוֹהִי בֵּי מִדְרָשָׁא וּמַקְשֵׁי: From the stories told about Reish Lakish throughout the Talmud, it is clear that he was an individual with a serious demeanor. It is recorded that once, when his daughter suggested that he sleep more comfortably, he responded: My belly serves as my pillow (*Gittin* 47a). It is likely that he took seriously the rabbinic dictum from tractate *Avot* (6:4): Such is the path of Torah: Eat bread dipped in salt, drink water in measure, sleep on the floor, live a life of travail, and toil in Torah. Therefore, Reish Lakish may have chosen to sleep in the study hall rather than on a comfortable bed, and while he was resting he raised a question that was the basis for rabbinic discussion for generations.

The sin offering of a woman who gave birth – חַטַּאת יוֹלֶדֶת: The Torah describes various *halakhot* that apply to a woman after giving birth. She is ritually impure for seven days if she gave birth to a boy, and for fourteen days if she gave birth to a girl. Later, after immersion in a ritual bath, she is ritually pure for the next thirty-three or sixty-six days, respectively, even if she experiences uterine bleeding. Nevertheless, during this period of forty days for a boy or eighty days for a girl, it is prohibited for her to enter the Temple or partake of the meat of offerings. After the fortieth or eightieth day, she brings a purification offering to the Temple. This offering consists of a lamb in its first year, which is brought as a burnt offering; and a pigeon or dove, which is brought as a sin offering. If she cannot afford the cost of a lamb for the burnt offering, she can bring two doves or two pigeons, one as a burnt offering and the other as a sin offering. She may then enter the Temple and partake of sacrificial foods (see Leviticus 12:1–8).

HALAKHA

A woman after childbirth who brought her sin offering and died – הָאִשָּׁה שֶׁהֵבִיאָה חַטָּאתָהּ וּמֵתָה: If a woman after childbirth brought her sin offering and then died, her heirs bring her burnt offering even if she did not designate a specific animal for this purpose, as her property is liened to this obligation (Rambam *Sefer Korbanot*, *Hilkhot Meḥusrei Kappara* 1:13).

NOTES

If they are fit let them propitiate God – אִם כְּשֵׁרִים הֵם יְרַצּוּ: The early commentaries explain that Reish Lakish's difficulty is parallel to the Gemara's earlier question: Say that in a case where one slaughtered them not for their sake, they are disqualified. He was initially unaware of the answer that the Gemara gave, and, as the Gemara will soon state, he subsequently gave that answer himself (see Rashi).

The heirs shall not bring her sin offering – לֹא יָבִיאוּ יוֹרְשִׁין חַטָּאתָהּ: Even if the woman had already consecrated an animal to bring as her sin offering the heirs may not bring it, as a sin offering whose owners have died is left to die (Rashi).

I concede to you with regard to a burnt offering, etc. – מוֹדֵינָא לָךְ בְּעוֹלָה וכו׳: Reish Lakish concedes not only that a burnt offering is fit even if it does not satisfy its owner's obligation, but that this *halakha* applies to any offering that is brought voluntarily (Rashi).

A guilt offering, which is not brought after its owner's death – אָשָׁם דְּלָא אָתֵי לְאַחַר מִיתָה: A guilt offering that was disqualified or whose owner died is left to graze until it becomes unfit, after which it is sold, and a burnt offering is acquired with the proceeds of the sale. A disqualified sin offering is left to die.

Your dispute is next to the opinion you find difficult – הֲרֵי מַחְלוֹקְתְּךָ בְּצִידּוֹ: Although this expression usually means: An opinion that disputes yours is written next to it, here it means: Your side of the dispute is written next to the opinion that you find difficult.

Great man [*adam gadol*] – אָדָם גָּדוֹל: *Adam gadol* in Hebrew, or *gavra rabba* in Aramaic, was an honorific reserved for a personality who is distinguished in the areas of Torah, ethical behavior, and excellent character traits.

This title was often used when a Sage would praise a colleague to others, sometimes citing the reason he is worthy of this description and other times not. There were instances when a Sage requested to be introduced as a great man to the residents of a certain locale to which he was traveling and where he was not familiar to them.

If one was introduced to a certain group as a great man, and his discourse or behavior then disappointed that group, they would sometimes ask: Is he the one of whom people say that he is a great man? Or: Is this the one whom you are praising?

אֶלָּא אֲמַר רֵישׁ לָקִישׁ, אֶפְתַּח אֲנָא פִּתְחָא לְנַפְשַׁאי: ״מוֹצָא שְׂפָתֶיךָ״ וגו׳, הַאי נְדָבָה? נֶדֶר הוּא כו׳, כִּדְלְעֵיל.

Rather, Reish Lakish said: I will introduce a solution[N] **to my own** difficulty. He then recited the exegesis stated above: The verse states: **"That which has gone out of your lips** you shall observe and do, **etc."** How can **this** be referring to **a gift** offering? **It is** already referred to as **a vow** offering; **and so on, as stated above.** In other words, it is derived from a verse that although the offering does not satisfy the obligation of its owner, it is fit to be sacrificed as a gift offering.

יָתֵיב רַבִּי זֵירָא וְרַבִּי יִצְחָק בַּר אַבָּא וְיָתֵיב אַבַּיֵּי גַּבַּיְיהוּ, וְיָתְבִי וְקָאָמְרִי: קַשְׁיָא לֵיהּ לְרֵישׁ לָקִישׁ אָשָׁם דְּלָא אָתֵי לְאַחַר מִיתָה, וְנָסֵיב לָהּ תַּלְמוּדָא ״מוֹצָא שְׂפָתֶיךָ״; אֵימָא: הַבָּא בְּנֵדֶר וּבִנְדָבָה לֵיְיתֵי וְלָא לִירַצֵּי, אָשָׁם לָא לֵיְיתֵי כְּלָל!

Rabbi Zeira and Rabbi Yitzḥak bar Abba were sitting,[N] **and Abaye was sitting with them. And they were sitting and saying:** The case of a **guilt offering was difficult for Reish Lakish,** as a guilt offering is **not brought after** the owner's **death, and he adduced the derivation** from the verse: **"That which has gone out of your lips,"** as a solution **to it.** This resolution is difficult: Why not **say** that only an offering **that is brought for a vow or a gift is brought** even in a case where it **does not propitiate,** since the verse mentions a vow and a gift; but **a guilt offering,** which is not brought voluntarily, **should not be brought at all** if it was slaughtered for the sake of the wrong type of offering. How does the verse resolve Reish Lakish's difficulty?

אֲמַר לְהוּ אַבַּיֵּי, רֵישׁ לָקִישׁ מֵהָכָא פָּתַח: ״וְשָׁחַט אוֹתָהּ לְחַטָּאת״, ״אוֹתָהּ״ – לִשְׁמָהּ כְּשֵׁרָה, שֶׁלֹּא לִשְׁמָהּ פְּסוּלָה, הָא שְׁאָר קָדָשִׁים שֶׁלֹּא לִשְׁמָן כְּשֵׁרִין; יָכוֹל יְרַצּוּ? תַּלְמוּד לוֹמַר: ״מוֹצָא שְׂפָתֶיךָ״.

Abaye said to them: Although **Reish Lakish** cited that verse, he actually **introduced** the solution to his difficulty **from here: "And slaughter it for a sin offering"** (Leviticus 4:33). It is derived from the word **"it"** in this verse that if a sin offering is slaughtered **for its sake,** it is **fit;** if it is slaughtered **not for its sake,** it is **unfit. Consequently, other offerings** slaughtered **not for their sake,** including a guilt offering, **are fit.** And since one **might** have thought that once they are fit, they also **propitiate** God, **the verse states: "That which has gone out of your lips,"** from which it is derived that such an offering does not satisfy its owner's obligation.

וְאֵימָא: הַבָּא בְּנֵדֶר וּנְדָבָה לֵיְיתֵי וְלָא לִירַצֵּי, אָשָׁם (נַמִי) אַרְצוּיֵי נַמִי לִירַצֵּי!

Rabbi Zeira and Rabbi Yitzḥak bar Abba asked him: **But** since the phrase in the verse "that which has gone out of your lips" is referring to offerings **brought for a vow or a gift,** why not **say** that only these offerings **do not propitiate** God even though **one must bring** them if slaughtered for the sake of the wrong offering, but **a guilt offering** slaughtered for the sake of the wrong offering **propitiates** God **as well?**

אֲמַר אַבַּיֵּי: אָשָׁם דְּמִירַצֵּי לָא מָצֵית אָמְרַתְּ, קַל וָחוֹמֶר מֵעוֹלָה: וּמָה עוֹלָה שֶׁאֵינָהּ מְכַפֶּרֶת אֵינָהּ מְרַצָּה, אָשָׁם שֶׁמְּכַפֵּר – אֵינוֹ דִּין שֶׁאֵינוֹ מְרַצֶּה?

Abaye said in response: **You cannot say that a guilt offering** that was slaughtered for the sake of the wrong offering **propitiates** God, due to an ***a fortiori*** inference **from a burnt offering: Just as a burnt offering, which does not atone**[N] for a sin as it is brought as a vow or gift offering, still **does not propitiate** God if it was slaughtered for the sake of the wrong offering, so too, with regard to **a guilt offering, which atones** for a sin and is therefore treated more stringently, **is it not logical that it does not propitiate** God?

NOTES

I will introduce a solution [*pitḥa*] – אֶפְתַּח אֲנָא פִּתְחָא: The Aramaic word *pitḥa*, or *petaḥ* in Hebrew, which literally means opening, is also a term in the *halakhot* of vows, meaning an extenuation. If one takes a vow and subsequently regrets it, he can go to a Sage, and the Sage will try to find an extenuation enabling the dissolution of the vow. For example, the Sage may conclude that when the individual took the vow, he did not take certain consequences of the vow into account. Sometimes, the one who took the vow suggests an extenuation himself. This is the context of the idiomatic statement of Reish Lakish.

Rabbi Zeira and Rabbi Yitzḥak bar Abba were sitting, etc. – יָתֵיב רַבִּי זֵירָא וְרַבִּי יִצְחָק בַּר אַבָּא וכו׳: The description of two or three Sages who were sitting and another Sage was sitting with them appears several times in the Talmud, and describes a setting where two or three prominent Sages were discussing a certain topic, perhaps in an official forum or court, and another Sage was present as their disciple or guest. Rav Sheshet, for example, is described in 5b as having sat with Rav Huna and Rav Naḥman, the prominent disciples of Rav, whereas in the subsequent story, Rav Ada bar Mattana, a younger Sage, is described as having sat with Rav Sheshet and Rav Naḥman. Abaye is described in several places as having sat with various combinations of Sages. Several Sages are mentioned as having sat with the panel of Rabbi Abbahu, Rabbi Ḥanina bar Pappi, and Rabbi Yitzḥak Nappaḥa.

A burnt offering, which does not atone – עוֹלָה שֶׁאֵינָהּ מְכַפֶּרֶת: Although the Sages taught that a burnt offering atones for not fulfilling a positive mitzva, one is not obligated by Torah law to bring a burnt offering to achieve atonement; it is considered a voluntary gift offering. A guilt offering, by contrast, is brought only by one who is obligated to bring one, usually to atone for a sin, e.g., robbery, misuse of consecrated property, or engaging in intercourse with a designated maidservant. Only a minority of guilt offerings are brought as part of a purification process.

מַה לְעוֹלָה שֶׁכֵּן כָּלִיל!

The Gemara challenges the inference: **What** is unique **about a burnt offering?** It is unique **in that it is** totally **consumed** on the altar. By contrast, the meat of a guilt offering is eaten by priests. Since in some ways a burnt offering is treated more stringently than a guilt offering, no *a fortiori* inference can be derived from one to the other.

שְׁלָמִים יוֹכִיחוּ.

The Gemara answers: **A peace offering can prove** that this aspect is not relevant, since it is not totally consumed on the altar, and still if slaughtered for the sake of the wrong offering it does not satisfy its owner's obligation. The inference can therefore be drawn from a peace offering rather than a burnt offering.

מַה לִשְׁלָמִים שֶׁכֵּן טְעוּנִין נְסָכִין וּתְנוּפַת חָזֶה וָשׁוֹק!

The Gemara rejects this as well: **What** is unique **about a peace offering?** It is unique **in that it requires libations, and the waving of** the **breast and** the right **hind leg.**

עוֹלָה תּוֹכִיחַ. וְחָזַר הַדִּין, לֹא רְאִי זֶה כִּרְאִי זֶה וְלֹא רְאִי זֶה כִּרְאִי זֶה, הַצַּד הַשָּׁוֶה שֶׁבָּהֶן שֶׁהֵן קֳדָשִׁים, וּשְׁחָטָן שֶׁלֹּא לִשְׁמָן – כְּשֵׁירִין וְאֵין מְרַצִּין, אַף אֲנִי אָבִיא אָשָׁם שֶׁהוּא קוֹדֶשׁ, וּשְׁחָטוֹ שֶׁלֹּא לִשְׁמוֹ – כָּשֵׁר וְאֵינוֹ מְרַצֶּה.

The Gemara answers: If so, **a burnt offering can prove**[N] the point, since these stringencies do not apply to it. **And the inference has reverted** to its starting point. At this stage the *halakha* is derived from a combination of the two sources: **The aspect of this** case, a burnt offering, **is not like the aspect of that** case,[B] the peace offering. **And the aspect of that** case **is not like the aspect of this** case. **Their common element is that they are offerings and** if one **slaughtered them not for their sake, they are fit but they do not propitiate. So too, I shall include a guilt offering** in this *halakha*, **as it is an offering, and** therefore if one **slaughtered it not for its sake,** it is **fit but it does not propitiate.**

מַה לְהַצַּד הַשָּׁוֶה שֶׁבָּהֶן, שֶׁכֵּן יֶשְׁנוֹ בְּצִיבּוּר!

The Gemara rejects this as well: **What** is unique **about their common element,** i.e., the common element of a burnt offering and a peace offering? These offerings are unique **in that they are** brought **by** the **public.** There are communal burnt offerings and peace offerings, but there are no communal guilt offerings.

תּוֹדָה תּוֹכִיחַ.

The Gemara responds: **A thanks offering can prove** the point, since there are no communal thanks offerings, and still a thanks offering slaughtered not for its sake does not satisfy its owner's obligation.

Perek **I**
Daf **5** Amud **b**

מַה לְתוֹדָה שֶׁכֵּן טְעוּנָה לֶחֶם!

The Gemara rejects this as well: **What** is unique **about a thanks offering?** It is unique **in that it requires** a meal offering of forty loaves of **bread.**

עוֹלָה וּשְׁלָמִים יוֹכִיחוּ. וְחָזַר הַדִּין, לֹא רְאִי זֶה כִּרְאִי זֶה, וְלֹא רְאִי זֶה כִּרְאִי זֶה, הַצַּד הַשָּׁוֶה שֶׁבָּהֶן – שֶׁהֵן קֳדָשִׁים, וּשְׁחָטָן שֶׁלֹּא לִשְׁמָן כָּשֵׁר וְאֵינוֹ מְרַצֶּה, אַף אֲנִי אָבִיא אָשָׁם שֶׁהוּא קֹדֶשׁ, וּשְׁחָטוֹ שֶׁלֹּא לִשְׁמוֹ – כָּשֵׁר וְאֵינוֹ מְרַצֶּה.

The Gemara answers: If so, **a burnt offering and a peace offering can prove** the point, as loaves are not brought with them. **And the inference has reverted** to its starting point. The *halakha* is derived from a combination of the two sources: **The aspect of this** case, a burnt offering and a peace offering, **is not like the aspect of that** case, a thanks offering, **and the aspect of that** case **is not like the aspect of this** case. **Their common element is that they are offerings, and** if one **slaughtered them not for their sake,** they are **fit but do not propitiate** God. **So too, I shall include a guilt offering** in this *halakha*, **as it is an offering, and** therefore if one **slaughtered it not for its sake,** it is **fit but does not propitiate** God.

מַה לְהַצַּד הַשָּׁוֶה שֶׁבָּהֶן שֶׁהֵן בָּאִין בְּנֶדֶר וּבִנְדָבָה!

The Gemara rejects this as well: **What** is unique **about the common element of** a thanks offering, a burnt offering, and a peace offering? It is unique in **that** these offerings **are brought** either **as a vow** offering **or as a gift** offering, whereas a guilt offering is brought only to fulfill an obligation.

NOTES

A burnt offering can prove – עוֹלָה תּוֹכִיחַ: Although the requirement of libations applies to most burnt offerings as well, it does not apply to a bird burnt offering.

BACKGROUND

The aspect of this case is not like the aspect of that case – לֹא רְאִי זֶה כִּרְאִי זֶה: This expression is used in halakhic midrash in formulating an analogy where a principle is derived on the basis of two *halakhot* mentioned in two different verses. First, the midrash articulates the difference between the two *halakhot*. Then it mentions the characteristic common to both. Any other case with that common element will then be subject to the same ruling.

אֶלָּא אָמַר רָבָא: "זֹאת הַתּוֹרָה" וגו' – הִקִּישׁוֹ הַכָּתוּב לִשְׁלָמִים, מָה שְׁלָמִים שֶׁהֵן קָדָשִׁים, וּשְׁחָטָן שֶׁלֹּא לִשְׁמָן – כְּשֵׁרִים וְאֵין מְרַצִּין, אַף אֲנִי אָבִיא אָשָׁם שֶׁהוּא קוֹדֶשׁ כו'.

Rather, Rava says: The verse: "This is the law of the burnt offering, of the meal offering, and of the sin offering, and of the guilt offering, and of the consecration offering, and of the sacrifice of peace offerings" (Leviticus 7:37), **juxtaposes** a guilt offering **with a peace offering,** indicating that **just as peace offerings are offerings and** if one **slaughtered them not for their sake, they are fit but do not propitiate, so too, I shall include a guilt offering, as it is an offering,** and therefore if it is slaughtered not for its sake, although it is fit, it does not satisfy the obligation of its owner.

מַאי חָזֵית דְּאַקַּשְׁתְּ לִשְׁלָמִים, אַקֵּישׁ לְחַטָּאת!

The Gemara asks: **What did you see,** i.e., why do you think it is reasonable, **that you compared** a guilt offering **to a peace offering?** Why not **compare** it **to a sin offering,** which is disqualified in such a case?

הָא מִיעֵט רַחֲמָנָא: "אוֹתָהּ".

The Gemara answers: **The Merciful One excluded** all other offerings from the *halakha* concerning a sin offering in this matter, as derived from the verse: "And slaughter **it** for a sin offering" (Leviticus 4:33).

(סִימָן: הנ"ש בש"ר).

The Gemara provides **a mnemonic** for the *amora'im* who participated in the two following discussions: ***Heh, nun, shin; beit, shin, reish.***

יָתֵיב רַב הוּנָא וְרַב נַחְמָן, וְיָתֵיב רַב שֵׁשֶׁת גַּבַּיְיהוּ, וְיָתְבִי וְקָאָמְרִי: קַשְׁיָא לֵיהּ לְרֵישׁ לָקִישׁ אָשָׁם דְּלָא אָתֵי לְאַחַר מִיתָה – לֵימָא לֵיהּ רַבִּי אֶלְעָזָר: אָשָׁם נַמִּי אָתֵי לְאַחַר מִיתָה!

Rav Huna and Rav Naḥman were sitting, and Rav Sheshet was sitting with them. And they were sitting and saying: Reish Lakish raised his **difficulty** with regard to **a guilt offering, since it is not brought after** its owner's **death. Let Rabbi Elazar say to him** that **a guilt offering is also** essentially **brought after** its owner's **death,** since it is sold once it develops a blemish, and the proceeds are used to buy a burnt offering.

אֲמַר לְהוּ רַב שֵׁשֶׁת: אָשָׁם לְמַאי קָרֵיב – לְמוֹתָרוֹ, חַטָּאת נַמִּי מִיקְרַב קָרְבָה מוֹתָרָהּ!

Rav Sheshet said to them: This claim can be refuted: **What** element **of a guilt offering is sacrificed** after its owner's death? Only **its remainder,** i.e., the money from its sale that is used to purchase an animal to be sacrificed. And if so, it is no different from **a sin offering, the remainder of which is also sacrificed,**[N] and a sin offering itself is entirely disqualified if slaughtered not for its sake.

חַטָּאת, אַף עַל גַּב דְּקָרְבָה מוֹתָרָהּ – מִיעֵט רַחֲמָנָא "הוּא".

Rav Huna and Rav Naḥman explained: **A sin offering** that was slaughtered not for its sake is disqualified **even though its remainder is sacrificed,** because **the Merciful One** specifically **excludes** a sin offering from being a fit offering if sacrificed not for its own sake, as derived from the verse: "And he shall lay his hand upon the head of the goat, and slaughter it in the place where they slaughter the burnt offering before the Lord; **it** is a sin offering" (Leviticus 4:24). The redundant phrase "it is a sin offering" teaches that a sin offering is disqualified if sacrificed not for its own sake.

אָשָׁם נַמִּי, כְּתִיב בֵּיהּ "הוּא"!

The Gemara asks: Isn't it **also written with regard to a guilt offering:** "And the priest shall make them smoke upon the altar for an offering made by fire unto the Lord; **it** is a guilt offering" (Leviticus 7:5)? Why is a guilt offering not disqualified when it is slaughtered not for its sake?

NOTES

A sin offering the remainder of which is also sacrificed – חַטָּאת נַמִּי מִיקְרַב קָרְבָה מוֹתָרָהּ: In principle, a sin offering whose owner is deceased must be left to die. Nevertheless, in a case where one designated two animals for an obligatory sin offering, with the intent that if one of them dies or is disqualified he will sacrifice the other, as soon as the first is sacrificed properly the second is rendered the remainder of a sin offering. It is therefore left to graze until it becomes unfit for sacrifice, and it is then sold, with the proceeds used to buy a burnt offering, which can be sacrificed even after the owner's death. Consequently, the status of the sin offering's remainder differs from that of the offering proper, since this second animal was consecrated initially as a sin offering only in the event that the other animal dies or is disqualified.

הַהוּא לְאַחַר הַקְטָרַת אֵימוּרִים הוּא דִּכְתִיב; כִּדְתַנְיָא: אֲבָל אָשָׁם לֹא נֶאֱמַר בּוֹ "הוּא" אֶלָּא לְאַחַר הַקְטָרַת אֵימוּרִין, וְהוּא עַצְמוֹ אִם לֹא הִקְטִירוּ אֵימוּרִין – כָּשֵׁר.

The Gemara answers: **That** verse **is written** not with regard to the main sacrificial rites, but with regard to the stage **after the burning of the** offering's **sacrificial portions** on the altar, **as it is taught** in a *baraita*: **But with regard to a guilt offering,** the term **"It** is a guilt offering" **is stated only after the burning of the sacrificial portions.**[B] **And** since the guilt offering **itself** is **fit** even **if the sacrificial portions were not burned** at all, it is certainly fit if they were burned not for the sake of a guilt offering.

וְאֶלָּא "הוּא" לָמָּה לִי? לְכִדְרַב הוּנָא אָמַר רַב, דְּאָמַר רַב הוּנָא אָמַר רַב: אָשָׁם שֶׁנִּיתַּק לִרְעִיָּה וּשְׁחָטוֹ סְתָם – כָּשֵׁר;

The Gemara asks: **But** if so, **why do I** need the term **"It** is a guilt offering" to be stated at all? The Gemara answers: It is necessary **for that which Rav Huna** says that **Rav says. As Rav Huna says** that **Rav says:** With regard to a **guilt offering** whose owner died or whose transgression was otherwise atoned for, and **that was** therefore **consigned** by the court **to grazing**[H] until it develops a blemish so that it can be sold and the proceeds used to purchase a burnt offering, if, before it developed a blemish, someone **slaughtered it without specification** of its purpose, it is **fit** as a burnt offering.

נִיתַּק – אִין, לֹא נִיתַּק – לָא, מַאי טַעְמָא? אָמַר קְרָא: "הוּא" – בַּהֲוָיָיתוֹ יְהֵא.

The Gemara infers: If **it was consigned** to grazing, **yes,** it is fit as a burnt offering if slaughtered. By inference, if **it was not consigned** to grazing, it is **not** fit.[N] **What is the reason** for this? **The verse states:** "**It** is a guilt offering," indicating that **it shall** remain **as it is,** i.e., as a guilt offering, unless it is consigned by the court to fulfill another purpose.

יָתְבִי רַב נַחְמָן וְרַב שֵׁשֶׁת, וְיָתֵיב רַב אַדָּא בַּר מַתָּנָה גַּבַּיְיהוּ, וְיָתְבִי וְקָאָמְרִי: הָא דְּקָאָמַר רַבִּי אֶלְעָזָר: מָצִינוּ בַּבָּאִין לְאַחַר מִיתָה שֶׁהֵן כְּשֵׁרִין וְאֵין מְרַצִּין – לֵימָא לֵיהּ רֵישׁ לָקִישׁ: הָנְהוּ נַמִי לַיְיתוּ וְלִירַצּוּ!

§ **Rav Naḥman and Rav Sheshet were sitting, and Rav Adda bar Mattana was sitting with them. And they were sitting and saying:** In response to **that which Rabbi Elazar said** to Reish Lakish: **We have found** a precedent for this situation **in the case of** offerings that **are brought after** their owners' **death, as they are fit but they do not propitiate** God, **let Reish Lakish say to him: These** offerings **should also be brought and propitiate** God with regard to the heirs. Why did Reish Lakish not challenge Rabbi Elazar's assumption?

אֲמַר לְהֶן רַב אַדָּא בַּר מַתָּנָה: יוֹלֶדֶת, אִם הִיא יָלְדָה, בָּנֶיהָ מִי יָלְדוּ?

Rav Adda bar Mattana said to them: How can the offering of a **woman after childbirth** propitiate God after her death? **If she gave birth, did her children give birth?**

מַתְקִיף לָהּ רַב אַסִי: וּמַאן לֵימָא לָן דְּאִי אִיכָּא כַּמָּה עֲשֵׂה גַּבָּהּ לָא מִיתְכַּפְּרָא? וְכֵיוָן דְּכִי אִיכָּא כַּמָּה עֲשֵׂה גַּבָּהּ מִיכַּפְּרָא – יוֹרְשֶׁיהָ נַמִי מִיכַּפַּר.

Rav Asi objects to this reasoning: **And who shall say to us that if** a woman **has several** violations of **positive mitzvot**[N] for which to atone, **she does not atone** by means of the burnt offering she brings after childbirth for her purification? Clearly, such offerings can atone for transgressions other than those for which they are brought. **And since, when she has several** violations of **positive mitzvot she atones** by means of the offering, **so too,** if she dies, **her heirs atone** by this offering for their own violations of positive mitzvot.

לְמֵימְרָא דְּקַנְיָא לְהוּ? וְהָאָמַר רַבִּי יוֹחָנָן: הִנִּיחַ מִנְחָה לִשְׁנֵי בָנָיו וּמֵת – קְרֵיבָה, וְאֵין בּוֹ שׁוּתָּפוּת; וְאִי סָלְקָא דַּעְתָּךְ קַנְיָא לְהוּ, "נֶפֶשׁ" אָמַר רַחֲמָנָא.

The Gemara asks: **Is this to say that** the offering is **acquired by** the heirs, and this is why it atones for their transgressions? **But doesn't Rabbi Yoḥanan say** that if one **left his two sons a meal offering**[H] **and** then **died,** the offering must be **sacrificed, and it does not have** the status of a meal offering brought in **partnership?**[H] **And if it enters your mind** that the offering is **acquired by** the heirs, it should be considered a meal offering brought in partnership, which is unfit, as **the Merciful One states** in the Torah: "And when **one** brings a meal offering unto the Lord" (Leviticus 2:1). The word "one" teaches that two people cannot bring a meal offering together. Clearly, the heirs do not inherit the offering, and if so, it should not atone for their transgressions.

BACKGROUND

Sacrificial portions – אֵימוּרִין: This term refers to the portions of sin offerings, guilt offerings, and peace offerings that are consumed on the altar, e.g., the fats, the kidneys, and the tail. Occasionally, the limbs of the burnt offering are also included in this expression.

NOTES

If it was not consigned to grazing it is not fit – לֹא נִיתַּק לָא: It appears from the Gemara that the consignation of a guilt offering to grazing is effective by Torah law. *Tosafot* and other early commentaries prove from other sources that this is a rabbinic decree; by Torah law, a guilt offering that is no longer fit to be sacrificed as such is automatically rendered a burnt offering. It is unnecessary for the court to consign it to grazing. Therefore, *Tosafot* emend the text, omitting the sentence: If it was consigned to grazing, yes, it is fit; but if it was not consigned to grazing, it is not fit. Accordingly, the term "it is a guilt offering" is cited as support for the *halakha* that if the animal was slaughtered, it is fit as a burnt offering. Since its designation is for it to be sold for the purchase of a burnt offering once it develops a blemish, it shall be as it will be, i.e., it is considered a burnt offering already.

If a woman has several violations of positive mitzvot, etc. – אִי אִיכָּא כַּמָּה עֲשֵׂה וכו׳: A burnt offering atones for transgressions for which there is no prescribed offering, e.g., failure to fulfill positive mitzvot, which are more common than standard transgressions. One burnt offering can atone for several violations of positive mitzvot. As Rashi explains (6a): Since the verse states of even one voluntary burnt offering: "It shall be accepted for him to atone for him" (Leviticus 1:4), clearly one burnt offering atones for all such transgressions. Accordingly, even the burnt offering of a woman after childbirth, which is brought as part of her purification process, atones for any positive mitzvot that she may have violated.

HALAKHA

A guilt offering that was consigned to grazing – אָשָׁם שֶׁנִּיתַּק לִרְעִיָּה: With regard to a guilt offering whose owner died or was atoned for, and was therefore consigned to grazing, if it was slaughtered for the sake of a burnt offering it is fit. The Sages decreed that it is not sacrificed for the sake of a burnt offering *ab initio*, lest one sacrifice a guilt offering for the sake of a burnt offering before its owner was atoned for (Rambam *Sefer Avoda, Hilkhot Pesulei HaMukdashin* 4:15).

If one left his two sons a meal offering – הִנִּיחַ מִנְחָה לִשְׁנֵי בָנָיו: If one died leaving a meal offering, his sons bring it (Rambam *Sefer Avoda, Hilkhot Ma'aseh HaKorbanot* 14:3).

And it does not have the status of a meal offering brought in partnership – וְאֵין בּוֹ שׁוּתָּפוּת: A meal offering is not brought by partners (Rambam *Sefer Avoda, Hilkhot Ma'aseh HaKorbanot* 14:2).

HALAKHA

If one left his two sons an animal offering – הִנִּיחַ בְּהֵמָה לִשְׁנֵי בָנָיו: If one who died left his two sons an animal that he consecrated to be an offering, his sons bring it to be sacrificed in the Temple. They cannot substitute another animal for it, as they are considered partners, and partners cannot effect substitution (Rambam *Sefer Korbanot, Hilkhot Temura* 1:5).

וְלָא קָנְיָא לְהוּ? וְהָאָמַר רַבִּי יוֹחָנָן: הִנִּיחַ בְּהֵמָה לִשְׁנֵי בָנָיו וּמֵת – קְרֵיבָה, וְאֵין מְמִירִין בָּהּ; אִי אָמְרַתְּ בִּשְׁלָמָא קָנְיָא לְהוּ – הַיְינוּ דְּאֵין מְמִירִין בָּהּ, דַּהֲוָיָא לְהוּ כְּשׁוּתָּפִין,

The Gemara asks: **And is the** offering **not acquired by them? But doesn't Rabbi Yoḥanan** himself **say** that if one **left his two sons an animal** offering[H] **and** then **died,** the offering must be **sacrificed, and they cannot effect substitution** of another animal **for it?**[B] Even if they declare another animal to be a substitute for it, that animal is not consecrated. **Granted, if you say** that the offering is **acquired by them, this is** the reason **that they cannot effect substitution** of another animal **for it:** It is **because they are like partners,**

BACKGROUND

They cannot effect substitution of another animal for it – אֵין מְמִירִין בָּהּ: The possibility of substitution is mentioned in the Torah (Leviticus 27:10), and a tractate of the Talmud, *Temura*, focuses on these *halakhot*. The main features of the concept of substitution are as follows: The Torah prohibits substituting any offering, whether whole or blemished, for another animal. One who does so violates a prohibition and is flogged as a punishment. Nevertheless, despite the fact that this act of substitution is prohibited, if it is performed, the second animal does acquire a measure of sanctity, while the first animal also remains sacred. All animals can be used as substitutes, whether they are whole or blemished, and the animal designated as a substitute can never be worked or redeemed. The fate of the substitute varies with the particular type of offering. In some instances, e.g., that of a substitute for a sin offering, the animal is left to die. In other cases, such as that of a guilt offering, the animal is put out to graze until it becomes blemished. Lastly, some substitutes, e.g., that of a peace offering, are consecrated for the altar along with the original animal.

Perek **I**
Daf **6** Amud **a**

NOTES

And partners cannot effect substitution – וְשׁוּתָּפִין לָא מָצוּ מְמִירִין: Rashi explains that this is derived from the consistent singular form of the verbs in the verse discussing substitution (see Leviticus 27:10). Therefore, two people who are partners in an offering are not able to effect substitution.

HALAKHA

And partners cannot effect substitution – וְשׁוּתָּפִין לָא מָצוּ מְמִירִין: If an individual substituted another animal for his offering, the substitute is consecrated. Although it is prohibited for partners and the general public to substitute another animal for their offering, if one substitutes another animal for a communal offering, or if an offering is owned by partners and one of them substitutes another animal for it, although he receives lashes for his transgression, the substitute does not become consecrated (Rambam *Sefer Korbanot, Hilkhot Temura* 1:1).

To include the heir – לְרַבּוֹת אֶת הַיּוֹרֵשׁ: One who inherited an offering is able to substitute another animal for it (Rambam *Sefer Korbanot, Hilkhot Temura* 1:5).

A man will redeem, serves to include the heir – גָּאֹל יִגְאַל לְרַבּוֹת אֶת הַיּוֹרֵשׁ: One who redeems his tithe must add one-fifth of its value to the funds, whether the tithe was separated from his own produce or from his inheritance (Rambam *Sefer Zera'im, Hilkhot Ma'aser Sheni* 5:1).

וְשׁוּתָּפִין לָא מָצוּ מְמִירִין. אֶלָּא אִי אָמְרַתְּ לָא קָנְיָא לְהוּ, אָמוֹרֵי נָמֵי לֵימְרוּ!

and partners cannot effect substitution[NH] of other animals for their offering. **But if you say** that it is **not acquired by them,** and the animal is the property solely of the deceased father, **let them also effect substitution** on his behalf, as heirs are able to affect substitution for their deceased parents' offerings.

שָׁאנֵי הָתָם, דְּאָמַר קְרָא: ״אִם הָמֵר יָמִיר״ – לְרַבּוֹת אֶת הַיּוֹרֵשׁ, אֶחָד מֵמִיר וְאֵין שְׁנַיִם מְמִירִין.

The Gemara answers: **There it is different,** as although **the verse states: "If he shall at all change** [*hamer yamir*] animal for animal" (Leviticus 27:10), the superfluous word *hamer* serving **to include the heir**[H] as one who is able to effect substitution, nevertheless the subject's singular form teaches that only **one** heir **can effect substitution, but two** heirs **cannot effect substitution.**

מַתְקִיף לַהּ רַב יַעֲקֹב מִנְּהַר פְּקוֹד: אֶלָּא מֵעַתָּה, גַּבֵּי מַעֲשֵׂר דִּכְתִיב: ״וְאִם גָּאֹל יִגְאַל״ – לְרַבּוֹת אֶת הַיּוֹרֵשׁ, הָכִי נָמֵי אֶחָד גּוֹאֵל וְאֵין שְׁנַיִם גּוֹאֲלִין!

Rav Ya'akov of Nehar Pekod objects to this derivation: **If that is so,** one should say the same **with regard to** the redemption of the second **tithe,**[B] **as it is written: "And if** a man **will redeem** [*gaol yigal*] any of his tithe, he shall add to it the fifth part thereof" (Leviticus 27:31), with the superfluous word *gaol* serving **to include the heir**[H] as one who must add the one-fifth. **So too,** it should be derived from the verb's singular form that if **one** heir **redeems** the tithe, he must add one-fifth of its value, **but** if **two** heirs **redeem** it, **they do not** need to add one-fifth. In fact, the *halakha* is that partners must also add one-fifth.

שָׁאנֵי מַעֲשֵׂר, דְּגַבֵּי אֲבוּהוֹן נָמֵי אִיתֵיהּ בְּשׁוּתָּפוּת.

The Gemara answers: Redemption of the **tithe is different,** as the **father had** the ability to redeem the tithe **even in partnership** with another when alive. Therefore, the heirs can do so as well. By contrast, substitution of an offering cannot be effected by partners.

אֲמַר לֵיהּ רַב אַסִּי לְרַב אָשֵׁי: וּמִינַּהּ, אִי אָמְרַתְּ בִּשְׁלָמָא קָנְיָא לְהוּ – הַיְינוּ דְּחַד מִיהָא מֵימַר. אֶלָּא אִי אָמְרַתְּ לָא קָנְיָא לְהוּ, הֵיכִי מֵימַר?

Rav Asi said to Rav Ashi: But from this *halakha* **itself,** that two heirs cannot effect substitution of an offering, it can be proven that they acquire the offering of the deceased. **Granted, if you say** it is **acquired by them, this is** the reason **that one** heir, **in any event, can effect substitution** of another animal for the offering. **But if you say** it is **not acquired by them, how can** even one heir **effect substitution?**

BACKGROUND

Redemption of the second tithe – פִּדְיוֹן מַעֲשֵׂר: The second tithe is one-tenth of the produce that remains after *teruma* has been given to the priests and the first tithe has been given to the Levites. The second tithe is separated during the first, second, fourth, and fifth years of the Sabbatical cycle. After the second tithe is set aside, it is brought to Jerusalem to be consumed there by its owner. If the journey to Jerusalem is too long, making it difficult to carry all the second-tithe produce there, or if the produce became ritually impure, it could be redeemed for an equivalent sum of money. If the owner redeems his own produce he has to add one-fifth of its value. This redemption money is brought to Jerusalem where it can be spent only on food.

וְהָאָמַר רַבִּי אַבָּהוּ אָמַר רַבִּי יוֹחָנָן: הַמַּקְדִּישׁ מוֹסִיף חוֹמֶשׁ, וּמִתְכַּפֵּר עוֹשֶׂה תְּמוּרָה, וְהַתּוֹרֵם מִשֶּׁלּוֹ עַל שֶׁל חֲבֵירוֹ טוֹבַת הֲנָאָה שֶׁלּוֹ!

But doesn't Rabbi Abbahu say that **Rabbi Yoḥanan says:** If one **consecrates** his own animal to atone for someone else and he then redeems it, he **adds one-fifth**[H] of its value, as he would for any other offering he owned, but if the one for whom it atones redeems it, he need not add one-fifth, since he is not the owner. Nevertheless, only the **one for whom** the offering **atones can render** another animal **a substitute**[H] for it, as in this respect only he is considered its owner. Rabbi Yoḥanan's statement concludes: **And** if **one separates *teruma***[B] **from his** own produce **to** exempt the produce **of another**[H] from the obligation to have teruma separated from it, **the benefit of discretion is his.**[N] Only the one who separated the *teruma* is entitled to determine which priest receives it. Since an heir is able to effect substitution, apparently the offering atones for his transgression. This supports the claim that the heir acquires the offering.

מִקִּיבְעָא לָא מְכַפְּרָא, מִקּוּפְיָא מְכַפְּרָא.

Rav Ashi responds: The offering **does not atone** for the transgressions of the heirs **by** its **essence,** as it was not consecrated for their atonement, and they do not acquire it. Therefore, two heirs of a meal offering can bring it, as explained above. Yet, it **does atone** for them **incidentally** [*mikkufeya*].[NL] Therefore, an heir can effect substitution of another animal for it.

אִיבַּעְיָא לְהוּ: כִּיפְּרוּ עַל מַה שֶּׁבָּאוּ אוֹ לֹא כִּיפְּרוּ?

§ With regard to the *halakha* that offerings slaughtered not for their sake are fit to be sacrificed but do not satisfy the obligations of their owners, **a dilemma was raised before** the Sages: After these offerings are sacrificed, **did they atone for** the sins for **which they came,**[N] **or did they not atone** for them?

אֲמַר רַב שֵׁשֶׁת בְּרֵיהּ דְּרַב אִידִי: מִסְתַּבְּרָא דְּלֹא כִּיפְּרוּ, דְּאִי סָלְקָא דַּעְתָּךְ כִּיפְּרוּ – שֵׁנִי לָמָּה הוּא בָּא?

Rav Sheshet, son of Rav Idi, said: It stands to reason that they did not atone, as, if it enters your mind that **they did atone, for what** purpose **is the second** offering **brought?**[N] Why is the owner required to bring another offering if the first atoned for his sin?

וְאֶלָּא מַאי, לֹא כִּיפְּרוּ? לָמָּה הוּא קָרֵב?

The Gemara challenges this reasoning: **Rather, what** is the alternative? That **they did not atone?** If so, **for what** purpose **is** the first offering **sacrificed?**

אֲמַר רַב אַשִׁי: רַב שֵׁישָׁא בְּרֵיהּ דְּרַב אִידִי הָכִי קָא קַשְׁיָא לֵיהּ: אִי אָמְרַתְּ בִּשְׁלָמָא לֹא כִּיפְּרוּ – שֶׁלֹּא לִשְׁמוֹ מִכֹּחַ לִשְׁמוֹ קָאָתֵי, וְשֵׁנִי לָמָּה הוּא בָּא – לְכַפֵּר; אֶלָּא אִי אָמְרַתְּ כִּיפְּרוּ, שֵׁנִי לָמָּה הוּא בָּא?

Rav Ashi said: This is what is **difficult for Rav Sheisha,** i.e., Rav Sheshet, **son of Rav Idi: Granted, if you say** that such an offering **did not atone,** it **is brought** even when slaughtered **not for its sake on the strength of** its prior consecration **for its sake. And** in that case, **for what** purpose **is the second** offering **brought?** It is brought **to atone** for the sin. **But if you say** that offerings that were slaughtered not for their sake **atoned** for the sin, **for what** purpose **is the second** offering **brought?**

NOTES

The benefit of discretion is his – טוֹבַת הֲנָאָה שֶׁלּוֹ: Although one who separates *teruma* may not receive payment for it from a priest, he still enjoys the benefit of discretion. Included in this is that he is entitled to determine which priest receives the *teruma* and that he may even receive payment from a third party to give it to a specific priest.

It does atone incidentally – מִקּוּפְיָא מְכַפְּרָא: Incidental atonement applies in a case where the offering is brought by someone other than the one obligated to bring it or seeking atonement. In a case where heirs bring the offering of the deceased, they do not have full ownership of it since it was not consecrated for their sake, and it therefore does not achieve atonement for them. Consequently, two heirs can bring a meal offering, even though a meal offering is not brought in partnership. By contrast, heirs do have a certain degree of ownership of the offering, as they are the ones obligated to bring it. They also have certain ownership rights, e.g., to partake of the meat if applicable. They therefore achieve incidental atonement, and can effect substitution, as the ability to effect substitution belongs not to the one who consecrated the offering but to the one for whom it atones.

Did they atone for the sins for which they came – כִּיפְּרוּ עַל מַה שֶּׁבָּאוּ: Why does it matter whether or not the offering atones for the sin, if the owner is in any event obligated to bring another offering? Rashi explains that if it atones for the sin, the owner does not need to be concerned about incurring retribution for the sin before he brings another offering.

For what purpose is the second offering brought – שֵׁנִי לָמָּה הוּא בָּא: Some commentaries explain that this dilemma relates specifically to a guilt offering, which is brought only for atonement. With regard to a burnt offering or a peace offering, the answer to Rav Sheshet's question is obvious, as those offerings can be brought as a gift, regardless of sin (*Tosefot Tukh*; see *Tosafot*). *Keren Ora* concludes that in the case of a guilt offering, the first offering evidently does not fully atone for the sin, as that would preclude the obligation to bring a second offering, since a guilt offering cannot be brought as a gift. Rather, the dilemma pertains to burnt offerings and peace offerings.

HALAKHA

If one consecrates he adds one-fifth – הַמַּקְדִּישׁ מוֹסִיף חוֹמֶשׁ: If an animal consecrated for sacrifice on the altar develops a blemish, the one who consecrated it adds one-fifth when he redeems it. If another person redeems it, even if the offering was designated to atone for him, he does not add one-fifth (Rambam *Sefer Hafla'a*, *Hilkhot Arakhin* 7:4).

The one for whom the offering atones can render another a substitute – וּמִתְכַּפֵּר עוֹשֶׂה תְּמוּרָה: If one consecrated an animal to atone for someone else, the beneficiary has the power of effecting substitution, not the one who consecrated the animal (Rambam *Sefer Korbanot*, *Hilkhot Temura* 1:4).

If one separates *teruma* from his produce to exempt the produce of another – הַתּוֹרֵם מִשֶּׁלּוֹ עַל שֶׁל חֲבֵירוֹ: With regard to *teruma*, it is permitted for one to separate produce from his own crops on behalf of someone else's yield, thereby exempting the beneficiary from further separation of *teruma*. The donor retains the benefit of determining who receives the *teruma*, which means he may give it to the priest of his choice (Rambam *Sefer Zera'im*, *Hilkhot Terumot* 4:2).

BACKGROUND

Separates *teruma* – תּוֹרֵם: Whenever the term *teruma* appears without qualification, it refers to *teruma gedola*. The Torah states: "All the best of the oil, and all the best of the wine, and of the grain, the first of them that they will give to the Lord, to you have I given them" (Numbers 18:12).

The Sages interpreted this verse to dictate that, after the first fruits have been set aside, a certain portion of all of one's produce must be set aside for the priests. The Torah does not specify the amount of *teruma* that must be set aside; one can fulfill his obligation even by separating a single kernel of grain from an entire crop. The Sages, however, established a measure: One-fortieth qualifies as a generous gift, one-fiftieth is an average gift, and one-sixtieth represents a miserly gift. One may not set aside the other tithes until he has set aside *teruma*. This mitzva applies only in Eretz Yisrael.

Teruma is considered sacred and may be eaten only by a priest and his household while they are in a state of ritual purity (see Leviticus 22:9–15). To emphasize the significance of that state of purity, the Sages required the priests to wash their hands before partaking of it. This is the source for the practice of washing one's hands prior to a meal. A ritually impure priest or a non-priest who partakes of *teruma* is subject to the penalty of death at the hand of Heaven.

If *teruma* contracts ritual impurity, it may no longer be eaten and must be destroyed. Nevertheless, it remains the property of the priest, and he may derive benefit from its destruction, such as from the heat produced by burning it. Nowadays, *teruma* is not given to the priests because they have no definite proof of their priestly lineage. Nevertheless, the obligation to separate *teruma* still remains, although only a small portion of the produce is separated.

LANGUAGE

Incidentally [*mikkufeya*] – מִקּוּפְיָא: According to Rashi, the word *kufeya* literally means floating, from the root *kuf*, *peh*, *alef*. Figuratively, it refers to an event that occurs incidentally, without intention or designation.

HALAKHA

If one deemed placing hands a non-essential mitzva – אִם עֲשָׂאָה לַסְּמִיכָה שִׁירֵי מִצְוָה: Placing one's hands on the head of the animal is not an essential sacrificial rite. Therefore, if the owner did not perform this rite, the offering is not invalidated, and it still atones for his sins. Nevertheless, the verse ascribes to him blame as though it did not atone for his sins (Rambam *Sefer Avoda, Hilkhot Ma'aseh HaKorbanot* 3:12).

אִיבַּעְיָא לְהוּ: אַעֲשֵׂה דִּלְאַחַר הַפְרָשָׁה מְכַפְּרָא אוֹ לָא מְכַפְּרָא?

§ **A dilemma was raised before** the Sages: When one brings a burnt offering, which atones for violations of positive mitzvot, **does it atone** even **for** a violation of **a positive mitzva that** one committed **after designating** the animal as an offering, **or does it not atone** for such a violation?

מִי אָמְרִינַן: מִידֵי דַּהֲוָה אַחַטָּאת; מָה חַטָּאת, דְּקוֹדֶם הַפְרָשָׁה – אִין, דִּלְאַחַר הַפְרָשָׁה – לָא, אַף הָכָא נָמֵי, דְּקוֹדֶם הַפְרָשָׁה – אִין, לְאַחַר הַפְרָשָׁה – לָא.

The Gemara elaborates: **Do we say** that the *halakha* in this case is **just as it is with regard to a sin offering,** in that **just as a sin offering does** atone for a sin **that** one committed **before designation** of the animal but does **not** atone for a sin **that** one committed **after designation, here too,** a burnt offering **does** atone for violations **that** one committed **before designation** but does **not** atone for those committed **after designation?**

אוֹ דִּלְמָא לָא דָּמְיָא לְחַטָּאת, דְּחַטָּאת עַל כׇּל חֵטְא וְחֵטְא בָּעֵי לְאֵיתוּיֵי חֲדָא חַטָּאת, וְהָכָא כֵּיוָן דְּאִיכָּא כַּמָּה עֲשֵׂה גַּבֵּיהּ מְכַפְּרָא, אַעֲשֵׂה דִּלְאַחַר הַפְרָשָׁה נָמֵי מְכַפְּרָא?

Or, perhaps a burnt offering is **not similar to a sin offering,** as with regard to **a sin offering one must bring one sin offering for each and every sin** he commits. **But here, since** a burnt offering **atones** even for one who **has** committed **several** violations of **positive mitzvot,** one may claim that **it also atones** even **for** the violation of **a positive mitzva that** one committed **after designation** of the animal.

תָּא שְׁמַע: ״וְסָמַךְ...וְנִרְצָה״, וְכִי סְמִיכָה מְכַפֶּרֶת? וַהֲלֹא אֵין כַּפָּרָה אֶלָּא בְּדָם, שֶׁנֶּאֱמַר: ״כִּי הַדָּם הוּא בַּנֶּפֶשׁ יְכַפֵּר״! אֶלָּא מָה תַּלְמוּד לוֹמַר: ״וְסָמַךְ...וְנִרְצָה לְכַפֵּר״? שֶׁאִם עֲשָׂאָה לַסְּמִיכָה שִׁירֵי מִצְוָה, מַעֲלֶה עָלָיו הַכָּתוּב כְּאִילּוּ לֹא כִּיפֵּר וְכִיפֵּר;

The Gemara suggests: **Come** and **hear** proof from a *baraita*: The verse states: **"And he shall place** his hand on the head of the burnt offering, **and it shall be accepted** for him to atone for him" (Leviticus 1:4). **And does placing hands atone** for one's sins? **But isn't atonement** achieved **only by** the sprinkling of **the blood, as it is stated: "For it is the blood that makes atonement by reason of the life"** (Leviticus 17:11)? **Rather, what** is the meaning when **the verse states: "And he shall place…and it shall be accepted** for him **to atone"?** This teaches **that if one deemed** the ritual of **placing hands** to be **a non-essential mitzva**[H] and consequently failed to perform it, **the verse ascribes to him** blame **as though** the offering **did not atone** for his sins; **and** nevertheless, the offering **atoned** for his sins.

מַאי לָאו דְּכִיפֵּר – עֲשֵׂה דְּקוֹדֶם הַפְרָשָׁה, לֹא כִּיפֵּר – אַעֲשֵׂה דִּסְמִיכָה, דַּהֲוָה לֵיהּ עֲשֵׂה דִּלְאַחַר הַפְרָשָׁה?

What, does the final clause of the *baraita* **not** mean **that** the offering **atoned** for the violation of any **positive mitzva that** the owner committed **before designation** of the animal, but **it did not atone for** violation of **the positive mitzva of placing hands** on the head of the offering, **as that constitutes** a violation of **a positive mitzva after designation** of the animal? Apparently, a burnt offering does not atone for the violations committed after the animal's designation.

אָמַר רָבָא: עֲשֵׂה דִּסְמִיכָה קָאָמְרַתְּ? שָׁאנֵי הָתָם, דְּכׇל כַּמָּה דְּלָא שָׁחֵיט בְּעָמוֹד וּסְמוֹךְ קָאֵי; אֵימַת קָא הָוֵי עֲשֵׂה? לְאַחַר שְׁחִיטָה, לְאַחַר שְׁחִיטָה לָא קָא מִיבַּעְיָא לַן.

Rava said in response: **You say** that **the positive mitzva of placing hands** is proof? **There it is different, since as long as he does not slaughter** the offering, **he remains** obligated **to stand and place** his **hands** on its head. He has not yet violated the mitzva. **When does** the violation of this **positive mitzva occur?** It occurs **after** the **slaughter,** at which point fulfillment of the mitzva is no longer possible. And with regard to a violation committed **after** the **slaughter, we do not raise the dilemma;** clearly a burnt offering does not atone for such a violation.

אֲמַר לֵיהּ רַב הוּנָא בַּר יְהוּדָה לְרָבָא, אֵימָא: ״כִּיפֵּר״ – גַּבְרָא,

Rav Huna bar Yehuda said to Rava: Say the *baraita* means that the offering **atoned**[N] for the transgression of **the person,**

NOTES

Say that the offering atoned, etc. – אֵימָא כִּיפֵּר וכו׳: Rav Huna bar Yehuda suggested an interpretation of the *baraita* according to which a burnt offering atones for transgressions that were committed after its designation as well. According to his interpretation, the distinction is not between transgressions that were committed before and after designation, but between different levels of atonement. The owner achieves a basic level of atonement, after which he is not required to bring another offering, even for violating the mitzva of placing his hands on the head of the animal. Despite this, he is not accepted by God as having completely atoned for his transgressions.

לֹא כִּיפֵּר – קַמֵּי שְׁמַיָּא!

but **it did not atone** for him **before Heaven,** i.e., it is not accepted by God as a perfect offering.

מִי לָא תְּנַן: "וְהַנּוֹתָר בַּשֶּׁמֶן אֲשֶׁר עַל כַּף וגו' לְכַפֵּר עָלָיו לִפְנֵי ה'", אִם נָתַן – כִּיפֵּר, וְאִם לֹא נָתַן – לֹא כִּיפֵּר, דִּבְרֵי רַבִּי עֲקִיבָא. רַבִּי יוֹחָנָן [בֶּן נוּרִי] אוֹמֵר: שְׁיָרֵי מִצְוָה הֵן, בֵּין נִיתַּן בֵּין שֶׁלֹּא נִיתַּן – כִּיפֵּר, וּמַעֲלִין עָלָיו כְּאִילּוּ לֹא כִּיפֵּר;

Didn't we learn in a mishna with regard to the purification process of a leper (*Nega'im* 14:10): The verse states: **"And the rest of the oil**[B] **that is in** the priest's **hand** he shall put upon the head of the one that is to be purified, **to make atonement for him before the Lord"** (Leviticus 14:18). This teaches that **if** the priest **placed** the oil on the leper's head, **it atoned** for him, and he is purified, **but if he did not place** the oil on his head,[H] **it did not atone** for him; this is **the statement of Rabbi Akiva. Rabbi Yoḥanan ben Nuri says:** Placement of the oil on the leper's head **is a non-essential mitzva.**[N] Therefore, **whether** the oil **was placed** on his head or **whether it was not placed** on his head, **it atoned** for him, **but** the verse **ascribes** the leper blame **as though it did not atone** for him.

מַאי "כְּאִילּוּ לֹא כִּיפֵּר"? אִילֵימָא דְּמִבָּעֵי לְאֵיתוּיֵי קׇרְבָּן אַחֲרִינָא – הָאָמְרַתְּ: בֵּין נִיתַּן בֵּין לֹא נִיתַּן כִּיפֵּר! אֶלָּא: כִּיפֵּר – גַּבְרָא, לֹא כִּיפֵּר – קַמֵּי שְׁמַיָּא. הָכָא נַמִי, כִּיפֵּר – כו'!

The Gemara comments: **What** is the meaning of the phrase: **As though it did not atone** for him? **If we say that it is necessary** for the leper **to bring another offering** of oil, **didn't you say** that **whether** the oil **was placed** on his head or **whether it was not placed** on his head, **it atoned** for him? **Rather,** the meaning of the statement is as follows: **It atoned** for **the person,** but **did not atone** for him **before Heaven. Here too,** with regard to one who sacrificed an offering without placing hands on its head, the *baraita* apparently means that the offering **atoned** for the owner's transgression, even if it did not atone for him before Heaven.

הָתָם נַמִי: כִּיפֵּר – מַתַּן בְּהוֹנוֹת, לֹא כִּיפֵּר – מַתְּנוֹת הָרֹאשׁ.

The Gemara rejects this suggestion: **There too,** with regard to the purification process of a leper, one can explain that the oil atoned for one matter and did not atone for another: It **atoned;** in other words, the **placement** of oil on the leper's right **thumb and big toe,**[N] which was performed, effected its atonement. But it **did not atone,** i.e., there still needs to be an atonement effected by **placement** of oil on **the** leper's **head,**[N] and another *log* of oil must be brought for the performance of that act.

תָּא שְׁמַע, רַבִּי שִׁמְעוֹן אוֹמֵר: כִּבְשֵׂי עֲצֶרֶת לָמָּה הֵן בָּאִין?

The Gemara returns to the matter of atonement for transgressions committed after the offering's designation. **Come and hear** another proof from a *baraita*: **Rabbi Shimon says:** With regard to the communal peace offering of two **lambs** that accompanies the two loaves on *Shavuot*,[B] **for what** sin **are they brought?**

כִּבְשֵׂי עֲצֶרֶת שְׁלָמִים נִינְהוּ! אֶלָּא: שְׂעִירֵי עֲצֶרֶת לָמָּה הֵן בָּאִין?

The Gemara interrupts the citation of the *baraita*: **The** two **lambs** sacrificed on *Shavuot* are not brought for a sin; **they are peace offerings** brought with the annual public offering of two loaves of new wheat. **Rather,** the *baraita* should be emended as follows: **For what** sin **are the goats** sacrificed on *Shavuot*[N] as a sin offering **brought?**

NOTES

Placement of the oil on the leper's head is a non-essential mitzva – שְׁיָרֵי מִצְוָה הֵן: Since this is the act performed with "the rest of the oil," it is comparable to the act of pouring the remainder of the blood of an offering on the base of the altar, which is a mitzva that is not essential to the sacrificial process.

There too it atoned in the placement of oil on the leper's right thumb and big toe – הָתָם נַמִי כִּיפֵּר מַתַּן בְּהוֹנוֹת: Just as the *baraita* concerning the placement of one's hands on the offering was interpreted to mean that the offering atones for transgressions that were committed until a certain point and does not atone for transgressions committed after that point, so too, this mishna means that the oil atones at an earlier stage of the rite, i.e., that of placing oil on the leper's thumb and toe, but does not atone with regard to the latter stage of placing the oil on his head.

It did not atone by placement of oil on the leper's head – לֹא כִּיפֵּר מַתְּנוֹת הָרֹאשׁ: Rashi explains that according to both opinions, the leper is required to bring another *log* of oil. The difference between them is that according to Rabbi Yoḥanan ben Nuri, oil must be applied only to his head; whereas Rabbi Akiva maintains that it must be applied again to his right thumb and big toe, as the oil that was already applied there is deemed ineffective.

The goats sacrificed on *Shavuot* – שְׂעִירֵי עֲצֶרֶת: It is stated in the portion of the Festivals in Leviticus that one goat must be sacrificed on *Shavuot* as a sin offering (Leviticus 23:19). In the portion of the additional offerings on Festivals recorded in Numbers, one sin offering goat is also mentioned (Numbers 28:30). From the fact that no other offerings mentioned in the portion of the Festivals in Leviticus are mentioned again in Numbers, the Sages derived that these are two separate obligations, and that two goats must be sacrificed on *Shavuot*.

BACKGROUND

The rest of the oil, etc. – הַנּוֹתָר בַּשֶּׁמֶן וכו': The purification process for lepers is detailed in the Torah (Leviticus, chapter 14). This includes the requirement that a priest sprinkle oil that has been sanctified for this purpose in the direction of the Holy of Holies seven times, after which he applies it to the leper's right earlobe, right big toe, and right thumb. The rest of the oil is applied to his head, as described in this verse.

The offering of lambs that accompanies the loaves on *Shavuot* – כִּבְשֵׂי עֲצֶרֶת: The Torah (see Leviticus 23:17–20) requires that two male lambs be sacrificed as communal peace offerings to accompany the two loaves of bread brought in the Temple on *Shavuot*. The loaves and the lambs are waved together in a special ceremony before the altar.

HALAKHA

If he did not place the oil on his head – אִם לֹא נָתַן: The Rambam writes in one place: After the priest cups his hand and fills it with oil, and sprinkles it in the direction of the Holy of Holies, he goes to the leper and applies oil to his right earlobe, thumb, and big toe. He places the remainder of the oil on the head of the leper being purified. If he did not place the remainder on the leper's head, it does not atone for him, in accordance with the opinion of Rabbi Akiva; the *halakha* follows Rabbi Akiva's opinion when he is in dispute with one of his colleagues.

In another place the Rambam writes: If the priest finished applying the oil to the leper's right thumb and big toe, and the *log* of oil then spilled before he managed to place the remainder of the oil in his hand on the head of the leper being purified, it is unnecessary for the leper to bring another *log* of oil; placing the remaining oil on his head is not essential.

Mahari Kurkus resolves the contradiction by distinguishing between a case where the oil did not spill and a case where the oil spilled. In the former case, not placing oil on the leper's head precludes purification; in the latter case, this action is considered unessential. The later commentaries discuss this contradiction extensively (Rambam *Sefer Korbanot*, *Hilkhot Meḥusrei Kappara* 4:2, 5:5).

BACKGROUND

The defiling of the Temple or its sacrificial foods – טוּמְאַת מִקְדָּשׁ וְקָדָשָׁיו: The Torah renders it prohibited for a person who is ritually impure to eat consecrated food (see Leviticus 7:19–20), and prohibits a person from entering the Temple while ritually impure (see Numbers 19:20). If one deliberately commits either of these transgressions, he is liable to be punished with excision from the World-to-Come [*karet*]. If he transgresses these mitzvot unwittingly, he must bring an offering as atonement. The nature of this offering depends on the financial state of the person bringing it.

There is a unique aspect to the unwitting transgression of these mitzvot. To be obligated to bring an offering, a person must have been aware before committing the transgression both of his personal status and of the sanctity of the Temple or of the sacrificial foods involved. He must then have forgotten one of these factors while committing the transgression, and he must remember it afterward. If he was unaware of both factors before committing the transgression, even if he became aware of them afterward, he does not bring an offering.

The sin offerings of the Festivals atone for incidents where one was unaware of one of these factors both before his unwitting transgression and afterward. Other cases are atoned for by the sin offerings brought on Yom Kippur.

Daily offering – תָּמִיד: The daily offering consisted of two lambs, one sacrificed in the morning and one in the afternoon of each day, and it served to open and close the daily sacrificial service in the Temple. No offerings were brought before the morning offering or following the afternoon offering. The one exception was the Paschal offering, which was sacrificed after the daily afternoon offering on Passover eve.

HALAKHA

The court makes a non-verbal stipulation about them – לֵב בֵּית דִּין קָמַתְנֶה עֲלֵיהֶן: In a case where a libation that was brought with a communal animal offering is consecrated by placement in a service vessel, and the animal offering is then disqualified from sacrifice, if there is another animal offering in the Temple at the time, the libation can be sacrificed with it. This is because the court makes a non-verbal stipulation that if a libation is not necessary for the communal offering with which it was brought, it is consecrated for sacrifice with another offering. A libation that is brought with the animal offering of an individual cannot be sacrificed with another offering; rather it is left overnight and thereby disqualified (Rambam *Sefer Avoda*, *Hilkhot Pesulei HaMukdashin* 12:6).

עַל טוּמְאַת מִקְדָּשׁ וְקָדָשָׁיו;

Rabbi Shimon answers: They are brought **for the defiling of** the **Temple,** by entering it while ritually impure, **or** for defiling **its sacrificial foods,**[B] by partaking of them while ritually impure.

נִזְרַק דָּמוֹ שֶׁל רִאשׁוֹן, שֵׁנִי לָמָּה קָרֵב? עַל טוּמְאָה שֶׁאוֹרְעָה בֵּין זֶה לָזֶה. אֱמוֹר מֵעַתָּה: רְאוּיִין הָיוּ יִשְׂרָאֵל לְהַקְרִיב קָרְבְּנוֹתֵיהֶן בְּכָל עֵת וּבְכָל שָׁעָה, אֶלָּא שֶׁחִיסֵּךְ הַכָּתוּב.

Rabbi Shimon continues: Once **the blood of** the **first** goat **is sprinkled** on the altar, thereby atoning for this defilement, **for what** sin is the **second one sacrificed?** It is sacrificed **for** any incident involving **impurity that** may have **occurred between** the sacrifice of **that** first goat **and** the sacrifice of **this** second goat. **Based on this, say** that **the Jewish people should have** had to **sacrifice their offerings at all times and at every moment,** as perhaps they sinned in the interim; **but the verse spared** them of this obligation.

וְהָא הָכָא, דַּעֲשֵׂה דִּלְאַחַר הַפְרָשָׁה, וְקָא מְכַפְּרָא!

The Gemara infers: **And here,** where an incident involving impurity occurred between the sacrifice of the two goats, is a case **where** the **positive mitzva** of distancing ritually impure people from the Temple was violated **after** the **designation** of the offering, as both goats were designated in advance. **And** nevertheless, the second goat **atones** for the violation. Evidently, an offering can atone for transgressions committed after its designation.

אִי דְּאַפְרְשִׁינְהוּ בְּבַת אַחַת – הָכִי נַמִי. הָכָא בְּמַאי עָסְקִינַן – דְּאַפְרְשִׁינְהוּ בָּזֶה אַחַר זֶה.

The Gemara rejects this inference: **If** both goats were **designated simultaneously,** this would **indeed** be evidence to that effect. But **here we are dealing with** a case **where** they were **designated sequentially,** and an incident involving impurity may have occurred between their respective designations.

וְלֵיקוּ וְלֵימָא לֵיהּ לִקְרָא דְּכִי כְּתִיבָא בָּזֶה אַחַר זֶה כְּתִיבָא?!

The Gemara challenges this assertion: **But shall we stand and say about the verse**[N] mandating these two sin offerings **that when it is written, it is written** specifically with regard to a case **where** they are designated **sequentially?**

אֲמַר רַב פַּפָּא: קָרְבְּנוֹת צִבּוּר קָאָמְרַתְּ? שָׁאנֵי קָרְבְּנוֹת צִבּוּר, דְּלֵב בֵּית דִּין קָמַתְנֶה עֲלֵיהֶן, כִּדְרַב יְהוּדָה אָמַר שְׁמוּאֵל, דְּאָמַר רַב יְהוּדָה אָמַר שְׁמוּאֵל: קָרְבְּנוֹת צִבּוּר – סַכִּין מוֹשַׁכְתָּן לְמַה שֶּׁהֵן.

Rav Pappa said the inference can be rejected for a different reason: **Do you say** that evidence can be adduced from **communal offerings? Communal offerings are different, as** the **court makes a non-verbal stipulation**[N] **about them,**[H] in accordance with what **Rav Yehuda** says that **Shmuel says. As Rav Yehuda** says that **Shmuel says:** With regard to **communal offerings,** the slaughtering **knife,** i.e., the act of slaughter, **designates them for what they are.**[N] The court stipulates that the second goat be consecrated as it is sacrificed, and it therefore atones for incidents of impurity that occur beforehand. Individual offerings, by contrast, are all designated in advance.

אֲמַר לֵיהּ רַב יוֹסֵף בְּרֵיהּ דְּרַב שְׁמוּאֵל לְרַב פַּפָּא: וּמִי אִית לֵיהּ לְרַבִּי שִׁמְעוֹן לֵב בֵּית דִּין מַתְנֶה עֲלֵיהֶן? הָאָמַר רַב אִידִי בַּר אָבִין אָמַר רַב עַמְרָם אָמַר רַבִּי יִצְחָק אָמַר רַבִּי יוֹחָנָן: תְּמִידִין שֶׁלֹּא הוּצְרְכוּ לַצִּבּוּר,

Rav Yosef, son of Rav Shmuel, said to Rav Pappa: But does Rabbi Shimon accept the opinion that **the court can make a non-verbal stipulation about** communal offerings? **Doesn't Rav Idi bar Avin say** that **Rav Amram says** that **Rabbi Yitzḥak says** that **Rabbi Yoḥanan says:** With regard to animals designated as **daily offerings**[B] but **which** in the end **were not necessary for** use by **the public,**

NOTES

But shall we stand and say about the verse – וְלֵיקוּ וְלֵימָא לֵיהּ לִקְרָא: Rashi explains that the Torah requires that two sin offering goats be brought every *Shavuot*, and it is implausible that they are required to be designated sequentially every year. Therefore, in the years when the goats are designated simultaneously, one of them is superfluous.

The court makes a non-verbal stipulation – לֵב בֵּית דִּין קָמַתְנֶה: The court decides when and under what conditions animals that are designated for communal offerings are consecrated. Accordingly, the court stipulates that animals that were acquired by the Temple treasury in order to be sacrificed as daily offerings and were eventually not required for that purpose do not have the status of offerings and can be redeemed even while they are unblemished. Furthermore, the court stipulates that the second goat sacrificed on *Shavuot* is consecrated only after the first goat is sacrificed.

The Ritva on *Shevuot* 11a infers from the expression: A non-verbal stipulation, that it is not necessary for the court to state these stipulations explicitly. Rather, it is presumed that the court operates with the intent that any communal consecration should take effect at the appropriate time and under the appropriate conditions.

The slaughtering knife designates them for what they are – סַכִּין מוֹשַׁכְתָּן לְמַה שֶּׁהֵן: The act of slaughter designates the offering for its appropriate purpose, e.g., a daily offering or a communal gift offering, according to the needs of the public, even if the one slaughtering the offering does not have that purpose in mind. Explicit designation is unnecessary.

לְדִבְרֵי רַבִּי שִׁמְעוֹן – אֵין נִפְדִּין תְּמִימִים, לְדִבְרֵי חֲכָמִים – נִפְדִּין תְּמִימִין!

according to the statement of Rabbi Shimon, they may not be redeemed as long as they are **unblemished,**[N] since they retain the status of offerings. But **according to the statement of the Rabbis, they may be redeemed** even when they are **unblemished,**[H] as the court initially stipulates that if they are not needed they will not assume the status of an offering. Apparently Rabbi Shimon does not accept the notion that the court can stipulate that there be a delay in the consecration of communal offerings, and the *baraita* can be adduced as evidence that offerings atone for transgressions committed after their designation as offerings.

וְעוֹד, הָא בְּעָא מִינֵּיהּ רַבִּי יִרְמְיָה מֵרַבִּי זֵירָא: שְׂעִירֵי עֲצֶרֶת שֶׁקִּבֵּל דָּמָן בִּשְׁנֵי כוֹסוֹת, וְנִזְרַק דָּמוֹ שֶׁל רִאשׁוֹן, שֵׁנִי לָמָּה הוּא בָא? עַל טוּמְאָה שֶׁאֵירְעָה בֵּין [זְרִיקָה שֶׁל] זֶה לָזֶה (נִזְרַק דָּמוֹ שֶׁל שֵׁנִי לָמָּה הוּא קְרֵיבִין);

And furthermore, continued Rav Yosef, son of Rav Shmuel, one can otherwise infer from the goats sacrificed on *Shavuot* that an offering can atone for transgressions committed after designation; as **Rabbi Yirmeya asked Rabbi Zeira:** If the **goats** sacrificed on ***Shavuot*** were slaughtered simultaneously and **their blood was collected in two cups, and the blood of** the **first** goat **was sprinkled, for what** sin is the **second** goat **brought?** There was no time in the interim for other transgressions to occur. Rabbi Zeira answered: It atones **for** any incident involving **impurity that occurred between the sprinkling** of the blood **of that** first goat **and** the sprinkling of the blood of **this** second goat.

עַד כָּאן לָא מִיבַּעְיָא לֵיהּ אֶלָּא עֲשֵׂה דִּלְאַחַר שְׁחִיטָה, אֲבָל עֲשֵׂה דִּלְאַחַר הַפְרָשָׁה – לָא קָא מִיבַּעְיָא לֵיהּ!

One can infer: Rabbi Yirmeya **raised the dilemma only** about whether or not an offering atones for the violation of **a positive mitzva** committed **after** its **slaughter** and before the sprinkling of the blood. **But** with regard to the violation of **a positive mitzva that** one committed **after** the **designation** of the offering, before its slaughter, **he did not raise the dilemma.** Apparently, it was obvious to him that the offering atones for such a violation.

דִּלְמָא "אִם תִּמְצֵי לוֹמַר" קָאָמַר.

The Gemara rejects this proof: **Perhaps** Rabbi Yirmeya's dilemma was also with regard to the violations committed after designation. He phrased his question to apply to violations committed after slaughter because **he was saying:** Even **if you say**[N] that an offering atones for violations committed after designation, does it atone for those violations committed after slaughter? It may be that neither issue was clear to him.

NOTES

They may not be redeemed as long as they are unblemished – אֵין נִפְדִּין תְּמִימִים: Generally speaking, animals that were consecrated for sacrifice on the altar cannot be redeemed unless they develop a blemish that renders them unfit for sacrifice. With regard to animals that were consecrated as communal offerings, the Rabbis hold that it is a stipulation of the court that if they are not needed for this purpose, their sanctity adheres only to their monetary value and not to the animals themselves, so that they can be redeemed. Rabbi Shimon does not accept the principle that the court makes stipulations with regard to communal offerings. Therefore, in his opinion, animals that were consecrated as daily offerings and were eventually deemed unnecessary are used for the repletion of the altar, i.e., they are sacrificed at times when no other offering is being sacrificed so that the altar will not be idle (see *Shevuot* 12a). Although the animals were not consecrated initially for this specific purpose, Rabbi Shimon maintains that as long as they are sacrificed as the type of offering for which they were initially consecrated, i.e., as burnt offerings, they may be sacrificed for a different purpose.

He was saying, even if you say – אִם תִּמְצֵי לוֹמַר קָאָמַר: Rashi explains that it was not clear to Rabbi Yirmeya that an offering can atone for a transgression committed after it was designated. Rather, he merely raised a dilemma based on that premise. Rashi continues that although Rabbi Zeira's answer clearly indicates that he maintains that an offering can atone for a transgression committed after it was designated, perhaps the *halakha* is not in accordance with his opinion. *Tosafot* assert that Rabbi Zeira's opinion on the matter is not obvious either; he may have merely reasoned that if an offering can atone for a transgression committed after it was designated, it can atone for a transgression committed after it was slaughtered as well, without expressing his opinion with regard to the premise.

HALAKHA

They may be redeemed even when unblemished – נִפְדִּין תְּמִימִין: From the first of Nisan onward, communal offerings are brought only from the new collection of money. If animals still exist that were designated for the daily offerings and were purchased from the previous collection, they are redeemed and are transferred to non-sacred status. This is the *halakha* even with regard to unblemished animals, as it is a stipulation of the court with regard to all animals that are purchased for the daily offerings that if they are not needed, they can be transferred to non-sacred status, in accordance with the opinion of the Rabbis (Rambam *Sefer Zemanim*, *Hilkhot Shekalim* 4:11).

איתמר, תודה ששחטה לשם תודת חבירו (כשרה) – רבה אמר: כשרה, רב חסדא אמר: פסולה.

§ **It was stated** with regard to **a thanks offering that one slaughtered**[N] **for the sake of another's thanks offering:**[NH] **Rabba says** that it is **fit** and satisfies its owner's obligation, **and Rav Ḥisda says** it is **unfit** in this regard.

רבה אמר: כשרה – תודה לשם תודה נשחטה; רב חסדא אמר: פסולה – לשום שלמים דידיה נשחטה בעינן.

Rabba says it is **fit** because the **thanks offering was slaughtered for the sake of a thanks offering. Rav Ḥisda says** it is **unfit** because **it must be slaughtered for the sake of his own peace offering.**[N]

אמר רבה: מנא אמינא לה? דתניא: "ובשר זבח תודת שלמיו ביום הקריבו את זבחו" וגו׳, אבא חנין אמר משום רבי אליעזר: בא ללמד, תודה ששחטה לשם שלמים – כשרה, שלמים שנשחטו לשם תודה – פסולים. ומה הפרש בין זה לזה? תודה קרויה שלמים, ואין שלמים קרויין תודה;

Rabba said: From where do I say that it is fit? It is **as it is taught** in a *baraita*: The verse states: **"And the meat of the sacrifice of his thanksgiving peace offering… on the day that he presents his offering** it shall be eaten" (Leviticus 7:15–16). **Abba Ḥanin said in the name of Rabbi Eliezer:** The verse **comes to teach** that **a thanks offering that one slaughtered for the sake of a peace offering**[H] **is fit,** whereas **a peace offering that was slaughtered for the sake of a thanks offering is unfit. And what is the difference between this** offering **and that** offering? **A thanks offering is called a peace offering** in the verse, **but a peace offering is not called a thanks offering.**

שלמים לשם תודה – פסולה, הא תודה לשם תודה – כשרה, מאי לאו דחבריה?

Rabba explains: The *baraita* indicates that **a peace offering** that was slaughtered **for the sake of a thanks offering is unfit, but a thanks offering** that was slaughtered **for the sake of** some other **thanks offering is fit. What, is it not** referring to the thanks offering **of another,** teaching that it satisfies its owner's obligation?

לא, דידיה.

The Gemara responds: **No,** it is referring to another thanks offering **of his own,** which he designated to give thanks for another incident of deliverance.

אבל דחבריה מאי, פסולה? אדתני: שלמים לשם תודה פסולה – ליתני: תודה לשם תודה, וכל שכן שלמים לשם תודה!

The Gemara asks: **But** if one slaughtered his thanks offering for the sake of **another's** thanks offering, **what** is the *halakha*? Is it **unfit,** i.e., it does it not satisfy the owner's obligation? If so, **rather than teaching** that **a peace offering** slaughtered **for the sake of a thanks offering is unfit, let** the *baraita* **teach** that **a thanks offering** that was slaughtered **for the sake of** another's **thanks offering** is unfit, **and** one could infer that **all the more so a peace offering** slaughtered **for the sake of a thanks offering** is unfit.

שלמים לשם תודה דידיה איצטריך ליה, סלקא דעתך אמינא: מדתודה קרויה שלמים – שלמים נמי קרויין תודה, וכי שחיט להו לשם תודה – ליכשרו, קא משמע לן.

The Gemara answers: **It was necessary** for the *baraita* to specify a case where **a peace offering** was slaughtered **for the sake of his own thanks offering.** Otherwise, it might **enter your mind to say** that **since a thanks offering is called a peace offering, a peace offering is called a thanks offering as well, and** therefore **when one slaughters** a peace offering **for the sake of a thanks offering it should be fit.** Therefore the *baraita* **teaches us** that this is not the case.

אמר רבא: חטאת ששחטה לשם חטאת – כשירה, לשם עולה – פסולה.

§ **Rava says: A sin offering that one slaughtered for the sake** of another **sin offering**[NH] he was obligated to bring is **fit;** but if one slaughtered it **for the sake of a burnt offering** it is **unfit.**

NOTES

A thanks offering that one slaughtered, etc. – תודה ששחטה וכו׳: *Tosafot* suggest that this dispute is specifically with regard to a thanks offering, as the verse refers to it as "the sacrifice of his thanks offering peace offering" (Leviticus 7:15), indicating that it must be sacrificed specifically for the sake of his thanks offering, and not for another's thanks offering. Rashi maintains that the dispute pertains to all offerings and is stated specifically with regard to a thanks offering merely because Rabba proves his opinion from a *baraita* that relates to a thanks offering.

For the sake of another's thanks offering – לשם תודת חבירו: Rashi clarifies that this is not a case where one slaughtered one person's thanks offering for the sake of another person, as that would constitute a change of owner, which is determined only by the intent of the one who slaughtered to sprinkle its blood for the sake of another person (see 4a). Rather, this is referring to a case where two people, Reuven and Shimon, designated animals as thanks offerings, and the one who slaughtered Reuven's thanks offering had Shimon's thanks offering in mind. This, according to Rav Ḥisda, is a case of changing the offering, and therefore the offering does not satisfy its owner's obligation.

The later commentaries find this explanation difficult, and some emend Rashi's wording. One interpretation of Rashi is that the one who slaughtered Reuven's thanks offering had in mind at the time of slaughter the reason for Shimon's thanks offering. For example, Reuven brought a thanks offering because he came out of a dangerous place, Shimon brought one because he was healed from illness, and the priest slaughtered Reuven's thanks offering having in mind healing from illness (*Birkat HaZevaḥ*; *Ḥok Natan*). Some explain Rashi as saying that the one who slaughtered Reuven's thanks offering had in mind at the time of slaughter the animal that was designated for Shimon's thanks offering (*Zevaḥ Toda*).

For the sake of his own peace offering – לשום שלמים דידיה: Rav Ḥisda uses the term peace offering even though the discussion is about a thanks offering because his opinion is derived from the verse: "The sacrifice of his thanks offering peace offering" (Leviticus 7:15).

A sin offering that one slaughtered for the sake of another sin offering – חטאת ששחטה לשם חטאת: For example, a sin offering that was consecrated to atone for consuming blood and was slaughtered to atone for eating forbidden fat is not disqualified, as this is not considered a change of the offering.

Rabbeinu Tam suggests that this refers to one person's sin offering that was slaughtered for the sake of another's sin offering.

HALAKHA

For the sake of another's thanks offering – לשם תודת חבירו: If Reuven's burnt offering was slaughtered for the sake of Shimon's burnt offering, the obligation of neither is satisfied, in accordance with the opinion of Rav Ḥisda, who was a greater scholar than Rabba (Rambam *Sefer Avoda, Hilkhot Pesulei HaMukdashin* 15:1, and see *Likkutei Halakhot*).

A thanks offering that one slaughtered for the sake of a peace offering – תודה ששחטה לשם שלמים: A thanks offering that was slaughtered for the sake of a peace offering has satisfied its owner's obligation. A peace offering that was slaughtered for the sake of a thanks offering has not satisfied its owner's obligation. This is because a thanks offering is referred to as a peace offering, but a peace offering is not referred to as a thanks offering (Rambam *Sefer Avoda, Hilkhot Pesulei HaMukdashin* 15:13).

A sin offering that one slaughtered for the sake of another sin offering – חטאת ששחטה לשם חטאת: If one designated a sin offering for one transgression and slaughtered it for another transgression for which he was also obligated to bring a sin offering, the offering is disqualified, in accordance with the opinion of Rav Aḥa, son of Rav Ika, stated subsequently (9a), contrary to the opinion of Rava stated here (Rambam *Sefer Avoda, Hilkhot Pesulei HaMukdashin* 15:6 and *Kesef Mishne* there).

מַאי טַעְמָא? ״וְשָׁחַט אוֹתָהּ לְחַטָּאת״ אָמַר רַחֲמָנָא, וַהֲרֵי חַטָּאת לְשֵׁם חַטָּאת נִשְׁחֲטָה. לְשֵׁם עוֹלָה – פְּסוּלָה.

What is the reason for this distinction? **The Merciful One states** in the Torah: **"And slaughter it for a sin offering"** (Leviticus 4:33), **and** therefore, as long as the **sin offering was slaughtered for the sake of a sin offering,** even another sin offering, it is fit. But if it was slaughtered **for the sake of a burnt offering** it is **unfit.**

וְאָמַר רָבָא: חַטָּאת שֶׁשְּׁחָטָהּ עַל מִי שֶׁמְּחוּיָּיב חַטָּאת – פְּסוּלָה, עַל מִי שֶׁמְּחוּיָּיב עוֹלָה – כְּשֵׁרָה.

And Rava says: A sin offering that one slaughtered for a person other than its owner, but **who** nevertheless was **obligated** to bring **a sin offering,**[H] is **unfit.** But if one slaughtered it **for** one **who** was **obligated** to bring **a burnt offering,**[H] it is **fit.**

מַאי טַעְמָא? ״וְכִפֶּר עָלָיו״, עָלָיו – וְלֹא עַל חֲבֵירוֹ; חֲבֵירוֹ דּוּמְיָא דִּידֵיהּ, בִּמְחוּיָּיב כַּפָּרָה כְּמוֹתוֹ.

What is the reason for this distinction? The Torah states: **"And he shall be forgiven"** (Leviticus 4:26), indicating that it must be specifically **he,** the owner, **who** shall be forgiven, **and not another** person. **The other** person to whom this is referring, with regard to whom the offering is disqualified, is presumably **similar to** the owner **in** that **he is** also **obligated** to achieve **atonement similar to** the owner's by bringing a sin offering. Whereas if the other person is obligated to bring a burnt offering, and not a sin offering, this disqualification does not apply.

וְאָמַר רָבָא: חַטָּאת שֶׁשְּׁחָטָהּ עַל מִי שֶׁאֵינוֹ מְחוּיָּיב כְּלוּם – פְּסוּלָה, שֶׁאֵין לְךָ אָדָם בְּיִשְׂרָאֵל שֶׁאֵינוֹ מְחוּיָּיב עֲשֵׂה.

And Rava says: A sin offering that one slaughtered for a person **who is not obligated** to bring **anything**[H] is **unfit, as there is no person among the Jewish people who is not obligated** to bring an offering for violating **a positive mitzva.** Therefore, the one for whom he slaughtered the offering is considered one who was obligated to bring a sin offering.

וְאָמַר רָבָא: חַטָּאת מְכַפֶּרֶת עַל חַיָּיבֵי עֲשֵׂה מִקַּל וָחוֹמֶר: עַל חַיָּיבֵי כָרֵיתוֹת מְכַפֶּרֶת, עַל חַיָּיבֵי עֲשֵׂה לֹא כׇּל שֶׁכֵּן?

And Rava says that **a sin offering atones for those obligated** to bring a burnt offering for violating **a positive mitzva, due to an *a fortiori*** inference: If a sin offering **atones for those who are liable** for transgressions for which one receives **excision from the World-to-Come**[B] if he performs them intentionally, **all the more so** is it **not** clear that it atones **for those liable** for failing to fulfill **a positive mitzva?**

לְמֵימְרָא דְּבַת מִינָהּ הִיא? וְהָאָמַר רָבָא: חַטָּאת שֶׁשְּׁחָטָהּ עַל מִי שֶׁמְּחוּיָּיב חַטָּאת – פְּסוּלָה, עַל מִי שֶׁמְּחוּיָּיב עוֹלָה – כְּשֵׁרָה!

The Gemara asks: **Is this to say that** the violation of a positive mitzva **is of the same type as** the sins atoned for by a sin offering? **But doesn't Rava say** that **a sin offering that one slaughtered for** a person other than its owner but **who** was **obligated** to bring **a sin offering** is **unfit,** but if it was slaughtered **for** a person **who is obligated** to bring **a burnt offering,** it is **fit,** as he is not obligated to provide a similar atonement? Given that burnt offerings atone for violations of positive mitzvot, apparently such atonement is of a different type than atonement for the transgression of prohibitions.

Perek **I**
Daf **7** Amud **b**

מִקִּיבְעָא לָא מְכַפְּרָא, מִקּוּפְיָא מְכַפְּרָא.

The Gemara answers: A sin offering **does not atone** for violating a positive mitzva **by** its **essence,**[N] since prohibitions and positive mitzvot are not of the same type, but it **atones** for it **incidentally.**

וְאָמַר רָבָא: עוֹלָה שֶׁשְּׁחָטָהּ שֶׁלֹּא לִשְׁמָהּ – אָסוּר לִזְרוֹק דָּמָהּ שֶׁלֹּא לִשְׁמָהּ,

And Rava says: As for **a burnt offering that one slaughtered not for its sake, it is** still **prohibited to sprinkle its blood not for its sake.**

HALAKHA

A sin offering that one slaughtered for a person who was obligated to bring a sin offering – חַטָּאת שֶׁשְּׁחָטָהּ עַל מִי שֶׁמְּחוּיָּיב חַטָּאת: If a sin offering was slaughtered for the sake of another person who is obligated to bring a sin offering, it is disqualified, whether the latter person is obligated to bring a standard sin offering or a sliding-scale sin offering (Rambam *Sefer Avoda*, *Hilkhot Pesulei HaMukdashin* 15:7).

For one who was obligated to bring a burnt offering – עַל מִי שֶׁמְּחוּיָּיב עוֹלָה: If a sin offering was slaughtered for the sake of another who was obligated to bring a burnt offering, it is still fit to be sacrificed but does not satisfy its owner's obligation (Rambam *Sefer Avoda*, *Hilkhot Pesulei HaMukdashin* 15:8).

For a person who is not obligated to bring anything – עַל מִי שֶׁאֵינוֹ מְחוּיָּיב כְּלוּם: The Rambam writes: If a sin offering was slaughtered for the sake of a person who is not obligated to bring an offering at all, it is disqualified, as that person may be obligated to bring an offering without knowing it, in accordance with Rava's statement. In another place, the Rambam writes: If a burnt offering was slaughtered for a person who is not obligated to bring an offering at all, it did not satisfy its owner's obligation, as that constitutes a change of owner. This is because there is no Jew who never violated a positive mitzva; every Jew is obligated to atone for his violations. These explanations are discussed in *Kesef Mishne* and in the later commentaries (Rambam *Sefer Avoda*, *Hilkhot Pesulei HaMukdashin* 15:9, 14).

BACKGROUND

Excision from the World-to-Come [*karet*] – כָּרֵת: *Karet* is a divine punishment for serious transgressions. The precise nature of the retribution is a matter of dispute among the commentaries, with opinions including premature or sudden death, barrenness, the death of the sinner's children, and excision of the soul from the World-to-Come. Tractate *Karetot* mentions thirty-six transgressions punishable by *karet*, all of which are violations of prohibitions, with two exceptions: Neglecting to sacrifice the Paschal offering and failure to undergo circumcision. *Karet* applies only to a person who intentionally commits a transgression. In certain instances, if the transgression was committed in the presence of witnesses, the transgressor is subject to execution by an earthly court or to the penalty of lashes. Anyone who unwittingly transgresses one of the prohibitions punishable by *karet* must bring a sin offering as atonement.

NOTES

Does not atone by its essence, etc. – מִקִּיבְעָא לָא מְכַפְּרָא וכו׳: Since the appropriate offering brought for violating a positive mitzva is a burnt offering, they are not generally atoned for with a sin offering. Therefore, if one slaughters a sin offering for the sake of one obligated to bring a burnt offering, it is fit, since there is no connection between the two that would lead to its disqualification. By contrast, if one does not know of any violation obligating him to bring a burnt offering, a sin offering does atone incidentally for his own unknown violations. Therefore, if one slaughters a sin offering for the sake of one who, to his own knowledge, is not obligated to bring any offering, the offering is disqualified. Since everyone is assumed to have unknown violations of positive mitzvot, the atonement of a sin offering is pertinent to him, and considered of his type in this respect.

אִיבָּעֵית אֵימָא קְרָא, אִיבָּעֵית אֵימָא סְבָרָא. אִיבָּעֵית אֵימָא קְרָא: "מוֹצָא שְׂפָתֶיךָ תִּשְׁמֹר" וגו׳, אִיבָּעֵית אֵימָא סְבָרָא: מִשּׁוּם דְּשַׁנֵּי בָּהּ כו׳, כִּדְרֵישׁ פִּירְקָא.

Why is this so? **If you wish, cite a verse;** and **if you wish, propose a logical argument.** The Gemara elaborates: **If you wish, cite a verse: "That which has gone out of your lips you shall observe** and do; according to what you have vowed freely to the Lord your God, even that which you have promised with your mouth" (Deuteronomy 23:24). The derivation from this verse was explained in 2a. **If you wish, propose a logical argument:** Just **because** one **deviated** from protocol **in its** slaughter, shall he continue to deviate from protocol in the rest of the sacrificial process? This is **as** it was stated at **the beginning of the chapter** (2a).

וְאָמַר רָבָא: עוֹלָה הַבָּאָה לְאַחַר מִיתָה, שְׁחָטָהּ בְּשִׁינּוּי קוֹדֶשׁ – פְּסוּלָה, בְּשִׁינּוּי בְּעָלִים – כְּשֵׁרָה, דְּאֵין בְּעָלִים לְאַחַר מִיתָה.

And Rava says: With regard to **a burnt offering that is brought** by its owner's heirs **after** his **death,**[H] if one **slaughtered it with a deviation** from the type of **offering,** i.e., for the sake of another type of offering, it is **unfit,** i.e., it does not satisfy the owner's obligation, and the heirs must therefore bring another offering. But if it was slaughtered **with a deviation** with regard to the **owner,** i.e., for the sake of another person, it is **fit, as** the offering **has no** legal **owner after** the owner's **death.**

וְרַב פִּנְחָס בְּרֵיהּ דְּרַב אַמֵּי אָמַר: יֵשׁ בְּעָלִים לְאַחַר מִיתָה. אֲמַר לֵיהּ רַב אָשֵׁי לְרַב פִּנְחָס בְּרֵיהּ דְּרַב אַמֵּי: דַּוְקָא קָאָמַר מָר יֵשׁ בְּעָלִים לְאַחַר מִיתָה, וּבָעֵי לְאֵיתוּיֵי עוֹלָה אַחֲרִיתִי, אוֹ דִּלְמָא דְּאִי אִיכָּא כַּמָּה עֲשֵׂה גַּבֵּיהּ מְכַפְּרָא?

And Rav Pineḥas, son of Rav Ami, says that an offering **has an owner after** its owner's **death,** specifically, the heir. **Rav Ashi said to Rav Pineḥas, son of Rav Ami: Is the Master saying** that an offering **actually**[N] **has an owner after** its owner's **death, and** that if it was slaughtered for the sake of the wrong owner, the heir **must bring another burnt offering,** contrary to the opinion of Rava? **Or perhaps** the Master is merely saying **that if** the heir **has several** violations of **positive mitzvot,** the offering **atones** for them, but still if it was slaughtered for the sake of the wrong owner, the heir is not required to bring another offering.

אֲמַר לֵיהּ: דַּוְקָא קָאָמֵינָא.

Rav Pineḥas **said to him: I am saying** that the heir is **actually**[N] the owner, and if the offering was slaughtered for someone else, he must bring another offering.

וְאָמַר רָבָא: עוֹלָה – דּוֹרוֹן הִיא. הֵיכִי דָּמֵי? אִי דְּלֵיכָּא תְּשׁוּבָה – "זֶבַח רְשָׁעִים תּוֹעֵבָה", וְאִי דְּאִיכָּא תְּשׁוּבָה – הָתַנְיָא: עָבַר עַל מִצְוַת עֲשֵׂה וְשָׁב, לֹא זָז מִשָּׁם עַד שֶׁמּוֹחֲלִים לוֹ! אֶלָּא שְׁמַע מִינָּהּ: דּוֹרוֹן הוּא.

And Rava says: A burnt offering is a gift [*doron*][L] to God; its essential purpose is not atonement. Rava supports his assertion: **What are the circumstances** under which a burnt offering atones for violating a positive mitzva? **If** one brings a burnt offering **without repentance** for his transgression, he may not sacrifice it at all, as **"the sacrifice of the wicked is an abomination"** (Proverbs 21:27). **And if there is repentance, isn't it taught** in a *baraita* that if one **violates a positive mitzva and repents,**[H] God **forgives him before he** even **moves from** his place? If so, why is he required to bring an offering? **Rather, conclude from it** that a burnt offering **is a gift** that one brings in order to appease God even after he is forgiven.

(חַטָּאת עַל מִי מְכַפֵּר, עוֹלָה לְאַחַר דּוֹרוֹן, סִימָן)

The Gemara states **a mnemonic** for this series of statements by Rava: **A sin offering atones for who, a burnt offering after a gift.**

תַּנְיָא נָמֵי הָכִי, אָמַר רַבִּי שִׁמְעוֹן: חַטָּאת לָמָּה בָּאָה? לָמָּה בָּאָה? לְכַפֵּר! אֶלָּא, לָמָּה בָּאָה לִפְנֵי עוֹלָה? לְפַרְקְלִיט שֶׁנִּכְנַס, [רִיצָּה פְּרַקְלִיט, נִכְנַס] דּוֹרוֹן אַחֲרָיו.

This last statement of Rava **is also taught** in a *baraita*: **Rabbi Shimon said: For what** purpose **is a sin offering brought?** The Gemara interrupts: **For what** purpose **is it brought?** Is it not brought **to atone** for a transgression? **Rather,** Rabbi Shimon clearly meant: **For what** reason **is it brought before a burnt offering** in all circumstances where both are brought? Rabbi Shimon answered: It is comparable **to an advocate** [*lifraklit*][L] **who enters** before the king to convince him to pardon the defendant. Once the **advocate has appeased** the king, the **gift is brought in after him.**

"חוּץ מִן הַפֶּסַח וְהַחַטָּאת" כו׳. פֶּסַח מְנָלַן?

§ The mishna teaches that all offerings are fit even if slaughtered not for their sake, **except for the Paschal offering and the sin offering.** The Gemara asks: **From where do we** derive that **a Paschal offering** is required to be slaughtered for its sake?

דִּכְתִיב: "שָׁמוֹר אֶת חֹדֶשׁ הָאָבִיב וְעָשִׂיתָ פֶּסַח", שֶׁיְּהוּ כׇּל עֲשִׂיּוֹתָיו לְשֵׁם פֶּסַח.

The Gemara answers: It is derived from a verse, **as it is written: "Observe the month of the spring and offer** [*ve'asita*] **the Paschal offering"** (Deuteronomy 16:1), teaching **that all of the actions** [*asiyyotav*] of the Paschal offering, all of its sacrificial rites, must be performed **for the sake of** the **Paschal offering.**

HALAKHA

A burnt offering that is brought by its owner's heirs after his death – עוֹלָה הַבָּאָה לְאַחַר מִיתָה: With regard to a burnt offering that is brought by its owner's heirs after his death, even if it is slaughtered for the wrong owner, it satisfies the owner's obligation. This is in accordance with the opinion of Rava, as it follows the opinion of Rabbi Yoḥanan (5b), and the Gemara (6a) accepts his opinion (Rambam *Sefer Avoda, Hilkhot Pesulei HaMukdashin* 15:15).

If one violates a positive mitzva and repents – עָבַר עַל מִצְוַת עֲשֵׂה וְשָׁב: One who violated a positive mitzva that is not punishable by *karet* and repented is forgiven immediately (Rambam *Sefer HaMadda, Hilkhot Teshuva* 1:4).

NOTES

Saying actually, etc. – דַּוְקָא קָאָמַר וכו׳: The question is whether, by saying that an offering has an owner after its owner's death, Rav Pineḥas meant to dispute Rava's statement, or to clarify that although the heir is not considered an owner with regard to the *halakha* requiring intent for the sake of the owner, the offering does atone for him (see *Sefat Emet*).

I am saying actually – דַּוְקָא קָאָמֵינָא: The *Hazon Ish* writes that although the heir is obligated to bring another offering if it was slaughtered for the wrong owner, his obligation is to bring it from the inheritance, not from his own property. Later commentaries note that the opinion of Rav Pineḥas apparently disagrees with Rabbi Yoḥanan's opinion (5b) that heirs are not considered to be owners of the offering.

LANGUAGE

Gift [*doron*] – דּוֹרוֹן: From the Greek δῶρον, *doron*, meaning gift or present.

Advocate [*peraklit*] – פְּרַקְלִיט: Derived from the Greek παράκλητος, *paraklētos*, meaning one who makes another's claim for him, i.e., a lawyer or advocate.

אַשְׁכְּחַן שִׁינּוּי קוֹדֶשׁ, שִׁינּוּי בְּעָלִים מְנָלַן?

The Gemara asks: **We found** a source for the *halakha* that **deviation** from the type of **offering** is prohibited. **From where do we** derive that **deviation** with regard to the **owner** is also prohibited?

דִּכְתִיב: ״וַאֲמַרְתֶּם זֶבַח פֶּסַח הוּא״, שֶׁתְּהֵא זְבִיחָה לְשֵׁם פֶּסַח; אִם אֵינוֹ עִנְיָן לְשִׁינּוּי קוֹדֶשׁ, תְּנֵיהוּ עִנְיָן לְשִׁינּוּי בְּעָלִים.

The Gemara answers that this is derived from a verse, **as it is written: "And you shall say: It is the sacrifice** [*zevaḥ*] **of the** Lord's **Passover"** (Exodus 12:27), which indicates **that** the **slaughter** [*zeviḥa*] **must be** performed **for the sake of** the **Paschal offering. If** the verse **is not** necessary in order **to** derive **the matter** of **deviation** from the type of **offering,** as that *halakha* is derived from Deuteronomy 16:1, **apply it** to the **matter of deviation** with regard to the **owner.**

אַשְׁכְּחַן לְמִצְוָה, לְעַכֵּב מְנָלַן?

The Gemara asks: **We found** a source **for the mitzva** to sacrifice the Paschal offering for its sake and for the sake of its owner. **From where do we** derive that these intentions are **indispensable**[B] and, if lacking, disqualify the offering?

אָמַר קְרָא: ״וְזָבַחְתָּ פֶּסַח לַה׳ אֱלֹהֶיךָ״ וגו׳.

The Gemara answers: **The verse states: "And you shall sacrifice** [*vezavaḥta*] **the Paschal offering unto the Lord, your God,** of the flock and the herd" (Deuteronomy 16:2). By repeating the mitzva to sacrifice the Paschal offering for its sake and for the sake of its owner, the Torah indicates that these two intentions are both indispensable to the sacrificial process.

מַתְקִיף לַהּ רַב סָפְרָא: הַאי ״וְזָבַחְתָּ״ לְהָכִי הוּא דְּאָתָא? הַאי מִיבְּעֵי לֵיהּ לְכִדְרַב נַחְמָן, דְּאָמַר רַב נַחְמָן אָמַר רַבָּה בַּר אֲבוּהּ: מִנַּיִן לְמוֹתַר פֶּסַח שֶׁקָּרֵב שְׁלָמִים? שֶׁנֶּאֱמַר: ״וְזָבַחְתָּ פֶּסַח לַה׳ אֱלֹהֶיךָ צֹאן וּבָקָר״, וַהֲלֹא אֵין פֶּסַח בָּא אֶלָּא מִן הַכְּבָשִׂים וּמִן הָעִזִּים! מִכָּאן לְמוֹתַר הַפֶּסַח שֶׁיְּהֵא לְדָבָר הַבָּא מִן הַצֹּאן וּמִן הַבָּקָר, וּמַאי נִיהוּ? שְׁלָמִים!

Rav Safra objects to this: Does this verse: **"And you shall sacrifice," come to** teach **this** *halakha*? **It is necessary for** the statement **of Rav Naḥman, as Rav Naḥman says** that **Rabba bar Avuh says: From where** is it derived **that a leftover Paschal offering,** an animal consecrated but not ultimately sacrificed on Passover eve, **is sacrificed as a peace offering** afterward? It is derived from **that** which **is stated: "And you shall sacrifice the Passover offering unto the Lord, your God, of the flock and the herd."** The verse is difficult: **But isn't a Paschal offering brought only from the lambs and from the goats? From here** it is derived **that a leftover Paschal offering**[H] **should be** sacrificed **as** an offering **brought** both **from the flock and from the herd.**[N] **And what is that?** It is **a peace offering.**

אֶלָּא אָמַר רַב סָפְרָא: ״וְזָבַחְתָּ פֶּסַח״ – לְכִדְרַב נַחְמָן, ״שָׁמוֹר אֶת חֹדֶשׁ הָאָבִיב״ – לְמִצְוָה בְּשִׁינּוּי קוֹדֶשׁ, ״וַאֲמַרְתֶּם זֶבַח פֶּסַח״ – בְּשִׁינּוּי בְּעָלִים לְמִצְוָה, ״הוּא״ – לְעַכֵּב בֵּין הָכָא וְהָכָא.

Rather, Rav Safra says that the verses should be expounded as follows: The verse **"And you shall sacrifice the Paschal offering"** teaches the statement **of Rav Naḥman,** that a leftover Paschal offering is sacrificed as a peace offering. The verse: **"Observe the month of the spring** and offer the Paschal offering" (Deuteronomy 16:1), teaches that there is **a mitzva** to sacrifice the Paschal offering without **deviation** from the type of **offering.** The verse: **"And you shall say:** It is **the sacrifice of** the Lord's **Passover"** (Exodus 12:27), teaches that there is **a mitzva** to slaughter it without **deviation** with regard to the **owner.** The term **"it is"** in the latter verse teaches that **both here and there,** i.e., with regard to both the offering and the owner, proper intent is **indispensable.**

וְאַשְׁכְּחַן זְבִיחָה, שְׁאָר עֲבוֹדוֹת מְנָלַן? הוֹאִיל וְגַלֵּי גַּלֵּי.

Rav Safra continues: **And we found** a source for **slaughter. From where do we** derive that **other** sacrificial **rites** must also be performed for the sake of the owner or the offering is disqualified? **Since** the Torah **revealed** that this intention is indispensable to the proper slaughter of the Paschal offering, it thereby **revealed**[N] that it is critical to proper performance of the other rites as well.

רַב אַשִׁי אָמַר: הוֹאִיל וְגַלֵּי לָא אָמְרִינַן. אֶלָּא [עֲבוֹדוֹת] מְנָלַן? דִּכְתִיב: ״זֹאת הַתּוֹרָה לָעֹלָה וְלַמִּנְחָה״ וגו׳,

Rav Ashi says: We do not say that **since** the Torah **revealed** that this *halakha* is indispensable to slaughter, it thereby **revealed** that it is indispensable to the other rites as well. **Rather, from where do we** derive that it is indispensable to the other sacrificial **rites?** It is derived from a verse, **as it is written: "This is the law of the burnt offering, and of the meal offering,** and of the sin offering, and of the guilt offering, and of the consecration offering, and of the sacrifice of peace offerings" (Leviticus 7:37), indicating that all offerings must, like a peace offering, be sacrificed for their own sake.

BACKGROUND

Indispensable – לְעַכֵּב: This is a concept encountered in many areas of *halakha*. There is often a particular, proper way of performing a mitzva, but one who does not perform the mitzva in this fashion nevertheless fulfills his obligation. With regard to other mitzvot, the failure to perform certain details may render the obligation unfulfilled. These details are deemed indispensable. The distinction between elements in the performance of a mitzva that are required *ab initio* and details that are deemed indispensable is encountered primarily in the *halakhot* of sacrifices.

HALAKHA

A leftover Paschal offering – מוֹתַר הַפֶּסַח: If one separated money to buy a Paschal offering and ultimately did not use all of the money, he should buy a peace offering with the remainder, in accordance with Rav Naḥman's statement (Rambam *Sefer Korbanot, Hilkhot Korban Pesaḥ* 4:10).

NOTES

As an offering brought from the flock and from the herd – לְדָבָר הַבָּא מִן הַצֹּאן וּמִן הַבָּקָר: Why is it assumed that this is referring to a peace offering, when a burnt offering is also brought from both the flock and from the herd? Rashi answers that the reference is to an offering that can be brought from both sexes of the flock or herd; a burnt offering is brought only from males. *Tosafot* add two other answers: One is that this matter is derived from other verses that relate specifically to a peace offering (see 9a), and the other is that the verse presumably refers to an offering of lesser sanctity, similar to a Paschal offering.

Since the Torah revealed it revealed – הוֹאִיל וְגַלֵּי גַּלֵּי: This reasoning is comparable to one of the fundamental talmudic principles of biblical exegesis, namely: A matter that was included in a general category but emerged to teach a *halakha*, emerged to teach not just about itself but to teach about the entire category. Since slaughter is included in the category of sacrificial rites involving the blood of the offering, the *halakha* taught with regard to slaughter pertains to the other rites as well.

ותניא: "ביום צותו את בני ישראל להקריב את קרבניהם" – זה בכור ומעשר ופסח,

And it is taught in a *baraita*: In the verse: **"In the day that he commanded the children of Israel to present their offerings"** (Leviticus 7:38), **this** word, i.e., "offerings," is referring to the **firstborn**[B] animal, the animal **tithe,**[B] **and** the **Paschal offering,** which are not mentioned in the previous verse.

הקישו הכתוב לשלמים: מה שלמים, בין שינוי קודש בין שינוי בעלים בעינן למצוה – אף כל, בין שינוי קודש בין שינוי בעלים למצוה;

The text juxtaposes all types of offerings mentioned in both verses **with a peace offering,** indicating that **just as** one who sacrifices a **peace offering is required** to do so with the proper intent, **both** concerning **deviation** from the **offering and** concerning **deviation** with regard to the **owner,** and in addition, the *halakha* of proper intent is only **as a mitzva,** not as an indispensable requirement, **so too,** in the case of **any** type of offering that must have proper intent, **both** concerning **deviation** from the **offering and** concerning **deviation** with regard to the **owner,** the *halakha* of proper intent is only **as a mitzva.** Therefore, the mitzva *ab initio* is derived from the *halakha* of a peace offering; and those verses mentioned earlier repeat the *halakha* to teach that it is indispensable with regard to slaughter.

וכשלמים: מה שלמים בין זביחה בין שאר עבודות לא חלקת בהן למצוה – אף פסח לא תחלוק בו בין זביחה לשאר עבודות לעכב (משום שנאמר "הוא" בזביחה אינו אלא לעכב).

And the juxtaposition of the peace offering with the Paschal offering indicates that a Paschal offering is **similar to a peace offering** in another respect: **Just as** with regard to **a peace offering, you did not distinguish between slaughter and** the **other rites with regard to** the **mitzva** *ab initio* of proper intent, **so too, with regard to** the **Paschal offering, do not distinguish between slaughter and** the **other** sacrificial **rites** with regard **to** the *halakha* that proper intent is **indispensable.**

אלא "הוא" למה לי?

The Gemara asks: **Rather,** since the indispensability of proper intent with regard to the Paschal offering is derived from its juxtaposition with the peace offering, **why do I** need the term **"it is"** to be written in Exodus 12:27? What is derived from there?

כדתניא: נאמר בפסח "הוא" בשחיטה – לעכב, אבל אשם לא נאמר בו "הוא" אלא לאחר הקטרת אימורין, והוא עצמו שלא הוקטרו אימוריו – כשר.

The Gemara answers: This is written to teach that this requirement is indispensable only in the case of a Paschal offering, and not in the case of a guilt offering. **As it is taught** in a *baraita*: **Concerning** the **Paschal offering,** the term **"it is" is stated with regard to slaughter** in Exodus 12:27 **to** teach that intent for the owner is **indispensable. But** concerning **a guilt offering,** the term **"it is" is stated only after** the verse mentions **the burning of** the **sacrificial portions, and** since a guilt offering **itself** is **fit** even **when its portions were not burned** on the altar at all, intent for the sake of the owner at this point is certainly not indispensable.

חטאת מנלן? דכתיב: "ושחט אתה לחטאת", שתהא שחיטה לשם חטאת.

§ The Gemara asks: **From where do we** derive that if **a sin offering** is sacrificed for the sake of the wrong type of offering or one other than its owner, it is disqualified? The Gemara answers: It is derived from this verse, **as it is written: "And slaughter it for a sin offering"** (Leviticus 4:33), teaching **that** the **slaughter must be** performed **for the sake of a sin offering.**

אשכחן שחיטה, קבלה מנלן? דכתיב:

The Gemara asks: **We found** a source with regard to **slaughter. From where do we** derive this with regard to **collection** of the blood? The Gemara answers: It is derived from this verse, **as it is written:**

BACKGROUND

Firstborn – בכור: The male firstborn of cattle, sheep, or goats belonging to a Jew is consecrated from birth and must be given to a priest to be sacrificed on the altar in the Temple, with its meat eaten by the priests and their families (see Numbers 18:17–18). If a firstborn animal develops a physical blemish that disqualifies it from being sacrificed as an offering, it may be slaughtered and eaten like any other non-sacred kosher animal. Nevertheless, it still has to be given to a priest as a gift.

Animal tithe – מעשר בהמה: On three occasions each year, the owner of a herd of kosher animals is required to gather into an enclosure all the animals born during the preceding period and to let them out one by one. These animals pass "under the rod" (see Leviticus 27:32), and every tenth animal is marked with red paint, to indicate that it is an animal tithe and is consecrated. If it is fit to be sacrificed, the animal tithe is brought to the Temple and sacrificed in a manner similar to that of a peace offering. Its blood is sprinkled on the altar, and its meat is eaten by its owner but not by the priests. The *halakhot* of animal tithes are elucidated in tractate *Bekhorot*.

״וְלָקַח הַכֹּהֵן מִדַּם הַחַטָּאת״ – שֶׁתְּהֵא קַבָּלָה לְשֵׁם חַטָּאת.

"**And the priest shall take of the blood of the sin offering**" (Leviticus 4:25), teaching **that** the **collection** of the blood **must be** performed **for the sake of a sin offering.**

וְאַשְׁכַּחַן שְׁחִיטָה וְקַבָּלָה, זְרִיקָה מְנָלַן? דְּאָמַר קְרָא ״וְכִפֶּר עָלָיו הַכֹּהֵן מֵחַטָּאתוֹ״ – שֶׁתְּהֵא כַּפָּרָה לְשֵׁם חַטָּאת.

The Gemara asks: **And we found** a source for the *halakha* that the **slaughter and collection**[N] must be performed for the sake of a sin offering. **From where do we** derive this *halakha* with regard to the **sprinkling** of the blood? The Gemara answers: It is derived from a verse, **as the verse states: "And the priest shall make atonement for him concerning his sin"** (Leviticus 4:26),[N] teaching **that** the **atonement must be** effected **for the sake of a sin offering,** as atonement is effected by the sprinkling of the blood.

אַשְׁכַּחַן שִׁנּוּי קֹדֶשׁ, שִׁנּוּי בְּעָלִים מְנָלַן? אָמַר קְרָא: ״עָלָיו״ – עָלָיו וְלֹא עַל חֲבֵירוֹ.

The Gemara asks: **We found** a source for the prohibition against **deviation** from the type of **offering. From where do we** derive the prohibition against **deviation** with regard to the **owner?** The Gemara answers: The aforementioned **verse states:** "And the priest shall make atonement **for him,**" indicating that the intent must be **for him, and not for another.**

אַשְׁכַּחַן לְמִצְוָה, לְעַכֵּב מְנָלַן? כִּדְאָמַר רַב הוּנָא בְּרֵיהּ דְּרַב יְהוֹשֻׁעַ: ״חַטָּאת״ ״חַטָּאתוֹ״, הָכָא נַמִּי – ״חַטָּאת״ ״חַטָּאתוֹ״.

The Gemara asks: **We found** a source **for the mitzva** to sprinkle the blood for the sake of the owner *ab initio*. **From where do we** derive that this is **indispensable** and disqualifies the offering if not fulfilled? The Gemara answers: It is **as Rav Huna, son of Rav Yehoshua, says** with regard to the sin offering of a nazirite: Since the verse could have simply stated: **Sin offering,** but instead stated: **"His sin offering"** (Numbers 6:16), it is inferred that the offering must be sacrificed for his, the owner's, sake. **Here too,** since the verse could have simply stated **"sin,"** but states **"his sin,"** one infers that if the blood of the sin offering is not sprinkled for the sake of its owner, it is disqualified.

אַשְׁכַּחַן מִצְוָה בְּשִׁנּוּי קֹדֶשׁ, וּזְרִיקָה בְּשִׁנּוּי בְּעָלִים בֵּין לְמִצְוָה בֵּין לְעַכֵּב; לְעַכֵּב בְּכׇל עֲבוֹדוֹת בְּשִׁנּוּי קֹדֶשׁ, וּבִשְׁאָר עֲבוֹדוֹת בְּשִׁנּוּי בְּעָלִים בֵּין לְמִצְוָה בֵּין לְעַכֵּב, מְנָלַן?

The Gemara asks: **We found** a source for the **mitzva of** sacrificing a sin offering without **deviation** from the type of **offering** *ab initio*, **and** with regard to **sprinkling** its blood without **deviation** with regard to the **owner** concerning **both** its **mitzva** *ab initio* **and** its **indispensability. From where do we** derive that performing **all** sacrificial **rites** without **deviation** from the type of **offering is an indispensable** requirement, **and** that performing **all other rites,** besides sprinkling the blood, without **deviation** with regard to the **owner is both a mitzva** *ab initio* **and indispensable?**

אָמַר רַבִּי יוֹנָה: אָתְיָא מֵחַטַּאת נָזִיר, דִּכְתִיב: ״וְהִקְרִיב הַכֹּהֵן לִפְנֵי ה׳ וְעָשָׂה אֶת חַטָּאתוֹ וְאֶת עֹלָתוֹ״, שֶׁיְּהוּ כׇּל עֲשִׂיּוֹתָיו לְשֵׁם חַטָּאת.

Rabbi Yona says: It is derived from the *halakha* concerning **the sin offering of a nazirite; as it is written** concerning a nazirite: **"And the priest shall bring them before the Lord, and shall offer** [*ve'asa*] **his sin offering, and his burnt offering"** (Numbers 6:16). The verse teaches **that all of its** sacrificial **actions** [*asiyyotav*] **must be** performed **for the sake of a sin offering.**

אַשְׁכַּחַן שִׁנּוּי קֹדֶשׁ, שִׁנּוּי בְּעָלִים מְנָלַן? (אִם אֵינוֹ עִנְיָן לְשִׁנּוּי קֹדֶשׁ, תְּנֵיהוּ עִנְיָן לְשִׁנּוּי בְּעָלִים. אַשְׁכַּחַן לְמִצְוָה, לְעַכֵּב מְנָלַן?)

The Gemara asks: **We found** a source for the *halakha* that a sin offering must be sacrificed without **deviation** from the type of **offering,** and that this requirement is indispensable. **From where do we** derive that sacrificing it without **deviation** with regard to the **owner** is also indispensable, even in rites other than the sprinkling of the blood?

אָמַר רַב הוּנָא בְּרֵיהּ דְּרַב יְהוֹשֻׁעַ: ״חַטָּאת״ ״חַטָּאתוֹ״.

Rav Huna, son of Rav Yehoshua, says: Since the verse concerning a nazirite could have simply stated: **Sin offering,** but instead states: **"His sin offering,"** one infers that the offering must be sacrificed for the owner's sake.

מַתְקִיף לָהּ רָבִינָא: אֶלָּא מֵעַתָּה, ״עוֹלַת״ ״עוֹלָתוֹ״ מַאי דָּרְשַׁתְּ בֵּיהּ?

Ravina objects to this: If that is so, what do you interpret from the fact that the same verse could have stated: **Burnt offering,** but instead states: **"His burnt offering"?**[N]

NOTES

And we found a source for slaughter and collection – וְאַשְׁכַּחַן שְׁחִיטָה וְקַבָּלָה: Finding a source for this *halakha* with regard to the conveying of the blood to the altar is unnecessary, as the *halakhot* of collecting the blood all apply with regard to conveying the blood as well (Rashi; see 4a).

And the priest shall make atonement for him concerning his sin [*meḥattato*] – וְכִפֶּר עָלָיו הַכֹּהֵן מֵחַטָּאתוֹ: The term "concerning his sin [*meḥattato*]" is interpreted exegetically in reference to a sin offering, which is also called a *ḥatat*, as the term *meḥattato* is superfluous.

The Gemara cites this verse even though it is stated with regard to the sin offering of a king, as with regard to the sin offering of an ordinary person the verse states: "And the priest shall make atonement for him concerning his sin that he has sinned" (Leviticus 4:35); the term "his sin that he has sinned" cannot be interpreted in reference to the offering.

Tosafot maintain that the verse cited in the Gemara is not from the passage about the ruler's sin offering (Leviticus 4:26), but from the passage about a sliding-scale sin offering (Leviticus 5:6). This is based on the fact that the verse concerning the ruler's sin offering is stated after the burning of the portions consumed on the altar, at a stage when the priest's intent can no longer disqualify the offering (see 5b). Furthermore, the verse states: "And the priest shall make atonement for him concerning his sin [*meḥattato*], and he shall be forgiven"; the phrase "and he shall be forgiven" precludes interpretation of the term of *ḥatat* in reference to the offering.

What do you interpret from the fact that it could have stated: Burnt offering, but instead states: His burnt offering – עוֹלַת עוֹלָתוֹ מַאי דָּרְשַׁתְּ בֵּיהּ: The term "his burnt offering" cannot be interpreted in the same manner as "his sin offering," as it is universally accepted that a burnt offering that was slaughtered for the sake of the wrong owner is not disqualified. Therefore, interpreting the term "his sin offering" in this manner is also problematic, as one cannot interpret a verse selectively.

וּלְרָבִינָא, "מִנְחַת" "מִנְחָתוֹ", "נֶסֶךְ" "נִסְכּוֹ", מַאי דָּרְשַׁתְּ בְּהוּ?

The Gemara asks: **And according to Ravina, what do you interpret** from the subsequent verse: "The priest shall offer also his meal offering and his libation" (Numbers 6:17)? Why does Ravina not mention that this verse could have stated: **Meal offering,** but instead states: **"His meal offering,"**[B] and that it could have stated: **Libation,** but instead states: **"His libation"?**

הַהוּא מִבָּעֵי לֵיהּ: "מִנְחָתָם וְנִסְכֵּיהֶם" – בַּלַּיְלָה, "מִנְחָתָם וְנִסְכֵּיהֶם" – אֲפִילּוּ לְמָחָר. אֶלָּא "עוֹלַת" "עוֹלָתוֹ" מַאי דָּרְשַׁתְּ בְּהוּ?

The Gemara answers: **That** language **is necessary;** it is just like the phrase: **"Their meal offering and their libations,"**[BN] which is mentioned many times in the portion of the Festival offerings (e.g., Numbers 29:37). It teaches that the meal offerings and libations that are brought with the additional animal offerings of the Festivals can be sacrificed even **at night** after the offering is brought. The phrase: **"Their meal offering and their libations,"** also teaches that they may be brought **even on the following day.** Likewise here, when stated with regard to a nazirite, the phrase teaches that they may be brought at night or the day after the offering is sacrificed. **But** there remains a difficulty: **What do you interpret** from the fact that the verse could have stated: **Burnt offering,** but instead states: **"His burnt offering"?**

וְתוּ, מִי גָּמְרִי מֵהֲדָדֵי? חַטַּאת חֵלֶב מֵחַטַּאת נָזִיר לָא גָּמְרָה – שֶׁכֵּן יֵשׁ עִמָּהּ דָּמִים אֲחֵרִים, חַטַּאת נָזִיר מֵחַטַּאת חֵלֶב לָא גָּמְרָה – שֶׁכֵּן כָּרֵת!

The Gemara raises an additional objection to the derivation from a nazirite's sin offering: **And furthermore,**[N] **can** the *halakhot* of a standard sin offering and of a nazirite's sin offering **be derived from one another?**[N] The *halakhot* of **a sin offering** brought for a transgression, e.g., eating forbidden **fat,**[BN] **cannot be derived from** the *halakhot* of **a nazirite's sin offering,** due to the unique element of stringency of the latter, **since there is other blood,** i.e., other offerings are brought, **with it.** Likewise, the *halakhot* of **a nazirite's sin offering cannot be derived from** the *halakhot* of **a sin offering** brought for eating forbidden **fat,** due to the unique element of stringency of the latter, **since** it atones for a transgression punishable by **excision from the World-to-Come** [*karet*].

BACKGROUND

Meal offerings – מְנָחוֹת: These include all offerings of flour or bread brought in the Temple. Among the meal offerings are the two loaves of bread brought on *Shavuot*, the Temple shewbread, the various kinds of voluntary meal offerings, the sinner's meal offering, the loaves of bread accompanying a thanks offering, the meal offerings that accompany libations, the meal offering of a woman suspected by her husband of having been unfaithful [*sota*], and the *omer* offering. Numerous complex *halakhot* apply to these meal offerings, and most of tractate *Menaḥot* is dedicated to a detailed discussion of them. Most of the meal offerings are brought from unleavened wheat flour. Likewise, most of them require removing a handful of the offering and burning it on the altar, an essential element in the sacrificial process. Many types of meal offerings have oil mixed with them or incense added to them at some stage of their preparation. The *halakhot* of meal offerings parallel the *halakhot* of animal sacrifices in numerous respects, and many of the acts that disqualify animal sacrifices disqualify meal offerings as well.

Meal offering brought with the libations – מִנְחַת נְסָכִים: Meal offerings are brought together with all animal burnt offerings and peace offerings, both individual and communal. These meal offerings are accompanied by libations of wine. Oil, but not frankincense, is added to the meal offering brought with the libations. The handful of flour is not removed from this meal offering, nor is it waved or brought near to the altar as are other types of meal offerings. The entire meal offering is burned on the altar, and none of it is eaten by the priests. The quantities of flour in the meal offering brought with libations are fixed by the Torah: Three-tenths of an ephah for a bull, two-tenths for a ram, and one-tenth for a lamb. One-tenth of an ephah is approximately 3 ℓ. The animal offerings accompanied by a meal offering brought with libations are not rendered unfit if the meal offering is not sacrificed. Likewise, although the meal offering brought with libations is supposed to be sacrificed together with the animal offering, the meal offering remains acceptable even if the libations are sacrificed later.

Forbidden fat – חֵלֶב: This refers to animal fat whose consumption is prohibited by Torah law, in contrast to permitted fat. Intentionally consuming the forbidden fat of kosher domesticated animals is punishable by *karet* (see Leviticus 7:22–25). A sin offering must be brought for partaking of it unwittingly. The fat of non-domesticated kosher animals and kosher birds may be eaten. Among the signs differentiating forbidden from permitted fat is that the forbidden fat lies above the meat and is not intertwined with it. It is enclosed by a thin membrane and is easily peeled away from the meat. Most of the forbidden fat of an animal offering is sacrificed on the altar.

NOTES

Their meal offering and their libations – מִנְחָתָם וְנִסְכֵּיהֶם: Rashi explains that this is referring not to a specific verse, but to the phrase "their meal offering and their libations," which is mentioned many times in the portion of the additional offerings of the Festivals. Since this phrase is superfluous, as a meal offering and libations are brought with every burnt offering, it is interpreted exegetically as indicating that the meal offering and libations that are brought with animal offerings do not have to be sacrificed on the same day that the animal offering is sacrificed. This is provided that they were not already consecrated by being put in Temple service vessel, as that would render them disqualified due to being left overnight. Rashi adds that the *halakha* that meal offerings and libations don't have to be sacrificed on the day that the animal offering is sacrificed is inferred from the wording of the phrase. Even if the meal offering and libations of an animal offering are brought on the following night or day, they are still considered "their" meal offering and libations.

Rabbeinu Tam in *Sefer HaYashar* rejects this explanation, and claims that this *halakha* is derived from the verse: "With their meal offering and their libations, even an offering of fire, of a pleasing aroma unto the Lord" (Leviticus 23:18), stated with regard to the animal offerings that are brought with the offering of the two loaves on *Shavuot*. This verse juxtaposes the meal offering and libations with the portions of the animal offerings consumed by the fire on the altar, indicating that just as these portions can be sacrificed all night after the offering is slaughtered and its blood is sprinkled, so too, the meal offering and libations can be sacrificed at night, after the animal offering is already sacrificed. It is unclear according to this explanation how it is derived that the meal offering and libations can be sacrificed the next day as well (see *Tosafot*).

A third explanation is that of *Tosefot Rabbeinu Peretz* (*Menaḥot* 44b; see *Shita Mekubbetzet* here), according to which the Gemara is referring to the verse stated with regard to the second day of *Sukkot*: "And their meal offering and their libation for the bulls, for the rams" (Numbers 29:18). It is derived from the fact that the meal offering and libations are mentioned before the animal offerings that the meal offering and libations of the animal offerings of the first day of *Sukkot* may be sacrificed on the next day, the second day of *Sukkot*.

And furthermore, etc. – וְתוּ וכו׳: This difficulty pertains not only to the statement of Rav Huna, son of Rav Yehoshua, who derived from the *halakha* of a nazirite's sin offering that it is indispensable for a sin offering to be sacrificed for its owner's sake, but also to Rabbi Yona's derivation that it is indispensable for a sin offering to be sacrificed for its own sake.

Can the ***halakhot*** **be derived from one another** – מִי גָּמְרִי מֵהֲדָדֵי: The derivation from a nazirite's sin offering assumes that since it is stated with regard to a standard sin offering that it must be sacrificed for its sake, this applies with regard to a nazirite's sin offering as well. Therefore, the allusion to this *halakha* in the verse concerning a nazirite's sin offering is superfluous, and so it is interpreted as indicating that this requirement is indispensable with regard to both types of sin offerings. The Gemara questions the presumption that the *halakhot* of these sin offerings can be derived from one another.

A sin offering brought for eating forbidden fat – חַטַּאת חֵלֶב: This refers to a standard sin offering, which is brought to atone for transgressing a prohibition that is punishable by *karet* when transgressed intentionally. A standard sin offering is referred to as a sin offering brought for eating forbidden fat because this was the most common unwitting transgression of a prohibition punishable by *karet*. One can easily confuse forbidden fat for permitted fat, as they look and taste similar.

אֶלָּא אָמַר רָבָא: אָתְיָא מֵחַטַּאת מְצוֹרָע, דִּכְתִיב: ״וְעָשָׂה הַכֹּהֵן אֶת הַחַטָּאת״, שֶׁיְּהוּ כׇּל עֲשִׂיּוֹתָיו לְשֵׁם חַטָּאת.

Rather, Rava says:[N] These *halakhot* are **derived from** the *halakha* of **the sin offering of a leper;**[B] **as it is written: "And the priest shall offer [*ve'asa*] the sin offering"** (Leviticus 14:19), teaching **that all** sacrificial **actions of [*asiyyotav*]** a sin offering **must be** performed **for the sake of a sin offering.**

וְאַשְׁכְּחַן שִׁנּוּי קֹדֶשׁ, שִׁנּוּי בְּעָלִים מְנָלֵיהּ? אָמַר קְרָא: ״וְכִפֶּר עַל הַמִּטַּהֵר״ וגו׳, עַל הַמִּטַּהֵר זֶה וְלֹא עַל הַמִּטַּהֵר חֲבֵירוֹ.

And we found a source for the *halakha* that a sin offering must be sacrificed without **deviation** from the type of **offering,** and that this is indispensable. **From where do we** derive that sacrificing a sin offering without **deviation** with regard to the **owner** is also indispensable? **The verse states: "And make atonement for the one that is to be purified** of his impurity" (Leviticus 14:19), indicating that the sin offering must be sacrificed **for** the sake of **this** person **who is being purified, and not for another** person **who is to be purified.**

וְאַכַּתִּי מִי יָלְפָא מֵהֲדָדֵי? חַטַּאת חֵלֶב מֵחַטַּאת מְצוֹרָע לָא יָלְפָא – שֶׁכֵּן יֵשׁ עִמָּהּ דָּמִים אֲחֵרִים, חַטַּאת מְצוֹרָע מֵחַטַּאת חֵלֶב לָא גָּמְרָה – שֶׁכֵּן כָּרֵת!

The Gemara asks: **But still, can** the *halakhot* of a standard sin offering and a leper's sin offering **be derived from one another?** This comparison is also problematic. The *halakhot* of **a sin offering** brought for eating forbidden **fat cannot be derived from** the *halakhot* of **a leper's sin offering, since there is other blood** that is brought **with** the latter, i.e., a burnt offering and a guilt offering; and the *halakhot* of **a leper's sin offering cannot be derived from** the *halakhot* of **a sin offering** brought for eating forbidden **fat, since** the latter atones for a transgression punishable by ***karet.***

מֵחֲדָא לָא אָתְיָא, תֵּיתֵי חֲדָא מִתַּרְתֵּי.

The Gemara answers: Indeed, the *halakhot* of a sin offering **cannot be derived from** the *halakhot* of **one** other type of sin offering alone. But one can **derive** the *halakhot* of **one** type of sin offering **from** the *halakhot* of the other **two.** The verses concerning a standard sin offering, that of a leper, and that of a nazirite all contain elements that indicate that the offering must be sacrificed for its own sake. Two of them together are sufficient to teach that this *halakha* applies to the third case. The third case is therefore apparently extraneous, and it is understood to teach that proper intent in this regard is indispensable for all the offering's rites.

בְּהֵי לָא לִכְתּוֹב? [לָא לִכְתּוֹב] רַחֲמָנָא בְּחַטַּאת חֵלֶב וְתֵיתֵי מֵהָנָךְ – מָה לְהָנָךְ שֶׁכֵּן יֵשׁ עִמָּהֶם דָּמִים אֲחֵרִים!

The Gemara asks: **With regard to which** type of sin offering **should** the Torah **not have written** this *halakha*, i.e., which of the three cases should be regarded as the extraneous case? If you say: **Let the Merciful One not write** it **with regard to a sin offering** brought for eating forbidden **fat, and** one can **derive** it **from these** other sin offerings, i.e., those of a nazirite and a leper, this can be refuted: **What** is notable **about these** other sin offerings? They are notable **in that there is other blood** brought **with them.** Therefore, the *halakha* should apply only to similar sin offerings.

לָא לִכְתּוֹב רַחֲמָנָא בְּחַטַּאת נָזִיר וְתֵיתֵי מֵהָנָךְ – מָה לְהָנָךְ שֶׁכֵּן אֵין לָהֶן שְׁאֵלָה!

If you say: **Let the Merciful One not write** it **with regard to a nazirite's sin offering, and** one can **derive** it **from these** other sin offerings, those of a leper and a sinner, this can also be refuted: **What** is notable **about these** other sin offerings? They are notable **in that** one **does not have** the option of obtaining an exemption through **a request** to a halakhic authority.[B] A nazirite, by contrast, can request of a halakhic authority to dissolve his vow of naziriteship, thereby nullifying his obligation.

NOTES

Rather Rava says – **אֶלָּא אָמַר רָבָא**: Like Rabbi Yona's explanation, Rava's derivation is based on the assumption that the requirement of sacrificing a sin offering for its sake and for its owner's sake is derived from the verses of a standard sin offering; Rava derives from the verse about a leper's sin offering that this requirement is indispensable to the sacrificial process, just as Rabbi Yona derives it from the verse about a nazirite's sin offering (Rashi).

The *Shita Mekubbetzet* explains that Rava accepts Rabbi Yona's derivation with regard to the obligation to sacrifice the offering for its own sake. Rava's derivation concerns only the requirement of sacrificing the offering for the sake of its owner.

BACKGROUND

Leper [*metzora*] – **מְצוֹרָע**: The *halakhot* of *tzara'at*, traditionally rendered as leprosy but not necessarily identified medically with that illness, are recorded in the Torah in Leviticus, chapters 13–14. They are detailed in tractate *Nega'im*, which deals exclusively with the different types of leprosy. The *halakha* distinguishes between the ritual impurity of a quarantined leper, i.e., a suspected leper, who is isolated for a period of up to two weeks until his status is clarified, and that of a confirmed leper. A confirmed leper must grow his hair long, rend his garments, and cover his head in a particular way. Part of the purification process involves removing all of his body hair.

Request to a halakhic authority – **שְׁאֵלָה**: If a person makes a vow or takes an oath, and afterward he regrets having done so, he may go to a halakhic authority and request that he dissolve his vow or oath. In certain instances, the halakhic authority has the power to dissolve the vow, abrogating it retroactively. There are certain vows that are automatically dissolved and do not require the intervention of a halakhic authority. Others can be dissolved only under specific conditions.

לָא לִכְתּוֹב רַחֲמָנָא בְּחַטַּאת מְצוֹרָע וְתֵיתֵי מֵהָנָךְ – מַה לְהָנָךְ שֶׁכֵּן אֵין בָּאִין בְּדַלּוּת!

If you say: **Let the Merciful One not write** it **with regard to a leper's sin offering, and** one can **derive** it **from these** other sin offerings, those of a nazirite and a sinner, this can also be refuted: **What** is notable **about these** other sin offerings? They are notable **in that they cannot be brought** from doves instead of sheep if the owner is **poor**, unlike a leper's sin offering (see Leviticus 14:21). Therefore, the *halakhot* of these different sin offerings cannot be derived from one another.

אֶלָּא אָמַר קְרָא: ״זֹאת הַתּוֹרָה לָעֹלָה וְלַמִּנְחָה״ וגו׳ – הִקִּישׁוֹ הַכָּתוּב לִשְׁלָמִים, מַה שְּׁלָמִים – בֵּין שִׁנּוּי קֹדֶשׁ בֵּין שִׁנּוּי בְּעָלִים בָּעֵינַן לִשְׁמָן לְמִצְוָה, אַף חַטָּאת – בֵּין שִׁנּוּי קֹדֶשׁ בֵּין שִׁנּוּי בְּעָלִים בָּעֵינַן לִשְׁמָן לְמִצְוָה.

Rather, the *halakha* is derived from that which **the verse states: "This is the law of the burnt offering, and of the meal offering,** and of the sin offering, and of the guilt offering, and of the consecration offering, and of the sacrifice of peace offerings" (Leviticus 7:37). **The verse juxtaposes** a sin offering **with a peace offering,** indicating that **just as** for **a peace offering we require** intent **for its sake, as a mitzva** *ab initio*, **both** concerning the **deviation** from the type of **offering and** concerning **deviation** with regard to the **owner, so too,** for **a sin offering we require** intent **for its sake as a mitzva, both** concerning **deviation** from the type of **offering and** concerning **deviation** with regard to the **owner.**

הִילְכָּךְ, מִצְוָה מִשְּׁלָמִים, וְהָנָךְ קְרָאֵי לְעַכֵּב.

Therefore, the **mitzva** *ab initio* is derived **from** the *halakha* of a **peace offering; and those verses** mentioned earlier, from which this requirement is derived with regard to each type of sin offering separately, repeat the *halakha* **to** teach that it is **indispensable.**

וְאַשְׁכַּחַן חַטַּאת חֵלֶב דִּכְתִיב בָּהּ ״לְחַטָּאת״,

The Gemara asks: **And we found** a source for these *halakhot* with regard to **a sin offering** brought for eating forbidden **fat, as it is written with regard to it:** "And slaughter it **for a sin offering**" (Leviticus 4:33), indicating that it must be slaughtered for the sake of a sin offering. Likewise, sources for this *halakha* with regard to the sin offerings of a nazirite and a leper have also been cited.

Perek **I**
Daf **8** Amud **b**

חַטָּאת דַּעֲבוֹדָה זָרָה, דִּשְׁמִיעַת הַקּוֹל וּבִטּוּי שְׂפָתַיִם, וְטוּמְאַת מִקְדָּשׁ וְקָדָשָׁיו, דְּלָא כְּתִיב בְּהוּ, מְנָלַן?

From where do we derive these *halakhot* with regard to **a sin offering** brought **for idol worship,**[N] which has unique *halakhot*, as detailed in Numbers 15:27–31, and with regard to which the term: For a sin offering, is not written? Likewise, from where do we derive them with regard to the sin offerings that are brought **for** the **hearing of the voice,**[B] **and for an utterance**[B] **of the lips, and** for the **defiling of** the **Temple or its sacrificial** foods, which also have unique *halakhot* (Leviticus 5:1–13), and **with regard to which** the term: For a sin offering, **is not written** either?

NOTES

A sin offering brought for idol worship – חַטָּאת דַּעֲבוֹדָה זָרָה: This is a reference to the type of sin offering recorded in Numbers 15:22–31, which, according to the tradition of the Sages, is brought by one who transgresses the prohibition of idol worship unwittingly. Its purpose is similar to that of a standard sin offering: It atones for transgressing a prohibition punishable by *karet* that was performed unwittingly. Nevertheless, its details are different. A standard individual sin offering is a goat or a lamb, and a standard sin offering for an unwitting communal sin is a bull. By contrast, an individual sin offering for idolatrous worship is specifically a goat, and a communal sin offering for idolatrous worship is also a goat, and is brought together with a bull burnt offering.

BACKGROUND

Hearing the voice – שְׁמִיעַת הַקּוֹל: If an individual is approached by a litigant who asks him to testify in a court on his behalf, the witness must participate in the trial. In the event that he denies having knowledge and takes a false oath to that effect, he will, upon subsequent confession of his sin, be required to bring a sliding-scale sin offering, i.e., a sin offering whose type depends on the financial status of the sinner. The halakhic obligation of witnesses to testify is called hearing the voice, based on the verse: "And if anyone sins, in that he hears the voice of adjuration, he being a witness, whether he has seen or known, if he does not utter it, then he shall bear his iniquity" (Leviticus 5:1). It is irrelevant if the false oath was taken intentionally or not.

An oath on an utterance – שְׁבוּעַת בִּיטּוּי: This expression is derived from the verse: "Or a person who takes an oath to express with lips to do harm or to do good, for everything that a person shall express in an oath, and it was hidden from him and he knew and he is guilty of one of these" (Leviticus 5:4). This oath, which one takes to obligate himself, is called an oath on an utterance, to distinguish it from other oaths, e.g., an oath of testimony. The details of its numerous and complex *halakhot* are articulated in tractate *Shevuot*. The *halakha* is that one who intentionally takes a false oath is not liable to receive *karet*, although he is in violation of a Torah prohibition. If he transgresses the prohibition unwittingly, he is liable to bring a sliding-scale sin offering.

חַטָּאת דַּעֲבוֹדָה זָרָה אָתְיָא מֵחַטַּאת חֵלֶב, שֶׁכֵּן כָּרֵת כְּמוֹתָהּ. וְהָנָךְ כּוּלְּהִי אָתְיָין בְּמָה הַצַּד.

The Gemara answers: With regard to **a sin offering** brought **for idol worship,** these *halakhot* are **derived from** the *halakhot* of a **sin offering** brought for eating forbidden **fat, as** idol worship is also punishable by ***karet*****, similar to** consumption of forbidden fat. **And** with regard to **all these** other sin offerings, which are brought for transgressions not punishable by *karet*, these *halakhot* **are derived by** analogy from **the common element**[N] of the aforementioned three sources, namely, a standard sin offering, the sin offering of a nazirite, and the sin offering of a leper.

תָּנוּ רַבָּנַן: פֶּסַח בִּזְמַנּוֹ, לִשְׁמוֹ – כָּשֵׁר, שֶׁלֹּא לִשְׁמוֹ – פָּסוּל; וּבִשְׁאָר יְמוֹת הַשָּׁנָה, לִשְׁמוֹ – פָּסוּל, שֶׁלֹּא לִשְׁמוֹ – כָּשֵׁר.

§ **The Sages taught:** When **a Paschal offering** is sacrificed **at its** appointed **time,** on Passover eve after noon, if it is sacrificed **for its sake,** it is **fit;** if it is sacrificed **not for its sake,** it is **unfit,** as stated in the mishna. **And** when an offering consecrated as a Paschal offering is sacrificed **during the rest of the days of the year,** if it is sacrificed **for its sake,**[H] it is **unfit;**[N] if it is sacrificed **not for its sake,** it is **fit.**[H]

(של"ו קבאיצ"ן ממה"ר בצ"א ב"א, סִימָן)

The Gemara presents **a mnemonic** for the names of the *amora'im* mentioned in this discussion: ***Shin, lamed, vav; kuf, beit, alef, yod, tzadi, nun; mem, mem, heh, reish; beit, tzadi, alef; beit, alef.***

מְנָא הָנֵי מִילֵּי? אָמַר אֲבוּהּ דִּשְׁמוּאֵל: אָמַר קְרָא "וְאִם מִן הַצֹּאן קָרְבָּנוֹ לְזֶבַח שְׁלָמִים לַה׳", דָּבָר הַבָּא מִן הַצֹּאן – יְהֵא לְזֶבַח שְׁלָמִים.

The Gemara asks: **From where are these matters** derived, i.e., that if a Paschal offering is sacrificed during the rest of the year it is fit if sacrificed not for its sake? **Shmuel's father says: The verse states: "And if his offering for a sacrifice of peace offerings unto the Lord is of the flock"** (Leviticus 3:6), indicating that an offering **that is brought** only **from the flock**[N] **will be a sacrifice of peace offerings.**[N] The Paschal offering fulfills this criterion.

אֵימָא: שְׁלָמִים – אִין, מִידֵּי אַחֲרִינָא – לָא! אָמַר רַבִּי אִילָא אָמַר רַבִּי יוֹחָנָן: "לְזֶבַח" – לְרַבּוֹת כָּל זֶבַח.

The Gemara challenges: **Say** that if it is sacrificed for the sake of **a peace offering, yes,** it is fit, but if it is sacrificed for the sake of **some other** offering, it is **not** fit. **Rabbi Ila says** that **Rabbi Yoḥanan says:** The redundant expression **"for a sacrifice"** in Leviticus 3:6 is stated **to include any** type of **sacrifice.**

אֵימָא: כָּל דְּשָׁחֵיט לֶיהֱוֵי כְּמוֹתָהּ!

The Gemara asks: If so, **say** that a Paschal offering **should be** rendered **as any** offering for **which** one **slaughters** it; for example, if it is slaughtered for the sake of a burnt offering, it should be rendered a burnt offering.

אִי הֲוָה כְּתִיב "לִשְׁלָמִים וְזֶבַח" – כִּדְקָאָמְרַתְּ, הַשְׁתָּא דִּכְתִיב "לְזֶבַח שְׁלָמִים" – לְכָל דְּשָׁחֵיט לֵיהּ שְׁלָמִים לֶיהֱוֵי.

The Gemara answers: **If** the phrase: **For peace offerings and a sacrifice, was written** in the verse, it would be **as you say. Now that it is written: "For a sacrifice of peace offerings,"** it indicates that **for whatever** type of offering one **slaughters it, it will be a peace offering.**

אֵימָא: "לְזֶבַח" – כְּלָל, "שְׁלָמִים" – פְּרָט, כְּלָל וּפְרָט – אֵין בִּכְלָל אֶלָּא מַה שֶּׁבַּפְּרָט: שְׁלָמִים – אִין, מִידֵּי אַחֲרִינָא – לָא!

The Gemara challenges: **Say** that: **"For a sacrifice,"** is **a generalization** and: **"Of peace offerings,"** is **a detail,** and according to the principles of biblical hermeneutics, wherever there is **a generalization and a detail, the generalization includes only that which is** specified **in the detail.** Accordingly, if the offering is sacrificed for the sake of **a peace offering, yes,** it is fit; but if it is sacrificed for the sake of **another** offering, it is **not** fit.

"לַה׳" הֲדַר וְכָלַל.

The Gemara answers: With the term: **"Unto the Lord,"** the verse **then generalized** again. Therefore, the verse is formulated as a generalization, a detail, and a generalization, as the Gemara will explain.

HALAKHA

A Paschal offering sacrificed during the rest of the days of the year for its sake – בִּשְׁאָר יְמוֹת הַשָּׁנָה לִשְׁמוֹ: A Paschal offering that was sacrificed for its sake, not at its appropriate time of sacrifice but during the rest of the year, is disqualified (Rambam *Sefer Avoda, Hilkhot Pesulei HaMukdashin* 15:12).

If sacrificed not for its sake it is fit – שֶׁלֹּא לִשְׁמוֹ כָּשֵׁר: A Paschal offering that was sacrificed on a day other than Passover eve, with a different type of offering in mind, is fit (Rambam *Sefer Avoda, Hilkhot Pesulei HaMukdashin* 15:11).

NOTES

These *halakhot* are derived by analogy from the common element – אָתְיָין בְּמָה הַצַּד: By deriving these *halakhot* from the common element, the unique element of stringency of each sin offering is neutralized. Consequently, although taking a false oath on testimony or on an utterance is not punishable by *karet*, the sin offering of a nazirite and a leper prove that this factor is irrelevant to the *halakha* of intent for the sake of the offering and its owner. Although it can be claimed that there is no comparison to the sin offering of a nazirite and a leper, as other offerings are also brought with it, a standard sin offering proves that this factor is irrelevant too. Although bringing a sin offering for taking an oath on an utterance can be avoided by making a request to a halakhic authority for the dissolution of the oath, a nazirite's sin offering proves this factor irrelevant, as that sin offering can be avoided in the same manner. And although the sin offering for all three of these transgressions is a sliding-scale sin offering, a leper's sin offering proves this factor irrelevant, as it is also a sliding-scale sin offering.

During the rest of the days of the year if it is sacrificed for its sake it is unfit – בִּשְׁאָר יְמוֹת הַשָּׁנָה לִשְׁמוֹ פָּסוּל: The Gemara proceeds to discuss the source for the *halakha* that if it is sacrificed not for its sake, it is fit. Yet the Gemara does not cite a source for the *halakha* that if it is sacrificed for its sake it is unfit. Rashi explains that the Torah states several times that the time for sacrificing the Paschal offering is the afternoon of Passover eve, indicating that if it is sacrificed at another time as a Paschal offering, it is disqualified. *Tosafot* cite a logical explanation: Since the offering cannot serve as a Paschal offering when it is sacrificed at a time other than Passover eve, sacrificing it for the sake of a Paschal offering disqualifies it.

An offering that is brought only from the flock – דָּבָר הַבָּא מִן הַצֹּאן: Rashi maintains that this is indicated by the content of the verse, not by its superfluity. The Gemara (9a) cites several difficulties with this interpretation of the verse; e.g., a guilt offering is also brought only from sheep. *Tosefot Tukh* adds that the verse states explicitly that the offering can be a male or a female of the flock, whereas a Paschal offering is specifically a male.

Tosafot disagree with Rashi. They explain that since the subsequent verses detail the *halakhot* of sacrificing a peace offering in the event that it is a lamb or a goat, the verse: "And if his offering… is of the flock" is superfluous, and is therefore interpreted exegetically in reference to a Paschal offering, which is brought only from the flock.

Will be a sacrifice of peace offerings – יְהֵא לְזֶבַח שְׁלָמִים: Why is it assumed that this is referring to a Paschal offering that is sacrificed during the rest of the year not for its sake? If a Paschal offering is sacrificed on Passover eve not for its sake, the offering is disqualified, as stated in the mishna (2a), and as derived from the verses (see 7b). Likewise, if it is sacrificed during the rest of the year for its sake, it is clearly disqualified for other reasons. Therefore, this verse certainly is referring to a Paschal offering that is sacrificed during the rest of the year not for its sake.

מַתְקִיף לָהּ רַב יַעֲקֹב מִנְּהַר פְּקוֹד: הָא לָא דָּמֵי כְּלָלָא בָּתְרָא לִכְלָלָא קַמָּא, כְּלָלָא קַמָּא מְרַבֵּי זְבָחִים וְתוּ לָא, כְּלָלָא בָּתְרָא "לַה'" – כָּל דְּלַה', וַאֲפִילּוּ לְעוֹפוֹת וַאֲפִילּוּ לִמְנָחוֹת!

Rav Ya'akov of Nehar Pekod objects to this suggestion: **But the latter generalization is dissimilar to the former generalization. The former generalization:** "For a sacrifice," **includes** only **slaughtered offerings and nothing more,** whereas **the latter generalization:** "**Unto the Lord,**" includes **any** offering **unto the Lord. And** accordingly, **even** if the Paschal offering was sacrificed **for** the sake of **bird offerings, or even for** the sake of **meal offerings,** it should be fit, as these are brought "unto the Lord."

הָא תָּנָא דְּבֵי רַבִּי יִשְׁמָעֵאל בִּכְלָלֵי וּפְרָטֵי דָּרֵישׁ כִּי הַאי גַּוְונָא.

The Gemara responds to this objection: **The school of Rabbi Yishmael taught generalizations and details** even in examples **like this** case.

כְּלָל וּפְרָט וּכְלָל – אִי אַתָּה דָן אֶלָּא כְּעֵין הַפְּרָט, מַה הַפְּרָט מְפוֹרָשׁ שֶׁהוּא שֶׁלֹּא לִשְׁמוֹ וְכָשֵׁר – אַף כָּל שֶׁהוּא שֶׁלֹּא לִשְׁמוֹ וְכָשֵׁר.

The Gemara explains: Since "unto the Lord" is a second generalization, the verse is formulated as **a generalization, and a detail, and a generalization,** and **you may deduce** that the verse is referring **only** to items **similar to the detail. Just as** the items mentioned in **the detail** are clearly **defined as** a case where a Paschal offering was sacrificed **not for its own sake, and** nevertheless it is **fit, so too,** in **any** case **where it** was sacrificed **not for its sake but** for the sake of another offering, it is **fit.**

אִי מַה הַפְּרָט מְפוֹרָשׁ, דָּבָר הַבָּא בְּנֶדֶר וּבִנְדָבָה – אַף כָּל הַבָּא בְּנֶדֶר וּבִנְדָבָה; עוֹלָה וּשְׁלָמִים – אִין, חַטָּאת וְאָשָׁם – לָא!

The Gemara asks: **If** the verse is referring only to actions similar to the detail, then **just as** the items mentioned in **the detail** are clearly **defined** as a peace offering, which is **a matter that is brought as a vow** offering **or as a gift** offering, **so too,** a Paschal offering should be fit only if it was sacrificed for the sake of **any** offering **that is brought as a vow** offering **or as a gift** offering. Accordingly, if it was sacrificed for the sake of **a burnt offering or a peace offering, yes,** it is fit, as these are brought as a vow offering or as a gift offering; but if it was sacrificed for the sake of **a sin offering or a guilt offering,** it is **not** fit, as these are not brought as a vow offering or as a gift offering.

אֶלָּא: "לְזֶבַח" רִבּוּיָא הוּא.

The Gemara therefore rejects the exegetical method of generalizations and details in favor of that of amplifications and restrictions: **Rather,** the term: **"For a sacrifice," is** not a generalization, but **an amplification,** which includes any type of offering. Therefore, if a Paschal offering is sacrificed for the sake of any type of offering during the rest of the year, it is fit.

אֵימָא: לְכָל דְּשָׁחֵיט לֵיהּ לֶהֱוֵי כְּוָותֵיהּ!

The Gemara challenges: If so, **say** that it adds that a Paschal offering **should be** rendered **as any** offering **for which** one **slaughters** it. Why does Shmuel's father interpret that it is rendered a peace offering specifically?

אָמַר רַבִּי אָבִין:

Rabbi Avin says:

Perek **I**
Daf **9** Amud **a**

דּוֹחִין קָדָשִׁים הַנֶּאֱכָלִים אֵצֶל קָדָשִׁים הַנֶּאֱכָלִין, וְאֵין דּוֹחִין קָדָשִׁים הַנֶּאֱכָלִין אֵצֶל קָדָשִׁים שֶׁאֵינָן נֶאֱכָלִין.

Offerings that are eaten, in this case the Paschal offering, **are diverted** when slaughtered not for their sake **to** serve as other types of **offerings that are eaten,** such as peace offerings. **But offerings that are eaten are not diverted to** serve as **offerings that are not eaten,** such as burnt offerings.

אַטּוּ חַטָּאת וְאָשָׁם מִי לָא מִיתְאַכְלִי?

The Gemara asks: **Is that to say** that **a sin offering and a guilt offering are not eaten?** Why does a Paschal offering receive the status of a peace offering and not that of a sin offering or a guilt offering, which are eaten by the priests?

אֶלָּא, דּוֹחִין קָדָשִׁים הַנֶּאֱכָלִין לְכָל אָדָם אֵצֶל קָדָשִׁים הַנֶּאֱכָלִין לְכָל אָדָם, וְאֵין דּוֹחִין קָדָשִׁים הַנֶּאֱכָלִין לְכָל אָדָם אֵצֶל קָדָשִׁים שֶׁאֵין נֶאֱכָלִין לְכָל אָדָם.

Rather, the answer should be emended: **Offerings that are eaten by every** Jewish **person are diverted to** serve as **offerings eaten by every** Jewish **person,** i.e., peace offerings. **But offerings eaten by every** Jewish **person are not diverted to** serve as **offerings not eaten by every** Jewish **person,** i.e., sin offerings and guilt offerings, which are eaten only by priests.

רַבִּי יוֹסֵי בְּרַבִּי אָבִין אָמַר: דּוֹחִין קָדָשִׁים קַלִּים אֵצֶל קָדָשִׁים קַלִּים, וְאֵין דּוֹחִין קָדָשִׁים קַלִּים אֵצֶל קָדְשֵׁי קָדָשִׁים.

Rabbi Yosei, son of Rabbi Avin, says that there is a different answer: **Offerings of lesser sanctity are diverted to** serve as **offerings of lesser sanctity,** i.e., peace offerings. **But offerings of lesser sanctity are not diverted to** serve as **offerings of the most sacred order,** i.e., burnt offerings, sin offerings, or guilt offerings.

מַתְקִיף לַהּ רַב יִצְחָק בְּרַבִּי סַבְרִיו, אֵימָא: שְׁחָטֵיהּ לְשֵׁם מַעֲשֵׂר – לֶיהֱוֵי מַעֲשֵׂר; לְמַאי הִילְכְתָא? דְּלָא לִיבְעֵי נְסָכִים, וּלְמִלְקָא עֲלֵיהּ (בְּ"לֹא יִמָּכֵר") בְּ"לֹא יִגָּאֵל"!

Rav Yitzḥak, son of Rabbi Savriyu, objects to this answer:[N] If so, **say** that if one **slaughtered** a Paschal offering **for the sake of** the animal **tithe, let it be** rendered animal **tithe,** which, like a Paschal offering, is an offering of lesser sanctity. The Gemara adds: **For what *halakha*** does it matter, practically speaking, that a Paschal offering has been rendered an animal tithe rather than a peace offering? It matters **because** if it is rendered an animal tithe, **it should not require libations. And** furthermore, if one sells it, he **should be flogged for** transgressing the prohibition: **"It shall not be redeemed"** (Leviticus 27:33),[N] which applies to the animal tithe even after its slaughter.

אָמַר קְרָא: "הָעֲשִׂירִי יִהְיֶה קֹּדֶשׁ" – זֶה מַעֲשֵׂר וְאֵין אַחֵר מַעֲשֵׂר.

The Gemara responds: **The verse states** with regard to the animal tithe: **"The tenth shall be sacred"** (Leviticus 27:32). The definite article indicates that **this,** the tenth animal, is the **tithe, but another** animal slaughtered for its sake is **not a tithe.**

אֵימָא: שְׁחָטֵיהּ לְשֵׁם בְּכוֹר – לֶיהֱוֵי כִּבְכוֹר; לְמַאי הִילְכְתָא? דְּלָא לִיבְעֵי נְסָכִים. אִי נַמִי, דְּלִיתְבֵיהּ לְכֹהֲנִים!

The Gemara challenges: Still, **say** that if one **slaughtered** a Paschal offering **for the sake of a firstborn** animal, **let it be** rendered **like a firstborn.** The Gemara adds: **For what *halakha*** does it matter, practically speaking, that it has been rendered a firstborn rather than a peace offering? It matters **because** if it is rendered a firstborn, **it should not require libations. Also,** this means **that one should give it to the priests.**

בְּכוֹר נַמִי, עֲבָרָה עֲבָרָה מִמַּעֲשֵׂר גָּמַר.

The Gemara answers: With regard to **a firstborn too,** the verse states: "That you shall set apart [*veha'avarta*] unto the Lord all that opens the womb" (Exodus 13:12). Since with regard to the animal tithe it is stated: "Whatever passes [*ya'avor*] under the rod, the tenth shall be holy" (Leviticus 27:32), it is **derived** by verbal analogy between the **passing** [*avara*] stated with regard to a firstborn and the **passing** [*avara*] stated with regard to the animal **tithe** that a Paschal offering cannot become a firstborn either.

וְאֵימָא: שְׁחָטֵיהּ לְשֵׁם תְּמוּרָה – לֶיהֱוֵי תְּמוּרָה; לְמַאי הִילְכְתָא – לְמִלְקָא עֲלֵיהּ. אִי נַמִי, לְמֵיקַם עֲלֵיהּ בְּ"לֹא יִמָּכֵר וְלֹא יִגָּאֵל"!

The Gemara challenges: **But say** that if one **slaughtered** a Paschal offering **for the sake of a substitute, let it be** rendered **a substitute.** The Gemara adds: **For what *halakha*** does it matter, practically speaking, that it has been rendered a substitute rather than a peace offering? The one who slaughtered it **should be flogged for** transgressing the prohibition of effecting substitution. **Also,** its sale **should be determined to** violate the prohibition: **"It shall not be sold or redeemed"** (Leviticus 27:28).[N]

אָמַר מָר זוּטְרָא בְּרֵיהּ דְּרַב נַחְמָן, אָמַר קְרָא: "וְהָיָה הוּא וּתְמוּרָתוֹ" – זוֹ תְּמוּרָה, וְאֵין אַחֵר תְּמוּרָה.

Mar Zutra, son of Rav Naḥman, says: It is derived from that which **the verse states** with regard to substitution: **"Then both it and that for which it is changed** shall be sacred" (Leviticus 27:33). The verse teaches that only **it,** the animal substituted, is **a substitute, but another** animal is **not a substitute.**

וְאֵימָא: שְׁחָטֵיהּ לְשֵׁם תּוֹדָה – לֶיהֱוֵי כִּי תוֹדָה; לְמַאי הִילְכְתָא – לְהַטְעִינוֹ לֶחֶם!

The Gemara challenges: **But say** that if one **slaughtered** a Paschal offering **for the sake of a thanks offering, let it be** rendered **like a thanks offering.** The Gemara adds: **For what *halakha*** does it practically matter that it has been rendered a thanks offering rather than a peace offering? If so, **it should require** a meal offering of forty loaves of **bread.**

מִי אִיכָּא מִידֵי דְּפֶסַח גּוּפֵיהּ לָא בָּעֵי לֶחֶם, וּמוֹתָרוֹ בָּעֵי לֶחֶם?

The Gemara answers: **Is there anything,** i.e., any situation, comparable to this suggestion **that a Paschal offering itself does not require bread, but its leftover,** an animal consecrated as a Paschal offering but ultimately not sacrificed on Passover eve, **requires bread** when slaughtered not for its sake? Such a suggestion is implausible.

NOTES

Rav Yitzḥak son of Rabbi Savriyu objects to this answer – מַתְקִיף לַהּ רַב יִצְחָק בְּרַבִּי סַבְרִיו: *Tosafot* comment that this objection is relevant to both answers, but the subsequent objection, concerning a Paschal offering that was slaughtered for the sake of a firstborn, pertains only to the answer of Rabbi Yosei, son of Rabbi Avin, which distinguishes between offerings of lesser sanctity and offerings of the most sacred order. This is because according to the previous answer, a firstborn is dissimilar to a Paschal offering, as a firstborn is consumed only by priests, whereas a Paschal offering is consumed by any Jew.

It shall not be redeemed – לֹא יִגָּאֵל: Although this verse is stated in reference to a substitute, the Sages derive from its juxtaposition with the verse concerning the animal tithe (Leviticus 27:32) that this prohibition applies with regard to the animal tithe as well. Furthermore, the Sages derive that in addition to the prohibition against redeeming a substitute or animal tithe, this verse also includes the prohibition against selling it.

It shall not be sold or redeemed – לֹא יִמָּכֵר וְלֹא יִגָּאֵל: Although this would render the wording of the cited verse imprecise, it seems reasonable to suggest that Gemara is referring to the verse: "Then both it and that for which it is changed shall be sacred; it shall not be redeemed" (Leviticus 27:33).

NOTES

The leftover of a thanks offering itself – מוֹתַר תּוֹדָה עַצְמָהּ: If one consecrated an animal as a thanks offering and the animal was lost, and he then consecrated another animal in its place and subsequently found the first animal, the first animal is sacrificed as a standard thanks offering, and the second is sacrificed as a thanks offering without the forty loaves of bread.

Here too the word *min* is stated to exclude – הָכָא נַמִּי מִן לְהוֹצִיא: With regard to the word *min*, the answer is that certain types of the flock are excluded from the Paschal offering, as it must be a male in its first year. The main proof that the verse indicates a Paschal offering and not a guilt offering is apparently that the term "of the flock" can refer to a Paschal offering, as it is brought from all species of the flock, i.e., lambs and goats, whereas a guilt offering is brought only from the rams, and therefore the term "of the flock" is inaccurate in its regard.

אִי הָכִי, הָשְׁתָּא נַמִּי מִי אִיכָּא מִידֵּי דְּפֶסַח גּוּפֵיהּ לָא בָּעֵי נְסָכִים, וּמוֹתָרוֹ בָּעֵי נְסָכִים?

The Gemara asks: **If so, now** that a leftover Paschal offering slaughtered for the sake of a peace offering becomes a peace offering, this objection can **also** be raised: **Is there anything** comparable to the suggestion **that a Paschal offering itself does not require libations, but its leftover requires libations** as a peace offering?

אֲנַן הָכִי קָאָמְרִינַן: מִי אִיכָּא מִידֵּי דְּמוֹתַר תּוֹדָה עַצְמָהּ לָא בָּעֵי לֶחֶם, וְאִילּוּ מוֹתָר דְּאָתְיָא לְהוּ מֵעָלְמָא בָּעְיָא לֶחֶם?

The Gemara explains its answer: **This** is what **we are saying: Is there anything** comparable to the suggestion **that the leftover of a thanks offering itself**[N] **does not require bread, but** the **leftover** of an offering **from** some **other** category **requires bread?**

מַתְקִיף לָהּ רַב [יֵימָר] בְּרֵיהּ דְּרַב הִילֵּל: וּמִמַּאי דִּבְמוֹתַר פֶּסַח כְּתִיב? דִּילְמָא בְּמוֹתַר אָשָׁם כְּתִיב!

§ It was taught that the verse: "And if his offering for a sacrifice of peace offerings unto the Lord is of the flock" (Leviticus 3:6), teaches that a Paschal offering sacrificed not on Passover eve is rendered a peace offering if sacrificed not for its sake. **Rav Yeimar, son of Rav Hillel, objects to this: But from where** is it derived **that** this verse **is written with regard to a leftover Paschal offering? Perhaps it is written with regard to a leftover guilt offering;** a guilt offering is also brought only from the flock.

אָמַר רָבָא, אָמַר קְרָא: "וְאִם מִן הַצֹּאן קָרְבָּנוֹ לְזֶבַח שְׁלָמִים", דָּבָר הַשָּׁוֶה בְּכָל הַצֹּאן.

Rava says: The verse states: "And if his offering for a sacrifice of peace offerings unto the Lord **is of** [*min*] **the flock,"** where the term "*min*" indicates **that** is brought **equally from all** species of the **flock,** i.e., from both sheep and goats. A guilt offering, by contrast, is brought only from rams, i.e., male sheep.

מַתְקִיף לָהּ רַבִּי אָבִין בַּר חִיָּיא, וְאִיתֵּימָא רַבִּי אָבִין בַּר כָּהֲנָא: בְּכָל אֲתַר אַתְּ אָמְרַתְּ "מִן" לְהוֹצִיא, וְכָאן "מִן" לְרַבּוֹת!

Rabbi Avin bar Ḥiyya, and some say Rabbi Avin bar Kahana, objects to this: You say everywhere that the word **"*min*"** is stated **to exclude** items, **but here** you claim that the word **"*min*"** is stated **to include** all species of the flock? You should say the opposite: The verse indicates an offering that is brought only from some species of the flock, i.e., a guilt offering.

אָמַר רַבִּי מָנִי: הָכָא נַמִּי "מִן" – לְהוֹצִיא, דְּלָא אָתֵי בֶּן שְׁתֵּי שָׁנִים וְלָא אָתֵי בִּנְקֵיבָה.

Rabbi Mani says: Here too, the word **"*min*"** is stated **to exclude**[N] certain categories of the flock, **as** a Paschal offering **is not brought** from an animal that is **in its second year, and is not brought from** the **female** animals of the flock.

מַתְקִיף לָהּ רַב חָנָא בַּגְדָּתָאָה: וּמִי מָצֵית אָמְרַתְּ דְּכִי כְּתִיב הַאי בְּמוֹתַר פֶּסַח כְּתִיב? וְהָא מִדִּכְתִיב: "אִם כֶּשֶׂב" "אִם עֵז" – מִכְּלָל דְּלָאו בְּמוֹתַר פֶּסַח כְּתִיב!

The Gemara cites another objection. **Rav Ḥana of Baghdad objects to this: How can you say that when this verse is written, it is written with regard to a leftover Paschal offering? But from** that **which is written** in the subsequent verses: "If he brings **a lamb**" (Leviticus 3:7), and "**if** his offering is **a goat**" (Leviticus 3:12), one learns **by inference that** the passage is **not written with regard to a leftover Paschal offering;** the Torah states elsewhere, in Exodus 12:5, that a Paschal offering is brought from both lambs and goats, and it is unnecessary to teach this again in Leviticus.

הַהוּא מִיבָּעֵי לֵיהּ לְכִדְתַנְיָא: "כֶּבֶשׂ" – לְרַבּוֹת אֶת הַפֶּסַח לְאַלְיָה,

The Gemara answers: **Those** verses **are necessary for that which is taught** in a *baraita*: The word **"lamb"** is written **to include the Paschal offering in** the requirement that the **tail**[B] be offered on the altar, which is written subsequently with regard to a peace offering (Leviticus 3:9), since this *halakha* is not mentioned in the verses concerning the Paschal offering.

BACKGROUND

Tail – אַלְיָה: This is the long, thick, fatty tail of the breed of sheep that was common in Eretz Yisrael and the surrounding regions during the Temple era. The tail covered the entire back of the sheep to the extent that it was difficult to ascertain its sex, particularly in younger animals. The Torah writes that when a lamb is brought as a peace offering, the tail is one of the parts of the animal consumed on the altar. This applies only to lambs, as other animals that are sacrificed, e.g., goats, do not have this kind of tail.

Fat-tailed sheep

כְּשֶׁהוּא אוֹמֵר: ״אִם כֶּבֶשׂ״ – לְרַבּוֹת פֶּסַח שֶׁעִיבְּרָה שְׁנָתָהּ, וּשְׁלָמִים הַבָּאִים מֵחֲמַת פֶּסַח, לְכׇל מִצְוֹת שְׁלָמִים, שֶׁיְּטָעֲנוּ סְמִיכָה וּנְסָכִים וּתְנוּפַת חָזֶה וָשׁוֹק. כְּשֶׁהוּא אוֹמֵר: ״אִם עֵז״ – הִפְסִיק הָעִנְיָן, לִימֵּד עַל הָעֵז שֶׁאֵינָהּ טְעוּנָה אַלְיָה.

The *baraita* continues: **When the verse states: "If** he brings **a lamb,"** it is **to include in all the mitzvot of peace offerings a Paschal offering whose** first **year has passed**[H] and is therefore too old to be sacrificed as a Paschal offering, **and peace offerings brought due to a Paschal offering.**[N] Specifically, this indicates **that they require placing hands** on the head of the offering, **libations, and the waving of** the **breast and thigh. And when** the verse **states:** "And **if** his offering is **a goat," it interrupted the** previous **matter**[N] and **taught that the** sacrificing of **a goat does not require** that the **tail** be burned on the altar.[HN]

וְהָא מֵהָכָא נָפְקָא? מִדַּאֲבוּהּ דִּשְׁמוּאֵל נָפְקָא! דְּאָמַר אֲבוּהּ דִּשְׁמוּאֵל: ״וְאִם מִן הַצֹּאן קׇרְבָּנוֹ לְזֶבַח שְׁלָמִים״ – דָּבָר הַבָּא מִן הַצֹּאן יְהֵא לְזֶבַח שְׁלָמִים.

The Gemara asks: **But is it derived from here** that a Paschal offering that is too old to be sacrificed as a Paschal offering is sacrificed as a peace offering? **It is derived from** the verse **that Shmuel's father**[P] cites, **as Shmuel's father says:** The verse: **"And if his offering for a sacrifice of peace offerings** unto the Lord **is of the flock"** (Leviticus 3:6), teaches that an offering **that is brought** only **from the flock,** i.e., the Paschal offering, **will be a sacrifice of peace offerings.**

וְאַכַּתִּי, מִדְּרַב נַחְמָן אָמַר רַבָּה בַּר אֲבוּהּ נָפְקָא, דְּאָמַר רַב נַחְמָן אָמַר רַבָּה בַּר אֲבוּהּ: מִנַּיִן לְמוֹתַר פֶּסַח שֶׁקָּרֵב שְׁלָמִים – שֶׁנֶּאֱמַר: ״וְזָבַחְתָּ פֶּסַח לַה׳ אֱלֹהֶיךָ צֹאן וּבָקָר״, וַהֲלֹא אֵין פֶּסַח בָּא אֶלָּא מִן הַכְּבָשִׂים וּמִן הָעִזִּים! אֶלָּא, מִכָּאן לְמוֹתַר הַפֶּסַח שֶׁיְּהֵא לְדָבָר הַבָּא מִן הַצֹּאן וּמִן הַבָּקָר, וּמַאי נִיהוּ – שְׁלָמִים!

The Gemara responds: **But** even without the *baraita*, Shmuel's father's statement is **still** superfluous, as that *halakha* is **derived from that which Rav Naḥman** says that **Rabba bar Avuh says. As Rav Naḥman says** that **Rabba bar Avuh says: From where** is it derived **that a leftover Paschal offering is sacrificed as a peace offering? As it is stated: "And you shall sacrifice the Passover offering unto the Lord, your God, of the flock and the herd"** (Deuteronomy 16:2). Why is the herd mentioned? **But isn't a Paschal offering brought only from the lambs and from the goats? Rather,** it is derived **from here that a leftover Paschal offering should be** sacrificed as an offering **brought** both **from the flock and from the herd. And what is that?** It is **a peace offering.**

אֶלָּא, תְּלָתָא קְרָאֵי כְּתִיבִי;

Rather, none of these derivations are superfluous, as **three verses are written** that teach the *halakha* that a Paschal offering that is sacrificed not on Passover eve is sacrificed as a peace offering.

HALAKHA

A Paschal offering whose first year has passed – פֶּסַח שֶׁעִיבְּרָה שְׁנָתָהּ: A Paschal offering that became one year old and a peace offering that is brought due to a Paschal offering have the status of a standard peace offering. They require placing hands on the head of the offering, libations, and the waving of the breast and thigh. These are not required in the sacrifice of a Paschal offering (Rambam *Sefer Korbanot, Hilkhot Korban Pesaḥ* 4:7).

A goat does not require that the tail be burned on the altar – הָעֵז שֶׁאֵינָהּ טְעוּנָה אַלְיָה: The portions of an ox or a goat that are consumed on the altar consist of the forbidden fat that covers the innards, the kidneys, and the lobe of the liver. In the sacrifice of a lamb offering, the tail is also consumed on the altar (Rambam *Sefer Avoda, Hilkhot Ma'aseh HaKorbanot* 1:18).

NOTES

Peace offerings brought due to a Paschal offering – שְׁלָמִים הַבָּאִים מֵחֲמַת פֶּסַח: Rashi explains that this is referring to a peace offering brought on the fourteenth of Nisan, Passover eve, together with the Paschal offering, so as to eat its meat before the Paschal offering and thereby eat the Paschal offering to become satiated. This peace offering was called the Festival peace offering of the fourteenth.

And if his offering is a goat, it interrupted the previous matter – אִם עֵז הִפְסִיק הָעִנְיָן: The only apparent difference between the sacrifice of a peace offering lamb and goat is that the tail is not mentioned with regard to a goat. By inference, the reason that a separate passage is devoted to the sacrifice of a peace offering goat is in order to teach that the tail of a goat is not burned (*Tosafot* on 96b, citing Riva).

A goat does not require that the tail be burned on the altar – הָעֵז שֶׁאֵינָהּ טְעוּנָה אַלְיָה: The tail that is burned on the altar is not merely the thick, fatty section found underneath the tail of a sheep. It also includes some of the bone and fat from the body of the animal itself and some sections of the rump bone. Therefore, it was necessary to state that this part of a goat is not burned on the altar even though it does not have an actual tail. Nevertheless, it does have the other parts of the body that are removed together with the tail.

PERSONALITIES

Shmuel's father – אֲבוּהּ דִּשְׁמוּאֵל: Shmuel's father was the first-generation *amora* Rabbi Abba bar Abba the priest. In the Babylonian Talmud he is nicknamed after his famous son, as the name Abba was very common. In the Jerusalem Talmud he is referred to as Rabbi Ba bar Va.

Rabbi Abba bar Abba was a distinguished personality in many respects. He was one of the greatest Sages in Babylonia and was a leader of the Jewish community there. When Rav came to Babylonia, he refused to accept leadership as long as Rabbi Abba bar Abba was still alive.

Rabbi Abba bar Abba apparently studied under the tutelage of the Babylonian Sages of the previous generation, including Rabbi Yehuda ben Beteira. He also studied under Rabbi Yehuda HaNasi in Eretz Yisrael, and asked him many questions, both in person and via letters.

The Sages of Eretz Yisrael had great respect for him, and even after he returned to Babylonia they would send him questions by letter. He had a close relationship with the Sage Levi ben Sisi, who moved from Eretz Yisrael to Babylonia. They would study together in the study hall of Neharde'a and would travel together, and they had a common halakhic approach. When Levi ben Sisi died, Rabbi Abba bar Abba delivered a long eulogy for him.

Rabbi Abba bar Abba was a cotton merchant whose commerce would send him to many different cities. He was a wealthy man and a landowner who was very active in charity and good deeds, e.g., redeeming hostages. He was also a priest from a prestigious family. Besides his famous son Shmuel, he had another son, Rabbi Pineḥas, who was also a Torah scholar.

חד לְעִיבְּרָה זְמַנּוֹ וְעִיבְּרָה שְׁנָתוֹ, וְחַד לְעִיבְּרָה זְמַנּוֹ וְלֹא שְׁנָתוֹ, וְחַד לְלֹא עִיבְּרָה לֹא זְמַנּוֹ וְלֹא שְׁנָתוֹ.

One verse teaches this *halakha* in a case where **its time** of sacrifice, Passover eve, **has passed, and its** first **year has** also **passed,** disqualifying it for sacrifice as a Paschal offering. **And one** verse teaches the *halakha* in a case where **its time** of sacrifice **has passed, but not its** first **year. And** the third **one** teaches a case where **neither its time** of sacrifice **nor its** first **year has passed,** but it was sacrificed before Passover eve.

וּצְרִיכִי, דְּאִי כְּתַב רַחֲמָנָא חַד, הֲוָה אָמֵינָא – הֵיכָא דְּעִיבְּרָה שְׁנָתוֹ וּזְמַנּוֹ, דְּאִידְּחֵי מִפֶּסַח לְגַמְרֵי, אֲבָל עִיבְּרָה זְמַנּוֹ וְלֹא שְׁנָתוֹ דַּחֲזֵי לְפֶסַח שֵׁנִי – אֵימָא לָא;

And all these verses **are necessary. As, had the Merciful One written** only **one** of the verses, **I would say** that it is referring to a case **where** both **its** first **year and its time** of sacrifice **have passed.** Only such a Paschal offering should be sacrificed as a peace offering, **as it was completely rejected from** its status as a **Paschal offering. But** in a case where **its time** of sacrifice **has passed, but its** first **year** has **not** passed, in **which** case it is still **fit to** be sacrificed as a Paschal offering on the **second** ***Pesaḥ*****,**[B] **I would say** that it is **not** sacrificed as a peace offering.

וְאִי כְּתַב רַחֲמָנָא הָנֵי תַּרְתֵּי – מִשּׁוּם דְּאִידְּחֵי לְהוּ מִמִּילְּתַיְיהוּ, אֲבָל הֵיכָא דְּלָא עָבַר לֹא זְמַנּוֹ וְלֹא שְׁנָתוֹ, דַּחֲזֵי לְפֶסַח – אֵימָא לָא, צְרִיכִי.

And had the Merciful One written only **these two** verses, one might assume that only these Paschal offerings are sacrificed as peace offerings, **as they were** both **rejected from their status** as Paschal offerings. **But** in a case **where neither its time** of sacrifice **nor its** first **year have passed,** in **which** case it is still **fit to** be sacrificed as a **Paschal offering** on Passover eve, **I would say** that it is **not** sacrificed as a peace offering. Therefore, all three verses **are necessary.**

אָמַר רַב מִשְּׁמֵיהּ דְּמָבוֹג: חַטָּאת שֶׁשְּׁחָטָהּ לְשׁוּם חַטַּאת נַחְשׁוֹן – כְּשֵׁירָה, דְּאָמַר קְרָא: ״זֹאת תּוֹרַת הַחַטָּאת״, תּוֹרָה אַחַת לְכָל הַחַטָּאוֹת.

§ **Rav says in the name of Mavog:**[L] **A sin offering that** one **slaughtered for the sake of a sin offering of Nahshon,** i.e., a sin offering similar to those brought by the princes during the dedication of the Tabernacle (see Numbers, chapter 7), not to atone for a sin but as a gift, **is fit** and satisfies its owner's obligation; **as the verse states: "This is the law of the sin offering"** (Leviticus 6:18), indicating that there is **one law for all the sin offerings.**

יָתֵיב רָבָא וְקָאָמַר לַהּ לְהָא שְׁמַעְתָּא. אֵיתִיבֵיהּ רַב מְשַׁרְשְׁיָא לְרָבָא, רַבִּי שִׁמְעוֹן אוֹמֵר: כָּל הַמְּנָחוֹת שֶׁנִּקְמְצוּ שֶׁלֹּא לִשְׁמָן – כְּשֵׁירוֹת וְעָלוּ לַבְּעָלִים לְשׁוּם חוֹבָה,

Rava sat and stated this *halakha* of Mavog. **Rav Mesharshiyya**[P] **raised an objection to Rava** from a *baraita*: **Rabbi Shimon says: All meal offerings from which a handful was removed not for their sake** but for the sake of another type of meal offering **are fit, and satisfied the obligation of the owner,** in contrast to animal offerings, which if slaughtered not for their sake do not satisfy their owners' obligations.

לְפִי שֶׁאֵין הַמְּנָחוֹת דּוֹמוֹת לִזְבָחִים, שֶׁהַקּוֹמֵץ מַחֲבַת לְשֵׁם מַרְחֶשֶׁת – מַעֲשֶׂיהָ מוֹכִיחִין עָלֶיהָ שֶׁהִיא מַחֲבַת, חֲרֵיבָה לְשֵׁם בְּלוּלָה – מַעֲשֶׂיהָ מוֹכִיחִין שֶׁהִיא חֲרֵיבָה.

This is **because meal offerings are not similar to slaughtered offerings. As, if one removes a handful** from a meal offering prepared in a shallow **pan**[B] **for the sake of** a meal offering prepared in **a deep pan,**[B] his intention is demonstrably incorrect, as **its** mode of **preparation proves that it is** a meal offering prepared in a shallow **pan.** Likewise, if one removes a handful from **a dry** meal offering **for the sake of** a meal offering **mixed** with oil,[N] his intention is demonstrably incorrect, as **its** mode of **preparation proves that it is a dry** meal offering. The demonstrably incorrect nature of the intention prevents it from affecting the status of the meal offering in any way.

BACKGROUND

Second *Pesaḥ* – פֶּסַח שֵׁנִי: One who did not bring a Paschal offering, e.g., one who was ritually impure or far from Jerusalem, can compensate by bringing the offering on the fourteenth of Iyyar. There is a tannaitic dispute as to whether one who was not obligated to bring a Paschal offering must bring a second *Pesaḥ* on the fourteenth of Iyyar. Many of the *halakhot* that apply to the sacrifice of the Paschal offering apply to the second *Pesaḥ*. Yet, there is no prohibition against eating or possessing leavened bread on that day. Nonetheless, leavened bread may not be eaten together with the second *Pesaḥ*.

Meal offering prepared in a shallow pan – מִנְחַת מַחֲבַת: This is a type of meal offering that is fried in a shallow pan. This offering can be voluntary. It is also sacrificed daily by the High Priest, as well as by every priest on his first day of service in the Temple.

Meal offering prepared in a deep pan – מִנְחַת מַרְחֶשֶׁת: This is a type of meal offering that is deep-fried in a container filled with oil. This offering is voluntary and has no parallel among the obligatory or communal offerings.

LANGUAGE

Mavog – מָבוֹג: Mavog was apparently a Sage who lived in Mavog, Syria, a city referred to in Latin sources as Mabbog and called Mambidj in modern times.

NOTES

A dry meal offering for the sake of a meal offering mixed with oil – חֲרֵיבָה לְשֵׁם בְּלוּלָה: Most meal offerings are mixed with oil, but a meal offering brought for a sin is not (see Leviticus 5:11).

PERSONALITIES

Rav Mesharshiyya – רַב מְשַׁרְשְׁיָא: Rav Mesharshiyya was a Babylonian *amora* of the fifth generation. He was a prominent disciple of Rava, to whom he would ask many questions, and whose questions he would often answer. He would also cite many statements of Rava, and add to them. Sometimes a statement is cited in the Gemara where it is uncertain whether it is the statement of Rava or Rav Mesharshiyya.

Rav Mesharshiyya was a colleague of Rav Pappa, whom he trusted with the education of his son. Ravina and Rav Zevid were also his colleagues. His father-in-law was Rav Kahana, and three of his sons, Rav Yitzḥak, Rav Ḥama, and Rava, studied under Rav Ashi. According to some opinions, Rav Mesharshiyya assisted Rav Ashi in founding his academy in Meḥasya. It is told that when he died, even the palm trees were in distress, and they grew thorns instead of fruit.

אֲבָל בִּזְבָחִים אֵינוֹ כֵּן, שְׁחִיטָה אַחַת לְכוּלָּן, קַבָּלָה אַחַת לְכוּלָּן, זְרִיקָה אַחַת לְכוּלָּן;

But with regard to slaughtered offerings this is not so. There is **one** mode of **slaughter for all of** the offerings, **one** mode of **collection** of the blood **for all of them,** and **one** mode of **sprinkling for all of them.** Therefore, improper intention affects the status of the offering; if a rite is performed for the sake of the wrong type of offering, the offering does not satisfy its owner's obligation.

טַעְמָא דְּמַעֲשֶׂיהָ מוֹכִיחִין, הָא אֵין מַעֲשֶׂיהָ מוֹכִיחִין – לָא, אַמַּאי? לֵימָא: "וְזֹאת תּוֹרַת הַמִּנְחָה", תּוֹרָה אַחַת לְכָל הַמְּנָחוֹת!

Rav Mesharshiyya inferred from the *baraita*: **The reason** a meal offering satisfies its owner's obligation even when one removed a handful for the sake of another type of meal offering **is that its** mode of **preparation proves** its true nature. **But if its** mode of **preparation does not prove** its nature, it does **not** satisfy its owner's obligation. **Why** not? If Mavog's derivation is correct, **let us say** likewise that the verse: **"This is the law of the meal offering"** (Leviticus 6:7), indicates that there is **one law for all of the meal offerings,** regardless of their mode of preparation.

אֶלָּא אִי אִיתְּמַר הָכִי אִיתְּמַר, אָמַר רַב מִשְּׁמֵיהּ דְּמָבוֹג: חַטָּאת שֶׁשְּׁחָטָהּ עַל מְנָת שֶׁיִּתְכַּפֵּר בָּהּ נַחְשׁוֹן – כְּשֵׁירָה, אֵין כַּפָּרָה לְמֵתִים.

Rather, if Mavog's statement **was stated, it was stated like this:**[B] **Rav says in the name of Mavog: A sin offering that one slaughtered on the condition that Nahshon,** the prince of Judah, **be atoned for by it is fit;** this is not considered a change of owner, as **there is no atonement for the dead.**[NH]

וְלֵימָא מֵת בְּעָלְמָא!

The Gemara challenges: **But** if this was Mavog's statement, why did he mention Nahshon? **Let him state** this *halakha* in reference to **a dead** person **in general.**

הָא קָא מַשְׁמַע לַן: טַעְמָא דְּמֵת, הָא דְּחַי דּוּמְיָא דְּנַחְשׁוֹן – פְּסוּלָה, וּמַאי נִיהוּ? חַטַּאת נָזִיר וְחַטַּאת מְצוֹרָע.

The Gemara answers: **This** statement of Mavog **teaches us** that **the reason** for the fitness of a sin offering slaughtered for the atonement of Nahshon **is that he is dead. Consequently,** if it was slaughtered for the sake of **a living** person obligated to bring a sin offering **similar to** that of **Nahshon,** it is **unfit. And what is that?** It is **a nazirite's sin offering or a leper's sin offering,** which are brought not to atone for a sin but to become ritually pure. Consequently, if one sacrifices a standard sin offering for the sake of one obligated to bring the sin offering of a nazirite or a leper, it is considered a change of owner, and the offering is unfit.

הָנֵי עוֹלוֹת נִינְהוּ!

The Gemara counters: Why is the offering disqualified? **These** sin offerings of a nazirite and a leper **are** equivalent to **burnt offerings,** since they are not brought for atonement. Sacrificing a sin offering for the sake of one obligated to bring a burnt offering is not considered deviation with regard to the owner and does not disqualify it (see 3b).

אֶלָּא אִי אִיתְּמַר הָכִי אִיתְּמַר, אָמַר רַב מִשְּׁמֵיהּ דְּמָבוֹג: חַטָּאת שֶׁשְּׁחָטָהּ עַל שֶׁמְּחוּיָּיב חַטָּאת כְּנַחְשׁוֹן – כְּשֵׁירָה, חַטַּאת נַחְשׁוֹן עוֹלָה הִיא.

The Gemara answers: **Rather, if** Mavog's statement **was stated, it was stated like this: Rav says in the name of Mavog: A sin offering that one slaughtered for one who is obligated to bring a sin offering similar to** that of **Nahshon** is **fit; Nahshon's sin offering is** equivalent to **a burnt offering.**

אִיכָּא דְּאָמַר, אָמַר רַב מִשְּׁמֵיהּ דְּמָבוֹג: חַטָּאת שֶׁשְּׁחָטָהּ לְשֵׁם חַטַּאת נַחְשׁוֹן – פְּסוּלָה, חַטַּאת נַחְשׁוֹן עוֹלָה הִיא.

There is one **who says** that **Rav says in the name of Mavog: A sin offering that one slaughtered for the sake of a sin offering of Nahshon** is **unfit.** This is because **a sin offering of Nahshon is** equivalent to **a burnt offering,** and he is therefore considered to have deviated from the type of offering.

וְלֵימָא: חַטַּאת נָזִיר וְחַטַּאת מְצוֹרָע! עִיקַּר חַטָּאת נָקַט.

The Gemara challenges: **But** why did Mavog mention a sin offering of Nahshon, which one cannot bring at all? **Let him say** this *halakha* with regard to **a nazirite's sin offering and a leper's sin offering,** which are also equivalent to burnt offerings. The Gemara explains: Mavog **cited the primary sin offering,** the first case of an individual sin offering recorded in the Bible.

אָמַר רַב: חַטַּאת חֵלֶב שֶׁשְּׁחָטָהּ לְשֵׁם חַטַּאת דָּם, לְשֵׁם חַטַּאת עֲבוֹדָה זָרָה – כְּשֵׁירָה;

§ **Rav says: A sin offering** brought for consuming forbidden **fat that one slaughtered for the sake of a sin offering** brought for consuming **blood,**[B] or **for the sake of a sin offering** brought for engaging in **idol worship, is fit;** it is not considered deviation from the type of offering.

BACKGROUND

If it was stated it was stated like this – אִי אִיתְּמַר הָכִי אִיתְּמַר: Sometimes, when an objection has been raised against an amoraic statement, the Gemara addresses the objection by suggesting that the remark of the *amora* was reported incorrectly and must be emended, introducing the corrected version with: If it was stated, it was stated like this.

Blood – דָּם: The Torah prohibits the consumption of animal blood (see Leviticus 7:26). This applies to the blood of both kosher and non-kosher domesticated animals, non-domesticated animals, and birds. One who willfully consumes their blood is subject to *karet*. If he does so unwittingly, he is required to bring a sin offering. Meat requires salting before it is cooked in order to remove its blood. Consuming blood from a living animal is prohibited beyond the general prohibition against consuming blood.

NOTES

There is no atonement for the dead – אֵין כַּפָּרָה לְמֵתִים: Intent for the sake of the wrong owner disqualifies a sin offering if the intent is for the sake of another person who requires similar atonement (Rashi; see 3b).

HALAKHA

There is no atonement for the dead – אֵין כַּפָּרָה לְמֵתִים: A sin offering that was slaughtered for the sake of a dead person is fit, as there is no atonement for the dead. It does not satisfy its owner's obligation (Rambam *Sefer Avoda*, *Hilkhot Pesulei HaMukdashin* 15:9).

לְשֵׁם חַטַּאת נָזִיר, לְשֵׁם חַטַּאת מְצוֹרָע – פְּסוּלָה, הָנֵי עוֹלוֹת נִינְהוּ.

But if it was slaughtered **for the sake of a nazirite's sin offering,** or **for the sake of a leper's sin offering,** it is **unfit; these** sin offerings **are** equivalent to **burnt offerings,** as they are not brought for atonement.

בָּעֵי רָבָא: חַטַּאת חֵלֶב שֶׁשְּׁחָטָהּ לְשֵׁם חַטָּאת דְּטוּמְאַת מִקְדָּשׁ וְקָדָשָׁיו, מַהוּ? מִי אָמְרִינַן כָּרֵת כְּמוֹתָהּ,

Rava raises a dilemma: In the case of **a sin offering** brought for consuming forbidden **fat that one slaughtered for the sake of a sin offering** brought **for** the **defiling of** the **Temple or its sacrificial** foods, **what is** the *halakha*? **Do we say** that the offering is fit, as the latter type of sin offering atones for a transgression punishable by ***karet*** when committed intentionally, **similar to** the transgression of consuming forbidden fat?

אוֹ דִּילְמָא אֵין קָבוּעַ כְּמוֹתָהּ?

Or perhaps is it unfit, as a sin offering brought for defiling the Temple is a sliding-scale sin offering, the contents of which vary with the financial situation of the transgressor (see Leviticus 5:3–13), and **not a set** sin offering, which is always an animal, **like** a sin offering brought for consuming forbidden fat?

רַב אַחָא בְּרֵיהּ דְּרָבָא מַתְנֵי כּוּלְּהוּ לִפְסוּלָא, מַאי טַעְמָא? "וְשָׁחַט אוֹתָהּ לְחַטָּאת" – לְשֵׁם אוֹתָהּ חַטָּאת.

Rav Aḥa, son of Rava, teaches a version of Rav's statement according to which in **all of** the cases he mentioned, including one where the sin offering was slaughtered for the sake of a sin offering brought for consuming blood or for engaging in idol worship, the offering is **unfit.**[H] **What is the reason?** It is derived from the verse: **"And slaughter it** [*otah*] **for a sin offering"** (Leviticus 4:33), that a sin offering must be slaughtered **for the sake of that** [*otah*] **sin offering,** and no other.

אֲמַר לֵיהּ רַב אַשִׁי לְרַב אַחָא בְּרֵיהּ דְּרָבָא: [בָּעֲיָא דְּרָבָא] הֵיכִי מַתְנִיתוּ לָהּ?

Rav Ashi said to Rav Aḥa, son of Rava: How do you teach Rava's dilemma? Rava appears to assume that if one slaughters a sin offering for the sake of some other types of sin offering it remains fit. How is this compatible with your version of Rav's statement, according to which slaughter for the sake of any other type of sin offering disqualifies it?

אֲמַר לֵיהּ: אֲנַן בְּשִׁינּוּי בְּעָלִים מַתְנִינַן לָהּ, [וְהָכִי מַתְנִינַן לָהּ], אָמַר רָבָא: חַטַּאת חֵלֶב שֶׁשְּׁחָטָהּ עַל מִי שֶׁמְּחוּיָּיב חַטַּאת דָּם וְחַטַּאת עֲבוֹדָה זָרָה – פְּסוּלָה, עַל מִי שֶׁמְּחוּיָּיב חַטַּאת נָזִיר וְחַטַּאת מְצוֹרָע – כְּשֵׁירָה.

Rav Aḥa **said to him: We teach** Rava's dilemma **with regard to deviation** with regard to the **owner** rather than from the type of offering. **And this is how we teach it:** First, **Rava says: A sin offering** brought for consuming forbidden **fat that one slaughtered for** the sake of one **who is obligated** to bring **a sin offering**[H] for consuming **blood, or** for the sake of one who is obligated to bring **a sin offering** for engaging in **idol worship,** is **unfit.** Since the other person is also obligated to bring a sin offering, this is considered deviation with regard to the owner. But if it was slaughtered **for one who is obligated** to bring **a nazirite's sin offering or a leper's sin offering,** it is **fit,** as these sin offerings are not brought for atonement. Deviation with regard to the owner disqualifies an offering only if the other owner is obligated to bring a similar offering.

וּבְעָיֵין לָהּ הָכִי, בָּעֵי רָבָא: חַטַּאת חֵלֶב שֶׁשְּׁחָטָהּ עַל מִי שֶׁמְּחוּיָּיב חַטַּאת דְּטוּמְאַת מִקְדָּשׁ וְקָדָשָׁיו, מַהוּ? מִי אָמְרִינַן כָּרֵת כְּמוֹתָהּ, אוֹ דִּילְמָא אֵין קָבוּעַ כְּמוֹתָהּ?

And then **we pose the dilemma like this: Rava raises a dilemma:** In the case of **a sin offering** brought for consuming forbidden **fat that one slaughtered for** the sake of **one who is obligated** to bring **a sin offering for** the **defiling of** the **Temple or its sacrificial** foods, **what is** the *halakha*? **Do we say** that the offering is unfit, as the one who defiled the Temple or its sacrificial foods is obligated to bring a sin offering for a transgression punishable by ***karet*, similar to** the transgression of the owner? **Or perhaps** it remains fit, as a sin offering brought for defiling the Temple is **not a set** sin offering **like** a sin offering brought for consuming forbidden fat?

HALAKHA

In all of the cases he mentioned the offering is unfit – כּוּלְּהוּ לִפְסוּלָא: A sin offering that was slaughtered for the sake of the wrong transgression, e.g., a sin offering brought for consuming forbidden fat that was slaughtered for consuming blood, is disqualified, in accordance with the version of Rav Aḥa, son of Rava. Rav Ashi, who was the later authority, apparently accepted his version. Furthermore, the Gemara in tractate *Karetot* (27b) follows his opinion (Rambam *Sefer Avoda, Hilkhot Pesulei HaMukdashin* 15:3, 6 and *Kesef Mishne* there).

That one slaughtered for one who is obligated to bring a sin offering, etc. – שֶׁשְּׁחָטָהּ עַל מִי שֶׁמְּחוּיָּיב חַטַּאת וכו׳: If a sin offering was slaughtered for the sake of another who is obligated to bring a sin offering for another sin, or even a sliding-scale sin offering, e.g., a sin offering for defiling the Temple or its sacrificial foods, it is disqualified (Rambam *Sefer Avoda, Hilkhot Pesulei HaMukdashin* 15:7).

תֵּיקוּ.

The Gemara concludes: The dilemma **shall stand** unresolved.[B]

אִיתְּמַר: שְׁחָטָה לִשְׁמָהּ לִזְרוֹק דָּמָהּ שֶׁלֹּא לִשְׁמָהּ – רַבִּי יוֹחָנָן אָמַר: פְּסוּלָה, וְרֵישׁ לָקִישׁ אָמַר: כְּשֵׁירָה.

§ **It was stated:** If one **slaughtered** a sin offering **for its sake** with intent **to sprinkle its blood**[H] **not for its sake** but for the sake of another type of offering, **Rabbi Yoḥanan says** that the offering is **unfit, and Reish Lakish says** it is **fit.**

רַבִּי יוֹחָנָן אָמַר פְּסוּלָה – מְחַשְּׁבִין מֵעֲבוֹדָה לַעֲבוֹדָה, וְיָלְפִינַן מִמַּחְשֶׁבֶת פִּיגּוּל.

Rabbi Yoḥanan says it is **unfit,** as in his opinion **one can have intention from** one **rite to** affect another **rite,** i.e., one can disqualify an offering by performing one rite with improper intent about a subsequent rite that he has not yet performed. **And we derive** this *halakha* **from intent of** ***piggul,***[BN] i.e., intent while performing one of the main rites to consume the offering after the appointed time, which disqualifies the offering.

וְרֵישׁ לָקִישׁ אָמַר כְּשֵׁירָה – אֵין מְחַשְּׁבִין מֵעֲבוֹדָה לַעֲבוֹדָה, וְלָא יָלְפִינַן מִמַּחְשֶׁבֶת פִּיגּוּל.

And Reish Lakish says that it is **fit,** as in his opinion **one cannot have intention from** one **rite to** affect another **rite,**[N] **and we do not derive** *halakhot* with regard to deviation from the type of offering **from intent of** ***piggul.***

וְאָזְדוּ לְטַעֲמַיְיהוּ, דְּאִיתְּמַר:

And Rabbi Yoḥanan and Reish Lakish each **follow** [***ve'azdu***][L] **their** general line of **reasoning** in this matter; **as it was stated:**

HALAKHA

Slaughtered a sin offering for its sake with intent to sprinkle its blood, etc. – **שְׁחָטָה לִשְׁמָהּ לִזְרוֹק דָּמָהּ וכו׳**: If one slaughtered a sin offering for its sake, but with the intent to sprinkle its blood not for its sake, the offering is disqualified; it is considered as though the blood was actually sprinkled with this intent, as one can have intention from one rite to affect another. This is in accordance with the opinion of Rabbi Yoḥanan, as his opinion is accepted in his disputes with Reish Lakish. Furthermore, Rava's conclusion is in accordance with his opinion (Rambam *Sefer Avoda, Hilkhot Pesulei HaMukdashin* 15:10 and *Kesef Mishne* there).

BACKGROUND

The dilemma shall stand unresolved [*teiku*] – **תֵּיקוּ**: Various explanations have been offered with regard to the etymology of this term. One explanation is that the word is an abbreviated version of *tikom*, it shall stand. Another is that its source is the word *tik*, a case or pouch, whose contents are unknown. Accordingly, the resolution is unknown to us as if it is hidden inside a case (*Arukh*). Although not the literal meaning, some raise the suggestion that the term alludes to an acrostic for the Hebrew phrase: *Tishbi yetaretz kushyot uve'ayot*, or: The Tishbite, i.e., Elijah the prophet, will resolve questions and dilemmas (*Tosefot Yom Tov*). This last idea refers to the tradition that when Elijah the prophet returns to the Jewish people to announce the advent of the Messiah, he will also reveal the solutions to outstanding halakhic difficulties.

Piggul – **פִּיגּוּל**: *Piggul* is a disqualifying intent in the sacrifice of an offering, whether an animal, a bird, or a meal offering. If, while engaged in sacrificing an offering, a priest expresses intent to sprinkle the blood of the offering, burn its fats on the altar, or consume its meat, after the designated time, that intent disqualifies the offering and renders it unfit due to improper intent. An offering that has assumed that status may not be sacrificed, and it does not satisfy the obligation of the one bringing it. Anyone who partakes of that offering intentionally is liable to receive *karet*. The Sages also decreed that an offering in that state imparts ritual impurity. The intent of the priest sacrificing the offering and not that of the one bringing it determines whether it is unfit due to improper intent or not.

NOTES

And we derive this *halakha* from intent of *piggul* – **וְיָלְפִינַן מִמַּחְשֶׁבֶת פִּיגּוּל**: *Tosafot* write that since *piggul* is the source of this *halakha*, the offering is disqualified only if the intent of the one slaughtering it was to sprinkle its blood not for its sake, and not if it was to collect the blood not for its sake, as *piggul* intent during the collection of the blood does not disqualify an offering (see 27b).

One cannot have intention from rite to rite, etc. – **אֵין מְחַשְּׁבִין מֵעֲבוֹדָה לַעֲבוֹדָה וכו׳**: Why doesn't Reish Lakish derive from the *halakha* concerning *piggul* that one can have intention while performing one rite about another rite? Rashi explains that *piggul* is not an example of having intention about one rite while performing another rite, but having intention during the performance of one rite to consuming the offering beyond its designated time (see also *Sefat Emet*). In *Or Same'aḥ* it is added that while *piggul* refers to intent to perform another rite in the wrong manner, the case here is of one who intends to perform another rite with the wrong intent. Therefore, the two cases cannot be compared.

LANGUAGE

Follow [*azdu*] – **אָזְדוּ**: The Aramaic word *azda* means to walk or go, as in the verse: "The thing has gone [*azda*] from me" (Daniel 2:5). It has the same meaning as the word *azla*; the letters *dalet*, *tet*, *lamed*, *nun*, and *tav* are frequently interchanged in Aramaic. Some claim that the word denotes power and might, similar to the Hebrew word *zadon*.

הַשּׁוֹחֵט אֶת הַבְּהֵמָה עַל מְנָת לִזְרוֹק דָּמָהּ לַעֲבוֹדָה זָרָה, וּלְהַקְטִיר חֶלְבָּהּ לַעֲבוֹדָה זָרָה – רַבִּי יוֹחָנָן אָמַר: אֲסוּרָה; מְחַשְּׁבִין מֵעֲבוֹדָה לַעֲבוֹדָה, וְיָלְפִינַן חוּץ מִבִּפְנִים.

With regard to **one who slaughters an animal**[H] **in order to sprinkle its blood for idol worship, or** in order **to burn its** forbidden **fat for idol worship, Rabbi Yoḥanan says:** Deriving benefit from the animal is **prohibited,** as it is considered an offering to idol worship, even if ultimately its blood was not sprinkled or its fat burned to that effect. This is because **one can have intention from** one **rite to** affect another **rite;** idolatrous intent while slaughtering the animal renders it forbidden, even if the intention pertains not to the slaughter itself but to the sprinkling of the blood or the burning of the forbidden fat. **And** this *halakha* is derived from the *halakhot* of *piggul*, as **we derive** *halakhot* of idol worship, which are applicable even **outside** the Temple, **from** *halakhot* concerning intent that apply **inside** the Temple.

רֵישׁ לָקִישׁ אָמַר: מוּתֶּרֶת; אֵין מְחַשְּׁבִין מֵעֲבוֹדָה לַעֲבוֹדָה, וְלָא יָלְפִינַן חוּץ מִפְּנִים.

Reish Lakish says: Deriving benefit from the animal is **permitted.**[N] **One cannot have intention from** one **rite to** affect another **rite, and we do not derive** *halakhot* applicable **outside** the Temple **from** *halakhot* that apply **inside** the Temple.

וְאִי אַשְׁמְעִינַן בְּהָא – בְּהָא אָמַר רֵישׁ לָקִישׁ, אֲבָל פְּנִים מִפְּנִים אֵימָא מוֹדֵי לֵיהּ לְרַבִּי יוֹחָנָן;

Although both disputes are essentially the same, each is necessary. **And if** the Sages **had taught us** the dispute only **with regard to that** issue, namely, an animal slaughtered with idolatrous intent, one would have reasoned that **Reish Lakish says** his opinion only **with regard to that** issue, as he maintains that *halakhot* applicable outside the Temple are not derived from *halakhot* applicable only inside the Temple. **But** with regard to an offering that was slaughtered with the intention of sprinkling its blood not for its sake, one might **say** that **he concedes to Rabbi Yoḥanan** that it is disqualified, as *halakhot* applicable **inside** the Temple can be derived **from** other *halakhot* applicable **inside** the Temple.

וְאִי אַשְׁמְעִינַן הָא – בְּהָא קָאָמַר רַבִּי יוֹחָנָן, אֲבָל בְּהַהִיא אֵימָא מוֹדֵי לֵיהּ לְרֵישׁ לָקִישׁ, צְרִיכִי.

And if the Sages **had taught us** the dispute only with regard to **this** issue, namely, an offering that was slaughtered with the intention of sprinkling its blood not for its sake, one might claim that **Rabbi Yoḥanan says** his opinion only **with regard to this** issue, which concerns *halakhot* applicable inside the Temple. **But with regard to that** issue, an animal that was slaughtered with idolatrous intent, one would **say** that **he concedes to** the opinion of **Reish Lakish** that *halakhot* applicable outside the Temple are not derived from *halakhot* applicable only inside the Temple. Therefore, both statements **are necessary.**

כִּי אֲתָא רַב דִּימִי אָמַר: מֵתִיב רַב יִרְמְיָה לְסִיּוּעֵיהּ לְרַבִּי יוֹחָנָן, וְרַבִּי אִילָא לְסִיּוּעֵיהּ לְרֵישׁ לָקִישׁ.

When Rav Dimi came[B] from Eretz Yisrael, **he said: Rav Yirmeya responds**[N] to this dispute by eliciting evidence **to support** the opinion of **Rabbi Yoḥanan; and Rabbi Ila** elicits evidence **to support** the opinion of **Reish Lakish.**

רַב יִרְמְיָה לְסִיּוּעֵיהּ לְרַבִּי יוֹחָנָן: וּמָה בְּמָקוֹם שֶׁאִם אָמַר ״הֲרֵינִי שׁוֹחֵט חוּץ לִזְמַנּוֹ״ שֶׁהוּא כָּשֵׁר, שְׁחָטוֹ עַל מְנָת לִזְרוֹק דָּמוֹ חוּץ לִזְמַנּוֹ – פָּסוּל, מָקוֹם שֶׁאִם אָמַר ״הֲרֵינִי שׁוֹחֵט שֶׁלֹּא לִשְׁמוֹ״ פָּסוּל, שְׁחָטוֹ עַל מְנָת לִזְרוֹק דָּמוֹ שֶׁלֹּא לִשְׁמוֹ – אֵינוֹ דִּין שֶׁיְּהֵא פָּסוּל?

Rav Dimi elaborated: **Rav Yirmeya** elicits evidence **to support** the opinion of **Rabbi Yoḥanan** by an *a fortiori* inference: **Just as in** the **case** of improper intent with regard to the offering's time, **where if** the one slaughtering the offering **said: I am hereby slaughtering** it **beyond its** designated **time,** it is **fit,**[N] and nevertheless, if he **slaughtered it in order to sprinkle its blood beyond its** designated **time,** it is **unfit,** so too, in the **case** of deviation from the type of offering, **where** even **if he said: I am hereby slaughtering** it **not for its sake,** it is **unfit, isn't it logical that if he slaughtered it in order to sprinkle its blood not for its sake, it should be unfit?**

מַתְקִיף לַהּ רָבָא בַּר אֲהִילַאי: מָה לְחוּץ לִזְמַנּוֹ שֶׁכֵּן כָּרֵת!

Rava bar Ahilai[P] **objects to this** inference: One cannot claim that deviation from the type of offering is a more severe transgression than intent to consume it or sprinkle its blood beyond its designated time, since the latter has its own element of stringency. **What** is notable **about** intent **beyond its** designated **time?** It is notable **in that** one who eats the meat of such an offering is liable to be punished with ***karet*,** whereas one who eats the meat of an offering disqualified due to deviation from the type of offering is not.

HALAKHA

One who slaughters an animal, etc. – **הַשּׁוֹחֵט אֶת הַבְּהֵמָה וכו׳:** If an animal is slaughtered with the intent to sprinkle its blood for idolatrous worship, deriving benefit from it is prohibited; *halakhot* concerning intent while slaughtering non-sacred animals outside the Temple are derived from *halakhot* concerning intent while slaughtering offerings inside the Temple, in accordance with the opinion of Rabbi Yoḥanan (Rambam *Sefer Kedusha, Hilkhot Sheḥita* 2:15; *Shulḥan Arukh, Yoreh De'a* 4:1).

NOTES

Reish Lakish says: Deriving benefit from the animal is permitted – **רֵישׁ לָקִישׁ אָמַר מוּתֶּרֶת:** *Tosafot* note that Reish Lakish concedes that the one who slaughtered the animal with this intent is liable to receive the death penalty, due to his idolatrous intent.

Rav Yirmeya responds [*metiv*] – **מֵתִיב רַב יִרְמְיָה:** The word *metiv* generally refers to an objection to the statement of an *amora*, usually from a mishna or *baraita*. Here, the reference is to a claim or proof. This sense of the word is common in the Jerusalem Talmud, e.g., *Pesaḥim* 5:2.

If he said, I am hereby slaughtering it beyond its designated time, it is fit – **אִם אָמַר הֲרֵינִי שׁוֹחֵט חוּץ לִזְמַנּוֹ שֶׁהוּא כָּשֵׁר:** This statement does not disqualify the offering, as he simultaneously contradicts it in practice by actually slaughtering it within its designated time. Furthermore, *piggul* applies only where one performs one of the main sacrificial rites with intent to consume it beyond the designated time. Intent to slaughter the offering beyond its designated time is of no consequence. See Rashi and the different versions of his comment printed in the Vilna edition.

BACKGROUND

When Rav Dimi came – **כִּי אֲתָא רַב דִּימִי:** Rav Dimi was one of the Sages who would often travel from Eretz Yisrael to Babylonia, primarily to transmit the Torah of the Sages in Eretz Yisrael to the Torah centers of the Diaspora. Occasionally he would travel for business purposes as well. Many questions, particularly those concerning the Torah of the Sages in Eretz Yisrael, remained unresolved in Babylonia, until a messenger from Eretz Yisrael would arrive and elucidate the *halakha*, the novel expression, or the unique circumstances pertaining to a particular statement that required clarification.

PERSONALITIES

Rava bar Ahilai – **רָבָא בַּר אֲהִילַאי:** Rava bar Ahilai, sometimes referred to as Rabba bar Ahilai, was a fifth-generation Babylonian *amora*. He is cited frequently as addressing the statements of the Sages before him, whether raising an objection, disagreeing altogether, or providing support. His statements are discussed by the *amora'im* of the subsequent generation.

אֶלָּא אָמַר רָבָא בַּר אֲהִילַאי, הָכִי קָאָמַר: וּמַה מָּקוֹם שֶׁאִם אָמַר ״הֲרֵינִי שׁוֹחֵט חוּץ לִמְקוֹמוֹ״ שֶׁהוּא כָּשֵׁר, שְׁחָטוֹ עַל מְנָת לִזְרוֹק דָּמוֹ חוּץ לִמְקוֹמוֹ – פָּסוּל, מָקוֹם שֶׁאִם אָמַר ״הֲרֵינִי שׁוֹחֵט שֶׁלֹּא לִשְׁמוֹ״ שֶׁהוּא פָּסוּל, [שְׁחָטוֹ עַל מְנָת] לִזְרוֹק דָּמוֹ שֶׁלֹּא לִשְׁמוֹ – אֵינוֹ דִּין שֶׁיְּהֵא פָּסוּל?

Rather, Rava bar Ahilai says: Rav Yirmeya was actually referring to improper intent with regard to the offering's designated area, since consumption of an offering thereby disqualified is not punishable by *karet*. And **this** is what **he is saying: Just as** in the **case** of improper intent with regard to the offering's designated area, **where if** the one slaughtering the offering **said: I am hereby slaughtering** it **outside its** designated **area,**[N] **it is fit,** and nevertheless, if he **slaughtered it in order to sprinkle its blood outside its** designated **area,** it is **unfit,** so too, in the **case** of deviation from the type of offering, **where** even **if he said: I am hereby slaughtering** it **not for its sake, it is unfit, isn't it logical that** if **he slaughtered it in order to sprinkle its blood not for its sake, it should be unfit?**

מַתְקִיף לָהּ רַב אַשִׁי: מַה לְּחוּץ לִמְקוֹמוֹ – שֶׁכֵּן נוֹהֵג בְּכׇל הַזְּבָחִים, תֹּאמַר בְּשֶׁלֹּא לִשְׁמוֹ – שֶׁאֵינוֹ נוֹהֵג אֶלָּא בְּפֶסַח וְחַטָּאת!

Rav Ashi objects to this inference: **What** is notable **about** intent to sprinkle the blood **outside its** designated **area?** It is notable **in that** the disqualification **applies to all slaughtered offerings. Can you say** that the same *halakhot* govern the disqualification of an offering sacrificed **not for its sake, which applies only to a Paschal offering and a sin offering?**

אֶלָּא אָמַר רַב אַשִׁי, הָכִי קָאָמַר: וּמַה בְּמָקוֹם שֶׁאִם אָמַר ״הֲרֵינִי שׁוֹחֵט לְשֵׁם פְּלוֹנִי״ שֶׁהוּא כָּשֵׁר, לִזְרוֹק דָּמוֹ (שֶׁלֹּא לִשְׁמוֹ) לְשֵׁם פְּלוֹנִי – פָּסוּל, מָקוֹם שֶׁאִם אָמַר ״הֲרֵינִי שׁוֹחֵט שֶׁלֹּא לִשְׁמָן״ שֶׁהוּא פָּסוּל, [שְׁחָטוֹ עַל מְנָת] לִזְרוֹק דָּמָן שֶׁלֹּא לִשְׁמָן – אֵינוֹ דִּין שֶׁיְּהֵא פָּסוּל?

Rather, Rav Ashi says: This is what Rav Yirmeya **is saying: Just as in** the **case** of deviation with regard to the owner, **where, if** the one slaughtering the offering **said: I am hereby slaughtering** it **for the sake of so-and-so,**[N] **it is fit,** and nevertheless, if he slaughtered it in order **to sprinkle its blood for the sake of so-and-so,** it is **unfit,** so too, in the **case** of deviation from the type of offering, **where** even **if he said: I am hereby slaughtering** it **not for its sake, it is unfit, isn't it logical that** if **he slaughtered it in order to sprinkle its blood not for its sake, it should be unfit?** The opinion of Rabbi Yoḥanan is supported by this logical line of reasoning.

רַבִּי אִילָּא לְסַיּוּעֵיהּ לְרֵישׁ לָקִישׁ: לֹא תֹּאמַר בִּזְרִיקָה, וְתֵיתֵי מִקַּל וָחוֹמֶר מִבֵּינַיָּיא, מִשְּׁחִיטָה וְקַבָּלָה, לְמַאי הִלְכְתָא כְּתַב רַחֲמָנָא? לוֹמַר, דְּאֵין מְחַשְּׁבִין מֵעֲבוֹדָה לַעֲבוֹדָה.

Rabbi Ila elicits evidence **to support** the opinion of **Reish Lakish,** that performance of one rite with improper intent with regard to another rite is of no consequence: The Torah **should not have stated** the requirement of sacrificing an offering for its own sake **with regard to sprinkling** of the blood, **and** rather **should have** let one **derive** it **by an *a fortiori*** inference **from the common** element **of** two other rites,[N] **from slaughter and collection** of the blood. If so, **for what *halakha* does the Merciful One write** this redundant requirement? It is in order **to say that one cannot have intention from** one **rite to** affect another **rite.**

מַתְקִיף לָהּ רַב פַּפָּא: וְדִלְמָא דִּמְחַשְּׁבִין מֵעֲבוֹדָה לַעֲבוֹדָה!

Rav Pappa objects to this derivation: **But perhaps** the requirement is written to teach the opposite, **that one can have intention from** one **rite to** affect another **rite.** A redundant requirement should expand, not reduce, the scope of actions that can disqualify the offering.

NOTES

Slaughtering it outside its designated area – שׁוֹחֵט חוּץ לִמְקוֹמוֹ: The *halakhot* of an offering sacrificed with intent to consume it outside its designated area are derived from the *halakhot* of *piggul* (see 28a). In both cases the offering is disqualified. The difference between them is that intent that the offering be consumed beyond its designated time renders it *piggul*, and one who consumes its meat is liable to be punished with *karet*, whereas in a case of intent to consume it outside its designated area it is not rendered *piggul*, and one who eats its meat is not liable to be punished with *karet*.

I am hereby slaughtering for the sake of so-and-so – הֲרֵינִי שׁוֹחֵט לְשֵׁם פְּלוֹנִי: Deviation with regard to the owner disqualifies the offering only if one's intent is to sprinkle the blood for someone else's sake. This is because the sprinkling of the blood is the rite that atones for the owner (see 4a and Rashi there).

By an *a fortiori* inference from the common element of two other rites – מִקַּל וָחוֹמֶר מִבֵּינַיָּיא: In other words, the requirement to sprinkle the blood of an offering for its own sake can be inferred *a fortiori* from the common element of slaughter and collection of the blood. Since only a priest can sprinkle the blood, whereas the offering can be slaughtered by a non-priest, it can be inferred *a fortiori* that if slaughter for the sake of the wrong offering disqualifies the offering, certainly sprinkling the blood for the sake of the wrong offering disqualifies it. This inference can be refuted, due to the fact that a Paschal offering is disqualified if slaughtered for the sake of those who are incapable of eating it. Evidently, slaughter has a unique element of stringency. Therefore, collection of the blood is cited to prove this factor irrelevant; although collecting the blood of a Paschal offering for the sake of those who are incapable of eating it does not disqualify the offering, nevertheless, this rite must be performed for the sake of the offering (Rashi).

אִם כֵּן, לִשְׁתּוֹק קְרָא מִינֵּיהּ, וְתֵיתֵי מִקַּל וָחוֹמֶר דְּרַב אַשִׁי.

The Gemara answers: **If that were so, let the verse remain silent with regard to** sprinkling the blood for the sake of the offering, **and one could derive** that one can have intention from one rite to affect another rite **from Rav Ashi's** aforementioned ***a fortiori*** inference. The verse must be meant to counteract that inference and teach that one cannot have intention from one rite to affect another rite.

וְאִידָּךְ, פָּרֵיךְ הָכִי: מַה לְּהָנָךְ, שֶׁכֵּן טְעוּנוֹת צָפוֹן וְיֶשְׁנָן בַּחַטָּאוֹת הַפְּנִימִיּוֹת.

And the other *amora*, Rabbi Yoḥanan, **would refute** Rabbi Ila's proof **like this:** It is necessary for the Torah to state the requirement with regard to sprinkling. It cannot be derived from the cases of slaughter and collection of the blood, since these two share an element of stringency that sprinkling lacks. **What** is notable **about these?** They are notable **in that** in offerings of the most sacred order **they must** be performed in the **north** of the Temple courtyard. **And** furthermore, **they are** performed **in the** sacrifice of **inner sin offerings** as well as external sin offerings, unlike the sprinkling of the blood on the external altar.

וְאִידָּךְ: הַשְׁתָּא מִיהָא בִּשְׁלָמִים קַיְימִין.

And the other *amora*, Reish Lakish, would respond that **now, in any event, we stand** in a discussion **with regard to peace offerings,** since the requirement of sacrifice for the offering's sake is derived from the verses concerning peace offerings. Peace offerings are neither offerings of the most sacred order nor inner sin offerings, and therefore the elements of stringency mentioned above are irrelevant.

אִיתְּמַר: שְׁחָטָהּ לִשְׁמָהּ לִזְרוֹק דָּמָהּ שֶׁלֹּא לִשְׁמָהּ – רַב נַחְמָן אָמַר: פְּסוּלָה, רַבָּה אָמַר: כְּשֵׁרָה. וַהֲדַר בֵּיהּ רַבָּה לְגַבֵּי רַב נַחְמָן מִקַּל וָחוֹמֶר דְּרַב אַשִׁי.

A parallel dispute **was stated:** If one **slaughtered** a sin offering **for its sake** but with intent **to sprinkle its blood not for its sake, Rav Naḥman says** that the offering is **unfit,** and **Rabba says** that it is **fit. And Rabba retracted his** opinion, and conceded **to Rav Naḥman, due to Rav Ashi's *a fortiori*** inference.

״רַבִּי אֱלִיעֶזֶר אוֹמֵר: אַף (אֶת) הָאָשָׁם״. תַּנְיָא, אָמַר רַבִּי אֱלִיעֶזֶר: חַטָּאת בָּאָה עַל חֵטְא וְאָשָׁם בָּא עַל חֵטְא, מַה חַטָּאת שֶׁלֹּא לִשְׁמָהּ – פְּסוּלָה, אַף אָשָׁם שֶׁלֹּא לִשְׁמוֹ – פָּסוּל.

§ The mishna teaches: **Rabbi Eliezer says: The guilt offering, too,** is unfit when sacrificed not for its sake. With regard to this **it is taught** in a *baraita*: **Rabbi Eliezer said: A sin offering is brought** for committing **a transgression and a guilt offering is brought** for committing **a transgression. Just as a sin offering** sacrificed **not for its sake is unfit, so too, a guilt offering** sacrificed **not for its sake** is **unfit.**

אָמַר לוֹ רַבִּי יְהוֹשֻׁעַ: לֹא, אִם אָמַרְתָּ בְּחַטָּאת שֶׁכֵּן דָּמָהּ לְמַעְלָה!

Rabbi Yehoshua said to him: The inference is **not** valid. **If you say** this **with regard to a sin offering, whose blood** is sprinkled **above** the red line[N] that encircles the altar, should you necessarily say the same with regard to a guilt offering, whose blood is sprinkled below that line, like most animal offerings?

אָמַר לוֹ רַבִּי אֱלִיעֶזֶר: פֶּסַח יוֹכִיחַ, שֶׁדָּמוֹ לְמַטָּה וּשְׁחָטוֹ שֶׁלֹּא לִשְׁמוֹ – פָּסוּל.

Rabbi Eliezer said to him: A Paschal offering can prove the point, **as its blood is** sprinkled **below** the red line, **and** nevertheless, if one **slaughtered it not for its sake** it is **unfit.**

אָמַר לוֹ רַבִּי יְהוֹשֻׁעַ: מַה לְּפֶסַח שֶׁכֵּן זְמַנּוֹ קָבוּעַ!

Rabbi Yehoshua said to him: A Paschal offering cannot serve as the source either, since it possesses a unique element of stringency. **What** is notable **about a Paschal offering?** It is notable **in that** its designated **time is fixed.** A guilt offering does not have a fixed time.

אָמַר לוֹ רַבִּי אֱלִיעֶזֶר: חַטָּאת תּוֹכִיחַ.

Rabbi Eliezer said to him: A sin offering can prove the point, as it does not have a fixed time, and nevertheless, it is disqualified if sacrificed not for its sake.

אָמַר לוֹ רַבִּי יְהוֹשֻׁעַ:

Rabbi Yehoshua said to him:

NOTES

Above the red line – לְמַעְלָה: A line was painted in red encircling the Temple altar at precisely half its height, just as a copper line encircled the altar in the Tabernacle (Rashi). This marking was necessary because the blood of animal sin offerings and birds brought as burnt offerings must be sprinkled on the upper portion of the altar, above the red line, whereas the blood of all other offerings must be sprinkled on the lower portion, below the red line.

חוֹזְרַנִי חֲלִילָה.

I return to my previous claim that a sin offering is unique since its blood is sprinkled above the red line. The discussion is going **around** [*ḥalila*][L] in circles.

חָזַר רַבִּי אֱלִיעֶזֶר וְדָנוֹ דִּין אַחֵר: חַטָּאת נֶאֱמַר בָּהּ "הִיא" בִּשְׁחִיטָה – הִיא לִשְׁמָהּ כְּשֵׁירָה, שֶׁלֹּא לִשְׁמָהּ פְּסוּלָה; וּפֶסַח נֶאֱמַר בּוֹ "הוּא" בִּזְבִיחָה – הוּא לִשְׁמוֹ כָּשֵׁר, שֶׁלֹּא לִשְׁמוֹ פָּסוּל;

Rabbi Eliezer then presented a different logical inference: With regard to a sin offering, the word **"it" is stated concerning slaughter,** in the verse: "And slaughter it in the place where they kill the burnt offering before the Lord; it is a sin offering" (Leviticus 4:24). The word "it" teaches that if **it** is sacrificed **for its sake** it is **fit;** if it is sacrificed **not for its sake** it is **unfit. And** similarly, **with regard to a Paschal offering,** the word **"it" is stated concerning slaughter** [*zeviḥa*], in the verse: "It is the sacrifice [*zevaḥ*] of the Lord's Passover" (Exodus 12:27). Here, the word "it" teaches that if **it** is sacrificed **for its sake** it is **fit;** if it is sacrificed **not for its sake** it is **unfit.**

אַף אָשָׁם נֶאֱמַר בּוֹ "הוּא", הוּא לִשְׁמוֹ – כָּשֵׁר, שֶׁלֹּא לִשְׁמוֹ – פָּסוּל.

And the word **"it" is stated with regard to a guilt offering as well,** in the verse: "It is a guilt offering" (Leviticus 7:5). Here too, say that the word "it" teaches that if **it** is sacrificed **for its sake** it is **fit;** if it is sacrificed **not for its sake** it is **unfit.**

אָמַר לוֹ רַבִּי יְהוֹשֻׁעַ: חַטָּאת נֶאֱמַר בָּהּ "הִיא" בִּשְׁחִיטָה – הִיא לִשְׁמָהּ כְּשֵׁרָה, שֶׁלֹּא לִשְׁמָהּ פְּסוּלָה; פֶּסַח נֶאֱמַר בּוֹ "הוּא" בִּזְבִיחָה – הוּא לִשְׁמוֹ כָּשֵׁר, שֶׁלֹּא לִשְׁמוֹ פָּסוּל. אֲבָל אָשָׁם לֹא נֶאֱמַר בּוֹ "הוּא" אֶלָּא לְאַחַר הַקְטָרַת אֵימוּרִין, וְהוּא עַצְמוֹ שֶׁלֹּא הוּקְטְרוּ אֵימוּרִין – כָּשֵׁר!

Rabbi Yehoshua said to him: With regard to a sin offering, the word **"it" is stated concerning slaughter,** teaching that if **it** is sacrificed **for its sake** it is **fit,** but if it is sacrificed **not for its sake** it is **unfit. With regard to a Paschal offering** too, the word **"it" is stated concerning slaughter,** likewise teaching that if **it** is sacrificed **for its sake** it is **fit,** but if it is sacrificed **not for its sake** it is **unfit. But with regard to a guilt offering,** the word **"it" is stated only after the burning of the sacrificial portions. And** since the offering **itself is fit** even if the **sacrificial portions were not burned** at all, it is certainly fit if they were burned not for the sake of a guilt offering.

אָמַר לוֹ רַבִּי אֱלִיעֶזֶר, הֲרֵי אוֹמֵר: "כַּחַטָּאת כָּאָשָׁם", מַה חַטָּאת שֶׁלֹּא לִשְׁמוֹ – פָּסוּל, אַף אָשָׁם שֶׁלֹּא לִשְׁמוֹ – פָּסוּל.

The *baraita* concludes: **Rabbi Eliezer said to him:** A sin offering and a guilt offering are juxtaposed in the verse that **states: "As is the sin offering, so is the guilt offering"** (Leviticus 7:7).[N] The verse teaches that **just as a sin offering** sacrificed **not for its sake** is **unfit, so too, a guilt offering** sacrificed **not for its sake** is **unfit.**

אָמַר מָר: אָמַר לוֹ רַבִּי יְהוֹשֻׁעַ: חוֹזְרַנִי חֲלִילָה. וּלְמִיהֲדַר דִּינָא וְלַיְיתֵי בְּ"מָה הַצַּד"!

§ The Gemara discusses the *baraita*. **The Master said: Rabbi Yehoshua said to him: I return** to my previous claim, that a sin offering is unique since its blood is sprinkled above the red line. The discussion is going **around** in circles. The Gemara asks: **And let the derivation revert** to its starting point, **and let** Rabbi Eliezer **derive** the point **by** analogy from **the common element** of the two sources, a sin offering and a Paschal offering. Together they can prove that a guilt offering sacrificed not for its sake is also unfit, since they share no element of stringency that the latter lacks.

מִשּׁוּם דְּאִיכָּא לְמִיפְרַךְ: מַה לְּהַצַּד הַשָּׁוֶה שֶׁבָּהֶן שֶׁכֵּן יֵשׁ בָּהֶן צַד כָּרֵת.

The Gemara answers: Even such a derivation is not valid, **as it can be refuted: What** is notable **about their common element?** A sin offering and a Paschal offering are notable **in that they** both **have an element of *karet*.** A sin offering is brought for a transgression punishable by *karet* when committed intentionally, and one who refrains intentionally from bringing a Paschal offering is liable to be punished with *karet*. A guilt offering, by contrast, has no element of *karet*.

"אָמַר לוֹ רַבִּי יְהוֹשֻׁעַ: לֹא, אִם אָמַרְתָּ בְּחַטָּאת שֶׁכֵּן דָּמָהּ לְמַעְלָה". וְלֵימָא לֵיהּ: לֹא, אִם אָמַרְתָּ בְּחַטָּאת שֶׁכֵּן נִכְנָס דָּמָהּ לִפְנַי וְלִפְנִים!

§ The *baraita* states: **Rabbi Yehoshua said to him:** Your comparison of a guilt offering to a sin offering is **not** valid. **If you say** a *halakha* **with regard to a sin offering, whose blood is** sprinkled **above** the red line, should you necessarily say the same with regard to a guilt offering, whose blood is sprinkled below that line? The Gemara challenges: **And let** Rabbi Yehoshua **say to him** another refutation: Your comparison is **not** valid, as **if you say** the *halakha* **with regard to a sin offering, whose blood enters the innermost sanctum,** i.e., the Holy of Holies, on Yom Kippur, must the same be said for a guilt offering, whose blood never enters the innermost sanctum?

LANGUAGE

Around [*halila*] – חֲלִילָה: This means to do the same thing again and again. Perhaps the word derives from the root *ḥet*, *vav*, *lamed*, as does the word *maḥol*, which means dancing in a circle.

NOTES

The verse states: As is the sin offering so is the guilt offering – **הֲרֵי אוֹמֵר כַּחַטָּאת כָּאָשָׁם**: This concludes the discussion, as a *halakha* that is derived from a juxtaposition cannot be refuted through logical reasoning. Rabbi Yehoshua does not deny the juxtaposition; rather, he derives another *halakha* from it, as explained on 11a (Rashi).

NOTES

The blood of all offerings requires four placements – כָּל הַדָּמִים טְעוּנָה אַרְבַּע מַתָּנוֹת: According to the majority of the Sages, the blood of all offerings other than sin offerings is sprinkled twice, once on the northeastern corner and once on the southwestern corner, so that blood is sprinkled on all four sides of the altar. Rabbi Yishmael maintains that although the blood is placed on only these two corners, it must be placed individually on each side of each corner, so that the blood is placed four times altogether. The reason the blood is not placed on all four corners is that it must be sprinkled on corners that have bases, and the southeastern corner does not have a base (see 53a).

בְּחַטָּאוֹת הַחִיצוֹנוֹת קָאָמְרִינַן.

The Gemara answers: **We are stating** a comparison of a guilt offering to a sin offering specifically **with regard to the external sin offerings,** whose blood does not enter the innermost sanctum.

שֶׁאִם נִכְנָס דָּמָהּ [לִפְנַי] וְלִפְנִים – פְּסוּלָה!

The Gemara counters: If so, Rabbi Yehoshua could have refuted the comparison by pointing out another difference between a sin offering and a guilt offering, **as, if the blood of** an external sin offering **enters the innermost sanctum,** it is **disqualified.** This is not so in the case of the blood of a guilt offering.

אִית לֵיהּ לְרַבִּי אֱלִיעֶזֶר אַף הָאָשָׁם.

The Gemara answers: **Rabbi Eliezer holds** that **a guilt offering** whose blood enters the innermost sanctum is **also** disqualified.

שֶׁכֵּן מְכַפֶּרֶת עַל חַיָּיבֵי כָּרֵיתוֹת!

The Gemara counters: Rabbi Yehoshua could have pointed out another distinction, **as** a sin offering **atones for** transgressions for which one is **liable to** receive *karet* if he committed them intentionally.

מֵחַטָּאת דִּשְׁמִיעַת הַקּוֹל.

The Gemara answers: Rabbi Eliezer derives the *halakha* specifically **from a sin offering** brought **for hearing the voice,** i.e., for falsely taking an oath that one is unable to testify in another's case. This transgression is not punishable by *karet.*

שֶׁכֵּן טְעוּנָה אַרְבַּע מַתָּנוֹת!

The Gemara counters: Rabbi Yehoshua could have pointed out another distinction, **that** the blood of a sin offering **requires four placements** on the altar, whereas the blood of a guilt offering requires only two.

כְּרַבִּי יִשְׁמָעֵאל, דְּאָמַר: כָּל הַדָּמִים טְעוּנָה אַרְבַּע מַתָּנוֹת.

The Gemara answers: Perhaps Rabbi Eliezer holds **in accordance with** the opinion of **Rabbi Yishmael, who says** that **the blood** of almost **all** offerings **requires four placements.**[N]

שֶׁכֵּן טְעוּנָה עַל אַרְבַּע קְרָנוֹת!

The Gemara counters: Rabbi Yehoshua could have pointed out another distinction, **that** a sin offering's blood **requires** placement **on** all **four corners** of the altar, whereas the blood of a guilt offering, even according to Rabbi Yishmael, is sprinkled on only two corners.

וְלִיטַעֲמִיךְ, הָאִיכָּא אֶצְבַּע, הָאִיכָּא קֶרֶן, הָאִיכָּא חוּדָּה! אֶלָּא, חַד מִתְּרֵי תְּלָת טַעֲמֵי נָקַט.

The Gemara answers: **And according to your reasoning,** why didn't Rabbi Yehoshua mention other distinctions between a sin offering and a guilt offering? **Isn't there** the requirement that a priest place a sin offering's blood on the altar with his **finger? Isn't there** the requirement to place a sin offering's blood on the **corner** of the altar? And even according to the opinion that it is not placed on the corner itself, **isn't there** the requirement to place it on **the edge of** the corner? None of these requirements pertain to any offering other than a sin offering. **Rather,** Rabbi Yehoshua **mentioned one of two** or **three** valid **claims** at his disposal.

אָמַר מָר: אָמַר לוֹ רַבִּי יְהוֹשֻׁעַ: לֹא, אִם אָמַרְתָּ. לֵימָא לֵיהּ רַבִּי אֱלִיעֶזֶר: אָשָׁם נַמִי דָּמוֹ לְמַעְלָה!

§ **The Master says: Rabbi Yehoshua said to him:** Your comparison is **not** valid. **If you say** this with regard to a sin offering, whose blood is sprinkled above the red line, should you necessarily say the same with regard to a guilt offering, whose blood is sprinkled below that line? The Gemara challenges: **Let Rabbi Eliezer say to him: The blood of a guilt offering is also** sprinkled **above** the red line,[B] since Rabbi Eliezer holds that the *halakhot* of a guilt offering and a sin offering are parallel.

BACKGROUND

Corners of the altar, the red line – קַרְנוֹת הַמִּזְבֵּחַ, חוּט הַסִּיקְרָא:

Diagram of the altar:

1. Base of the altar
2. Red line
3. Surrounding ledge
4. Corners of the altar
5. Location of the ash mound
6. Location of the arrangement of the wood
7. Location of the arrangement of the incense
8. Special arrangement of wood for Yom Kippur
9. Location of the perpetual fire
10. Ramp
11. Cavities

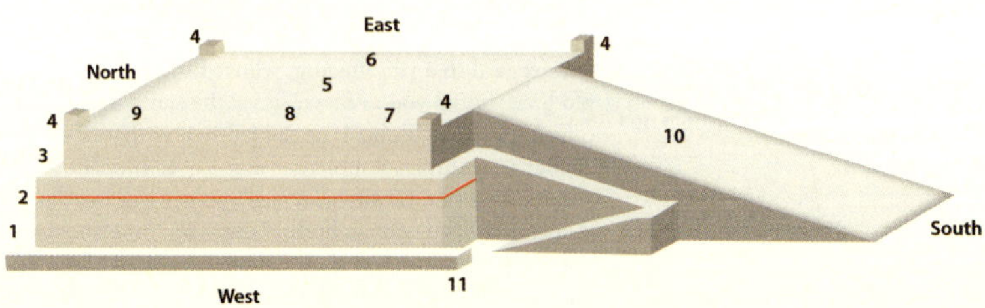

אָמַר אַבָּיֵי: אָשָׁם דָּמוֹ לְמַעְלָה לָא מָצֵית אָמְרַתְּ, קַל וָחוֹמֶר מֵעוֹלָה: וּמָה עוֹלָה שֶׁהִיא כָּלִיל – דָּמָהּ לְמַטָּה, אָשָׁם שֶׁאֵינוֹ כָּלִיל לֹא כׇּל שֶׁכֵּן?

Abaye said: You cannot say that **the blood of a guilt offering** is presented **above** the red line,[H] due to **an *a fortiori* inference from** the case of **a burnt offering:**[N] **Just as** in the case of **a burnt offering, which is** treated stringently in that it is totally **consumed** on the altar, **its blood** is presented **below** the red line, **all the more so** is it **not** clear that in the case of **a guilt offering, which is not** totally **consumed** on the altar, its blood is presented below the red line?

מָה לְעוֹלָה שֶׁכֵּן אֵינָהּ מְכַפֶּרֶת!

The Gemara rejects the inference: **What** is notable **about a burnt offering?** It is notable **in that it does not atone** for a sin, unlike a guilt offering. Perhaps this is why its blood is presented below the red line.

חַטַּאת הָעוֹף תּוֹכִיחַ.

The Gemara answers: **A bird sin offering can prove** the point, as it atones for a sin, and still its blood is presented below the red line.

מָה לְחַטַּאת הָעוֹף שֶׁכֵּן אֵינָהּ מִין זֶבַח!

The Gemara rejects this as well: **What** is notable **about a bird sin offering?** It is notable **in that it is not a type of offering** that is **slaughtered**; it is killed by pinching the nape of its neck. Perhaps this is why its blood is presented below the red line.

עוֹלָה תּוֹכִיחַ. לֹא רְאִי זֶה כִּרְאִי זֶה וְלֹא רְאִי זֶה כִּרְאִי זֶה, הַצַּד הַשָּׁוֶה שֶׁבָּהֶן – שֶׁהֵן קׇדְשֵׁי קֳדָשִׁים וְדָמָן לְמַטָּה, אַף אֲנִי אָבִיא אָשָׁם שֶׁהוּא קוֹדֶשׁ קֳדָשִׁים וְדָמוֹ לְמַטָּה.

The Gemara answers: If so, **a burnt offering can prove** the point, since it is slaughtered, and its blood is still presented below the red line. Therefore, the *halakha* is derived from a combination of the *halakhot* of a burnt offering and a bird sin offering: **The aspect of this** case **is not like the aspect of that** case **and the aspect of that** case **is not like the aspect of this** case. **Their common element is that they are offerings of the most sacred order, and their blood** is presented **below** the red line. **So too, I shall include a guilt offering** in this *halakha*, **as it is an offering of the most sacred order,** and therefore **its blood is** presented **below** the red line.

אֲמַר לֵיהּ רָבָא מִפַּרְזִקְיָא לְרַב אָשֵׁי, וְלִפְרוֹךְ: מָה לְהַצַּד הַשָּׁוֶה שֶׁבָּהֶן שֶׁכֵּן אֵין לָהֶן קִצְבָה, תֹּאמַר בְּאָשָׁם שֶׁיֵּשׁ לוֹ קִצְבָה!

Rava of Parzakya[P] **said to Rav Ashi: Let** Rabbi Eliezer **refute** this inference: **What** is notable **about the common element of** the two cases? It is notable **in that neither** a burnt offering nor a bird sin offering **has a fixed** value. Need **you say** that the same *halakhot* apply **to a guilt offering, which has a fixed** value of two silver shekels (see Leviticus 5:15)?

אֶלָּא הַיְינוּ טַעְמָא דְּרַבִּי אֱלִיעֶזֶר, דְּאָמַר קְרָא: ״הַכֹּהֵן הַמְחַטֵּא אוֹתָהּ״ – אוֹתָהּ דָּמָהּ לְמַעְלָה, וְאֵין דָּמוֹ שֶׁל אַחֵר לְמַעְלָה.

Rather, this is Rabbi Eliezer's reason for not claiming that the blood of a guilt offering is presented below the red line: **As the verse states** with regard to the presenting of the blood of a sin offering: **"The priest who offers it"** (Leviticus 6:19). The word "it" indicates that **its blood** is presented **above** the red line, **but the blood of another** slaughtered offering is **not** presented **above** the red line.

אִי הָכִי, חַטָּאת נָמֵי נֵימָא: ״אוֹתָהּ״ – לִשְׁמָהּ כְּשֵׁרָה, שֶׁלֹּא לִשְׁמָהּ פְּסוּלָה; הָא שְׁאָר זְבָחִים, בֵּין לִשְׁמָן בֵּין שֶׁלֹּא לִשְׁמָן – כְּשֵׁרִין!

The Gemara asks: **If so,** if Rabbi Eliezer accepts that the word "it" indicates exclusivity, **let him also say** that the verse: "And slaughter **it** for a sin offering" (Leviticus 4:33), teaches that only **a sin offering is fit** if slaughtered **for its sake,** and **unfit** if slaughtered **not for its sake. Consequently, other slaughtered offerings, whether** slaughtered **for their sake or not for their sake, are fit.** Why then does Rabbi Eliezer deem a guilt offering unfit if slaughtered not for its sake?

הַהוּא ״אוֹתָהּ״ לָאו דַּוְקָא, דְּהָא שַׁיַּיר פֶּסַח.

The Gemara answers: **That** instance of the word **"it"** does **not** indicate that the *halakha* applies **specifically** to a sin offering and to no other offerings, **as** the Torah **excludes** the **Paschal offering** from such a generalization. A Paschal offering is certainly disqualified if sacrificed not for its sake.

הָכָא נָמֵי לָאו דַּוְקָא, דְּהָא שַׁיַּיר עוֹלַת הָעוֹף!

The Gemara counters: If so, **here too,** with regard to the presenting of the blood above the red line, one must say the word "it" does **not** indicate that this *halakha* applies **specifically** to a sin offering and no other offerings, **as** the Torah **excludes a bird burnt offering** from such a generalization. The blood of a bird burnt offering is presented above the red line.

HALAKHA

You cannot say the blood of a guilt offering is presented above the red line – אָשָׁם דָּמוֹ לְמַעְלָה לָא מָצֵית אָמְרַתְּ: The blood of a burnt offering, a guilt offering, and a peace offering is sprinkled on the altar in the same manner: The priest takes the blood in the cup and sprinkles it twice, on the lower half of the northeastern and the southwestern corners of the altar. The priest sprinkles the blood on the corner so that it reaches both sides of the corner. This way, blood is sprinkled on all four sides of the altar (Rambam *Sefer Avoda, Hilkhot Ma'aseh HaKorbanot* 5:6).

NOTES

An *a fortiori* inference from a burnt offering – קַל וָחוֹמֶר מֵעוֹלָה: The source for the *halakha* that the blood of a burnt offering is sprinkled below the red line is unclear. Although the Gemara derives from the verse: "And slaughter it for a sin offering" (Leviticus 4:33), that only the blood of a sin offering is placed above the red line and the blood of all other offerings is placed below the red line, that derivation is apparently based on the premise that the blood of a burnt offering is placed below the red line.

Rashi explains on 10a that since the Torah mentions that blood is required to be placed on the corners of the altar only with regard to a sin offering, it is assumed that the blood of the other offerings is sprinkled on the lower portion of the altar.

In the Rambam's Commentary on the Mishna (5:6) it is suggested that this *halakha* is derived from a logical inference based on the distinction between a bird burnt offering and a bird sin offering. Since the blood of a bird burnt offering is placed above the red line and the blood of a bird sin offering is placed below the red line, and the blood of an animal sin offering is placed above the red line, apparently the blood of an animal burnt offering is placed below the red line. Furthermore, the base of the altar is referred to several times in the Torah as the base of the burnt offering altar, which indicates that the blood of a burnt offering is sprinkled close to the base of the altar.

PERSONALITIES

Rava of Parzakya – רָבָא מִפַּרְזִקְיָא: Rava of Parzakya, sometimes referred to erroneously as Ravina of Parzakya, was a Sage who lived in the sixth generation of Babylonian *amora'im*. He was a halakhic authority, and he participated in Rav Ashi's compilation of the Talmud, along with other Sages. He engaged in many halakhic discussions with Rav Ashi. Nothing is known of his family other than the fact that he had a son named Huna, who was a Torah scholar and who also engaged in discussions with Rav Ashi. The identity of his town Parzakya is unknown.

LANGUAGE

Red [*sikra*] – סִיקְרָא: This word means red in Persian. In the Bible the word appears in the form of a verb, e.g., "Painting [*mesakkerot*] their eyes" (Isaiah 3:16). This color red was used for painting items or parts of the body and for writing, among other uses. It was apparently based on minium, or lead oxide.

NOTES

Any blood…only the blood of a sin offering – כָּל דָּמִים...חַטָּאת בִּלְבַד: This *halakha* is derived from the verse: "And any sin offering, any of whose blood is brought into the Tent of Meeting to atone in the Sanctuary, shall not be eaten" (Leviticus 6:23). Although the straightforward meaning of the verse is that the flesh of inner sin offerings is not eaten but burned, the Sages derive an additional *halakha*, that if the blood of an external sin offering enters the Sanctuary, the offering is disqualified, and its flesh may not be eaten (see 82a and Ramban's Commentary on the Torah, Leviticus 6:23).

HALAKHA

Only the blood of a sin offering – חַטָּאת בִּלְבַד: If one brings the blood of an outer sin offering into the Sanctuary, the offering is disqualified, in accordance with the opinion of the Rabbis (Rambam *Sefer Avoda*, *Hilkhot Pesulei HaMukdashin* 2:13).

בִּזְבִיחָה מִיהָא לָא שַׁיֵּיר מִידֵּי.

The Gemara answers: **With regard to** offerings that require **slaughter, in any event,** the Torah **excluded nothing** from the generalization. Bird offerings are irrelevant, as they are killed by the pinching of the nape.

וְאִי בָּעֵית אֵימָא: הָא מַנִּי? רַבִּי אֶלְעָזָר בְּרַבִּי שִׁמְעוֹן הִיא, דְּאָמַר: הַאי מָקוֹם לְחוּד וְהַאי מָקוֹם לְחוּד,

And if you wish, say instead that even the blood of a bird burnt offering is presented in a manner different from that of a sin offering. In accordance with **whose** opinion **is this** suggestion? **It is** in accordance with the opinion of **Rabbi Elazar, son of Rabbi Shimon, who says: This place** where the blood of a sin offering is presented is **discrete, and that place** where the blood of a bird burnt offering is presented is **discrete.**

דְּתַנְיָא: דָּמִים הַתַּחְתּוֹנִים נִיתָּנִין מִחוּט הַסִּיקְרָא וּלְמַטָּה, וְהָעֶלְיוֹנִים – מִחוּט הַסִּיקְרָא וּלְמַעְלָה. אָמַר רַבִּי אֶלְעָזָר בְּרַבִּי שִׁמְעוֹן: בַּמֶּה דְּבָרִים אֲמוּרִין – בְּעוֹלַת הָעוֹף, אֲבָל בְּחַטַּאת בְּהֵמָה – הִיא עַצְמָהּ אֵין נַעֲשָׂה אֶלָּא עַל גּוּפָהּ שֶׁל קֶרֶן.

As it is taught in a *baraita*: **The blood** that must be placed on **the lower** half of the altar **is placed** anywhere **from the red** [*hasikra*][L] **line and below, and** the blood that must be placed on **the upper** half is placed anywhere **from the red line and above. Rabbi Elazar, son of Rabbi Shimon, said: In what case is this statement said?** It is said **with regard to a bird burnt offering. But** the placement of the blood of **an animal sin offering is itself performed only on the actual corner** of the altar.

תְּנַן הָתָם, שֶׁהָיָה רַבִּי עֲקִיבָא אוֹמֵר: כָּל דָּמִים שֶׁנִּכְנְסוּ לְהֵיכָל לְכַפֵּר – פְּסוּלִים. וַחֲכָמִים אוֹמְרִים: חַטָּאת בִּלְבַד. רַבִּי אֱלִיעֶזֶר אוֹמֵר: אַף הָאָשָׁם, שֶׁנֶּאֱמַר: ״כַּחַטָּאת כָּאָשָׁם״.

§ **We learned** in a mishna **elsewhere** (81b): **As Rabbi Akiva would say: Any blood that** should have been sprinkled on the external altar but instead **entered to atone in the Sanctuary** is **unfit. And the Rabbis say:** That is the *halakha* **only** with regard to the blood of **a sin offering.**[NH] **Rabbi Eliezer says:** The halakhic status of **a guilt offering** is **also** like that of a sin offering, **as it is stated: "As is the sin offering, so is the guilt offering"** (Leviticus 7:7).

בִּשְׁלָמָא רַבִּי אֱלִיעֶזֶר כִּדְקָאָמַר טַעְמָא, אֶלָּא רַבָּנַן מַאי טַעְמָא?

The Gemara asks: **Granted,** the opinion of **Rabbi Eliezer** is understandable, **as he states the reason** for his opinion. **But what is the reason** for the opinion of **the Rabbis?**

אָמַר רָבָא: אָשָׁם נִכְנַס דָּמוֹ לִפְנִים פָּסוּל לָא מָצֵית אָמְרַתְּ, קַל וָחוֹמֶר מֵעוֹלָה: מָה

Rava said: You cannot say that **the blood of a guilt offering that entered into** the Sanctuary **is disqualified,** due to **an *a fortiori*** inference **from** the case of **a burnt offering: Just as**

Perek **I**
Daf **11** Amud **a**

NOTES

The meal offering of a sinner – מִנְחַת חוֹטֵא: This refers to a sliding-scale sin offering. A person in extreme poverty who is obligated to bring a sliding-scale sin offering brings a meal offering (see Leviticus 5:11).

A bird sin offering is a dilemma raised by Rabbi Avin – חַטַּאת הָעוֹף בְּעָיָא דְּרַבִּי אָבִין הִיא: The dilemma stems from the fact that the blood of a bird sin offering is not collected in a bowl; rather, it is sprinkled by holding the bird itself. Since blood can be disqualified by entering the Sanctuary only after being collected in a bowl, Rabbi Avin raised a dilemma as to whether the neck of the bird is considered to be like a service vessel, as its blood is sprinkled on the altar from its neck, or it is considered to be like the flesh of an offering, which is not disqualified by entering the Sanctuary.

עוֹלָה שֶׁהִיא כָּלִיל, נִכְנַס דָּמָהּ לִפְנִים – כְּשֵׁרָה, אָשָׁם שֶׁאֵינוֹ כָּלִיל – לֹא כׇּל שֶׁכֵּן?

with regard to **a burnt offering, which is** totally **consumed** by the fire on the altar, nevertheless, even if **its blood enters into** the Sanctuary it is **fit,** with regard to **a guilt offering, which is not** entirely **consumed** on the altar, **all the more so** is it **not** clear that even if its blood enters the Sanctuary it remains fit?

מָה לְעוֹלָה, שֶׁכֵּן אֵינָהּ מְכַפֶּרֶת.

The Gemara refutes this inference: **What** is notable **about a burnt offering?** It is notable **in that it does not atone** for a sin. Perhaps this is why its blood is not disqualified if it enters the sanctuary.

מִנְחַת חוֹטֵא תּוֹכִיחַ.

The Gemara responds: **The meal offering of a sinner**[N] **can prove** the point, as it is not disqualified by entering the Sanctuary, even though it atones for a sin.

וְלֵימָא: חַטַּאת הָעוֹף תּוֹכִיחַ! חַטַּאת הָעוֹף בְּעָיָא דְּרַבִּי אָבִין הִיא.

The Gemara interjects: **But let us say** that **a bird sin offering can prove** the point, as it too atones for a sin but is not disqualified by entering the Sanctuary. This case is more similar to that of a guilt offering, as a bird has blood, unlike a meal offering. The Gemara answers: It is not certain that **a bird sin offering** is not disqualified by entering the Sanctuary; this **is a dilemma** raised **by Rabbi Avin.**[N]

וְלִפְרוֹךְ: מָה לְמִנְחַת חוֹטֵא, שֶׁכֵּן אֵינָהּ מִין זֶבַח!

The Gemara asks: **But let us refute** the above response as follows: **What** is notable **about a sinner's meal offering?** It is notable **in that it is not a type of slaughtered offering.**

עוֹלָה תּוֹכִיחַ. וְחָזַר הַדִּין, לֹא רְאִי זֶה כִּרְאִי זֶה, וְלֹא רְאִי זֶה כִּרְאִי זֶה, הַצַּד הַשָּׁוֶה שֶׁבָּהֶן – שֶׁהֵן קָדְשֵׁי קָדָשִׁים וְנִכְנָס (דָּמָן) לִפְנִים כְּשֵׁרִין, אַף אֲנִי אָבִיא אָשָׁם שֶׁהוּא קוֹדֶשׁ קָדָשִׁים, וְנִכְנָס דָּמוֹ לִפְנִים כָּשֵׁר.

The Gemara answers: If so, **a burnt offering can prove** the point, since it is a slaughtered offering, and still if its blood enters the Sanctuary, it is not disqualified. **And the inference has reverted** to its starting point. The *halakha* is derived from the *halakhot* of a burnt offering and a sinner's meal offering: **The aspect of this** case **is not like the aspect of that** case **and the aspect of that** case **is not like the aspect of this** case. **Their common element is that they are offerings of the most sacred order, and if** they **enter into** the Sanctuary **they are** still **fit. So too, I shall include a guilt offering** and infer that **since it is** also **an offering of the most sacred order,** if **its blood enters into** the Sanctuary it is still **fit.**

אֲמַר לֵיהּ רָבָא מִבַּרְנִישׁ לְרַב אַשִׁי, וְלִפְרוֹךְ: מַה לְהַצַּד הַשָּׁוֶה שֶׁבָּהֶן – שֶׁכֵּן אֵין לָהֶן קִצְבָּה, תֹּאמַר בְּאָשָׁם שֶׁיֵּשׁ לוֹ קִצְבָּה!

Rava of Barnish[BP] **said to Rav Ashi: But let us refute** this inference: **What** is notable **about their common element?** It is notable **in that neither** a burnt offering nor a sinner's meal offering **has a fixed** value. **Should you say** the same *halakhot* apply **to a guilt offering, which has a fixed** value?

אֶלָּא הַיְינוּ טַעֲמַיְיהוּ דְּרַבָּנַן, דְּאָמַר קְרָא: "דָּמָהּ" – דָּמָהּ שֶׁל זוֹ, וְלֹא דָּמָהּ שֶׁל אַחֵר.

Rather, this is the reason for the opinion **of the Rabbis: As the verse states:** "And any sin offering, any of **whose blood** is brought into the Tent of Meeting to atone in the Sanctuary, shall not be eaten" (Leviticus 6:23). The term "whose blood" teaches that **the blood of this** offering, i.e., a sin offering, **and not the blood of another** offering, is disqualified in this manner.

וְאִידָךְ? "דָּמָהּ" – וְלֹא בְּשָׂרָהּ.

And how does **the other** *tanna*, Rabbi Eliezer, interpret this term? He derives from it that only **its blood** is disqualified by entering the Sanctuary, **but not its flesh.**

וְאִידָךְ? "דָּם" "דָּמָהּ".

And from where do **the other** Rabbis derive that the flesh of a sin offering is not disqualified by entering the Sanctuary? They maintain that both *halakhot* are derived from this term, as the verse could have simply stated: **Blood,** but stated: **"Whose blood."** The redundancy excludes not only the flesh, but also other offerings.

וְאִידָךְ? "דָּם" "דָּמָהּ" לָא דָּרֵישׁ.

And the other *tanna*, Rabbi Eliezer, **does not interpret** the redundancy indicated by the change from: **Blood,** to: **"Whose blood,"** to be significant. Once the word blood is mentioned, it is grammatically necessary for the verse to state "whose blood."

בִּשְׁלָמָא לְרַבָּנַן, דְּאָמְרִי: אָשָׁם שֶׁשְּׁחָטוֹ שֶׁלֹּא לִשְׁמוֹ כָּשֵׁר – הַיְינוּ דְּאִיתְקַשׁ מִנְחָה לְחַטָּאת מִנְחָה לְאָשָׁם.

§ The Gemara resumes its discussion of the dispute in the mishna between Rabbi Eliezer and the Rabbis. **Granted, according to the Rabbis, who say** that **a guilt offering that one slaughtered not for its sake is fit, that is why a meal offering is juxtaposed with a sin offering,** and **a meal offering** is also juxtaposed **with a guilt offering.**

דְּתַנְיָא, רַבִּי שִׁמְעוֹן אוֹמֵר: "קֹדֶשׁ קָדָשִׁים הוּא כַּחַטָּאת וְכָאָשָׁם", מִנְחַת חוֹטֵא הֲרֵי הִיא כְּחַטָּאת – לְפִיכָךְ קְמָצָהּ שֶׁלֹּא לִשְׁמָהּ פְּסוּלָה, מִנְחַת נְדָבָה הֲרֵי הִיא כְּאָשָׁם – לְפִיכָךְ קְמָצָהּ שֶׁלֹּא לִשְׁמָהּ כְּשֵׁרָה;

This is **as it is taught** in a *baraita*: **Rabbi Shimon says:** The verse states with regard to a meal offering: **"It is most sacred, as the sin offering, and as the guilt offering"** (Leviticus 6:10), teaching that **a meal offering of a sinner is like a sin offering. Therefore,** if one **removed its handful not for its sake,** it is **disqualified.** And the verse also teaches that **a voluntary meal offering is like a guilt offering. Therefore,** if one **removed its handful not for its sake,**[H] it is still **fit.** This accords with the opinion of the Rabbis, that a guilt offering slaughtered not for its sake is fit.

אֶלָּא לְרַבִּי אֱלִיעֶזֶר, לְמַאי הִלְכְתָא אִיתְקַשׁ מִנְחָה לְחַטָּאת וּמִנְחָה לְאָשָׁם?

But according to Rabbi Eliezer, for what *halakha* is a meal offering juxtaposed with a sin offering, and a meal offering juxtaposed **with a guilt offering?**

לְכִי אִידָךְ דְּרַבִּי שִׁמְעוֹן, דִּתְנַן: שֶׁלֹּא בִּכְלִי שָׁרֵת – פְּסוּלָה, וְרַבִּי שִׁמְעוֹן מַכְשִׁיר;

The Gemara answers: They are juxtaposed **to** teach **the other** *halakha* derived **by Rabbi Shimon** from this verse; **as we learned** in a mishna (*Menaḥot* 26a): If the handful of a meal offering is conveyed to the altar **not in a service vessel,**[H] the offering is **unfit. And Rabbi Shimon deems** it **fit.**

BACKGROUND

Barnish – בַּרְנִישׁ: Barnish was a city located near the cities of Sura and Meḥasya. Some suggest a connection between the name of the city and the Burnitz, or Barnitz, River, which supplied drinking water to Meḥasya. Others interpret the name Barnish as denoting a leader or elder. It is similar to the Hebrew word *parnas* and other words in ancient languages that carry this meaning.

Approximately nine miles away from Barnish was a synagogue called Daniel's Synagogue where, according to a local tradition, the prophet Daniel would pray. Jews from Barnish would go there to pray on Shabbat due to the synagogue's extra sanctity. This was halakhically permitted despite the long distance, as there were several towns along the way, the remains of which exist to this day.

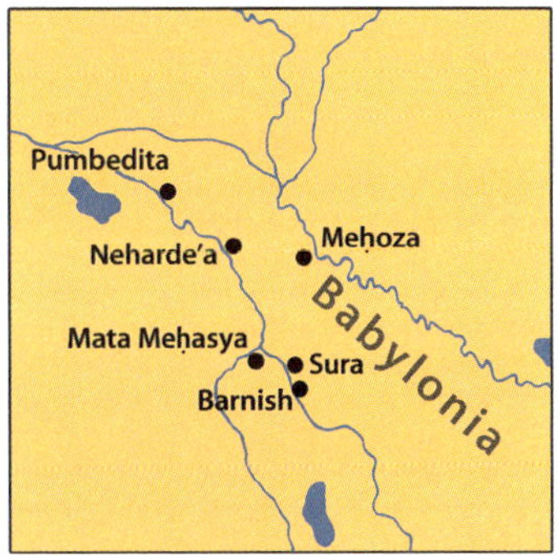

Location of Barnish

PERSONALITIES

Rava of Barnish – רָבָא מִבַּרְנִישׁ: This Sage lived in the sixth generation of Babylonian *amora'im*. He had many discussions with Rav Ashi, in which he raised difficulties with the statements and actions of Rav Ashi and other Sages. Nothing is known about his family. The city where he lived, Barnish, was adjacent to Meḥasya, where Rav Ashi served as head of the yeshiva.

HALAKHA

If one removed its handful not for its own sake – קְמָצָהּ שֶׁלֹּא לִשְׁמָהּ: If a handful was removed from any meal offering with the wrong type of meal offering in mind, the offering is still fit, but it does not satisfy its owner's obligation. A sinner's meal offering and a meal offering of jealousy are exceptions to this *halakha*: If one of their four main rites was performed with the wrong type of meal offering in mind, they are disqualified (Rambam *Sefer Avoda, Hilkhot Pesulei HaMukdashin* 15:2).

A meal offering not in a service vessel – שֶׁלֹּא בִּכְלִי שָׁרֵת: If the meal offering was not in a service vessel when the handful was removed from it, or if the handful was not put in a service vessel, or if it was conveyed to the altar without a service vessel, it is disqualified, in accordance with the opinion of the first *tanna* (Rambam *Sefer Avoda, Hilkhot Pesulei HaMukdashin* 11:6).

HALAKHA

With his left hand – בִּשְׂמֹאל: Sacrificial service is performed only with one's right hand; if one performs the service with his left hand his service is not valid. This is in accordance with the unattributed opinion in the mishna on 15b (Rambam *Sefer Avoda, Hilkhot Biat HaMikdash* 5:18).

A Paschal offering whose first year has passed – הַפֶּסַח שֶׁעָבְרָה שְׁנָתוֹ: A Paschal offering whose first year has passed that was slaughtered on Passover eve after noon for the sake of a Paschal offering is fit, but it does not satisfy its owner's obligation. The *halakha* is the same with regard to another offering that was slaughtered on Passover eve for the sake of a Paschal offering. This is in accordance with the opinion of Rabbi Yehoshua, whose opinion is generally accepted when he is in dispute with Rabbi Eliezer (Rambam *Sefer Avoda, Hilkhot Pesulei HaMukdashin* 15:12).

NOTES

They disagree with regard to other offerings slaughtered for the sake of a sin offering – בַּאֲחֵרִים לְשֵׁם חַטָּאת פְּלִיגִי: Rabbeinu Tam (*Tosafot* 11b) cites a version of the text that reads as follows: And they disagree, etc., In other words, Rabba was not in disagreement with the statement of Rabbi Yoḥanan that Yosef ben Ḥoni and Rabbi Eliezer said the same thing; rather, he was explaining that Rabbi Yoḥanan was referring only to the case of an offering that is slaughtered for the sake of a Paschal offering, and not to the case of an offering that is slaughtered for the sake of a sin offering.

As it is taught in a *baraita*, etc. – דְּתַנְיָא וכו׳: The *baraita* is apparently cited as a source for Rabba's opinion that Rabbi Eliezer agrees with Yosef ben Ḥoni with regard to a Paschal offering but disagrees with him with regard to a sin offering, as it is apparent from the *baraita* that Rabbi Eliezer concedes that a burnt offering that is sacrificed for the sake of a sin offering is fit. Rashi maintains that Rabbi Yoḥanan also derives his opinion from this *baraita*.

וְאָמַר רַב יְהוּדָה בְּרֵיהּ דְּרַבִּי חִיָּיא: מַאי טַעְמָא דְּרַבִּי שִׁמְעוֹן? אָמַר קְרָא: ״קֹדֶשׁ קָדָשִׁים הוּא כַּחַטָּאת וְכָאָשָׁם״, בָּא לְעוֹבְדָהּ בְּיָד – עוֹבְדָהּ בְּיָמִין כְּחַטָּאת, בִּכְלִי – עוֹבְדָהּ בִּשְׂמֹאל כְּאָשָׁם.

And Rav Yehuda, son of Rabbi Ḥiyya, says: What is the reasoning of Rabbi Shimon? The verse states with regard to a meal offering: **"It is most sacred, as the sin offering, and as the guilt offering,"** teaching that if a priest **comes to perform** its sacrificial rites **by hand, he must perform** them **with** his **right** hand, **like** one performs the rites of **a sin offering.** And if he performs them **with a vessel, he may perform** them **with** his **left** hand,[H] **like** one performs the rites of **a guilt offering,** since Rabbi Shimon maintains this is permitted in the case of a guilt offering.

וְרַבִּי שִׁמְעוֹן, הַאי קְרָא מַפֵּיק לֵיהּ לְהָכִי וּמַפֵּיק לֵיהּ לְהָכִי?

The Gemara asks: **And** as for **Rabbi Shimon** himself, **does he expound this verse for this** purpose, concerning one who if one removes its handful not for its sake, **and expound it for that** purpose, concerning conveying the handful with one's hand?

עִיקַּר קְרָא לְכִדְרַב יְהוּדָה בְּרֵיהּ דְּרַבִּי חִיָּיא הוּא דַּאֲתָא. וּמִנְחַת חוֹטֵא דִּפְסוּלָה שֶׁלֹּא לִשְׁמָהּ – [טַעְמָא אַחֲרִינָא הוּא:] חַטָּאת טַעְמָא מַאי? דִּכְתִיב בָּהּ: ״הִיא״, מִנְחַת חוֹטֵא נָמֵי כְּתִיב בָּהּ: ״הִיא״.

The Gemara answers: **The verse comes mainly to** teach **that which Rav Yehuda, son of Rabbi Ḥiyya,** explained. **And** the *halakha* **that a meal offering of a sinner** whose handful was removed **not for its sake is unfit** is due to **another reason: What is the reason a sin offering** sacrificed not for its sake is disqualified? The reason is **that** the word **"it" is written with regard to it** in the verse: "It is a sin offering" (Leviticus 4:24). Since the word **"it" is also written with regard to the meal offering of a sinner,** in the verse: "For it is a sin offering" (Leviticus 5:11), the same applies in that case.

וּלְרַבָּנַן, לְמַאי הִלְכְתָא אִיתְקַשׁ אָשָׁם לְחַטָּאת? לוֹמַר לָךְ: מָה חַטָּאת טְעוּנָה סְמִיכָה, אַף אָשָׁם טָעוּן סְמִיכָה.

In the mishna, Rabbi Eliezer cites the verse: "As is the sin offering, so is the guilt offering" (Leviticus 7:7), as a source for his opinion. The Gemara asks: **And according to the Rabbis, for what** *halakha* **is a guilt offering juxtaposed with a sin offering?** The Gemara answers: They are juxtaposed **to tell you** that **just as a sin offering requires placing hands** on the head of the offering, **so too, a guilt offering requires placing hands** on the head of the offering.

״יוֹסֵף בֶּן חוֹנִי אוֹמֵר: הַנִּשְׁחָטִין״ כו׳. אָמַר רַבִּי יוֹחָנָן: יוֹסֵף בֶּן חוֹנִי וְרַבִּי אֱלִיעֶזֶר אָמְרוּ דָּבָר אֶחָד.

§ The mishna teaches: **Yosef ben Ḥoni says:** Other offerings **that are slaughtered** for the sake of a Paschal offering or a sin offering are unfit. **Rabbi Yoḥanan says: Yosef ben Ḥoni and Rabbi Eliezer said the same thing,** i.e., Rabbi Eliezer agrees with Yosef ben Ḥoni.

רַבָּה אָמַר: בַּאֲחֵרִים לְשֵׁם חַטָּאת פְּלִיגִי.

Rabba says: Although they agree that other offerings slaughtered for the sake of a Paschal offering are unfit, **they disagree with regard to other** offerings slaughtered **for the sake of a sin offering.**[N] Whereas Yosef ben Ḥoni holds that they are unfit, Rabbi Eliezer maintains that they are fit.

דְּתַנְיָא: הַפֶּסַח שֶׁעָבְרָה שְׁנָתוֹ וּשְׁחָטוֹ בִּזְמַנּוֹ לִשְׁמוֹ, וְכֵן הַשּׁוֹחֵט אֲחֵרִים לְשֵׁם פֶּסַח בִּזְמַנּוֹ – רַבִּי אֱלִיעֶזֶר פּוֹסֵל, וְרַבִּי יְהוֹשֻׁעַ מַכְשִׁיר.

This is **as it is taught** in a *baraita*:[N] In the case of **a Paschal offering whose first year has passed,**[H] and it must therefore be sacrificed as a peace offering, **and one slaughtered it at its** designated **time** on Passover eve **for its own sake** as a Paschal offering, **and likewise,** if **one slaughtered other** offerings **for the sake of a Paschal offering at its** designated **time,** the *tanna'im* disagree as to the status of the offering. **Rabbi Eliezer deems it** unfit, **and Rabbi Yehoshua deems** it **fit.**

אָמַר רַבִּי יְהוֹשֻׁעַ: אִם בִּשְׁאָר יְמוֹת הַשָּׁנָה שֶׁאֵינוֹ כָּשֵׁר לִשְׁמוֹ – אֲחֵרִים כְּשֵׁרִים לִשְׁמוֹ, בִּזְמַנּוֹ שֶׁהוּא כָּשֵׁר לִשְׁמוֹ – אֵינוֹ דִּין שֶׁיִּכְשְׁרוּ אֲחֵרִים לִשְׁמוֹ?

Rabbi Yehoshua said: If, during the rest of the days of the year, when a Paschal offering **is not fit** if it is slaughtered **for its own sake,** nevertheless, **other** offerings that are slaughtered **for its sake are fit,** then **at its** designated **time, when** a Paschal offering **is fit** if it is slaughtered **for its own sake, isn't it logical that other** offerings slaughtered **for its sake should be fit?**

אָמַר לוֹ רַבִּי אֱלִיעֶזֶר: אוֹ חִילּוּף הַדְּבָרִים, וּמָה אִם בִּשְׁאָר יְמוֹת הַשָּׁנָה שֶׁאֵינוֹ כָּשֵׁר לִשְׁמוֹ – כָּשֵׁר הוּא לְשֵׁם אֲחֵרִים, בִּזְמַנּוֹ שֶׁהוּא כָּשֵׁר לִשְׁמוֹ – אֵינוֹ דִּין שֶׁיּוּכְשַׁר לְשֵׁם אֲחֵרִים? וְיוּכְשַׁר פֶּסַח בְּאַרְבָּעָה עָשָׂר שֶׁלֹּא לִשְׁמוֹ!

Rabbi Eliezer said to him: Or conversely, just as during the rest of the days of the year, when a Paschal offering **is not fit** if it is slaughtered **for its own sake, it is fit** if slaughtered **for the sake of other** offerings, so too, **at its** designated **time, when it is fit** if slaughtered **for its own sake, isn't it logical that it should be fit** if slaughtered **for the sake of other** offerings? **And** accordingly, **a Paschal offering** slaughtered **not for its own sake on the fourteenth** of Nisan **should be deemed fit,** which contradicts the *halakha*. Clearly, this line of reasoning leads to incorrect conclusions.

וְכָךְ אַתָּה אוֹמֵר? מַה לִּי הוּכְשְׁרוּ אֲחֵרִים בִּשְׁאָר יְמוֹת הַשָּׁנָה לִשְׁמוֹ – שֶׁכֵּן הוּא כָּשֵׁר לְשֵׁם אֲחֵרִים, וְיוּכְשְׁרוּ אֲחֵרִים בִּזְמַנּוֹ לִשְׁמוֹ? שֶׁכֵּן הוּא פָּסוּל לְשֵׁם אֲחֵרִים!

Furthermore, Rabbi Eliezer refuted Rabbi Yehoshua's logic as follows: **And do you say this** derivation? **What** does it matter **to me** that **other** offerings slaughtered **during the rest of the days of the year for the sake of** a Paschal offering **are deemed fit? After all,** a Paschal offering slaughtered **for the sake of other** offerings **is** also **fit. But** must you say that **other** offerings slaughtered **at** its designated **time for its sake should be deemed fit? After all,** at its designated time, a Paschal offering slaughtered **for the sake of other** offerings **is unfit.**[N]

אָמַר לוֹ רַבִּי יְהוֹשֻׁעַ: אִם כֵּן, הוֹרַעְתָּה כֹּחַ פֶּסַח וְנָתַתָּ כֹּחַ בִּשְׁלָמִים!

Rabbi Yehoshua said to him: If, as you maintain, other offerings slaughtered on Passover eve for the sake of a Paschal offering are disqualified, **you have diminished the force** of the requirement that **a Paschal offering** be sacrificed for its own sake, **and you have given** more **force to** the requirement that **a peace offering** be sacrificed for its own sake. A Paschal offering sacrificed at the proper time, i.e., during the rest of the year, for the sake of a peace offering, is fit, whereas a peace offering sacrificed on Passover eve for the sake of a Paschal offering is unfit.

חָזַר רַבִּי אֱלִיעֶזֶר וְדָנוֹ דִּין אַחֵר: מָצִינוּ מוֹתַר פֶּסַח בָּא שְׁלָמִים, וְאֵין מוֹתַר שְׁלָמִים בָּא פֶּסַח.

The *baraita* continues: **Rabbi Eliezer then presented a different logical inference: We find** that **a leftover Paschal offering,** an animal consecrated as a Paschal offering but ultimately not sacrificed on Passover eve, is **brought** as **a peace offering; but a leftover peace offering,** one bought with money left over from funds dedicated toward the acquisition of a peace offering, is **not brought** as **a Paschal offering.** A Paschal offering is a potential peace offering, but a peace offering is not a potential Paschal offering.

וּמַה פֶּסַח שֶׁמּוֹתָרוֹ בָּא שְׁלָמִים, שְׁחָטוֹ בִּזְמַנּוֹ לְשׁוּם שְׁלָמִים – פָּסוּל, שְׁלָמִים שֶׁאֵין מוֹתָרָן בָּא פֶּסַח, אִם שְׁחָטָם לְשֵׁם פֶּסַח בִּזְמַנּוֹ – אֵינוֹ דִּין שֶׁיְּהוּ פְּסוּלִין?

And if so, one may infer *a fortiori*: **Just as** with regard to **a Paschal offering, whose leftover** offering **is brought** as **a peace offering,** and nevertheless, if one **slaughtered it at its** designated **time for the sake of a peace offering** it is **unfit,** so too, with regard to **a peace offering, whose leftover** offering **is not brought** as a Paschal offering, **if** one **slaughtered** it **for the sake of a Paschal offering at its** designated **time, isn't it logical that** it **should be unfit?**

NOTES

After all a Paschal offering slaughtered for the sake of other offerings is unfit – שֶׁכֵּן הוּא פָּסוּל לְשֵׁם אֲחֵרִים: Rashi claims that it is from here that Rabbi Yoḥanan inferred that Rabbi Eliezer also disqualifies an offering that is sacrificed for the sake of a sin offering. Since a sin offering that is sacrificed for the sake of another offering is unfit all year round, the same should apply with regard to another offering that is sacrificed for the sake of a sin offering. Rabba, by contrast, infers from the fact that Rabbi Eliezer subsequently suggests a different line of reasoning that he retracted this reasoning.

Perek I
Daf 11 Amud b

אָמַר לוֹ רַבִּי יְהוֹשֻׁעַ: מָצִינוּ מוֹתַר חַטָּאת בָּא עוֹלָה, וְאֵין מוֹתַר עוֹלָה בָּא חַטָּאת;

Rabbi Yehoshua said to him: This inference is not valid, as **we find** that **a leftover sin offering,** e.g., one bought with money left over from funds dedicated to the acquisition of a sin offering, **is brought** as **a burnt offering,** whereas **a leftover burnt offering is not brought** as **a sin offering.**

וּמַה חַטָּאת שֶׁמּוֹתָרָהּ בָּא עוֹלָה, שְׁחָטָהּ לְשֵׁם עוֹלָה – פְּסוּלָה, עוֹלָה שֶׁאֵין מוֹתָרָהּ בָּא חַטָּאת, שְׁחָטָהּ לְשֵׁם חַטָּאת – אֵינוֹ דִּין שֶׁתְּהֵא פְּסוּלָה?

And according to Rabbi Eliezer's logic, one should derive *a fortiori*: **Just as** with regard to **a sin offering, whose leftover is brought** as **a burnt offering,** nevertheless, if one **slaughtered it for the sake of a burnt offering** it is **unfit,** so too, with regard to **a burnt offering, whose leftover is not brought** as **a sin offering,** if one **slaughtered it for the sake of a sin offering, isn't it logical that it should be unfit?** Yet, the *halakha* is that a burnt offering slaughtered for the sake of a sin offering is fit.

אָמַר לוֹ רַבִּי אֱלִיעֶזֶר: לֹא, אִם אָמַרְתָּ בְּחַטָּאת – שֶׁכֵּן כְּשֵׁרָה לִשְׁמָהּ כׇּל הַשָּׁנָה כּוּלָּהּ, תֹּאמַר בְּפֶסַח – שֶׁאֵינוֹ כָּשֵׁר לִשְׁמוֹ אֶלָּא בִּזְמַנּוֹ? הוֹאִיל וְהוּא פָּסוּל לִשְׁמוֹ, דִּין הוּא שֶׁיִּפָּסְלוּ אֲחֵרִים לִשְׁמוֹ.

Rabbi Eliezer said to him: No, if you said that this is the *halakha* **with regard to a sin offering,**[N] that another offering sacrificed for its sake is fit, this is only **because** a sin offering **is fit** when sacrificed **for its sake all year long. Shall you** also **say** that this is the *halakha* **with regard to a Paschal offering, which is fit** when sacrificed **for its sake only at its** designated **time? Since** a Paschal offering **is unfit** when sacrificed **for its sake** during the rest of the year, **it is logical that other** offerings **should be disqualified** when sacrificed **for its sake** at its designated time.

NOTES

No, if you said that with regard to a sin offering, etc. – לֹא אִם אָמַרְתָּ בְּחַטָּאת וכו׳: From the fact that Rabbi Eliezer does not dispute the premise that if another offering is sacrificed for the sake of a sin offering it is still fit, it is apparent that he accepts this premise, in accordance with the opinion of Rabba. *Tosafot*, citing Rabbeinu Tam, maintain that Rabbi Yoḥanan agrees. Rashi explains that this is not conclusive proof that Rabbi Eliezer accepts this premise, as perhaps his claim was that even if another offering that is sacrificed for the sake of a sin offering is still fit, another offering that is sacrificed for the sake of a Paschal offering is not.

HALAKHA

One who eats untithed produce – **אוֹכֵל אֶת הַטֶּבֶל**: One who eats an olive-bulk of produce from which *teruma* and *teruma* of the tithe have not been separated is liable to receive the penalty of death at the hand of Heaven (Rambam *Sefer Kedusha, Hilkhot Ma'akhalot Assurot* 10:19).

״שִׁמְעוֹן אֲחִי עֲזַרְיָה אוֹמֵר״ כו׳.

§ The mishna teaches: **Shimon, brother of Azarya, says** that this is the distinction: With regard to all offerings, if one slaughtered them for the sake of an offering whose sanctity is greater than theirs, they are fit; if one slaughtered them for the sake of an offering whose sanctity is less than theirs, they are unfit.

רַב אַשִׁי מַתְנֵי מִשְּׁמֵיהּ דְּרַבִּי יוֹחָנָן, וְרַב אַחָא בְּרֵיהּ דְּרָבָא מַתְנֵי מִשְּׁמֵיהּ דְּרַבִּי יַנַּאי: מַאי טַעְמָא דְּשִׁמְעוֹן אֲחִי עֲזַרְיָה? דְּאָמַר קְרָא: ״וְלֹא יְחַלְּלוּ אֶת קׇדְשֵׁי בְּנֵי יִשְׂרָאֵל אֵת אֲשֶׁר יָרִימוּ לַה׳״ – בְּמוּרָם מֵהֶן אֵין מִתְחַלְּלִין, בְּנָמוּךְ מֵהֶם מִתְחַלְּלִין.

Rav Ashi teaches in the name of Rabbi Yoḥanan, and Rav Aḥa, son of Rava, teaches the same statement **in the name of Rabbi Yannai: What is the reason** for the opinion **of Shimon, brother of Azarya?** It is derived from that **which the verse states: "And they shall not profane the holy things of the children of Israel, which they will set apart** [*yarimu*] **unto the Lord"** (Leviticus 22:15). The verse is interpreted not as a prohibition but as a halakhic axiom, teaching that offerings **are not profaned,** i.e., disqualified, **by** sacrifice for the sake of offerings whose sanctity is **more elevated** [*muram*] **than theirs; they are profaned** only **by** sacrifice for the sake of offerings whose sanctity is **less than theirs.**

וְהַאי לְהָכִי הוּא דְּאָתָא? וְהָא מִיבְּעֵי לֵיהּ לְכִדְשְׁמוּאֵל, דְּאָמַר שְׁמוּאֵל: מִנַּיִן לְאוֹכֵל אֶת הַטֶּבֶל שֶׁהוּא בְּמִיתָה? שֶׁנֶּאֱמַר: ״וְלֹא יְחַלְּלוּ אֶת קׇדְשֵׁי בְּנֵי יִשְׂרָאֵל אֵת אֲשֶׁר יָרִימוּ לַה׳״, בַּעֲתִידִים לְהָרוּם הַכָּתוּב מְדַבֵּר!

The Gemara asks: **And does that** verse **come to** teach **this** *halakha*? **But isn't it necessary for Shmuel's** derivation? **As Shmuel says: From where** is it derived **that one who eats untithed produce**[H] **is** liable **to** be punished with **death**[N] at the hand of Heaven? **As it is stated: "And they shall not profane the holy things of the children of Israel, which they will set apart unto the Lord."** The term: "Will set apart," indicates that **the verse is speaking of** holy items **that are to be set apart in the future,** i.e., untithed produce, which includes the portion designated for the priest [*teruma*].

אִם כֵּן, לִכְתּוֹב קְרָא ״אֲשֶׁר הוּרְמוּ״, מַאי ״אֲשֶׁר יָרִימוּ״? שְׁמַע מִינַּהּ תַּרְתֵּי.

The Gemara answers: **If so,** if **the verse** taught only one *halakha*, the *halakha* of Shimon, brother of Azarya, it **should have written: Which they have set apart. What** is the reason the verse states: **"Which they will set apart,"** in the future tense? **Conclude from it** that the verse teaches **two** *halakhot*: An offering sacrificed for the sake of an offering of greater sanctity is fit, and consumption of untithed produce is punishable by death at the hand of Heaven.

בָּעֵי רַבִּי זֵירָא: כְּשֵׁרִין וְאֵין מְרַצִּין, וְכִי פָּלֵיג – בַּחֲדָא פָּלֵיג; אוֹ דִּלְמָא כְּשֵׁרִין וּמְרַצִּין, וּבְתַרְתֵּי פְּלִיגִי?

Rabbi Zeira raises a dilemma: According to Shimon, brother of Azaria, who says that less sacred offerings sacrificed for the sake of more sacred offerings are fit, perhaps they **are fit but do not propitiate** God, i.e., they do not fulfill the owner's obligation, as the Rabbis hold. If so, **when** Shimon, brother of Azaria, **disagrees** with the first *tanna* in the mishna, **he disagrees** only **with regard to one** matter, i.e., that more sacred offerings sacrificed for the sake of less sacred ones are disqualified altogether. **Alternatively, perhaps** Shimon, brother of Azaria, holds that if less sacred offerings are sacrificed for the sake of more sacred offerings they are both **fit and propitiate** God, **and they disagree** with the Rabbis **about two** matters.[N]

אָמַר אַבַּיֵי וְאִיתֵּימָא רַבִּי זְרִיקָא, תָּא שְׁמַע: הַבְּכוֹר וְהַמַּעֲשֵׂר שֶׁשְּׁחָטָן לְשֵׁם שְׁלָמִים – כְּשֵׁרִים, שְׁלָמִים שֶׁשְּׁחָטָן לְשֵׁם בְּכוֹר אוֹ לְשֵׁם מַעֲשֵׂר – פְּסוּלִין;

Abaye, and some say Rabbi Zerika, said: Come and **hear** proof that they do not satisfy the owners' obligation: Shimon, brother of Azarya, elaborated on his opinion in the mishna: **A firstborn** animal **and the** animal **tithe that one slaughtered for the sake of peace offerings are fit,** as the sanctity of peace offerings is greater. **Peace offerings that one slaughtered for the sake of a firstborn** animal **or for the sake of** the animal **tithe are unfit.**

NOTES

Is liable to be punished with death – **שֶׁהוּא בְּמִיתָה**: Although the penalty of death at the hand of Heaven is not mentioned in this verse, it is derived from a verbal analogy between the phrase "And they shall not profane" here and the same phrase in the verse concerning those who partake of *teruma* in a state of ritual impurity: "Lest they bear sin for it, and die there if they profane it" (Leviticus 22:9).

And they disagree about two matters – **וּבְתַרְתֵּי פְּלִיגִי**: According to the first *tanna*, any offering that is sacrificed for the sake of another type of offering is fit but does not satisfy its owner's obligation. Shimon, brother of Azarya, maintains, according to this suggestion, that an offering that is sacrificed for the sake of an offering of greater sanctity than it is fit and satisfies its owner's obligation, whereas an offering that is sacrificed for the sake of an offering of lesser sanctity than it is disqualified (Rashi).

וְאִי סָלְקָא דַעְתָּךְ כְּשֵׁרִין וּמְרַצִּין, בְּכוֹר בַּר רִיצּוּיֵי הוּא? אֶלָּא כְּשֵׁרִין וְאֵין מְרַצִּין; וּמִדְּסֵיפָא כְּשֵׁרִין וְאֵין מְרַצִּין, רֵישָׁא נַמִּי כְּשֵׁרִין וְאֵין מְרַצִּין.

And if it enters your mind that offerings sacrificed for the sake of offerings of greater sanctity are both **fit and propitiate** God, **is a firstborn** an offering that **propitiates?** Sacrificing a firstborn does not serve to propitiate God; **rather,** conclude that such offerings **are fit but do not propitiate. And** one can infer that **since** in **the latter clause they are fit but do not propitiate,** in **the former clause as well,** concerning all offerings of lesser sanctity slaughtered for the sake of offerings of the most sacred order, **they are fit but do not propitiate.**

מִידֵּי אִירְיָא? הָא כִּדְאִיתָא וְהָא כִּדְאִיתָא.

The Gemara responds: **Are the cases comparable? This** case is **as it is, and that** case is **as it is.** Perhaps Shimon, brother of Azarya, holds that offerings of lesser sanctity slaughtered for the sake of offerings of the most sacred order propitiate God, but a firstborn animal and animal tithe slaughtered for the sake of peace offerings do not propitiate God.

אֶלָּא מַאי קָא מַשְׁמַע לָן? גָּבוֹהַּ וְנָמוּךְ קָא מַשְׁמַע לָן? תָּנֵינָא: כֵּיצַד? קָדְשֵׁי קָדָשִׁים שֶׁשְּׁחָטָן לְשֵׁם קָדָשִׁים קַלִּים כו'!

The Gemara asks: **Rather, what is** the latter clause concerning a firstborn and animal tithe **teaching us,** if not that no offerings of lesser sanctity propitiate God when sacrificed for the sake of offerings of greater sanctity? How is the clause not redundant? **Does it teach us** an example of offerings of **higher** sanctity **and** offerings of **lower** sanctity? **We** already **learn** such an example in the former clause, which teaches: **How so? Offerings of the most sacred order that one slaughtered for the sake of offerings of lesser sanctity** are unfit; offerings of lesser sanctity slaughtered for the sake of offerings of the most sacred order are fit.

מַהוּ דְּתֵימָא: קָדְשֵׁי קָדָשִׁים וְקָדָשִׁים קַלִּים הוּא דְּאִיכָּא גָּבוֹהַּ וְנָמוּךְ, אֲבָל קַלִּים וְקַלִּים לָא.

The Gemara answers: It is stated **lest you say that** the *halakha* of offerings of **higher** sanctity **and** offerings of **lower** sanctity **applies only** when the difference is between **offerings of the most sacred order and offerings of lesser sanctity, but** with regard to offerings of **lesser** sanctity **and** other offerings of **lesser** sanctity this *halakha* does **not** apply, as they are all considered to possess the same level of sanctity. Therefore the mishna adds the example of a firstborn animal and animal tithe slaughtered for the sake of peace offerings, to clarify that one can distinguish between different offerings of lesser sanctity as well.

הָא נַמִּי תָּנֵינָא: שְׁלָמִים קוֹדְמִים אֶת הַבְּכוֹר, מִפְּנֵי שֶׁהֵן טְעוּנִין מַתַּן אַרְבַּע וּסְמִיכָה וּנְסָכִים וּתְנוּפַת חָזֶה וְשׁוֹק!

The Gemara raises an objection to this answer: **We** already **learn this as well,** in another mishna (89a): The **peace offering precedes** sacrifice of **the firstborn because** the peace offering **requires placement** of its blood twice so as to be visible on **four** sides of the altar, **placing hands** on the head of the offering, **libations, and waving** of the **breast and thigh** by the priest and the owner, none of which is required for the firstborn.

הָא עִיקָּר, הַהִיא אַגְּרָרָא נְסַבָהּ.

The Gemara answers: The **primary** mention of the distinction is in **this** mishna; **that** mishna **cites it incidentally,** in discussing the order of precedence of offerings.

מתני׳ הַפֶּסַח שֶׁשְּׁחָטוֹ שַׁחֲרִית בְּאַרְבָּעָה עָשָׂר שֶׁלֹּא לִשְׁמוֹ – רַבִּי יְהוֹשֻׁעַ מַכְשִׁיר, כְּאִילּוּ נִשְׁחַט בִּשְׁלֹשָׁה עָשָׂר; בֶּן בְּתֵירָא פּוֹסֵל, כְּאִילּוּ נִשְׁחַט בֵּין הָעַרְבַּיִם.

MISHNA With regard to **the Paschal offering that one slaughtered** on the **morning of** the **fourteenth** of Nisan, the day when the Paschal offering should be slaughtered in the afternoon, if he did so **not for its sake,**[H] **Rabbi Yehoshua deems it fit as though it were slaughtered on the thirteenth** of Nisan. An animal consecrated as a Paschal offering that was slaughtered not at its designated time for the sake of a different offering is fit for sacrifice as a peace offering. **Ben Beteira deems it unfit as though it were slaughtered** in the **afternoon** of the fourteenth.

HALAKHA

The Paschal offering that one slaughtered on the morning… not for its sake – הַפֶּסַח שֶׁשְּׁחָטוֹ שַׁחֲרִית...שֶׁלֹּא לִשְׁמוֹ: If a Paschal offering was slaughtered at its designated time, namely, the fourteenth of Nisan, not for its sake, it is disqualified. The Rambam rules that it is disqualified even if it was slaughtered in the morning, in accordance with the opinion of ben Beteira, as his opinion is discussed by the *amora'im* (*Kesef Mishne*). The Ra'avad rules in accordance with the opinion of Rabbi Yehoshua, that if it was slaughtered in the morning it is fit (Rambam *Sefer Avoda*, *Hilkhot Pesulei HaMukdashin* 15:11).

אָמַר שִׁמְעוֹן בֶּן עַזַּאי: מְקוּבָּל אֲנִי מִפִּי שִׁבְעִים וּשְׁנַיִם זָקֵן בַּיּוֹם שֶׁהוֹשִׁיבוּ אֶת רַבִּי אֶלְעָזָר בַּיְשִׁיבָה, שֶׁכׇּל הַזְּבָחִים הַנֶּאֱכָלִין שֶׁנִּזְבְּחוּ שֶׁלֹּא לִשְׁמָן – כְּשֵׁרִין, אֶלָּא שֶׁלֹּא עָלוּ לַבְּעָלִים מִשּׁוּם חוֹבָה, חוּץ מִן הַפֶּסַח וּמִן הַחַטָּאת. וְלֹא הוֹסִיף בֶּן עַזַּאי אֶלָּא הָעוֹלָה, וְלֹא הוֹדוּ לוֹ חֲכָמִים.

Shimon ben Azzai said: I received a tradition **from seventy-two elders,**[N] as the Sanhedrin deliberated and decided **on the day that they installed Rabbi Elazar** ben Azarya **at** the head of **the yeshiva**[N] and ruled **that all the slaughtered offerings that are eaten that were slaughtered not for their sake are fit, but** these offerings **did not satisfy the obligation of the owner, except for the Paschal offering and the sin offering.** Based on that version, **ben Azzai added** to the *halakha* cited in the first mishna **only the burnt offering,** which is not eaten, **and the Rabbis** disagreed and **did not concede to him.**

גמ׳ אָמַר רַבִּי אֶלְעָזָר אָמַר רַבִּי אוֹשַׁעְיָא: מַכְשִׁיר הָיָה בֶּן בְּתֵירָא בְּפֶסַח שֶׁשְּׁחָטוֹ שַׁחֲרִית בְּאַרְבָּעָה עָשָׂר לִשְׁמוֹ, דְּכוּלֵּיהּ יוֹמָא זִימְנֵיהּ הוּא.

GEMARA **Rabbi Elazar says that Rabbi Oshaya says: With regard to a Paschal offering that one slaughtered** on the **morning of** the **fourteenth** of Nisan **for its sake, ben Beteira would deem** it **fit,** as he held that **the entire day,** not only the afternoon, **is its** designated **time.**

וּמַאי ״כְּאִילּוּ״?

The Gemara asks: **And what** is the reason the mishna states that according to ben Beteira, a Paschal offering slaughtered on the morning of the fourteenth is considered **as though** it were slaughtered in the afternoon? This language seems to indicate that it does not have the same status as a Paschal offering actually slaughtered in the afternoon.

אַיְּידֵי דְּאָמַר רַבִּי יְהוֹשֻׁעַ ״כְּאִילּוּ״, אָמַר אִיהוּ נָמֵי ״כְּאִילּוּ״.

The Gemara responds: **Since Rabbi Yehoshua says** the term: **As though** it were slaughtered on the thirteenth, ben Beteira **also says** the term: **As though** it were slaughtered in the afternoon. But in fact he maintains that there is no difference between a Paschal offering slaughtered on the morning of the fourteenth and one slaughtered in the afternoon.

אִי הָכִי, אַדְּמִיפַּלְגִי בְּשֶׁלֹּא לִשְׁמוֹ, לִיפְלְגוּ בְּלִשְׁמוֹ!

The Gemara asks: **If so, rather than disagreeing** in the mishna **with regard to** a Paschal offering that was slaughtered on the morning of the fourteenth **not for its sake, let them disagree with regard to** one slaughtered **for its sake;** ben Beteira holds that it is fit, and Rabbi Yehoshua holds that it is unfit.

אִי אִיפַּלְגוּ בְּלִשְׁמוֹ, הֲוָה אָמִינָא: אֲבָל בְּשֶׁלֹּא לִשְׁמוֹ מוֹדֵי רַבִּי יְהוֹשֻׁעַ לְבֶן בְּתֵירָא, הוֹאִיל וּמִקְצָתוֹ רָאוּי, קָא מַשְׁמַע לַן.

The Gemara answers: **If** the mishna were to write only that **they disagree with regard to** a Paschal offering slaughtered **for its sake, I would say: But in** a case where it was slaughtered **not for its sake, Rabbi Yehoshua concedes to ben Beteira** that it is disqualified, even though it was slaughtered in the morning, **since** at least **part of** the day, the afternoon, is **fit** for its sacrifice as a Paschal offering. Therefore, the mishna **teaches us** that they disagree with regard to this case as well.

וְהָכְתִיב: ״בֵּין הָעַרְבַּיִם״!

The Gemara asks: How can ben Beteira claim that a Paschal offering may be slaughtered in the morning? **But isn't it written:** "And the whole assembly of the congregation of Israel shall slaughter it **in the afternoon** [*bein ha'arbayim*]" (Exodus 12:6)?

אָמַר עוּלָּא בְּרֵיהּ דְּרַב עִילַּאי: בֵּין שְׁנֵי עֲרָבִים.

Ulla, son of Rav Ilai, says: Ben Beteira interprets the phrase *bein ha'arbayim* literally: **Between two evenings,**[N] i.e., between the eve of the fourteenth and the night after the fourteenth. Accordingly, the Paschal offering may be sacrificed all day long.

NOTES

Seventy-two elders – שִׁבְעִים וּשְׁנַיִם זָקֵן: The Rid explains that the Sanhedrin of Yavne had seventy-two members, including seventy-one common judges and a president.

On the day that they installed Rabbi Elazar at the head of the yeshiva – בַּיּוֹם שֶׁהוֹשִׁיבוּ אֶת רַבִּי אֶלְעָזָר בַּיְשִׁיבָה: The removal of Rabban Gamliel from his post as head of the yeshiva and the installation of Rabbi Elazar in his place are described extensively in tractate *Berakhot* (27b–28a). Many *halakhot* were established on that day, and according to tradition, the testimonies in tractate *Eduyyot* were transmitted on that day.

Between two evenings – בֵּין שְׁנֵי עֲרָבִים: The literal meaning of *erev* is evening, so *bein ha'arbayim* means between the two evenings. The common interpretation of the phrase is that it refers to the afternoon, which is between the point when the sun starts to turn toward the evening and the actual evening. Ben Beteira interprets the phrase as referring to the entire day, from the end of the previous evening until the evening, i.e., from dawn until sunset of the fourteenth (Rashi on Exodus 12:6).

תָּמִיד, דִּכְתִיב בֵּיהּ ״בֵּין הָעַרְבַּיִם״, הָכִי נַמִי דְּכוּלֵּי יוֹמָא כָּשֵׁר?

The Gemara asks: If so, with regard to the **daily offering, concerning which it is written:** "The one lamb you shall offer in the morning, and the other lamb you shall offer ***bein ha'arbayim***" (Numbers 28:4), is **the entire day fit** for sacrifice **also?**

הָתָם, מִדִּכְתִיב: ״אֶת הַכֶּבֶשׂ אֶחָד תַּעֲשֶׂה בַבֹּקֶר״, מִכְּלָל דְּבֵין הָעַרְבַּיִם – בֵּין הָעַרְבַּיִם מַמָּשׁ.

The Gemara answers: **There, since it is written: "The one lamb you shall offer in the morning," by inference,** the term ***bein ha'arbayim*** is referring to the **actual afternoon.**

אֵימָא: חַד בַּבֹּקֶר, אִידָּךְ כּוּלֵּיהּ יוֹמָא!

The Gemara counters: **Say** that **one** of the lambs should be sacrificed **in the morning,** and **the other** one can be sacrificed **all day.** Why is it evident from the requirement that one be sacrificed in the morning that the other must be sacrificed in the afternoon?

אֶחָד בַּבֹּקֶר, וְלֹא שְׁנַיִם בַּבֹּקֶר.

The Gemara answers: The clause **"One** lamb you shall offer **in the morning"** indicates that **two** lambs are **not** sacrificed **in the morning;** the other must perforce be sacrificed in the afternoon.

נֵרוֹת, דִּכְתִיב ״בֵּין הָעַרְבַּיִם״, הָכִי נַמִי דְּכוּלֵּי יוֹמָא כָּשֵׁר!

The Gemara asks: With regard to the **lamps**[B] of the Candelabrum, one should say the same, **as it is written:** "And when Aaron lights the lamps ***bein ha'arbayim***" (Exodus 30:8). Is **the entire day fit** for lighting **also,** according to the opinion of ben Beteira?

שָׁאנֵי הָתָם, דִּכְתִיב: ״מֵעֶרֶב וְעַד בֹּקֶר״, וְתַנְיָא: ״מֵעֶרֶב וְעַד בֹּקֶר״ – תֵּן לָהּ מִדָּתָהּ שֶׁתְּהֵא דּוֹלֶקֶת וְהוֹלֶכֶת מֵעֶרֶב וְעַד בֹּקֶר. דָּבָר אַחֵר: אֵין לְךָ עֲבוֹדָה כְּשֵׁרָה מֵעֶרֶב וְעַד בֹּקֶר אֶלָּא זוֹ בִּלְבַד.

The Gemara answers: **There it is different, as it is written:** "To burn **from evening to morning"** (Exodus 27:21). **And it is taught** in a *baraita*: The phrase **"from evening to morning"** indicates that you must **allocate** the Candelabrum **its measure**[NH] of oil so **that it will burn from evening until morning. Alternatively,** the same verse can be interpreted as follows: **Only this rite is valid from evening until morning,** since all other rites must be performed during the day. Therefore, the Candelabrum is lit only at the end of the day.

קְטוֹרֶת דִּכְתִיב בָּהּ: ״בֵּין הָעַרְבַּיִם״, הָכִי נַמִי דְּכוּלֵּי יוֹמָא כָּשֵׁר!

The Gemara asks: With regard to the **incense,**[B] one should say likewise, **as it is written with regard to it: *"Bein ha'arbayim*** he shall burn it" (Exodus 30:8). Is **the entire day also fit** for burning the incense according to the opinion of ben Beteira?

שָׁאנֵי קְטֹרֶת,

The Gemara answers: The **incense is different,**

NOTES

You must allocate the Candelabrum its measure, etc. – תֵּן לָהּ מִדָּתָהּ וכו׳: It is difficult to assess the exact amount of oil necessary for every night, as the length of the night changes over the course of the year. Therefore, half a *log* was put in every night, as the Sages assessed that that amount was enough to burn all night on the longest nights of the year. Consequently, during the summer the Candelabrum would be lit during the early hours of the morning as well (see Rashi).

HALAKHA

You must allocate the Candelabrum its measure – תֵּן לָהּ מִדָּתָהּ: Half a *log* of oil is put into each lamp of the Candelabrum every night, an amount that allows it to stay lit from evening to morning (Rambam *Sefer Avoda, Hilkhot Temidin UMusafin* 3:11).

BACKGROUND

Lamps – נֵרוֹת: The Candelabrum is one of the sacred utensils in the Temple. It is made of gold and stands on the south side of the Sanctuary. Its seven decorated branches hold lamps, containers for oil, into which wicks are inserted. The Candelabrum is lit in the evening, and fueled with sufficient oil so that it burns until the morning, no matter how long the night lasts. The Candelabrum is eighteen handbreadths high, a little less than two meters, and in front of it stands a small platform with three steps for the priest who lights and cleans it. In exigent circumstances, it is permitted to fashion the Candelabrum out of metals other than gold, but it is still required to have seven branches.

Lighting the Candelabrum in the Sanctuary

Incense – קְטוֹרֶת: The incense is a mixture of ingredients placed on the golden altar in the Temple and burned each morning and evening. The incense contains eleven ingredients in fixed proportions. As with all other offerings, some salt is added to the incense. A special herb smolders and emits a column of smoke that rises straight up. Generally the incense is prepared in sufficient quantity for an entire solar year, including the amounts required daily and the additional requirements for the Yom Kippur service. It is prohibited to prepare incense according to the Temple formula for use outside the Temple, and one who does so is liable to be punished with *karet*.

NOTES

As it is juxtaposed with the lighting of the lamps – דְּאִיתְקַשׁ לְנֵרוֹת: That the incense is burned at the same time that the Candelabrum is lit is not only derived from a juxtaposition; it is explicit in the verse, which states: "And when Aaron lights the lamps *bein ha'arbayim* he shall burn it, a perpetual incense before the Lord" (Exodus 30:8).

דְּאִיתְקַשׁ לְנֵרוֹת.

as it is juxtaposed with the lighting of the **lamps** (see Exodus 30:8).[N] Evidently, it is burned in the afternoon as well.

הָתָם נַמִי כְּתִיב: ״שָׁם תִּזְבַּח אֶת הַפֶּסַח בָּעֶרֶב״!

The Gemara asks: Just as it is written explicitly that the Candelabrum must be lit in the evening, **there too,** with regard to a Paschal offering, **it is written: "There you shall sacrifice the Passover offering at evening"** (Deuteronomy 16:6). How can ben Beteira claim that it may be sacrificed all day long?

הַהוּא לְ״יֵאוֹחַר דָּבָר״ הוּא דַּאֲתָא, דְּתַנְיָא: ״יֵאוֹחַר דָּבָר שֶׁנֶּאֱמַר בּוֹ ״בָּעֶרֶב״ וּ״בֵין הָעַרְבַּיִם״, לְדָבָר שֶׁלֹּא נֶאֱמַר בּוֹ אֶלָּא ״בֵּין הָעַרְבַּיִם״ בִּלְבַד.

The Gemara answers: **That** verse **comes to** teach a different *halakha*, that a certain **item should be** sacrificed **after** another item. **As it is taught** in a *baraita* with regard to the order of precedence between the Paschal offering and the daily afternoon offering: **An item,** i.e., the Paschal offering, **with regard to which** both the expressions: **"In the evening,"** and: **"*Bein ha'arbayim,*"** are **stated, should be** sacrificed **after an item,** the daily afternoon offering, **with regard to which only "*bein ha'arbayim*" is stated.**

וּמִי אִיכָּא מִידֵּי, דְּאִילּוּ שָׁחֵיט לֵיהּ מִצַּפְרָא, אָמְרַתְּ: זִימְנֵיהּ הוּא, וְכִי מָטֵי בֵּין הָעַרְבַּיִם, אָמְרַתְּ: ״יֵאוֹחַר דָּבָר״?

The Gemara asks: **But is there anything** comparable to ben Beteira's suggestion, **that if one slaughters it in the morning, you say** that **it is** its designated **time** and it is fit; **but when afternoon comes, you say** that the **item should be** sacrificed only **after** the daily afternoon offering?

אִין, דְּהָאָמַר רַבִּי יוֹחָנָן: הֲלָכָה, מִתְפַּלֵּל שֶׁל מִנְחָה וְאַחַר כָּךְ מִתְפַּלֵּל שֶׁל מוּסָפִין.

The Gemara answers: **Yes,** there is a precedent; **as Rabbi Yoḥanan says:** If one did not recite the additional prayers of Shabbat, the New Moon, or a Festival, which should be recited in the morning, until it is time for the afternoon prayer, the ***halakha*** is that he should first **recite the afternoon prayer, and recite the additional prayers thereafter.**[H]

וּ״בֵין הָעַרְבַּיִם״ דִּכְתִיב גַּבֵּי קְטֹרֶת וְנֵרוֹת לָמָּה לִי?

The Gemara asks: **But** if the term **"*bein ha'arbayim*"** is referring to the entire day, as ben Beteira maintains, **why do I** need those instances of the expression **that are written with regard to** burning **incense and** lighting the **lamps,** which are not performed all day?

וְעוֹד, הֵשִׁיב רַבִּי תַּחַת בֶּן בְּתֵירָא לְדִבְרֵי רַבִּי יְהוֹשֻׁעַ: לֹא, אִם אָמַרְתָּ בִּשְׁלֹשָׁה עָשָׂר – שֶׁאֵין מִקְצָתוֹ רָאוּי, תֹּאמַר בְּאַרְבָּעָה עָשָׂר שֶׁמִּקְצָתוֹ רָאוּי;

Furthermore, this interpretation of the opinion of ben Beteira is difficult, as **Rabbi** Yehuda HaNasi **responded on behalf of ben Beteira to the statement of Rabbi Yehoshua** that a Paschal offering slaughtered not for its sake on the morning of the fourteenth of Nisan is fit, as though it were slaughtered on the thirteenth: **No, if you said** that this is the *halakha* **with regard to the thirteenth, as no part of** the day is **fit** for sacrificing the Paschal offering, **shall you** also **say** that this is the *halakha* **with regard to** the **fourteenth, part of which is fit** for sacrificing the Paschal offering? Since it can be sacrificed in the afternoon of the fourteenth, if it is slaughtered in the morning not for its sake, it is disqualified.

וְאִם אִיתָא – כּוּלּוֹ רָאוּי הוּא!

The Gemara concludes: **And if it is so** that a Paschal offering can be sacrificed throughout the day of the fourteenth, **all of it is fit,** not only part of it.

אֶלָּא אָמַר רַבִּי יוֹחָנָן: פּוֹסֵל הָיָה בֶּן בְּתֵירָא בְּפֶסַח שֶׁשְּׁחָטוֹ בְּאַרְבָּעָה עָשָׂר שַׁחֲרִית, בֵּין לִשְׁמוֹ בֵּין שֶׁלֹּא לִשְׁמוֹ, הוֹאִיל וּמִקְצָתוֹ רָאוּי.

Rather, Rabbi Oshaya's interpretation of ben Beteira's opinion is rejected. Instead, **Rabbi Yoḥanan says: With regard to a Paschal offering that one slaughtered on the fourteenth**[H] **in the morning, ben Beteira would deem** it **unfit, whether** it was slaughtered **for its sake or not for its sake.** It is unfit even if it was slaughtered not for its sake, **since part of** the day is **fit** for its sacrifice as a Paschal offering.

HALAKHA

Recite the afternoon prayer and recite the additional prayers thereafter – מִתְפַּלֵּל שֶׁל מִנְחָה וְאַחַר כָּךְ מִתְפַּלֵּל שֶׁל מוּסָפִין: If one is obligated to recite both the additional prayer and the afternoon prayer, as he did not recite the additional prayer until it was time to recite the afternoon prayer, i.e., after six and a half hours of the day, he must first recite the afternoon prayer and then the additional prayer. Even if he recited the additional prayer first he has fulfilled his obligation (Rambam *Sefer Ahava, Hilkhot Tefilla* 3:11; *Shulḥan Arukh, Oraḥ Ḥayyim* 286:4).

A Paschal offering that one slaughtered on the fourteenth, etc. – פֶּסַח שֶׁשְּׁחָטוֹ בְּאַרְבַּע עָשָׂר וכו׳: A Paschal offering that was slaughtered on the fourteenth of Nisan before noon is disqualified, as that is not its designated time of sacrifice, in accordance with the opinion of Rabbi Yoḥanan (Rambam *Sefer Avoda, Hilkhot Pesulei HaMukdashin* 15:12).

מְגַדֵּף בָּהּ רַבִּי אַבָּהוּ: אִם כֵּן, פֶּסַח כָּשֵׁר לְבֶן בְּתֵירָא הֵיכִי מַשְׁכַּחַתְּ לַהּ? אִי דְּאַפְרְשֵׁיהּ הָאִידָּנָא – דָּחוּי מֵעִיקָּרוֹ הוּא, וְאִי דְּאַפְרְשִׁינְהוּ מֵאֶתְמוֹל – נִרְאֶה וְנִדְחֶה הוּא!

Rabbi Abbahu ridiculed [***megaddef***][L] this interpretation: **If so, how can you find a fit Paschal offering according to ben Beteira? If** its owner **designated** an animal **now,** on the morning of the fourteenth, as a Paschal offering, **it is disqualified from the outset,** as it cannot be sacrificed at all, either for its sake or not for its sake. **And even if** its owner **designated it the previous day,** when it was fit to be sacrificed not for its sake, **it was fit and** then **disqualified** the next morning, when it was no longer fit to be sacrificed until the afternoon. Once an offering is disqualified, it can no longer become fit.

אֶלָּא אָמַר רַבִּי אַבָּהוּ: תְּהֵא לְאַחַר חֲצוֹת.

Rather, Rabbi Abbahu says: Let the Paschal offering **be** fit when it is designated on the fourteenth **after noon,** when it may already be sacrificed as a Paschal offering.

אַבָּיֵי אָמַר: אֲפִילּוּ תֵּימָא מִצַּפְרָא, אֵין מְחוּסַּר זְמַן לְבוֹ בַּיּוֹם.

Abaye says: You may **even say** that it is fit if designated **in the morning,** as an offering is **not** disqualified due to the fact that it is an offering **whose time has not yet** arrived if its time will arrive **on that same day.**

רַב פַּפָּא אָמַר: אֲפִילּוּ תֵּימָא מֵאוּרְתָּא, לַיְלָה אֵין מְחוּסַּר זְמַן; דְּתָנֵי דְּבֵי רַבִּי יִשְׁמָעֵאל: לֵיל שְׁמִינִי נִכְנָס לַדִּיר לְהִתְעַשֵּׂר.

Rav Pappa says: You may **even say** that it is fit if designated **from** the previous **night,** as an offering that was designated at **night** and may be sacrificed the following day is **not** considered an offering **whose time has not yet** arrived,[N] **as it is taught in the school of Rabbi Yishmael:** Although an animal is unfit for sacrifice until its eighth day, on the **night** before its **eighth** day it may already **enter the den to be tithed.**[NH]

וְכִדְרַבִּי אַפְּטוֹרִיקִי, דְּרַבִּי אַפְּטוֹרִיקִי רָמֵי, כְּתִיב: "וְהָיָה שִׁבְעַת יָמִים תַּחַת אִמּוֹ" – הָא לַיְלָה חָזֵי, וּכְתִיב: "וּמִיּוֹם הַשְּׁמִינִי וָהָלְאָה יֵרָצֶה" – הָא לַיְלָה לָא חָזֵי!

And this is **in accordance with** the statement **of Rabbi Appetoriki,**[LP] as **Rabbi Appetoriki raises a contradiction: It is written:** "When a bull or a sheep or a goat is born, **then it shall be seven days with its mother**" (Leviticus 22:27); **consequently,** on the following **night,** i.e., the night before the eighth day, **it is fit** for sacrifice. **And it is written** subsequently in that verse: **"But from the eighth day and on it may be accepted** for an offering made by fire unto the Lord"; **consequently,** on the previous **night,** i.e., the night before the eighth day, **it is not** yet **fit.**

הָא כֵּיצַד? לַיְלָה לִקְדוּשָּׁה, וְיוֹם לְהַרְצָאָה.

How can **these** texts be reconciled? At **night** it is fit **for consecration, and** the following **day** it is fit **for effecting acceptance,** i.e., for sacrifice. Apparently, an offering that may be sacrificed the following day can be consecrated the previous night, even though it may not be sacrificed at night, and it is not considered an offering whose time has not yet arrived.

LANGUAGE

Ridiculed [*megaddef*] – מְגַדֵּף: The root *gimmel, dalet, peh* means to denigrate, in biblical Hebrew as well as in Aramaic. Similarly, in Arabic, the root جدف, *jdf*, also means to denigrate. It is used in reference to one who curses God. The phrase *megaddef bah*, which appears in amoraic discussions, means to ridicule a prior statement. Although it would appear inappropriate for a student to speak this way about the statement of his teacher, as Rabbi Abbahu was a disciple of Rabbi Yoḥanan, the later commentaries explain that the objective of the Sages was only to seek the truth, and therefore they did not object to their students speaking about their statements in this manner.

Some *ge'onim* interpret this expression based on the root *gimmel, reish, peh*, as the letters *dalet* and *reish* are frequently interchanged in Aramaic. They suggest that the word *megaddef* literally means swept, from the word *gerifa*, or diminished, from the word *geria*. Accordingly, the expression *megaddef bah* means that the previous statement should be removed or swept away. Other *ge'onim* interpret it as making a gesture with one's hand that expresses astonishment and protest.

Appetoriki – אַפְּטוֹרִיקִי: This name apparently derives from the Latin name Patricus, which means nobleman, or a person with distinguished lineage.

NOTES

An offering designated at night is not an offering whose time has not yet arrived – לַיְלָה אֵין מְחוּסַּר זְמַן: This pertains only to the consecration of the offering. If an offering is sacrificed before its time, even if it will be fit for sacrifice on that same day, Rav Pappa concedes that it is disqualified.

On the night before its eighth day it may enter the den to be tithed – לֵיל שְׁמִינִי נִכְנָס לַדִּיר לְהִתְעַשֵּׂר: The Torah states that an animal may be sacrificed as an offering starting the eighth day after its birth (see Leviticus 22:27). An animal that is not yet old enough to be sacrificed is not included in the selection of one-tenth of one's animals for tithe. Nevertheless, on the night prior to an animal's eighth day it is included in the selection, during which it can potentially be consecrated as an offering.

HALAKHA

On the night before its eighth day it may enter the den to be tithed – לֵיל שְׁמִינִי נִכְנָס לַדִּיר לְהִתְעַשֵּׂר: The Rambam omits this *halakha*. Some commentaries explain that the Rambam follows the ruling that he indicates elsewhere, that on the night before an animal is eligible to be sacrificed it is considered an animal whose time has not yet arrived. The *Kesef Mishne* writes that he does not know why the Rambam omits this *halakha*, apparently because there is no reason to assume that the Rambam would rule that way with regard to the animal's consecration (see Rambam *Sefer Korbanot, Hilkhot Ḥagiga* 2:5, *Hilkhot Meḥusrei Kappara* 3:4, and *Hilkhot Bekhorot* 6:14).

PERSONALITIES

Rabbi Appetoriki – רַבִּי אַפְּטוֹרִיקִי: Rabbi Appetoriki was a second-generation *amora* in Eretz Yisrael. His father, Dostai, who taught *baraitot* in Rabbi Ḥiyya's study hall, was honored with the title: Rabbi Appetoriki's father, due to his distinguished son. A small number of Rabbi Appetoriki's statements concerning the *halakhot* of offerings and the kashrut of eggs are cited in the Talmud.

NOTES

Shall we say that Rabbi Yoḥanan holds, etc. – לֵימָא קָסָבַר רַבִּי יוֹחָנָן וכו׳: The difficulty raised by Rabbi Abbahu, that according to Rabbi Yoḥanan a Paschal offering is disqualified permanently when it is consecrated, is based on the principle that once an offering is disqualified from being sacrificed, it cannot become fit again. Since there is a dispute as to whether this principle applies to offerings that were not yet slaughtered, Rabbi Zeira asked Rabbi Abbahu whether or not he assumes that Rabbi Yoḥanan holds that the principle applies to living offerings as well.

An animal belonging to two partners – בְּהֵמָה שֶׁל שְׁנֵי שׁוּתָּפִין: Rabbi Yoḥanan referred specifically to the case of an animal that is owned by partners, because if the sole owner of an animal consecrates half of it, the entire animal is consecrated automatically. It is possible to consecrate half an animal only when it belongs to partners, as one cannot consecrate the share belonging to his partner (Rashi).

But it may not be sacrificed – וְאֵינָהּ קְרֵיבָה: The animal can never be sacrificed. It is left to graze until it develops a blemish, after which its owner must redeem it and bring another offering purchased with the money (Rashi).

אֲמַר לֵיהּ רַבִּי זֵירָא לְרַבִּי אַבָּהוּ: לֵימָא קָסָבַר רַבִּי יוֹחָנָן: בַּעֲלֵי חַיִּים נִדְחִין?

§ Rabbi Abbahu presumes that an animal consecrated before it may be sacrificed is disqualified. With regard to this, **Rabbi Zeira said to Rabbi Abbahu: Shall we say that Rabbi Yoḥanan holds**[N] that consecrated **animals** that cannot be sacrificed at any given moment **are disqualified** from ever being sacrificed?

אֲמַר לֵיהּ: אִין. דְּאָמַר רַבִּי יוֹחָנָן: בְּהֵמָה שֶׁל שְׁנֵי שׁוּתָּפִין, הִקְדִּישׁ חֶצְיָהּ, וְחָזַר וְלָקַח חֶצְיָהּ וְהִקְדִּישָׁהּ – קְדוֹשָׁה וְאֵינָהּ קְרֵיבָה,

Rabbi Abbahu **said to him: Yes, as Rabbi Yoḥanan says:** With regard to **an animal belonging to two partners,**[NH] if one of them **consecrated** the **half of it** that belongs to him, **and then purchased** the other **half of it** from his partner **and consecrated it, it is consecrated,** despite the fact that it was consecrated piecemeal. **But it may not be sacrificed,**[N] since when he first consecrated it, the consecration did not extend to his partner's half. Since the animal was not fit to be sacrificed then, it is disqualified permanently.

וְעוֹשָׂה תְּמוּרָה, וּתְמוּרָתָהּ כַּיּוֹצֵא בָּהּ.

But as it is consecrated now, it can **render** consecrated as **a substitute** a non-sacred animal that is exchanged for it. If the owner substitutes a non-sacred animal for this one, the second animal becomes consecrated as well. **And** yet **its substitute is like it;** it too is consecrated but cannot be sacrificed.

וּשְׁמַע מִינַּהּ תְּלָת; שְׁמַע מִינַּהּ: בַּעֲלֵי חַיִּים נִדְחִין, וּשְׁמַע מִינַּהּ: דִּחוּי מֵעִיקָּרָא הָוֵה דִּחוּי, וּשְׁמַע מִינַּהּ:

And one can **conclude three** points **from** this statement: **Conclude from it** that **animals** that cannot be sacrificed **are** permanently **disqualified; and conclude from it** that **disqualification from the outset,** i.e., from the time the offering is consecrated, **is** permanent **disqualification; and conclude from it** that

HALAKHA

An animal belonging to two partners – בְּהֵמָה שֶׁל שְׁנֵי שׁוּתָּפִין: If an animal belonged to two partners, and one of them consecrated his half and then purchased the other half from his partner and consecrated it too, the animal is entirely consecrated and can be sacrificed on the altar. Although it was disqualified from being sacrificed at the outset, this does not cause permanent disqualification, as living animals that are disqualified from being sacrificed are not disqualified permanently. The owner can also effect substitution of the offering. This is contrary to the opinion of Rabbi Yoḥanan and in accordance with the opinion of those who disagree with him (Rambam *Sefer Avoda, Hilkhot Ma'aseh HaKorbanot* 15:4).

Perek **I**
Daf **12** Amud **b**

יֵשׁ דִּחוּי בְּדָמִים.

there is permanent **disqualification** even **in** a case where the animal possesses sanctity that inheres in its **monetary**[N] value, rather than inherent sanctity.

NOTES

There is disqualification in its monetary value – יֵשׁ דִּחוּי בְּדָמִים: Rashi explains that the concept of permanent disqualification applies even with regard to an item that contains not inherent sanctity but sanctity that inheres in its monetary value, such as the case under discussion, where the consecrated animal was not fit for sacrifice and was therefore designated for sale, with the proceeds from the sale used to purchase an animal to be sacrificed as an offering. The animal is disqualified from ever being sacrificed, even after the reason for its disqualification no longer applies, despite the fact that it was never rendered an offering to begin with.

The early commentaries find this interpretation difficult, as it is seemingly identical to the conclusion that an item that is disqualified from the outset is permanently disqualified. An animal that is disqualified from the time it was consecrated contains, by definition, sanctity that inheres in its monetary value, as it cannot be sacrificed as an offering.

Tosafot resolve this difficulty by finding a case where an item is disqualified from the outset but still has inherent sanctity: If a priest collects the blood of an offering in a bowl that has water in it, every drop of blood that falls into the bowl is disqualified for sacrifice due to the fact that the water constitutes the majority of liquid in the bowl, and the contents do not become fit again when the blood becomes the majority. In this case, the blood is disqualified from the outset, although it contains inherent sanctity. The Ramban on *Kiddushin* 7b adds that it is also possible for an item whose sanctity inheres in its monetary value to be disqualified after it is consecrated. Therefore, the two conclusions are not identical.

Tosafot, citing Rabbeinu Ḥayyim, add that the novel element of the conclusion that permanent disqualification applies to monetary value is that although it is not an offering, substitution applies to it.

Rabbeinu Ḥananel interprets this conclusion differently: If one dedicates money to buying an offering and is then disqualified from bringing it, the money is permanently disqualified from being used for this purpose. This opinion is discussed extensively in *Tosafot* and *Shita Mekubbetzet* (see also the early commentaries on *Kiddushin* 7a).

אָמַר עוּלָּא אָמַר רַבִּי יוֹחָנָן: אָכַל חֵלֶב וְהִפְרִישׁ קׇרְבָּן, וְנִשְׁתַּמֵּד, וְחָזַר בּוֹ – הוֹאִיל וְנִדְחֶה – יִדָּחֶה.

§ **Ulla says that Rabbi Yoḥanan says:** If one **ate** forbidden **fat and designated an offering** to atone for the transgression, **and** then **apostatized,**[HNL] thereby disqualifying himself from bringing an offering, **and** later **recanted** his apostasy, **since** the offering was already **disqualified, it shall be disqualified** permanently.

אִיתְּמַר נַמִּי, אָמַר רַבִּי יִרְמְיָה אָמַר רַבִּי אַבָּהוּ אָמַר רַבִּי יוֹחָנָן: אָכַל חֵלֶב וְהִפְרִישׁ קׇרְבָּן, וְנִשְׁתַּטָּה, וְחָזַר וְנִשְׁתַּפָּה, הוֹאִיל וְנִדְחֶה – יִדָּחֶה.

It was also stated that **Rabbi Yirmeya says** that **Rabbi Abbahu says** that **Rabbi Yoḥanan says:** If one **ate** forbidden **fat and designated an offering** to atone for his transgression, **and** then **became an imbecile,**[N] who is unfit to bring an offering, **and** then **again became** halakhically **competent, since** the offering was already **disqualified, it shall be disqualified** permanently.

וּצְרִיכִי: דְּאִי אַשְׁמְעִינַן קַמַּיְיתָא – מִשּׁוּם דְּהוּא דָּחֵי נַפְשֵׁיהּ בְּיָדַיִם, אֲבָל הָכָא דְּמִמֵּילָא אִידְּחֵי – כְּיָשֵׁן דָּמֵי.

The Gemara notes: **And** both statements **are necessary. As, if** Rabbi Yoḥanan **had taught us** only **the first** statement, concerning an apostate, one might have reasoned that the offering is permanently disqualified **because he disqualified himself by** his own **action, but here,** in the case of one who became an imbecile, **where he was disqualified** through a process that occurs **by itself,** when he becomes competent again he may bring his sacrifice, as it is **considered as** though he were **asleep.**[N] If one designated an offering and fell asleep, this certainly does not disqualify it.

וְאִי אַשְׁמְעִינַן הָכָא – מִשּׁוּם דְּאֵין בְּיָדוֹ לַחֲזוֹר, אֲבָל הָכָא דְּיֵשׁ בְּיָדוֹ לַחֲזוֹר – אֵימָא לָא, צְרִיכָא.

And if Rabbi Yoḥanan **had taught us** only the statement **here,** with regard to one who became an imbecile, one might have reasoned that the offering is permanently disqualified **because it is not in his power to return** to competence, **but here,** in the case of an apostate, **since it is in his power to recant** his apostasy, **I would say** that the offering is **not** permanently disqualified. Therefore, both statements are **necessary.**

בָּעֵי רַבִּי יִרְמְיָה: אָכַל חֵלֶב וְהִפְרִישׁ קׇרְבָּן, וְהוֹרוּ בֵּית דִּין שֶׁחֵלֶב מוּתָּר, וְחָזְרוּ בָּהֶן, מַהוּ? מִי הָוֵי דָּחוּי, אוֹ לָא הָוֵי דָּחוּי?

Rabbi Yirmeya raises a dilemma: If one **ate** forbidden **fat and designated an offering** for the transgression, **and** then the **court ruled that** the type of **fat** he ate is **permitted,** thereby rendering the offering unnecessary, **and** the court subsequently **retracted** its ruling, in this case, **what is the** *halakha*? **Is** the offering permanently **disqualified, or is it not** permanently **disqualified?**

אֲמַר לֵיהּ הַהוּא סָבָא: כִּי פְּתַח רַבִּי יוֹחָנָן בִּדְחוּיִין – מֵהָא פְּתַח. מַאי טַעְמָא? הָתָם – גַּבְרָא אִידְּחֵי, קׇרְבָּן לָא אִידְּחֵי. הָכָא – קׇרְבָּן נַמִּי אִידְּחֵי.

A certain elder [*hahu sava*][L] **said to** Rabbi Yirmeya: **When Rabbi Yoḥanan introduced**[N] the topic of permanently **disqualified** offerings, **he introduced** it **with this** case. **What is the reason? There,** in the case of one who apostatized or became an imbecile, although **the person was disqualified,**[N] the **offering** itself **was not disqualified.** Consequently, it is less evident that the offering will be disqualified permanently. But **here,** in a case where the court ruled that the fat is permitted, the **offering** itself **was also disqualified,** as it was rendered unnecessary. Therefore, this is a more obvious example.

"אָמַר שִׁמְעוֹן בֶּן עַזַּאי: מְקוּבְּלַנִי מִפִּי שִׁבְעִים וּשְׁנַיִם זָקֵן" כו׳. לָמָּה לִי לְמִתְנָא "שִׁבְעִים וּשְׁנַיִם זָקֵן"? דְּכוּלְּהוּ בַּחֲדָא שִׁיטְתָא הָווּ קַיְימִי.

§ The mishna teaches: **Shimon ben Azzai said: I received** a tradition **from seventy-two elders** [*zaken*] that all slaughtered offerings that are eaten, if slaughtered not for their sake, are fit. The Gemara asks: **Why do I** need to **teach** the phrase **seventy-two** elders using the singular form: ***Zaken,*** rather than the plural form: *Zekenim*? The Gemara answers: **Because they all maintained one opinion,** i.e., they all agreed with this *halakha*.

"לֹא הוֹסִיף בֶּן עַזַּאי אֶלָּא הָעוֹלָה".

The mishna continues: **Ben Azzai added only the burnt offering** to the sin offering and the Paschal offering, which are mentioned in the first mishna as disqualified when sacrificed not for their sake.

HALAKHA

If one ate forbidden fat and designated an offering and then apostatized – אָכַל חֵלֶב וְהִפְרִישׁ קׇרְבָּן וְנִשְׁתַּמֵּד: If one committed a transgression unwittingly, and consecrated an offering to atone for his sin, and subsequently became an apostate or an imbecile, the offering is disqualified. If he later recanted his apostasy or became competent again, the offering is fit to be sacrificed, as living animals are not permanently disqualified (Rambam *Sefer Korbanot*, *Hilkhot Shegagot* 3:8).

NOTES

And apostatized – וְנִשְׁתַּמֵּד: It is derived from the verses that an apostate cannot bring an offering, as the verse states (Proverbs 21:27): "The sacrifice of the wicked is an abomination" (see *Ḥullin* 5a and *Shita Mekubbetzet* here). The Rambam writes that this was a tradition. The Gemara (*Ḥullin* 5a) defines an apostate in this regard as one who worships idols, desecrates Shabbat in public, or transgresses the entire Torah. If one does not fit this definition but transgresses certain prohibitions regularly, offerings for those particular transgressions are not accepted from him.

And became an imbecile – וְנִשְׁתַּטָּה: Since the one bringing the offering must have proper intent (see *Arakhin* 21a), one who is incompetent cannot bring an offering.

As though he were asleep – כְּיָשֵׁן דָּמֵי: *Tosafot* on *Sanhedrin* 47a note that this is only a partial comparison, as one's offering can be sacrificed by the priests while he is asleep, which is certainly not the case with regard to an imbecile. An imbecile is compared to one who is asleep in that both his becoming an imbecile and his becoming competent again are not accomplished through his own actions.

When Rabbi Yoḥanan introduced, etc. – כִּי פְּתַח רַבִּי יוֹחָנָן וכו׳: Rashi explains that Rabbi Yoḥanan introduced the topic of permanently disqualified offerings with this case because it is more obvious than the previously mentioned cases (see *Shita Mekubbetzet*). Rabbeinu Tam explains that Rabbi Yoḥanan started with this case for didactic reasons, specifically because it is more novel than the previous cases.

There the person was disqualified, etc. – הָתָם גַּבְרָא אִידְּחֵי וכו׳: Rashi explains that this is referring to the case of an individual who became an apostate or an imbecile. The disqualification in these cases relates to the status of the individual, not the offering. But in the case where the court deemed the fat permitted, the offering itself was deemed irrelevant. Rabbeinu Tam offers the opposite interpretation: There, in the case where the court deemed the fat permitted, only the individual, who was subject to the court's ruling, was disqualified from bringing the offering; the offering itself was not disqualified, as the court was mistaken. By contrast, in the case of one who became an apostate or an imbecile, the offering was objectively disqualified due to its owner's status.

LANGUAGE

Apostatized [*nishtammed*] – נִשְׁתַּמֵּד: This term clearly is referring to apostasy, i.e., the act of abandoning one's religion. Its literal meaning is unclear. Some of the *ge'onim* explain that it derives from the Syriac root *ayin, mem, dalet*, which refers to being baptized. The *Ḥatam Sofer* suggests that the term stems from the Aramaic *ishtemodda*, which means becoming estranged. Others maintain that the word is from the Aramaic root *shin, mem, dalet*, which denotes a curse or excommunication, similar to the Hebrew root *shin, mem, tav*. Accordingly, an apostate [*meshumad*] is literally a cursed or excommunicated person.

A certain elder [*hahu sava*] – הַהוּא סָבָא: The literal meaning of this term is: That grandfather. The word *sava*, grandfather, is used in reference to any elderly individual and is also used in reference to a Torah scholar. *Hahu sava* is often mentioned as participating in halakhic discussions and teaching *baraitot*. Some later commentaries assert that *hahu sava* alludes to the prophet Elijah, who would reveal himself to the Sages as an elderly man.

אֲמַר רַב הוּנָא: מַאי טַעְמָא דְּבֶן עַזַּאי? ״עוֹלָה הוּא אִשֵּׁה רֵיחַ נִיחֹחַ לַה׳״, הִיא – לִשְׁמָהּ כְּשֵׁרָה, שֶׁלֹּא לִשְׁמָהּ פְּסוּלָה.

Rav Huna said: What is the reason for the opinion **of ben Azzai?** The verse states: **"It is a burnt offering, an offering made by fire, of a pleasing aroma unto the Lord"** (Leviticus 1:13). The word **"it"** teaches that if it is sacrificed **for its sake,** it is **fit;** if sacrificed **not for its sake,** it is **unfit.**

אָשָׁם נַמִי כְּתִיב בֵּיהּ ״הוּא״!

The Gemara asks: Isn't the word **"it" written with regard to a guilt offering as well,** in the verse: "It is a guilt offering" (Leviticus 7:5)? Nevertheless, a guilt offering sacrificed not for its sake is not disqualified.

הַהוּא לְאַחַר הַקְטָרַת אֵימוּרִים הוּא דִּכְתִיב.

The Gemara answers: **That** verse **is written after the burning of** the **sacrificial portions** on the altar. Since the offering is fit even if these portions are not burned at all, it is certainly fit if they are burned not for the sake of a guilt offering.

הַאי נַמִי לְאַחַר הַקְטָרַת אֵימוּרִים הוּא דִּכְתִיב!

The Gemara asks: Isn't **this** mention of the word "it" with regard to a burnt offering **also written after the burning of** the **sacrificial portions** on the altar?

תְּרֵי ״הוּא״ כְּתִיבִי.

The Gemara answers: The word **"it" is written** with regard to a burnt offering in **two** places, both in Leviticus 1:13 and in Exodus 29:18. Although both are written after the burning of the portions consumed on the altar, one of them is superfluous, and is therefore interpreted in reference to the main sacrificial rites, performed before the burning of the portions. The verse therefore teaches that the offering is fit only if these rites are performed for its sake.

גַּבֵּי אָשָׁם נַמִי תְּרֵי ״הוּא״ כְּתִיבִי!

The Gemara asks: **With regard to a guilt offering as well,** isn't the word **"it" written** in **two** places, Leviticus 5:9 and Leviticus 7:5?

אֶלָּא, בֶּן עַזַּאי בְּקַל וָחוֹמֶר מַיְיתֵי לַהּ: וּמַה חַטָּאת שֶׁאֵינָהּ כָּלִיל, שְׁחָטָהּ שֶׁלֹּא לִשְׁמָהּ – פְּסוּלָה, עוֹלָה שֶׁהִיא כָּלִיל – לֹא כָּל שֶׁכֵּן?

Rather, ben Azzai derives his *halakha* not from a verse, but **by an *a fortiori* inference: Just as** with regard to **a sin offering, which is not** totally **consumed** on the altar but partially eaten by priests, if **one slaughtered it not for its sake** it is **disqualified,** so too, with regard to **a burnt offering, which is** treated more strictly in that it is totally **consumed** on the altar, **all the more so** is it **not** clear that if it is slaughtered not for its sake it is disqualified?

מַה לְּחַטָּאת שֶׁכֵּן מְכַפֶּרֶת!

The Gemara rejects this inference: **What** is notable **about a sin offering?** It is notable **in that it atones** for sin, in contrast to a burnt offering, which is not brought for atonement. Therefore, only a sin offering is disqualified when sacrificed not for its sake.

פֶּסַח יוֹכִיחַ.

The Gemara suggests: **A Paschal offering can prove** the point, as it is not brought for atonement, yet it is disqualified if sacrificed not for its sake.

מַה לְּפֶסַח שֶׁכֵּן זְמַנּוֹ קָבוּעַ!

The Gemara rejects this as well: **What** is notable **about a Paschal offering?** It is notable **in that its time is set** at Passover eve, in contrast to a burnt offering, which does not have a designated time.

חַטָּאת תּוֹכִיחַ. וְחָזַר הַדִּין, לֹא רְאִי זֶה כִּרְאִי זֶה, וְלֹא רְאִי זֶה כִּרְאִי זֶה, הַצַּד הַשָּׁוֶה שֶׁבָּהֶן – שֶׁהֵן קֳדָשִׁים וּשְׁחָטָן שֶׁלֹּא לִשְׁמָן פָּסוּל, אַף אֲנִי אָבִיא עוֹלָה שֶׁהִיא קֳדָשִׁים, וּשְׁחָטָהּ שֶׁלֹּא לִשְׁמָהּ פְּסוּלָה.

The Gemara suggests: If so, **a sin offering can prove** the point, since it has no set time. **And the inference has reverted** to its starting point. The *halakha* is derived from the common element of the two sources: **The aspect of this** case **is not like the aspect of that** case **and the aspect of that** case **is not like the aspect of this** case. **Their common element is that they are offerings, and** if one **slaughtered them not for their sake,** they are **disqualified. So too, I shall include a burnt offering** in this *halakha,* **as it is an offering, and** therefore if one **slaughtered it not for its sake,** it is **disqualified.**

מַה לְּהַצַּד הַשָּׁוֶה שֶׁבָּהֶן, שֶׁיֵּשׁ בָּהֶן צַד כָּרֵת!

The Gemara rejects this as well: **What** is notable **about their common element?** It is notable in **that they** both **have an element of *karet*.** A sin offering is brought for a transgression punishable by *karet* when committed intentionally, and one who refrains intentionally from bringing a Paschal offering is liable to be punished with *karet.* A burnt offering does not have an element of *karet.*

בֶּן עַזַּאי

The Gemara answers: **Ben Azzai**

צַד כָּרֵת לָא פָּרֵיךְ.

does not refute the inference by citing a common **element of** ***karet*****,**[N] as the elements of *karet* in a sin offering and in a Paschal offering are not parallel.

אָשָׁם נַמִי לֵיתֵי!

The Gemara asks: If so, **let it be derived** from this inference that **a guilt offering** is **also** disqualified if sacrificed not for its sake.

אָשָׁם, פָּרֵיךְ: מָה לְהַצַּד הַשָּׁוֶה שֶׁבָּהֶן – שֶׁכֵּן יֶשְׁנָן בְּצִבּוּר כְּבְיָחִיד.

The Gemara answers: With regard to **a guilt offering,** ben Azzai **refutes** the inference as follows: **What** is notable **about the common element of** a sin offering and a Paschal offering? It is notable **in that there are communal** offerings **as well as individual** offerings[N] of these types, as well as communal burnt offerings, whereas there is no communal guilt offering.

וְאִיבָּעֵית אֵימָא: צַד כָּרֵת נַמִי פָּרֵיךְ, וּבֶן עַזַּאי גְּמָרָא גְּמִיר לַהּ, וְהָא דְּקָאָמַר רַב הוּנָא קַל וָחוֹמֶר – לֹא אֲמָרָהּ אֶלָּא לְחַדֵּד בָּהּ תַּלְמִידָיו.

And if you wish, say instead that actually, ben Azzai **also refutes** the entire inference, because a sin offering and a Paschal offering uniquely share **an element of** ***karet*****. And** the reason **ben Azzai** maintains that a burnt offering sacrificed not for its sake is disqualified is that **he learned it** as **a tradition. And** as for the fact **that Rav Huna cites an** ***a fortiori*** inference, he does not believe it to be the true source for ben Azzai's *halakha*; **he said it only to sharpen** the minds of **his students with it,** challenging them to refute it.

מתני׳ הַפֶּסַח וְהַחַטָּאת שֶׁשְּׁחָטָן שֶׁלֹּא לִשְׁמָן, קִבֵּל וְהָלַךְ וְזָרַק שֶׁלֹּא לִשְׁמָן, אוֹ לִשְׁמָן וְשֶׁלֹּא לִשְׁמָן, אוֹ שֶׁלֹּא לִשְׁמָן וְלִשְׁמָן – פְּסוּלִים.

MISHNA With regard to **the Paschal offering and the sin offering,**[H] where one **slaughtered them not for their sake,** or where he **collected** their blood in a vessel, **conveyed** this blood to the altar, **or sprinkled** this blood on the altar **not for their sake, or** where he performed one of these sacrificial rites **for their sake and not for their sake,**[H] **or not for their sake and for their sake,** in all these cases the offerings **are unfit.**

כֵּיצַד לִשְׁמָן וְשֶׁלֹּא לִשְׁמָן? לְשֵׁם פֶּסַח וּלְשֵׁם שְׁלָמִים. שֶׁלֹּא לִשְׁמָן וְלִשְׁמָן – לְשֵׁם שְׁלָמִים וּלְשֵׁם פֶּסַח.

How are these rites performed **for their sake and not for their sake?** In a case where one slaughtered the Paschal offering **for the sake of a Paschal offering and for the sake of a peace offering.** How are these rites performed **not for their sake and for their sake?** In a case where one slaughtered the Paschal offering **for the sake of a peace offering and for the sake of a Paschal offering.**

שֶׁהַזֶּבַח נִפְסָל בְּאַרְבָּעָה דְּבָרִים: בִּשְׁחִיטָה, וּבְקִבּוּל, וּבְהִילּוּךְ, וּבִזְרִיקָה.

The offering is unfit **because a slaughtered offering is disqualified** due to prohibited intent **in four matters:**[H] **In** the performance of the sacrificial rites of **slaughtering** the animal, **in collecting** the blood, **in conveying** the blood, **and in sprinkling** the blood.

רַבִּי שִׁמְעוֹן מַכְשִׁיר בְּהִילּוּךְ, שֶׁהָיָה אוֹמֵר: אִי אֶפְשָׁר שֶׁלֹּא בִּשְׁחִיטָה וְשֶׁלֹּא בְקַבָּלָה וְשֶׁלֹּא בִזְרִיקָה, אֲבָל אֶפְשָׁר בְּלֹא הִילּוּךְ – שׁוֹחֵט בְּצַד הַמִּזְבֵּחַ וְזוֹרֵק.

Rabbi Shimon deems the offering **fit** if the prohibited intent was **during** the rite of **conveying** the blood, **as he would say: It is impossible** to sacrifice an offering **without slaughtering** the animal, **or without collection** of the blood, **or without sprinkling** the blood, **but it is possible** to sacrifice an offering **without conveying** the blood to the altar. How so? If one **slaughters** the animal **alongside the altar and sprinkles** the blood, the blood does not need to be conveyed. Therefore, the rite of conveying the blood is not significant enough to cause the offering to be disqualified due to prohibited intent while performing it.

רַבִּי אֱלִיעֶזֶר אוֹמֵר: הַמְהַלֵּךְ בְּמָקוֹם שֶׁהוּא צָרִיךְ לְהַלֵּךְ – מַחְשָׁבָה פּוֹסֶלֶת, בְּמָקוֹם שֶׁאֵינוֹ צָרִיךְ לְהַלֵּךְ – אֵין מַחְשָׁבָה פּוֹסֶלֶת.

Rabbi Eliezer says: With regard to **one who conveys** the blood **in a situation where he is required to convey** it, prohibited **intent** while conveying it **disqualifies** the offering. If he conveys the blood **in a situation where he is not required to convey** it, prohibited **intent** while conveying it **does not disqualify** the offering.

גמ׳ וְקַבָּלָה מִי פָּסְלָה?

GEMARA The mishna teaches that a slaughtered offering is disqualified due to prohibited intent while performing four rites, including collection of the blood. The Gemara asks: **And does collection** of the blood with prohibited intent **disqualify** the offering?

NOTES

Does not refute the inference by citing a common element of ***karet*** – צַד כָּרֵת לָא פָּרֵיךְ: A sin offering atones for a transgression punishable by *karet*, but one who refrains from fulfilling his obligation to bring a sin offering is not punished with *karet*. Conversely, one who refrains from bringing a Paschal offering is punished with *karet*, but a Paschal offering does not atone for a sin punishable by *karet*. Since the connection of each of these offerings to *karet* is dissimilar, this is not considered a common element of theirs.

There are communal as well as individual offerings – יֶשְׁנָן בְּצִבּוּר כְּבְיָחִיד: This element pertains to a burnt offering as well; there are daily communal burnt offerings and additional ones on the Festivals. Communal sin offerings include those brought on New Moons and Festivals. A Paschal offering is an individual offering, but it contains certain characteristics of communal offerings. For example, it is brought by the entire Jewish people at the same time, and it is brought in a state of ritual impurity when the majority of the public is impure.

HALAKHA

The Paschal offering and the sin offering – הַפֶּסַח וְהַחַטָּאת: If a Paschal offering or a sin offering is slaughtered for the sake of the wrong offering, it is disqualified. This also applies to collecting the blood, conveying it to the altar, and sprinkling it (Rambam *Sefer Avoda*, *Hilkhot Pesulei HaMukdashin* 15:1).

For their sake and not for their sake – לִשְׁמָן וְשֶׁלֹּא לִשְׁמָן: If one slaughters an offering or performs any other of its four main rites not for the sake of the offering, it is disqualified. This is the *halakha* even if one slaughters the offering for its sake and not for its sake, e.g., one slaughters a burnt offering for the sake of a burnt offering and for the sake of a peace offering, or if he slaughters it not for its sake and for its sake, e.g., for the sake of a peace offering and for the sake of a burnt offering (Rambam *Sefer Avoda*, *Hilkhot Pesulei HaMukdashin* 13:1).

A slaughtered offering is disqualified in four matters – הַזֶּבַח נִפְסָל בְּאַרְבָּעָה דְּבָרִים: An offering is disqualified due to prohibited intent while performing one of the following four rites: Slaughter, collecting the blood, conveying the blood to the altar, and sprinkling the blood on the altar (Rambam *Sefer Avoda*, *Hilkhot Pesulei HaMukdashin* 13:4, 15:1).

וְהָתַנְיָא: "וְהִקְרִיבוּ" – זוֹ קַבָּלַת הַדָּם. אַתָּה אוֹמֵר: קַבָּלַת הַדָּם, אוֹ אֵינוֹ אֶלָּא זְרִיקָה? כְּשֶׁהוּא אוֹמֵר: "וְזָרְקוּ" – הֲרֵי זְרִיקָה אָמוּר, הָא מָה אֲנִי מְקַיֵּים "וְהִקְרִיבוּ" – זוֹ קַבָּלַת הַדָּם. "בְּנֵי אַהֲרֹן הַכֹּהֲנִים" – שֶׁתְּהֵא בְּכֹהֵן כָּשֵׁר וּבִכְלֵי שָׁרֵת.

But isn't it taught in a *baraita*: The verse states: **"And** the sons of Aaron, the priests, **shall present** the blood" (Leviticus 1:5); **this is** referring to **collection of the blood.**[N] **Do you say** it is referring to **collection of the blood, or is it** referring to **only sprinkling** the blood? **When it states** immediately afterward: **"And sprinkle** the blood roundabout against the altar," **sprinkling** the blood **is** thereby **stated.** If so, **how do I realize** the meaning of: **"And** the sons of Aaron, the priests, **shall present"? This** is referring to **collection of the blood.** And the phrase **"the sons of Aaron, the priests"** teaches **that** collection of the blood **must be** performed **by a fit priest,**[H] i.e., one who has no blemish and who was not disqualified due to flawed lineage, **and** that he must do so while he is wearing priestly **service vestments.**[BN]

אָמַר רַבִּי עֲקִיבָא: מִנַּיִן לְקַבָּלָה שֶׁלֹּא תְּהֵא אֶלָּא בְּכֹהֵן כָּשֵׁר וּבִכְלֵי שָׁרֵת? נֶאֱמַר כָּאן: "בְּנֵי אַהֲרֹן", וְנֶאֱמַר לְהַלָּן: "אֵלֶּה שְׁמוֹת בְּנֵי אַהֲרֹן הַכֹּהֲנִים הַמְּשֻׁחִים", מַה לְּהַלָּן בְּכֹהֵן כָּשֵׁר וּבִכְלֵי שָׁרֵת – אַף כָּאן בְּכֹהֵן כָּשֵׁר וּבִכְלֵי שָׁרֵת.

The *baraita* continues: **Rabbi Akiva said: From where** is it derived **that collection** of the blood **may be** performed **only by a fit priest and** while he is wearing **service vestments?** The expression **"the sons of Aaron" is stated here** in the verse in Leviticus, **and it is stated there: "These are the names of the sons of Aaron, the priests that were anointed,** whom he consecrated to minister in the priest's office" (Numbers 3:3). **Just as there,** in the verse in Numbers, it mentions the word "priests" **with regard to fit priests,** i.e., Aaron's sons, **and with regard to** priests who were consecrated to serve by being dressed with **service vestments** (see Exodus 29:30), **so too here,** the reference is **to a fit priest and with regard to** one who is wearing **service vestments.**

אָמַר רַבִּי טַרְפוֹן: אֲקַפַּח אֶת בָּנַיי, אִם לֹא שָׁמַעְתִּי לְהַבְחִין הֶפְרֵשׁ בֵּין קַבָּלָה לִזְרִיקָה, וְאֵין לִי לְפָרֵשׁ.

Rabbi Tarfon[P] **said: I will bury my sons if I did not hear** a *halakha* from my teachers **discerning a distinction between collection** of **and sprinkling** the blood, **but I cannot explicate** the distinction, as I do not remember what it was.

אָמַר רַבִּי עֲקִיבָא, אֲנִי אֲפָרֵשׁ: קַבָּלָה – לֹא עָשָׂה בָּהּ מַחֲשָׁבָה כְּמַעֲשֶׂה, זְרִיקָה – עָשָׂה בָּהּ מַחֲשָׁבָה כְּמַעֲשֶׂה; קִבְּלוֹ בַּחוּץ – אֵינוֹ חַיָּיב כָּרֵת, זְרָקוֹ בַּחוּץ – עָנוּשׁ כָּרֵת; קִבְּלוּהוּ פְּסוּלִין – אֵין חַיָּיבִין עָלָיו, זְרָקוּהוּ פְּסוּלִין – חַיָּיבִין עָלָיו.

The *baraita* continues: **Rabbi Akiva said: I will explicate:** With regard to **collection,** the Torah **does not render intent like action.** Collecting the blood with prohibited intent does not disqualify the offering. But with regard to **sprinkling,** the Torah **does render intent like action.** Furthermore, if one **collected** the blood **outside**[H] the Temple, **he is not liable** to be punished with ***karet.***[N] But if one **sprinkled** the blood **outside** the Temple, **he is punished** with ***karet.*** Moreover, if those who are **unfit** for the Temple service **collected** the blood,[HN] **they are not liable for** that action. But if those who are **unfit** for the Temple service **sprinkled** the blood, **they are liable** to receive the penalty of death at the hand of Heaven **for that** action.

HALAKHA

Collection of the blood…must be performed by a fit priest, etc. – **קַבָּלַת הַדָּם...תְּהֵא בְּכֹהֵן כָּשֵׁר וכו׳**: All sacrificial rites from the collection of the blood onward are performed by priests wearing service vestments (Rambam *Sefer Avoda, Hilkhot Ma'aseh HaKorbanot* 5:1).

Collected the blood outside – **קִבְּלוֹ בַּחוּץ**: One who sacrifices outside the Temple an item that is fit to be sacrificed on the altar is liable. Therefore, one who sprinkles the blood of an offering outside the Temple is liable. One who collects the blood of an offering outside the Temple is exempt from liability, as that is not a complete rite, but a preparatory rite (Rambam *Sefer Avoda, Hilkhot Ma'aseh HaKorbanot* 19:3, 6).

If those who are unfit collected the blood, etc. – **קִבְּלוּהוּ פְּסוּלִין וכו׳**: If a non-priest performs one of the sacrificial rites of the priests, his performance is not valid. For performing one of the following four rites, a non-priest is liable to receive the penalty of death at the hand of Heaven: Sprinkling the blood, burning the portions of an animal offering or the handful of a meal offering, pouring the wine libation, and pouring the water libation on *Sukkot*. A non-priest who collects the blood of an offering is not liable to receive death at the hand of Heaven even though his performance is not valid (Rambam *Sefer Avoda, Hilkhot Biat HaMikdash* 9:1, 5).

BACKGROUND

Service vestments – **כְּלֵי שָׁרֵת**: An ordinary priest wears four vestments for service: A tunic, trousers, a mitre, and a belt. These vestments are made of white linen, except for the belt, which is made of linen and wool. Each thread is made up of six intertwined threads. The High Priest wears the four vestments of an ordinary priest plus four additional vestments: A robe, an ephod, a breastplate, and a frontplate.

Priestly vestments

PERSONALITIES

Rabbi Tarfon – **רַבִּי טַרְפוֹן**: Rabbi Tarfon was one of the great *tanna'im* in the generation following the destruction of the Second Temple. Rabbi Tarfon was a priest, and although he was young in the days when the Temple still stood, it appears that he served as a priest in the Temple.

Rabbi Tarfon was apparently the same age as the students of Rabbi Yoḥanan ben Zakkai and may have studied under him as well. He is mentioned as having been on close terms with Rabbi Eliezer and Rabbi Yehoshua, with the latter calling him: Tarfon, my brother.

He spent much time in the great academy of Yavne, engaging in halakhic discussions with its important Sages. Rabbi Akiva was his disciple, and after having grown in stature, his colleague. In fact, Rabbi Akiva and Rabbi Tarfon regularly engaged in discussions, and Rabbi Tarfon honored and esteemed him greatly. Several of the Sages of the next generation were disciples of Rabbi Tarfon, including Rabbi Yehuda, his preeminent disciple.

Apparently, Rabbi Tarfon lived in the town of Lod. He was very wealthy and spent much money on charity and other acts of kindness. He was known for his humility and his seeking of truth. Many incidents are recorded about his pious behavior, and particularly about the way he honored his mother.

NOTES

And the sons of Aaron shall present the blood, this is collection of the blood – **וְהִקְרִיבוּ זוֹ קַבָּלַת הַדָּם**: Although the straightforward meaning of the word "present" in the verse is referring to conveying the blood to the altar, the Sages reason that it must be referring to collecting the blood. The reason is that while conveying the blood is not an indispensable rite, collecting the blood is both indispensable and mentioned in the Torah elsewhere: "And Moses took half the blood and put it in basins" (Exodus 24:6). Since the slaughter and the sprinkling of the blood are mentioned in the verse explicitly: "And he shall slaughter the bull before the Lord, and Aaron's sons, the priests, shall present the blood, and sprinkle the blood roundabout against the altar," collecting the blood is perforce indicated in the word "present." Nevertheless, since the straightforward meaning refers to conveying, the Sages derive that the *halakhot* of collecting apply to conveying as well (see 4a).

Service vestments [*kelei sharet*] – **כְּלֵי שָׁרֵת**: In the commentary of Rabbeinu Hillel on *Torat Kohanim*, the phrase *kelei sharet* is interpreted in reference to service vessels, i.e., the blood must be collected with a consecrated bowl. It is unclear how this requirement is derived from the phrase "the sons of Aaron, the priests." Therefore, Rashi and other commentaries interpret *kelei sharet* in reference to the priestly vestments, with which Aaron's sons were consecrated; as stated: "Seven days shall the son that is priest in his stead put them on, he who comes into the Tent of Meeting to minister in the holy place" (Exodus 29:30).

If one collected the blood outside the Temple he is not liable to be punished with *karet* – **קִבְּלוֹ בַּחוּץ אֵינוֹ חַיָּיב כָּרֵת**: The penalty of *karet* for sacrificing an offering outside the Temple is mentioned explicitly in the Torah only with regard to the slaughter of the animal and the burning of the portions that are consumed on the altar (see Leviticus 17:3–4, 8–9). It is derived that this punishment applies to sprinkling the blood outside the Temple as well (see 107a). It does not apply to other sacrificial rites.

If those unfit for Temple service collected the blood – **קִבְּלוּהוּ פְּסוּלִין**: These include both non-priests and priests who are unfit to serve, e.g., a priest who has a blemish or who recently drank wine. A non-priest who performs a complete rite, i.e., one that does not serve as a preparatory rite for another rite, is liable to be punished with death at the hand of Heaven. Complete rites include sprinkling the blood, which finishes the sacrifice of the blood, and burning the portions that are consumed on the altar, which completes the sacrifice of the flesh. Although the performance of other rites is also prohibited to non-priests, e.g., collecting the blood, one who does so is not liable to receive the punishment of death at the hand of Heaven. With regard to a priest who serves in the Temple when he is unfit, in some cases, e.g., if he drinks wine, his vestments are torn, or his hair is too long, he is liable to receive death at the hand of Heaven, and in other cases, e.g., if he serves without wearing his priestly vestments, or if he does not wash his hands and feet before serving, he is liable to receive lashes.

אָמַר לוֹ רַבִּי טַרְפוֹן: הָעֲבוֹדָה, אַתְּ הִטִּיתָ יָמִין וּשְׂמֹאל, אֲנִי שָׁמַעְתִּי וְאֵין לִי לְפָרֵשׁ, אַתָּה דּוֹרֵשׁ וּמַסְכִּים לַשְּׁמוּעָה. בַּלָּשׁוֹן הַזֶּה אָמַר לוֹ: עֲקִיבָא! כׇּל הַפּוֹרֵשׁ מִמְּךָ כְּפוֹרֵשׁ מֵחַיָּיו.

Rabbi Tarfon said to him excitedly: I take an oath by **the** Temple **service** that **you have** not **deviated left or right** from what I heard from my teachers. **I** myself **heard** them **and I cannot explicate** what they taught, whereas **you teach** this *halakha* on your own **in concurrence with the *halakha*** I heard. **He said to** Rabbi Akiva, **using this language: Akiva, anyone who leaves you is like one who leaves his life.** In any event, Rabbi Akiva's statement in the *baraita* apparently contradicts the mishna with regard to the matter of whether the collection of the blood with prohibited intent disqualifies the offering.

אָמַר רָבָא: לָא קַשְׁיָא, כָּאן – בְּמַחְשֶׁבֶת פִּיגּוּל, כָּאן – בְּמַחְשֶׁבֶת שֶׁלֹּא לִשְׁמָהּ.

Rava said: It is **not difficult.** The *baraita* **here** is referring **to intent of *piggul*,** i.e., intent to consume or burn the offering after its appointed time. The mishna **there** is referring **to intent not for the sake of** the offering.

דַּיְקָא נָמֵי, דְּקָתָנֵי: ״שֶׁהַזֶּבַח נִפְסָל״, וְלָא קָתָנֵי ״מִתְפַּגֵּל״, שְׁמַע מִינַּהּ.

The Gemara adds: The language of the mishna **is also precise, as it teaches that a slaughtered offering is disqualified** in this manner, **and it does not teach** that an offering **is rendered *piggul*** in this manner. Apparently, the mishna is referring to intent that merely disqualifies the offering without rendering it *piggul,* one who partakes of which is liable to receive *karet*. The Gemara concludes: **Conclude from** the mishna's language that this interpretation is correct.

וּמַחְשֶׁבֶת פִּיגּוּל לָא פָּסְלָה בְּקַבָּלָה?

The Gemara asks: **And does intent of *piggul* during** the **collection** of the blood **not disqualify** the offering?

וְהָתַנְיָא: יָכוֹל לֹא תְּהֵא מַחְשָׁבָה מוֹעֶלֶת אֶלָּא בִּזְרִיקָה בִּלְבַד, מִנַּיִן לְרַבּוֹת שְׁחִיטָה וְקַבָּלָה? תַּלְמוּד לוֹמַר: ״וְאִם הֵאָכֹל יֵאָכֵל מִבְּשַׂר זֶבַח שְׁלָמָיו (פִּיגּוּל הוּא) בַּיּוֹם הַשְּׁלִישִׁי לֹא יֵרָצֶה״ – בִּדְבָרִים הַמְבִיאִין לִידֵי אֲכִילָה הַכָּתוּב מְדַבֵּר.

But isn't it taught in a *baraita*: One **might** have thought that **intent** to consume an offering after its designated time **is effective** to render the offering *piggul* **only** when one has that intent **during sprinkling. From where** is it derived **to include slaughter and collection** of the blood in this *halakha*? **The verse states: "And if any of the flesh of the sacrifice of his peace offerings is at all eaten on the third day, it shall not be accepted,** neither shall it be imputed to the one who offers it; it shall be an abhorred thing [*piggul*]" (Leviticus 7:18). As derived on 29a, the verse is referring to performance of the sacrificial rites with intent to consume the offering after its designated time. The phrase "is at all eaten" teaches that **the verse speaks of matters that lead to consumption,**[H] i.e., those sacrificial rites that enable consumption of the offering, including slaughter of the animal and collecting the blood.

יָכוֹל שֶׁאֲנִי מְרַבֶּה אַף שְׁפִיכַת שִׁירַיִים וְהַקְטָרַת אֵימוּרִין?

The *baraita* continues: One **might** have thought **that I** should **include even** the **pouring of** the **remainder** of the blood on the base of the altar, after its sprinkling, **and** the **burning of** the **sacrificial portions** on the altar.

תַּלְמוּד לוֹמַר: ״בַּיּוֹם הַשְּׁלִישִׁי לֹא יֵרָצֶה הַמַּקְרִיב אוֹתוֹ לֹא יֵחָשֵׁב״, זְרִיקָה בִּכְלָל הָיְתָה, וְלָמָּה יָצְתָה – לְהַקִּישׁ אֵלֶיהָ, לוֹמַר לָךְ: מָה זְרִיקָה מְיוּחֶדֶת שֶׁהִיא עֲבוֹדָה (וּמְכַפֶּרֶת) וּמְעַכֶּבֶת כַּפָּרָה – אַף כׇּל עֲבוֹדָה וּמְעַכֶּבֶת כַּפָּרָה, יָצְאוּ שְׁפִיכַת שִׁירַיִים וְהַקְטָרַת אֵימוּרִין, שֶׁאֵין מְעַכְּבִין אֶת הַכַּפָּרָה!

Therefore, **the verse states: "On the third day, it shall not be accepted, neither shall it be imputed to the one who offers it"** (Leviticus 7:18).[N] The phrase "the one who offers it" indicates the sprinkling of the blood. **Sprinkling was included** in the general category of rites that enable consumption. **And for what** purpose **was it singled out? To compare** other *halakhot* **to it,** i.e., **to say to you: Just as sprinkling is unique, as it is a rite and** if not performed **it prevents atonement, so too, any rite** that **prevents atonement** if not performed is included in the *halakha* of *piggul*. **Pouring** the **remainder** of the blood **and burning** the **sacrificial portions are** therefore **excluded, as they do not prevent atonement** if not performed. Evidently, intent of *piggul* applies to the collection of the blood, contrary to Rava's resolution of the contradiction between the mishna and the *baraita*.

HALAKHA

Matters that lead to consumption – דְּבָרִים הַמְבִיאִין לִידֵי אֲכִילָה: An offering is rendered *piggul* only by prohibited intent while performing a rite that enables consumption of the offering. This refers both to consumption of the meat of the offering by man, and to consumption of the portions that are burned on the altar (Rambam *Sefer Avoda, Hilkhot Pesulei HaMukdashin* 3:3).

NOTES

Neither shall it be imputed to the one who offers it – הַמַּקְרִיב אוֹתוֹ לֹא יֵחָשֵׁב: The commentaries explain that the phrase "the one who offers it" indicates the sprinkling of the blood (see Rashi and *Torat Kohanim*). Furthermore, the phrase "It shall not be accepted" indicates the sprinkling of the blood, as it is this rite that atones for the owner and satisfies his obligation (see 4b).

HALAKHA

In order to pour the remainder tomorrow – עַל מְנָת לִשְׁפּוֹךְ שִׁירַיִם לְמָחָר: If one slaughters an offering in the Temple courtyard with intent to pour the remainder of its blood on the altar the next day, or to burn its portions on the altar the next day, the offering is *piggul* (Rambam *Sefer Avoda, Hilkhot Pesulei HaMukdashin* 17:6).

Pouring the remainder in order to burn the sacrificial portions tomorrow – שׁוֹפֵךְ שִׁירַיִם עַל מְנָת לְהַקְטִיר אֵימוּרִין לְמָחָר: Performing one of the following sacrificial rites: Flaying the animal, cutting the animal into pieces, and taking its portions up to the altar for burning, with the wrong offering in mind, or with intent to consume it beyond its designated time, or with intent to consume it outside the Temple, does not disqualify the offering (Rambam *Sefer Avoda, Hilkhot Pesulei HaMukdashin* 13:7).

Dipping one's finger renders the offering *piggul* – טְבִילַת אֶצְבַּע מְפַגֶּלֶת: If, while dipping his finger in the blood of an inner sin offering, the priest had in mind that the offering will be consumed after its designated time, the offering is *piggul*, just as it would be if the priest had this intent while sprinkling the blood, in accordance with the opinion of Rabbi Yehoshua ben Levi (Rambam *Sefer Avoda, Hilkhot Pesulei HaMukdashin* 17:3, and see *Mishne LaMelekh* and other commentaries there).

PERSONALITIES

Ilfa – אִילְפָא: In the Jerusalem Talmud this *amora* appears as Ḥilfei. A first-generation *amora* in Eretz Yisrael, Ilfa was apparently one of the younger students of Rabbi Yehuda HaNasi and studied under his prominent students as well. Years later, he became a good friend of Rabbi Yoḥanan, although Rabbi Yoḥanan was older. Still later, due to dire economic straits, he was forced to leave Eretz Yisrael and travel overseas on business. During his absence, Rabbi Yoḥanan was chosen to head the yeshiva in Eretz Yisrael.

Ilfa was famous for his sharp intelligence and the depth of his understanding both in Mishna and in the various collections of *baraitot* attributed to the students of Rabbi Yehuda HaNasi. Rabbi Yoḥanan treated him with great respect and cited Torah statements in his name. The Gemara also relates stories of his righteousness and great piety.

אֶלָּא לָא קַשְׁיָא, הָא – דְּאָמַר: ״הֲרֵינִי שׁוֹחֵט עַל מְנָת לְקַבֵּל דָּמָהּ לְמָחָר״, הָא – דְּאָמַר: ״הֲרֵינִי מְקַבֵּל דָּמָהּ עַל מְנָת לִשְׁפּוֹךְ שִׁירַיִם לְמָחָר״.

The Gemara answers: **Rather,** it is **not difficult. This** statement of Rava, that intent of *piggul* does not apply to collection, is referring to a case **where** the one slaughtering the offering **says: I am hereby slaughtering** this offering **in order to collect its blood tomorrow.** Because the collection of the blood is not considered consumption, such intent does not render the offering *piggul.* **That** statement of the *baraita* is referring to a case **where** the one collecting the blood **says: I am hereby collecting its blood in order to pour** the **remainder** of the blood on the base of the altar **tomorrow.**[H] Since pouring the remains is considered consumption of the blood on the altar, such intent renders the offering *piggul.*

אֲמַר לֵיהּ הַהוּא מֵרַבָּנַן לְרָבָא: וּשְׁפִיכַת שִׁירַיִם וְהַקְטָרַת אֵימוּרִין לָא פָּסְלָה בְּהוּ מַחֲשָׁבָה?

One of the Sages said to Rava: And does prohibited **intent with regard to** the **pouring** of the **remainder** of the blood **and** the **burning** of the **sacrificial portions not disqualify** the offering, as this explanation of the *baraita* seems to indicate?

וְהָתְנַן: יָכוֹל לֹא תְּהֵא מַחֲשָׁבָה מוֹעֶלֶת אֶלָּא בַּאֲכִילַת בָּשָׂר, מִנַּיִן לְרַבּוֹת שְׁפִיכַת שִׁירַיִם וְהַקְטָרַת אֵימוּרִים? תַּלְמוּד לוֹמַר: ״וְאִם הֵאָכֹל יֵאָכֵל״ – בִּשְׁתֵּי אֲכִילוֹת הַכָּתוּב מְדַבֵּר, אַחַת אֲכִילַת אָדָם, וְאַחַת אֲכִילַת מִזְבֵּחַ!

But didn't we learn in a *baraita*: One **might** have thought that **only** prohibited **intent with regard to consumption of the meat is effective** to render the offering *piggul.* **From where** is it derived **to include** the **pouring of** the **remainder** of the blood **and** the **burning of** the **sacrificial portions? The verse states: "And if** any of the flesh of the sacrifice of his peace offerings **is at all eaten** [*he'akhol ye'akhel*] on the third day, it shall not be accepted" (Leviticus 7:18). It is derived from the repeated verb that **the verse speaks of two** types of **consumption: One is consumption** of the meat **by man,** i.e., by the priests or the owner of the offering, **and** the other **one is consumption** of the blood and the sacrificial portions **on the altar.**

לָא קַשְׁיָא: הָא – דְּאָמַר: ״הֲרֵינִי זוֹרֵק עַל מְנָת לִשְׁפּוֹךְ שִׁירַיִם לְמָחָר״, הָא – דְּאָמַר: ״הֲרֵינִי שׁוֹפֵךְ שִׁירַיִם עַל מְנָת לְהַקְטִיר אֵימוּרִין לְמָחָר״.

The Gemara answers: It is **not difficult. This** case, where intent renders the offering *piggul,* is **where** the one sprinkling the blood **says: I am hereby sprinkling** the blood **in order to pour** the **remainder tomorrow.** Since sprinkling the blood is necessary for atonement, if it is performed with the intent that consumption occur beyond its designated time, the offering is rendered *piggul.* **That** case, where intent does not render the offering *piggul,* is **where he says: I am hereby pouring** the **remainder in order to burn** the **sacrificial portions tomorrow.**[H] Although burning the portions is considered consumption, pouring the remainder of the blood is not indispensable for atonement, and therefore the offering is not rendered *piggul.*

אָמַר רַבִּי יְהוּדָה בְּרֵיהּ דְּרַבִּי חִיָּיא: שָׁמַעְתִּי, שֶׁטְּבִילַת אֶצְבַּע מְפַגֶּלֶת בְּחַטָּאת פְּנִימִית.

§ **Rabbi Yehuda, son of Rabbi Ḥiyya, says: I heard that with regard to an inner sin offering,** whose blood is sprinkled on the curtain separating the Sanctuary and Holy of Holies, **dipping** one's **finger** in the blood in order to sprinkle it, if he does so with the intent of burning the offering on the altar the following day, **renders** the offering ***piggul.***[H]

שְׁמַעָהּ אִילְפָא, אֲמָרָהּ קַמֵּיהּ דְּרַב פַּדָּא. אֲמַר: כְּלוּם לָמַדְנוּ פִּיגּוּל אֶלָּא מִשְּׁלָמִים, מַה שְּׁלָמִים אֵין טְבִילַת אֶצְבַּע מְפַגֶּלֶת בָּהֶן – אַף חַטָּאת אֵין טְבִילַת אֶצְבַּע מְפַגֶּלֶת בָּהֶן!

Ilfa[P] **heard** this statement and **said it before Rav Padda.**[P] Rav Padda **said** in response: **Did we derive** the *halakha* of ***piggul*** with regard to all offerings **from anything but a peace offering?** The source for the *halakha* of *piggul* is the verse stated with regard to peace offerings (Leviticus 7:18). Therefore, **just as** with regard to **a peace offering,** prohibited intent while **dipping** one's **finger** in the blood to sprinkle it on the altar **does not render it *piggul,*** as there is no requirement to sprinkle the blood of a peace offering with one's finger rather than the containing vessel, **so too,** with regard to **a sin offering,** prohibited intent while **dipping** one's **finger** in the blood **does not render it *piggul.***

PERSONALITIES

Rav Padda – רַב פַּדָּא: This Sage is Rabbi Yehuda bar Pedaiah, generally known as bar Padda. He was the son of bar Kappara's sister and one of Rabbi Yehuda HaNasi's younger disciples. Rabbi Yehuda bar Pedaiah was considered one of the Sages of the South, living in Judea, perhaps in the town of Lod. All of the great second- and third-generation *amora'im* in Eretz Yisrael studied under him, and his statements are cited by the Sages Rabbi Yehoshua ben Levi, Rabbi Yoḥanan, and Reish Lakish. His contributions to *halakha* and *aggada* are found throughout both the Babylonian Talmud and the Jerusalem Talmud, and in aggadic *midrashim.*

וְכִי הַכֹּל מִשְּׁלָמִים לָמְדוּ? אִי מַה שְּׁלָמִים שֶׁלֹּא לִשְׁמָן אֵין מוֹצִיא מִידֵי פִּיגּוּל – אַף חַטָּאת שֶׁלֹּא לִשְׁמָהּ אֵין מוֹצִיא מִידֵי פִּיגּוּל!

The Gemara challenges: **But are all** of the *halakhot* of *piggul* **derived from** the *halakha* of **a peace offering? If** that is so, then **just as** sacrifice of **a peace offering not for its sake does not preclude** its being rendered ***piggul***, as it is still fit, **so too,** the *halakha* should be that sacrifice of **a sin offering not for its sake does not preclude** its being rendered ***piggul***. In fact, the *halakha* is that a sin offering sacrificed not for its sake cannot become *piggul*.

אֶלָּא מַאי אִית לָךְ לְמֵימַר – מֵרִבּוּיָא דִּקְרָאֵי קָאָתְיָא, הָכָא נַמִי – מֵרִבּוּיָא דִּקְרָא קָאָתֵי.

Rather, what have you to say to explain this *halakha*? You must say that it is **derived from an amplification of the verse.**[N] **Here too,** the *halakha* that prohibited intent while dipping one's finger in the blood of an inner sin offering renders it *piggul* is **derived from an amplification of the verse.**

אָמַר רַבִּי יְהוֹשֻׁעַ בֶּן לֵוִי: בַּעֲלִיָּה זוֹ שָׁמַעְתִּי, שֶׁטְּבִילַת אֶצְבַּע מְפַגֶּלֶת. תָּהֵי בָּהּ רַבִּי שִׁמְעוֹן בֶּן לָקִישׁ: כְּלוּם לָמְדוּ פִּיגּוּל אֶלָּא מִשְּׁלָמִים, מַה שְּׁלָמִים אֵין טְבִילַת אֶצְבַּע מְפַגֶּלֶת בָּהֶן – אַף חַטָּאת אֵין טְבִילַת אֶצְבַּע מְפַגֶּלֶת בָּהֶן!

Similarly, **Rabbi Yehoshua ben Levi says: I heard in this upper story**[B] **that** prohibited intent while **dipping** one's **finger** in the blood of an inner sin offering **renders** it ***piggul***. **Rabbi Shimon ben Lakish wondered** [***tahei***][L] **at this** *halakha*: **Did** the Sages **derive** the *halakha* of ***piggul*** **from anything but a peace offering? Just as** with regard to **a peace offering,** prohibited intent while **dipping** one's **finger** in the blood **does not render it *piggul*, so too,** with regard to **a sin offering,** the *halakha* should be that prohibited intent while **dipping** one's **finger** in the blood **does not render it *piggul*.**

וְכִי הַכֹּל מִשְּׁלָמִים לָמְדוּ? אִי מַה שְּׁלָמִים שֶׁלֹּא לִשְׁמָן אֵין מוֹצִיא מִידֵי פִּיגּוּל – אַף חַטָּאת שֶׁלֹּא לִשְׁמָהּ אֵין מוֹצִיא מִידֵי פִּיגּוּל!

The Gemara responds: **But are all** of the *halakhot* of *piggul* **derived** from those **of a peace offering? If** so, **just as** sacrifice of **a peace offering not for its sake does not preclude** its being rendered ***piggul*, so too,** the *halakha* should be that sacrifice of **a sin offering not for its sake does not preclude** its being rendered ***piggul***.

אֲמַר רַבִּי יוֹסֵי בְּרַבִּי חֲנִינָא: אִין, הַכֹּל מִשְּׁלָמִים לָמְדוּ, הוֹאִיל וְחוּץ לִמְקוֹמוֹ פּוֹסֵל בִּשְׁלָמִים, וְשֶׁלֹּא לִשְׁמוֹ פּוֹסֵל בְּחַטָּאת; מַה חוּץ לִמְקוֹמוֹ הַפּוֹסֵל בִּשְׁלָמִים מוֹצִיא מִידֵי פִּיגּוּל, אַף שֶׁלֹּא לִשְׁמוֹ הַפּוֹסֵל בְּחַטָּאת מוֹצִיאָהּ מִידֵי פִּיגּוּל.

Rabbi Yosei, son of Rabbi Ḥanina, said: Indeed, all of the *halakhot* of *piggul*, even this one, **are derived from a peace offering. Since in** the case of a **peace offering,** intent to consume it **outside** its designated **area disqualifies** it, **and in** the case of **a sin offering,** sacrifice **not for its sake disqualifies** it, one can infer that **just as** intent to consume the offering **outside its** designated **area, which disqualifies a peace offering, precludes** its being rendered ***piggul*, so too,** sacrifice **not for its sake, which disqualifies a sin offering, precludes its** being rendered ***piggul***. By contrast, dipping one's finger in the blood of an inner sin offering with intent to consume it after its designated time does not render it *piggul*, as there is no parallel *halakha* with regard to a peace offering.

אָמַר רַבִּי יִרְמְיָה: מִצְּדָּהּ תַּבְרָא; מַה לְּחוּץ לִמְקוֹמוֹ הַפּוֹסֵל בִּשְׁלָמִים – שֶׁכֵּן נוֹהֵג בְּכָל הַזְּבָחִים, תֹּאמַר בְּשֶׁלֹּא לִשְׁמוֹ, שֶׁאֵינוֹ נוֹהֵג אֶלָּא בְּפֶסַח וְחַטָּאת בִּלְבַד!

Rabbi Yirmeya says: This inference is **inherently disjointed: What** is notable **about** intent to consume the offering **outside its** designated **area, which disqualifies a peace offering?** It is notable **in that** its disqualification **applies to all slaughtered offerings.** This is why it precludes the offering from becoming *piggul*. Need **you say** the same **with regard to** disqualification by sacrifice **not for its sake, which applies only to a Paschal offering and a sin offering?**

אֶלָּא מַאי אִית לָךְ לְמֵימַר? דָּבָר הַפּוֹסֵל בָּהֶן – מוֹצִיאָם מִידֵי פִּיגּוּל, דָּבָר הַמְעַכֵּב בָּהֶן – מְבִיאָן לִידֵי פִּיגּוּל;

Rather, what have you to say to explain this derivation? One must say that it is not based on a case-to-case comparison, but on a principle that is derived from a peace offering, namely: Any **matter that disqualifies** a peace offering, e.g., intent to consume it outside its designated area, **precludes its** being rendered ***piggul***, and any **matter that prevents** atonement if not performed **renders** the offering ***piggul*** if performed with intent to consume it beyond its designated time.

הָכָא נַמִי, דָּבָר הַפּוֹסֵל בָּהּ – מוֹצִיא מִידֵי פִּיגּוּל, דָּבָר הַמְעַכֵּב בָּהּ – מְבִיאָהּ לִידֵי פִּיגּוּל.

One infers therefore that **here too,** with regard to an inner sin offering, any **matter that disqualifies it,** e.g., sacrifice not for its sake, **precludes** its being rendered ***piggul***, and any **matter that prevents** atonement if not performed **renders it *piggul*** if it is performed with intent to consume it beyond its designated time. Accordingly, dipping one's finger in the blood with intent to consume the offering beyond its designated time renders it *piggul*, as this rite is indispensable.

NOTES

It is derived from an amplification of the verse – מֵרִבּוּיָא דִּקְרָאֵי קָאָתְיָא: This may be referring to the specific *halakhot* under discussion. In other words, the general *halakha* of *piggul* with regard to the sin offering is derived from the peace offering, but several of its details are derived from amplifications indicated in the verse's language. Rashi explains that the *halakha* of *piggul* with regard to the sin offering in general is not derived directly from the peace offering, as explained in the Gemara (28b), but rather from an amplification in the verse, as expounded in *Torat Kohanim*.

BACKGROUND

Upper story – עֲלִיָּה: In the era of the Mishna and Talmud people would live in two-story houses. The bottom floor, referred to as the house, was the main living area. The upper floor had more privacy. For this reason, the Sages would often seclude themselves there in order to concentrate, study, or even to convene large meetings, which were sometimes held in secret.

LANGUAGE

Wondered [*tahei*] – תָּהֵי: While this verb is usually understood to mean wonder, some early commentaries interpret it as meaning question, or regret. The expression: Wondered at this [*tahei bah*] is used in reference to several *amora'im*, and is generally followed by a question that expresses an element of surprise.

אָמַר רַב מָרִי: אַף אֲנַן נַמִּי תָּנֵינָא: זֶה הַכְּלָל, כָּל הַקּוֹמֵץ וְנוֹתֵן בִּכְלִי וְהַמּוֹלִיךְ וְהַמַּקְטִיר;

Rav Mari says: We learn in a mishna **as well** that dipping one's finger in the blood of an inner sin offering with intent to consume it beyond its designated time renders the offering *piggul* (*Menaḥot* 12a): **This is the principle:** With regard to **anyone who removes a handful**[HB] from a meal offering, **or** who **places** the handful **in a vessel, or who conveys** the handful to the altar, **or who burns** it on the altar, if he does so with intent that the offering will be consumed after its designated time the offering is *piggul*.

בִּשְׁלָמָא קוֹמֵץ – הַיְינוּ שׁוֹחֵט, מוֹלִיךְ – הַיְינוּ מוֹלִיךְ, מַקְטִיר נַמִּי – הַיְינוּ זוֹרֵק, אֶלָּא נוֹתֵן בִּכְלִי מַאי נִיהוּ?

Since the *halakhot* of *piggul* are derived from those of a peace offering, one can ask: **Granted,** the one who **removes** a handful of a meal offering can render the offering *piggul*, as he **is** considered equivalent to the one who **slaughters** a peace offering. Just as the blood is the essential part of an animal offering, and it is removed by slaughter, so too, the handful of a meal offering is its essential part. Likewise, the one who **conveys** the handful **is** equivalent to the one who **conveys** the blood of a peace offering, and the one who **burns** the handful **is** equivalent to the one who **sprinkles** the blood **too. But** to **what is** the one who **places** the handful **in a vessel** equivalent? From where is it derived that he, too, can render the offering *piggul*?

אִילֵימָא דְּדָמֵי לְקַבָּלָה, מִי דָּמֵי? הָתָם – מִמֵּילָא, הָכָא – אִיהוּ קָא שָׁקֵיל וְרָמֵי!

If we say that placing the handful in a vessel is **comparable to collection** of the blood, as both rites involve placing the essential part of the offering in a vessel, one may respond: **Are** these rites actually **comparable? There,** in the case of a peace offering, the collection of the blood is performed passively. The blood spills into the vessel **by itself. Here,** in the case of a meal offering, the priest **takes** the handful himself **and places** it in a vessel. Clearly, placing the handful in a vessel is not equivalent to any specific rite in the sacrifice of a peace offering.

אֶלָּא, כֵּיוָן דְּלָא סַגִּי דְּלָא יָהֵיב – עַל כָּרְחֵיהּ עֲבוֹדָה חֲשׁוּבָה הִיא; הָכָא נַמִּי, כֵּיוָן דְּלָא סַגִּי דְּלָא עָבֵיד לָהּ – עַל כָּרְחֵיהּ הַיְינוּ הוֹלָכָה.

Rather, since it is not sufficient[N] for the handful to be sacrificed **without** first **placing** it in a service vessel, **it is, perforce, an important rite.** One who performs it can therefore render the offering *piggul* like those who perform other essential rites. **Here too,** with regard to dipping one's finger in the blood of an inner sin offering, although it has no equivalent in the sacrifice of a peace offering, **since it is not sufficient** if the priest **does not perform it, it is perforce** considered part of the **conveying** of the blood, and the priest can render the offering *piggul* while performing it.

לָא, לְעוֹלָם דְּדָמֵי לְקַבָּלָה. וּדְקָאָמְרַתְּ: הָכָא מִמֵּילָא, הָתָם אִיהוּ קָא שָׁקֵיל וְיָהֵיב; כֵּיוָן דְּאִידִי וְאִידִי מַתַּן כְּלִי הוּא – מַה לִּי מִמֵּילָא, מַה לִּי קָא שָׁקֵיל וְיָהֵיב.

The Gemara responds: **No, actually,** placing the handful in a vessel is **comparable to** the **collection** of the blood. **And** despite the distinction **that you say,** namely, that **here,** in the case of a peace offering, the blood spills **by itself,** while **there,** in the case of a meal offering, the priest **takes** the handful himself **and places** it in the vessel, nevertheless, **since** both **this** rite **and that** rite involve **placement** of the essential part of the offering in **a vessel,** they are equivalent. **What** difference is it **to me** if the blood spills into the vessel **by itself,** and **what** difference is it **to me** if the priest **takes** the handful himself **and places** it in the vessel? By contrast, dipping one's finger in the blood of an inner sin offering has no equivalent in a peace offering. Therefore, *piggul* does not apply to it.

לֵימָא כְּתַנָּאֵי, דְּתָנֵי חֲדָא: טְבִילַת אֶצְבַּע מְפַגֶּלֶת בְּחַטָּאת, וְתַנְיָא אִידָךְ: לֹא מְפַגֶּלֶת וְלֹא מִתְפַּגֶּלֶת; מַאי לָאו תַּנָּאֵי הִיא?

The Gemara suggests: **Let us say** that the principle that dipping one's finger in the blood is considered part of conveying it to the curtain is **the subject of** a dispute between ***tanna'im*. As it is taught** in **one** *baraita*: **With regard to** an inner **sin offering, dipping** one's **finger** in the blood with intent that it be consumed beyond its designated time **renders it** ***piggul*. And it is taught** in **another** *baraita*: Dipping one's finger in the blood with intent that it be consumed beyond its designated time **does not render** it ***piggul*, and neither does** slaughtering the animal with the intent to dip his finger in the blood the next day **render it** ***piggul*. What, is it not** that this matter is a dispute between ***tanna'im***?

HALAKHA

Anyone who removes a handful, etc. – כָּל הַקּוֹמֵץ וכו׳: With regard to removing the handful from the meal offering, placing it in a vessel, conveying it to the altar, and burning it on the altar, if one performs one of these rites with intent that the offering will be consumed outside its designated area, the offering is disqualified. If one does so with intent that it will be consumed after its designated time, the offering is *piggul* (Rambam *Sefer Avoda, Hilkhot Pesulei HaMukdashin* 13:6).

BACKGROUND

Handful – קוֹמֶץ: For most meal offerings a priest must take a handful and burn it on the altar. This rite can be performed only by a priest. According to many authorities, the priest scoops the flour out with the three middle fingers of his right hand, using his thumb and little finger to remove any surplus flour. He then consecrates the flour by placing it in a service vessel. Since the priest has to scoop out an exact handful of flour, no more and no less, removing the handful is considered one of the more difficult services in the Temple to perform correctly. After the handful is placed in a service vessel, it is conveyed to the altar and burned on the altar.

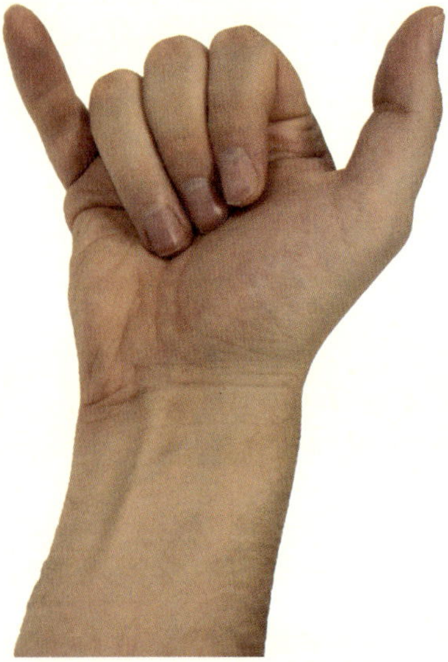

Position of the priest's hand when taking the handful

NOTES

Rather since it is not sufficient, etc. – אֶלָּא כֵּיוָן דְּלָא סַגִּי וכו׳: Rashi explains according to the Gemara in tractate *Sota* (14b) that this is not referring to the technical capability of sacrificing the handful on the altar without first placing it in a vessel. Rather, it is referring to the sacrificial requirement to sanctify the handful a second time, after it has already been sanctified with the rest of the meal offering, by placing it in another service vessel before burning it on the altar. This is derived from the *halakha* with regard to the blood of an animal offering, which is sanctified once together with the rest of the animal by slaughter, and is sanctified again when it is collected in a service vessel.

לָא, הָא – רַבָּנַן, הָא – רַבִּי שִׁמְעוֹן.

The Gemara responds: **No,** both *tanna'im* agree that dipping one's finger in the blood of an inner sin offering is part of conveying it to the curtain. Rather, **this** *baraita,* which states that a priest can render the offering *piggul* while dipping his finger in its blood, is in accordance with the opinion of **the Rabbis** in the mishna (13a), who hold that one can render the offering *piggul* while conveying the blood to the altar. **That** *baraita,* which states the opposite, is in accordance with the opinion of **Rabbi Shimon** in the mishna, who holds that one cannot render the offering *piggul* while conveying the blood.

אִי רַבִּי שִׁמְעוֹן – מַאי אִירְיָא טְבִילַת אֶצְבַּע? הָאָמַר

The Gemara asks: **If** the latter *baraita* is in accordance with the opinion of **Rabbi Shimon, why** is it referring **specifically** to **dipping** one's **finger? Doesn't he say**

Perek **I**
Daf **14** Amud **a**

כָּל שֶׁאֵינוֹ עַל מִזְבֵּחַ הַחִיצוֹן כִּשְׁלָמִים אֵין בּוֹ מִשּׁוּם פִּיגּוּל!

that **any** offering **whose** blood **is not** sprinkled **on the external altar like a peace offering is not subject to** the *halakhot* of ***piggul***? If so, *piggul* does not apply to inner sin offerings at all.

אֶלָּא, הָא וְהָא רַבָּנַן, וְלָא קַשְׁיָא: כָּאן – בְּחַטָּאוֹת הַחִיצוֹנוֹת, כָּאן – בְּחַטָּאוֹת הַפְּנִימִיּוֹת.

Rather, both **this** *baraita* **and that** *baraita* are in accordance with the opinion of **the Rabbis; and** the apparent contradiction between them is **not difficult. Here,** the *baraita* that maintains that one cannot render the offering *piggul* while dipping his finger in the blood is referring **to the external sin offerings,** since dipping one's finger in order to sprinkle the blood on the external altar is not considered an essential rite. **There,** the *baraita* that maintains that one can render the offering *piggul* while performing this rite is referring **to the inner sin offerings.**

חַטָּאוֹת הַחִיצוֹנוֹת פְּשִׁיטָא, לָא כְּתִיב בְּהוּ ״וְטָבַל״!

The Gemara asks: Isn't it **obvious** that one cannot render the offering *piggul* while dipping his finger in the blood of **the external sin offerings?** The statement: **"And** the priest **shall dip** his finger in the blood" (Leviticus 4:6), **is not written with regard to** these offerings. Since it is clearly not an essential rite, why was it necessary for the *baraita* to teach that improper intent while performing it cannot render the offering *piggul*?

אִצְטְרִיךְ, סָלְקָא דַּעְתָּךְ אָמִינָא: הוֹאִיל וּכְתִיב ״וְלָקַח״, וְאִי אָתֵי קוֹף רָמֵי לְהוּ אַיְּדֵיהּ, בָּעֵי לְמִישְׁקַל זִימְנָא אַחֲרִיתִי – כְּמַאן דִּכְתִיב ״וְטָבַל״ דָּמֵי;

The Gemara answers: It **was necessary** for the *baraita* to teach this, as otherwise it might **enter your mind to say** that **since it is written** with regard to an external sin offering: **"And** the priest **shall take**[N] of the blood of the sin offering with his finger" (Leviticus 4:34), **and** therefore **if a monkey comes** and **places** blood **on the hand of** the priest the priest **must take** blood from the vessel **again** to perform the mitzva as stated in the verse, **it is considered as though** the statement: **And** the priest **shall dip** his finger in the blood, **is written** with regard to an external sin offering as well.

קָא מַשְׁמַע לָן: לְהָכִי לָא כְּתִיב ״וְטָבַל״, דְּמַשְׁמַע הָכִי וּמַשְׁמַע הָכִי.

Therefore, the *baraita* **teaches us** that dipping one's finger in the blood of an external sin offering is an inessential rite and one cannot render the offering *piggul* while performing it. As it is **for this** reason that the phrase: **And** the priest **shall dip** his finger in the blood, **is not written** with regard to this offering, but rather: And the priest shall take of the blood of the sin offering with his finger, **which indicates this** *halakha*, that the priest must actively take the blood in his hand, **and** also **indicates that** *halakha*, that dipping one's finger in the blood is not an essential rite and cannot render the offering *piggul*.

NOTES

Since it is written: And the priest shall take, etc. – **הוֹאִיל וּכְתִיב וְלָקַח וכו׳**: In other words, since the priest is required to take blood with his finger, dipping his finger in the blood is necessary.

״רַבִּי שִׁמְעוֹן מַכְשִׁיר בְּהִילּוּךְ״. אָמַר רַבִּי שִׁמְעוֹן בֶּן לָקִישׁ: מוֹדֶה רַבִּי שִׁמְעוֹן בְּהוֹלָכַת חַטָּאוֹת הַפְּנִימִיּוֹת שֶׁמַּחֲשָׁבָה פּוֹסֶלֶת בְּהוּ, הוֹאִיל וַעֲבוֹדָה שֶׁאֵין יָכוֹל לְבַטְּלָהּ.

§ The mishna teaches that **Rabbi Shimon deems** the offering **fit** if the prohibited intent was **during** the rite of **conveying** the blood to the altar. **Rabbi Shimon ben Lakish says: Rabbi Shimon concedes**[N] **that** prohibited **intent during the conveying of** the blood of **the inner sin offerings disqualifies them, since** with regard to those offerings, it is **an indispensable rite.** Because the blood must be sprinkled inside the Sanctuary and the offering cannot be slaughtered inside the Sanctuary, conveying the blood into the Sanctuary is always necessary for such offerings.

וְהָאָמַר רַבִּי שִׁמְעוֹן: כָּל שֶׁאֵינוֹ עַל מִזְבֵּחַ הַחִיצוֹן כִּשְׁלָמִים אֵין חַיָּיבִין עָלָיו מִשּׁוּם פִּיגּוּל!

The Gemara asks: **But doesn't Rabbi Shimon say** that with regard to **any** offering **whose** blood **is not** sprinkled **on the external altar like a peace offering, one is not liable** to be punished with *karet* **for** eating **it, due to** the prohibition of ***piggul***? In other words, the *halakha* of *piggul* does not apply to inner sin offerings at all.

אָמַר רַבִּי יוֹסֵי בְּרַבִּי חֲנִינָא: מוֹדֶה הָיָה לִפְסוֹל, מִקַּל וָחוֹמֶר; וּמַה שֶּׁלֹּא לִשְׁמָן שֶׁהוּכְשְׁרוּ בִּשְׁלָמִים – פָּסוּל בְּחַטָּאת, חוּץ לִזְמַנּוֹ שֶׁפּוֹסֵל בִּשְׁלָמִים – אֵינוֹ דִּין שֶׁיִּפְסוֹל בְּחַטָּאוֹת?

Rabbi Yosei, son of Rabbi Ḥanina, says: Rabbi Shimon **concedes** that although intent to consume an inner sin offering after its designated time does not render it *piggul*, it **disqualifies** the offering, **due to an *a fortiori* inference: Just as** sacrifice **not for its sake, which is valid in** the case of **a peace offering,** is nevertheless **not valid in** the case of **a sin offering,** as stated in the mishna (2a), so too, **isn't it logical that** sacrifice with intent to consume it **beyond its** designated **time, which disqualifies peace offerings, should disqualify sin offerings?**

וְאַשְׁכְּחַן חוּץ לִזְמַנּוֹ, חוּץ לִמְקוֹמוֹ מְנָלַן?

The Gemara asks: **And we found** a source for the *halakha* that intent to consume an inner sin offering **beyond its** designated **time** disqualifies it according to Rabbi Shimon. **From where do we** derive that intent to consume it **outside its** designated **area** also disqualifies it?

אִי מִחוּץ לִזְמַנּוֹ – מַה לְּחוּץ לִזְמַנּוֹ שֶׁכֵּן כָּרֵת,

If we derive it **from** the case of intent to consume it **beyond its** designated **time,** one may respond: **What** is notable **about** intent to consume it **beyond its** designated **time?** It is notable **in that** it can render an offering *piggul*, for partaking of which one is liable to receive ***karet***.

אִי מִשֶּׁלֹּא לִשְׁמָהּ – שֶׁכֵּן נוֹהֵג בְּבָמָה!

If we derive it **from** the case of intent **not for its sake,** one may respond: What is notable about sacrifice not for its sake? It is notable **in that** this disqualification **applies** even **to** sacrifice on a private **altar**[B] during the era when such altars were permitted. By contrast, intent to consume the offering outside its designated area is irrelevant to sacrifice on a private altar, which has no designated area.

(חִיּוּב) שֶׁלֹּא לִשְׁמָן בְּמַאי נוֹהֵג? בְּפֶסַח וְחַטָּאת, פֶּסַח וְחַטָּאת בְּבָמָה לֹא קָרְבוּ.

The Gemara answers: **With regard to what** offering **does** disqualification due to intent **not for its sake apply?** It applies **to a Paschal offering and a sin offering.** Since **a Paschal offering and a sin offering may not be sacrificed on** a private **altar,**[NH] this factor is irrelevant. One may therefore derive from the case of intent not for its sake that intent to consume the offering outside its designated area disqualifies it.

וְאִיבָּעֵית אֵימָא, הֶיקֵּישָׁא הוּא: ״שְׁלִישִׁי״ – זֶה חוּץ לִזְמַנּוֹ, ״פִּיגּוּל״ – זֶה חוּץ לִמְקוֹמוֹ.

And if you wish, say that **it is** derived from the **juxtaposition** of the *halakha* of intent to consume the offering beyond its designated time with the *halakha* of intent to consume it outside its designated area. The verse states: "And if any of the flesh of the sacrifice of his peace offerings is at all eaten on the third day, it shall not be accepted, neither shall it be imputed to the one who offers it; it shall be an abhorred thing [*piggul*]" (Leviticus 7:18). **This** statement: "On the **third** day, it shall not be accepted," is referring to intent to consume the offering **beyond its** designated **time;** and **this** seemingly superfluous statement: "Neither shall it be imputed to the one who offers it; it shall be ***piggul***," is referring to intent to consume it **outside its** designated **area.** Such juxtaposition indicates that there are parallel *halakhot* in the two cases even if they are dissimilar.

NOTES

Rabbi Shimon concedes, etc. – מוֹדֶה רַבִּי שִׁמְעוֹן וכו׳: Rashi explains that slaughtering an animal in the Sanctuary is disrespectful. Therefore, it is necessary to convey the blood of inner sin offerings into the Sanctuary.

A Paschal offering and a sin offering may not be sacrificed on a private altar – פֶּסַח וְחַטָּאת בְּבָמָה לֹא קָרְבוּ: Only voluntary offerings were sacrificed on private altars (see 117a). Obligatory offerings, such as Paschal offerings, were sacrificed on the public altar. With regard to sin offerings and other obligatory offerings that do not have a designated time, there is a tannaitic dispute as to whether they were sacrificed on the public altar or not at all (see 119a and *Keren Ora*).

BACKGROUND

Private altars – בָּמוֹת: Before the Temple was built, there were periods when sacrificing offerings on private altars was permitted. It was permitted for any Jew, even an Israelite, to construct an altar and sacrifice certain offerings, primarily voluntary burnt offerings and peace offerings. Several of the requirements that pertain to the sacrificial process in the Temple did not apply to these altars, including the requirement to consume the meat of the offering within a certain boundary. During this period, only obligatory offerings and public offerings were brought on the public altar, such as the one in Nov or Gibeon. After the construction of the Temple in Jerusalem, private altars were prohibited forever. Still, for many generations people continued to transgress this prohibition and bring offerings to God upon private altars.

HALAKHA

A Paschal offering on a private altar – פֶּסַח בְּבָמָה: Even during the era when it was permitted to sacrifice offerings on a private altar, the Paschal offering was sacrificed only on the public altar (Rambam *Sefer Korbanot*, *Hilkhot Korban Pesaḥ* 1:3).

אָמַר רָבָא: אִם תִּימְצֵי לוֹמַר רַבִּי שִׁמְעוֹן סָבַר לָהּ כִּבְרֵיהּ, דְּאָמַר: בֵּין הָאוּלָם וְלַמִּזְבֵּחַ צָפוֹן – אֵין מַחֲשָׁבָה מוֹעֶלֶת בְּהוֹלָכַת חַטָּאוֹת הַפְּנִימִיּוֹת אֶלָּא מִפֶּתַח אוּלָם וְלִפְנִים;

§ **Rava says: If you say** that **Rabbi Shimon holds in accordance with** the opinion of **his son** Rabbi Elazar, **who says** that the area **between the Entrance Hall and the altar**[B] is considered part of the **north**[N] of the Temple courtyard, the only place where a sin offering may be slaughtered, he must also hold that prohibited **intent while conveying** the blood of **the inner sin offerings is effective** to disqualify them **only from the doorway of the Entrance Hall inward.** Prohibited intent before the priest reaches the doorway of the Entrance Hall does not disqualify the offering, as conveying the blood to the doorway is not necessary; the offering could have been slaughtered at the doorway in the first place.

וְאִם תִּמְצֵי לוֹמַר סָבַר לָהּ כְּרַבִּי יְהוּדָה, דְּאָמַר: תּוֹךְ עֲזָרָה מְקַדֵּשׁ – אֵין מַחֲשָׁבָה מוֹעֶלֶת בְּהוֹלָכַת סִילּוּק בָּזִיכִין אֶלָּא מִפֶּתַח הֵיכָל וְלַחוּץ;

And if you say that Rabbi Shimon **holds in accordance with** the opinion of **Rabbi Yehuda, who says** that the **interior of the Temple courtyard sanctifies**[N] offerings, i.e., that offerings can be sacrificed on the courtyard floor as if it were part of the altar, prohibited **intent while conveying** the **removed bowls** of frankincense[N] from the table in the Sanctuary to burn them on the external altar **is effective** to disqualify them **only** while **conveying** them **from the doorway of the Sanctuary outward** to the Entrance Hall. Since the table can be placed anywhere in the Sanctuary, conveying the bowls of frankincense in the Sanctuary itself is unnecessary, and once the priest exits the Entrance Hall to the Temple courtyard, the frankincense could theoretically be burned immediately.

וְאִם תִּמְצֵי לוֹמַר סָבַר: קְדוּשַּׁת הֵיכָל וְאוּלָם חֲדָא הִיא – אֵין מַחֲשָׁבָה מוֹעֶלֶת אֶלָּא מִפֶּתַח אוּלָם וְלַחוּץ;

Rava continues: **And if you say** that Rabbi Shimon also **holds** that **the sanctity of the Sanctuary and the Entrance Hall are one** and the same, and the table can be placed in the Entrance Hall as well, prohibited **intent is effective only** while conveying the frankincense **from the doorway of the Entrance Hall outward,**[N] i.e., in the doorway of the Entrance Hall itself.

וְאִם תִּמְצֵי לוֹמַר: תּוֹךְ הַפֶּתַח כְּלִפְנִים – אֵין מַחֲשָׁבָה מוֹעֶלֶת אֲפִילּוּ פְּסִיעָה אַחַת אֶלָּא בִּכְדֵי הוֹשָׁטַת יָדוֹ;

And if you say that he also **holds** that **inside the doorway is** considered **like inside** the Entrance Hall, then the table can be placed in the doorway too, and prohibited **intent is not effective** while conveying the frankincense **even one step. Rather,** it is effective only during the moment when the frankincense is taken out of the doorway to the courtyard, the time it takes the priest **to stretch out his hand** to place the bowls on the courtyard floor.

וְאִם תִּמְצֵי לוֹמַר סָבַר: הוֹלָכָה שֶׁלֹּא בָּרֶגֶל לָא שְׁמָהּ הוֹלָכָה – אֵין מַחֲשָׁבָה מוֹעֶלֶת כְּלָל.

And if you say that he also **holds** that **conveying** an offering **not by foot is not considered conveying,** prohibited **intent is not effective at all** while conveying the bowls of frankincense.

BACKGROUND

Between the Entrance Hall and the altar – בֵּין הָאוּלָם וְלַמִּזְבֵּחַ: This image depicts the main sections of the Temple: The Sanctuary, the Entrance Hall, the altar, the ramp to the altar, the area between the Entrance Hall and the altar, and the different courtyards.

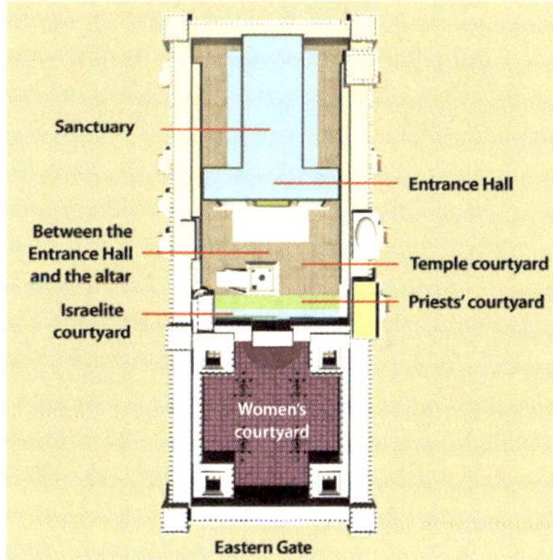

Main sections of the Temple

NOTES

Between the Entrance Hall and the altar is considered north – בֵּין הָאוּלָם וְלַמִּזְבֵּחַ צָפוֹן: Offerings of the most sacred order, including sin offerings, are required to be slaughtered: "On the side of the altar northward" (Leviticus 1:11). The Sages disagree (20a) as to what area is included in this description. Rabbi Yosei, son of Rabbi Yehuda, holds that only the area between the altar itself and the northern edge of the courtyard is included. Rabbi Elazar, son of Rabbi Shimon, adds the part of the northern half of the courtyard that is between the Entrance Hall and the altar. Rabbi Yehuda HaNasi also adds the part of the northern half of the courtyard that is between the altar and the eastern edge of the courtyard.

The interior of the Temple courtyard sanctifies – תּוֹךְ עֲזָרָה מְקַדֵּשׁ: According to Rabbi Yehuda, when King Solomon consecrated the First Temple, he consecrated the floor of the courtyard with the same degree of sanctity as the altar. Therefore, although offerings are required to be sacrificed on the altar *ab initio*, it is possible to sacrifice them on the courtyard floor.

While conveying the removed bowls of frankincense – בְּהוֹלָכַת סִילּוּק בָּזִיכִין: Every Shabbat, the shewbread and frankincense on the table in the Sanctuary are replaced. After the frankincense of that week is burned on the altar, the shewbread of the previous week may be eaten by the priests. This is parallel to the *halakha* that it is permitted to partake of animal offerings after the blood is sprinkled on the altar, and meal offerings are eaten after the handful is burned. Therefore, conveying the frankincense to the altar is parallel to conveying the blood of an animal offering or the handful of a meal offering, and if the one conveying it has intent to burn it or to eat the shewbread after its designated time, it is rendered *piggul*. According to Rabbi Shimon, this is the *halakha* only if conveying the frankincense to the altar is an indispensable stage in its sacrifice.

From the doorway of the Entrance Hall outward – מִפֶּתַח אוּלָם וְלַחוּץ: The doorway of the Entrance Hall is five cubits thick (*Middot* 4:7).

אָמַר לֵיהּ אַבָּיֵי לְאָמוֹרֵיהּ דְּרַב חִסְדָּא, בְּעֵי מִינֵּיהּ מֵרַב חִסְדָּא: הוֹלָכָה בְּזָר, מַהוּ?

§ **Abaye said to Rav Ḥisda's interpreter:**[B] **Ask Rav Ḥisda** for me: **What is the** *halakha* with regard to **a non-priest conveying** the blood?[H] Is the offering disqualified, as in a case where a non-priest performs any other sacrificial rite that may be performed only by priests?

אָמַר לֵיהּ: כְּשֵׁרָה, וּמִקְרָא מְסַיְּיעֵנִי: ״וַיִּשְׁחֲטוּ אֶת הַפָּסַח וַיִּזְרְקוּ הַכֹּהֲנִים אֶת הַדָּם מִיָּדָם וְהַלְוִיִּם מַפְשִׁיטִים״.

Rav Ḥisda **said to him:** The offering remains **fit, and a verse supports my** ruling: **"And they slaughtered the Paschal offering, and the priests sprinkled the blood, which they received of their hand, and the Levites flayed them"** (II Chronicles 35:11). Apparently, priests are required only for the sprinkling of the blood on the altar and later rites. Just as slaughter may be performed by non-priests, so can the collection and conveying of the blood be performed by them.

מֵתִיב רַב שֵׁשֶׁת: זָר וְאוֹנֵן

Rav Sheshet raises an objection from a *baraita*: **If a non-priest,**[H] **or an acute mourner,**[HB]

HALAKHA

A non-priest conveying the blood – הוֹלָכָה בְּזָר: If one unfit to perform the Temple service conveys the blood to the altar, even if a priest performs the beginning or end of the conveying, the offering is disqualified; in accordance with the conclusion of the discussion in the Gemara (Rambam *Sefer Avoda, Hilkhot Pesulei HaMukdashin* 1:27).

Service of a non-priest – זָר בַּעֲבוֹדָה: If a non-priest performs one of the sacrificial rites of the priests, his performance is not valid. A non-priest is liable to receive the penalty of death at the hand of Heaven for performing one of the following four rites: Sprinkling the blood, burning the portions of an animal offering or the handful of a meal offering, pouring a wine libation, and pouring a water libation on *Sukkot* (Rambam *Sefer Avoda, Hilkhot Biat HaMikdash* 9:1–2).

Service of an acute mourner – אוֹנֵן בַּעֲבוֹדָה: If a priest serves in the Temple while he is obligated by Torah law to observe the period of acute mourning, he has desecrated the offering in whose sacrifice he has participated, whether it is a communal or an individual offering (Rambam *Sefer Avoda, Hilkhot Biat HaMikdash* 2:6–7).

BACKGROUND

Rav Ḥisda's interpreter [*amora*] – אָמוֹרֵיהּ דְּרַב חִסְדָּא: The literal meaning of the word *amora* is identical to that of the mishnaic Hebrew word *meturgeman*. The interpreter was a Torah scholar who would stand alongside a Sage during his lecture and repeat his words loudly, translating them from Hebrew to Aramaic for the listeners. Often the interpreter would expound a short statement of the Sage, elucidating it for the benefit of the public. It is for this reason that the Sages of the Talmud chose to call themselves *amora'im*; they considered themselves interpreters, so to speak, of the Sages of the Mishna.

Acute mourner – אוֹנֵן: The period of acute mourning is observed on the day of the death of a wife or husband, father, mother, son, daughter, brother, or sister. The mourner is exempt from all positive mitzvot from the time of the death of the close relative until after the burial. At that point, or according to some opinions, the morning after the burial, his status changes from that of an acute mourner to that of a mourner. An ordinary priest is unfit to serve in the Temple while observing the period of acute mourning. A High Priest serves in the Temple even when he is an acute mourner, and his service is valid.

Perek **I**
Daf **14** Amud **b**

שִׁיכּוֹר וּבַעַל מוּם, בְּקַבָּלָה בְּהוֹלָכָה בִּזְרִיקָה – פָּסוּל, וְכֵן יוֹשֵׁב, וְכֵן שְׂמֹאל! תְּיוּבְתָּא.

a drunk priest,[H] **or a blemished**[B] priest[H] performs the rites of **collection, conveying** or **sprinkling**[H] the blood, the offering is **disqualified. And likewise,** it is disqualified if a priest performs any of these rites while **sitting.**[H] **And** this is **likewise** the *halakha* if a priest performs any of these rites with his **left** hand.[H] The Gemara concludes: This is **a conclusive refutation** of Rav Ḥisda's ruling; if a non-priest conveys the blood, it is disqualified.

וְהָא רַב חִסְדָּא קְרָא קָאָמַר.

The Gemara asks: **But didn't Rav Ḥisda state a verse** as proof that the offering is not disqualified? The verse states that the priests sprinkled the blood after receiving it from non-priests.

BACKGROUND

Blemished – בַּעַל מוּם: Certain types of blemishes render a priest unfit to serve in the Temple. The *halakhot* of these blemishes are discussed in tractate *Bekhorot*. Many of the blemishes that render animals unfit as offerings render priests unfit for Temple service (see Leviticus 21:16–24). Although it is prohibited for priests with blemishes to perform the Temple service, they may be employed in certain secondary tasks. One such task is ensuring that the wood for the altar is suitable for the service.

HALAKHA

Service of a drunk priest – שִׁכּוֹר בַּעֲבוֹדָה: It is prohibited for a priest who drank wine to enter the area in the Temple from the altar inward. If he enters this area and serves, his service is not valid, and he is liable to receive the punishment of death at the hand of Heaven. The definition of a priest who drank wine is one who drank at once a quarter-*log* of undiluted wine that is less than forty days old counting from the time it was pressed. He may not serve until the effect of the wine has passed (Rambam *Sefer Avoda, Hilkhot Biat HaMikdash* 1:1, 9:15).

Service of a blemished priest – בַּעַל מוּם בַּעֲבוֹדָה: It is prohibited for a priest who has a blemish to enter the area in the Temple from the altar inward. If he enters this area, he is liable to receive lashes, even if he did not serve. If he serves in the Temple he has desecrated the service, and he is flogged with two sets of lashes, one for entering and one for serving (Rambam *Sefer Avoda, Hilkhot Biat HaMikdash* 6:1, 9:15).

Collection, conveying, or sprinkling – בְּקַבָּלָה בְּהוֹלָכָה בִּזְרִיקָה: If one who is unfit to serve collects the blood of an offering, conveys the blood to the altar, or sprinkles it on the altar in its correct manner, the offering is disqualified (Rambam *Sefer Avoda, Hilkhot Pesulei HaMukdashin* 1:27).

Service while sitting – יוֹשֵׁב בַּעֲבוֹדָה: If one performs one of the sacrificial rites sitting down, his service is not valid. He is not liable to receive lashes, as this prohibition stems from a positive mitzva (Rambam *Sefer Avoda, Hilkhot Biat HaMikdash* 5:17).

Service with one's left hand – עֲבוֹדָה בִּשְׂמֹאל: The Temple service is performed with one's right hand. If one performs a rite with his left hand, his service is not valid. He is not liable to receive lashes, as this prohibition is not explicitly mentioned in the Torah (Rambam *Sefer Avoda, Hilkhot Biat HaMikdash* 5:18 and *Kesef Mishne* there).

דְּעָבִיד מַעֲשֵׂה אִיצְטַבָּא.

The Gemara answers: The verse described a case **where** the non-priests **served as a bench** [*itztaba*].[L] The priests would give the blood to the non-priests to hold it for them and would then take it and sprinkle the blood. The non-priests would not convey the blood to the altar.

רַבָּה וְרַב יוֹסֵף דְּאָמְרִי תַּרְוַיְיהוּ: הוֹלָכָה בְּזָר – מַחְלוֹקֶת רַבִּי שִׁמְעוֹן וְרַבָּנַן; רַבִּי שִׁמְעוֹן דְּאָמַר: עֲבוֹדָה שֶׁאֶפְשָׁר לְבַטְּלָהּ לָאו עֲבוֹדָה הִיא – כְּשֵׁרָה בְּזָר, לְרַבָּנַן – פְּסוּלָה.

Rabba and Rav Yosef both say that the case of **a non-priest conveying** the blood is subject to **a dispute** between **Rabbi Shimon and the Rabbis.** According to **Rabbi Shimon, who says** that **a dispensable rite is not** classified as a true **rite** and therefore does not disqualify the offering if performed with prohibited intent, the offering is **fit** even if the conveying of the blood is performed **by a non-priest. According to the Rabbis,** who hold that a dispensable rite is classified as a true rite, the conveying of the blood is **not valid**[N] if performed by a non-priest.

אֲמַר לֵיהּ אַבָּיֵי: וְהָא שְׁחִיטָה, דַּעֲבוֹדָה שֶׁאִי אֶפְשָׁר לְבַטְּלָהּ, וּכְשֵׁרָה בְּזָר! אֲמַר לֵיהּ: שְׁחִיטָה לָאו עֲבוֹדָה הִיא.

Abaye said to him: But what about **slaughter, which is an indispensable rite, and** yet the offering is **fit** even if it is performed **by a non-priest? He said to** Abaye: **Slaughter,** though indispensable, **is not** classified as a sacrificial **rite** at all. Therefore it need not be performed by a priest.

וְלָא? וְהָאָמַר רַבִּי זֵירָא אָמַר רַב: שְׁחִיטַת פָּרָה בְּזָר – פְּסוּלָה; וְאָמַר רַב עֲלַהּ: ״אֶלְעָזָר״ ״וְחוּקָּה״ כְּתִיב בָּהּ!

The Gemara asks: **And is it not? But doesn't Rabbi Zeira say** that **Rav says:** If **the slaughter of** a red **heifer**[B] is performed **by a non-priest,**[H] it is **not valid? And Rav said about this** *halakha*: It is derived from the phrases: **"Elazar** the priest" (Numbers 19:3), **and: "Statute"** (Numbers 19:2), which **are written with regard to** the red heifer. The mention of Elazar indicates that slaughter must be performed by a priest, and the term "statute" indicates that one may not deviate from any of the details of the service as delineated in the verses. If one does, the heifer is disqualified.

שָׁאנֵי פָּרָה, דְּקָדְשֵׁי בֶּדֶק הַבַּיִת הִיא.

The Gemara answers: The red **heifer is different, as it is** not an offering; it has the sanctity of items **consecrated for Temple maintenance.**[B] The *halakhot* that govern its service therefore differ from those of offerings proper.

וְלָאו כׇּל דְּכֵן הוּא: קׇדְשֵׁי בֶּדֶק הַבַּיִת – הָוְיָא עֲבוֹדָה, קׇדְשֵׁי מִזְבֵּחַ לָאו עֲבוֹדָה הִיא?

The Gemara asks: **But does this not** prove the point **all the more?** If slaughtering an animal **consecrated for Temple maintenance is** tantamount to a sacrificial **rite,** can slaughtering **offerings,** which are sacrificed on the **altar, not be** considered a sacrificial **rite?**

אָמַר רַב שֵׁישָׁא בְּרֵיהּ דְּרַב אִידִי: מִידֵּי דַּהֲוָה אַמַּרְאוֹת נְגָעִים, דְּלָאו עֲבוֹדָה הִיא, וּבָעֲיָא כְּהוּנָּה.

Rav Sheisha, son of Rav Idi, said: The slaughter of a red heifer is considered **just as it is in** the case of **shades of** leprous **marks, which** are deemed ritually pure or impure by a priest. Although this is **not** a sacrificial **rite,** it still **requires** a member of the **priesthood** to perform it. Therefore, the requirement that the red heifer be slaughtered by a priest does not prove that it is classified as a sacrificial rite.

וַהֲרֵי הוֹלָכַת אֵבָרִים לַכֶּבֶשׁ, דַּעֲבוֹדָה שֶׁאֶפְשָׁר לְבַטְּלָהּ הִיא, וּפְסוּלָה בְּזָר, דִּכְתִיב: ״וְהִקְרִיב הַכֹּהֵן אֶת הַכֹּל וְהִקְטִיר הַמִּזְבֵּחָה״, וְאָמַר מָר: זוֹ הוֹלָכַת אֵבָרִים לַכֶּבֶשׁ!

The Gemara further challenges the premise of Rabba and Rav Yosef that a dispensable rite can be performed by a non-priest: **But** what about **conveying** the **limbs** of the offering **to the ramp,**[H] **which is a dispensable rite,** as the offering can be slaughtered next to the ramp? **And** nevertheless, if it is performed **by a non-priest,** the offering is **disqualified, as it is written: "And the priest shall sacrifice the whole, and make it smoke upon the altar"** (Leviticus 1:13); **and the Master says: This** is referring to **conveying** the **limbs to the ramp.**

LANGUAGE

Bench [*itztaba*] – אִצְטַבָּא: The primary source of this word, which appears in several different forms, is the Greek στοά, *stoa*, which has several related definitions: Column, colonnade, shed, and warehouse. The Sages also employed this term in different ways. In this case, the reference is to a type of bench or shelf upon which items are placed.

NOTES

According to the Rabbis the conveying of the blood is not valid – לְרַבָּנַן פְּסוּלָה: Rashi explains that Rabba and Rav Yosef maintain that if a non-priest conveys the blood, the Rabbis deem the offering unfit, as they consider conveying an indispensable rite. Therefore, Abaye challenges this suggestion from the *halakha* that a non-priest can slaughter the offering, despite the fact that this is an indispensable rite. *Tosafot* claim that the offering is disqualified because all sacrificial rites from the collection of the blood onward must be performed by priests (see 32a). Rather, Abaye's objection is to the premise that according to Rabbi Shimon, the fact that conveying is not indispensable renders it unnecessary for it to be performed specifically by a priest. This understanding can be inferred from the wording of the statement of Rabba and Rav Yosef: Whereas they reason that Rabbi Shimon deems the offering fit because conveying is a dispensable rite, they do not state the reason why the Rabbis deem it unfit.

HALAKHA

If the slaughter of a red heifer is performed by a non-priest – שְׁחִיטַת פָּרָה בְּזָר: A red heifer that is slaughtered by a non-priest is fit, as a priest is never required for slaughter, in accordance with the opinion of Shmuel and Rabbi Yoḥanan in tractate *Yoma* 42a (Rambam *Sefer Avoda, Hilkhot Pesulei HaMukdashin* 1:2).

Conveying the limbs to the ramp – הוֹלָכַת אֵיבָרִים לַכֶּבֶשׁ: The limbs of an offering may be conveyed to the altar only by a priest who is fit for service (Rambam *Sefer Avoda, Hilkhot Pesulei HaMukdashin* 1:22).

Burning of the red heifer

BACKGROUND

Red heifer – פָּרָה: To eliminate the ritual impurity imparted by a human corpse, purification is achieved by means of water mixed with the ashes of a red heifer (see Numbers, chapter 19). The hairs of this heifer must be entirely red. Even two black hairs disqualify it for this ritual. Similarly, it may not have any blemishes, nor may it have been used for any labor. The red heifer is slaughtered on the Mount of Olives outside Jerusalem, and its blood is sprinkled seven times in the direction of the Temple. Its body is then burned on a special pyre, to which cedarwood, hyssop, and crimson wool are added (see Numbers 19:6). The ashes from this pyre are then gathered and mixed in a vessel with water drawn from a spring. Three hyssop branches are dipped in the water, which is then sprinkled on the impure individual. A single drop from the mixture suffices to transform him from an impure person to a pure one, and it is insignificant where the water lands on the body in order to purify him.

It has the sanctity of items consecrated for Temple maintenance – קׇדְשֵׁי בֶּדֶק הַבַּיִת הִיא: The red heifer is not considered an offering. This is evidenced by its not being slaughtered in the Temple courtyard but rather on the Mount of Olives. Therefore, the distinction that generally applies to offerings, between sacrificial rites that must be performed by a priest and required actions that may be performed by a non-priest, does not apply. Rather, all of the stages of the rite of the red heifer are similar in this regard and must be performed by a priest. Since the red heifer is consecrated, it certainly has sanctity and a status no lower than that of items consecrated for Temple maintenance. Nevertheless, unlike other items consecrated for Temple maintenance, it is slaughtered for a sacred purpose. Consequently, many of the *halakhot* of offerings also apply to it (Meiri).

הֵיכָא דְּגַלֵּי – גַּלֵּי, וְהֵיכָא דְּלָא גַּלֵּי – לָא גַּלֵּי.

The Gemara answers: In a case **where** the verse explicitly **revealed** that a rite must be performed by a priest, it **revealed** it; **but** in a case **where** the Torah **did not reveal** it, it **did not reveal** it. With regard to conveying the blood, the Torah does not state explicitly that a priest is required.

וְלָאו כׇּל דְּכֵן הוּא: וּמַה הוֹלָכַת אֵבָרִים לַכֶּבֶשׁ, דְּלָא מְעַכְּבָא כַּפָּרָה – בָּעֲיָא כְּהוּנָּה, הוֹלָכַת דָּם דִּמְעַכְּבָא כַּפָּרָה – [לֹא כׇּל שֶׁכֵּן]? (מִיבַּעְיָא).

The Gemara challenges: **But is it not all the more so** obvious? **Just as conveying the limbs to the ramp requires** that the conveyor be a member of the **priesthood,** even though it **does not prevent atonement** if not performed at all, since atonement was already effected by sprinkling the blood, **all the more so** is it **not** clear that concerning **conveying** the **blood** and sprinkling it on the altar, **where** the failure to convey it and sprinkle it on the altar **prevents atonement,** it must be that the conveyor be a member of the priesthood? This difficulty remains unresolved.

אִיתְּמַר נַמִי, אָמַר עוּלָּא אָמַר רַבִּי אֶלְעָזָר: הוֹלָכָה בְּזָר פְּסוּלָה, אֲפִילּוּ לְרַבִּי שִׁמְעוֹן.

It was also stated that **Ulla says** that **Rabbi Elazar says:** In a case where **conveying** the blood is performed **by a non-priest,** the offering is **disqualified, even according to Rabbi Shimon.**[N]

אִיבַּעְיָא לְהוּ: הוֹלָכָה שֶׁלֹּא בָּרֶגֶל, שְׁמָהּ הוֹלָכָה, אוֹ לֹא שְׁמָהּ הוֹלָכָה?

§ **A dilemma was raised before** the Sages: Is **conveying** the blood **not by foot**[H] but rather by passing it by hand to another priest **considered conveying, or is it not considered conveying?** Can the rite be performed in this manner?

תָּא שְׁמַע: וְכֵן יוֹשֵׁב, וְכֵן שְׂמֹאל – פָּסוּל; הָא עוֹמֵד דּוּמְיָא דְּיוֹשֵׁב – כָּשֵׁר.

The Gemara suggests: **Come** and **hear** evidence from the *baraita*: **And likewise,** if the priest collected, conveyed, or sprinkled the blood while **sitting, and likewise,** if he performed any of these rites with his **left** hand, the offering is **disqualified.** Since only sitting is listed, one **consequently** infers that if the priest conveyed the blood while **standing** but in a manner **similar to sitting,** i.e., by outstretching his hand without walking, the offering is **fit.** Evidently, conveying the blood does not require walking.

דִּלְמָא יוֹשֵׁב – דְּקָשָׁיֵיף מֵישָׁף, עוֹמֵד – דּוּמְיָא דְּיוֹשֵׁב, דְּנָיֵיד פּוּרְתָּא.

The Gemara rejects this inference: **Perhaps** when the *baraita* states: **Sitting,** it is referring to one who conveys the blood by moving toward the altar while sitting on the ground in such a manner **that he rubs** himself against the floor of the courtyard as he pulls himself forward. If so, the parallel case of **standing** in a manner **similar to sitting** is a case **where** the priest **moves** forward **a bit.** Perhaps if he does not move at all and merely outstretches his hand, the rite is not valid.

תָּא שְׁמַע: שָׁחַט יִשְׂרָאֵל וְקִבֵּל הַכֹּהֵן, נְתָנוֹ לַחֲבֵירוֹ, וַחֲבֵרוֹ לַחֲבֵירוֹ.

The Gemara suggests: **Come** and **hear** a proof from a mishna (*Pesaḥim* 64a): **An Israelite would slaughter** the Paschal offering, **and a priest would collect**[H] the blood. The priests would be lined up from the place where the lamb was slaughtered until the altar. The priest who collected the blood would immediately **hand it to another** priest standing next to him, **and the other** priest would pass it **to another,** and so forth, until it would reach the altar. Evidently, the blood can be passed from hand to hand; it need not be conveyed by foot.

הָתָם נַמִי, דְּנָיְידִי פּוּרְתָּא. וּמַאי קָא מַשְׁמַע לַן? ״בְּרׇב עָם הַדְרַת מֶלֶךְ״.

The Gemara answers: **There, too,** the priests **would move a bit** with their feet while passing the blood forward. The Gemara asks: **But what is** the mishna **teaching us** in this description, if not that the blood need not be conveyed by foot? The Gemara answers: It teaches that: **"In the multitude of people is the king's glory"** (Proverbs 14:28). It honors God when the Temple service is performed by a multitude of priests.

תָּא שְׁמַע: קִבֵּל הַכָּשֵׁר וְנָתַן לַפָּסוּל – יַחֲזִיר לַכָּשֵׁר.

The Gemara suggests: **Come** and **hear** another resolution from a mishna (32a): If a priest who is **fit** for Temple service **collected**[H] the blood in a vessel **and gave** it **to an unfit** individual standing next to the altar, that individual **should return** it **to the fit** priest,[N] so that he may perform a complete act of conveying the blood to the altar. Evidently, the blood must be conveyed to the altar by foot. If conveying by hand were valid, another priest could simply take the blood from the unfit person and complete the conveying of the blood to the altar.

NOTES

Even according to Rabbi Shimon – אֲפִילּוּ לְרַבִּי שִׁמְעוֹן: Rashi explains that Rabbi Shimon concedes that conveying is classified as a sacrificial rite of the priests. Therefore, if it is performed by a non-priest, the offering is disqualified. Nevertheless, conveying the blood with prohibited intent does not disqualify the offering, as this rite is not necessary for rendering the offering permitted for consumption (see 13a).

That individual should return it to the fit priest – יַחֲזִיר לַכָּשֵׁר: Rashi explains that there are two proofs from this mishna that conveying the blood by hand is not valid. One proof is from the fact that the blood must be returned to the location where it was collected; apparently, the act of giving the blood to the unfit individual was not valid, as it was performed by hand. Secondly, if the unfit individual can return the blood to the priest without disqualifying it, despite the *halakha* that a non-priest who conveys the blood disqualifies the offering, then apparently conveying the blood by hand is not considered performance of the rite of conveying. The Gemara's response is that in fact, the mishna is saying that the fit priest should take back the blood from the unfit person himself, and convey it to the altar without necessarily returning it to the place where the animal was slaughtered.

HALAKHA

Conveying not by foot – הוֹלָכָה שֶׁלֹּא בָּרֶגֶל: Conveying the blood not by foot is not considered performance of the rite of conveying. Therefore, if a priest collects the blood and sprinkles it on the altar from his location, without walking with it to the altar, the offering is disqualified, as the mitzva of conveying was not performed, in accordance with the opinion of Rabbi Yoḥanan (Rambam *Sefer Avoda*, *Hilkhot Pesulei HaMukdashin* 1:23).

An Israelite would slaughter and a priest would collect, etc. – שָׁחַט יִשְׂרָאֵל וְקִבֵּל הַכֹּהֵן וכו׳: After the Paschal offering is slaughtered, a priest collects the blood and hands it to another priest, who then hands it to another priest, allowing many priests to participate in the mitzva. Every priest moves slightly with his feet while passing the blood, in accordance with the conclusion of the Gemara (Rambam *Sefer Korbanot*, *Hilkhot Korban Pesaḥ* 1:14 and *Leḥem Mishne* there).

If a priest who is fit for service collected, etc. – קִבֵּל הַכָּשֵׁר וכו׳: If a fit priest collected the blood and handed it to an unfit person, and the unfit person did not walk with it but remained in his position, he should return it to the fit priest, and the offering is still fit (Rambam *Sefer Korbanot*, *Hilkhot Pesulei HaMukdashin* 1:27 and *Leḥem Mishne* there).

אֵימָא: יַחֲזוֹר הַכָּשֵׁר וִיקַבְּלֶנּוּ.

The Gemara rejects this inference: **Say** that the wording of the mishna should be emended; instead of stating that the unfit person should return the vessel to the fit priest, it should state that **the fit** priest, even another priest, **should then receive it** from the unfit person. If so, the mishna proves nothing about conveying by hand.

אִיתְּמַר, אָמַר עוּלָּא אָמַר רַבִּי יוֹחָנָן: הוֹלָכָה שֶׁלֹּא בָּרֶגֶל – לֹא שְׁמָהּ הוֹלָכָה.

It was stated: Ulla says that **Rabbi Yoḥanan says: Conveying** the blood **not by foot is not considered conveying.**

Perek **I**
Daf **15** Amud **a**

אֶפְשָׁר לְתַקּוֹנָהּ, אוֹ לָא אֶפְשָׁר לְתַקּוֹנָהּ?

The Gemara asks: If the blood was conveyed by hand, is it **possible to correct it**[H] by conveying it again properly, **or** is it **not possible to correct it,** and the offering is disqualified permanently?

תָּא שְׁמַע: קִבֵּל הַכָּשֵׁר וְנָתַן לְפָסוּל – יַחְזִיר לְכָשֵׁר.

The Gemara suggests: **Come** and **hear** proof from the aforementioned mishna: If a priest **fit** for Temple service **collected** the blood in a vessel **and gave** the vessel **to an unfit** person standing next to the altar, the latter **should return** it **to the fit** priest. Apparently, even after the blood is conveyed in an inappropriate manner, it can be corrected.

וְנִהֲי נַמִי דְּיַחֲזוֹר הַכָּשֵׁר וִיקַבְּלֶנּוּ, אִי סָלְקָא דַּעְתָּךְ לָא אֶפְשָׁר לְתַקּוֹנָהּ, אִיפַּסְלָא לַהּ!

And though one can **indeed** explain **that the fit** priest **should then receive it** from him, as posited above, **if it enters your mind** that if the blood is conveyed incorrectly it is **not possible to correct it,** the offering **was** already **disqualified** when the priest gave the blood to the unfit person. Taking it back is of no consequence.

מִי סָבְרַתְּ דְּקָאֵי זָר גַּוַּאי, לָא, דְּקָאֵי זָר בָּרַאי.

The Gemara rejects this inference: **Do you maintain that** this is referring to a case where the **non-priest is standing inside,** between the fit priest and the altar? **No,** it is a case **where** the **non-priest is standing outside,** farther away from the altar than the priest. Therefore, when the priest gave him the blood, he was not conveying it toward the altar at all; he was moving it farther away from the altar.

אִיתְּמַר, אָמַר עוּלָּא אָמַר רַבִּי יוֹחָנָן: הוֹלָכָה שֶׁלֹּא בָּרֶגֶל – פְּסוּלָה; אַלְמָא לָא אֶפְשָׁר לְתַקּוֹנָהּ.

It was stated: Ulla says that **Rabbi Yoḥanan says: Conveying** the blood **not by foot** renders the offering **unfit. Apparently, it is not possible to correct it,** as otherwise Rabbi Yoḥanan would have merely stated that it is not considered conveying, as in his earlier statement (14b).

אֵיתִיבֵיהּ רַב נַחְמָן לְעוּלָּא: נִשְׁפַּךְ מִן הַכְּלִי עַל הָרִצְפָּה וַאֲסָפוֹ – כָּשֵׁר!

Rav Naḥman raised an objection to Ulla from a mishna (32a): If the blood **spilled from the vessel onto the floor**[H] **and one collected it** from the floor, it is **fit** for sacrifice. Apparently, although spilling the blood on the floor constitutes a not valid conveying toward the altar, it can still be corrected after the fact.

הָכָא בְּמַאי עָסְקִינַן – כְּשֶׁיָּצָא לַחוּץ.

The Gemara explains: **Here we are dealing with** a case **where** the blood that spilled **went outward,** i.e., away from the altar, so it did not constitute conveying at all.

לְבָרַאי נָפֵיק, לְגַוַּאי לָא עָיֵיל? בִּמְקוֹם מִדְרוֹן. אִיבָּעֵית אֵימָא: בְּגוּמָּא, וְאִיבָּעֵית אֵימָא: בִּסְמִיכָא.

The Gemara asks: Can spilled blood **go outward** and **not come inward?** Clearly, spilled blood spreads to all sides. The Gemara answers: It is a case where the blood spilled **on an inclined plane,** and it therefore spilled only outward, away from the altar. **And if you wish, say** instead that it spilled **into a hole** in the ground, so it did not spread in any direction. **And if you wish, say** instead that it is a case **where** the blood is **thick,** so it did not spread in all directions.

HALAKHA

Possible to correct it – אֶפְשָׁר לְתַקּוֹנָהּ: The Rambam does not rule in this case explicitly. The *Kesef Mishne* explains that the Rambam accepts the opinion of Rabbi Yoḥanan that the offering is permanently disqualified, as he rules in that manner with regard to a case where a non-priest conveys the blood (*Mishne LaMelekh*). The *Leḥem Mishne* claims that the two cases are not comparable, as conveying by hand is a meaningless action, and should not disqualify the offering permanently; rather, it can be corrected by conveying the blood again properly, in accordance with the conclusion of the Gemara. The later authorities agree with this opinion (Rambam *Sefer Avoda, Hilkhot Pesulei HaMukdashin* 1:27).

Spilled from the vessel onto the floor – נִשְׁפַּךְ מִן הַכְּלִי עַל הָרִצְפָּה: If the blood spilled from the vessel onto the floor, and one collected it from the floor, it is fit (Rambam *Sefer Avoda, Hilkhot Pesulei HaMukdashin* 1:25).

LANGUAGE

Go to all that trouble [*ikhpal*] – **אִיכְּפַל**: It appears from Rashi's commentary elsewhere (see *Shabbat* 5a) that the word *ikhpal* is an extension of the root *alef*, *kaf*, *peh*, meaning to make a strenuous effort. Some explain the word *ikhpat*, or care, as deriving from the same root.

וְאִיכְּפַל תַּנָּא לְאַשְׁמוֹעִינַן כָּל הָנֵי? וְעוֹד, אַדְּתָנֵי בְּאִידָּךְ פִּירְקִין: נִשְׁפַּךְ עַל הָרִצְפָּה וַאֲסָפוֹ פָּסוּל; לִיפְלוֹג בְּדִידֵיהּ: בַּמֶּה דְּבָרִים אֲמוּרִים – כְּשֶׁיָּצָא לַחוּץ, אֲבָל נִכְנַס לִפְנִים – פָּסוּל! תְּיוּבְתָּא.

The Gemara asks: **But did the** ***tanna*** **go to all that trouble** [*ikhpal*][LN] just **to teach us all these** unlikely cases? **And furthermore, rather than teaching in another chapter** (see 25a) that if the blood **spilled** from the animal's neck **onto the floor and one collected it** in a vessel from the floor it is **unfit, let** the mishna **teach a distinction within** the case where the blood spilled from the vessel **itself: In what** case **is this statement,** that the blood is fit, **said?** In a case **where** the spilled blood **went outward,** away from the altar, **but** if it **came inward** it is **unfit.** The Gemara concludes: This is **a conclusive refutation;** if the blood is conveyed in a not valid manner, it can be corrected.

אִתְּמַר: הוֹלָכָה שֶׁלֹּא בָּרֶגֶל מַחֲלוֹקֶת רַבִּי שִׁמְעוֹן וְרַבָּנַן. בְּהוֹלָכָה רַבָּתִי – דְּכוּלֵּי עָלְמָא לָא פְּלִיגִי דִּפְסוּלָה, כִּי פְּלִיגִי – בְּהוֹלָכָה זוּטַרְתִּי.

§ **It was stated:** The **dispute** in the mishna (13a) between **Rabbi Shimon and the Rabbis** as to whether improper intent while conveying the blood disqualifies the offering is only with regard to **conveying** the blood **not by foot.**[N] **With regard to greater conveying,** i.e., conveying the blood by moving the feet, **everyone agrees that** if one performs it with prohibited intent, the offering is **unfit. When they disagree,** it is **with regard to lesser conveying,** i.e., conveying the blood by hand without moving the feet, in a case where the offering was slaughtered next to the altar.

מַחְכוּ עֲלַהּ בְּמַעֲרָבָא: אֶלָּא חַטַּאת הָעוֹף דִּפְסוּלָה בָּהּ מַחֲשָׁבָה, לְרַבִּי שִׁמְעוֹן הֵיכִי מַשְׁכַּחַתְּ לַהּ? אִי דַּחֲשִׁיב עֲלַהּ מִקַּמֵּי דְּלֵיפּוֹק דָּם – לָאו כְּלוּם הִיא, וְאִי בָּתַר דִּנְפַק דָּם – אִיתְעֲבִידָא לֵיהּ מִצְוָתוֹ!

They laughed at this statement[N] **in the West,** Eretz Yisrael, saying: **But** if so, one encounters difficulty with regard to **a bird sin offering,**[N] **which** is killed through pinching its nape on the altar and whose blood is sprinkled directly from its neck. It is known that if one sprinkled its blood with prohibited **intent,** the offering is **unfit. And according to Rabbi Shimon,** who holds that prohibited intent while conveying the blood by hand does not disqualify the offering, **how can you find these** circumstances?[N] **If** the priest **has** prohibited **intent with regard to** the offering **before** the **blood comes out** of the bird, this intent **is nothing,** since his waving it is like conveying by hand. **And if** he has such intent **after the blood came out, its mitzva was** already **performed,** as the blood already reached the altar.

NOTES

But did the ***tanna*** **go to all that trouble, etc.** – **וְאִיכְּפַל תַּנָּא וכו׳**: Although it is possible for the blood to spill on an inclined plane or in a hole, or for the blood to be thick, it is unlikely that the mishna was referring to these unusual cases without specification; the floor of the Temple courtyard is generally flat and straight, and blood that spills out of a slaughtered animal is liquid. Although the Gemara often interprets statements of the Mishna in reference to specific cases, this is done only when necessary, and only in reference to common cases.

Conveying not by foot – **הוֹלָכָה שֶׁלֹּא בָּרֶגֶל**: The commentaries find this discussion difficult to understand. The various possible interpretations are discussed extensively in *Mishne LaMelekh*. According to Rashi, and apparently the Rambam too, the dispute in the mishna is specifically with regard to a case where the offering was slaughtered next to the altar, so conveying the blood by foot is unnecessary. But in a case where the offering was not slaughtered next to the altar, they agree that prohibited intent while conveying the blood to the altar by foot disqualifies the offering, as in this case, conveying is necessary. According to this interpretation, major and minor conveying refer to conveying by foot and by hand, respectively.

Rabbeinu Peretz (see *Shita Mekubbetzet*) agrees that the Gemara distinguishes between a case where the offering was slaughtered next to the altar and a case where it was slaughtered farther away. He maintains that both major and minor conveying refer to conveying by foot. Rabbi Shimon holds that in a case where the offering was slaughtered next to the altar, since conveying the blood by foot is unnecessary, and conveying it by hand is not a sacrificial rite that can cause the offering to be disqualified due to prohibited intent, even if the priest conveys the blood by foot, the offering cannot be disqualified. The Rabbis hold that conveying the blood by hand is a valid manner of conveying, and therefore the offering can be disqualified due to prohibited intent. This suggestion is raised in *Mishne LaMelekh* as well.

In *Panim Meirot* it is suggested that both major and minor conveying refer to conveying not by foot. Minor conveying refers to a case where the offering was slaughtered next to the altar, so that conveying by foot is unnecessary. The Rabbis hold that since conveying by hand is valid in this case, if one does so with prohibited intent, the offering is disqualified, whereas Rabbi Shimon maintains that the offering is not disqualified, as the rite of conveying refers to conveying by foot. Major conveying refers to a case where it is necessary to walk the blood to the altar, but one conveys it to the altar not by foot. In this case, Rabbi Shimon concedes that the offering is disqualified, as the requirement of conveying was not fulfilled.

They laughed at this statement – **מַחְכוּ עֲלַהּ**: This expression is attributed to certain *amora'im* in Eretz Yisrael (see *Sanhedrin* 17b) who would occasionally treat a halakhic statement with disdain, assuming that it was not thoroughly examined.

Bird sin offering – **חַטַּאת הָעוֹף**: The blood of a bird sin offering is not collected in a vessel; rather, the priest pinches its nape next to the altar and then sprinkles its blood on the altar by holding its body and waving it. The rest of the blood is squeezed out onto the base of the altar. As explained in the Gemara (65a), a bird sin offering is disqualified due to prohibited intent during the performance of two rites: Pinching its nape and squeezing out its blood. The latter rite includes the sprinkling of its blood.

How can you find these circumstances – **הֵיכִי מַשְׁכַּחַתְּ לַהּ**: This is difficult only according to the suggestion that Rabbi Shimon holds that conveying by hand is not disqualified due to prohibited intent. If Rabbi Shimon disagrees with the Rabbis with regard to conveying by foot, but maintains that conveying by hand is considered a sacrificial rite and prohibited intent disqualifies it, the *halakha* is the same with regard to waving a bird sin offering to sprinkle its blood on the altar.

מַאי קוּשְׁיָא? דִּלְמָא מִדְּפָרֵישׁ וְעַד דְּמָטֵא לַמִּזְבֵּחַ.

The Gemara asks: **What is the difficulty? Perhaps** the offering is disqualified due to prohibited intent **from** the moment the blood **leaves** the bird **until** the moment **it reaches the altar.**

דְּהָא בְּעָא מִינֵּיהּ רַבִּי יִרְמְיָה מֵרַבִּי זֵירָא: הָיָה מַזֶּה, וְנִקְטְעָה יָדוֹ שֶׁל מַזֶּה עַד שֶׁלֹּא הִגִּיעַ דָּם לַאֲוִיר הַמִּזְבֵּחַ, מַהוּ? וַאֲמַר לֵיהּ: פְּסוּלָה, מַאי טַעְמָא? ״וְהִזָּה...וְנָתַן״ בָּעֵינַן!

This is as **Rabbi Yirmeya asked Rabbi Zeira:** If the priest **was sprinkling** the blood, **and the hand of the one sprinkling was severed**[H] **before** the **blood reached the airspace of the altar, what is** the *halakha*? Is the sprinkling not valid since it was performed by a blemished priest, or is it valid because the blood left the bird before he was blemished? **And** Rabbi Zeira **said to him:** It is **not valid. What is the reason? We require** that the verse: **"And sprinkle** of the blood" (Leviticus 4:6), be fulfilled in the same manner as the verse that follows it: **"And** the priest shall **place**[N] of the blood upon the corners of the altar" (Leviticus 4:7), namely, that the blood reach the altar. Therefore, the blood can be disqualified anytime until it reaches the altar, whether through the priest becoming blemished or through prohibited intent.

כִּי אֲתוֹ רַב פָּפָּא וְרַב הוּנָא בְּרֵיהּ דְּרַב יְהוֹשֻׁעַ מִבֵּי רַב, אָמְרִי: הַיְינוּ חוּכָא, וּבְהוֹלָכָה רַבָּתִי לָא פְּלִיגִי? וְהָא כִּי פְּלִיגִי – בְּהוֹלָכָה רַבָּתִי פְּלִיגִי!

When Rav Pappa and Rav Huna, son of Rav Yehoshua, came from the study hall, they said: This is the reason for **the laughter** of the scholars of Eretz Yisrael: **With regard to greater conveying,** i.e., conveying by foot, can one say Rabbi Shimon and the Rabbis **do not disagree?** Clearly, **when they disagree** in the mishna, **they disagree with regard to greater conveying,** as Rabbi Shimon reasons that conveying is a dispensable rite. Only conveying by foot is dispensable, since even if the offering is slaughtered next to the altar, the priest will need to move its blood somewhat with his hand.

אֶלָּא, בְּהוֹלָכָה זוּטַרְתִּי – כּוּלֵּי עָלְמָא לָא פְּלִיגִי דְּלָא פָּסְלָה, כִּי פְּלִיגִי – בְּהוֹלָכָה רַבָּתִי.

Rather, the statement under discussion should be emended to say: **With regard to lesser conveying,** i.e., conveying the blood by hand, **everyone agrees that it does not disqualify**[N] the offering due to prohibited intent. **When they disagree,** it is **with regard to greater conveying,** i.e., conveying the blood for a distance by foot. Rabbi Shimon holds that improper intent even then does not disqualify the offering, as the rite is dispensable, and the Rabbis maintain that it does disqualify it.

הוֹלִיכוֹ זָר, וְהֶחֱזִירוֹ כֹּהֵן וְחָזַר וְהוֹלִיכוֹ – פְּלִיגִי בַּהּ בְּנֵי רַבִּי חִיָּיא וְרַבִּי יַנַּאי, חַד אָמַר: כָּשֵׁר, וְחַד אָמַר: פָּסוּל. מָר סָבַר: אֶפְשָׁר לְתַקּוֹנָה, וּמָר סָבַר: לָא אֶפְשָׁר לְתַקּוֹנָה.

§ If **a non-priest conveyed** the blood to the altar, **and a priest returned it**[H] to its original location, **and** a priest then **conveyed it again** to the altar, **the sons of Rabbi Ḥiyya and Rabbi Yannai disagree with regard to** the *halakha*. **One says** that the offering is **fit, and one says** it is **unfit.** This is because one **Sage holds** that if the blood is conveyed improperly, it is **possible to correct it, and** one **Sage holds** that it is **not possible to correct it.**

הוֹלִיכוֹ כֹּהֵן וְהֶחֱזִירוֹ, וְחָזַר וְהוֹלִיכוֹ זָר, אָמַר רַב שִׁימִי בַּר אַשִׁי: לְדִבְרֵי הַמַּכְשִׁיר – פָּסוּל, לְדִבְרֵי הַפּוֹסֵל – מַכְשִׁיר.

If **a priest conveyed it** to the altar, **and** then **returned it, and a non-priest** then **conveyed it again, Rav Shimi bar Ashi says: According to the statement of the one who deems** the offering **fit** in the previous case, where a non-priest conveyed it the first time and a priest conveyed it the second time, in this case the offering is **unfit,** as a non-priest conveyed it the second time. **According to the statement of the one who deems** the offering **unfit** in the previous case, as a non-priest conveyed it the first time, in this case, where a priest conveyed it the first time, **he deems** the offering **fit.**

רָבָא אָמַר: אַף לְדִבְרֵי הַפּוֹסֵל פָּסוּל. מַאי טַעְמָא – דְּהָא צָרִיךְ

Rava says: Even according to the statement of the one who deems the offering **unfit** in a case where a non-priest conveyed it the first time, it is **unfit** in this case as well, where a priest conveyed it the first time and a non-priest conveyed it the second time. **What is the reason? Because** after the blood is returned to its original location, **it is necessary**

NOTES

And sprinkle, and place – וְהִזָּה וְנָתַן: These verses are stated with regard to the sin offering of the anointed priest: "And the priest shall dip his finger in the blood, and sprinkle of the blood seven times before the Lord, in front of the Curtain of the Sanctuary. And the priest shall place of the blood upon the corners of the altar of sweet incense before the Lord" (Leviticus 4:6–7). It is derived from the juxtaposition of the two verses that just as blood must be placed on the altar of incense, so too, the blood that is sprinkled must actually reach the curtain. It is further derived that the same *halakha* applies to a bird sin offering: When its blood is sprinkled on the external altar, it must actually reach the altar.

Everyone agrees that it does not disqualify – כּוּלֵּי עָלְמָא לָא פְּלִיגִי דְּלָא פָּסְלָה: Rashi emends the text so that is reads: Everyone agrees that it disqualifies. He explains that because minor conveying is indispensable, it is considered a complete sacrificial rite, and prohibited intent while performing it therefore disqualifies the offering. Later commentaries note that this conclusion contradicts the Rambam's ruling that it is required to convey the blood by foot. Rashi explains the Gemara according to the standard version of the text as well: Everyone agrees that minor conveying does not disqualify the offering due to prohibited intent, as it is too minor an act to be considered a separate rite; it is actually part of the rite of sprinkling.

HALAKHA

The hand of the one sprinkling was severed – נִקְטְעָה יָדוֹ שֶׁל מַזֶּה: If the hand of the one sprinkling the blood is severed before the blood reaches the airspace of the altar, the sprinkling is not valid, in accordance with the opinion of Rabbi Zeira (Rambam *Sefer Avoda, Hilkhot Pesulei HaMukdashin* 2:7).

A non-priest conveyed the blood and a priest returned it – הוֹלִיכוֹ זָר וְהֶחֱזִירוֹ כֹּהֵן: If a fit priest collected the blood and handed it to an unfit person, and the latter did not walk with it but rather remained in his position, he should return it to the fit priest, and the offering is still fit. If the unfit person conveyed the blood, even if he then brought it back to the fit priest, and the latter conveyed it again, the offering is disqualified, as a not valid conveying cannot be corrected, in accordance with the opinion of Rava. If a fit priest conveyed the blood initially, but then brought it back and gave it to an unfit person, who then conveyed it again, the offering is disqualified (Rambam *Sefer Avoda, Hilkhot Pesulei HaMukdashin* 1:27).

HALAKHA

Unnecessary conveying – הִילּוּךְ שֶׁאֵין צָרִיךְ לְהַלֵּךְ: Conveying the blood is a sacrificial rite during which prohibited intent disqualifies the offering, even when it is unnecessary. For example, if the one who collected the blood then took it farther away from the altar and meanwhile had in mind that the offering would be consumed after its designated time, it is disqualified. This is in accordance with the opinion of the first *tanna* in the mishna, according to the Gemara's understanding at the end of the discussion (Rambam *Sefer Avoda, Hilkhot Pesulei HaMukdashin* 13:9, and Ra'avad and *Mishne LaMelekh* there).

NOTES

If this *baraita* is taught it is taught – אִי תַּנְיָא תַּנְיָא: Although Abaye's inference is not taught explicitly in the *baraita*, Rava concedes that it is correct, as though it were taught explicitly. According to another version of the text, Abaye's inference is, in fact, explicit in the *baraita*.

Rashi writes that according to this *baraita*, there is no dispute between the Rabbis and Rabbi Eliezer. Both agree that any conveying toward the altar is considered a sacrificial rite and can cause the offering to be disqualified due to prohibited intent, whereas conveying in the opposite direction is not considered a sacrificial rite. Rabbi Eliezer's statement in the mishna is merely stated in contrast to the opinion of Rabbi Shimon that prohibited intent during the conveying of the blood does not disqualify the offering.

The Rambam writes that prohibited intent disqualifies the offering even while conveying the blood away from the altar. He clearly maintains that the Rabbis do not accept Rabbi Eliezer's distinction. This is indicated by the fact that the first *tanna* in the mishna renders conveying in general a rite during which the offering can be disqualified (*Korban Aharon* on *Torat Kohanim*).

לְאַמְטוּיֵיהּ.

to bring it again. Therefore, the second conveying must also be performed by a priest.

אֲמַר לֵיהּ רַבִּי יִרְמְיָה לְרַב אַשִׁי: הָכִי אֲמַר רַב יִרְמְיָה מִדִּיפְתִּי, הָא צָרִיךְ לְאַמְטוּיֵיהּ – מַחְלוֹקֶת רַבִּי אֱלִיעֶזֶר וְרַבָּנַן.

Rabbi Yirmeya said to Rav Ashi: This is what **Rav Yirmeya of Difti said** when he stated **that it is necessary to bring** the blood to the altar again, and that therefore the second conveying is considered a sacrificial rite and must be performed by a priest: He meant that this principle is subject to **a dispute** between **Rabbi Eliezer and the Rabbis.**

דִּתְנַן, רַבִּי אֱלִיעֶזֶר אוֹמֵר: הַמְהַלֵּךְ בְּמָקוֹם שֶׁצָּרִיךְ לְהַלֵּךְ – מַחְשָׁבָה פּוֹסֶלֶת, מָקוֹם שֶׁאֵין צָרִיךְ לְהַלֵּךְ – אֵין מַחְשָׁבָה פּוֹסֶלֶת.

This is **as we learned** in the mishna (13a): **Rabbi Eliezer says:** With regard to **one who conveys** the blood **in a situation where he is required to convey** it, prohibited **intent** while conveying it **disqualifies** the offering. If he conveys the blood **in a situation where he is not required to convey** it, prohibited **intent** while conveying it **does not disqualify** the offering.

וְאָמַר רָבָא: הַכֹּל מוֹדִים, קִבְּלוֹ בַּחוּץ וְהִכְנִיסוֹ בִּפְנִים – זֶהוּ הִילּוּךְ שֶׁצָּרִיךְ לְהַלֵּךְ. קִבְּלוֹ בִּפְנִים וְהוֹצִיאוֹ לַחוּץ – זֶהוּ הִילּוּךְ שֶׁאֵין צָרִיךְ לְהַלֵּךְ.

And Rava says: All of the *tanna'im* **concede** that if one **collected** the blood **outside,** i.e., at a distance from the altar, **and he brought it inside,** close to the altar, **that is** considered **necessary conveying. If** one **collected it inside and took it outside, that is** considered **unnecessary conveying.**[H]

לֹא נֶחְלְקוּ אֶלָּא כְּשֶׁהִכְנִיסוֹ וְחָזַר וְהוֹצִיאוֹ, מָר סָבַר: הָא צָרִיךְ לְאַמְטוּיֵיהּ, וּמָר סָבַר: לָאו כְּהִילּוּךְ הַצָּרִיךְ לַעֲבוֹדָה דָּמֵי.

They disagree only with regard to a case **where he brought it in and took it out again.** One **Sage,** the first *tanna,* **holds** that since **it is necessary to bring it** back to the altar, it is considered necessary conveying, and prohibited intent while performing it disqualifies the offering. **And** one **Sage,** Rabbi Eliezer, **holds** that since the rite of conveying to the altar was already performed, **it is not considered conveying that is necessary for the** sacrificial **service,** and prohibited intent while performing it does not disqualify the offering. Apparently, the same dispute applies to a case where a non-priest conveyed the blood the second time.

אֵיתִיבֵיהּ אַבָּיֵי, רַבִּי אֱלִיעֶזֶר אוֹמֵר: הַמְהַלֵּךְ מָקוֹם שֶׁצָּרִיךְ לְהַלֵּךְ – מַחְשָׁבָה פּוֹסֶלֶת, כֵּיצַד? קִבְּלוֹ בַּחוּץ וְהִכְנִיסוֹ לִפְנִים – זֶהוּ הִילּוּךְ שֶׁצָּרִיךְ לְהַלֵּךְ, קִבְּלוֹ בִּפְנִים וְהוֹצִיאוֹ לַחוּץ – זֶהוּ הִילּוּךְ שֶׁאֵין צָרִיךְ לֵילֵךְ; וְהָא חָזַר וְהִכְנִיסוֹ, הִילּוּךְ שֶׁצָּרִיךְ לְהַלֵּךְ הוּא!

Abaye raised an objection to Rava's interpretation from a *baraita*: **Rabbi Eliezer says:** With regard to **one who conveys** the blood **in a situation where he is required to convey** it, prohibited **intent** while conveying it **disqualifies** the offering. **How so? If** one **collected** the blood **outside,** at a distance from the altar, **and he brought it inside,** close to the altar, **that is** considered **necessary conveying.** If one **collected it inside and took it outside, that is** considered **unnecessary conveying. And consequently,** one infers that if **he brought it in again, it is** considered **necessary conveying** even according to Rabbi Eliezer.

אֲמַר לֵיהּ: אִי תַּנְיָא – תַּנְיָא.

Rava said to him: If this *baraita* **is taught, it is taught,**[N] and I cannot disagree with it.

הדרן עלך כל הזבחים

Summary of **Perek I**

The central topic of the chapter is the status of offerings sacrificed for the sake of the wrong type of offering, or for the wrong person. Any offering sacrificed in this manner does not satisfy its owner's obligation, and the owner is required to bring another offering; this applies to communal as well as individual offerings. Most offerings are not completely disqualified due to the prohibited intent of the one sacrificing them, and their sacrificial process continues. The sacrificial portions of the offering are burned on the altar, its meat is eaten by those fit to eat it, and its hide is given to the priests. These *halakhot* are all derived from verses in the Torah that discuss peace offerings. Sin offerings and Paschal offerings are completely disqualified if they are sacrificed for the sake of the wrong type of offering, as derived from other verses that address these offerings specifically.

Prohibited intent affects the status of an offering only while one is performing one of four necessary sacrificial rites: Slaughter, collecting the blood, conveying the blood to the altar, and presenting it on the altar. If one performs one of the first three rites with intent that the blood be presented for the sake of the wrong type of offering, or for the wrong person, the status of the offering is also affected: It does not satisfy the obligation of the one who brought it, and if it is a sin offering or a Paschal offering, it is disqualified. This is the *halakha* even if the blood is not ultimately sprinkled with the wrong intent.

The status of the offering is affected even in a case where only part of a rite was performed with prohibited intent and the rest of the same rite was performed with the proper intent.

Image **Credits**

All images are copyright © Koren Publishers Jerusalem Ltd., except:

p1 © HaRav Menachem Makover, courtesy of *Harenu Bevinyano*; **p14** left image © Michael Caviglia; **p14** right image © Myrabella; **p18** both images © **courtesy of the Temple Institute**; **p48** © hopenfox; **p67** © **courtesy of the Temple Institute**; **p74** © **courtesy of the Temple Institute**, and Koren Publishers Jerusalem Ltd.; **p81** © HaRav Menachem Makover, courtesy of *Harenu Bevinyano*.

My Notes

My Notes

My Notes

My Notes

Koren Talmud Bavli

THE NOÉ EDITION

ZEVAḤIM

Steinsaltz Center

KOREN

תלמוד בבלי

הוצאת קורן ירושלים

מהדורת נאה

מסכת זבחים

דף ב. עד דף טו:

COMMENTARY BY

Rabbi Adin Even-Israel
Steinsaltz

EDITOR-IN-CHIEF

Rabbi Dr Tzvi Hersh Weinreb

EXECUTIVE EDITOR

Rabbi Joshua Schreier

•

STEINSALTZ CENTER
KOREN PUBLISHERS JERUSALEM

עין משפט נר מצוה

א א מיי' פט"ו מהל' פסה"מ הל"א סמג לאוין שלו:
ב ב מיי' שם הל"ג:

גליון הש"ס

מתני' חוץ מן הפסח. עיין מנחות דף מח ע"ב תוס' ד"ה כבשי: **תוס'** ד"ה כל וכו' ובפ' המפקיד פירשתי. עיין לקמן דף ד' ע"ב תוס' ד"ה מחשבה ודף מא ע"ב רש"י ד"ה כגון שנתן ובמנחות דף ב ע"ב רש"י ד"ה אבל מחשבה למינכרא ובפסחים דף סג ע"א תוס' ד"ה ר"מ סבר ובחולין דף לט ע"א תוס' ד"ה אלא זביחה:

וגי' רש"ק נמי פריך בפירקין כו' מנא לן דהא מיירי בהן כו' וגי' נ"ק ולהכי נמי לא מפרש בפירקין הנך כו'

כל

מתני' *הַזְּבָחִים אשֶׁנִּזְבְּחוּ שֶׁלֹּא לִשְׁמָן – כְּשֵׁרִים, א] אֶלָּא שֶׁלֹּא עָלוּ לַבְּעָלִים לְשֵׁם חוֹבָה, בחוּץ מִן הַפֶּסַח וְהַחַטָּאת, ב] הַפֶּסַח בִּזְמַנּוֹ, וְהַחַטָּאת בְּכָל זְמַן; רַבִּי אֱלִיעֶזֶר אוֹמֵר: אַף הָאָשָׁם, הַפֶּסַח בִּזְמַנּוֹ, וְהַחַטָּאת וְהָאָשָׁם בְּכָל זְמַן. אָמַר רַבִּי אֱלִיעֶזֶר: הַחַטָּאת בָּאָה עַל חֵטְא וְהָאָשָׁם בָּא עַל חֵטְא, מַה חַטָּאת פְּסוּלָה שֶׁלֹּא לִשְׁמָהּ, אַף הָאָשָׁם פָּסוּל שֶׁלֹּא לִשְׁמוֹ. *יוֹסֵי בֶּן חוֹנִי אוֹמֵר: הַנִּשְׁחָטִין לְשֵׁם פֶּסַח וּלְשֵׁם חַטָּאת – פְּסוּלִין; שִׁמְעוֹן אֲחִי עֲזַרְיָה אוֹמֵר: שְׁחָטָן לְשֵׁם גָּבוֹהַּ מֵהֶן – כְּשֵׁרִין, לְשֵׁם נָמוּךְ מֵהֶן – פְּסוּלִין. כֵּיצַד? קָדְשֵׁי קָדָשִׁים שֶׁשְּׁחָטָן לְשֵׁם קָדָשִׁים קַלִּים – פְּסוּלִין, קָדָשִׁים קַלִּים שֶׁשְּׁחָטָן לְשֵׁם קָדְשֵׁי קָדָשִׁים – כְּשֵׁרִין; הַבְּכוֹר וְהַמַּעֲשֵׂר שֶׁשְּׁחָטָן לְשֵׁם שְׁלָמִים – כְּשֵׁרִין, שְׁלָמִים שֶׁשְּׁחָטָן לְשֵׁם בְּכוֹר וּלְשֵׁם מַעֲשֵׂר – פְּסוּלִין.§ **גמ'** *לָמָּה לִי לְמִיתְנָא: ג] "אֶלָּא שֶׁלֹּא עָלוּ"? לִיתְנֵי: "וְלֹא עָלוּ לַבְּעָלִים לְשֵׁם חוֹבָה"! הָא קמ"ל: לַבְּעָלִים הוּא דְּלֹא עָלוּ לְשֵׁם חוֹבָה, אֲבָל בִּקְדוּשָּׁתַיְיהוּ קָיְימִי וְאָסוּר לְשַׁנּוּיֵי בְּהוּ, וְכִדְרָבָא, *דְּאָמַר רָבָא: געוֹלָה שֶׁשְּׁחָטָהּ שֶׁלֹּא לִשְׁמָהּ – אָסוּר לִזְרוֹק דָּמָהּ שֶׁלֹּא לִשְׁמָהּ. *אִיבָּעֵית אֵימָא סְבָרָא, אִיבָּעֵית אֵימָא קְרָא. אִיבָּעֵית אֵימָא סְבָרָא: מִשּׁוּם דְּשַׁנֵּי בָּהּ, כָּל הָנֵי לִישַׁנֵּי בָּהּ וְלֵיזִיל? אִיבָּעֵית אֵימָא קְרָא: דברים כג °"מוֹצָא שְׂפָתֶיךָ תִּשְׁמוֹר וְעָשִׂיתָ כַּאֲשֶׁר נָדַרְתָּ לַה' אֱלֹהֶיךָ נְדָבָה" וגו', *הַאי "נְדָבָה"? נֶדֶר

רש"י

כל הַזְּבָחִים שֶׁנִּזְבְּחוּ שֶׁלֹּא לִשְׁמָן. שֶׁשָּׁחַט עוֹלָה לְשֵׁם שְׁלָמִים. כְּשֵׁרִים. לִזְרוֹק דָּמָן, וּלְהַקְטִיר אֵימוּרֵיהֶם, וְלֶאֱכוֹל אֶת הַנֶּאֱכָלִין. אע"פ שֶׁמִּצְוָתָן לְשׁוֹחֲטָן לִשְׁמָן כִּדְיָלֵיף בַּגְּמָ'. **אֶלָּא שֶׁלֹּא עָלוּ וכו'.** וְצָרִיךְ לְהָבִיא אַחֵר לְחוֹבָתוֹ אוֹ לְנִדְרוֹ וְיִשְׁחָטֶנּוּ לִשְׁמוֹ. **חוּץ מִן הַפֶּסַח וְהַחַטָּאת.** שֶׁהֵן פְּסוּלִין לְגַמְרֵי. וְיָלֵיף לָהּ בַּגְּמָ'. *הַפֶּסַח בִּזְמַנּוֹ. [פָּסוּל] שֶׁלֹּא לִשְׁמוֹ כָּל זְמַן שְׁחִיטָתוֹ, דְּהַיְינוּ מֵחֲצוֹת הַיּוֹם שֶׁל עֶרֶב פֶּסַח עַד הָעֶרֶב. אֲבָל קוֹדֶם לָכֵן וְאַחַר מִכָּאן – קַיְימָא לָן (לקמן דף ז:) דְּפֶסַח בִּשְׁאָר יְמוֹת הַשָּׁנָה [שְׁלָמִים] הוּא, וְכָל דִּינוֹ כִּשְׁלָמִים, וְאָמְרִינַן לְעֵיל דִּשְׁאָר זְבָחִים כְּשֵׁרִין שֶׁלֹּא לִשְׁמָן, וּבַגְּמָ' יָלֵיף לָהּ מִקְּרָאֵי. **אַף הָאָשָׁם.** כִּדְמְפָרֵשׁ טַעְמָא וְאָזֵיל. **הַנִּשְׁחָטִין לְשֵׁם פֶּסַח.** כָּל שְׁאָר זְבָחִים שֶׁנִּזְבְּחוּ בְּי"ד בְּנִיסָן לְשֵׁם פֶּסַח, אוֹ שֶׁנִּזְבְּחוּ לְשֵׁם חַטָּאת בְּכָל זְמַן – פְּסוּלִין, כִּי הֵיכִי דְּאִינְהוּ פְּסוּלִין לְשֵׁם אֲחֵרִים. וּבַגְּמָרָא יָלֵיף טַעְמָא דַּאֲחֵרִים לְשֵׁם פֶּסַח בַּבָּרַיְיתָא. **שִׁמְעוֹן אֲחִי עֲזַרְיָה.** עַל שֵׁם שֶׁעֲזַרְיָה עָסַק בְּפְּרַקְמַטְיָא וְסִיפֵּק צָרְכֵי שִׁמְעוֹן אָחִיו בְּשָׁעָה שֶׁהָיָה עוֹסֵק בַּתּוֹרָה, וְהִתְנוּ בֵּינֵיהֶן שֶׁיְּהֵא חֵלֶק לַעֲזַרְיָה בִּשְׂכַר תַּלְמוּדוֹ שֶׁל שִׁמְעוֹן, כִּדְאָמְרִי' בְּסוֹטָה (דף כא.): "אִם יִתֵּן אִישׁ אֶת כָּל הוֹן בֵּיתוֹ" וגו' – לֹא כְּשִׁמְעוֹן אֲחִי עֲזַרְיָה, לְפִיכָךְ נִקְרָא עַל שְׁמוֹ, שֶׁלִּמֵּד עַל יָדוֹ. **שְׁחָטָן.** לִשְׁאָר זְבָחִים לְשֵׁם גָּבוֹהַּ מֵהֶן – כְּשֵׁרִין, כִּדְמְפָרֵשׁ וְאָזֵיל. וּבַגְּמָרָא (לקמן דף יא:) יָלֵיף לָהּ, וּמְפָרֵשׁ לְהַאי "כְּשֵׁרִין", אִי כְּשֵׁרִין [וְעָלוּ] קָאָמַר וּבְתַרְתֵּי *פְּלִיגִי, אִי כְּשֵׁרִין וְלֹא עָלוּ קָאָמַר, וּבְגָבוֹהַּ וּבְנָמוּךְ הוּא דִּפְלִיגִי. **לְשֵׁם נָמוּךְ מֵהֶן פְּסוּלִין.** לְגַמְרֵי. **בְּכוֹר וּמַעֲשֵׂר** בְּהֵמָה נְמוּכִין מִשְּׁלָמִים, כִּדְאָמְרִינַן בְּפֶ' "כָּל הַתָּדִיר" (לקמן דף פט.): מִפְּנֵי שֶׁהַשְּׁלָמִים טְעוּנִין מַתַּן אַרְבַּע, סְמִיכָה, וּנְסָכִים, וּתְנוּפַת חָזֶה וָשׁוֹק. **גמ'** לָמָּה לִי לְמִיתְנֵי **אֶלָּא.** לְהַאֲרִיךְ בִּלְשׁוֹנוֹ? לִיתְנֵי: וְלֹא עָלוּ לַבְּעָלִים כו' – לָשׁוֹן קְצָרָה, כִּדְקַיְימָא לָן (פסחים דף ג:): לְעוֹלָם יִשְׁנֶה אָדָם לְתַלְמִידוֹ דֶּרֶךְ קְצָרָה. **הָא קמ"ל.** שֶׁאֵין בָּהֶם שׁוּם יְרִידָה אֶלָּא אוֹתָהּ לְבַדּוֹ. **אֲבָל בִּקְדוּשָּׁתַיְיהוּ קָיְימִי וְאָסוּר לְשַׁנּוּיֵי בְּהוּ.** תּוּ שִׁינּוּיָא אַחֲרִינָא, לַעֲבוֹד אַחַת מִשְּׁאָר עֲבוֹדוֹת לְכַתְּחִלָּה שֶׁלֹּא לִשְׁמָהּ. מִיהוּ, אִם עָבַר וְשִׁינָּה – כָּשֵׁר. **מִשּׁוּם דְּשַׁנֵּי בָּהּ.** חֲדָא זִימְנָא, לִישַׁנֵּי בָּהּ כָּל הָנֵי וְנֵיזִיל?

תוספות

כל הזבחים שנזבחו כו'. עבודה קמייתא נקט, והוא הדין קבלה והולכה וזריקה כדקתני סיפא (לקמן ד' יג.). ושינוי קודש שייך בהנך ארבע עבודות, כגון עולה לשם שלמים. אבל שינוי בעלים לא שייך אלא בזריקה, כגון שוחט או מקבל או מוליך קרבן ראובן ע"מ לזרוק דמו לשם שמעון, כדמוכח לקמן בפירקין (דף י.). וצריך לדקדק: מנא ליה להתלמוד שינוי בעלים? דקבעי לקמן בפרקין (דף ד.): מנא לן דבעינן זביחה לשמה כו', והדר קאמר: אשכחנא שינוי קודש, שינוי בעלים מנא לן – משמע דאמתניתין קאי וכולה מתניתין לא מישתמעא כלל שינוי בעלים, דלישנא ד"לשמן" משמע לאפוקי שינוי קודש, וכולה מתניתין לא נקיט אלא שינוי קודש, דקתני נמי בסיפא (שם דף יג.): כיצד לשמן ושלא לשמן – לשם פסח לשם שלמים! ונראה דסמך אמתניתין דלקמן פרק "בית שמאי" (דף מו:), דתנן: לשם ששה דברים הזבח נזבח: לשם זבח, לשם זובח. וכן פירש בקונטרס בגמ'. וא"ת: אי אההיא קאי, א"כ הוה ליה לפרושי נמי מנא לן לשם השם, לשם אישים, [לשם ריח] לשם ניחוח! וי"ל: דלא אתי לפרושי אלא בהני דכשירין ולא עלו לשם חובה, אבל הנך כשירין ומרצין ועלו לשם חובה, כמו שאפרש. ועוד יש לומר: ד"שלא לשמן" דמתניתין – משמע בין שינוי קודש בין שינוי בעלים. כמו ברייתא דרבי שמעון "קמלה שלא לשמה", דמוקי ריש פ"ק דמנחות (דף ג:) בשינוי בעלים. ולהכי *נמי [לא פריך] בפירקין דהנך ארבעה דברים מנא לן, דלא מיירי בהן במתני'. ומיהו, רבה דווקא מוקי לה בשינוי בעלים, אבל רבא ורב אשי לא מוקמי לה הכי התם. ואם תאמר: והא בפרק "בית שמאי" (לקמן דף מו:) דריש להו מדכתיב: "עולה אשה ריח ניחוח לה'" עולה לשם עולה, והיינו שינוי קודש. ובפירקין בגמ' (לקמן דף ד.) דריש שינוי קודש מקרא אחרינא! ויש לומר: דקרא דהתם בהקטרת אימורים, והכא בעבודת הדם. ואע"ג דקתני: "לשם ו' דברים הזבח נזבח" – הוא הדין הזבח נקטר, דהא קרא דמייתי התם בהקטרה מיירי. ומ"מ שפיר דריש מקרא דהתם זביחה לשם ו' דברים, מדאיתקש אל שם זבח, דלשם זבח, דהיינו שינוי קודש, הוי בין בעבודת דם [כדיליף] מקראי דפירקין, בין בהקטרה [כדיליף] מקרא דהתם – ה"ה שאר *חמשה דברים יהו בזביחה כמו בהקטרה. ומיהו, הא לא מצינן למילף מהיקישא דנימא ולא עלו לשם חובה – ואינה מרצה *בכל (מקום) הנך ו' דברים, דההוא קרא כתיב בהקטרת אימורים, והוא עצמו שלא הוקטרו אימורים – כשר. ולקמן דמייתי קרא לשם זבח דהיינו שינוי קודש לא מייתי נמי קרא לשם זובח דהיינו שינוי בעלים *משום דהנהו ו' דברים לא שייך לפרש בשעת הקטרה דבשעת הקטרה לא משכחת לשם זובח דשינוי בעלים ליתיה אלא בשוחט ע"מ לזרוק או מקבל ומוליך ע"מ לזרוק, כדמוכח בפירקין (לקמן ד' ח.), ובשעת הקטרה כבר נזרק הדם, ואם כן מהיכא תיתי הקטרה לשם זובח? דבההוא קרא "לעולה אשה ריח ניחוח" לא כתיב. ומעבודת דם לא אתי, דעבודת דם גופיה ליתיה אלא בע"מ לזרוק, כדפרישית. והשתא זביחה לשם ששה דברים, והקטרה לשם חמשה. אי נמי: הא דקאמר זביחה לשם ששה דברים – לא שחישב בשעת שחיטה לשם ו' דברים, אלא כלומר הזבח נעשה לשם ו' דברים, וכל אחת בשעתה. ●ובפ' "המפקיד" (ב"מ דף מג:) פירשתי הא דמחשבה פוסלת בקדשים אי בדיבור הזבח נעשה [שלא] לשמה, או אפילו במחשבה. **הפסח** בזמנו. אבל שלא בזמנו לא, ואפי' שוחטו לשם עולה. ואפילו למ"ד בעי עקירה – מ"מ הוי שלמים, כדדרשינן: "ואם מן הצאן קרבנו לזבח שלמים" – כל דשחיט ליה שלמים ליהוי, לקמן בפירקין (דף ח:). **החטאת** באה על חטא והאשם בא על החטא. איכא חטאת ואשם נמי דאין באין על חטא, כגון חטאת יולדת ואשם מצורע. אלא משום דרובא אתו על חטא משוו להו אהדדי. **לשם** גבוה מהן כשירין. בגמרא* מיבעי לן אי בעי למימר כשירין ומרצין ופליגי בתרתי, או כשירין ואין מרצין ולא פליגי אלא בחדא. [משמע דלא מספקא אלא בחדא] כגון *בגבוה, אבל בנמוך – פשיטא ליה דפסולין לגמרי קאמר. ותימה: מנא ליה? דילמא פסול ולא עלו קאמר. דאשכחן [בברייתא] כי האי גוונא, דתניא (לקמן דף ד.): שלמים ששחטן לשם תודה – פסולין. והיינו פסולין ולא עלו, ולא פסולין לגמרי! ויש לומר: משום דדרשינן טעמא דשמעתא בגמרא (שם דף יא:) מדכתיב: "ולא יחללו את קדשי בני ישראל אשר ירימו" – במורם [מהם] אין מתחללין, בנמוך מהם מתחללין, וחילול משמע פסול גמור. ואע"ג דדרשינן בגמרא:* קדשים מחללין קדשים ואין חולין מחללין קדשים, ולא מיפסלו שאר קדשים שלא לשמן – מכל מקום שייך בהן חילול משום פסח וחטאת דמיפסלו. *ועוד יש לדקדק מגופה דמתניתין: הבכור והמעשר ששחטן לשם שלמים כשירין – משום דהוי לשם גבוה, דאי לשם נמוך – מיפסלי. והיינו לענין פסול גמור, דבבכור ובמעשר לא שייך לא עלו לבעלים לשם חובה.

ואסור לשנויי. יש מקומות שהתנא [אינו] חושש לאשמעינן חידוש זה. ובפרק "התכלת" (מנחות דף מח:) גבי שאר שלמי נזיר, וגבי אשם נזיר ואשם מצורע, דקתני: "כשירין ולא עלו", ולא קתני "אלא". **קרי** ליה נדר וקרי ליה נדבה. משמע הכא דכל היכא דכתיב "נדר" – נדר דוקא, נדבה נדבה דוקא וכן בפרק קמא דר"ה (דף ו.) לענין, "בל תאחר". ואפילו לר"מ בפ"ק דחולין (דף ב.) דדריש: "טוב אשר לא תדור" – טוב מזה ומזה שאינו נודר כל עיקר, אלמא קרי לנדבה נדר – שאני הכא דדריש, מדשני קרא בדיבוריה. אי נמי, בחולין דריש, דכיון דחייש קרא לתקלה – לא שנא נדר לא שנא נדבה, דבתרווייהו איכא למיחש. אי נמי: משום דנדר נפקא לן מקרא ד"כי תחדל לנדור", ש"מ ד"טוב אשר לא תדור" לנדבה אתא.

ואם

שיטה מקובצת
(כתב יד)

הגהות נפלאות אמתיות לרבינו בצלאל אשכנזי ז"ל מתוך גפ"ת כ"י שהי' לפניו. וגם חדושים ושיטות הראשונים ז"ל שקבצן וכתבן על גליון הש"ס שלו ד' ווינציאה רפ"ב.

א] אלא שלא עלו כו'. וצריך להביא אחר לחובתו או לנדרו כדפי' בקונטרס ודוקא נדר שהוא חייב באחריותו אבל נדבה אם שחט שלא לשמה אין צריך להביא אחר דהא אפי' אם נאבד אינו חייב באחריותו. תוס' הר"פ: ב] הפסח בזמנו. פסול שלא לשמו כל זמן שחיטה דהיינו מחצות היום של ערב פסח עד הערב אבל קודם זמנו ואחר זמנו קי"ל דהוי שלמים דפסח בשאר ימות השנה שלמים הוי וכל דינו כשלמים וא"כ כי שחטו נמי לשם עולה או לשם קרבן אחר כשר הוא ודינו כשלמים כדקיי"ל כל הזבחים שנזבחו שלא לשמן כשרים ומ"מ קודם זמנו ולאחר זמנו אינם שוים דאחר זמנו לא בעי עקירה ואפי' שחטו סתם כשר ואפי' שחטו לשם פסח בפירוש כשר ושלמי' לשם פסח קשחיט כדאמרי' במס' חולין בפ' השוחט אבל קודם זמנו אם שחטו סתם פסול כיון דמסתמא לשם פסח קאי לכך בעי עקירה שיעקרנו בפירוש משם פסח לשם אחר וא"ת מאי איריא דפסח בזמנו דפסול שלא לשמו אפי' קודם זמנו נמי דהא אם שחטו קודם זמנו לשם פסח או סתמא נמי פסול אע"ג דדינו להיות כשלמים וי"ל דהתם לאו משום דשלא לשמו הוא דמיפסל אלא משום דקודם זמנו שם פסח עליו לגמרי כיון דלפסח קאי וכי שחיט ליה לשם פסח או סתמא הו"ל פסח ששחטו קודם חצות דמיפסל משום דבין הערבים אמר רחמנא ושנה הכתוב לעכב חד בפ' החדש הזה לכם וחד בפ' ויעשו בני ישראל את הפסח במועדו ואע"ג דאיכא קראי בגמרא נמי דקודם זמנו הוי שלמים היינו דוקא ע"י עקירה כדדריש ליה בגמרא ע"י כלל ופרט וכלל ואף למאי דמסיק לובה ריבויא הוא מ"מ ממעיט לשמו כמו שאפרש בגמרא בעז"ה והילכך קודם זמנו לעולם שם פסח עליו עד דעקר ליה שם פסח לשם שלמים ולכך מיפסל לשם פסח או סתמא מטעם פסח ששחטו קודם חצות כדפי' רש"י אבל שחטו לאחר הפסח לשם אחר הוי שלמים כיון דנפק ליה משם פסח ואפי' שחטו לשם עולה הוי שלא לשמו אפ"ה כשר דמידי דהוה אזבחים דכשרין שלא לשמן לא משכחת שלא לשמו פסול בפסח אלא בזמנו דוקא ותדע דפסח ששחט קודם זמנו לשם פסח לאו משום שינוי קודש הוא דמיפסל דהא נמי אם שחטו סתמא פסול וכל הזבחים דפסולין משום שינוי קודש כששחטן שלא לשמן אם שחטן סתמא כשרים כדמוכח בגמרא תוס' טו"ך: ג] אלא כלומר משמע שיש בו כשרות אחר שלא וכו' אבל בקדושתייהו קיימי פי' בשם קדושה ראשונה דעדיין שם הראשון עליהם ואסור לשנויי בהו גם מכאן ואילך תוס' טו"ך:

מסורת הש"ס

וגי' נ"ק בשם ס"י הפסח בזמנו כל זמן כו' ומוחק כל הני תיבות

מנחות ד: ידים פ"ד מ"ב

פסחים עג: ע"ש

מנחות ב.

נ"א פליגי בגבוה ונמוך או כשירין ולא עלו קאמר ובנמוך הוא כו'

[לקמן ז:]

[ברכות ז: וש"נ]

לקמן ד: מנחות ב.

נ"א ד' נ"ק נ"א מכל

נ"א משום דשינוי בעלים לא שייך כו' נ"ק בשם ס"י

לקמן יא:

נ"א בנמוך

לקמן ג:

נ"ע דלקמן בגמרא רוצה לדייק כן ממלת כשירין ודחי דילמא הא כדאיתא כו' וא"כ מפסולים יוכל לחות ג"כ

אלא

נֶדֶר, הוּא! אֶלָּא, אִם כְּמָה שֶׁנָּדַרְתָּ עָשִׂיתָ – יְהֵא נֶדֶר, וְאִם לֹא – נְדָבָה יְהֵא, וּנְדָבָה מִי שָׁרֵי לְשַׁנּוּיֵי בָּהּ? אֲמַר לֵיהּ רָבִינָא לְרַב פָּפָּא: לָא הֲוֵית גַּבָּן בְּאוּרְתָּא בִּתְחוּמָא בֵּי חַרְמָךְ, דְּרָמֵי רָבָא מִילֵּי מַעַלְּיָיתָא אַהֲדָדֵי וְשַׁנֵּי לְהוּ. מַאי מִילֵּי מַעַלְּיָיתָא? תְּנַן: כָּל הַזְּבָחִים שֶׁנִּזְבְּחוּ שֶׁלֹּא לִשְׁמָן כו'; טַעְמָא דְּשֶׁלֹּא לִשְׁמָן, הָא ^א סְתָמָא – עָלוּ נַמִי לַבְּעָלִים לְשֵׁם חוֹבָה, אַלְמָא סְתָמָא נַמִי כְּלִשְׁמָן דָּמֵי; וּרְמִינְהִי: * ^ב כָּל הַגֵּט שֶׁנִּכְתַּב שֶׁלֹּא לְשֵׁם אִשָּׁה – פָּסוּל, ^ג וּסְתָמָא נַמִי פָּסוּל! וְשַׁנֵּי: זְבָחִים בִּסְתָמָא לִשְׁמָן עוֹמְדִין, אִשָּׁה בִּסְתָמָא לָאו לְגֵירוּשִׁין עוֹמֶדֶת. וּזְבָחִים בִּסְתָמָא כְּשֵׁירִין, מְנָלַן? אִילֵימָא מֵהָא דִּתְנַן: כָּל הַזְּבָחִים שֶׁנִּזְבְּחוּ שֶׁלֹּא לִשְׁמָן כו', וְלָא קָתָנֵי "שֶׁלֹּא נִזְבְּחוּ לִשְׁמָן"; גַּבֵּי גֵּט נַמִי הָקָתָנֵי: כָּל הַגֵּט שֶׁנִּכְתַּב שֶׁלֹּא לְשֵׁם אִשָּׁה – פָּסוּל, וְלָא קָתָנֵי "שֶׁלֹּא נִכְתַּב לְשֵׁם אִשָּׁה – פָּסוּל"! אֶלָּא מֵהָא, א] (א) *דִּתְנַן: כֵּיצַד לִשְׁמָן וְשֶׁלֹּא לִשְׁמָן – לְשֵׁם פֶּסַח וּלְשֵׁם שְׁלָמִים; טַעְמָא דְּאָמַר לְשֵׁם פֶּסַח וּלְשֵׁם שְׁלָמִים, הָא לְשֵׁם פֶּסַח וּסְתָמָא – כָּשֵׁר, אַלְמָא סְתָמָן כְּלִשְׁמָן דָּמֵי; דִּילְמָא שָׁאנֵי הָתָם, דְּאָמַר: ^ה כָּל הָעוֹשֶׂה – עַל דַּעַת רִאשׁוֹנָה הוּא עוֹשֶׂה! אֶלָּא מִסֵּיפָא: שֶׁלֹּא לִשְׁמָן וְלִשְׁמָן – לְשֵׁם שְׁלָמִים וּלְשֵׁם פֶּסַח; טַעְמָא דְּאָמַר לְשֵׁם שְׁלָמִים וּלְשֵׁם פֶּסַח, הָא סְתָמָא וּלְשֵׁם פֶּסַח – כָּשֵׁר; דִּילְמָא שָׁאנֵי הָתָם, דְּאָמַר: *יוֹכִיחַ סוֹפוֹ עַל תְּחִילָּתוֹ! אִי נַמִי, אַיְּידֵי דִּתְנָא "לִשְׁמָן וְשֶׁלֹּא לִשְׁמָן", תְּנָא נַמִי: "שֶׁלֹּא לִשְׁמָן וְלִשְׁמָן"! אֶלָּא מֵהָא, *לְשֵׁם שִׁשָּׁה דְּבָרִים הַזֶּבַח נִזְבָּח: לְשֵׁם זֶבַח, לְשֵׁם זוֹבֵחַ, לְשֵׁם (ב) שֵׁם, לְשֵׁם אִשִּׁים, לְשֵׁם רֵיחַ, לְשֵׁם נִיחוֹחַ, וְהַחַטָּאת וְאָשָׁם לְשֵׁם חֵטְא. א"ר יוֹסֵי: אַף מִי שֶׁלֹּא הָיָה בְּלִבּוֹ לְשֵׁם אַחַת מִכָּל אֵלּוּ – כָּשֵׁר, שֶׁתְּנַאי בֵּית דִּין הוּא; אַתְנוּ בֵּית דִּין דְּלָא לֵימָא לִשְׁמוֹ, דִּילְמָא אָתֵי לְמֵימַר שֶׁלֹּא לִשְׁמוֹ. וְאִי סָלְקָא דַּעְתָּךְ סְתָמָא פָּסוּל, קָיְימִי בֵּית דִּין וּמַתְנִי מִילְּתָא דְּמִיפְּסִיל בֵּיהּ? וְגַבֵּי גֵּט דִּסְתָמָא פָּסוּל מְנָלַן? אִילֵימָא מֵהָא דִּתְנַן: * ^ד הָיָה עוֹבֵר בַּשּׁוּק וְשָׁמַע (ג) סוֹפְרִים מַקְרִין: "אִישׁ פְּלוֹנִי גֵּירֵשׁ פְּלוֹנִית מִמָּקוֹם פְּלוֹנִי", וְאָמַר: זֶה שְׁמִי וְזֶה שֵׁם אִשְׁתִּי – פָּסוּל לְגָרֵשׁ בּוֹ; דִּילְמָא כִּדְרַב פָּפָּא, דְּאָמַר *רַב פָּפָּא: הָכָא בְּסוֹפְרִים הָעֲשׂוּיִין לְהִתְלַמֵּד עָסְקִינַן, וְלָא אִיכְּתוּב לְשׁוּם כְּרִיתוּת כְּלָל! אֶלָּא מֵהָא:
יָתֵר

רש"י

נֶדֶר הוּא. דְּהָא "כַּאֲשֶׁר נָדַרְתָּ" כְּתִיב. וְיֵשׁ חִילּוּק בֵּין נֶדֶר לִנְדָבָה, נֶדֶר – דְּאָמַר "הֲרֵי עָלַי", וּנְדָבָה – "הֲרֵי זוֹ". אִם כְּמָה שֶׁנָּדַרְתָּ עָשִׂיתָ. שֶׁעָבַד עֲבוֹדוֹתֶיהָ לִשְׁמָהּ. יְהֵא נֶדֶר. וְיַעֲלֶה זֶה לְנִדְרְךָ. וְאִם לָאו יְהֵא לִנְדָבָה. כְּאִילּוּ הִתְנַדַּבְתָּ לָזֶה נְדָבָה אַחֶרֶת, וְלֹא לְשֵׁם הָרִאשׁוֹנָה. וּנְדָבָה מִי שָׁרֵי לְשַׁנּוּיֵי בָּהּ. וְכֵיוָן דְּרַחֲמָנָא קַרְיֵיהּ נְדָבָה, מִי שָׁרֵי לְשַׁנּוּיֵי בָּהּ? הָא אָמְרִינַן בְּפֶ' שֵׁנִי (לקמן ד' כט:): אָסוּר לְחַשֵּׁב בְּקָדָשִׁים, וְיָלֵיף מִקְּרָא דְּ"לֹא יֵחָשֵׁב". וְהָכִי מִידְּרַשׁ קְרָא: אִם מוֹצָא שְׂפָתֶיךָ תִּשְׁמוֹר וְעָשִׂיתָ – אָז יִהְיֶה נֶדֶר אֲשֶׁר נָדַרְתָּ, וְאִם לָאו – נְדָבָה. (מִפִּי הַשְּׁמוּעָה בִּמְנָחוֹת עַד כָּאן). לָא הֲוֵית גַּבָּן בְּאוּרְתָּא בִּתְחוּמָא. כְּלוֹמַר, חֲבָל עַל שֶׁלֹּא הָיִיתָ אֶמֶשׁ בְּשַׁבָּת אֶצְלֵנוּ בְּתוֹךְ הַתְּחוּם, שֶׁתּוּכַל לָבֹא לְבֵית הַמִּדְרָשׁ וְלִשְׁמוֹעַ. בֵּי חַרְמָךְ. שֵׁם מָקוֹם. וְשַׁנֵּי לְהוּ. וּפֵירְקָן. שֶׁלֹּא לִשְׁמָן. מַשְׁמַע דְּעָקַר שְׁמַיְיהוּ בְּהֶדְיָא. שֶׁלֹּא לְשֵׁם אִשָּׁה. הָאִשָּׁה הַזֹּאת שֶׁנִּכְתַּב לְשׁוּם אַחֶרֶת שֶׁשְּׁמָהּ כְּשֵׁם זוֹ – פָּסוּל, דִּכְתִיב: "וְכָתַב לָהּ" – לִשְׁמָהּ. וּסְתָמָא נַמִי פָּסוּל. כְּגוֹן אִם כְּתָבוֹ הַסּוֹפֵר [סְתָם] לְשֵׁם לֵאָה, שֶׁיְּהֵא מְזוּמָּן לִכְשֶׁיָּבֹא אָדָם אֶצְלוֹ שֶׁשְּׁמוֹ וְשֵׁם אִשְׁתּוֹ (שָׁוִין) כֵּן, וְיִתְּנֶנּוּ לוֹ. וּלְקַמָּן מְפָרֵשׁ מְנָלַן מַתְנִי' דִּסְתָם פָּסוּל. וְשַׁנֵּי. וְתָרִיץ רָבָא גּוּפֵיהּ דְּרָמִינְהוּ אַהֲדָדֵי. בִּסְתָמָן לִשְׁמָן עוֹמְדִין. הִילְכָּךְ כָּל כַּמָּה דְּלָא עָקַר שְׁמַיְיהוּ בְּהֶדְיָא הָווּ לִשְׁמָן. מְנָלַן. *מִמַּתְנִי'? הֵיכִי שָׁמַע לֵיהּ רָבָא דְּתִיקְשֶׁה לֵיהּ? שֶׁנִּזְבְּחוּ שֶׁלֹּא לִשְׁמָן. מַשְׁמַע דְּעָקַר שְׁמָן מֵהֶן. שֶׁלֹּא נִזְבְּחוּ לִשְׁמָן. מַשְׁמַע שֶׁלֹּא הִזְכִּיר שְׁמָן עֲלַיְיהוּ, דְּהַיְינוּ סְתָמָא. שֶׁנִּכְתַּב שֶׁלֹּא לְשֵׁם אִשָּׁה זוֹ. מַשְׁמַע שֶׁנִּכְתַּב לְשֵׁם אַחֶרֶת בְּפֵירוּשׁ. כֵּיצַד לִשְׁמָן כו'. מַתְנִי' הִיא. לְשֵׁם פֶּסַח וּלְשֵׁם שְׁלָמִים. כָּךְ חִישֵּׁב עָלָיו. הָא לְשֵׁם פֶּסַח וּסְתָמָא. שֶׁלֹּא חִישֵּׁב אַחֲרָיו לְשֵׁם שְׁלָמִים – כָּשֵׁר, וְאַע"ג דְּסוֹף שְׁחִיטָה סְתָמָא אִישְׁתְּחִיט. אַלְמָא סְתָמָן כְּלִשְׁמָן דָּמֵי. דְּאִי כְּשֶׁלֹּא לִשְׁמָן דָּמֵי, הָוְיָא לֵיהּ כְּאִילּוּ אָמַר לְשֵׁם פֶּסַח וּלְשֵׁם שְׁלָמִים. עַל דַּעַת [רִאשׁוֹנָה. אֲבָל] הֵיכָא דִּשְׁחָטֵיהּ כּוּלֵּיהּ סְתָמָא, אֵימָא לָךְ דְּפָסוּל! הָא סְתָמָא [וּלְשֵׁם] פֶּסַח. תְּחִילָּה שְׁחָטָהּ סְתָם, וְסוֹפָהּ לְשֵׁם פֶּסַח – כָּשֵׁר, וְלָא מִיפְּסִיל מִשּׁוּם תְּחִילָּתָהּ. אַלְמָא סְתָמָא כְּלִשְׁמָן. א"נ אַיְּידֵי כו'. כְּלוֹמַר, לְעוֹלָם לֹא תֵּידוֹק מִינֵּיהּ: הָא סְתָמָא וּלְשֵׁם פֶּסַח כָּשֵׁר. דִּלְעוֹלָם אֵימָא לָךְ פָּסוּל, דִּסְתָמָא כְּשֶׁלֹּא לִשְׁמוֹ. וְהַאי דְּקָתָנֵי לְשֵׁם שְׁלָמִים, אַיְּידֵי דִּפְרֵישׁ בְּלִשְׁמָן וְלֹא לִשְׁמָן לְשֵׁם שְׁלָמִים – דְּהָתָם דַּוְוקָא הוּא, דְּאִילּוּ סְתָמָא הֲוֵי כָּשֵׁר, דְּעַל דַּעַת רִאשׁוֹנָה הוּא עוֹשֶׂה – פָּרֵישׁ נַמִי תַּנָּא דְּמַתְנִי' בְּשֶׁלֹּא לִשְׁמוֹ וְלִשְׁמוֹ לְשֵׁם שְׁלָמִים וּלְשֵׁם פֶּסַח. וְלָאו דַּוְוקָא, דְּה"ה לִסְתָמָא וּלְשֵׁם פֶּסַח דְּמִיפְּסַל בִּתְחִילַּת שְׁחִיטָה. לְשֵׁם שִׁשָּׁה דְּבָרִים. מִשְׁנָה בְּפֶרֶק "ב"ש", וּמִקְּרָאֵי יָלֵיף לְהוּ. לְשֵׁם זֶבַח. לְשֵׁם מַה שֶּׁהוּקְדַּשׁ. לְשֵׁם זוֹבֵחַ. שֶׁיִּתְכַּפֵּר בּוֹ בְּעָלָיו, וְלֹא שֶׁיִּתְכַּפֵּר בּוֹ אַחֵר. לְשֵׁם (ד) שֵׁם. (לְנַחַת רוּחַ) לְהקב"ה שֶׁאָמַר (*וְנַעֲשָׂה רְצוֹנוֹ). לְשֵׁם אִשִּׁים. לְהַקְטִירָם, וְלֹא לַעֲשׂוֹתָם צְלִי עַל הַמִּזְבֵּחַ, קרבוניי"ש בְּלַעַ"ז. לְשֵׁם רֵיחַ. לְאַפּוּקֵי אֵיבָרִים שֶׁצְּלָאָן וְהֶעֱלָן, דְּשׁוּב אֵין בָּהֶן רֵיחַ. וְהָכִי מְפָרֵשׁ לְהוּ הָתָם. לְשֵׁם נִיחוֹחַ. לְשֵׁם הֲנָחַת רוּחַ לְהקב"ה, שֶׁאָמַר וְנַעֲשָׂה רְצוֹנוֹ. שֶׁלֹּא הָיָה בְּלִבּוֹ. לִשְׁמוֹ, אֶלָּא סְתָם, וְלֹא הִזְכִּיר אֶחָד מֵאֵלֶּה. שֶׁתְּנַאי בֵּית דִּין הוּא. שֶׁיִּשְׁחֲטוּ סְתָם וְלֹא יַזְכִּירוּ בִּשְׁחִיטָתָן לִשְׁמוֹ, כִּדְמְפָרֵשׁ טַעְמָא וְאָזֵיל: אַתְנוּ ב"ד דְּלָא לֵימָא לִשְׁמָן כו'. וְגַבֵּי גֵּט דִּסְתָמָא פָּסוּל מְנָא לֵיהּ. כְּלוֹמַר, הֵיכִי שָׁמַע לֵיהּ רָבָא מַתְנִי' דְּגִיטִּין דְּפָסוּל, דְּתִיקְשֶׁה לֵיהּ, וּרְמִינְהִי אַהֲדָדֵי? מַקְרִין. אֶת הַתַּלְמִידִין, שֶׁמְּלַמְּדִין אוֹתָן לִכְתּוֹב טוֹפְסֵי גִיטִּין. דְּלָא אִיכְּתוּב לְשֵׁם כְּרִיתוּת כְּלָל. אֲבָל הֵיכָא דְּאִיכְּתַב ב] לְשֵׁם כְּרִיתוּת, שֶׁיְּהֵא מְזוּמָּן לוֹ לִכְשֶׁיִּזְדַּמֵּן לוֹ *מְגָרֵשׁ שֶׁשְּׁמוֹ וְשֵׁם אִשְׁתּוֹ ג] שָׁוִין בּוֹ – כָּשֵׁר. וְנִמְלַךְ

תוספות

ואם לאו יהא נדבה. אע"ג דבפ"ק דר"ה (דף ו.) דריש ליה לענין "בל תאחר" דלא שייך לאחר שחיטה, הכא דריש מפשטיה דקרא, דמשמע דקרי ליה לנדר נדבה. **זבחים** בסתם לשמן הן עומדין. ואינו פסול עד שיכוין שלא לשמן. [וא"ת: בפ"ק דחולין (דף יב:) בעי ר"י אי קטן יש לו מחשבה וכו', ופי' בקונטרס: כגון בשחיטת קדשים, דיליף בריש זבחים דבעי לשמה, ושחט קטן עולה לשמה מי הוי כוונה או לא? הא משמע הכא דמסתמא נמי כשר, ואינו פסול עד שיכוין שלא לשמן!] וי"ל: דסתמא דקטן גרע, דאין לו דעת להבין שהן קדשים, וסבור שהן חולין, והוה ליה מתעסק, ופסול, כדאמר בפרק "בית שמאי" (לקמן דף מו:): לשם חולין – כשירין, משום חולין – פסולה. והאי קטן, אפילו אומר: יודע אני שהן קדשים ולשמן אני מתכוין – מיבעיא לן אי כוונתו כוונה, או דילמא לא מהני אם אין מעשיו מוכיחין. **סתם** אשה לאו לגירושין עומדת. ואפי' זינתה תחת בעלה, מכל מקום לאו להתגרש בגט זה עומדת. וגם, אם לא ירצה הבעל – לא יגרשנה, *אלא שלא תשמשנו. ומתוך הא מילתא מיתרצא מה שמקשים בסוף פרק שני דגיטין (דף כג.) דאמר: גוי אדעתא דנפשיה עביד, ואינו כשר לכתוב את הגט. ובפ' שני דעבודה זרה (דף כו:) אמרי': ימול ארמאי ואל ימול כותי, משום דכותי מתכוין לשם הר גריזים. [והתם נמי] בעינן לשמה, כדדרשינן (שם דף כז.) מ"לה' המול" (ימול), ואפי' הכי מכשרינן ארמאי. דיש לחלק בין גט למילה, כמו שמחלק כאן בין זבחים לגט: *הא סתמא פסול משום דסתם אשה לאו לגירושין קיימא, ולכך נמי [בגוי] פסול אע"ג דעביד סתם. אבל מילה – סתמא לשמה קיימא, כמו זבחים, הילכך גוי כשר אע"ג דעביד סתם. **הא** לשם פסח וסתמא כשר. פי' בקונטרס: ד] דסוף שחיטה סתמא אישתחיט. ותימה: כיון דאמר בתחילת שחיטה לשם פסח, *וכי כל שעה יש לו לדבר עד שיגמר שחיטתו? ונראה לפרש דבשתי עבודות איירי, כגון דשחיט לשם פסח וקיבל סתם. ומיהו בפרק "תמיד נשחט" (פסחים דף נט:) מיבעי לן אי בעבודה אחת תנן או בשתי עבודות, ועבודה אחת היינו כדפירש הקונטרס! ויש ליישב: דאפילו אם תימצי לומר לשם פסח וסתמא פסול, [אפ"ה] אין צריך לדבר כל שעה, אלא שבתחילת שחיטה יאמר שעושה כל השחיטה לשם שחיטת פסח.

אתנו בית דין דלא לימא לשמה דילמא אתי למימר שלא לשמה. בשמעתא קמייתא דגיטין (דף ג.) דמפרש דלכך לא תיקנו לומר "בפני נכתב לשמה" למ"ד לפי שאין בקיאין לשמה – משום דאי מפשת ליה לדיבורא אתי למיגזייה – לא הוי מצי למימר דילמא אתי למימר שלא לשמה, דמי הוא שוטה כל כך שנותן גט לאשה זו שנכתב לשמה והוא אומר שלשם אחרת נכתב? אבל אדם השוחט קרבן, פעמים שטועה וסבור שהוא קרבן אחר, וכן המקבל ומוליך וזורק. *)**קיימי** בית דין ומתני כו'. יש תימה: למה לו להאריך כל זה? הא בהדיא אמר סתמא כשר! ונראה לפרש: ד"מי שלא היה בלבו" היינו שלא אמר בהדיא לשם אחד ה] מכל אלו, אבל חישב בלבו למה שדינו להיות. הא סתמא פסול. **) להכי [דייק] מתנאי בית דין וכי מתנו בית דין: דלא לימא בהדיא, ובמחשבה סגי? ושמא אתי לידי פסול, שלא יחשב כלל וישחוט סתמא, ויפסל! **בסופרים** העשויין להתלמד עסקינן. ואפילו למאן דאמר בפרק קמא דעירובין (דף יג.) גבי מגילת סוטה דמוחקין אותה מן התורה, אף על גב דבעינן לשמה, ואף על גב דתורה

*) עיין נ"ק **) ועי' רש"ק

עין משפט נר מצוה

ג א מיי' פ"ד מהל' מעה"ק הלכה י ועיין רש"ק:
ד ב ג ד מיי' פ"ג מהל' גירושין הל"א סמג עשין נ טוש"ע אה"ע סי' קלא סעיף א:

הגהות הב"ח

(א) גמ' אלא מהא כיצד לשמן כו' ותיבות דתנן נמחק: (ב) שם לשם השם: (ג) שם ושמע קול סופרים מקרין איש פלוני מגרש את פלונית: (ד) רש"י ד"ה לשם שאמר ונעשה רצונו. נ"ב לאו היינו לשם ניחוח וכן מבואר לקמן דף מו ע"ב וי"ל שהוא שוחט לשם הקב"ה וממילא הוא נחת רוח כו' מה שא"כ לשם ניחוח שצריך לשחוט עבור נחת רוח וק"ל:

גליון הש"ס

גמ' כל העושה על דעת ראשונה. לקמן דף מא ע"ב שבת דף נא ע"א: תום' ד"ה סתם וכו' אלא שלא תשמשנו. עיין בתשובת הר"ם אלשקר סי' פח:

שיטה מקובצת

א] אלא מהא כיצד לשמן כו' וא"ת והמקשה מאי ס"ד וכי תעלה על דעתך דלעולם יעמוד ויאמר לשם פסח וי"מ דאה"נ דבכל עבודה ועבודה יש לו לפרש לשם פסח והשתא לפי' זה הוי פי' דמתני' דלשמו ושלא לשמו בשתי עבודות כמו בשחיטה וקבלה ששחט לשם פסח וקבל לשם שלמים ולא נהירא דע"כ דלשמו ושלא לשמו דמתני' ר"ל הכל בעבודה אחת כדפ"ה לקמן דאי בשתי עבודות היינו רישא הפסח והחטאת ששחטו שלא לשמו וקבל והלך וזרק שלא לשמו דאו או קאמר כדפ"ה לקמן דליכא למימר דעשה כל העבודות שלא לשמו דלמה לי כולי האי בחדא סגי אלא ע"כ או או קאמר וא"כ סיפא דקתני לשמו ושלא לשמו ר"ל בעבודה אחת ששחט לשם פסח ולשם שלמים וא"כ הדרא קושיא

מסורת הש"ס

גיטין כד. · לקמן יג. פסחים נט. · גי' הג"ה היכא שמעינן ממתניתין דסתמא כשר דתיקשי ליה לרבא · [גיטין סו. נדרים מח. חולין לט:] · לקמן מו. · גיטין כד. · [שם:] · ס"א ל"ג · ס"א והיה הטעם · נ"א נגרש למי · נ"א דהתם · נ"א לנ"ל בסוף שחיטה לשם פסח

לדוכתיה ר"ל דמשחיטה פריך דמשמע ליה לשמו ושלא לשמו בשחיטה ששחט סימן ראשון לשם פסח ושני לשם שלמים ולהכי דייק הא לשם פסח וסתמא כשר אלמא סתמא כלשמו דמי דאי כשלא לשמו דמי נהי דאין צריך לעמוד ולומר לשם פסח מ"מ בכל סימן וסימן היה לו להזכיר לשם פסח. תוס' טוך: ב] דאיכתב ליה לשם אשתו: ג] כן כשר ותיבות שוין בו נמחק: ד] בקונטרס פי' וכו' ותוס' טוך תירצו דמשחיטה פריך דמשמע ליה לשמו ושלא לשמו בשחיטה ששחט סימן אחד לשם פסח וסימן ב' לשם שלמים ולכך דייק הא לשם פסח וסתמא כשר אלמא סתמא כלשמן דמי דאי כשלא לשמן דמי נהי דא"צ לזבוח לעולם לשם פסח מ"מ בכל סימן וסימן היה לו להזכיר לשם פסח ע"כ: ה] לשם אחד והא דקאמר ר"י שלא היה בלבו היינו שלא היה ניכר וידוע לשומעין אם היה בלבו לכך לכך והיינו (דשני) [דשחט] בשתיקה כלומר שלא נדר בשפתיו מה שחשב בלבו והא דפריך בגמרא ואי ס"ד סתמא פסול קיימי ב"ד ומתני מילתא דמיפסל ביה. ה"פ מילתא שיבא לידי פסול דהיינו ע"י שתיקה דמתוך ששתוק אולי ישכח ולא יכוון גם בלבו ומיפסל אי סתמא פסול דיותר יבא שלא יחשוב כלל כשהוא מחשב בלבו מאם לטעות ולומר שלא לשמו אם הוא אומר לשמו בפירוש. תוס' טוך:

*יתר על כן, כתב לגרש את אשתו ונמלך, מצאו בן עירו ואמר לו: "שמי כשמך ושם אשתי כשם אשתך" – פסול לגרש בו; דילמא שאני התם, דאינתיק ליה לשם גירושין דההוא! אלא מהא: *יתר על כן, יש לו שתי נשים ששמותיהן שוות, כתב לגרש את הגדולה – לא יגרש בו את הקטנה; דילמא שאני התם, דאינתיק ליה לשם גירושין דההיא! אלא מהא: יתר על כן, אמר ללבלר: "כתוב, ולאיזה שארצה אגרש" – פסול לגרש בו; דילמא שאני התם, דאין ברירה! אלא מהא: *הכותב טופסי גיטין – צריך שיניח מקום האיש ומקום האשה *ומקום העדים ומקום הזמן; ואמר רב יהודה אמר שמואל: אף צריך שיניח מקום "הרי את מותרת לכל אדם". תו רמי מילתא אחריתי. מי *אמר רב יהודה אמר רב: חטאת ששחטה לשם עולה – פסולה, שחטה לשם חולין – כשירה; אלמא דמינה מחריב בה, דלאו מינה לא מחריב בה? ורמינהי: כל הגט שנכתב שלא לשם אשה – פסול; א] ואפי' לשם גויה נמי פסול! ושני: גט, דל גויה מיניה – הוה ליה סתמא, וסתמא פסול. קדשים, דל חולין מינייהו – הוה ליה סתמא, וסתמא כשירים. ורמא מילתא אחריתי. מי אמר רב יהודה אמר רב: חטאת ששחטה לשם עולה – פסולה, שחטה לשם חולין – כשירה; אלמא דמינה מחריב בה, דלא מינה לא מחריב בה? והתניא: *°"תוכו" – ולא תוך תוכו, ואפי' כלי שטף מציל! ושני: עשו חולין אצל קדשים כמחיצה אצל תנור, מה מחיצה אצל תנור לא מהניא לה כלל, אף חולין אצל קדשים לא מהניא ליה כלל. *דתנן: תנור שחצצו בנסרים או ביריעות, ונמצא שרץ במקום אחד – הכל טמא. *כוורת שהיא פחותה ופקוקה בקש ומשולשלת לאויר התנור, שרץ בתוכה – התנור טמא, שרץ בתנור – אוכלין שבתוכה טמאין, ורבי אליעזר מטהר. אמר רבי אליעזר: קל וחומר, אם הציל במת החמור, לא תציל בכלי חרס הקל? אמרו לו: לא, אם

רש"י

ונמלך. שלא יגרשנה. דילמא שאני התם. דלאו סתמא הוא, אלא שלא לשמה ממש. דאינתיק. משאר כל האנשים והנשים [לשם] גירושין של זה ושל זו. אלא מהא. דעדיפא מקמייתא, דהכא חד גברא הוא. דאין ברירה. וגריעה מקמייתא. דשמא בשעה שנכתב לא היה בדעתו של בעל לזו, ואינתק לשם האחרת. הכותב טופסי גיטין. שיהו מזומנין לו. טופס – לשון טפוס, מול"ל בלע"ז. מקום הרי את כו'. דזהו עיקר גופו. אלמא: סתמא פסול ואף על גב דאיכתב לשם כריתות לכשיזדמן לו. תו רמי מילתא אחריתי. אדרבינא ורב פפא קאי, דקאמר ב] דרמי רבא אהדדי ושנינהו. דרב יהודה אמר רב. לקמן בפרק "בית שמאי" (דף מו:). לשם חולין כשירה. קס"ד סברא דידיה היא, כדמפרש: דמינה מחריב בה, דבר שהוא מינו מועיל ג] בו לעקור את שמו. דלאו מינה. כגון חולין, שאינו מין קדשים – לא מחריב בה, ואין שמו נתפס על הזבח לעקור שמו ממנו. פסול. לגרש בו אשה אחרת. ואפי' לשם גויה. דהא "שלא לשם האשה" קתני, דמשמע שלא לשם אשה זו אלא לשום אשה אחרת כל דהו. ואע"ג דגויה לאו בת גירושין היא – מהניא לפסול, אלמא דלאו מינה ד] [מחריב] בה. דל גויה מיניה. ואימא נמי דלאו מינה לא מחריב בה – אפילו הכי פסול, דהוה ליה סתמא, דמיהו לאו לשם אשה זו נכתב. דל חולין מינייהו. כדסבירא לן דלא חייל ולא מחריב ביה, דלא מיניה הוה – הוו להו שחוטין סתם, ואמרן לעיל: סתמא כשירה. תוכו. ה] "כל כלי חרס" וגו' (ויקרא יא) ולא תוך תוכו. כלי המונח בתנור ופיו למעלה מן פי התנור, ואוכלין ומשקין בתוכו, ושרץ בתנור – אוכלין שבכלים טהורין, והכי אמרינן בת"כ. אבל היה פיו בתוך התנור – "תוכו" קרינן ביה. ואפי' כלי שטף מציל. כלומר, לא מיבעיא כלי חרס המונח בתנור דמציל על האוכלין שבתוכו, דהא תוך תוכו הוא. וכלי גופיה ליכא למימר דמיטמא ו] באויר ויטמא אוכלין שבו, דאין כלי חרס מיטמא מגבו. אלא אפי' כלי שטף שמיטמא מגבו – הכא טהור ומציל, דאמר [בפ' קמא דפסחים] (דף כ:): אוכלין ז] מיטמאים מאויר כלי חרס, ואין כלי מיטמא מאויר כלי חרס. ומדקתני "כלי שטף מציל" – אלמא דלאו מיניה חייך ביה, ח] [ומבטל את שם תוכו], הכא נמי, ליחול שם חולין וליפסל! ושני *הכא עשו חולין אצל קדשים כו'. כלומר, לעולם דלאו מינה לאו מחריב ביה. וכלי שטף אצל כלי חרס – מיניה הוא, דהא מנא והא מנא. אבל חולין אצל קדשים הוי דלאו מיניה, כמחיצה אצל תנור, דאמרינן ביה לקמן דלא מהניא ביה להיות חציצה בין שרץ לאוכלין, כדאמרן: דלאו מיניה לא מחריב בה. שחצצו בנסרים. שעשה מחיצה באמצעו, וחלקו עד למעלה מפיו – הכל טמא, אפילו אוכלין שבעבר השני של מחיצה. כוורת שהיא פחותה. גרסינן בטהרות. ולהכי נקט פחותה – דלאו כלי הוא, (א) דאי הואי שלימה הוה מצלת על אוכלין שבתוכה, כדאמרן: ט] אפי' כלי שטף מציל. אבל השתא דלאו כלי הוא – הויא כמחיצה בעלמא. ופקוקה בקש. רבותא נקט, דאע"ג דפקוקה פחיתתה בקש – לא הוי כלי, ואפי' פיה למעלה מפי י] תנור לא מצלת על אוכלין שבתוכה. ומשולשלת = תלויה. אוכלין שבתוכה טמאים. והיינו דאמרן: דלא מינה, כגון מחיצה – לא מחריב בה, לבטל שם תוכו ממנו. אם

תוספות

דתורה להתלמד עבידא, כדקאמר התם – לענין גט מודה, כדפרישית שם ובפ"ב דגיטין (דף כ.). וס"ת נמי פסלינן [בגט], בפ"ב דגיטין (דף יט:) כדמוכח בעובדא דההוא גברא דעל לבי כנישתא שקל ספר תורה ויהב לדביתהו. **כתב** לגרש את אשתו ונמלך כו'. תימה: מה ענין זה אצל סתם? ויש לומר, יא] דס"ד: כיון דנמלך – אם כן מסתמא כתבו מתחילה שאם יחזור בו יגרש מי שירצה. **הכותב** טופסי גיטין כו'. כל הנך משניות בפ' "כל הגט" (גיטין דף כו.). ותימה: דלא קתני בהך "יתר על כן". דעל כרחין יתר הוא, דמכל הנך קמייתא לא מצי למידק סתמא פסול אלא מהך! ויש לומר: דמשום דאמר ללבלר דקתני ברישא, *דהך יתר כמו כן, *דייקינן מזאת [סתמא], ודייקינן מינה אין ברירה.* וקשה לה"ר יצחק: דפ"ק דפסחים (דף יד.) תנן "הוסיף ר"ע", אף ע"ג דלמאן דמוקי מילתא דר' חנינא בולד [וולד] הטומאה דרבנן לא שמעינן לה ממילתיה דר' עקיבא, דמיירי בפסולא [דאורייתא]. מיהו, יש לומר: *אע"ג דקתני "הוסיף", אי לא הוה תני ליה – לא הוה *[קמשמע לן] מידי. **ואמר** רב יהודה אמר שמואל אף צריך שיניח כו'. איצטריך לאיתויי דרב יהודה, משום דמינה דייקינן בגיטין דאתיא כרבי אלעזר דאמר עדי מסירה כרתי, דקי"ל כוותיה. ואיכא דמוקי לה התם כר"מ, ומפרש: מפני התקנה, משום קטטה. ולדידיה ליכא למידק מינה סתמא פסול יב]. **ואפילו** לשם עבודה זרה נמי פסול. מדקתני "שנכתב שלא לשם אשה", דמשמע (על [כל] נשים בכלל. ולא דמי לשלא לשמן ד"כל הזבחים", דלא אמרינן אפי' חולין בכלל. דהתם איכא לפרושי שנזבחו שלא לשם זבח זה אלא לשם זבח אחר. **ורמינהו** תוכו ולא תוך תוכו ואפי' כלי שטף מציל. מפרש בקונטרס: שרץ בחילון ואוכלין בפנימי. לא מיבעיא כלי חרס דאין מיטמא מגבו, אלא אפי' כלי שטף דמיטמא מגבו – אין אוכלין שבתוכו יג] [טמאים], שגם כלי שטף אינו מקבל טומאה מאויר כלי חרס, כדאמר בפ' קמא דפסחים (דף כ:): אוכלין מקבלין טומאה מאויר כלי חרס ואין כלים מקבלים טומאה מאויר כלי חרס. וקשה לפירושו: דאם כן, מה חידוש יותר בכלי שטף מכלי חרס? ועודף דאיכא חידוש יותר בכלי חרס, כגון אם שרץ באויר כלי חרס פנימי, ואוכלין בכלי חרס חיצון יד] – טהורין, אע"פ שהפנימי טמא! טו] ונראה לפרש: דכל רבותא של כלי שטף היינו משום דלאו מינה הוא, וס"ד דלא מחריב בה וטמא, קמ"ל. טז] [ודוקא בכלי שטף שאינו מינו היה טמא אי לאו קרא], אבל תוך תוכו, שהכל הוא של חרס מינו – פשיטא שהוא טהור בלא פסוק, ד"תוך" דוקא אמר רחמנא. וכן מוכח לקמן דכלי שטף דוקא איצטריך קרא, דפריך: ומי אמר רבא חטאת ששחטה על מי שמחוייב עולה כשירה, אלמא לאו מינה לא מחריב בה. והתניא: "תוכו" ולא תוך תוכו, ואפי' כלי שטף מציל! ומשני: ארבעה "תוכו" כתיבי, חד תוכו ולא תוך תוכו. פי': אפי' לא כתב אלא "תוך" – הוה מיעטנא כלי חרס פנימי, שאין אוכלין שבתוכו מקבלין טומאה ע"י שרץ שבחילון, שהרי אין השרץ תוכו. ודוקא כלי חרס פנימי דהוי דומיא דידיה מעיטנא, דמינה מחריב בה ומציל. להכי כתב וי"ו של "תוכו", למימר דאפי' לאו מינה, כגון כלי שטף *מחריב בה ומציל. יז] ותימה, אמאי לא שני בשמעתין נמי הכי: שאני התם דאמר קרא "תוכו" ולא תוך תוכו, ולא איצטריך אלא לכלי שטף! וי"ל: דעדיפא משני הכא, דקאי על חטאת לשם חולין כשירה. ועל זה תירך: עשו חולין אצל קדשים, דאין מינם כלל ולכך לא מחריב בה, כמחיצה אצל תנור – יח] כמו מחיצה, וכמו כוורת הקש פחותה שאינה כלי כלל ואינה מצלת כלל. אבל כלי שטף קרוי מינו קצת, שיש לו שם כלי עליו, ולכך מחריב ומציל. אבל לקמן קאי על חטאת ששחטה לשם מחוייב עולה – כשירה, דאע"ג שהוא קדשים קרוי אינו מינו, ולא מחריב בה. ועל זה פריך: מאי שנא מכלי שטף שהוא כלי, ואינו מינו, ומחריב? ועל זה צריך לתרץ משום קרא "תוכו" ולא תוך תוכו. אבל לא מצי לתרץ עשוהו כמחיצה אצל תנור – דההוא אינו כלי כלל. והשתא הכא ולקמן מתרץ דומה בדומה (ודוקא בכלי שטף שאינו מינו היה טמא אי לאו קרא, אבל תוך יט] שהכל חרס – טהור בלא פסוק, דחד "תוך" אמר רחמנא). שכן

שיטה מקובצת

א] ואפי' לשם גויה נמי פסול. דהלשון משמע שלא לשם אותה אשה ותימה דממתניתין נמי נידוק הכי שנזבחו שלא לשמן ואפי' לשם חולין נמי לא עלו וכ"ת משום דמתני' מפרש בהדיא בסיפא שלא לשמן היינו לשם שלמים גבי שלמים ושלא לשמו גבי גיטין נמי מפרש בהדיא ונמלך ומצאו בן עירו וכו' דאין זה לשם גויה וי"ל דוודאי אי הוה תני במתניתין שלא לשם זבח כי ההיא דקתני שלא לשם אשה אז היה משתמע הכי אבל השתא דקתני שנזבחו שלא לשמן משמע שפיר שלא לשם זבח זה אלא לשם זבח אחר. תום' טוך: ב] דקאמר ליה מילי דרמי: ג] תיבת בו נמחק: ד] דלאו מינה נמי מחריב בה: ה] של כלי חרס ותיבות כל וגו' נמחק: ו] דמיטמא מאויר אות ב' נמחק: ז] אוכלין ומשקין מיטמאים: ח] ביה לבטל את שם תוכו: ט] כדאמרן דאפי' כלי: י] מפי התנור לא: יא] דס"ד כיון שהוא בעיר מי ששמו כשמו אם כן היה דעת הסופר שאם ימלך זה לגרש בו יגרש אחר ועוד כיון דמצאו בן עירו מיד ואמר לו שמו כשמי אלמא קטטה ביניהם מקודם לכן ולכך כתב לו הסופר סתמא גם לצרכו. הכי הוה ס"ד ודחי ליה מ"מ אנתיק. תום' טוך: יב] סתמא פסול והס"ד פי' שאם יכתבו שם האשה תבא אשה מן השוק שיהיה שמה כך ותהיה סבורה שבעלה צוה לגרש ויבא לידי קטטה בין איש לאשתו ולכך אתינן מילתא דרב יהודה דמוקי לה כר"א דבעי כתיבה לשמה מדאצטריך גם להניח הרי את מותרת לכל אדם דמשום קטטה לא שייך לומר. תום' טוך: יג] שבתוכו טמאין שגם: יד] חיצון דטהורים אע"פ: טו] טמא דהוי רבותא טפי מבכלי שטף דאינו מקבל טומאה מאויר ונראה: טז] תיבות ודוקא בכלי כו' עד לאו קרא נמחק: יז] ומציל וא"ת הא קיי"ל כל דבר המקבל טומאה אינו חוצץ בפני הטומאה וי"ל משום דגלי קרא דאין הכלים מטמאין מאויר כ"ח כדאיתא בפ"ח דכלים משנה ד' וקשה דסוף סוף הדרא קושיא לדוכתיה כגון דאין כלים שבעולם מטמא מאויר כ"ח א"כ מה לי כ"ח ומה לי כלי (עץ) [שטף] לעולם כו' ומאי אפילו ונראה דלא מבעיא כ"ח דמינה הוא אלא אף כלי שטף דלאו מינה הוא ומחריב בה ובקונטר' נמי פי' כך בסוף ההלכה גבי ד' תוכו כתיב כו' ופי' שם אלא בא ללמד על כלי שטף שאף הוא מציל דלא תימא דלאו מינה לא מחריב וא"ת לישני הכא ד' תוכו כתיב כדמשני לקמן וי"ל דמ"מ קשיא ליליף מינייהו לענין לשמה דלאו מינה מחריב בה כגון חולין כו' כמו לענין תוך תוכו ומשני עשו חולין אצל קדשים כמחיצה אצל תנור כלומר ליכא לדמויי כלל חולין לכלי שטף דכלי שטף חשיב שפיר מינה כיון דאידי ואידי כלי הוא אלא למחיצה דמיא ולאו מצלא משום דלאו מינה הוא וחולין אצל קדשים לא שנא. ולישנא עשו חולין אצל קדשים מוכח קצת דמעיקרא הוי בעי למילף חולין מיתורא דתוך תוכו דכלי שטף. אבל ליכא לשנויי דהשתא לא ידע מיתורא דד' תוכו כתיבי כדמשני לקמן שהרי בסמוך בסוף סוגיין משמע שידע ליה ליתורא דקאמר דהכא נמי לייתי תוכו ליפקו מק"ו כמו שפי' שם בקונטרס. והא ליכא למימר דשפיר ידע יתורא דתוך תוכו לגבי כ"ח דהוי מינה ולאו לגבי כלי שטף דלאו מינה הוא והוי ס"ד דהא דקאמר אפי' כלי שטף מסברא קאמר והשתא פריך שפיר גם זה אינו כדמוכח בפ' הקונטרס גבי ד' תוכו כתיב דכל עיקר היתור לא איצטריך לכ"ח לכך נראה דעדיפא (א) כו' וא"ת אמאי לא משני כדלעיל גבי גט דל גויה מינה כו' נהי דלאו מינה לא מחריב ב) שניה תוך תוכו והוי סתמא מ"מ תוכו ולא תוך תוכו ולכך מציל וי"ל (דאפ"ה) [דאם] אינו חשוב תוך תוכו סתמא א"כ הוי בכלל תוכו וכן משמע לישנא דברייתא דקאמר ולא תוך תוכו ואפילו כלי שטף דמשמע [דממיעוטא] תוך תוכו מציל בכלי שטף הוא מטעם יתור כדפי' תום' טוך: יח] תיבות כמו מחיצה נמחק: יט] אבל תוך תוכו שבכלי חרס טהור כו' דחד תוכו אמר:

הגהות הב"ח

(א) רש"י ד"ה כוורת וכו' דלאו כלי הוא וכמחיצה הויא דאי הואי:

גליון הש"ס

תום' ד"ה הכותב וכו' דהך יתר כמו כן. ע' בכורות... אבן חגיגה ד' כג ע"ב ד"ה וקתני:

א) כוון לדברי התוס' בד"ה ורמינהו דכתבו שם וי"ל דעדיפא משני הכא וכו'. ב) נראה דצ"ל לא מחריב לבטל שם תוכו מ"מ הוי סתמא ולא הוי בכלל תוכו ולכך מציל.

עין משפט נר מצוה

ה א מיי' פ"ג מהל' גירושין הל"ב טוש"ע אה"ע סי' קלא סעי' כ:
ו ב מיי' שם הל"ג טוש"ע שם סעי' ג:
ז ג מיי' שם הל"ד טוש"ע שם סעי' ז:
ח ד מיי' פ"ג מהל' גירושין:
ט ה מיי' פט"ו מהל' פסה"מ הל"ב:
י ו מיי' פי"ד מהל' כלים הל' ח ט:
יא ז מיי' שם הל"ו:
יב ח מיי' שם הלי"ח:

נ"א דדייקינן מזאת דייקינן מינה כו' [וע"ע תוס' גיטין כד: סד"ה יתר מכן]

נ"א אפי' הכי קתני הוסיף דאי לאו כו' נ"ק [רש"ק נ"י קשה ליה]

מסורת הש"ס

[גיטין כד.] [שם:] גיטין כו. ע"ש [וקצת משולל הכונה ובמשנה דגיטין ליתא] [לקמן מו:] חולין כה. כלים פ"ח מ"א תוספתא ב"ק דכלים פ"ו ס"א ס"א נ"א רבא ל"ג

אם הציל במת חמור – שכן א] חלוקה באוהלין, תציל בכלי חרש הקל – ב] שאין חלוקין *באוהלין? התינח לרבנן, לרבי אליעזר מאי איכא למימר? ר' אליעזר קל וחומר קאמר. אי הכי, ג] *התם נמי לימא קל וחומר: קדשים מחללין קדשים, חולין לא כל שכן? אלא, ד] טעמא דרב כרבי ה] אלעזר, *דאמר רבי אלעזר: מאי טעמא דרב? °"ולא יחללו את קדשי בני ישראל ו] את אשר ירימו לה'" – קדשים מחללין קדשים, ואין חולין מחללין קדשים. אלמא, אתא קרא אפקיה מקל וחומר, ז] הכא נמי: ליתי "תוכו" לפקיה מק"ו! האי "תוכו" מיבעי ליה לאוכלין שגיבלן בטיט והכניסן לאויר תנור; סד"א: הואיל ובנגיעה לא מטמא, באוירו נמי לא מטמו, [קמ"ל]. ח] ורבנן: הנך לא צריכי קרא.§ רב יוסף בר אמי רמי שינוי קודש אשינוי בעלים, ומשני. מי אמר *רב: חטאת ששחטה לשם חטאת – כשירה, לשם עולה – פסולה; אלמא דלאו מינה מחריב בה, דמינה לא מחריב בה? והאמר רב: *חטאת ששחטה על מי שמחוייב חטאת – פסולה, על מי שמחוייב עולה – כשרה; אלמא דבר מינה מחריב בה, דלאו מינה לא מחריב בה! ומשני: *התם °"ושחט אותה לחטאת" אמר רחמנא, והרי חטאת לשם חטאת נשחטה; *הכא "וכפר עליו" כתיב, עליו – *ולא על חבירו, •חבירו דומיא דידיה, שמחוייב כפרה (א) כמותה. רב חביבא רמי שינוי בעלים א"תוך תוכו", ומשני. ומי אמר רב: חטאת ששחטה על מי שמחוייב [חטאת – פסולה, על מי שמחוייב] עולה – כשירה; אלמא, דמינה מחריב בה, (ב) לאו מינה לא מחריב בה? והתניא: "תוכו" – ולא תוך תוכו, אפילו כלי שטף מציל! ומשני: ט] *ארבעה "תוכו" כתיבי (תוכו) תוך, תוכו, תוך, תוכו; חד – לגופיה, וחד – לגזירה שוה, חד – תוכו של זה ולא תוכו של אחר, אידך – תוכו ולא תוך תוכו, ואפילו כלי שטף מציל.§ מנלן

רש"י

אם הציל. המחיצה במת החמור – באהל המת, שהמחיצה מפסקת י] וכלים שמעבר השני טהורין, דכתיב (במדבר יט): "כל אשר באהל יטמא", והני לאו בההוא אהל נינהו. שכן חולקין. דרך בני אדם לחלוק אוהלין במחיצה, הלכך אהל אחרינא הוא. תציל בכלי חרס. יא] [בתמיה. שאין חולקין כלי חרס] במחיצות, הלכך "תוכו" קרינא ביה. התינח לרבנן. דאמרי מחיצה לא מצלא, איתא לדרב דאמר דלאו מיניה לא מחריב ביה. אלא לר' אליעזר מאי איכא למימר. לימא דרב תנאי היא? ר' אליעזר קל וחומר קאמר. לעולם בעלמא ר' אליעזר כרב סבירא ליה, כגון חולין וקדשים. אבל לענין מחיצה – מקל וחומר יליף, כיון דבמת החמור מצלא – קל וחומר לכלי חרס הקל, שהשרץ קל מן המת. הכי גרסינן: אלא טעמא דרב כר' יב] אלעזר "ולא יחללו את קדשי" הכי דריש ליה: אין יג] דבר אחר מחלל את קדשי בני ישראל, וגזירת הכתוב היא. ופרכינן: אלמא לר' אלעזר דבעית לאוקמה לדרב אליביה, אתא קרא ד"לא יחללו" ואפקיה מק"ו, דהוה לן למידרש: קדשים מחללין קדשים יד] כו'. ה"נ ליתי תוכו. קרא יתירא, דדרשינן לקמן: "תוכו" ולא תוך תוכו טו] (וקאמרת מקרא למידק למידרש תוכו ולא תוך תוכו) וקאמרת מסברא דלא ממעט אלא תוך כלי אחר, אבל מחיצה דלאו בת מיניה – לית ליה לאיתרובי, אי לאו משום קל וחומר. ואמאי אמרת קל וחומר? ליתי "תוכו" וליפקיה, דמדמעט תוך תוכו – מכלל דתוכו לעולם טמא. דאי מחיצה טז] (*בעלמא) מצלא – למה לי קרא למעוטי תוך תוכו? השתא תוכו מציל, תוך תוכו מבעיא? והאי שבעבר המחיצה תוכו הוא לרב, דהאמרת דלאו מיניה לא מחריב ביה. אמר לך ר' אלעזר האי תוכו דאתי למעוטי תוך תוכו, ובעית למידק מיניה מחיצה לא מצלא. מיבעי ליה לאוכלין שגיבלן. ואיפן בטיט סביב, שאין השרץ יכול ליגע בהן, והכניסן לאויר התנור. והני הוא דאיתרבו לטומאה מדרשא דלא תוך תוכו הוא, כדקאמרת: תוך תוכו הוא דמציל, אבל הקפת טיט – לא מיחרבא ביה לבטולי שם תוכו, יז] *דלאו מיניה כה"ג לא מחריב ביה. דס"ד אמינא: הואיל וא"א להם ליטמא במגע שרץ – לא נטמאו נמי מתורת אויר כלי חרס, *קמ"ל מיעוטא יח] דלא, תוך תוכו הוא (דאמר) דלא מטמא, אבל הני מיטמו. ומיהו, מחיצה אע"ג דלאו מיניה הוא – אתא ק"ו ורבייה לאיתרובי ביה. ורבנן יט] הני. אוכלין לא צריכי קרא. הך וי"ו יתירא דדריש לקמן למעוטי תוך תוכו, ואיתרבו הנך כ] [דלאו] מיניה נינהו – לא איצטריך קרא לרבויינהו, דהני מ"תוך" נפקי, דהא בתוך נינהו, ומהיכא תיתי לך לטהרינהו? והא דקאמר הואיל ובנגיעה לא מטמאו – לאו אירייא היא לטהרינהו מדין אויר. שינוי קודש. חטאת לשם עולה. שינוי בעלים. חטאת ראובן כא] ששחט לשם שמעון להתכפר בה שמעון, דקי"ל [לקמן] דפסולה, דכתיב: "לכפר עליו" כב] ולא על חבירו. חטאת ששחטה לשם חטאת. חטאת חלב ששחטה לשם חטאת דם. והא מילתא לקמן בפירקין (דף ז.). והאמר רב. בשינוי בעלים: חטאת ראובן ששחטה להתכפר בה שמעון, אם שמעון מחוייב חטאת כג] (הוה) – פסולה, אבל אם מחוייב עולה ולא חטאת – כשרה. אלמא: לאו מיניה לאו מחריב ביה! התם. כד] שינוי קודש נפקא לן [לפסולא מ"ושחט] אותה לחטאת" – שתהא שחיטה לשם חטאת, וכאן הרי חטאת לשם חטאת נשחטה. הכא. בשינוי בעלים, פסולה נפקא לן מ"עליו" ולא על חבירו. והילכך, חבירו דומיא דידיה, דבר מיניה הוא דמחריב ביה לבטולי שמיה. ארבעה תוכו כתיבי. כיצד? "תוכו" תרי זימני, ודרוש "תוך" ודרוש "תוכו", דהוה מצי למיכתב "אל תוך" וכתיב "תוכו" למיעוטא, וכן בחבירו. חד לגופיה. שיטמא [*אוכלין] מאוירן. וחד לג"ש. שיטמא שרץ את הכלי ואע"פ שלא נגע כה] כו', כדיליף ליה ב"הכל שוחטין" (חולין דף כד:): נאמר "תוכו" ליטמא, ונאמר "תוכו" לטמא. ולא תוכו של אחר. למעוטי כלי שטף מטומאת אויר, אא"כ נגע. וחד תוכו ולא תוך תוכו. כדפרישית לעיל. וע"כ עיקר קרא לכלי שטף אתא, דאי למעוטי כלי חרס שבתוך התנור, ופיו למעלה מפי התנור, שיציל על האוכלין שבתוכו – למה לי וי"ו יתירא למעוטי? לכתוב "כל אשר כו] [בתוך] יטמא", ומהיכא תיתי לטמויי אוכלים שבפנימי? הא לאו תוכו נינהו! אלא, ללמד על כלי שטף שאף הוא יציל, דלא תימא דלאו מיניה לאו מחריב ביה. הילכך גזירת הכתוב היא. ומנלן

תוספות

*שכן חולקין אוהלים. פי' בקונטרס: שכן דרך בני אדם לחלוק אהלים במחילה, הילכך אהל אחרינא הוא. אבל תנור – אין דרך לחלקו. משמע לפירושו דפליגי אף בתנור שחללו בנסרים או ביריעות. ובתורת כהנים משמע דבכוורת פחותה ופקוקה ומשולשלת לאויר תנור דוקא פליגי, ולא כשחללו בנסרים. וטעמא, משום דכוורת שיש לה ד' מחילות חיילא, דדמי לכלי, ולכך מטהר. אבל מחילה אחת בתנור – מודה ר' אליעזר דלא חיילא, וטמא. והכי איתא בפרשת "ויהי ביום השמיני" גבי "תוכו" ולא תוך תוכו, כיצד? חבית שנתנוה בתנור ופיה למעלה מן התנור כו' מיכן אמרו: כוורת שהיא פחותה כו'. ור' אליעזר אומר: מצלת. אמר ר' אליעזר: אם הצילה במת חמור – לא תציל בכלי חרס הקל? אמרו לו: אם הצילה במת חמור – מקום שהמחילה מצלת, תציל בכלי חרס הקל שאין כו] מחילה מצלת? משמע ד"שכן חולקים אהלים" דאמרו לו דשמעתין – היינו נמי פירושו ד"אמרו לו" דתורת כהנים! לכך נראה לרבינו הקדוש לפרש הכי: אם הציל כוורת פחותה ופקוקה באהל המת – שכן חולקין אהלים, פירוש: שכן מחילה אחת המפסקת מצלת, תאמר בכלי חרס שתחוך כוורת – שאין חולקין אהלים, פי': שמחילה אחת המפסקת בתנור אינה מצלת! אלמא בתנור שחללו לא פליגי. והא דמסיים בתורת כהנים בתר הכי, כח] וקתני בלשון שמועתינו, שאמר לו ר' יוחנן בן נורי: [אם הציל אהלים מיד אוהלים במת כט] חמור – שכן חולקים אוהלים, יצילו אוהלים מיד ל] אוהלים בשרץ, שכן אין חולקים כלי חרס? אמר רבי יוסי: אמרתי לר' יוחנן בן נורי]: תמיה אני אם קיבל ממך רבי אליעזר תשובה, מפני שהוא הנדון. פירש לא] ר"ש שגם שם פליג ר' אליעזר, ועל זה ל"ע. ונראה לי ברוך: גם מהכא משמע לב] בפירוש ד"חולקים אהלים" דקאמר ר' יוחנן בן נורי – לג] היינו מחילה של תנור, ועל זה אמר לו רבי יוסי: הלא גם שם פליג רבי אליעזר. והשתא פירכא ד"אמרו לו" ופירכא דר' יוחנן בן נורי – הכל אחד, אלא דמר אמר בהאי לישנא ומר אמר בהאי לישנא. ואין להפך לד] הגירסא כמו שיש א) [מקצת ספר] בתורת כהנים, ולגרוס ב"אמרו לו": שכן חולקים אהלים, ולפרש כפי' ר"ש, ועל ר' יוחנן בן נורי נגרוס: שכן מחילה מצלת, ועל זה יתיישב ר' יוסי שאומר: הלא הוא הנדון. אין לומר כן, שהרי בתוספתא דמסכת כלים לה] ב) מוכחא, כי ליכא מילתא ד"אמרו לו" כלל, כי אם דברי ר' יוחנן בן נורי: שכן חולקין אהלים, ועלה א"ר יוסי: הלא הוא הנדון. והתם אין לשנות הגירסא, כיון ד"אמרו לו" לא איירי התם – ש"מ ד"חולקין אהלים" הוי פירושן לו] גבי כלי חרס מחילה המפסקת בתנור כמו פירכא דמחילה [מצלת] ד"אמרו לו", שניהן סוברין שרבי אליעזר לז] הודה [במחילה] גבי תנור, ועל זה אמר ר' יוסי: הוא הנדון, גם שם פליג ר"א. ברו"ך.

לח] הכא נמי נימא קל וחומר מחללין קדשים כו'. יש תימה: דעד השתא אסיקנא איפכא מתוך הסברא, דאדרבה בשביל שהם קדשים ומינה – לכך מחריב בה. אבל חולין, דלאו בר מינה – לא מחריבו! ונראה לפרש דעביד קל וחומר משום דמה קדשים שאין מחללין, כגון בשוחט חטאת סתם וכסבור שהיא עולה – דכשירה, ואפ"ה מחללין קדשים בשוחט לשם עולה. חולין שמחללין, כגון בכסבור שהן חולין, דאמר בסוף "בית שמאי" (לקמן דף מו:) משום חולין פסולה, לא כל שכן שמחללין קדשים בשוחטן לשם חולין? לא יחללו את קדשי בני ישראל. אע"ג דהאי קרא כתיב בטבל ובתרומה, כדמוכח לקמן (דף יא:) בגמרא דשמעון אחי עזריה, דילמא "קדשי" מיותר קדרים, דהוה מצי למיכתב: ולא יחללו את אשר ירימו.

א) נ"ל טעות סופר ב) נ"ל מוכחא דליכא מילתא כו' נ"ק

מה

א] שכן חולקין אהלים (תיבות חלוקה באוהלין נמחק) משמע שכן חילוק מחיצה מועילה (באהלים) [באוהל המת] להציל תאמר בכ"ח דלא וקשה דהוא הדין והוא התשובה דבמחיצה נמי פליגי כדפירש"י אלא נראה כפרש"י ז"ל שכן חולקין אהלים כלומר שכן דרך בני אדם לחלוק אהלים כו' וא"ת וכי בדרך בני אדם תליא מילת' ור"י מפרש דאה"נ דכי אמר רחמנא כל אשר באהל יטמא ולא מה שבאהל (אחרים) [אחר] זהו לפי דרך בני אדם וא"ת התינח דליכא למילף שרץ ממת כדאמרי' שכן חולקים אהלים אבל כוורת פקוקה המצלת במת מטעם צמיד פתיל ולא מטעם מחיצה א"כ נילף שרץ ממת מק"ו ואמאי פליגי רבנן בכוורת וי"ל דכיון דלענין מחיצה נדחה הק"ו דשרץ ממת תו ליכא למילף בכוורת דאיכא למפרך מה למת שכן מחיצה מצלת כך יש לפרש לפי שיטת הקונטרס דפי' דרבנן פליגי בין בכוורת בין במחיצה מיהו קשה דבת"כ משמע דר"א בר פלוגתייהו דרבנן לא פליג במחיצה דקתני במלתייהו דרבנן אמרו לו אם הצילה במת החמור שכן מחיצה מצלת כו' משמע דבמחיצה כ"ע מודו דלא מצלא בכ"ח לכך נ"ל דאה"נ דבמחיצה מודו כ"ע ושכן חולקין אהלים ר"ל שכן מועיל חילוק אהלים דמצלת מחיצה גבי מת מה שאין כן בשרץ דכ"ע מודו דהיינו כי הא דת"כ וק"ו דר"א ה"ק אם הצילה במת החמור מטע' מוקף צמיד פתיל ואכוורת קאי דוקא ותימה לר"א מחיצה גופה נילף מהאי דינא ק"ו ממת לשרץ וצ"ל דפשיטא ליה דליכא למילף מחיצה מק"ו לפי שדרך בני אדם לחלוק אהלים כמו שפי' רבינו יחיאל נ"ע זה תירוץ נוכל לומר מבחוץ. תוס' טוך: ב] שאין חולקין בכלי חרס תיבות חלוקין באוהלין נמחק: ג] אי הכי. התם תיבת הכא נמחק: ד] אלא היינו טעמא. וגרסינן אלא משום דהשתא לא צריכנא להא שינויי דלעיל דעשו חולין כמחיצה דאפילו באת לדמות חולין לכלי שטף מ"מ ניחא משום דגבי חולין אצל קדשים גלי קרא ולכך לא ילפינן מהתם ומהאי טעמא ניחא בין לר"א ובין לרבנן. תוס' טוך: ה] כרבי אלעאי תיבת אלעזר נמחק: ו] תיבות את אשר ירימו לה' נמחק: ז] עי' בהשמטות בסוף המסכת: ח] ורבנן הנך לא צריכי קרא פ"ה האי וי"ו יתירא דדריש לקמן למעוטי תוך תוכו ואתרבו הנך (מיניה דתוכו נינהו) [אוכלין שגבלן בטיט] לא איצטרי' [קרא לרבויינהו] דהני מתוך נפקי דהא בתוך נינהו ואי משום דאמרת הואיל ובנגיעה לא מטמא לאו [אירייא] היא דאין לדמות נגיעה לאויר הילכך הא דאיצטריך תוך תוכו לגלויי דתוכו טמא אפי' בהפסקה היינו להפסקה דמחיצה וכוורת לאפוקי מק"ו דר"א וא"ת לרבנן למה לי האי טעמא תיפוק ליה דאינהו פרכי ליה (לקמן) לר' אליעזר כדקאמרי רבנן לעיל שכן חולקין אהלים ויש לומר למאי דפרישית לעיל ניחא דאיכא תנא דקאמר לא קיבל ר"א התשובה ונשאר הק"ו ולפי' השני נאמר דלדברי רבי אליעזר קאמרי רבנן כלומר לדבריך נמי דאית לך הק"ו לייתי א) תוכו בשביל אוכלין שגבלן בטיט דהנך לא צריכי קרא. תוס' טוך: ט] עי' בהשמטות בסוף המסכת: י] מפסקת דכלים שמעבר: יא] בתמיה שאין חולקין כלי חרס: יב] כר' אלעאי תיבת אלעזר נמחק: יג] תיבת ב) דבר נמחק מחלל רק: יד] קדשים חולין לא כ"ש הס"ד ותיבת כו' נמחק: טו] מתיבת וקאמרת כו' עד תיבת וקאמרת נמחק: טז] תיבת בעלמא או הג"א תיבת מעליא נמחק: יז] שם תוכו דלאו מינה: יח] דלא דוקא תוך תוכו אבל הני והשאר נמחק: יט] ורבנן הנך אוכלין: כ] הנך אוכלין שגבלן בטיט ולא איצטריך ותיבות דלאו מיניה נינהו נמחק: כא] (ראובן) שנשחט להתכפר בה ותיבות ששחט לשם שמעון נמחק: כב] עליו. עליו ולא: כג] חטאת הוא פסולה: כד] בשינוי קודש דפסולה נפקא לן מושחט אותה: כה] נגע בו ותיבת כו' נמחק: כו] אשר בתוך יטמא: כז] שאין המחיצה מצלת: כח] תיבת וקתני נמחק: כט] במת החמור שכן: ל] מיד אהלים באהל השרץ שכן אין: לא] פירש רבי תיבות ר"ש ל"ש ונמחק: לב] משמע דפי' אות ב' נמחק: לג] דהיינו מחיצה מצלת תיבות של תנור נמחק: לד] להפך הגירסא כמו שיש במעט ספרים בתורת כהנים: לה] תיבות מוכחא כי נמחק: לו] הוי פירושן דמפסקת ומצלת כמו. והשאר נמחק: לז] אלעזר מודה גבי אות ה' נמחק ותיבת במחיצה ל"ש: לח] מה"ד התם נמי ותיבת הכא נמחק:

א) נראה דל"ל ליתי תוכו ומפיק מק"ו דבשביל אוכלין וכו'. ב) אולי נ"ל אין חולין מחלל את קדשי בני ישראל רק קדשים ותיבת דבר נמחק.

מסורת הש"ס / הגהות

נ"א בכלי חרס

נ"ל הכא

לקמן מו:

ויקרא כב

[לקמן ז. איתא רבא וכצ"ל ועי' זבחים ט: ומנחות ג: ותוס' זבחים ז. ד"ה אמר רבא]

[שם]

שם ז

נ"א הכא

לקמן ד: ז. ח. פסחים סב.

נ"א מעליא ומגלא

חולין כה.

נ"א דלאו כה"ג מחריב

ס"א קמ"ל מיעוטא דוקא תוך תוכו הוא כו' אבל הני מיטמי

וגי' נ"ק אוכלין ומשקין שבאוירן

הגהות הב"ח

(א) גמ' שמחוייב כפרה כמותו: (ב) שם דלאו מינה לא:

גליון הש"ס

גמ' חבירו דומיא דידיה. עיין חולין דף לב ע"א תוס' ד"ה אבל:

וּמְנָלַן דְּבָעֵינַן זְבִיחָה לִשְׁמָהּ. לְכַתְּחִילָּה. דְּאִי מִ"מוֹצָא שְׂפָתֶיךָ" – לָא מִיפָּרְשִׁי בֵּיהּ* עֲבוֹדוֹת. מַמַּאי דִּלְעִנְיַן שְׁחִיטָה יג] קְרוּי זֶבַח [דִּלְמָא] הַיְינוּ שְׁמַיְיהוּ. "זֶבַח שְׁלָמִים", וְלָא נֶאֱמַר "זֶבַח" מִשּׁוּם שְׁחִיטָה! מַה לִּזְבִיחָה שֶׁכֵּן יד] פּוֹסֶלֶת שֶׁלֹּא לְשֵׁם אוֹכְלִין בְּפֶסַח. שֶׁאִם שְׁחָטוֹ שֶׁלֹּא לְאוֹכְלִין, כְּגוֹן לְחוֹלֶה וּלְזָקֵן שֶׁאֵין יְכוֹלִין לֶאֱכוֹל כְּזַיִת – פָּסוּל, וַאֲפִילּוּ הֵן בְּעָלָיו, דִּכְתִיב: "אִישׁ לְפִי אָכְלוֹ" אֲכִילָה בִּכְזַיִת. וּשְׁאָר עֲבוֹדוֹת לָא פָּסְלֵי שֶׁלֹּא לְאוֹכְלִין, דִּכְתִיב: "תָּכוֹסּוּ", וְתַנְיָא (פסחים דף סא.), רַבִּי אוֹמֵר: לְשׁוֹן סוּרְסִי הוּא זֶה, כְּאָדָם הָאוֹמֵר לַחֲבֵירוֹ "כּוֹס לִי טָלֶה זֶה". וְהָכִי אָמְרִינַן בִּפְסָחִים (דף עח:) דְּאֵין (מַחֲשָׁבָה) *אוֹכְלִין בִּזְרִיקָה. הַמַּקְרִיב. קַבָּלָה הוּא, דְּתַנְיָא: "וְהִקְרִיבוּ" – טו] זֶה קַבָּלַת הַדָּם. שֶׁכֵּן פְּסוּלָה בְּזָר. לְאַפּוֹקֵי שְׁחִיטָה שֶׁכְּשֵׁירָה בְּזָר, כִּדְלְקַמָּן בְּפֶרֶק שְׁלִישִׁי (דף לב.). שְׁחִיטָה וְקַבָּלָה טְעוּנוֹת צָפוֹן – בְּפ' "אֵיזֶהוּ מְקוֹמָן" (לקמן דף מח.) יָלֵיף לְהוּ מִקְּרָאֵי. וְיֶשְׁנָן בַּחַטָּאוֹת הַפְּנִימִיּוֹת. אֲבָל זְרִיקַת מִזְבַּח הַחִיצוֹן לֵית בְּהוּ. זְרִיקָה זָר חַיָּיב עָלֶיהָ מִיתָה. אֲבָל שְׁחִיטָה כְּשֵׁרָה בְּזָר. וְקַבָּלָה וְהוֹלָכָה, אַע"פ שֶׁפְּסוּלָה בְּזָר – אֵין חַיָּיב עָלֶיהָ מִיתָה, כִּדְאָמְרִי' בְּסֵדֶר יוֹמָא (דף כד.): אַרְבָּעָה עֲבוֹדוֹת זָר חַיָּיב עֲלֵיהֶם מִיתָה: זְרִיקָה וְהַקְטָרָה וְנִיסּוּךְ הַמַּיִם וְהַיַּיִן. דִּכְתִיב גַּבֵּי "וְהַזָּר הַקָּרֵב יוּמָת" – "וַעֲבַדְתֶּם עֲבוֹדַת מַתָּנָה", וְדָרְשִׁינַן: עֲבוֹדַת מַתָּנָה וְלֹא עֲבוֹדַת סִילּוּק, "וַעֲבַדְתֶּם" – עֲבוֹדָה תַּמָּה, וְלֹא עֲבוֹדָה שֶׁיֵּשׁ אַחֲרֶיהָ עֲבוֹדָה, וְהָנֵי כּוּלְּהוּ יֵשׁ אַחֲרֵיהֶם עֲבוֹדָה. מִכּוּלְּהוּ. בַּמֶּה הַצַּד הַשָּׁוֶה שֶׁבָּהֶן, שֶׁהֵן עֲבוֹדָה וּצְרִיכָה לִשְׁמָהּ – אַף אֲנִי אָבִיא הוֹלָכָה. הוֹלָכָה אֶפְשָׁר לְבַטְּלָהּ. שֶׁאִם רָצָה – שׁוֹחֵט בְּצַד הַמִּזְבֵּחַ וְזוֹרֵק, כִּדְתַנְיָא בְּמַתְנִיתִין (לקמן דף יג.). וְהִקְרִיבוּ זוֹ קַבָּלַת הַדָּם. "וְשָׁחַט אֶת בֶּן הַבָּקָר וְהִקְרִיבוּ בְּנֵי אַהֲרֹן הַכֹּהֲנִים" – זוֹ קַבָּלָה, דְּהָא בָּתַר שְׁחִיטָה כְּתִיב. *וְלָא אֶפְשָׁר לְאוֹקוּמֵיהּ בְּהוֹלָכָה, וְאַף עַל גַּב דִּלְשׁוֹן הוֹלָכָה הוּא, כְּדַחֲזֵינַן בְּהוֹלָכַת אֵבָרִים דִּכְתִיב בֵּיהּ הַקְרָבָה, וּלְשׁוֹן הוֹלָכָה הִיא. טז] ה"ג: וְאַפְקֵיהּ רַחֲמָנָא קַבָּלָה בִּלְשׁוֹן הוֹלָכָה לְמֵימְרָא דְּהוֹלָכָה לָא תַּפְקָה מִכְּלַל קַבָּלָה. שִׁינּוּי בְּעָלִים מְנָלַן. שֶׁצָּרִיךְ לְשׁוֹחֲטוֹ עַל מְנָת שֶׁיִּתְכַּפְּרוּ בּוֹ בְּעָלָיו וְלֹא שֶׁיִּתְכַּפֵּר בּוֹ אַחֵר, דְּקָתָנֵי לְקַמָּן (דף מו:): לְשֵׁם שִׁשָּׁה דְּבָרִים הַזֶּבַח נִזְבָּח, לְשֵׁם זוֹבֵחַ – יז] מְנָלַן דְּבָעֵינַן לְשֵׁם זוֹבֵחַ? זֶבַח תּוֹדַת שְׁלָמָיו. שֶׁתְּהֵא זְבִיחָתוֹ לְשֵׁם תּוֹדָה. כְּשֵׁרָה. וְעָלוּ לְשֵׁם חוֹבָה. פְּסוּלָה. כְּלוֹמַר, לֹא עָלוּ לְשֵׁם חוֹבָה. תּוֹדָה קְרוּיָה שְׁלָמִים. כִּדְכְתִיב: "תּוֹדַת שְׁלָמָיו", כְּמוֹ: "חַטַּאת הַקָּהָל" (ויקרא ד), "תּוֹרַת מֹשֶׁה עַבְדִּי" (מלאכי ג). אֲנַן מִזֶּבַח תּוֹדָה קָאָמְרִי'. דְּרָשָׁא דִּידַן, יח] וְאַבָּא חָנָן מִ"תּוֹדַת שְׁלָמָיו". חַטָּאת וְאָשָׁם מִנַּיִן. בְּת"כ קָתָנֵי לַהּ, גַּבֵּי הַאי קְרָא "וּבְשַׂר זֶבַח תּוֹדַת שְׁלָמָיו בְּיוֹם קָרְבָּנוֹ יֵאָכֵל" – לָמַדְנוּ לְתוֹדָה שֶׁנֶּאֱכֶלֶת לְיוֹם וָלַיְלָה. חַטָּאת וְאָשָׁם מִנַּיִן. ת"ל "זֶבַח". א"כ. דִּלְהַךְ דְּרָשָׁא לְחוּדֵיהּ אָתָא, לְרַבּוֹת חַטָּאת וְאָשָׁם שֶׁתְּהֵא אֲכִילָתוֹ לְיוֹם וָלַיְלָה – יט] לִכְתּוֹב לְ"זֶבַח" לְבַסּוֹף, לְגַבֵּי אֲכִילָה. לֹא חָלַקְתָּ. דְּהָא כּוּלְּהוּ אִיתְרַבּוּ לְעֵיל. שֶׁכֵּן פְּסוּלוֹ בְּגוּפוֹ. לְקַמָּן מְפָרֵשׁ לַהּ וְאָזֵיל. וְיֶשְׁנוֹ בְּד' עֲבוֹדוֹת. שֶׁאִם שָׁחַט שֶׁלֹּא לִשְׁמוֹ, אוֹ קִיבֵּל וְהָלַךְ וְזָרַק שֶׁלֹּא לִשְׁמוֹ, אע"פ שֶׁלֹּא חִישֵּׁב כ] אֶלָּא עַל הַשְּׁחִיטָה שֶׁלֹּא לִשְׁמוֹ – פָּסוּל, כִּדְרַבֵּינַן לְהוּ לְעֵיל. אֲבָל שִׁינּוּי בְּעָלִים – לֹא שַׁיָּיךְ אֶלָּא בִּזְרִיקָה, דְּהָא דְּרַבֵּינַן שְׁחִיטָה לִפְסוֹל בְּשִׁינּוּי בְּעָלִים אֵינוֹ אֶלָּא כְּגוֹן שֶׁשָּׁחַט עַל מְנָת לִזְרוֹק לְהִתְכַּפֵּר בּוֹ אַחֵר, אֲבָל שָׁחַט שֶׁלֹּא לְשֵׁם בְּעָלָיו, וְלֹא הִזְכִּיר עַל מְנָת לִזְרוֹק – אֵין זוֹ מַחֲשָׁבָה, דְּשִׁנּוּי בְּעָלִים לֹא שַׁיָּיךְ בְּקָרְבָּן אֶלָּא לְהִתְכַּפֵּר בּוֹ, וְכַפָּרָה בִּזְרִיקָה הִיא. וְהָכִי אָמְרִי' לְקַמָּן בְּפִרְקִין (דף י.): שֶׁאִם אָמַר "הֲרֵינִי שׁוֹחֵט לְשֵׁם פְּלוֹנִי" – כָּשֵׁר, שְׁחָטוֹ עַל מְנָת לִזְרוֹק לְשֵׁם פְּלוֹנִי – פָּסוּל. וְכֵן לְעִנְיַן קַבָּלָה וְהוֹלָכָה, לֹא שַׁיָּיךְ שִׁינּוּי בְּעָלִים אא"כ חִישֵּׁב לְקַבֵּל עַל מְנָת לִזְרוֹק לְשֵׁם אַחֵר. וְיֶשְׁנוֹ לְאַחַר מִיתָה. הַמַּפְרִישׁ קָרְבָּנוֹ וָמֵת, וְהַיּוֹרֵשׁ מַקְרִיבוֹ – שַׁיָּיךְ בּוֹ שִׁינּוּי קֹדֶשׁ, אֲבָל לֹא שִׁינּוּי בְּעָלִים, שֶׁהֲרֵי מֵתוּ בְּעָלָיו. וְיֶשְׁנוֹ בְּצִבּוּר. אֲבָל שִׁנּוּי בְּעָלִים לֹא שַׁיָּיךְ בְּקָרְבַּן צִבּוּר, שֶׁהֲרֵי הַכֹּל בְּעָלָיו.
וְאע"ג

תורה אור

א] מְנָלַן אדְּבָעֵינַן זְבִיחָה לִשְׁמָהּ? דְּאָמַר קְרָא: °"וְאִם זֶבַח שְׁלָמִים קָרְבָּנוֹ" – שֶׁתְּהֵא זְבִיחָה לְשֵׁם [שְׁלָמִים]. וְדִילְמָא הַיְינוּ שְׁמַיְיהוּ! *מִדִּכְתִיב: °"הַמַּקְרִיב אֶת דַּם הַשְּׁלָמִים" °"הַזּוֹרֵק אֶת דַּם הַשְּׁלָמִים", וְלָא כְּתִיב "זֶבַח", וְהָכָא כְּתִיב "זֶבַח" – שְׁמַע מִינַּהּ: שֶׁתְּהֵא זְבִיחָה לְשֵׁם שְׁלָמִים. אַשְׁכְּחַן זְבִיחָה, שְׁאָר עֲבוֹדוֹת מְנָלַן? וְכִי תֵּימָא: לֵילַף מִזְּבִיחָה; ב] *מַה לִּזְבִיחָה שֶׁכֵּן (א) נִפְסֶלֶת שֶׁלֹּא לְשֵׁם אוֹכְלִין בְּפֶסַח! אֶלָּא אָמַר קְרָא: "הַמַּקְרִיב אֶת דַּם הַשְּׁלָמִים" – שֶׁתְּהֵא קַבָּלָה לְשֵׁם שְׁלָמִים. וְלִכְתּוֹב רַחֲמָנָא בְּקַבָּלָה, וְלֵילַף שְׁחִיטָה מִינַּהּ! מִשּׁוּם דְּאִיכָּא לְמִיפְרַךְ: מַה לְּקַבָּלָה שֶׁכֵּן פְּסוּלָה בְּזָר ג] וְאִשָּׁה. אַשְׁכְּחַן שְׁחִיטָה וְקַבָּלָה, זְרִיקָה מְנָלַן? וְכִי תֵּימָא לֵילַף (ב) מֵהָנֵי – מַה לְּהָנֵי שֶׁכֵּן טְעוּנוֹת צָפוֹן, וְיֶשְׁנָן בַּחַטָּאוֹת הַפְּנִימִיּוֹת! אֶלָּא אָמַר קְרָא: "הַזּוֹרֵק אֶת דַּם הַשְּׁלָמִים" – שֶׁתְּהֵא זְרִיקָה לְשֵׁם שְׁלָמִים. וְלִכְתּוֹב רַחֲמָנָא בִּזְרִיקָה וְלֵילַף מִינַּהּ! מִשּׁוּם דְּאִיכָּא לְמִיפְרַךְ: מַה לִּזְרִיקָה – שֶׁכֵּן חַיָּיב עָלֶיהָ זָר מִיתָה. אַשְׁכְּחַן כּוּלְּהוּ, הוֹלָכָה מְנָלַן? וְכִי תֵּימָא לֵילַף מִכּוּלְּהוּ – מַה לְּכוּלְּהוּ שֶׁכֵּן עֲבוֹדָה שֶׁאִי אֶפְשָׁר לְבַטְּלָהּ, תֹּאמַר בְּהוֹלָכָה שֶׁאֶפְשָׁר לְבַטְּלָהּ! אֶלָּא אָמַר קְרָא: °"וְהִקְרִיב ד] אֶת הַכֹּל הַמִּזְבֵּחָה", *וְאָמַר מָר: זוֹ הוֹלָכַת אֵבָרִים לַכֶּבֶשׁ; וְתַנְיָא: ה] °"וְהִקְרִיבוּ" – *זוֹ קַבָּלַת הַדָּם; ו] (ג) וְאַפְּקִיהּ רַחֲמָנָא בִּלְשׁוֹן הוֹלָכָה, לְמֵימְרָא דְּהוֹלָכָה לָא תַּפְקָה מִכְּלַל קַבָּלָה. ז] וְאַשְׁכְּחַן שִׁנּוּי קוֹדֶשׁ, בשִׁנּוּי בְּעָלִים מְנָלַן? אָמַר רַב פִּנְחָס בְּרֵיהּ דְּרַב אַמִי, אָמַר קְרָא: °"וּבְשַׂר זֶבַח תּוֹדַת שְׁלָמָיו" – שֶׁתְּהֵא זְבִיחָה לְשֵׁם תּוֹדָה; אִם אֵינוֹ עִנְיָן לְשִׁינּוּי קוֹדֶשׁ, דְּנָפְקָא לַן מֵהָתָם – תְּנֵהוּ עִנְיָן לְשִׁינּוּי בְּעָלִים. וְהַאי לְהָכִי הוּא דְּאָתָא? הָא מִיבְּעֵי לֵיהּ *לִכְדְתַנְיָא: "וּבְשַׂר זֶבַח תּוֹדַת שְׁלָמָיו", אַבָּא חָנִין אוֹמֵר מִשּׁוּם רַבִּי אֱלִיעֶזֶר, בָּא לְלַמֵּד: תּוֹדָה שֶׁשְּׁחָטָהּ לְשֵׁם שְׁלָמִים – כְּשֵׁרָה, שְׁלָמִים שֶׁשְּׁחָטָן לְשֵׁם תּוֹדָה – פְּסוּלָה. מַה הֶפְרֵשׁ בֵּין זֶה לָזֶה? תּוֹדָה קְרוּיָה שְׁלָמִים, וְאֵין שְׁלָמִים קְרוּיָה תּוֹדָה! אֲנַן מִ"זֶּבַח" ח] קָאָמְרִינַן. וְאַכַּתִּי מִיבְּעֵי לֵיהּ: חַטָּאת וְאָשָׁם מִנַּיִן? תַּלְמוּד לוֹמַר: "זֶבַח"! אִם כֵּן, ט] נִכְתּוֹב קְרָא "וּבְשַׂר תּוֹדַת שְׁלָמָיו" י] [זֶבַח], מַאי "זֶבַח"? שְׁמַע מִינַּהּ תַּרְתֵּי. אַשְׁכְּחַן זְבִיחָה, שְׁאָר עֲבוֹדוֹת מְנָלַן? וְכִי תֵּימָא לֵילַף מִזְּבִיחָה; מַה לִּזְבִיחָה שֶׁכֵּן פּוֹסֵל שֶׁלֹּא לְשֵׁם אוֹכְלִין בְּפֶסַח! נֶאֶמְרָה זְבִיחָה בְּשִׁינּוּי קוֹדֶשׁ, וְנֶאֶמְרָה זְבִיחָה בְּשִׁינּוּי בְּעָלִים; מַה זְּבִיחָה הָאֲמוּרָה בְּשִׁינּוּי קוֹדֶשׁ – לֹא חָלַקְתָּ בֵּין זְבִיחָה לִשְׁאָר עֲבוֹדוֹת, אַף זְבִיחָה הָאֲמוּרָה בְּשִׁינּוּי בְּעָלִים – לֹא תַּחְלֵק בָּהֶן בֵּין זְבִיחָה לִשְׁאָר עֲבוֹדוֹת. אִיכָּא לְמִיפְרַךְ: *מַה לְּשִׁינּוּי קוֹדֶשׁ, יא] שֶׁכֵּן (ד) פְּסוּלָה בְּגוּפָהּ, וְיֶשְׁנוֹ בְּאַרְבַּע עֲבוֹדוֹת, יב] וְיֶשְׁנוֹ לְאַחַר מִיתָה, וְיֶשְׁנוֹ גבְּצִיבּוּר כְּבְיָחִיד!
וְאע"ג

מה לזביחה שכן פוסל שלא לשם אוכלין בפסח. וא"ת: זריקה נמי תפסול מק"ו דשחיטה, שאינו פוסל בשינוי בעלים אלא על מנת לזרוק, ופוסלת על מנת שלא לשם אוכלין – ק"ו זריקה שפוסלת בזורק שלא לשם בעלים, שתפסול שלא לשם אוכלין! וי"ל: דאיכא למיפרך, מה לזביחה – שכן טעונה צפון וישנה בחטאות הפנימיות. מיהו, אכתי לא קמא ליה הך פירכא עד בסמוך. לכך י"ל: דהכא לא יליף מזביחה אלא קבלה והולכה. ברו"ך. ועוד נראה: דבפ' "תמיד נשחט" (פסחים דף סא.) ממעט שאר עבודות שלא [פסול] לשם אוכלין. מה לזריקה שכן חייב עליה זר כו'. וא"ת: ונילף קבלה והולכה משחיטה וזריקה! וי"ל: מה להנך שכן חייבין בחוץ, כדלקמן בשמעתין. דהולכה לא תפקה מכלל קבלה. וזריקה לא אתיא מכולהו, שישנן בחטאות הפנימיות. בא ללמד תודה ששחטה לשם שלמים כשרה. תימה: דבסוף "כל הפסולין" (לקמן דף לו.) דרשי' מיניה: מנין לרבות שלמי נזיר ושלמי פסח – ת"ל "שלמיו", פי': דנאכלין ליום ולילה! וי"ל: דהתם דריש מדכתביה גבי אכילה. ש"מ תרתי. וא"ת: ואימא כוליה [להכי] הוא דאתא, שתהא זביחה לשם תודה! וי"ל: דאיכא לרבויי חטאת ואשם, מדכתיב *ביה אכילה. וישנן לאחר מיתה. אבל שינוי בעלים אינן לאחר מיתה. בפסחים (דף סא.) הקשה רבינו: (דלמא מאחר) דשיעבודא לאו דאורייתא – כמו כן אין שינוי קודש לאחר מיתה, דמאי נפקא מינה דלא עלו לשם חובה? הא לא מיחייבי יורשין להביא אחר! דפלוגתא היא בקדושין בפ"ק (דף יג:) גבי האשה שהביאה חטאתה ומתה יביאו יורשין עולתה, דקאמר שמואל: והוא שהפרישתה מחיים, *ורב אשי אמר: אפי' שלא הפרישתה מחיים. והל"ל הכא: למ"ד שיעבודא [לאו] דאורייתא, שאין שנוי קודש לאחר מיתה – *תרתי מיהא דווקא! ויש לומר: דנפקא מינה אם הפריש שתי שלמים או שתי עולות לאחריות, ופירש שאם אחת מתה או אבודה – השניה תהיה קריבה עולה כדין הראשונה, ואם קרבה הראשונה כתקונה – השניה תהיה חולין. וכי מתו בעלים ועשה יורש אחת שלא לשמה – הרי היא כאילו נאבדה, וקרבה שניה תחתיה, ואם עשה הראשונה כתיקנה – אז השניה חולין. אבל אם לא פירש כלום, אלא סתם הפריש שתים *לאחריות, אז אפילו נעשית הראשונה כתיקנה – הוי שניה רועה ודמיה קרבי עולה, כמו גבי מפריש שתי חטאות לאחריות, כדאיתא לקמן (דף יא:): מותר חטאת קרב עולה. *)והכי נמי הוי בהפריש שתי שלמים או שתי עולות לאחריות. ועי"ל: דלאחר מיתה הוי [איסור] בשינוי קודש כשמשנהו, אבל ליכא איסורא בשינוי בעלים כיון דליכא בעלים. מיהו, אכתי לא ידע דרשא ד"מוצא שפתיך" דמינה נפקא איסור לשינוי קודש, מדמייתי לה בסמוך. הגה"ה. וישנן בציבור. משא"כ בשינוי בעלים, דאם שחט **)לשמו התמיד – הרי הוא בעליו, ואפי' לשם גוי לא מיפסיל, דבעינן חבירו דומיא דידיה, מחוייב כפרה כמותו. ברו"ך.

*) ונראה נמי דהכא **) נ"א לשם היחיד

מחשבה

נ"א עבודות לשמו

רש"ק מ"ז ונ"א דאין מחשבת אוכלין בזריקה ולא בקבלה והולכה אלא בשחיטה כל"ל

הגהות הב"ח

(א) גמ' מה לזביחה שכן פוסלת שלא לשם: (ב) שם זריקה מנ"ל וכ"ת ליליף מהני כ"ב ע"ל דף י ע"א: (ג) שם ואפקה רחמנא לקבלה בלשון הולכה: (ד) שם מה לשינוי קודש שכן פסולו בגופו וישנו:

[עירובין קד. יומא כז. מנחות י.] חגיגה יא. פסחים סה: לקמן יב: ודף כד: לה.

[עמ"ש תוס' יומא כז. ד"ה והקריבו וכו' על פירש"י דהכא]

לקמן ז.

יג א ב מיי' פ"ד מהל' מעשה הק' הל' י ופי"ג מהלכות פסה"מ הל' א:
יד ג מיי' פט"ו מהל' פסה"מ הלכה א:

נ"א לא ס"ד מדכתיב כו'

[לקמן קז.]

[נ"ל גבי]

נ"א דלמ"ד

[נ"ל והקריב הכהן את הכל והקטיר]

לקמן יג. וקדושין לו: חגיגה יא.]

[נ"ל ורב אשי]

גי' נ"ק חדא

נ"א שלמים או עולות הפריש שתים

שיטה מקובצת

א] מנלן דבעינן זביחה [לשמה] פי' הקונטרס ואי ממוצא שפתיך תשמור לא מפרשי כלל בד' עבודות של דם וקשה דהא ועשית כתיב בהאי קרא דמוצא שפתיך ועשית משמע [בעבודת] הדם וכן קשה הא דאמר תלמודא גבי לא ידענא במאי דפי' לא ידענא במאי אמר הא אמר רחמנא מוצא שפתיך תשמור ועשית וי"ל פי' שלא ישנה ממוצא שפתיו ודלמא לאו לענין לשמה משתעי קרא (וה"ה דאף) ואף כי ישנה באחת במחשבה שלא לשמה מקרי שפיר מוצא שפתיך כיון דבשאר עבודות לא שינה. ת' מהר"פ: ב] עי' בהשמטות בסוף המסכת: ג] תיבת ואשה נמחק: ד] והקריב הכהן את הכל: ה] עי' בהשמטות בסוף המסכת: ו] הדם והולכה היא ואפקיה. ה"ג ואפקיה רחמנא בלשון הולכה למימרא כו' פי' לשון הולכה היא כמו שמוכיח מקרא דוהקריב הכהן את הכל המזבחה ואמת הוא דע"כ זו קבלת הדם כדפי' ואפקיה רחמנא בלשון הולכה כלומר למה אפקיה רחמנא בלשון הולכה כיון שהוא קבלה למימרא דלא תפקיה כו' ויש להקשות נילף זריקה משחיטה וקבלה והולכה ולישתוק מזריקה דמאי פרכת שכן טעונה צפון הולכה לא בעי צפון וי"ל דמ"מ איכא למיפרך שכן ישנן בחטאות הפנימיות דהולכה נמי הוי בחטאות הפנימיות שהיה מוליך את הדם עד להיכל ועד לפרכת. תוס' טוך: ז] עי' בהשמטות בסוף המסכת: ח] מזבח תודת קאמרינן: ט] אם כן לכתוב קרא תודת שלמיו זבח ללמד על חטאת (ושלמים) [ואשם] שנאכלין ליום ולילה ומדאקדמיה זבח לתודה ש"מ זבח לשם תודה. וא"ת ואימא כוליה לזביחה לשם תודה הוא דאתא ומנלן לרבות חטאת ואשם (הנאכל) [דנאכל] ליום ולילה ויש לומר מדכתביה להאי קרא גבי אכילה שמע מינה לרבות נמי חטאת ואשם לאכול יום ולילה. תוס' טוך: י] שלמיו זבח מאי זבח תודת שלמיו שמע מינה: יא] שכן פסולו בגופו וישנן בד' עבודות משא"כ בשינוי בעלים וא"ת והלא לקמן מוכח מקראי פסול בכל ד' עבודות בשינוי בעלים ותירץ בקונטרס דאינו אלא בשוחט ע"מ לזרוק בשינוי בעלים או מקבל ע"מ כו' ויש להקשות דהלא אנו באים ללמוד דלא חלקת בין שינוי בעלים לשינוי קודש וא"כ נימא כמו דבשינוי קודש מיפסל בכל ד' העבודות [אפילו אם לא חישב] ע"מ לזרוק כמו כן שינוי בעלים נמי ולפי' הקונטרס דפי' דאחד ששחט שלא לשם בעליו ולא הזכיר ע"מ לזרוק אין זו מחשבה דשם בעלים לא שייך בקרבן אלא להתכפר בו וכפרה בזריקה והשתא ניחא שפיר דאין למילף משינוי קודש כי אם עבודות דשייכא בה מחשבת שינוי בעלים ובשחיטה וקבלה והולכה לא שייכא מחשבת שינוי אלא א"כ דחשב ע"מ לזרוק. תוס' טוך: יב] וישנו לאחר מיתה. פי' (המקריב) [המפריש] קרבנו ומת היורש מקריבו ושייך בו שינוי קודש ולא שינוי בעלים דאין בעלים לאחר מיתה דקדק ריב"א דהכא אתיא כמ"ד שעבודא דאורייתא דלמ"ד שעבודא לאו דאורייתא אפי' משינוי קודש לא יביאו יורשין אחר (מיתה) וא"כ שינוי קודש נמי אינו (אלא) לאחר מיתה ואומר רבי דאתיא נמי כמ"ד שעבודא לאו דאורייתא ואפ"ה ישנו שינוי קודש לאחר מיתה כגון שהפריש שתי (חטאות) [שלמים או עולות] לאחריות וכשמשנה בזה לא יעלה זה לשם חובה וצריך להקריב השני. תוס' טוך: יג] שחיטה וזריקה קאי זבח ותיבת קרוי נמחק: יד] שכן נפסלת שלא לשם כו' שחטו שלא לשם אוכלין כגון: טו] זו קבלת: טז] היא הס"ד ומה"ד והולכה היא ה"ג ואפקיה רחמנא לקבלה: יז] תיבות מנלן דבעינן לשם זובח נמחק: יח] דידן ודאבא חנן: יט] לכתבינהו לזבח: כ] חישב ע"מ לזרוק שלא לשמו (תיבות אלא על השחיטה נמחק) ס"א אלא על השחיטה או על הקבלה והולכה שלא לשמה פסול כדרבינן להו לעיל:

וְאע"ג דְּתַרְתֵּי לָאו דַּוְקָא, תַּרְתֵּי מִיהָא דַּוְקָא. מַאי שְׁנָא שִׁינּוּי בְּעָלִים דְּלָא הָוֵי פְּסוּלוֹ בְּגוּפוֹ? מַחֲשָׁבָה בְּעָלְמָא; שִׁינּוּי קוֹדֶשׁ נַמִי מַחֲשָׁבָה בְּעָלְמָא הוּא. אֶלָּא, כֵּיוָן דְּאַחְשְׁבָהּ פְּסָלָהּ — ה"נ כֵּיוָן דְּאַחְשְׁבָהּ פְּסָלָהּ! וּלְרַב פִּנְחָס בְּרֵיהּ דְּרַב מָרִי, *דְּאָמַר: יֵשׁ שִׁינּוּי בְּעָלִים לְאַחַר מִיתָה. תַּרְתֵּי מִיהָא אִיכָּא לְמִיפְרַךְ! אֶלָּא אָמַר רַב א] אַשִׁי, אָמַר קְרָא: °"וְנִרְצָה לוֹ לְכַפֵּר עָלָיו" — (ויקרא א) *וְלֹא עַל חֲבֵירוֹ. וְהַאי לְהָכִי הוּא דְּאָתָא? הַאי מִיבְּעֵי לֵיהּ לְכִדְתַנְיָא: "וְנִרְצָה לוֹ לְכַפֵּר עָלָיו", ב] רַבִּי שִׁמְעוֹן אוֹמֵר: אֶת שֶׁעָלָיו — חַיָּיב בְּאַחֲרָיוּתוֹ, וְאֶת שֶׁאֵינוֹ עָלָיו — אֵינוֹ חַיָּיב בְּאַחֲרָיוּתוֹ; ג] וְאָמַר רַב יִצְחָק בַּר אַבְדִּימִי: מַאי טַעְמָא? כֵּיוָן דְּאָמַר "עָלַי" — כְּמַאן דְּטָעוּן לֵיהּ אַכַּתְפֵּיהּ דָּמֵי! רַב אַשִׁי מִ"וְנִרְצָה לוֹ לְכַפֵּר" קָאָמַר.§ אַשְׁכַּחַן זְבִיחָה וּזְרִיקָה, קַבָּלָה מְנָלַן? וְכִי תֵּימָא לֵילַף מִזְּבִיחָה וּזְרִיקָה — מַה לִּזְבִיחָה וּזְרִיקָה שֶׁכֵּן עֲבוֹדָה שֶׁחַיָּיבִין עָלֶיהָ בַּחוּץ! אֶלָּא אָמַר ד] רַב אַשִׁי: אָתְיָא מֵאֵיל נָזִיר, דִּכְתִיב: °"וְאֶת הָאַיִל יַעֲשֶׂה (במדבר ו) זֶבַח שְׁלָמִים" — *שֶׁתְּהֵא עֲשִׂיָּיתוֹ לְשֵׁם שְׁלָמִים; וְאִם אֵינוֹ עִנְיָן לְשִׁינּוּי קוֹדֶשׁ, דְּנָפְקָא לֵיהּ מֵהָתָם — תְּנֵהוּ עִנְיָן לְשִׁינּוּי בְּעָלִים. אֲמַר לֵיהּ רַב אַחָא בַּר אַבָּא לְרָבָא, אֵימָא: "יַעֲשֶׂה" — כְּלָל, "זֶבַח" — פְּרָט, כְּלָל וּפְרָט — אֵין בַּכְּלָל אֶלָּא מַה שֶּׁבַּפְּרָט, זְבִיחָה אִין, מִידֵּי אַחֲרִינָא לָא! אִי כְּתִיב "יַעֲשֶׂה שְׁלָמִים זֶבַח" — כִּדְקָאָמְרַתְּ, הַשְׁתָּא דִּכְתִיב: "יַעֲשֶׂה זֶבַח שְׁלָמִים" — הֲוָה לֵיהּ כְּלָל שֶׁאֵינוֹ (א) מָלֵא, וְכָל כְּלָל שֶׁאֵינוֹ מָלֵא — אֵין דָּנִין אוֹתוֹ בִּכְלָל וּפְרָט. רָבִינָא אָמַר: לְעוֹלָם דָּנִין, וְ"לַה'" — חָזַר וְכָלַל. אֲמַר לֵיהּ רַב אַחָא (ב) מִדִּיפְתִּי לְרָבִינָא: וְהָא לָא דָּמֵי כְּלָלָא קַמָּא לִכְלָלָא בַּתְרָא, כְּלָלָא קַמָּא מְרַבֶּה עֲשִׂיּוֹת וְתוּ לָא, כְּלָלָא בַּתְרָא — כָּל לַה', וַאֲפִילּוּ שְׁפִיכַת שִׁירַיִים וְהַקְטָרַת אֵימוּרִין! *הָא תָּנָא דְּבֵי רַבִּי יִשְׁמָעֵאל ה] בִּכְלָלֵי וּפְרָטֵי (ג) דָּרֵישׁ כִּי הַאי גַּוְונָא: כְּלָל וּפְרָט וּכְלָל — אִי אַתָּה דָּן אֶלָּא כְּעֵין הַפְּרָט, מַה הַפְּרָט מְפוֹרָשׁ — עֲבוֹדָה וּבָעֵינַן לִשְׁמָן, אַף כֹּל — עֲבוֹדָה וּבָעֵינַן לִשְׁמָן. אִי מַה הַפְּרָט מְפוֹרָשׁ — עֲבוֹדָה וְחַיָּיבִין עָלֶיהָ בַּחוּץ, אַף כָּל עֲבוֹדָה וְחַיָּיבִין עָלֶיהָ בַּחוּץ; שְׁחִיטָה וּזְרִיקָה אִין, קַבָּלָה וְהוֹלָכָה לָא! אִי נַמִי, מַה הַפְּרָט מְפוֹרָשׁ — דָּבָר הַטָּעוּן צָפוֹן וְיֶשְׁנוֹ בַּחַטָּאוֹת (ד) הַפְּנִימִיּוֹת, אַף כָּל הַטָּעוּן צָפוֹן וְיֶשְׁנוֹ בַּחַטָּאוֹת הַפְּנִימִיּוֹת; שְׁחִיטָה וְקַבָּלָה אִין, זְרִיקָה לָא! אִיכָּא לְמֵימַר הָכִי, וְאִיכָּא לְמֵימַר הָכִי, *שְׁקוּלִין הֵן וְיָבֹאוּ שְׁנֵיהֶן. לִישָּׁנָא אַחֲרִינָא: ו] וְחָדָא חֲדָא תֵּיקוּ בְּמִילְּתָא. אִיבָּעֵית אֵימָא: זְרִיקָה ז] מִדְּרַב אַשִׁי נָפְקָא. אַשְׁכַּחַן אֵיל נָזִיר, שְׁאָר שְׁלָמִים מְנָלַן? וְכִי תֵּימָא נֵילַף מֵאֵיל נָזִיר, מַה לְּאֵיל נָזִיר שֶׁכֵּן יֵשׁ ח] עִמָּהֶן דָּמִים אֲחֵרִים! א"כ, נִכְתּוֹב ט] "שַׁלְמֵי", מַאי "שְׁלָמִים"? לְרַבּוֹת כָּל שְׁלָמִים. אַשְׁכַּחַן שְׁלָמִים, שְׁאָר כָּל קָדָשִׁים מְנָלַן? וְכִי תֵּימָא, נֵילַף מִשְּׁלָמִים — מַה לִּשְׁלָמִים שֶׁכֵּן טְעוּנִין סְמִיכָה וּנְסָכִים וּתְנוּפַת חָזֶה וָשׁוֹק! אֶלָּא, אָמַר קְרָא: °"זֹאת הַתּוֹרָה לָעוֹלָה לַמִּנְחָה וְלַחַטָּאת (ויקרא ז) וְלָאָשָׁם וְלַמִּלּוּאִים וּלְזֶבַח הַשְּׁלָמִים", הִקִּישָׁן הַכָּתוּב לִשְׁלָמִים: מַה שְּׁלָמִים — בֵּין שִׁינּוּי קוֹדֶשׁ בֵּין שִׁינּוּי בְּעָלִים בָּעֵינַן לִשְׁמָהּ, אַף כֹּל — בֵּין שִׁינּוּי קוֹדֶשׁ בֵּין שִׁינּוּי בְּעָלִים בָּעֵינַן לִשְׁמָהּ. י] אֵימָא: הֵיכָא דְּשָׁחֵיט לְהוּ שֶׁלֹּא לִשְׁמָהּ לִיפַּסְלוּ! אָמַר קְרָא: °"מוֹצָא שְׂפָתֶיךָ תִּשְׁמֹר וְעָשִׂיתָ כַּאֲשֶׁר נָדַרְתָּ" וגו', (דברים כג) *"הַאי נְדָבָה? נֶדֶר הוּא! יא] [אֶלָּא] אִם כְּמָה שֶׁנָּדַרְתָּ עָשִׂיתָ — יְהֵא נֶדֶר, וְאִם לָאו — יְהֵא נְדָבָה. וְאִיצְטְרִיךְ "מוֹצָא שְׂפָתֶיךָ" וְאִיצְטְרִיךְ "זֹאת הַתּוֹרָה"; דְּאִי כָּתַב רַחֲמָנָא "מוֹצָא", (ה) יב] (הֲוָה אָמֵינָא: לָא

רש"י

יג] ואע"ג דתרתי לאו דוקא תרתי דוקא. *אע"ג דמותבינן ארבעה יד] פרכי, איכא תרתי שאין עיקר, כדמפרש ואזיל. תרתי מיהא דוקא. והשתא מפרש אמאי תרתי לאו דוקא. ולרב פנחס כו'. ולקמן בשילהי שמעתין אזלה לה הך פירכא דלאחר מיתה. לכפר עליו. היינו זריקה. אלמא זריקה לשם בעלים בעיא. את שעליו. כגון נדר, דאמר "הרי עלי עולה" — חייב באחריותו, אם הפריש בהמה לנדרו אם מתה או נגנבה. דהכי משמע: אותו שעליו יקריב אותו ונרצה לו, ועד שיקריבנו — לא נרצה, ולא נפטר. את שאינו עליו. כגון דאמר "הרי זו עולה". מונרצה לו טו] לכפר קאמר. דהכי משמע: לו לכפר, ולא טז] לחבירו. שכן עבודה שחייבין עליה בחוץ. יז] דכתיב (ויקרא יז): "אשר ישחט מחוץ למחנה". וזורק נמי מרבינן ליה לקמן בפ' "השוחט" (דף קז.): "דם שפך" — לרבות הזורק. תאמר בקבלה והולכה שאין חייבין עליה בחוץ — דתנן בפ' בתרא (שם קיב:): והיולך והבולל כו' והמקבל דמים בחוץ — פטור. יעשה כלל. שיהו כל עשיותיו לשם שלמים. זבח פרט. שחיטה הוא דבעי לשמה. אי כתיב יעשה שלמים זבח כדקאמרת. דמשמע כללא, שיהו עשייתו יח] שלמים. השתא דכתיב יעשה זבח שלמים. לא גמר הכלל את דבריו ולא נשלם להשמיענו על מה הוזכרו כאן העשיות, יט] עד שבא "זבח" והפסיק את הדבר. כלל שאינו מלא. כ] ולא נתמלא דבריו להשלים. מלא — פרלאשיי"ן בלע"ז. לה'. יעשה זבח שלמים לה'. כא] עשייתו. עבודות המיוחדות, שחיטה וזריקה קבלה והולכה. שפיכת שירים. שנשפכין שירי הדם ליסוד כב] [אחר] שנתן ארבע מתנות, ואינן מעכבין כפרה. הא תנא דבי רבי ישמעאל כו'. בשילהי "אלו טריפות" (חולין דף סו.) גבי פרשת חגבים. איכא למימר הכי. עבודה וחייבין עליה בחוץ, ואתיא לה זריקה. ואיכא למימר הכי. עבודה שטעונה צפון, ואתיא לה קבלה. שקולין הן. המדות שוות, והי מינייהו מפקת? אי דרשת הא — אחנא דרישנא לאידך, הלכך יבאו שניהם. והולכה על כרחך לא תפקה מכלל קבלה. מדרב אשי. מ"ונרצה לו לכפר". וכלל ופרט לאיתויי קבלה, דאי לזריקה — לא איצטריך. שכן יש עמו דמים אחרים. שבאין עמו חטאת ועולה. אשכחן שלמים. בין בשינוי קודש בין בשינוי בעלים. שכן טעונין כו'. ושאר זבחים יש מהן שאין טעונים סמיכה ולא נסכים, כגון בכור ומעשר ופסח. ויש מהן שאין טעונין נסכים, כגון חטאת ואשם. כג] ובכולן אין אחד שיהא טעון חזה ושוק. ליפסלו. שהרי לא נעשו כהלכתן, ואין זריקתן מתרת בשרן לאכילה. ואיצטריך. למיכתב "זאת התורה" למיגמר משלמים, ולא תימא מ"מוצא שפתיך" נפקא דלכתחילה בעינן לשמה. לא

תוספות

מחשבה בעלמא. *ואפי' יהא צריך דיבור, כיון דליכא מעשה הוי כמחשבה בעלמא. ויש תימה: דהכא משוי להו, ובפ' "תמיד נשחט" (פסחים סב:) משמע שיש חילוק, דמפרש: מה בין כד] לשמן לשלא לשמן, לאוכליו ושלא לאוכליו — זה פסולו בגופו, וזה אין פסולו בגופו! וי"ל: דכיון דלא מיפסיל אלא מפני שאין יכול לאכול כזית, כגון לשם חולה וזקן — [א]חשיב טפי פסולו בקודש מחמת דבר אחר, כיון דאם היה יכול לאכול — היה כשר. וקשה: דעל כרחין שלא למנוין ולערלים ולטמאין צריך לומר דלא חשיבי פסולן בגופו, כי היכי דלא תיקשי לן נמי מה בין לשמן ושלא לשמן, למנוין ושלא למנוין למולין ולערלים לטמאין ולטהורים! וי"ל: דשינוי בעלים חשבינן פסולו בגופו, משום דתלוי [ב] בזריקה כה] (בכפרה) ושם בעלים [על הכפרה] אבל שלא לאוכלין ושלא למנויין — תלוי בשחיטה, ואין שם בעלים על השחיטה. אי נמי: שלא לאוכלין כו] [ושלא למנויין] יכול לקיים מחשבתו בהיתר [באותן] שיהיו מנויין עליו, כז] אם אינם חולים וזקנים. אבל שלא לשמה — אינו יכול לקיימו, לכך קרוי פסולו בגופו.

הגה"ה ה"ג במגילה (דף ח.): מאי [משמע] אמר רב יצחק בר אבדימי. רב אשי כח] (אמר) מונרצה לו קאמר. תימה: למה לי קרא לשינוי בעלים בזריקה? הא אפי' שאר עבודות לא מיפסלי אלא בשוחט על מנת לזרוק, כ"ש זורק כט] *עצמו, [דבעינן] שם בעלים!

(נ"י רש"ק מנמו שלא לשם בעלים כצ"ל)

שכן עבודה וחייבים ל]. פירוש: עבודה שחייבין עליה בחוץ.

שקולים הם ויבאו שניהם. אע"ג דהכא תרתי והכא חדא — חשיב להו שקולין. והקשה הרב רבי חיים: דהשתא משמע דהיכא דלא ידע הי מינייהו לרבוי — מרבי תרווייהו. וכן בריש ב"ק (דף ג.) דמרבי מ"ושלח" שן ורגל, משום דשקולין הן. וכן בפ"ק דערכין (דף ד:) גבי "נפשות". ואילו בפרק "כל האסורים" (תמורה דף כח:) ופרק "שור שנגח ארבעה וה'" (ב"ק דף מ:) דרשינן: "מן הבהמה" — להוציא את הרובע, "ומן הצאן" — להוציא את הנוגח. וקאמר: מפני שיש ברובע מה שאין בנוגח ויש בנוגח מה שאין ברובע, הוצרך לומר רובע והוצרך לומר נוגח! ותירץ: דהיכא דאיכא משמעות בריבוי — מרבינן כל השקולים כי הכא, ד"זבח" משמע לרבוי כעין זביחה כל שהיא עבודה, וכן "ושלח" יש במשמע רגל ושן, ו"נפשות" נמי משמע הכל. אבל "מן" לא משמע למעוטי שניהם*).

אימא היכא דשחיט שלא לשמן ליפסלו. תימה: הא בכל דוכתא בעינן בקדשים לא] [שינה] לעכב, והכא לא שינה! וי"ל: דפריך משינוי קודש, דאיכא תרי קראי, ואמרי' לעיל: אם אינו ענין לשינוי קודש — תנהו ענין לשינוי בעלים. ופריך: לב] דהשתא אימר תרווייהו בשינוי קודש ולעכב. וקשה, מאי משני: אמר קרא "מוצא שפתיך"? דלמא ההוא קרא אתא לשינוי בעלים, דלא אשכחן ששינה בהן הכתוב! ולא קשה מידי, ד"מוצא שפתיך" לא משמע שינוי בעלים. [הג"ה]: [ג] ונראה דפריך מכח סברא, כעין קושיא דר"ל לג] דלקמיה, דאימא דליפסלו כיון דאמרת דלא עלו לשם חובה, או נימא דיעלו, (רש"ק) דאם כשרין הן — ירצו, ואם אין מרצין — למה באין? לד] [ומיהו] לא דמי, דריש לקיש פריך יהו כשרין גמורין כמו שאר קדשים, דלא שנה לעכב לה] *בו ליפסלו. והכא לא הוה ליה למיפרך שלא לשמה ליפסלו, אלא הוה ליה למימר: וליתכשרו, ויעלו לחובה כשאר קדשים

*) [ועי' היטיב תוס' ב"ק מ: ד"ה ויש]

שיטה מקובצת

א] רב אמי תיבת אשי נמחק: ב] רבי שמעון אומר את שעליו חייב כו'. ודייק ממשמעות דקרא ונרצה לו לכפר עליו אימתי נרצה לו כשהוא לכפר ואז לא יביא אחר הא אם לא כיפר יביא אחר ואימתי אני אומר שיביא אחר לכפר כשאמר עליו שאז עליו אחריות. תוס' טוך ותוס' ר"פ: ג] באחריותו מאי משמע אמר רב יצחק: ד] אמר רבא ותיבות רב אשי נמחק: ה] ישמעאל הוא דדריש כללי ופרטי כי האי גוונא: ו] אחרינא שקול הוא וכל חדא וחדא תיקו אמילתיה אב"א: ז] מדרב אשי נפקי. כלומר והולכה לא תפקיה (מהולכה) [מכלל קבלה] וזריקה אתיא מדרב אשי ונרצה לו לכפר וא"ת למה לי קרא למיפסל שינוי בעלים בזריקה (או) [הא] מקבל ע"מ לזרוק שלא לשם בעלים [פסול] כדפ"ה לעיל א"כ כ"ש זורק עצמו וי"ל [דהו"א] דגזירת הכתוב הוא ובעינן זורק ע"מ להקטיר או ע"מ לשפוך שירים דלעולם בעינן ב' עבודות בענין [שלא לשם בעלים דהא חזינן] דשחיטה וקבלה דלא מהניא כי אם [במחשב מעבודה לעבודה] הוא א) דכותיה אשכחן גבי פיגול דאינו [מפגל כי אם] במחשב מעבודה לעבודה. תוס' טוך: ח] יש עמו דמים: ט] נכתוב שלמיו מאי: י] אימא היכא דשחיט להו שלא לשמה ליפסלו. פי' בתוס' אע"ג דלא שינה הכתוב לעכב מ"מ ליפסלו מסברא כיון דשינה בלשמן כאילו חסר העבודה ששינה בה [וא"ת הא] מדשינה הכתוב לעכב בחטאת ש"מ היכא שלא שינה הכתוב דאינו פסול ותירצו בתוס' דאדרבה הייתי אומר אם [שינה בכל] הקרבנות לפיסולא מהיקשא דחטאת דאתקש כולהו לחטאת בהיקשא דזאת התורה וכ"ת א"כ הייתי מקשה פסח למה לי דשינה [לפסול] תיפוק ליה מהיקשא דחטאת י"ל כיון דפסח לא הוי בהדיא כתוב בההוא ענינא (דמשום ביום) [דמביום] צוותו נפקא כדאמרינן לקמן (דף ז ע"ב) הייתי אומר [דלאו להכי אתא] דה"נ הוה ס"ד תלמודא לקמן וי"מ דמכח מה ראית פריך כלומר בפסח וחטאת נמי לא שינה בהם הכתוב וליכא אלא חד קרא [דבעינן לשמה והא] דמוכח עיכובא היינו משום דילפינן פסח וחטאת לשמה למצוה מהיקשא דשלמים א"כ קרא דלשמה דכתיב גבי פסח [וחטאת לעכב] אתא כיון דלמצוה [ילפי' מהיקשא] דשלמים ופריך הכא הכי [מנא לי] למיקם קרא [דגבי] פסח וחטאת לעיכובא [והא דכתיב] הכא גבי [שלמים למצוה] איפוך אנא [דהא] דכתיב גבי [פסח וחטאת למצוה] וקרא [דכתיב] גבי שלמים לעיכובא [אכן] אינו נראה [דמשמע] דפריך (מהיכא) [הכא] דשלא לשמה בכל [הקרבנות] לפסול לכן נראה כדפי' וא"ת לפי מה דפי' שסברא הוא [אף] בלא שינה הכתוב דחסר בעבודה א"כ למה שינה הכתוב בפסח וחטאת תיפוק ליה מהאי סברא דפרישנא וי"ל דהיינו לפי מה דמכשירין בכל הקרבנות ממוצא כו' לכך אצטריך שינה לעכב דלא תילף הכשרה בפסח וחטאת [מהיקשא] דשלמים. תוס' הר"פ: יא] הוא אלא: יב] מוצא שפתיך הוה אמינא: יג] ה"ג ואע"ג דתרתי לאו דוקא תרתי מיהו דוקא אע"ג דמהני ארבעה תיבת דמותבינן נמחק: יד] פירכא איכא: טו] תיבת לכפר נמחק: טז] לכפר ולא על חבירו הס"ד: יז] בחוץ כלומר שכן עבודה חשובה להתחייב עליה בחוץ דכתיב: יח] עשייתו לשם שלמים: יט] תיבת עד נמחק: כ] מלא לא אות ו' נמחק: כא] מה"ד עשיות. עבודות המיוחדים שחיטה: כב] ליסוד אחר: כג] ואשם ואין בכולן שיהא אות ו' ותיבות אין אחד נמחק: [illegible]

מסורת הש"ס

נ"א אע"ג דמהני ארבעה דפרכינן איכא כו' נ"ק

לקמן ז: ע"ש פסחים סח. ע"ש

[לעיל ג: וש"נ]

מגילה ח.

לקמן ח: [ב"ק סד. חולין סו. כריתות כח.]

[נזיר נח: ב"ק ג. ערכין ד:]

נ"ל שלמיו מאי שלמים כו' רש"ק [וכ"ה בילקוט פ' ויקרא רמז תנ"ה ע"ש]

[נ"ל או ליפסלו וכ"ה בס"י]

[לעיל ב. מנחות ב.]

הגהות הב"ח

(א) גמרא כלל שאינו מלא נ"ב לישנא דקרא בכסף מלא: (ב) שם א"ל רב אחא מדיפתי נ"ב ע"ל דף ח ע"ב: (ג) שם בכללי ופרטי כי האי גוונא דריש כלל: (ד) שם ויענו בחטאת הפנימיות נ"ב משמע דהולכה אינו טעון צפון ואינו בחטאות הפנימיות וקשה א"כ לא ליכתב קרא גבי זריקה דשינוי קודש ותיליף מבינתים משחיטה קבלה והולכה וצ"ל דכ"ז לפי הה"א דמקשן אבל לפי המסקנא [דלעיל דהולכה] לא תפקה מכלל קבלה א"כ לפ"ז גם הולכה טעון צפון ויענו בחטאות הפנימיות ודו"ק: (ה) שם דאי כתב רחמנא מוצא שפתיך ה"א לא ידענא במאי:

גליון הש"ס

גמ' שתהא עשייתו לשם שלמים. עי' מנחות דף מז ע"א תוס' ד"ה במה: תוס' ד"ה מחשבה וכו' ואפי' יהא צריך דבור. עי' לעיל דף ב' ע"א תוס' ד"ה כל בסה"ד:

א) אולי צ"ל וה"ה לזריקה נמי לכוונתה הוא ולכוונתה אשכחן וכו':

הגהות צ"ק [א] חשיב טפי פסולו מחמת דבר אחר כו': [ב] מריקה ועיקר כפרה מריקה ושם בעלים על הזריקה כו' כצ"ל: [ג] ואין נראה לומר דפריך כו':

אם

תורה אור

לָא יָדַע בְּמַאי — כְּתַב רַחֲמָנָא: "זֹאת הַתּוֹרָה", וְאִי כָּתַב רַחֲמָנָא "זֹאת הַתּוֹרָה", הֲוָה אָמֵינָא לִיפַּסְלוּ — כְּתַב רַחֲמָנָא: "מוֹצָא שְׂפָתֶיךָ". רָמֵי רֵישׁ לָקִישׁ עַל מְעוֹהִי בֵּי מִדְרָשָׁא וּמַקְשֵׁי: א] אִם כְּשֵׁרִים הֵם — יֵרָצוּ, וְאִם אֵין מְרַצִּין — לָמָּה בָּאִין? אָמַר לוֹ ר' *אֱלִיעֶזֶר: מָצִינוּ בַּבָּאִין לְאַחַר מִיתָה שֶׁהֵן כְּשֵׁרִין וְאֵין מְרַצִּין, דִּתְנַן: *אהָאִשָּׁה שֶׁהֵבִיאָה חַטָּאתָהּ וּמֵתָה — יָבִיאוּ יוֹרְשִׁין עוֹלָתָהּ, עוֹלָתָהּ וּמֵתָה — לֹא יָבִיאוּ יוֹרְשִׁין חַטָּאתָהּ. א"ל: מוֹדֵינָא לָךְ בְּעוֹלָה, דְּאָתְיָא לְאַחַר מִיתָה, אָשָׁם דְּלָא אָתֵי לְאַחַר מִיתָה מְנָלַן? א"ל: הֲרֵי מַחְלוֹקְתְּךָ בְּצִידּוֹ, רַבִּי אֱלִיעֶזֶר אוֹמֵר: אַף הָאָשָׁם. אָמַר: זֶהוּ שֶׁאוֹמְרִין עָלָיו אָדָם גָּדוֹל הוּא? קָאָמֵינָא אֲנָא מִשְׁנָה שְׁלֵימָה, וְאַתְּ אָמְרַתְּ לִי ר' אֱלִיעֶזֶר! אֶלָּא אָמַר רֵישׁ לָקִישׁ, אֶפְתַּח אֲנָא פִּתְחָא לְנַפְשַׁאי: דברים כג °"מוֹצָא שְׂפָתֶיךָ" וגו', הַאי נְדָבָה? נֶדֶר הוּא כו', כִּדְלְעֵיל. יָתֵיב רַבִּי זֵירָא וְרַבִּי יִצְחָק בַּר אַבָּא וְיָתֵיב אַבַּיֵי גַּבַּיְיהוּ, וְיָתְבִי וְקָאָמְרִי: קַשְׁיָא לֵיהּ לְרֵישׁ לָקִישׁ אָשָׁם דְּלָא אָתֵי לְאַחַר מִיתָה, וְנָסֵיב לָהּ תַּלְמוּדָא "מוֹצָא שְׂפָתֶיךָ"; ב] אֵימָא: הַבָּא בְּנֶדֶר וּבִנְדָבָה לַיְיתֵי וְלָא לִירַצֵּי, אָשָׁם לָא לַיְיתֵי כְּלָל! ויקרא ד אֲמַר לְהוּ אַבַּיֵי, רֵישׁ לָקִישׁ מֵהָכָא פָּתַח: °"וְשָׁחַט אוֹתָהּ לְחַטָּאת", "אוֹתָהּ" — לִשְׁמָהּ כְּשֵׁרָה, שֶׁלֹּא לִשְׁמָהּ פְּסוּלָה, הָא שְׁאָר קָדָשִׁים שֶׁלֹּא לִשְׁמָן כְּשֵׁירִין; ג] יָכוֹל יֵרָצוּ? ת"ל: "מוֹצָא שְׂפָתֶיךָ". וְאֵימָא: ל"ג הַבָּא בְּנֶדֶר וּנְדָבָה לַיְיתֵי וְלָא לִירַצֵּי, אָשָׁם ד] (נַמִי) אַרְצוּיֵי נַמִי לִירַצֵּי! אָמַר אַבַּיֵי: אָשָׁם דְּמִירַצֵּי לָא מָצֵית אָמְרַתְּ, קַל וָחוֹמֶר מֵעוֹלָה: וּמָה עוֹלָה שֶׁאֵינָהּ מְכַפֶּרֶת אֵינָהּ מְרַצָּה, אָשָׁם שֶׁמְּכַפֵּר — אֵינוֹ דִּין שֶׁאֵינוֹ מְרַצֶּה? מַה לְּעוֹלָה שֶׁכֵּן כָּלִיל! שְׁלָמִים יוֹכִיחוּ. מַה לִּשְׁלָמִים שֶׁכֵּן טְעוּנִין ה] נְסָכִין וּתְנוּפַת חָזֶה וָשׁוֹק! °עוֹלָה תּוֹכִיחַ. *וְחָזַר הַדִּין, לֹא רְאִי זֶה כִּרְאִי זֶה וְלֹא רְאִי זֶה כִּרְאִי זֶה, הַצַּד הַשָּׁוֶה שֶׁבָּהֶן שֶׁהֵן קָדָשִׁים, וּשְׁחָטָן שֶׁלֹּא לִשְׁמָן — כְּשֵׁירִין וְאֵין מְרַצִּין, אַף אֲנִי אָבִיא אָשָׁם שֶׁהוּא קוֹדֶשׁ, וּשְׁחָטוֹ שֶׁלֹּא לִשְׁמוֹ — כָּשֵׁר וְאֵינוֹ מְרַצֶּה. מַה לְּהַצַּד הַשָּׁוֶה שֶׁבָּהֶן, שֶׁכֵּן יֶשְׁנוֹ בְּצִיבּוּר! תּוֹדָה תּוֹכִיחַ.

מַה

לָא יָדְעִינַן בְּמַאי. קָאָמַר רַחֲמָנָא "מוֹצָא שְׂפָתֶיךָ תִּשְׁמוֹר", דְּהָא לָא כְּתִיב בְּהֶדְיָא בְּהַאי קְרָא עֲבוֹדוֹת לִשְׁמָן, וְדִלְמָא לָאו בְּלִשְׁמָן מִשְׁתָּעֵי קְרָא – כָּתַב רַחֲמָנָא "זֹאת הַתּוֹרָה" לְמֵילַף מִשְּׁלָמִים, דִּמְפָרְשָׁה בְּהוּ לִשְׁמָן. ו] הָכִי גָּרְסִי': רָמֵי רֵישׁ לָקִישׁ עַל מְעוֹהִי. שׁוֹכֵב עַל בִּטְנוֹ פָּנָיו ז] (*עַל) כְּלַפֵּי קַרְקַע. לָמָּה הֵן בָּאִין. וְאַהָכִי לָא ח] קָמָא לֵיהּ טַעְמָא דְּמַתְנִי', דְּיָלְפִינַן מִ"מוֹצָא שְׂפָתֶיךָ". וְאֵין מְרַצִּין. שֶׁאֵין כַּפָּרָה לַמֵּתִים. וְאַף אַתָּה אַל תִּתְמַהּ עַל אֵלּוּ. הָאִשָּׁה. יוֹלֶדֶת. ט] לֹא יָבִיאוּ יוֹרְשִׁין חַטָּאתָהּ. דַּהֲוְיָא לָהּ חַטָּאת שֶׁמֵּתוּ בְּעָלֶיהָ, וְהִלְכְתָא גְּמִירִי לָהּ דְּלְמִיתָה אָזְלָה י]. מוֹדֵינָא לָךְ בְּעוֹלָה. שֶׁאִם שְׁחָטָהּ שֶׁלֹּא יא] לִשְׁמָן שֶׁתִּתְקָרֵב אע"פ שֶׁאֵינָהּ מְרַצָּה, הוֹאִיל וּמָצִינוּ שֶׁבָּאָה לְאַחַר מִיתָה וְאֵינָהּ מְרַצָּה. וְה"ה לִשְׁלָמִים וּשְׁאָר קָרְבָּנוֹת חוּץ מֵחַטָּאת. (א) *וְאָשָׁם מִיהוּ דְּלָא אָתֵי לְאַחַר מִיתָה, דְּקי"ל (תמורה דף יח.) דְּכָל שֶׁבְּחַטָּאת מֵתָה בְּאָשָׁם רוֹעָה, מְנָא לָן דְּקָרֵב שֶׁלֹּא לִשְׁמָן, הוֹאִיל וְאֵינוֹ מְרַצֶּה? דְּלָא אַפֵּיק תַּנָּא דְּמַתְנִי' אֶלָּא פֶּסַח וְחַטָּאת. מַחְלוֹקְתְּךָ יב]. *וְסִיַּיעְתָּךְ, דְּאִיכָּא רַבִּי אֱלִיעֶזֶר דְּקָאֵי כְּוָותָךְ. מִשְׁנָה שְׁלֵימָה. סְתָם מַתְנִי', דְּלָא פָּסַל אֶלָּא חַטָּאת (ב). פִּתְחָא לְנַפְשַׁאי. מְנָלַן (ג) דְּקָרְבִי. יָתֵיב רַבִּי זֵירָא וכו'. וְקָמַתְמַהּ אַפֵּירוּקֵיהּ דר"ל. וְקַשְׁיָא לֵיהּ לְרֵישׁ לָקִישׁ אָשָׁם. אַמַּאי קָרֵב שֶׁלֹּא לִשְׁמוֹ שֶׁלֹּא לְרַצּוֹת? הָא לָא אָתֵי לְאַחַר מִיתָה. וְנָסֵיב יג] תַּלְמוּדָא. כְּלוֹמַר נָסֵיב קְרָא לְתַלְמוּדָא דְּמִילְּתֵיהּ. אֵימָא הַבָּא בְּנֶדֶר וּנְדָבָה. כִּדְמַשְׁמַע קְרָא, לַיְיתוּ וְלָא לִירַצּוּ כו'. רֵישׁ לָקִישׁ מֵהָכָא פָּתַח. לָהּ. (ד) (מֵהָכָא) לָא נָפְקָא לֵיהּ מִ"מוֹצָא שְׂפָתֶיךָ" דְּלִיקְרַב, אֶלָּא דְּלָא לִירַצֵּי. וְהַקְרָבָתוֹ מֵהַאי קְרָא יָלֵיף: "וְשָׁחַט אוֹתָהּ לְחַטָּאת", "אוֹתָהּ" – מִיעוּטָא הוּא, אוֹתָהּ הוּא דְּבָעֵינַן לִשְׁמָהּ, וְאִי לָא – פְּסוּלָה, כִּדְיָלְפִינַן לְקַמָּן. הָא שְׁאָר קָדָשִׁים כו'. אַרְצוּיֵי נַמִי לִירַצּוּ. כֵּיוָן דְּנָפְקָא לָן הַקְרָבָתָן מֵ"אוֹתָהּ". אֵינָהּ מְרַצָּה. כִּדְאָמַר: אִם לָאו יְהֵא נְדָבָה. אָשָׁם שֶׁמְּכַפֵּר. עַל לָאוִין הָאֲמוּרִים בִּשְׁבוּעַת הַפִּקָּדוֹן, וְהֶקְדֵּשׁ, וְשִׁפְחָה חֲרוּפָה. שֶׁכֵּן טְעוּנִים נְסָכִים. וְלָא גָּרַס סְמִיכָה, דְּאָשָׁם נַמִי טָעוּן סְמִיכָה. שְׁלָמִים יֶשְׁנוֹ בְּצִבּוּר. כִּבְשֵׂי עֲצֶרֶת.

הִקִּישׁ

קדשים שלא שנה לעכב, כל כמה דאכתי לא ידע קרא ד"מוצא שפתיך". ואי פריך: ליפסלו, דנגמר מחטאת יד] *[ופסח] בהיקישא ד"זאת התורה" כדפרישית בסמוך, אי ב"מה מצינו" – איכא למיפרך: שכן כרת. ואי בהקישא ד"זאת התורה" – א"כ ליכתוב חדא, או טו] לחטאת גרידא או פסח גרידא. ואי נאמר דבכל דוכתא דמצרכינן שנה לעכב היינו מהכא, טז] [מדכתיב] "מוצא שפתיך" וגו' – א"כ אתי שפיר הא דפריך וליפסלו כו'. ע"כ הג"ה.

הג"ה מצינו בבאין לאחר מיתה שכשרין ואין מרצין. וא"ת: מי דמי? הני לא עלו, אבל באין לאחר מיתה – עלו לגמרי לשם חובה. דלמ"ד שיעבודא דאורייתא, אם היה הקרבן נפסל – היו היורשין זקוקין להביא אחר. ואפילו למ"ד לאו דאורייתא, אם הפריש שניהם לאחריות, אם נפסל הראשון – חייבין להקריב את השני, נמצא דבאין לאחר מיתה מרצין לענין שעולין לשם חובה, משא"כ בשינוי קודש! י"ל דמ"מ דמיא קצת להדדי לענין דאין מרצין רצוי גמור, דאין כפרה למת, ולאו בר חיוב הבאה הוא, אלא *שנתחייב מחיים. ובשינוי קודש ובעלים נמי אין רצוי גמור. וא"ת: ומה ראיה מייתי מבאין לאחר מיתה? אטו מי ילפינן מינה בכל מקום שלא שנה הכתוב דאינו אלא למצוה, דנימא כשרין ולא עלו? וי"ל: דדוקא שנוי קודש ושנוי בעלים יז] דוקא מדמי, דהוי באין לאחר מיתה שאין לו בעלים, וכמו שלשם כשר ואינו מרצה – כמו כן כאן ששנה אותו מבעליו והוי כאין לו בעלים יח].

עולתה ומתה לא יביאו יורשין חטאתה. משמע: *אבל אם היתה יט] יכולה להביא חטאתה אחר *עולתה – עלתה לה עולתה לשם עולה. וכן משמע בתורת כהנים בפרשת "אשה כי תזריע" שאם הביאה עולתה תחילה – תביא חטאתה ממין עולתה. וכן במס' קינים (ספ"ב) ותימה: דבפרק "תמיד נשחט" (פסחים דף נט.) אמרי': זה בנין אב, שכל חטאות קודמות לעולת כ] העוף, אפי' חטאת העוף לעולת בהמה. ואפי' דיעבד קאמר דפסול, מדמשני: שאני עולת מצורע דרחמנא אמר "והעלה" שהעלה כבר. והיינו דיעבד, דלכתחילה חטאת קודמת, כדכתיב בהדיא בקרא. כא] ש"מ דבעלמא דיעבד לא! ותירץ ה"ר חיים: דה"ה דבעלמא כשר דיעבד, והא דבעי קרא במצורע – משום דכתיב ביה הוויה "זאת תהיה" – בהוויתו יהא, דמשמע עיכובא, כדאמר פ"ק דמנחות (דף ה.). ונראה לי: דילפי' חטאת ועולה של יולדת מחטאת ועולה של מצורע, דגילה הכתוב דאם עשה עולה תחלה כשירה מ"והעלה" כדאיתא בפ' "תמיד נשחט" (פסחים נט.). ואי לא קרא ד"והעלה" דמכשר – היה פוסל בכל מקום מטעם דיש מחוסר זמן לבו ביום, שאמר הכתוב להקריב חטאת קודם לעולה, אפי' בעלמא דליכא "תהיה" דמשמע עיכובא. תדע, דתניא בפ"ק דמנחות (דף ה.): הקדיש חטאתו לאשמו – לא יהא אחד ממרס בדמו, אלא תלא לבית השריפה. וקאמר: הא דמיפסיל – לאו משום "תהיה", דהא לא קאי אשחיטה, משום דלאו עבודה היא, אלא מטעם דיש מחוסר זמן לבו ביום, שאמר הכתוב להקדיש אשם תחילה, וזה הטעם למה לא יהיה גבי חטאת ועולה בעלמא. ולכך איצטריך "והעלה" במצורע להכשיר. וגמרינן מיניה בעלמא (פסחים דף נט.) להכשיר אם הקדיש עולה לחטאת, אבל לא גמרינן מיניה בחטאת ואשם כי אם קרבנות כמותם. ברוך. **לא** יביאו יורשין חטאתה. הגירסא משובשת בתורת כהנים, ופירשתי במנחות בפ"ק (דף ד:). **אשם** דלא אתא לאחר מיתה מנא לן. תימה: כיון דעולה ושלמים ניחא ליה, נילף אשם מינייהו בהיקישא ד"זאת התורה", ולמה לי "מוצא שפתיך"? וי"ל: דאדרבה, הוה אמינא איפכא, דנילף שאר קדשים מאשם דלא אתו כלל. **אשם** לא ליתי כלל. תימה: הא לא איצטריך "מוצא שפתיך" כלל אלא לאשם, דלשאר קדשים אתו מסברא, כדאמרינן דלא צריכי קרא, דהא אתו לאחר מיתה! וי"ל: דהשתא הדר ביה מההוא טעמא. דאע"ג דאמר ליה "מודינא לך בעולה" – לא היה אומר כן אלא מתוך דוחק. *הא שאר כל הקדשים אפילו שלא לשמן כשירין. ואם תאמר: *ל"ל "אותה"? הא מדלריכי קראי לעכב בפסח וחטאת – מכלל דשאר קדשים כשרין! וכי תימא נילף מינייהו – מה להנך שכן לד כרת. ובהיקישא ד"זאת התורה" נמי לא אתו, דא"כ לא ליכתוב עיכובא אלא באחד, בפסח או בחטאת, ואידך לייתו מהיקשא. **מה** לשלמים שכן טעונין נסכים. לא גרסינן סמיכה, דאשם נמי טעון סמיכה, כדאמר לקמן בפירקין (דף יא.). וה"ר חיים פירש: דמשום אשם מצורע מלי למינקט סמיכה, למ"ד בריש "כל הפסולים" (לקמן דף לג.): כב] סמיכה לאו דאורייתא. **תודה** כג] יוכיח. אע"ג דאשכחן עולה שבאה בנדבת ציבור שמקיילין בהן את המזבח, (תודה) ושלמים לא אתו בנדבת ציבור, דהא ממעטינן להו בתורת כהנים בפרשת "ואם מן הצאן קרבנו לזבח שלמים".

חטאת

עין משפט נר מצוה

נ"א ופסח וקסה כדפריך בסמוך

טו א מיי' פ"א מהל' מחוסרי כפרה הל' יג:

מנחות ד: קדושין יג: קינין סוף פ"ב

נ"א שנתחייב הקרבן מחיים נ"ק

אבל הוא אם היתה חיה יכולה כו' נ"ק

עולתה ועולתה לה כו'

[קדושין ה: כה. וש"נ]

מסורת הש"ס

נ"א למטה נ"ק

נ"ל אלעזר

ס"א מיהו אשם דלא אתי כו'

ס"א מחלוקת המסייעתך

הגהות הב"ח

(א) רש"י ד"ה מודינא וכו' חוץ מחטאת ופסח מיהו אשם דלא אתי: (ב) ד"ה משנה וכו' חטאת ופסח הס"ד: (ג) ד"ה פתחא וכו' דקרב כצ"ל ואות י' נמחק: (ד) ד"ה ר"ל מהכא פתח לה פתחא לא נפקא:

גליון הש"ס

גמ' א"ל ר"א מצינו. עי' נדה דף ע ע"ב תוס' ד"ה ור"א: **שם** עולה תוכיח. תמוה לי הא גם עולה צריכה נסכים ואי דעולת עוף יוכיח א"כ איך פרכינן עלה מה לעולה שיש בציבור הא עולת עוף אינה בציבור ואי דשם עולה איתא בצבור הכי נמי נימא דשם עולה טעונה נסכים וצריך עיון:

עי' רש"ק

[עמ"ש בס"ד לקמן מח. על הגליון בתוס' ד"ה ואתא]

נ"ק מ"ז

שיטה מקובצת

א] אם כשרים הם ירצו כו'. עיקר הקושיא דרשב"ל בא מהא דקאמר אם אינם מרצים למה באים כדמשמע סוגיין וזהו כעין קושיא דלעיל שהקשה [אימא היכא] דשחיט להו שלא לשמה ליפסלו ומיהו קשה למה לא הקשה בפשיטות כמו לעיל ונראה דרשב"ל היה עושה עצמו כאילו היה [מסופק אם קרא] לעכב או למצוה והיה קשה לו מה נפשך אי כשרים הם ונאמר דהנך קראי דלשמה למצוה בעלמא נינהו לכך הם כשרים א"כ ירצו [כיון] דלמצוה בעלמא נינהו לענין כשרות הקרבנות ה"נ נימא לענין ריצוי ואם אינם מרצים למה באים כלומר ואם נפשך [לומר] לעכב אע"ג שלא שינה בו הכתוב כדפי' לעיל ולכך אין מרצין למה באים כי היכי דקראי אתו לעכב לענין ריצוי [הכי נמי נימא לענין כשרות הקרבן דהא] עיקר [מכה ממה נפשך] אתא לאקשויי כך פי' מורי שי'. תוס' הר"פ: ב] ע' בהשמטות בסוף המסכת: ג] ע' בהשמטות בסוף המסכת: ד] אשם ארצוי נמי לירצו (תיבת נמי נמחק) אין להקשות דלעיל מקשה אשם לא לייתי כלל דמסברא יש לנו לפסול באשם [יותר] משאר קרבנות והכא מקשה מסברא יש להכשיר באשם [יותר] משאר קרבנות וי"ל דלעיל לא היה יודע מדרשא דאותה ויש לפסול מסברא באשם יותר משאר קרבנות ממה מצינו בחטאת אבל עתה דאנו יודעים [מדרשא דאותה אף] דיכולים לפסול באשם כיון דאשם בא לכפר ולא שייך ביה ואם לאו יהא נדבה י"ל דאין להכשירו לחצאין וכי גלי קרא באשם אותה לגמרי אכשרי אפי' לרצות ולכפר: ה] שכן טעונין סמיכה. לא גרסינן סמיכה דאשם נמי טעון סמיכה כדנפקא לן לקמן [דף יא ע"א] מכחטאת וכאשם [ואפשר] דגרסי' [משום] אשם מצורע שאינו טעון סמיכה ואם תאמר אי מיירי באשם מצורע הא אשם מצורע טעון נסכים ומאי מקשה שכן טעונין סמיכה ונסכים [וי"ל דהכי פריך מה לשלמים] שכן כולן טעונין סמיכה ונסכים אבל אין כל האשמות טעונין סמיכה ונסכים ותימה מאי קאמר [עולה תוכיח] הא בעולה כתיב וסמך וי"ל דר"ל [עולת העוף וא"ת] מאי פריך בסמוך שכן ישנן בצבור כביחיד והלא עולת העוף אינה באה בצבור וי"ל דמ"מ פריך משם עולה שישנו בצבור [דעל מה מצינו אף] פרכא כל דהו פרכינן. תוס' טוך: ו] תיבות הכי גרסינן נמחק: ז] תיבת על נמחק: ח] לא קיימי: ט] יולדת הס"ד ומה"ד יביאו יורשיה עולתה דשעבודא דאורייתא הס"ד: י] אולה. א) וטעם זה מועיל דוקא היכא דמעכב הריצוי חיסרון בעלים כמו הכא אבל בהרבה מקומות כשירין ומרצין: יא] שלא לשמה שתקריב: יב] מחלוקתך מחלוקת המסייעתך: יג] ונסיב לה: יד] מחטאת ומפסח דאי במה מצינו איכא למיפרך: טו] או חטאת אות ל' נמחק: טז] מהכא מדאיצטריך מוצא: יז] ושנוי בעלים דהוי שינוי בעלים כבאין לאחר: יח] בעלים ושינוי קודש נמי יליף משינוי בעלים הס"ד: יט] היתה חיה: כ] תיבת העוף נמחק: כא] בקרא ואחר ישחט את העולה ש"מ דבעלמא אפילו דיעבד: כב] הפסולים סמיכת אשם מצורע: כג] תודה תוכיח:

א) כוונתו בזה לתרץ מה שהקשו התוס' ד"ה הגה"ה וא"ת ומאי ראי' וכו' ודו"ק:

באן

מה לתודה שכן טעונה לחם! עולה ושלמים יוכיחו. וחזר הדין, לא ראי זה כראי זה, ולא ראי זה כראי זה, הצד השוה שבהן — שהן קדשים, ושחטן שלא לשמן כשר ואינו מרצה, אף אני אביא אשם שהוא קדש, ושחטו שלא לשמו — כשר ואינו מרצה. מה להצד השוה שבהן שהן א] באין בנדר ובנדבה! אלא אמר רבא: "זאת התורה" וגו' — הקישו הכתוב לשלמים, מה שלמים שהן קדשים, ושחטן שלא לשמן — כשרים ואין מרצין, אף אני אביא אשם שהוא קודש כו'. ב] מאי חזית דאקשת לשלמים, אקיש לחטאת! הא מיעט רחמנא: "אותה". (סימן: הג"ש *בש"ר). יתיב רב הונא ורב נחמן, ויתיב רב ששת גבייהו, ויתבי וקאמרי: ג] קשיא ליה לריש לקיש אשם דלא אתי לאחר מיתה — לימא ליה ר"א: אשם נמי אתי לאחר מיתה! אמר להו רב ששת: אשם למאי קרב — למותרו, חטאת נמי מיקרב קרבה מותרה! חטאת, אף ע"ג דקרבה מותרה — מיעט רחמנא "הוא". *אשם נמי, כתיב ביה "הוא"! ההוא לאחר הקטרת אימורים הוא דכתיב; *כדתניא: אבל אשם לא נאמר בו "הוא" אלא לאחר הקטרת אימורין, והוא עצמו ד] אם לא (א) הקטירו אימורין — כשר. ואלא "הוא" למה לי? לכדרב הונא אמר רב, *דאמר רב הונא אמר רב: אשם שניתק [א]לרעיה ושחטו סתם — כשר; ניתק — אין, לא ניתק — לא, מאי טעמא? אמר קרא: "הוא" — בהווייתו יהא. יתבי רב נחמן ורב ששת, ויתיב רב אדא בר מתנה גבייהו, ויתבי וקאמרי: הא דקאמר רבי אלעזר: מצינו בבאין לאחר מיתה שהן כשרין ואין מרצין — לימא ליה ריש לקיש: הנהו נמי לייתו ולירצו! אמר להן רב אדא בר מתנה: יולדת, אם היא ילדה, בניה מי ילדו? מתקיף לה רב ה] אסי: ומאן לימא לן דאי איכא כמה עשה גבה לא מיתכפרא? וכיון דכי איכא כמה עשה גבה מיכפרא — יורשיה נמי מיכפרי. למימרא דקניא להו? והאמר רבי יוחנן: [ב]הניח מנחה לשני בניו ומת — קריבה, [ג]ואין בו שותפות; ואי ס"ד קניא להו, ו] ° "נפש" אמר רחמנא. ולא קניא להו? והאמר ר' יוחנן: [ד]הניח בהמה לשני בניו ומת — קריבה, ואין ממירין בה; אי אמרת בשלמא קניא להו — היינו דאין ממירין בה, דהויא להו ז] כשותפין, ושותפין

ר"ת שלמה יצחק | נ"א לאחר | ויקרא ב

תורה אור

הקיש הכתוב. אשם לשלמים, ואין משיבין על ההיקש. אקיש לחטאת. דפסול. קשיא ליה לריש לקיש אשם משום דלא אתי לאחר מיתה לימא ליה ר' אליעזר אשם נמי אתי לאחר מיתה. ח] שהאשם שמתו בעליו — רועה, ודמיו נופלין לקיץ המזבח. למותרו. שדמיו נופלין לנדבה, כדפרישית. חטאת נמי. מותרו נדבה הוא. כגון הפריש שתי חטאות לאחריות — מתכפר באחת מהן והשניה תרעה (יומא סה.). והיא קריבה לאחר מיתת בעלים, שהרי נתכפר בחבירתה בחייו, ואין זו חטאת שמתו בעליה. אלמא אתיא חטאת לאחר מיתה, ואפי' הכי פסולה שלא לשמה, ואשם נמי ליפסול! מיעט רחמנא הוא. בשעיר נשיא כתיב בשחיטתו (ויקרא ד): "ושחט אותו במקום אשר ישחט את העולה לפני ה' חטאת הוא" — שישחטנו לשם חטאת, ואם לאו — פסול, ד"הוא" משמע בהווייתו יהא, אם בהווייתו ט] יהא — כשר, ואם לאו — פסול. ומינה ילפי' פסול דחטאת לקמן בפרקין (דף י:). אשם נמי כתיב ביה אשם הוא. כ"ש את אהרן": (ג) י] "והקטירו המזבח אשה לה' אשם הוא", בזמן שהוא לשם אשם — כשר, ואם לאו — פסול! ההוא לאחר הקטרת אימורין (ג). דלא ילפינן מיניה, כדתניא לקמן בפ"ק: אבל אשם לא נאמר בו "הוא" אלא לאחר הקטרת אימורין. וליכא למימר בהקטרה יא] דמבעי לשמו לעכב, דהוא עצמו שלא הוקטרו יב] אימורין כשר, דאין כפרה אלא בדם. ואע"ג דכתיב באשם: "קדש קדשים הוא" יג] (ויקרא ו) קודם שחיטה — לא ילפינן מיניה, דלא משמע לשמו אלא כשכתוב "הוא" עם שם הקרבן, כגון "חטאת הוא" "אשם הוא", והיכא דכתיב גבי אחת מעבודת הדם. שניתק לרעייה. שמתו בעליו או שנתכפרו באחר, וניתק מדין אשם לרעייה, שאמרו לו ב"ד: יד] הוציאו וירעה. ושחטו סתם כשר. לעולה, הואיל וסופו לקיץ המזבח, שהוא עולה. ניתק אין. דמיעקר שם אשם מיניה משנמסר לרועה, וקם סתמיה לעולה. לא ניתק — לא הוי סתמיה לעולה, דאמר קרא: "אשם הוא" — בהווייתו יהא טו]. הנהו נמי לייתו ולירצו. איורשים. יולדת. עולת יולדת, דאייתי ראיה מיניה: יביאו יורשים עולתה — מאי לייתו ולירצו היכא? אם היא ילדה כו'. מאן לימא דאי איכא כמה עשה גבה. דיולדת, דלא מיכפרא עולתה עלייהו אם טז] הביאה מחיים? עולה מכפרת על עשה ועל לא תעשה שניתק לעשה, דתניא גבי עולת נדבה בת"כ: (ד) "ונרצה לו" — מלמד שהמקום מרוצה לו. ועל מה המקום מרוצה לו? אם תאמר דברים שחייבין עליהם מיתת ב"ד, מיתה בידי שמים, כרת (בידי שמים), מלקות ארבעים, חטאות יז] אשמות — הרי עונשן אמור. הא אין עולה באה אלא על עשה ועל לא תעשה שניתק לעשה. למימרא דקני להו. ליורשין בהמת קרבן אביהן, דקפרכת: תכפר עלייהו. אין בה משום שותפות. דאמרינן ב"המנחות והנסכים" (מנחות קד:): הכל בא בשותפות, לא חילק הכתוב אלא מנחה, שנאמר בו "נפש". ה"ג: [נפש] אמר רחמנא. "ונפש כי תקריב קרבן מנחה" וגו' (ויקרא ג). דאין ממירין בה. אם המיר יח] אינו תמורה.

ושותפין

חטאת נמי מיקרב קרבה מותרה. ואפי' הכי פסולה שלא לשמה, כיון דאינה באה לאחר מיתה לשם חטאת כי אם לשם עולה. אשם נמי, כיון דאינו קרב להדיא לשם אשם אלא לשם עולה — לא דמי לשאר קדשים*. [ומקשה]: חטאת אע"ג דקרב מותרה, מיעט רחמנא "הוא"! למסקנא זו משמע שעומד מוקשה דלימא ליה ר' אליעזר אשם נמי כו'. נ"ל דגרס "וחטאת" בוי"ו, וכל זה מדברי רב ששת, וה"פ: וחטאת, אע"ג דקרב מותרה — מיעט רחמנא "הוא", שלא תכשירנה מדאתיא לאחר מיתה כמו מחיים, ומשום הכי איצטריך לריש לקיש לעיל "אותה". והא דפריך: אשם נמי כתיב ביה "הוא" — לאו לסתור דבריו של רב ששת קאתי, אלא הכי קאמר: היכי ממעטת ליה מפסול שלא לשמן מ"אותה"? הא כתיב בה "הוא" יט]* לפוסלן!

מיעט רחמנא היא. בכמה מקומות משמע דמדכתיב "היא" בחטאת נפקא לן עיכובא. דלקמן בגמ' (דף י:) דרבי אליעזר אומר אף האשם, כ] א"ל ר' יהושע: חטאת נאמר בה "היא" בשחיטה [וכו']. ובפ"ק דמנחות (דף ד.): כא] חטאת טעמא מאי — דכתיב בה "היא". ותימה: דלקמן בפירקין (דף ז:) כב] *גמרא חוץ מן הפסח והחטאת, ויליף לה מקראי אחריני! וה"ר חיים מפרש: דצריכי תרי קראי, חד לחטאת ששחטה לשם עולה, וחד לחטאת חלב ששחטה לשם חטאת נזיר ומצורע. אע"ג דכולן שמן חטאת מ"מ פסולה, כיון דאינן באין לכפר — דינן כמו עולות, כדאמרינן לקמן, ולא דמי לחטאת חלב ששחטה לשם חטאת [דם] דכשרה. וקצת קשה מהא דפריך בריש מנחות (דף ג:) גבי חטאת חלב לשם חטאת נזיר ומצורע: ליתכפר, דכתיב "זאת תורת", ומאי פירכא? והלא גלי קרא דכתיב בה "היא"! ונראה: דאיצטריך "היא" גבי חטאת לגלויי אמנחת חוטא *ואמנחת קנאות כג] *ואשמה, דכתב בה "היא". וכמו בפסח (והיינו) דאמר לקמן גבי פסח: אלא "הוא" למה ליה? לכדתניא: כל מקום שנאמר בו "הוא" כו'. ורבינו *ש"י מוחקו, משום דליתיה בברייתא דלקמן. ובחנם מחק, דשמא היא ברייתא בתוספתא. ומיהו, קצת תימה: אמאי צריך תרי כד] קראי, חד לחטאת וחד כה] לפסח? וה"ר יצחק מפרש: חד לחטאת נקבה דלא אתי מותרה גופה עולה, אלא תרעה עד שתסתאב, ויביא בדמיה עולה, ולהכי פסולה בשנוי קודש. וחד בשעיר נשיא דהוי זכר, ומותרו גופיה הוי עולה כי הפריש שתים לאחריות, ואימא דלא ליפסול בשלא לשמן. ויש שום צריכותא דלא מצינן למילף חד מחבריה, דאי הוי כתיב בנשיא בדידיה סגי, וצ"ע.

הגה"ה ניתק אין לא ניתק לא אמר קרא הוא בהווייתו יהא. משמע הכא דניתק לרעייה דאורייתא. ותימה: דבפסחים בסוף "אלו דברים" (דף עג.) משמע דהוי דרבנן, דמפרש התם: דוקא שחטו סתם דיעבד, אבל לכתחלה — לא, גזירה לאחר כפרה אטו לפני כפרה. ולא קאמר גזירה לאחר ניתוק אטו קודם ניתוק! וי"ל, דה"פ: בהווייתו יהא קודם כפרה, הלכך כו] *איכא כפרה נמי בעי ניתוק, גזירה אטו לפני כפרה. ור"ת לא גריס כאן "ניתק אין לא ניתק לא". כז] וכן בפ"ק דמנחות (דף ד.). ולקמן ליתיה בפ' "פרת חטאת" (קטו:) ולא בתמורה פ' "ואלו קדשים" כח] (דף יח.). ובא לפרש טעם למה הוא כשר, כיון דגמירי דבאשם רועה, ומפרש: משום דכתיב "הוא", דמשמע בהווייתו יהא. פירוש בהווייתו — מה שסופו להיות, דהיינו עולה, שסופו עומד לכך כשיסתאב ויפלו דמיו לנדבה. °ואין לחוש אי קאי קרא אהלכתא, כט] דכי האי גוונא אשכחן בפ' "הלוקח עובר פרתו" (בכורות דף טז.) דאיצטריך קרא ואיצטריך הלכתא. והשתא, הא דנקט בכל דוכתא: כל שבחטאת מתה באשם רועה — לא נקט רעיה אלא לפי שתיקנוה חכמים, וכי גמירי הכי גמירי: כל שבחטאת מתה — באשם קרב עולה, דרעיה דרבנן היא.

נפש אמר רחמנא. ומשמע דמ"נפש" קדריש. וכן בסוף "המנחות והנסכים" (מנחות קד:) קתני: הכל בא בשותפות חוץ ממנחה, דכתיב "נפש". ותימה: דבתורת כהנים דריש "נפש" — ולא ליבור, "קרבנו" — ולא שותפין! ונראה דרישא דקרא מייתי בכל מקום. *ולא קניא להו והאמר רבי יוחנן. דרבי יוחנן אדרבי יוחנן הוי מצי לאקשויי.

אחד

טז א מיי' פ"ד מהל' פסה"מ הלכה טו:
יז ב מיי' פי"ד מהלכות מעה"ק הל' ג:
גי' צ"ק קדשים הס"ד ואח"כ מה"ד חטאת
יח ג מיי' שם הל' ב:
יט ד מיי' פ"א מהלכות תמורה הל' ה:

נ"ל אמר צ"ק

[אולי צ"ל בס"ד]

גי' הצ"ק ואמנחת קנאות דמעכבי דכתיב בה נמי היא ועי"ל דהיא דחטאת אתיא לגלויי אהוא דאשם דלא מעכב כהוא דפסח והיינו דאמר לקמן כו' כצ"ל ועי' בתום' במנחות דף ד ע"א תוספות ד"ה חטאת

הגהות הב"ח

(א) גמ' והוא עצמו אם לא הוקטרו אימוריו כשר ואלא הוא: (ב) רש"י ד"ה אשם נמי וכו' והקטיר אותם הכהן המזבחה אשה לה': (ג) ד"ה ההוא וכו' אימורין הוא דכתיב דלא וכו' וליכא למימר בהקטרת אימורין דבעי לשמו וכו' אימוריו כשר: (ד) ד"ה מאן לימא וכו' בת"כ נ"ב פרשה ג' פ"ד:

[מנחות ד.]

לקמן ז: י: [מנחות ד.]

לקמן קיב. קטו: פסחים עג. נזיר כה: ע"ש מנחות ד. תמורה יח.

עיין צ"ק

גליון הש"ס

תוס' ד"ה הג"ה וכו' ואין לחוש אי קאי קרא אהלכתא. עי' נזיר דף סא ע"ב תוס' ד"ה ואימא. וצע"ק:

שיטה מקובצת

א] באין בנדר ובנדבה. ולעיל אעולה [לא פריך האי פירכא] לפי דעדיפא [פריך שכן כליל] א"נ דהוי פירכא כ"ד משום דבאה בנדר ונדבה איכא נמי קולא [במה שהיא כשרה] ואינה מכפרת [ובחד] מחד לא פרכינן פירכא כל דהו [ופרכא כל דהו] מיהו הוי ולא לגמרי כי [פרכא כל דהו כמו] תורת הזמה לא פריך בב"מ. תוס' טוך: אלא אמר רבא זאת כו'. הלכך מכח היקשא דזאת לא מצית למימר דאשם לייתי ולירצי דהא איתקש לשלמים אבל גבי פירכא קמייתא דהוי פריך אשם לא לייתי כלל לא מצי לשנויי מהאי היקשא דהכא דאדרבה דהו"א ליקשינן לחטאת כדפריך הכא דעדיין לא הי' יודע דרשא דאותה ומיהו קשה לייתי לעיל מהאי היקשא דשלמים [וכי פריך] ליה ליקשי לחטאת יתרץ ליה מאותה כדעבד השתא אלא נראה דמעיקרא דהוי פריך אשם לא לייתי כלל מכח דכיון דלא שייך ביה סברא דאם לאו יהא נדבה מסתבר לדמויי לחטאת הוא כיון דשניהם באים לכפרה ואפי' בלא היקשא והלכך לא אתיא הך היקשא דשלמים ומפקא מהך סברא כיון דכשרות [לא ידעינן] באשם לכך אייתי אותה להכשיר אשם ולאפקא מהאי סברא ואכתי קשה אשם ארצויי נמי לירצי ועל אותה קושיא שייך שפיר להביא היקשא דשלמים [כיון דאפיקתיה] מהך סברא דמדמינן ליה לחטאת כך נראה למורי ואע"ג דגם עתה סברא הוא דכיון דכשר ירצה כדפי' לעיל דאין לומר דכשר לחצאין [כיון דבא] לכפרה דלא שייך ביה ואם לאו יהא נדבה אפ"ה אמרי' השתא דמפקינן מהיקשא דשלמים לומר שאינו מרצה דמ"מ כבר יצא [לתרץ על] עיקר [הקושיא דלא לייתי כלל לפרכא] דכיון דבא לכפר כחטאת הלכך אמרינן היקשא משלמים: ב] מאי חזית כו' אאשם פריך דלא פריך אשר קרבנות [דהא בהו כתיב] מוצא שפתיך ואם כמו שנדרת כו': ג] וקאמרי קא קשיא: ד] עצמו שלא הוקטרו אימורין: ה] רב אשי תיבת אסי נמחק: ו] אמר רחמנא נפש ולא: ז] להו דשותפין אות כ' נמחק: ח] מיתה דקי"ל כל שבחטאת מתה באשם רועה: ט] בהווייתו הוא יהא: י] והקטיר אותם הכהן המזבחה: יא] בהקטרה דנבעי לשמו: יב] אימוריו כשר: יג] הוא. גליון וא"ת הא כתיב כחטאת כאשם הוא ולגבי עבודות כתבי וי"ל דלא הוי מיעוט כיון דכתיב האשם הוא ולא כתב אשם הוא כמו חטאת הוא בלא ה' ועוד דאיצטריך לומר האשם הוא דטעון צפון והוי כאילו לא כתיב בה הוא ע"כ: יד] ב"ד הוציאוהו: טו] יהא והווייתו אשם ואין אשם בא בנדבה הס"ד: טז] אם הביאתה: יז] חטאות ואשמות: יח] המיר בה: יט] הוא דמשמע פסול ונהי [דאותה בא] לסתור היקשא מ"מ לא בא לסתור מה שכתוב בהדיא ולא לסתור דברי רב ששת פריך אלא פריך לפי המסקנא היאך מכשירין מטעם אותה הא כתיב הוא לפוסלן ומשני האי הוא בתר הקטרה: כ] האשם אמרינן אמר לו ר' יהושע: כא] דמנחות אמרינן: כב] בפירקין בגמ' דחוץ: כג] קנאות דכתב בהו הוא כמו בחטאת וכמו בפסח ותיבת ואשמה ל"ש ונמחק: כד] תרי הוא תיבת קראי נמחק: כה] וחד בפסח אות ל נמחק: כו] הילכך לאחר פרה ותיבת איכא נמחק: כז] לא ובפ"ק תיבת וכן ל"ש ונמחק: כח] קדשים אלא גרסי' אשם פי' שמתו בעליו או שנתכפר באחר ושחטה סתם כשר לעולה הוא בהווייתו יהא עולה כיון שמתו בעליו או שנתכפרו באחר וכ"ת והלא גמירי דבאשם: כט] אהילכתא לפי' ר"ת דפירש דהלכה נישנית כל שבחטאת מתה באשם (עולה) [רועה]:

תורה אור

ושותפין לא מצו ממירין. אלא אי אמרת לא קניא להו, א] אמורי נמי לימרו! שאני התם, *דאמר קרא: °"אם המר ימיר" — לרבות את היורש, אחד ממיר ואין שנים ממירין. מתקיף לה רב יעקב מנהר פקוד: אלא מעתה, גבי מעשר דכתיב: °"ואם גאל יגאל" — *לרבות את היורש, הכי נמי אחד גואל ואין שנים גואלין! שאני מעשר, דגבי אבוהון נמי איתיה בשותפות. אמר ליה רב אסי לרב אשי: ומינה, אי אמרת בשלמא קניא להו — היינו דחד מיהא מימר. אלא אי אמרת לא קניא להו, היכי מימר? והאמר רבי אבהו אמר ר' יוחנן: *המקדיש מוסיף חומש, ומתכפר עושה תמורה, והתורם משלו על של חבירו — טובת הנאה שלו! מקיבעא לא מכפרא, מקופיא מכפרא.§ איבעיא להו: כיפרו על מה שבאו או לא כיפרו? אמר רב (א) ששת בריה דרב אידי: מסתברא דלא כיפרו, דאי סלקא דעתך כיפרו — שני למה הוא בא? ואלא מאי, לא כיפרו? למה הוא קרב? אמר רב אשי: רב ששא בריה דרב אידי הכי קא קשיא ליה: אי אמרת בשלמא לא כיפרו — שלא לשמו מכח לשמו קאתי, ושני (ב) למה הוא בא — לכפר; אלא ב] אי אמרת כיפרו, שני למה הוא בא?§ איבעיא להו: אעשה *דלאחר הפרשה מכפרא או לא מכפרא? מי אמרינן: מידי דהוה אחטאת; מה חטאת, דקודם הפרשה — אין, דלאחר הפרשה — לא, אף הכא נמי, דקודם הפרשה — אין, לאחר הפרשה — לא. או דלמא לא דמיא לחטאת, דחטאת על כל חטא וחטא בעי לאיתויי חדא חטאת, והכא כיון (ג) דאיכא כמה עשה גביה מכפרא, אעשה דלאחר הפרשה נמי מכפרא? תא שמע:* °"וסמך ונרצה", (ד) וכי סמיכה מכפרת? והלא אין כפרה אלא בדם, שנאמר: °"כי הדם הוא בנפש יכפר"! אלא מה תלמוד לומר: "וסמך ונרצה לכפר"? ג] שאם עשאה לסמיכה שירי מצוה, מעלה עליו הכתוב כאילו לא כיפר וכיפר; (ה) ד] מאי לאו דכיפר — עשה דקודם הפרשה, לא כיפר — אעשה דסמיכה, דהוה ליה עשה דלאחר הפרשה? אמר רבא: עשה דסמיכה קאמרת? שאני התם, דכל כמה דלא שחיט בעמוד וסמוך קאי; אימת (ו) קא הוי עשה? לאחר שחיטה, לאחר שחיטה לא קא מיבעיא לן. א"ל רב הונא בר יהודה לרבא, אימא: "כיפר" — גברא,

לא

(ויקרא כז) (שם) (שם א) (שם יז)

רש"י

ושותפין לא מצו ממירין. דתניא: הכל ממירין [חוץ מן השותפים]. לפי שכל הפרשה כולה נאמרה בלשון יחיד, כמו "לא יחליפנו ולא ימיר אותו", "ואם המר ימיר" — אחד מימר ולא שנים ממירין. שאני התם. אע"ג דלא קניא להו, גזירת הכתוב הוא דשני יורשין אין ממירין זבח שהפריש אביהן. אחד ממיר. דהא דיורש ממיר בקרבן אביו מהכא נפקא לן: "אם המר" — לרבות את היורש, דהוה מצי למיכתב "אם ימר". והכא נמי בלשון יחיד כתביה. אם ה] יגאל איש ממעשרו לרבות יורש. שמוסיף חומש, ופודה את מעשר אביו. איתיה בשותפות. דלא אשכחן דמימעט שותפין מפדיון מעשר שני. ותמורה היינו טעמא — משום דכל הפרשה נאמרה בלשון יחיד. המקדיש מוסיף חומש כו'. אדם שנדר קרבן, והפרישו חבירו משלו להתכפר בו הנודר, והומם, ובא לחללו; אם המפריש מחללו — מוסיף חומש, ואם המתכפר מחללו — אינו מוסיף חומש. דתלייה רחמנא לחומש במקדיש, דכתיב (ויקרא כז): "ואם המקדיש יגאל את ביתו ויסף חמישיתו", "ואם גאל יגאל את השדה [המקדיש אותו]". ומתכפר עושה תמורה. דאיהו הוה בעלים דידיה. ובמסכת תמורה יליף טעמא בפ"ק. והתורם. תרומה משלו על הכרי של חבירו טובת הנאה של מפריש הוא, בידו לתתה ו] לכהן שירצה. ואם בא ישראל ואמר לו "הילך סלע זו ותן תרומתך לבן בתי כהן" — אותה ז] סלע טובת הנאה של מפריש הוא. ויליף התם טעמא: ח] "את כל מעשר תבואתך ונתת" (דברים כו) מי שהפרישה מתבואתו — בידו לתתה. ומשני: מקיבעא לא מכפרא מקופיא מכפרא. ט] כפרה קבועה, שיהא יורש בעליו ממש — אין להן. הלכך, גבי מנחה — כשרה ליקרב, דלא י] *דשותפין היא. אבל כפרה קופיא ורפה ממילא — יש להן בו, והלכך ממיר. "קופיא" — לשון צף, כמו (חגיגה טז:): אקפו ידייכו, וכמו (מלכים ב ו): "ויצף הברזל" תרגום: וקפא ברזלא. ויש לו יא] דומה במסכת יומא (דף טז:). כיפרו על מה שבאו. קדשים שנזבחו שלא לשמן יב] יקרבו, ותנן: לא עלו לבעלים לשם חובה, וצריך להביא אחר. מיהו, מבעיא יג] ליה אם כפרו על החטא שהופרשו עליו. ונפקא מיניה שלא ידאג מן היסורין בינתיים. אמר רב אשי רב ששא בריה דרב אידי. דיליף יד] לא כיפרו, מדבעי לאיתויי שני. הכי טו] קשיא ליה. בהבאת שני, טפי מהקרבת ראשון. אי אמרת בשלמא לא כיפרו. אפילו הכי מיקרב טז] קרבי — דשלא לשמו מכח לשמו קאתי, דמתחילתו לשמו הוקדש. ושני בא לכפר על החטא, כגון אם עולה היא — מכפרת על עשה או אם אשם הוא יכפר על אשמו. אעשה דלאחר הפרשה כו'. אסתם יז] עולה קאי, שנזבחו לשמן. אחטאת. דלא מכפרא יח] אלא שגגת כרת דקודם הפרשה, דכתיב: "או הודע אליו חטאתו" וגו' (ויקרא ד). כיון דאי איכא כמה עשה גביה מכפרא. שהרי לא חייב הכתוב (ז) להביאו, יט] שמתחייב על כל עשה ועשה, אלא דורון בעלמא. כ] וכתיב "ונרצה לו" — מלמד שנתרצה להקדוש ברוך הוא (בת"כ פ' ויקרא), אלמא כולן נתכפרו. שירי מצוה. שלא נחשבה בעיניו ולא עשאה. כאילו לא כיפר וכיפר. כלומר, אף על פי כן כיפר. מאי כיפר ומאי לא כיפר — (ח) לאו, כיפר — עשה קמא דקודם הפרשה, ולא כיפר — עשה דסמיכה דהוה ליה לאחר הפרשה. בעמוד וסמוך קאי. ואכתי כל כמה דלא שחטיה — לא עבר עליה. כיפר גברא. על כל עשה שבידו, וינצל מן היסורין כא].

לא

תוספות

אחד מימר ואין שנים ממירין. משמע דלרבי יוחנן יורש מימר. ותימה: דבפ' "מי שהוציאוהו" (עירובין מו:) קאמר רבי יוחנן: רבי מאיר ורבי יהודה — הלכה כרבי יהודה, ובריש תמורה (דף ב.) וערכין (דף ב.) פליגי בה רבי מאיר ורבי יהודה, וקאמר רבי יהודה: יורש אינו מימר! וי"ל: משום דר' יוחנן אית ליה הלכה כסתם משנה, ובריש תמורה וערכין אומר: הכל ממירין — לאתויי יורש. **מתכפר** עושה תמורה. והא דתניא בפ' קמא דתמורה (דף ט.): "לא יחליפנו" בשל אחרים — הא מפרש התם: כגון דאמר מריה דבהמה דהקדש "כל הרוצה להמיר בבהמתו ימיר". **מקופיא** מכפרא. תימה: דבפ' קמא דתמורה (דף י.) ילפינן דמתכפר עושה תמורה מנזיר, והיא כפרה קבועה היא! וי"ל: דלא יליף מנזיר אלא דמפריש אינו מימר, אבל מתכפר עושה תמורה אפי' מקופיא. וא"ת: דיורש בקופיא גרידא כב] קרי מתכפר ומימר, וכי הוו שנים יורשים מיקרו שותפין ולא ממירין? והא ביומא פרק "הוציאו לו" (דף נ:) קבעי בפר כה"ג שאחיו הכהנים מתכפרים, אי בקביעותא מתכפרין — והוו שותפין ולא מצי ממיר, או מקופיא מתכפרין — וכולו של כהן גדול, ומצי מימר דיחיד הוא אלמא לא חשיב מתכפר כשהוא מקופיא, מדכהן גדול מימר ולא מיקרו שותפין מה שאחיו מתכפרין בו בקופיא! וי"ל: כג] דבשמעתא שניהם היורשין הוו מקופיא, לכך מיקרו שותפין ולא ממירין. אבל התם, כיון דאיכא השתא בהאי קרבן כפרת כהן גדול דקביעא — לא חשיבא לגביה אחיו כמו שותפין על ידי כפרת קופיא. **דאי** ס"ד כיפרו שני למה הוא בא. תימה: כמה קרבנות אדם מתנדב ומביא זה אחר זה מיד, אע"פ שכיפר הראשון שנעשה לשמו! וי"ל דפריך: שני למה חייב להביא. ואם תאמר: מאי קאמר שני למה הוא בא? דלמא קאתי לכפר אמחשבה דשלא לשמן, דחשיב עשה לאחר שחיטה, כמו סמיכה דבסמוך! ומיהו כד] יש לומר, דמחשבה תלויה בעובד, וקרבן לא מכפר אלא על בעליה. ונראה דמאשם קדייק, שאינו בא נדבה. **אלא** מאי לא כיפרו למה הוא קרב. נ"ע: דהיינו קשיא דריש לקיש, דאם כשירין הם — ירצו, ואם אינן מרצין — למה הן באין! **או** דלמא לא דמיא לחטאת. תימה: דנפשוט ממתני' דפ"ק דשבועות (דף ב:), דאפי' לר' שמעון דלית ליה (שם יא:) לב בית דין מתנה עליהן, שעיר שלא קרב כה] עליו ברגל זה — יקרב ברגל אחר. אע"פ שמרגל שעברו נתכפרו כבר אטומאת מקדש וקדשיו דקודם הפרשה, כו] דקאתי האי שעיר מכפר אטומאה שאחר כך! ויש לומר: כיון שאבד וקרב אחר תחתיו — איגלאי מילתא שלא היתה הפרשתן הפרשה עד רגל אחר דשחטי ליה. **והלא** אין כפרה אלא בדם. כז] בפרק "תמיד נשחט" (פסחים נט:) אמרי': כל כמה דלא אכלי כהנים — בשר לא מצי מכפר, דכתיב: "ואכלו אותם אשר כופר בהם" — מלמד שהכהנים אוכלין בשר ובעלים מתכפרים. כח] אבל מכל מקום, עיקר כפרה אינה אלא בדם. **לאחר** שחיטה לא קא מיבעיא לן. בסוף הסוגיא בעי רבי ירמיה אפילו לאחר שחיטה.

לא

עין משפט נר מצוה

כ א מיי' פ"א מהל' תמורה הלכה א:
כא ב מיי' שם הלכה ה:
כב ג מיי' פ"ו מהלכות ערכין הלכה ב ופ"ה מהל' מעשר שני הלכה ח:
כג ד מיי' פ"ו מהלכות ערכין הלכה ז:
כד ה מיי' פ"ו מהלכות תמורה הלכה ז:
כה ו מיי' פ"ו מהלכות תרומות הלכה ב:
כו ז מיי' פ"ג מהלכות מעשה"ק הלכה יב:

מסורת הש"ס

תמורה ב.
ת"כ פרשה בחקותי
יומא נ: תמורה י. נדרים לו:
נ"א חל שותפין אהא
[עי' תוספות שבת עב. ד"ה כי אתא]
יומא ה. מנחות צג:

הגהות הב"ח

(א) גמ' אמר רב שישא בריה דר' אידי מסתברא: (ב) שם מכח לשמו קאתי ושני הוא כל"ל ותיבת למה נמחק: (ג) שם והכא כיון דאי איכא כמה: (ד) שם ת"ש וסמך ונרצה לו לכפר עליו וכי סמיכה: (ה) שם כאילו לא כיפר וכיפר מאי לאו: (ו) שם אימת הוי כל"ל ותיבת קא נמחק: (ז) רש"י ד"ה כיון דאי וכו' לא חייב כתוב להביאו שמתחייב וכו' בעלמא הס"ד ואח"כ מ"ה ונרצה לו לכפר עליו מלמד וכו' אלמא כולן נתכפרו: (ח) ד"ה מאי כיפר וכו' כיפר מאי לאו:

שיטה מקובצת

א] להו ממורי אות א' נמחק: ב] אי אמרת כיפרו שני למה הוא בא. תימה מאי פריך הא גלי קרא ואם לאו יהא נדבה למדנו שלא עלו לשם חובה וצריך להביא אחר וצ"ל דה"ק למה הוא בא [על מה מכפר מה] שלא כיפר הראשון ומיבעיא באשם דאי בעולה ושלמים מאי בעי ליה שני למה בא הלא הוא בא בנדבה והלא אדם מתנדב שלמים ועולה כמה שירצה וא"ת לפי מה שפרש"י דכפרו כדי להגין עליו מן היסורין מאי פריך למה הוא בא א) להגין עליו מן היסורים וי"ל דה"פ כיון דכפרו עליו להגין מן היסורין שני למה הוא מביא: איבעי' להו אעשה דלאחר הפרשה מכפרא. אעולה קא בעי דמכפרת על עשה כדפרש"י לעיל. תוס' טוך: ג] לכפר לומר לך שאם: ד] וכיפר מאי כיפר מאי לא כיפר: ה] אם גאל יגאל: ו] לתתה לכל כהן אות ל' נמחק: ז] תיבת סלע נמחק: ח] טעמא מדכתיב את: ט] מכפרא כלומר כפרה קבועה שיהא

היורש: י] דלא חל שותפין אהא וכן לענין מרצין ס"א וכן לענין שאלתא דרב אשי לעיל: יא] ויש לו דמיון במסכת: יב] וקרבו אות י' נמחק: יג] מבעיא לן: יד] דיליף שלא: טו] הכי קא קשיא ליה בהקרבת שני [טפי] מהקרבת: טז] מקרב קרב אלא על שגגת: יז] אסתם אות י' נמחק: יח] דלא מכפרא אלא על שגגת: יט] להביאו שהתחייב עשה: כ] בעלמא הוא ונרצה וכתיב ונרצה לו מלמד שנתרצה מכל להקב"ה: כא] ונינצל מן היסורין. גליון פי' ואפי' לאחר הפרשה: כב] גרידא קאמרת הכא דמתכפר ומימר: כג] וי"ל ס"א דשאני התם לפי [שהוא מקבעא] לכהן הגדול ולכך [גם] כפרה דכהנים [דקופיא לא חשיבא] אבל הכא דמת דקבעא [לכן דקופיא חשיבא]: כד] ומיהו בזה: כה] תיבת עליו נמחק: כו] וקאתי אות ד' נמחק: כז] ברם ועי"ג דבפרק: כח] תיבת אבל נמחק:

א) נראה דל"ל נימא דבא השני ג"כ להגין מן היסורים.

כז א מיי' פ"ד מהלכות מחוסרי כפרה הלכה ג:

כח ב מיי' פי"ב מהלכות פסולי המוקדשין הלכה ו:

[במשנה איתא מן השמן והיינו קרא דכתיב בפרשת מצורע יד פסוק כט והנותר מן השמן אשר על כף וגו' לכפר עליו לפני ה' וכן העתיקו התוס' ודע דלעיל בקרא יח כתיב והנותר בשמן אשר על כף וגו' וכפר עליו הכהן לפני ה']

תורה אור (ויקרא יד)

לא כיפר — קמי שמיא! מי לא *תנן: °"והנותר *בשמן אשר על כף (א) וגו' לכפר עליו לפני ה'", אאם נתן — כיפר, ואם לא נתן — לא כיפר, דברי ר"ע. ר' יוחנן א] [בן נורי] אומר: שירי מצוה הן, בין ניתן בין שלא ניתן — כיפר, ומעלין עליו כאילו לא כיפר; מאי "כאילו לא כיפר"? אילימא דמבעי (ב) לאיתויי קרבן אחרינא — האמרת: בין ניתן בין לא ניתן כיפר! אלא: כיפר — גברא, לא כיפר — קמי שמיא. הכא נמי, כיפר כו'! התם נמי: כיפר — מתן בהונות, ב] לא כיפר — מתנות הראש. ת"ש, ר' שמעון אומר: *כבשי עצרת למה הן באין? כבשי עצרת שלמים נינהו! אלא: שעירי עצרת למה הן באין? על טומאת מקדש וקדשיו; נזרק דמו של ראשון, שני למה קרב? על טומאה שאורעה בין זה לזה. אמור מעתה: ראויין היו ישראל להקריב קרבנותיהן בכל עת ובכל שעה, אלא שחיסך הכתוב. ג] והא הכא, דעשה דלאחר הפרשה, (ג) וקא מכפרא! אי דאפרשינהו בבת אחת — הכי נמי. הכא במאי עסקינן — דאפרשינהו בזה אחר זה. ד] וליקו ולימא ליה לקרא דכי כתיבא בזה אחר זה כתיבא?! אמר רב פפא: קרבנות צבור קאמרת? בשאני קרבנות צבור, דלב בית דין קמתנה עליהן, כדרב יהודה אמר שמואל, *דאמר רב יהודה אמר שמואל: קרבנות צבור — ה] סכין מושכתן למה שהן. אמר ליה רב יוסף בריה דרב ו] שמואל לרב פפא: *ומי אית ליה לרבי שמעון לב בית דין מתנה עליהן? *והאמר רב אידי בר אבין אמר רב עמרם אמר רבי יצחק אמר רבי יוחנן: תמידין שלא הוצרכו לצבור, לדברי

לא כיפר קמי שמיא. לנחת רוח לקונו, דלא עבד מלוה מן המובחר. **אם נתן.** שיריים על ראש מצורע כיפר ז] כו', דכפרה אמתנות הראש כתיבא. **שירי מצוה הן.** דכתיב "והנותר", הלכך הוי כשפיכת שירי הדם דחטאת דלא מעכבי, כדלקמן (דף נב.). **לא כיפר מתנות הראש.** ויביא לוג אחר, ויתן מתנות הראש. ולר' עקיבא צריך שיתחיל בבהונות. **כבשי עצרת שלמים נינהו.** והיכי תנא סיפא דמילתיה על טומאת מקדש וקדשיו? והלא חובה ללחם הן באין, להתיר את החדש במקדש למנחות ולבכורים! **שעירי עצרת.** גבי עצרת כתיבי שני שעירים, חד בתורת כהנים: "ועשיתם שעיר עזים אחד לחטאת", וחד בחומש הפקודים למוספין. וקיימא לן במסכת שבועות (דף ב.): שעירי הרגלים באין על טומאת מקדש וקדשיו שאין בה ידיעה לא בתחילה ולא בסוף. **שני למה קרב.** והלא ראשון כיפר ח] לטומאה שלפניו! בין זה לזה. קס"ד בין הקרבתו של זה להקרבתו של זה. [ראויים היו ישראל כו'. דכל שעה] בספק חוטאין קיימי. **אלא שחיסך הכתוב.** ט] *חסך מעונותיהם, ולא דקדק אחריהם, לפי שחס על ממונם. וחבירו במסכת מנחות (דף עו:): מפני החיסכון. ומפרש: מאי "מפני החיסכון" – התורה חסה על ממונם של ישראל. **והא הכא.** דטומאה שאירעה בין זה לזה – עשה דלאחר הפרשה הוא, שהרי מאתמול הופרשו, וקתני דשני מכפר! טומאת מקדש וקדשיו עשה נמי הוא, דכתיב: "וישלחו מן המחנה" וגו' (במדבר ה). **אי דאפרשינהו בבת אחת הכי נמי.** דלא מכפר שני תמידי, ואין צריך י] לבא. **הכא במאי עסקינן.** דהולרך שני לבא – יא] דאפרשינן בזה אחר זה. והאי "שאורעה בין זה לזה" דקתני – שאורעה אתמול, בין הפרשתו של זה להפרשתו של זה. ולעולם אעשה דלאחר הפרשה לא מכפר. **וליקום ולימא ליה כו'.** בתמיה: אפשר שלא בא הכתוב אלא לכך? והלא בכל שנה הצריכו יב] שנים! לב בית דין. יג] (העם) העוסקין בצרכי צבור מתנה עליהן, שאפי' יפרישו הכהנים בבת אחת – לא תהא הפרשת האחרון הפרשה עד סמוך להקרבתו, כדי שיהא ראוי שני זה לבא על טומאה שאורעה בינתיים. **קרבנות צבור סכין.** השוחטן, מושכתן למה שהן ראויים ועומדין, ואפילו לא ידע השוחט מה הן. יד] (או) כגון תמידין שלא הוצרכו לצבור, שניקחו מתרומה ישנה, והגיע אחד בניסן שמצוה להביא מן החדש כדאמרינן בראש השנה (דף ז.) – שוחטן, וכשרין לקיץ המזבח, כדין שאר מותר תרומת כסף הנשאר בקופות טו] התרומה, כשמגיע אחד בניסן שמקיילין בו את המזבח. ואע"ג דלשם תמידין נלקחו, ולא לשם עולת נדבת צבור, כגון קיץ המזבח, הואיל ולא חזו לתמידין – קרבי למאי דחזו, משום דלב ב"ד מתנה עליהן: אם (ד) הוצרכו, ואם לאו – יקיילו בהן את המזבח. ונראה בעיני דלא גרסי לה להא דשמואל הכא, דהא מוקמינן ליה בפ"ק דשבועות (דף יב:) אליבא דמאן דלית ליה לב בית דין מתנה עליהן. לדברי

לא כיפר מתנות הראש. פי' בקונט': ויביא לוג אחר ויתן מתנות הראש. ולר' עקיבא צריך להתחיל בבהונות. ותימה: דבסוף "הוציאו לו" (יומא דף סא.) משמע דלכולי עלמא אין מתנות הראש מעכבות, ואפילו נשפך הלוג. דפליגי התם ר"א ור"ש ורבנן בנתן מקצת מתנות שבבהונות ונשפך הלוג, וקתני סיפא: גמר מתנות שבבהונות ונשפך הלוג – דברי הכל מתנות שבראש אינן מעכבות טז] כלל, דאין צריך להביא אחר. דבענין אחר אי אפשר לפרש. וזהו דלא כתנאי דהכא! וצ"ל: דלר' יוחנן בן נורי נמי אין מעכבות כלל ואין צריך לעשותן. ומעיקרא ס"ד: לא כיפר קמי שמיא – אפילו מה שעשה כבר, כגון מתנות בהונות עצמן, אע"פ שנתנן – אין בהן ריצוי גמור לפי שחיסר מתנות הראש, אע"ג דלא מעכבי. כמו שאמר לעיל שקרבן שעשה לא כיפר קמי שמיא בשביל סמיכה שלא עשה, אע"ג דלא מעכבת, והדר מסיק: יז] ומתן בהונות שכבר עשה – כיפר לגמרי, שיש בהן ריצוי גמור. אבל מתנות הראש – לא כיפר קמי שמיא, ואין צריך לעשותן, דכתיב "והנותר" וגו'. וכן הקרבן כשר וכיפר על כל עשה שקודם לכן, אבל סמיכה לא כיפר, דהויא לאחר הפרשה, עד שיביא קרבן אחר. אבל קשה על זה, דלא הוי ליה לתרץ רק: התם כתיב "והנותר", וגבי סמיכה לא כתיב והנותר! וצ"ל דהתם ה"פ: מתנות הראש לא מעכבי – דכיון שקיבל מדם האשם ומן השמן על הבהונות אינו קרוי עוד מחוסר כפורים, אלא מותר לאכול בקדשים וליכנס למקדש. דמתן שמן נמי קרוי קרבן, כדאמר פרק "בית שמאי" (לקמן מד:): "לכל קרבנם" – לרבות לוג שמן של מצורע. ולכן לכל הפחות *צריך ליתן על הבהונות קודם שיהא מותר בקדשים. נרו"ך.

וליקו ולימא ליה לקרא דכי כתיבא בזה אחר זה כתיבא. הא לא פריך דלימא ליה לקרא שלא חייב להביא שנים אלא כשהפריש בזה אחר זה, אבל הפריש שנים בבת אחת יח] [אינו חייב]. שזו אינו קושיא, דאפי' הפריש שנים בבת אחת, נהי כשקרב האחד לא מהני השני שהופרש עמו, מכל מקום יכול יט] להפריש אחר כן ולהקריב, ומועיל, דלעולם חייבה תורה להביא שנים. אלא הכי פריך: דאטו מי לימא ליה לקרא כ] דכי משתעי [שצריך להקריב ב' – דוקא *כשמפריש בזה אחר זה? וקשה: ליפרך נמי, דאטו מי לימא ליה לקרא דכי משתעי] ע"י לב ב"ד! ונראה, דבלאו קרא הוה קשיא ליה משעירי עצרת שעושין כל שנה, שדוחק הוא להעמידם ולומר שהיו מפרישין אותן בזה אחר זה. **סכין** מושכתן למה שהן. בסוף פרק קמא דשבועות (דף יב:) אמרינן דשמואל סבר להא דר' יוחנן כא] דהתם, ובסמוך מייתי לה, (ה) אמר רבי יוחנן: תמידין שלא הוצרכו לצבור, לדברי ר"ש אין נפדין תמימים. פירוש: אלא מקילין בגופן את המזבח, כדקאמר התם לר' שמעון. ופי' שם בקונט' דשמואל סבר לה להא דאמר רבי יוחנן: כב] לדברי ר"ש אין נפדין תמימים ומקילין בהן את המזבח, דאמר שמואל: סכין מושכתן למה שהן, פי': סכין כג] השוחטן סתם מושכתן לקרבן שהופרשו מתחילה, כד] כגון עולת תמיד לעולת קיץ, אע"פ שאין זה אותו קרבן, כיון דמעיקרא עולה והשתא עולה. והשתא קשה: מאי מייתי התם "תניא נמי הכי" מברייתא? הלא ממתני' דהתם הוה ליה לאיתויי! ועוד: דהדיא מוכח בשמעתין דמילתיה דשמואל דווקא כרבנן דפליגי עליה דרבי שמעון, דאית להו לב בית דין מתנה עליהן! ויש פירושים ברש"י שמוגה בהן: נראה בעיני דלא גרסינן הא דשמואל הכא, דהא בפרק קמא דשבועות מוקמינן לה אליבא דמאן דלית ליה לב בית דין מתנה עליהן. וזהו דוחק למחוק כל מילתיה דשמואל מן הספרים. ועוד נראה, שדברי הקונטרס סותרים זה את זה, שפירש: סכין מושכתן למה שהן ראויין ועומדין, כגון תמידין שלא הוצרכו לצבור שנקחו מתרומה ישנה, והגיע אחד בניסן – מקילין בהן את המזבח. ואף על גב דלשם תמידין נלקחו ולא לשם עולות נדבת צבור, הואיל ולא חזו תו לציבור – קרבי למאי דחזו, משום דלב בית דין מתנה עליהן: אם הוצרכו – הוצרכו, ואם לאו – יקילו בהן. אלמא לפירושו לא מהני תנאי בית דין למיקרב תו לתמידין. ואחר כך פירש: לדברי חכמים נפדין תמימים, דאית להו לב בית דין מתנה עליהן להכשירן לתמידי שנה הבאה, שאם לא הוצרכו – יהיו לדמיהן, שיפדו אותן ממעות חולין בלא מום, ויוציאום לחולין, ויפלו דמיהן למותר תרומה, ואחר כך יקחו אותן מתרומה חדשה ויוכשרו לתמידים. ונראה כפירוש הערוך,* וזה לשונו: סכין מושכתן למה שהן, פירוש: למה שהן, אם תמידין אם מוספין – סכין מושכתן להיות כן. אבל טרם שמושכתן הסכין, אין לומר איזה תמיד ואיזה מוספין, אלא תלויין ועומדין בתנאי לב בית דין, שכך מתנה עליהן לב בית דין: אף על פי שאמרו שהן תמידין, אם ירצו להקריבן לשם זבח אחר – רשאין, לפי שבזמן שמשך כה] הסכין לשחיטת התמיד – הרי הוא תמיד, ובזמן שמשך זה הסכין לשל מוסף – הרי הוא מוסף. וזה סייעתא לר' יוחנן [דאמר] שאם לא הוצרכו להן [אליבא דרבנן] נפדין תמימים, שלא משכתן סכין (ו) לעולם. והשתא להאי פירושא לא גרסינן "תניא נמי הכי", דמילתא דשמואל כרבנן, אלא גרסי': תניא מודה ר' שמעון כו' וטעמא

ולכן לכל הפחות א"ל ליתן על הראש קודם כו' צ"ק

צ"ל כשמפרישים בזה אחר זה ומתשני לקרא משתעי ע"י לב ב"ד כו' רש"ק ועי"ש וגי' צ"ק כשמפרישים בזא"ז אך ק' א"כ מאי מסני לב ב"ד וכי משתעי קרא ע"י לב ב"ד ונראה דבלאו קרא כו'

נגעים פי"ד משנה י

תוספתא דשבועות פ"א

נ"א חסך על עוונותיהם ולא כו' צ"ק

שבועות יב:

מנחות עט:

[שבועות יא: מנחות סד]

[בערך משך]

הגהות הב"ח

(א) גמ' על כף וגו' וכפר עליו הכהן לפני ה' אם נתן: (ב) שם דמיבעי ליה לאיתויי: (ג) שם דלאחר הפרשה הוא וקא: (ד) רש"י ד"ה קרבנות וכו' אם הוצרכו הוצרכו ואם לאו: (ה) תום' ד"ה סכין וכו' מייתי לה לאמר ר' יוחנן: (ו) בא"ד שלא משכתן סכין מעולם וכו':

שיטה מקובצת

א] יוחנן בן נורי: ב] לא כיפר מתנות הראש. פי' הקונטרס ויביאו לוג אחר כו' ולא נהירא דהא אמרינן בפ' הוציאו לו (דף ס"א) נשפך הלוג אחר שגמר מתנותיו של בהונות דברי הכל מתנות הראש לא מעכבות [אלא נראה] דמעיקרא (הקשה) [פירש] כיפר גברא להגין מן היסורין לא כיפר קמי שמיא שלא עשה מן המובחר ודחי [דזה] לא מקרי לא כיפר בשביל כך [אלא כיפר מתן בהונות לא כיפר] מתנות הראש קמי שמיא ולא עשה בהם נחת רוח ליוצרו אבל להביא לוג אחר לכ"ע לא צריך: ג] והא הכא דעשה דלאחר הפרשה הוא. פ"ה [דטומאה שארעה בין זה כו' וקשה] מ"מ מאי פשיט אבעייתו הוא בעי מדבר שאין בו כרת ופשיט ליה מכרת וי"ל דהוא פשיט מכ"ש מדקאמר שהוא מכפר בדבר שיש בו כרת כ"ש [בדבר שאין בו כי אם עשה לבדו] מ"מ קשה דתפשוט כמו כן בחטאת דעשה דלאחר הפרשה מכפרת ולעיל משמע דפשיטא ליה בחטאת [לא] מהני. ועוד קשה דכרת ולאו איכא נמי הכא דכתיב ולא יטמאו את מחניהם וכתיב את מקדש ה' טמא ונכרתה וגו' גבי קדשים בטומאת הגוף (כרת איכא) אבל עשה ליכא כלל לכך נראה למורי דפריך משעירי עצרת אעשה דעולה דיש לספק לזה כמו לזה דטעמא מאי מספקא לן בעולה משום [דבא] על עשה טובא שעירי עצרת נמי מכפרת על טומאת מקדש וקדשיו שארעה בין רגל לרגל שעבר ושעירי הרגלים מכפרים על אין בה ידיעה לא בתחלה ולא בסוף והא דקאמר אעשה דלאחר הפרשה לאו דוקא אלא כלומר כמו עשה דעולה כדפי' תוס' הר"פ ז"ל: ד] וליקו ולימא לקרא כי כתיב בזה כו'. לא מיירי קרא כי אם שהפריש שניהם בזה אחר זה אבל אם הפרישם בבת אחת אין צריך להקריב השני כך פרש"י וקשה דגם אם הפרישם בבת אחת יניח להשני ויפריש אחר [ויקרבנו] וא"כ מיירי שפיר בכל ענין שיביא אותם שני שעירים אף כשהפרישם בבת אחת א) תוס' טוך: ה] ע' בהשמטות בסוף המסכת: ו] דרב שמעיה תיבת שמואל נמחק: ז] כיפר ואם לא נתן לא כיפר תיבת כו' נמחק: ח] כיפר על מה שלפניו ותיבת לטומאה ל"ש ונמחק: ט] חשך הכתוב על עונותם: י] להביא אחר תיבת לבא נמחק: יא] דאפרשינהו: יב] הצריכו הכתוב: יג] תיבת העם נמחק: יד] תיבת או נמחק: טו] בקופות של תרומה אות ה' נמחק: טז] מעכבות וכעין זה קתני התם גבי מתנות של פר ושעיר של יוה"כ והיינו דאינן מעכבות כלל: יז] מסיק דמתן אות ו' נמחק: יח] בבת אחת אינו חייב אלא אחת: יט] יכול להביא השני שהפריש ולהפריש אחר אחר כך ולהקריבו: כ] לקרא דשנים שחייבה [תורה] לאותן שהופרשו [שלא] בבת אחת יש תימה אי קא מהני לב ב"ד דאטו מי לימא קרא דכי: כא] יוחנן דאמר התם ובסמוך מייתי לה תמידין ותיבות אמר ר' יוחנן נמחק: כב] יוחנן דלדברי: כג] סכין השוחטת סתם: כד] מתחילה לכך: כה] שמשך זה הסכין של תמיד הרי ותיבת לשחיטת ואות ה' נמחק:

א) וכתוס' ד"ה וליקו כתבו לייסב זה.

כט א מיי' פ"ד מהל' שקלים הלכה יא:
ל ב מיי' פט"ו מהלכות פסה"מ הלכה יג:
לא ג מיי' שם הלכה ז:
לב ד מיי' שם הלכה ח:
לג ה מיי' שם הלכה ט והלכה יד:

לְדִבְרֵי ר' שִׁמְעוֹן — אֵין נִפְדִּין תְּמִימִים, *לְדִבְרֵי חֲכָמִים — אנִפְדִּין תְּמִימִין! וְעוֹד, הָא בְּעָא מִינֵּיהּ ר' יִרְמְיָה מֵר' זֵירָא: שְׂעִירֵי עֲצֶרֶת שֶׁקִּבֵּל דָּמָן בִּשְׁנֵי כוֹסוֹת, וְנִזְרַק דָּמוֹ שֶׁל רִאשׁוֹן, שֵׁנִי לָמָּה הוּא א] בָּא? עַל טוּמְאָה שֶׁאוֹרְעָה בֵּין [זְרִיקָה שֶׁל] זֶה לָזֶה (נִזְרַק דָּמוֹ שֶׁל שֵׁנִי לָמָּה הוּא קְרֵיבִין) עַד כָּאן לָא מִיבַּעְיָא לֵיהּ אֶלָּא עֲשֵׂה דִּלְאַחַר שְׁחִיטָה, אֲבָל עֲשֵׂה דִּלְאַחַר הַפְרָשָׁה — לָא קָא מִיבַּעְיָא לֵיהּ! דִּלְמָא "אִם תִּימְצֵי לוֹמַר" קָאָמַר. אִיתְּמַר, תּוֹדָה שֶׁשְּׁחָטָהּ לְשֵׁם תּוֹדַת חֲבֵירוֹ ב] (כְּשֵׁרָה) — רַבָּה אָמַר: כְּשֵׁרָה, רַב חִסְדָּא אָמַר: פְּסוּלָה. רַבָּה אָמַר: כְּשֵׁרָה — תּוֹדָה לְשֵׁם תּוֹדָה נִשְׁחֲטָה; רַב חִסְדָּא אָמַר: פְּסוּלָה (א) — ג] לְשׁוּם שְׁלָמִים דִּידֵיהּ ד] נִשְׁחֲטָה בָּעֵינַן. (ויקרא ז) אָמַר רַבָּה: מְנָא אָמֵינָא לַהּ? *דְּתַנְיָא: °"וּבְשַׂר זֶבַח תּוֹדַת שְׁלָמָיו בְּיוֹם הַקְרִיבוֹ אֶת זִבְחוֹ" וגו', אַבָּא חָנִין אָמַר מִשּׁוּם ר' אֱלִיעֶזֶר: בָּא לְלַמֵּד, בתּוֹדָה שֶׁשְּׁחָטָהּ לְשֵׁם שְׁלָמִים — כְּשֵׁרָה, שְׁלָמִים שֶׁנִּשְׁחֲטוּ לְשֵׁם תּוֹדָה — פְּסוּלִים. וּמָה הֶפְרֵשׁ בֵּין זֶה לָזֶה? גתּוֹדָה קְרוּיָה שְׁלָמִים, וְאֵין שְׁלָמִים קְרוּיִין תּוֹדָה; שְׁלָמִים לְשֵׁם תּוֹדָה — פְּסוּלָה, הָא תּוֹדָה לְשֵׁם תּוֹדָה — כְּשֵׁרָה, מַאי לָאו דְּחַבְרֵיהּ? לָא, דִּידֵיהּ. אֲבָל דְּחַבְרֵיהּ מַאי, פְּסוּלָה? אַדְּתָנֵי: שְׁלָמִים ה] לְשֵׁם תּוֹדָה פְּסוּלָה — לִיתְנֵי: תּוֹדָה לְשֵׁם תּוֹדָה, וְכ"ש שְׁלָמִים לְשֵׁם תּוֹדָה! שְׁלָמִים לְשֵׁם תּוֹדָה דִּידֵיהּ אִיצְטְרִיךְ לֵיהּ, סָלְקָא דַּעְתָּךְ אָמֵינָא: מִדְּתוֹדָה קְרוּיָה שְׁלָמִים — שְׁלָמִים נַמִי קְרוּיִין תּוֹדָה, וְכִי שָׁחֵיט לְהוּ לְשֵׁם תּוֹדָה — לִיכַּשְׁרוּ, קָא מַשְׁמַע לָן.§ אָמַר *רָבָא: דחַטָּאת שֶׁשְּׁחָטָהּ לְשֵׁם חַטָּאת — כְּשֵׁירָה, (ויקרא ד) לְשֵׁם עוֹלָה — ו] פְּסוּלָה. מַאי טַעְמָא? °"וְשָׁחַט אוֹתָהּ לְחַטָּאת" אָמַר רַחֲמָנָא, וַהֲרֵי חַטָּאת לְשֵׁם חַטָּאת נִשְׁחֲטָה. לְשֵׁם עוֹלָה — פְּסוּלָה. וְאָמַר רָבָא: *הְחַטָּאת שֶׁשְּׁחָטָהּ עַל מִי שֶׁמְּחוּיָּיב חַטָּאת — פְּסוּלָה, וְעַל מִי שֶׁמְּחוּיָּיב עוֹלָה — כְּשֵׁרָה. מַאי טַעְמָא? "וְכִפֶּר עָלָיו", *"עָלָיו" — וְלֹא עַל חֲבֵירוֹ; חֲבֵירוֹ דּוּמְיָא דִּידֵיהּ, בִּמְחוּיָּיב כַּפָּרָה כְּמוֹתוֹ. וְאָמַר רָבָא: *חַטָּאת זשֶׁשְּׁחָטָהּ ז] עַל מִי שֶׁאֵינוֹ מְחוּיָּיב כְּלוּם — פְּסוּלָה, שֶׁאֵין לְךָ אָדָם בְּיִשְׂרָאֵל שֶׁאֵינוֹ מְחוּיָּיב עֲשֵׂה. וְאָמַר רָבָא: חַטָּאת מְכַפֶּרֶת עַל חַיָּיבֵי עֲשֵׂה מִק"ו: עַל חַיָּיבֵי כְּרֵיתוֹת מְכַפֶּרֶת, עַל חַיָּיבֵי עֲשֵׂה לֹא כׇּל שֶׁכֵּן? לְמֵימְרָא דְּבַת מִינָהּ הִיא? וְהָאָמַר רָבָא: חַטָּאת שֶׁשְּׁחָטָהּ עַל מִי שֶׁמְּחוּיָּיב חַטָּאת — פְּסוּלָה, ח] עַל מִי שֶׁמְּחוּיָּיב עוֹלָה — כְּשֵׁרָה!

מִקִּיבְעָא

רש"י

לְדִבְרֵי רַבִּי שִׁמְעוֹן אֵין נִפְדִּין תְּמִימִין. דְּהָכִי גָּמַר לָהּ רַבִּי יוֹחָנָן מֵרַבֵּיהּ דִּפְלִיגִי בָּהּ רַבִּי שִׁמְעוֹן וְרַבָּנַן, לְרַבִּי שִׁמְעוֹן – לֵית לֵיהּ לֵב ב"ד מַתְנֶה עֲלֵיהֶן ט] לְהַכְשִׁירָן לִתְמִידֵי שָׁנָה הַבָּאָה, [לוֹמַר]: אִם הוּצְרְכוּ הוּצְרְכוּ, וְאִם לָאו יְהֵא קְדוֹשִׁים לִדְמֵיהֶן, שֶׁיִּפְדּוּ אוֹתָן מִמְּעוֹת חוּלִּין בְּלֹא מוּם, וְיוֹצִיאֵם לְחוֹל וְיִפְּלוּ דְּמֵיהֶם לְמוֹתַר תְּרוּמָה, וְאַחַר כָּךְ יַחְזְרוּ וְיִקְחוּ אוֹתָם מִתְּרוּמָה חֲדָשָׁה י] וְיוּכְשְׁרוּ לִתְמִידִין. וּלְדִבְרֵי חֲכָמִים נִפְדִּין תְּמִימִים, דְּאִית לְהוּ לֵב בֵּית דִּין מַתְנֶה עֲלֵיהֶן תְּנַאי זֶה. אַלְמָא: לֵית לֵיהּ לְרַבִּי שִׁמְעוֹן לֵב בֵּית דִּין מַתְנֶה עֲלֵיהֶן, יא] (בָּהֶן) דְּאִי אִית לֵיהּ יוּכְשְׁרוּ לִתְמִידִין, וְלֹא יְקַיְּילוּ. יב] *אֶלָּא לֵית [לֵיהּ לֵב ב"ד מַתְנֶה] כָּךְ שָׁמַעְתִּי בִּשְׁבוּעוֹת. וְעוֹד. אִי נַמִי בָּעֵית לְמֵימַר דִּקְרָא דָּחִיק, וּמוֹקֵי אַנַּפְשֵׁיהּ כְּשֶׁהִפְרִישָׁן בְּזֶה אַחַר זֶה, וּבְטוּמְאָה דְּעֶרֶב יוֹם טוֹב קָאָמַר – מִי מָצֵית לְמֵימַר דְּכִי קָתָנֵי "שֶׁאֵירְעָה בֵּין זֶה לָזֶה" בְּהַפְרָשָׁה קָאָמַר? וְהָא בְּעָא מִינֵּיהּ כו'. בִּשְׁתֵּי כוֹסוֹת. יג] נִשְׁחָטִין כְּאֶחָד, וְאֵין שָׁהוּת לְאוֹרוּעֵי טוּמְאָה בֵּין שְׁחִיטָתֵיהֶן, וְנִזְרַק דָּמוֹ שֶׁל רִאשׁוֹן – שֵׁנִי לָמָּה קָרֵב לְר' שִׁמְעוֹן? הֲרֵי אֵין יד] טוּמְאָה בֵּין זֶה לָזֶה! וְאָמַר לֵיהּ: לְטוּמְאָה שֶׁאוֹרְעָה בֵּין זְרִיקָתוֹ שֶׁל זֶה לִזְרִיקָתוֹ שֶׁל זֶה. ע"כ לָא מִיבַּעְיָא טו] כו'. אֲפִילּוּ לְרַבִּי יִרְמְיָה לָא טז] מְתַמַּהּ אֶלָּא אִי מְכַפֵּר אַעֲשֵׂה דִּלְאַחַר שְׁחִיטָתוֹ אִי לָא, מִכְּלָל דִּפְשִׁיטָא לֵיהּ דְּ"בֵין זֶה לָזֶה" דְּקָאָמַר רַבִּי שִׁמְעוֹן – בְּטוּמְאַת י"ט קָאָמַר, יז] בֵּין שְׁחִיטָתוֹ שֶׁל זֶה לִשְׁחִיטָתוֹ שֶׁל יח] זֶה! דִּלְמָא אִם תִּמְצָא לוֹמַר קָאָמַר. דִּלְמָא תַּרְוַיְיהוּ קָמִיבַּעְיָא לֵיהּ. וְהָכִי קָמִיבַּעְיָא לֵיהּ: הַאי "בֵּין זֶה לָזֶה" דְּקָאָמַר רַבִּי שִׁמְעוֹן, קוֹדֶם הַפְרָשָׁה קָאֵי אוֹ לְאַחַר הַפְרָשָׁה קָאֵי? וְאִם תִּימְצֵי לוֹמַר יט] אַחַר הַפְרָשָׁה נַמִי קָאֵי, קוֹדֶם שְׁחִיטָה אוֹ אֲפִילּוּ לְאַחַר שְׁחִיטָה עַד זְרִיקָה? וְאַהְדַּר לֵיהּ אִיהוּ: אֲפִילּוּ עַד זְרִיקָה. כ] וְדִלְמָא לָא קַיְימָא לָן כְּר' זֵירָא, וְלָא אִיפְשִׁיטָא בַּעְיָין. תּוֹדָה שֶׁשְּׁחָטָהּ לְשֵׁם תּוֹדַת חֲבֵירוֹ. לֹא שֶׁשְּׁחָטָהּ ע"מ שֶׁיִּתְכַּפֵּר בָּהּ מִי שֶׁאֵינוֹ בְּעָלֶיהָ.* כא] וְאֵין זֶה שִׁינּוּי בְּעָלִים *אֶלָּא שִׁינּוּי קוֹדֶשׁ, שֶׁהָיְתָה לִרְאוּבֵן תּוֹדָה וּלְשִׁמְעוֹן תּוֹדָה אַחֶרֶת, וְשָׁחַט אֶת תּוֹדָתוֹ שֶׁל זֶה לְשֵׁם תּוֹדָתוֹ שֶׁל זֶה. כב] *[וְה"ה] בְּשׁוֹחֵט חַטַּאת חֵלֶב לְשֵׁם חַטַּאת דָּם. כְּשֵׁרָה. וְעוֹלָה לַבְּעָלִים, דַּאֲפִי' שִׁינּוּי קֹדֶשׁ אֵין כָּאן. פְּסוּלָה. כג] לֹא עָלְתָה לַבְּעָלִים, דְּשִׁינּוּי קֹדֶשׁ הוּא. לְשֵׁם שְׁלָמִים דִּידֵיהּ בָּעֵינַן. דִּכְתִיב: "זֶבַח תּוֹדַת שְׁלָמָיו". וְהַאי דְּאִיפְלוּג בְּתוֹדָה – מִשּׁוּם דְּמִינָּהּ מַיְיתֵי רַבָּה סַיְיעְתָּא לְמִילְּתֵיהּ מִדְּאַבָּא חָנָן, וּמִיהוּ ה"ה לִשְׁאָר זְבָחִים. כְּשֵׁרָה. עָלְתָה לַבְּעָלִים. פְּסוּלִין. לֹא עָלוּ. לָא דִּידֵיהּ. כד] וְאַע"פ שֶׁלֹּא בָּאוּ עַל הוֹדָיָיה אַחַת. דְּאַרְבָּעָה צְרִיכִין לְהוֹדוֹת, כִּדְאָמְרִינַן בִּבְרָכוֹת (דף נד:) וּכְתִיב בְּהוּ (תהלים קז): "וְיִזְבְּחוּ זִבְחֵי תוֹדָה". וְשָׁחַט תּוֹדָה בִּשְׁעַת עֲלִיָּיתוֹ מִן הַיָּם לְשֵׁם תּוֹדָה שֶׁהִפְרִישׁ עַל יְצִיאָתוֹ מִבֵּית הָאֲסוּרִין כה]. חַטָּאת שֶׁשְּׁחָטָהּ לְשֵׁם חַטָּאת. כְּגוֹן חַטַּאת חֵלֶב שֶׁנִּשְׁחֲטָה לְשֵׁם חַטַּאת דָּם. כְּשֵׁרָה. וְעָלְתָה לוֹ. פְּסוּלָה. פְּסוּלָה לְגַמְרֵי, כְּדִתְנַן: חוּץ מִן הַפֶּסַח וְהַחַטָּאת. עַל מִי שֶׁמְּחוּיָּיב חַטָּאת. בְּשִׁינּוּי בְּעָלִים, עַל מְנָת לִזְרוֹק דָּמָהּ לְשֵׁם חֲבֵירוֹ הַמְחוּיָּיב חַטָּאת כְּמוֹתוֹ. שֶׁאֵינוֹ מְחוּיָּיב עֲשֵׂה. שֶׁלֹּא עָבַר כו] עֲשֵׂה. וּבַעֲשֵׂה שַׁיָּיךְ לְמֵימַר חַטָּאת, כִּדְמְפָרֵשׁ וְאָזֵיל. וְאָמַר רָבָא חַטָּאת מְכַפֶּרֶת עַל חַיָּיבֵי עֲשֵׂה. הִלְכָּךְ מְחוּיָּיב כַּפָּרָה כְּמוֹתוֹ הוּא. לְמֵימְרָא. דַּעֲשֵׂה בַּת מִינָּהּ דְּחַטָּאת הִיא. וְהָאָמַר רָבָא כו' עַל מִי שֶׁמְּחוּיָּיב עוֹלָה כְּשֵׁרָה. כז] אַלְמָא לָאו מִינֵּיהּ הוּא, דְּהָא כח] עֲבֵירוֹת עֲשֵׂה בְּיָדוֹ שֶׁהִפְרִישׁ עוֹלָה עֲלֵיהֶן.

מִקִּיבְעָא

תוספות

וטעמא, משום דבאין לכפר על [טומאת] מקדש וקדשיו (ב) כמתניתין דהתם, ובברייתא חידש טפי ממתניתין. והא דקתני: שתחלתו לא בא אלא לכפר על מזבח החיצון – לאפוקי שעיר הפנימי, דבעינן תרתי: טומאת מקדש ומזבח החיצון. ואף על גב דמשמע התם דאי כט] לא משום גזירה (ג) הוי מקילין בגופן אפי' במותר חטאות הפנימיות – היינו משום דהכי גמירי, דמותר חטאות לבור לעולה. ורבינו חננאל מפרש כפירוש הערוך, וגרים התם: תניא נמי הכי. *וקאי אמילתא דרבי יוחנן, דאמר דלרבי שמעון מקילין בהן בגופן, הואיל ומעיקרא עולה והשתא עולה, אבל לא במותר חטאת כו'. ותימה: אמאי נטר עד לסוף? דלעיל הוה ליה לאתויי!

דלמא אם תימצי לומר קאמר. ורבי זירא נמי שהשיב נמי לרבי ירמיה על טומאה שאירעה בין זו לזו, כמו כן "אם תימצי לומר" קאמר. וקושיא ראשונה "ומי אית ליה לרבי שמעון לב בית דין מתנה" – לא חש לתרץ, דאיכא למימר דאפרשינהו בזה אחר זה, ואינו חושש בקושיא ד"ליקו ולימא ליה לקרא" כו'. *ועוד: דהיכא דלית ליה תקנתא ברעייה אית ליה לרבי שמעון לב בית דין מתנה, כדמוכח במנחות פ' "התודה" (עט:). ומיהו, הא מוכח דהיכא דאית ליה תקנתא ברעייה – לית ליה לב בית דין מתנה, וכאן אית ליה תקנתא ברעייה.

תודה ששחטה לשם תודת חבירו ל] כשרה. ועולה לשם חובה. משום שנוי בעלים לא מיפסלא, דאין שינוי בעלים אלא (א"כ) בזריקה. ורב חסדא אמר: פסולה – פירוש: לא עלתה לשם חובה, משום דהוי שינוי קודש כשאמר תודת פלוני לשם תודה אחרת של פלוני. אבל אמר "תודה זו לשם פלוני" – כשרה גמורה, לפי שהוא שינוי בעלים בשחיטה, *דכשירה גמורה. **הגה"ה** רב חסדא אמר פסולה. נראה דוקא בתודה פליג, משום דכתיב לא] בהן קרא "שלמיו". ובקונטרס פירש דהוא הדין בשאר קרבנות.

אמר רבא חטאת ששחטה לשם חטאת כשרה. פירש רבינו תם: *דרבה כרב חסדא ס"ל, דהא דרבה אידחי. וטעמא דתודה – משום *שלמים משמע דר"ל דאיירי ששחטה לשם חטאת חבירו. ונראה דלאו בהכי מיירי, מדלא קאמר בהדיא "חבירו", אלא מיירי בחטאת חלב לשם חטאת דם, לב] כדאמר רבא לקמן בפירקין (דף ט:): חטאת חלב ששחטה לשם חטאת דם לשם חטאת עבודה זרה – כשרה, לשם חטאת נזיר לשם חטאת מצורע – פסולה, הני עולות נינהו. ואם תאמר: ותרתי *דרבה למה לי? ויש לומר: דהך דהכא נקט לאשמועינן דשינוי קודש איפכא משינוי בעלים. אע"ג דרבא לא פירש הפסוקים כדבריו, מדאמר בריש פירקין (לעיל דף ג:) דרב יוסף בר אמי רמי שינוי קודש*) לג] ומשני. [והא] דלקמן נקט לחלק בחטאות, וגם משום בעיא דאחר כך דבעי רבא חטאת חלב ששחטה לשם חטאת דטומאת מקדש וקדשיו מהו.

חטאת ששחטה על מי שמחוייב עולה כשרה. וכגון שלא הפרישה עדיין, דאי הפרישה – הוה ליה כעל מי שאינו מחוייב כלום, אם תימצי לומר דלא מכפרא אעשה דלאחר הפרשה, דמסתמא עולה יביא ויכפר על הכל. א"נ, דאמר "הרי עלי עולה", דכשיפרישנה יכפר על כל עשה שעבר.

על מי שאינו מחוייב כלום פסולה. **) אי דגרסינן בהא מימרא עולה, דגבי עולה נמי כתיב "לכפר עליו". דאי גרסינן הכא חטאת, ל"ל אידך מילתא דרבא דחטאת מכפרת על חייבי עשה? מהכא שמעינן לה.

על חייבי עשה לא כל שכן. מהאי קל וחומר הוה לן למימר דאפילו מקיבעא מכפרא. אלא דאינה מכפרא הואיל ועיקרא למילתא אחריתי קאתיא, ואהני קל וחומר לקופיא.

*) נ"ל אשינוי בעלים **) נ"א אית דגרסי נ"ק

עולה

מסורת הש"ס

שבועות י.

מהרש"ק מ"ז

ולא יקיילו אלא לייתו בדמיהן נ"ק

[לעיל ז.]

[לעיל ג: איתא רב]

וקאי אמילתא דרב שמואל בר יצחק דאמר לדר"ש דוקא תמידין מקילין בהם כו'

גירסת הג"ק ועוד דהיכא דלית ליה תקנתא בקרון המזבח איתא לר"ש לב ב"ד מתנה ומיהו הא מוכח במנחות בפ' התודה דהיכא דאית ליה תקנתא ברעייה וכו' כנ"ל

שנוי בעלים בשחיטה הס"ד

[לעיל ג.]

[לעיל ג: ז: לקמן ח. פסחים סב.]

[נ"ל דרבא]

[נ"ל שלמיו דידיה]

הגהות הב"ח

(א) גמ' רב חסדא אמר פסולה נשחטה לשם שלמים דידיה בעינן: (ב) תד"ה (בד"ה הקודם) סכין כו' מקדש וקדשיו דתני במתני' התם ובברייתא חידש טפי ממתניתין דקתני כנ"ל ותיבת והא נמחק: (ג) שם דאי לאו משום גזרה הוו מקילין:

וגי' הג"ק בעלים דזהו שינוי בעלים אלא דאיירי בשינוי קודש כו' כנ"ל

תודתו של זה הס"ד ואח"כ ד"ה כשרה ועולה לבעלים דאפי' ש"ק אין כאן דהוי כשוחט תודתו לשם תודת חבירו ואח"כ ד"ה פסולה כו'

גליון הש"ס

גמ' תודה קרויה שלמים. כעין זה מנחות דף עו ע"א ועיין לקמן דף כג ע"ב תוס' ד"ה במנחות ובמנחו' דף יז ע"ב תוס' ד"ה מהלכתינהו: שם חטאת ששחטה לשם חטאת כשרה. עיין נזיר דף כו ע"ב תוס' ד"ה שהרי:

שיטה מקובצת

א] הוא קרב על טומאה שאורעה בין זה לזה עד כאן לא מיבעיא כו' והשאר נמחק: ב] תיבת כשרה נמחק: ג] לשם שלמים: ד] תיבת נשחטה נמחק: ה] שלמים דידיה לשם: ו] עולה ודאי פסולה: ז] על מי שאינו מחויב כלום פסולה. דהוי שפיר מחויב כפרה כמותו כדמפרש ואזיל ואמר רבא כו' ולפרושי מלתא קמייתא אתא: ח] על מי שמחויב עולה כשרה. אלמא לאו מינה הוא והא הכא עבירת עשה בידו שהפריש עולה עליה ומשני מקיבעא לא מכפרא כו' כך פי' הקונטרס ומ"מ קשה היאך פשיטא ליה לרבא דפסול והא לקמן מספקא ליה לרבא אפי' על חטאת חלב ששחטה על מי שמחויב חטאת דטומאת מקדש וקדשיו דשמא לא הוי מחויב כפרה כמותו לפי שאינה קבועה כמותה כ"ש על מי שאינו מחויב כלום לכך נ"ל דגרסי' עולה ששחטה על מי שאינו מחויב כו' דגבי עולה הוא דכתיב וכיפר עליה הכהן ואמר רבא חטאת כו' ועלה פריך למימרא דבת מינה היא ולא בעי לשנויי דלכך כי שחטה על מי שמחוייב עולה כשרה משום דלא גרע מטומאת מקדש וקדשיו משום דלא בעי למיפשט בעיא דרבא דלקמן ולכך משני משום דמקיבעא לא מכפרי תוס' תוך: ט] עליהן להכשיר: י] חדשה ויתכשרו לתמידין זה לא נאמר אלא יעשה מהן קיץ למזבח: יא] תיבת בהן ל"ש ונמחק: יב] יקיצו בהן אלא בדמיהן כך שמעתי בשבועות והשאר ל"ש ונמחק: יג] ששחטן תיבת נשחטין נמחק: יד] אין כאן טומאה: טו] מבעיא כלומר: טז] לא מבעיא תיבת מתמה נמחק: יז] קאמר שהייתה: יח] של האחר והיינו עשה דלאחר הפרשה הס"ד: יט] לומר לאחר: כ] זריקה ס"א ואין למיפשט בעיין מתשובת ר' זירא [דאפשר] דהשיב באת"ל [דאת"ל] דאינו מכפר על עשה דלאחר הפרשה כמו [כן שעירי עצרת דמכפרין] על טומאת מקדש וקדשיו [ליכא למבעיא על טומאה שבין] שחיטה לשחיטה [דהא דהשיב] רבי זירא על [הבעיא] דלעיל דאמר [על טומאה שאירעה] לאחר שחיטת הראשון לא למיפשט האבעיא דאבעיא לן לדודאי ר' זירא לא פליג ארבא [דסבר דליכא למיפשט

מִקִּיבְעָא לָא מְכַפְּרָא, מִקּוּפְיָא מְכַפְּרָא. *וְאָמַר רָבָא: עוֹלָה שֶׁשְּׁחָטָהּ שֶׁלֹּא לִשְׁמָהּ — אָסוּר לִזְרוֹק דָּמָהּ שֶׁלֹּא לִשְׁמָהּ, אִיבָּעֵית אֵימָא קְרָא, אִיבָּעֵית אֵימָא סְבָרָא. אִיבָּעֵית אֵימָא קְרָא: °"מוֹצָא שְׂפָתֶיךָ תִּשְׁמוֹר" וגו', אִיבָּעֵית אֵימָא סְבָרָא: מִשּׁוּם דְּשַׁנֵּי בָּהּ כו', כִּדְרֵישׁ (א) פִּירְקָא. וְאָמַר רָבָא: עוֹלָה הַבָּאָה לְאַחַר מִיתָה, שְׁחָטָהּ בְּשִׁינּוּי קוֹדֶשׁ — פְּסוּלָה, אבְּשִׁינּוּי בְּעָלִים — כְּשֵׁרָה, דְּאֵין בְּעָלִים לְאַחַר מִיתָה. *וְרַב פִּנְחָס בְּרֵיהּ דְּרַב אַמִּי אָמַר: יֵשׁ בְּעָלִים לְאַחַר מִיתָה. אֲמַר לֵיהּ רַב אַשִׁי לְרַב פִּנְחָס בְּרֵיהּ דְּרַב אַמִּי: דַּוְקָא קָאָמַר מָר יֵשׁ בְּעָלִים לְאַחַר מִיתָה, וּבָעֵי לְאִיתּוּיֵי עוֹלָה אַחֲרִיתִי, אוֹ דִּלְמָא דְּאִי אִיכָּא כַּמָּה עֲשֵׂה גַּבֵּיהּ מְכַפְּרָא? א"ל: דַּוְקָא קָאָמִינָא. וְאָמַר רָבָא: עוֹלָה — דּוֹרוֹן הִיא. הֵיכִי דָּמֵי? אִי דְּלֵיכָּא תְּשׁוּבָה — °"זֶבַח רְשָׁעִים תּוֹעֵבָה", וְאִי דְּאִיכָּא תְּשׁוּבָה — א] *הָתַנְיָא: בעָבַר עַל מִצְוַת עֲשֵׂה וְשָׁב, לֹא זָז מִשָּׁם עַד שֶׁמּוֹחֲלִים לוֹ! אֶלָּא ש"מ: דּוֹרוֹן הוּא. (חטא"ת ע"ל מ"י מכפ"ר עול"ה לאח"ר דורו"ן, סימ"ן) תַּנְיָא נַמִּי הָכִי, א"ר שִׁמְעוֹן: חַטָּאת לָמָּה בָּאָה? לְכַפֵּר! אֶלָּא, גלָמָּה בָּאָה לִפְנֵי עוֹלָה? *לְפְרַקְלִיט שֶׁנִּכְנַס, ב] [רִיצָה פְּרַקְלִיט, נִכְנַס] דּוֹרוֹן אַחֲרָיו.§ "חוּץ מִן דהַפֶּסַח וְהַחַטָּאת" כו'.§ פֶּסַח מְנָלַן? דִּכְתִיב: °"שָׁמוֹר אֶת חֹדֶשׁ הָאָבִיב וְעָשִׂיתָ פֶּסַח", שֶׁיְּהוּ כָּל עֲשִׂיּוֹתָיו לְשֵׁם פֶּסַח. ג] אַשְׁכַּחַן שִׁינּוּי קוֹדֶשׁ, שִׁינּוּי בְּעָלִים מְנָלַן? דִּכְתִיב: °"וַאֲמַרְתֶּם זֶבַח פֶּסַח הוּא", שֶׁתְּהֵא זְבִיחָה לְשֵׁם פֶּסַח; אִם אֵינוֹ עִנְיָן לְשִׁינּוּי קוֹדֶשׁ, תְּנֵיהוּ עִנְיָן לְשִׁינּוּי בְּעָלִים. אַשְׁכַּחַן לְמִצְוָה, לְעַכֵּב מְנָלַן? אָמַר קְרָא: °"וְזָבַחְתָּ פֶּסַח לַה' אֱלֹהֶיךָ" וגו'. מַתְקִיף לָהּ רַב סָפְרָא: הַאי "וְזָבַחְתָּ" לְהָכִי הוּא דְּאָתָא? הַאי מִיבָּעֵי לֵיהּ לְכִדְרַב נַחְמָן, דְּאָמַר רַב נַחְמָן אָמַר רַבָּה בַּר אֲבוּהּ: מִנַּיִן *)לְמוֹתַר יפֶּסַח שֶׁקָּרֵב שְׁלָמִים? שֶׁנֶּאֱמַר: °"וְזָבַחְתָּ פֶּסַח לַה' אֱלֹהֶיךָ צֹאן וּבָקָר", וַהֲלֹא אֵין פֶּסַח בָּא אֶלָּא מִן הַכְּבָשִׂים וּמִן הָעִזִּים! ד] מִכָּאן לְמוֹתַר הַפֶּסַח שֶׁיְּהֵא לְדָבָר הַבָּא מִן הַצֹּאן וּמִן הַבָּקָר, וּמַאי נִיהוּ? שְׁלָמִים! אֶלָּא אָמַר רַב סָפְרָא: "וְזָבַחְתָּ פֶּסַח" — לְכִדְרַב נַחְמָן, "שָׁמוֹר אֶת חֹדֶשׁ הָאָבִיב" — (ב) לְמִצְוָה בְּשִׁינּוּי קוֹדֶשׁ, "וַאֲמַרְתֶּם זֶבַח פֶּסַח" — ה] בְּשִׁינּוּי בְּעָלִים לְמִצְוָה, "הוּא" — לְעַכֵּב בֵּין הָכָא וְהָכָא. וְאַשְׁכַּחַן זְבִיחָה, שְׁאָר עֲבוֹדוֹת מְנָלַן? הוֹאִיל *וְגַלֵּי גַּלֵּי. רַב אַשִׁי אָמַר: הוֹאִיל וְגַלֵּי גַּלֵּי לָא אָמְרִינַן. אֶלָּא [עֲבוֹדוֹת] מְנָלַן? דִּכְתִיב: °"זֹאת הַתּוֹרָה לָעוֹלָה וְלַמִּנְחָה" וגו', וְתַנְיָא: °"בְּיוֹם צַוֹּתוֹ אֶת בְּנֵי יִשְׂרָאֵל לְהַקְרִיב אֶת קָרְבְּנֵיהֶם" — זֶה בְּכוֹר וּמַעֲשֵׂר וּפֶסַח, הִקִּישׁוֹ הַכָּתוּב לִשְׁלָמִים: מַה שְּׁלָמִים, בֵּין שִׁינּוּי קוֹדֶשׁ בֵּין שִׁינּוּי בְּעָלִים בָּעֵינַן לְמִצְוָה — אַף כֹּל, בֵּין שִׁינּוּי קוֹדֶשׁ בֵּין שִׁינּוּי בְּעָלִים לְמִצְוָה; *וְכִשְׁלָמִים: מַה שְּׁלָמִים בֵּין זְבִיחָה בֵּין שְׁאָר עֲבוֹדוֹת לֹא חִלַּקְתָּ בָּהֶן לְמִצְוָה — אַף פֶּסַח לֹא תַּחֲלוֹק בּוֹ בֵּין זְבִיחָה לִשְׁאָר עֲבוֹדוֹת לְעַכֵּב ו] (מִשּׁוּם שֶׁנֶּאֱמַר "הוּא" בִּזְבִיחָה אֵינוֹ אֶלָּא לְעַכֵּב). אֶלָּא "הוּא" לָמָּה לִי? (ג) כִּדְתַנְיָא: ז] נֶאֱמַר בְּפֶסַח "הוּא" בִּשְׁחִיטָה — לְעַכֵּב, *אֲבָל אָשָׁם לֹא נֶאֱמַר בּוֹ "הוּא" אֶלָּא לְאַחַר הַקְטָרַת אֵימוּרִין, וְהוּא עַצְמוֹ שֶׁלֹּא הוּקְטְרוּ אֵימוּרָיו — כָּשֵׁר.§ חַטָּאת מְנָלַן? דִּכְתִיב: °"וְשָׁחַט אוֹתָהּ לְחַטָּאת", שֶׁתְּהֵא שְׁחִיטָה לְשֵׁם חַטָּאת. אַשְׁכַּחַן שְׁחִיטָה, קַבָּלָה מְנָלַן? דִּכְתִיב:
וְלָקַח

תורה אור: דברים כג | משלי כא | דברים טז | שמות יב | דברים טז | שם | ויקרא ז | שם | שם ד

רש"י

מִקִּיבְעָא לָא מְכַפְּרָא. חַטָּאת אַעֲשֵׂה. מִקּוּפְיָא מְכַפְּרָא. הִלְכָּךְ, עַל מִי שֶׁמְּחוּיָּיב עוֹלָה כְּשֵׁרָה, ח] כֵּיוָן [דְּהִפְרִישׁ] עוֹלָה — שָׁיְיכִי כּוּלְּהוּ עֲשֵׂה שֶׁבְּיָדוֹ אַעוֹלָה, וְתוּ לָא שַׁיָּיךְ חַטָּאת גַּבֵּיהּ. אֲבָל מִי שֶׁלֹּא הִפְרִישׁ כְּלוּם, וַעֲבֵירוֹת עֲשֵׂה בְּיָדוֹ — שַׁיָּיךְ חַטָּאת גַּבֵּיהּ, דְּאִילּוּ הֲוָה מִתְחַיֵּיב חַטָּאת — מְכַפֵּר עֲשֵׂה מִקּוּפְיָא, הִלְכָּךְ חָיֵיל שְׁמֵיהּ אַחַטָּאתוֹ שֶׁנִּשְׁחֲטָה לִשְׁמוֹ, לְפוֹסְלָהּ. לְאַחַר מִיתָה. שֶׁמֵּת בְּעָלֶיהָ וְהִקְרִיבָהּ הַיּוֹרֵשׁ. פְּסוּלָה. לֹא עָלְתָה, (ד) וְצָרִיךְ הַיּוֹרֵשׁ לְהָבִיא אַחֶרֶת. יֵשׁ בְּעָלִים. שֶׁהַיּוֹרֵשׁ הוּא בְּעָלֶיהָ. דַּוְקָא קָאָמַר מָר. *אִי פְּלִיגֵי אַדְּרָבָא וּבָעֵי לְאַתּוּיֵי אַחֲרִיתִי. אוֹ דִּלְמָא דְּאִי אִיכָּא כַּמָּה עֲשֵׂה גַּבֵּיהּ ט] דְּיוֹרֵשׁ — מְכַפְּרָא אִם לֹא שִׁינָּה בָּהּ, וּמִיהוּ הֵיכָא דְּשַׁנֵּי — לָא בָּעֵי לְאִיתּוּיֵי אַחֲרִיתִי, דְּהָא אִיהוּ לָא נָדַר מִידֵּי. עוֹלָה דּוֹרוֹן הִיא. אֵינָהּ בָּאָה לְכַפֵּר עַל עֲשֵׂה כַּפָּרָה מַמָּשׁ, אֶלָּא אַחַר שֶׁכִּפְּרָה הַתְּשׁוּבָה עַל הָעֲשֵׂה — הִיא בָּאָה לְהַקְבָּלַת פָּנִים. כְּאָדָם שֶׁסָּרַח בַּמֶּלֶךְ וְרִיצָּהוּ ע"י פְּרַקְלִיטִין, וּכְשֶׁבָּא לְהַקְבִּיל פָּנָיו מֵבִיא דּוֹרוֹן בְּיָדוֹ. הֵיכִי דָּמֵי. כְּלוֹמַר, י] הֵיכִי דָּמֵי שֶׁתְּהֵא בָּאָה לְכַפָּרָה? אִי דְּלֵיכָּא תְּשׁוּבָה. אַעֲבֵירוֹת עֲשֵׂה שֶׁבְּיָדוֹ. זֶבַח רְשָׁעִים תּוֹעֵבָה. פָּסוּק הוּא בְּמִשְׁלֵי (כא). לָמָּה בָּאָה לִפְנֵי עוֹלָה. כָּל מָקוֹם שֶׁמֵּבִיא חַטָּאת וְעוֹלָה — חַטָּאת קוֹדֶם, כִּדְיָלֵיף לְקַמָּן בְּפֶרֶק "כָּל הַתָּדִיר" (דף פט:). פְּרַקְלִיט = מֵלִיץ טוֹב. פֶּסַח מְנָלַן (ה). בֵּין לְמִצְוָה בֵּין לְעַכֵּב. יא] דְּקס"ד לָא אָתֵי לָן כִּשְׁאָר זְבָחִים מִשְּׁלָמִים, דְּלָא כְּתִיב בְּהַהוּא קְרָא ד"זֹאת הַתּוֹרָה" דְּאִיתְרַבִּי כָּל הַזְּבָחִים מִינֵּיהּ לְמִצְוָה. מוֹתַר הַפֶּסַח. שֶׁאָבַד, יב] *וְנִתְכַּפֵּר בְּאַחֵר, וְנִמְצָא הָרִאשׁוֹן. לְדָבָר הַבָּא מִן הַצֹּאן וּמִן הַבָּקָר. הַיְינוּ שְׁלָמִים, שֶׁהֵן בָּאִין מִכָּל צֹאן וּמִכָּל בָּקָר, בֵּין זְכָרִים בֵּין נְקֵבוֹת. מַה שֶּׁאֵין כֵּן בִּשְׁאָר זְבָחִים שֶׁהוּקְבְּעוּ אוֹ בְּזָכָר אוֹ בִּנְקֵבָה, עוֹלָה וְאָשָׁם הוּקְבְּעוּ בִּזְכָרִים, חַטָּאת הוּקְבַּע בִּנְקֵבוֹת וְהוּקְבַּע בִּזְכָרִים, כְּגוֹן שְׂעִיר נָשִׂיא אֵינוֹ בָּא יג] בִּנְקֵבָה. לְמִצְוָה בְּשִׁינּוּי קוֹדֶשׁ. יד] בְּכוּלְּהוּ עֲשִׂיּוֹת יָלְפִינַן מִינֵּיהּ, דְּהָא כְּתִיב "וְעָשִׂיתָ". הוּא טו]. מַשְׁמַע: פֶּסַח הוּא — בַּהֲוָיָיתוֹ, לִשְׁמוֹ כָּשֵׁר, שֶׁלֹּא לִשְׁמוֹ פָּסוּל. טז] דְּהָכָא וְהָכָא. בְּשִׁינּוּי קוֹדֶשׁ וּבְשִׁינּוּי בְּעָלִים, ד"הוּא" מַשְׁמַע אַתַּרְוַויְיהוּ, כְּשֶׁהוּא עָשׂוּי כְּמִצְוָתוֹ מַשְׁמַע. וְאַשְׁכַּחַן זְבִיחָה. בְּשִׁינּוּי [קוֹדֶשׁ וּבְשִׁינּוּי] בְּעָלִים. בְּיוֹם צַוּוֹתוֹ. יז] סָמוּךְ לְ"זֹאת הַתּוֹרָה", וְדָרְשִׁינַן סְמוּכִין: "בְּיוֹם צַוּוֹתוֹ לְהַקְרִיב אֶת קָרְבְּנֵיהֶם" — לְרַבּוֹת קָרְבָּנוֹת שֶׁלֹּא הוּזְכְּרוּ בַּמִּקְרָא בָּעִנְיָן שֶׁלְּמַעְלָה. אַף כֹּל כו'. הִלְכָּךְ, (ו) מִצְוָה בְּפֶסַח יָלְפִינַן מִשְּׁלָמִים, דְּרַבִּינַן לְהוּ לְעֵיל לְשִׁינּוּי קוֹדֶשׁ וּלְשִׁינּוּי בְּעָלִים. ("וְעָשִׂיתָ פֶּסַח" — לְעַכֵּב בְּכָל עֲשִׂיּוֹתָיו בְּשִׁינּוּי קֹדֶשׁ, "וַאֲמַרְתֶּם זֶבַח פֶּסַח" — לְעַכֵּב בִּזְבִיחָה בְּשִׁינּוּי בְּעָלִים). וּכִשְׁלָמִים. כְּלוֹמַ', כֵּיוָן דְּגַלֵּי קְרָא עִכּוּבָא בִּזְבִיחָה, יָלְפִינַן שְׁאָר עֲבוֹדוֹת לְעִכּוּבָא מֵהֶיקֵּשָׁא דְּמִצְוָה כִּשְׁלָמִים: מַה שְּׁלָמִים כו'. הָכִי גָּרְסִי': אֶלָּא הוּא לָמָּה לִי לְכִדְתַנְיָא יח] [וכו'] אֲבָל אָשָׁם לֹא נֶאֱמַר כו'. וְל"ג: "כָּל מָקוֹם שֶׁנֶּאֱמַר יט] בִּזְבִיחָה (ז) אֵינוֹ אֶלָּא לְעַכֵּב", דְּהַךְ בָּרַיְיתָא לְקַמָּן הִיא בְּפִירְקִין בְּדִינָא ר' אֱלִיעֶזֶר וְרַבִּי יְהוֹשֻׁעַ וְל"ג לֵיהּ. לְכִדְתַנְיָא. כְּלוֹמַר, לְגַלּוּיֵי עַל "הוּא" דְּגַבֵּי אָשָׁם דְּלָא יָלְפִינַן פָּסוּל מִינֵּיהּ. כִּדְמַהְדַּר לֵיהּ רַבִּי יְהוֹשֻׁעַ לְר' אֱלִיעֶזֶר לְקַמָּן בְּפִירְקִין (דף י:), שֶׁהָיָה דּוֹרֵשׁ: "אָשָׁם הוּא", לִשְׁמוֹ כָּשֵׁר שֶׁלֹּא לִשְׁמוֹ פָּסוּל, וְקָא מַהְדַּר לֵיהּ רַבִּי יְהוֹשֻׁעַ: פֶּסַח נֶאֱמַר בּוֹ "הוּא" בִּשְׁחִיטָה, לְפִיכָךְ שֶׁלֹּא לִשְׁמוֹ פָּסוּל, אֲבָל אָשָׁם כו'.
וְלָקַח

תוספות

עולה דורון היא. אע"ג דלעשה מכפרת יותר מחטאת, דהא מכפרא מקיבעא. **ריצה** פרקליט. אע"ג דאיכא עולת יולדת ומצורע ונזיר, דלא מייתי קרבן אלא לאישתרויי בקדשים, כדאמר בפרק בתרא דכריתות (דף כו.) — *ואפילו הם חטאתם קודמת לעולה, דלא חלקה תורה.

ואמרתם זבח פסח. האי קרא כתיב ברישא, ו"שמור את חודש האביב" הוה ליה לאוקומי כ] [בשינוי בעלים] באם אינו ענין. אלא משום דכייל בה כל עבודות, דכתיב: "ועשית פסח" כא] [דמשמע] מסתמא כל עשיות — הלכך מוקי ליה לשינוי קודש כב]. **וזבחת** פסח. בסוף "התודה" (מנחות פג.) דריש לה במשנה לדבר שבחובה [שהיא באה מן החולין]. והתם בגמרא כג] נמי מייתי דרשא דהכא. **ומאי** ניהו שלמים. דעולה ליכא למימר, דאינה באה מכל צאן ובקר, כדפי' בקונטרס דאינה באה נקבה. ועוד: איכא לקמן תלתא קראי, וההוא ד"אם כבש" מוכח בהדיא דהוי שלמים. ועוד: דדוחין קדשים קלים אבל קדשים קלים ולא אבל קדשי קדשים, כדלקמן (דף ט.). **וזבחת** פסח לכדרב נחמן. בסיפרי פרשת "עשר תעשר" דריש כולהו בשנוי קודש. והכי איתא התם: *"וזבחת" — אין לי אלא זביחה, שאר עבודות מנין? כד] ואשינוי [קודש] קאי — ת"ל: "ועשית". יכול אף הקטר חלבו? ת"ל: "וזבחת". ואין זה בסוגיא שלנו. **הוא** לעכב בין הכא בין הכא. בשינוי קודש — בכל עבודות, בשינוי בעלים — בזביחה. אע"ג ד"הוא" בזביחה כתיב כה] בפרשת "בא אל פרעה", וקרא ד"ועשית" בפרשת "ראה אנכי", מכל מקום משמע "הוא" — בהוייתו, כשהוא עשוי כמלותו, כדפי' בקונטרס. והשתא הא דקאמר: אשכחן זביחה, שאר עבודות מנא לן — אשינוי בעלים קאי. עוד יש לפרש: דבין בשינוי קודש בין בשינוי בעלים קבעי מנא לן לעכב. ד"הוא" קאי דוקא אזביחה, ומדאפקיה רחמנא לשינוי בעלים בלשון שינוי קודש, אית לן לאוקומי כו] הא דזביחה לעכב בין בשינוי בעלים בין בשינוי קודש. ושינויא ד"הואיל וגלי גלי" — לא ניחא להאי פירושא כמו לפירוש קמא. **מה** שלמים בין בזביחה בין בשאר עבודות לא חלקת בהן. *וא"ת: כיון דכתיב "ועשית פסח" לעכב בשינוי קודש בכל עשיות — לשתוק קרא כז] מזביחה ותיתי משלמים, דמה שלמים לא חלקת בין בשינוי קודש לשינוי בעלים למצוה — אף לפסח לא תחלוק לעכב! **אלא** הוא למה לי. לקמן בפרק "בית שמאי" (דף לז:) ובפסחים פרק "מי שהיה טמא" (דף צו.) דריש "הוא" דפסח למעוטי תמורת פסח, ותרי "הוא" כתיבי. ובפסחים בסוף "תמיד נשחט" (דף סג:) דריש רבי אליעזר מ"הוא" דפסח: לא הוא כשר לשם אחרים, ולא אחרים כשרין לשמו. ורבי אליעזר לטעמיה, דאית ליה עכובא באשם, ולא מוקי ליה למימר: אבל אשם לא נאמר בו "הוא" כו'. **כל** מקום שנאמר הוא בזביחה. פירש בקונטרס: ולא גרסינן ליה, משום דליתיה בברייתא דלקמן. ואין למחוק בשביל כך הספרים, דאפשר שהיא בברייתא בשום מקום בתוספתא כח].
זריקה

*) פסחים ע: מנחות פג: [לקמן ט.]

עין משפט נר מצוה

לד א מיי' פט"ו מהל' פסה"מ הלכה טו:
לה ב מיי' פ"א מהל' תשובה הלכה ד:
לו ג סמג עשין רעג:
לז ד מיי' פט"ו מהלכות פסה"מ הלכה א והלכה ד:
לח ה מיי' שם הלכה ה והלכה ד:
לט ו מיי' פ"ד מהלכות קרבן פסח הלכה ו:

נ"ל אפי' הכי חטאתם כו' נ"ק

נ"ל וזבחת פסח שתהא שחיטתו לשם פסח שחטו שלא לשמו פסול אין לי אלא זביחה כו' נ"ק

מסורת הש"ס

[לעיל ו.]

נ"א לאתפלוגי אהדדי והס"ד נ"ק

לעיל ז: ע"ש פסחים סח. ע"ש

יומא פו. [שבועות יב:]

[גי' הערוך לפרקליט שנכנס לרצות ריצה הפרקליט ונכנס דורון. מליצי רעי (איוב טז) תרגום פרקליטי חבריי]

נ"א ונתכפר אחר

[ועי' לקמן יז: מנחות נב: מ"ק ז:]

ס"א ל"ג

ס"א הלכך למצוה משלמים והנך קראי אם אינו ענין למצוה דנפקא לן מהתם תנהו ענין לעבב

לעיל ה: ולקמן י: [מנחות ז.]

הגהות הב"ח

(א) גמ' כדריש פירקא נ"ב דף כ' סוף ע"א: (ב) שם חדש האביב ועשית למצוה: (ג) שם למה לי לכדתניא פסח נאמר בו הוא בשחיטה: (ד) רש"י ד"ה פסולה לא עלתה לו וצריך: (ה) ד"ה פסח מנלן בין לשמו בין למצוה: (ו) ד"ה אף כל וכו' הלכך למצוה בפסח ילפינן משלמים וכצי קראי לדרבינן: (ז) ד"ה הכי גרסינן וכו' בזביחה הוא אינו וכו' ור' יהושע הס"ד ותיבות ול"ג ליה נמחק:

שיטה מקובצת

א] תשובה למה לי עולה והתניא: ב] שנכנס לרצות ריצה פרקליט נכנס: ג] אשכחן שינוי קודש [אא"ה כאן חסר שורה שלימה ההתחלה ועוד משורה שניה כמה תיבות רק הענין מובן להמעיין] כדמוכח בסמוך וא"ת למצוה תיפוק ליה מהיקשא דשלמים דהא כתיב בהדיא בקרא לחטאת וי"ל דלא [הוי מצי למילף] מעיקרא [למצוה מהיקשא דשלמים כיון דלא מצא] לאשכוחי קרא בגופיה כך פרש"י ומורי פירש דס"ד דתלמודא דהיקשא לא הוי לענין פסח וחטאת [כיון דאין באים בנדר ונדבה] ולא הוי [דומיא] דשלמים אלא דבר שבא בנדר ונדבה דומיא דשלמים ומ"מ כי לא משכח קרא בגופייהו מסיק [דלמצוה] מהיקשא נפיק כיון דשלמים למצוה נפקא ממוצא שפתיך ניחא טפי לאוקמי ההיקש לגמרי למצוה ועיכובא נפקא לן מקראי דכתיבי בגופייהו תוס' אחרות: ד] אלא מכאן: ה] פסח למצוה בשינוי בעלים הוא לעבב: ו] לעבב הלכך למצוה משלמים והנך קראי אם אינו ענין למצוה דנפקא לה מהתם תנהו ענין לעבב ותיבות משום שנאמר הוא בזביחה אינו אלא לעבב נמחק: ז] תיבות נאמר בפסח הוא בשחיטה לעבב נמחק: ח] כשרה דכיון שנדר תיבת שהפריש ל"ש ונמחק: ט] גביה דהיורש: י] כלומר דהיכי דמי: יא] לעבב א] בשינוי בעלים: יב] שאבד הפסח: יג] בא נקבה הס"ד: יד] קודש וכולהו: טו] הוא ס"א הוא לעבב בין הכא ובין הכא כלומר בין בשינוי קודש ובין בשינוי בעלים דפסח הוא משמע בהוייתו יהא לשמו כשר שלא לשמו פסול והוא תרוייהו הוויות משמע כלומר כשהוא עשוי כמצוותן: טז] מה"ד הכא והכא: יז] צוותו כו': יח] תיבת וכו' נמחק: יט] שנאמר הוא בזביחה אינו בא אלא: כ] לאוקמי בשינוי בעלים: כא] פסח דמשתמע כל ותיבת מסתמא נמחק: כב] קודש ז"ל תוס' הר"פ וי"ל דאותו פסוק דועשית משתמע שינוי קודש דמשמע כל עשיותיו דפסח ואיזה שינוי דפוסל בכל עבודות שינוי קודש הוא דשינוי בעלים אינו בד' עבודות כי אם ע"מ לזרוק: כג] בגמרא מייתי נמי הא דהכא ותיבת דרשא ל"ש ונמחק: כד] תיבות ואשינוי קודש ל"ש ונמחק ותיבת קאי ג"כ נמחק: כה] ע' בהשמטות בסוף המסכת: כו] הוא דזביחה: כז] קרא מואמרתם זבח פסח ותיתי תיבת מזביחה ל"ש ונמחק: כח] בתוספתא או בת"כ הס"ד:

א) נראה דל"ל בשינוי קודש ובשינוי בעלים דקס"ד וכו'.

"ולקח הכהן מדם החטאת" — שתהא קבלה לשם חטאת. ואשכחן שחיטה וקבלה, זריקה מנלן? א] דאמר קרא: "וכפר עליו הכהן מחטאתו" — שתהא כפרה לשם חטאת. אשכחן שנוי קדש, שנוי בעלים מנלן? אמר קרא: "עליו" — *עליו ולא על חבירו. אשכחן למצוה, לעכב מנלן? כדאמר רב הונא בריה דרב יהושע: "חטאת" "חטאתו", הכא נמי — "חטאת" "חטאתו". אשכחן מצוה בשנוי קדש, וזריקה בשנוי בעלים בין למצוה בין לעכב; לעכב ב] בכל עבודות בשנוי קדש, ג] ובשאר עבודות בשנוי בעלים בין למצוה בין לעכב, מנלן? אמר ר' יונה: אתיא מחטאת נזיר, דכתיב: "והקריב הכהן לפני ה' ד] ועשה את חטאתו ואת עולתו", שיהו כל עשיותיו לשם חטאת. ה] אשכחן שנוי קדש, שנוי בעלים מנלן? (א) ו] (אם אינו ענין לשנוי קדש, תניהו ענין לשנוי בעלים. אשכחן למצוה, לעכב מנלן?) אמר רב הונא ז] [בריה דר"י]: "חטאת" "חטאתו". מתקיף לה רבינא: אלא מעתה, "עולת" "עולתו" מאי דרשת ביה? ולרבינא, "מנחת" "מנחתו", "נסך" "נסכו", מאי דרשת בהו? ח] ההוא *מבעי ליה: "מנחתם ונסכיהם" — בלילה, "מנחתם ונסכיהם" — אפי' למחר. אלא "עולת" "עולתו" מאי דרשת (ב) בהו? ותו, מי גמרי מהדדי? חטאת חלב מחטאת נזיר לא גמרה — שכן יש עמה דמים אחרים, חטאת נזיר מחטאת חלב לא גמרה — שכן כרת! ט] אלא אמר רבא: אתיא מחטאת מצורע, דכתיב: "ועשה הכהן את החטאת", שיהו כל עשיותיו לשם חטאת. ואשכחן שנוי קדש, שנוי בעלים מנליה? אמר קרא: "וכפר על המטהר" וגו', על המטהר זה ולא על המטהר חבירו. ואכתי מי ילפא מהדדי? חטאת חלב מחטאת מצורע לא ילפא — שכן יש עמה דמים אחרים, חטאת מצורע מחטאת חלב לא גמרה — שכן כרת! י] מחדא לא אתיא, תיתי חדא מתרתי. בהי לא לכתוב? [לא לכתוב] רחמנא בחטאת חלב ותיתי מהנך — מה להנך שכן יש עמהם דמים אחרים! לא לכתוב רחמנא בחטאת נזיר ותיתי מהנך — מה להנך שכן אין להן שאלה! לא לכתוב רחמנא בחטאת מצורע ותיתי מהנך — מה להנך שכן אין באין בדלות! אלא אמר קרא: "זאת התורה לעולה ולמנחה" וגו' — הקישו הכתוב לשלמים, מה שלמים — בין שנוי קדש בין שנוי בעלים בעינן לשמן למצוה, אף חטאת — בין שנוי קדש בין שנוי בעלים בעינן לשמן למצוה. הילכך, מצוה משלמים, והנך קראי לעכב. ואשכחן חטאת חלב דכתיב בה "לחטאת", חטאת

רש"י

ולקח הכהן. לשון קבלה הוא. וכפר. היינו בזריקה. הולכה לא אצטריך קרא, דבכלל קבלה יא] היא מתרביא ליה. אשכחן למצוה כו'. ואי קשיא: מצוה מהיקשא ד"זאת התורה" משלמים אתיא, כשאר כל הזבחים! אין הכי נמי, ומסקנא מהתם יליף לה לקמיה. ומעיקרא הוא דמהדרינן דנכתבו פולהו בגופיה. כדאמר רב הונא כו'. לקמן בשמעתין. חטאתו. "וכפר עליו הכהן מחטאתו" (כשנזרק דמו לשמו. חטאת חטאתו). מדהוה ליה למכתב "מחטאת", וכתיב וי"ו יתירא למדרש בה לשם בעלים. אשכחן מצוה בשנוי קדש. בכל עבודות, וזריקה אשכחן בה מצוה ועכוב בשנוי בעלים, דהאי "מחטאתו" יב] נמי בזריקה כתיב, שהיא הכפרה. לעכב בכל עבודות בשנוי קדש. שלא למדנו לאחד מהן, ושאר עבודות לבד מזריקה בשנוי בעלים, בין למצוה בין לעכב, מנלן? שיהו כל עשיותיו לשם חטאת. ולמצוה לא אצטריך קרא, דהא נפקא לן משאר חטאות, והאי לעכובא. [ה"ג בס"א:] אשכחן שנוי קדש שנוי בעלים מנלן. אמר רב הונא כו'. גבי נזיר כתיב: "ועשה את חטאתו ואת עולתו" — יג] הרי למצוה. וכשלמים, מה שלמים לא חלקת בהן בין זריקה לשאר עבודות בשנוי בעלים למצוה — אף חטאת לא תחלק בין זריקה לשאר עבודות לעכב. הרי לך מצוה ועכוב בין בשנוי קדש בין בשנוי בעלים, כך נ"ל. וכן יש לפרש גבי חטאת מצורע לקמן, נ"ל. ולרבינא. דלא קשיא ליה אלא "עולת" "עולתו", "מנחתו" ו"נסכו" דכתיבי נמי גבי נזיר אמאי לא קשיא ליה? ההוא מיבעי ליה. כי היכי דדרשינן לכל "מנחתם *ונסכיהם" — יד] בלילה, ואפי' למחר, שיוכשרו טו] לבא למחר (ג) לבא בלילה — טז] הכי נמי דרשינן להאי "ועשה את מנחתו" — יז] כל זמן שיעשנו הוא קרוי מנחתו ונסכו של זה, אע"פ שלא קרבו עם זבחו. מי גמרי. שאר חטאות וחטאת נזיר מהדדי, דתמצי לומר חד למצוה וחד לעכב? סתם "חטאת" קרי חטאת חלב, משום דשכיחא טפי. שכן כרת. מכפרת על חייבי כרת. הלכך, לא גמרי מהדדי, וכיון דלא גמרי מהדדי — תרווייהו למצוה אצטריכו. ואשכחן שנוי קדש. ולעכב, דהא נפקא לן מצוה לעיל בשאר חטאות. וכפר על המטהר. סיפיה ד"ועשה הכהן את החטאת" הוא, יח] ו"על המטהר" — אכולהו עשיות קאי. ותיתי מהנך. נזיר ומצורע. שאלה. נזיר נשאל לחכם ועוקר נזירתו, ופטור מן הקרבן. שכן אין באין בדלות גרסינן. שאין יט] *חטאות יורדות בעניות להביא עוף. והנך קראי לעכב. וכשלמים: מה שלמים לא חלקת בהן למצוה — אף חטאת לא תחלוק בו לעכב. וכיון דכתיב עכובא בזריקה — אתיא להו כ] לכולהו עבודות בהך דרשא מהיקשא דשלמים. אשכחן חטאת חלב דכתיב ביה לחטאת. "ושחט אותה לחטאת", בסתם חטאת כתיב, (ד) כא] "אם נפש כי תחטא" וגו'. חטאת

תוספות

זריקה מנלן מוכפר עליו הכהן מחטאתו. הרבה יש תימה: דהני קראי דשחיטה וקבלה: "ושחט אותה לחטאת", "ולקח הכהן", כתיבי בסתם חטאת, כגון חטאת חלב בפרשת "ויקרא" גבי כשבה. והאי קרא ד"וכפר עליו הכהן מחטאתו" כתיב בחטאת דשמיעת קול וביטוי שפתים, אבל בחטאת חלב לא כתיב "מחטאתו", אלא "על חטאתו" כתיב. ובתורת כהנים באותה פרשה עצמה דחטאת חלב דריש מקרא ד"מחטאתו" אע"ג דלא כתיב בההיא פרשתא, וזהו תימה דשביק קרא ד"על חטאתו" דכתיב בההיא פרשתא! ושמא משום ד"על חטאתו" לאחר הקטרת אימורים הוא דכתיב. אבל תימה: דלקמן משמע דכל הני קראי דהכא בחטאת חלב כתיבי, דקאמר: אשכחנא חטאת חלב, כב] אבל חטאת דשמיעת קול וביטוי שפתים מנא לן? וי"ל, דהכי קאמר לקמן: אשכחנא חטאת חלב עכובא שחיטה וקבלה בשנוי קדש, ושאר עבודות נילף כדאמר לעיל: מה שלמים לא חלקת בין זביחה לשאר עבודות למצוה — אף כאן לא תחלוק לעכב. וקבלה נמי לא הוצרך לכתוב. אבל שמיעת קול מנא לן? דאע"ג דכתיב ביה: "וכפר עליו מחטאתו", ודרשינן לעיל: לשם חטאת — היינו שנוי קדש בזריקה. ו"לא חלקת" לא נימא בזריקה, לפי שהיא עיקר כפרה. ושנוי בעלים בחטאת חלב נגמר משמיעת קול דליכא פירכא. וי"מ: ד"מחטאתו" דקאמר — היינו בשעיר נשיא דכתיב ביה נמי "מחטאתו", כג] וקאי גם אחטאת חלב. וקשה: דכתיב לאחר הקטרת אימורים. נראה לי, ברו"ך. ועוד נ"ל: דלא הוה מצי למדרש מ"וכפר על חטאתו אשר חטא" דכתיב בחטאת חלב, משום דהכי קאמר: על פשעו אשר חטא כד] *) (ולא בשמיעת קול איירי בחטאת קרבנו). ולא כה] משעיר נשיא, דכתיב: "מחטאתו ונסלח לו" — והיינו מפשעו וחטאתו שלו, ונסלח לו. אבל בשמיעת קול לא כתיב כו] זה ולא זו, אלא "מחטאתו" היינו מקרבנו. ברו"ך.

וזריקה בשנוי בעלים בין למצוה בין לעכב. תימה: דמהאי קרא כז] "וכפר עליו הכהן מחטאתו" דרשינן תרווייהו, זריקה בשנוי קדש ושנוי בעלים. ואם כן מ"חטאת" "חטאתו" תיפוק ליה נמי עכובא בשנוי קדש כמו בשנוי בעלים, דאתרווייהו קאי!

ועשה את חטאתו שיהו כל עשיותיו לשם חטאת. אשכחנא שנוי קדש שנוי בעלים מנ"ל אמר רב הונא בריה דרב יהושע חטאת חטאתו. כך גירסת הקונטרס. ולגירסא זו מוקי ברישא לעכב בשנוי קדש, קודם שנעמיד למצוה בשנוי בעלים ב"אם אינו ענין". ואינו משמע כן בכולי פירקא לעיל גבי שלמים ופסח, דקאמר: אשכחנא שנוי קדש, שנוי בעלים מנא לן? ומוקי ברישא בשנוי בעלים ב"אם אינו ענין" קודם שיעמיד קרא לעכב. ומיהו, י"ל: דשאני הכא, דכבר אשכחנא קרא לזריקה בשנוי בעלים. ואית ספרים דגרסי: אם אינו ענין לשנוי קדש, דנפקא ליה מהתם, תניהו ענין לשנוי בעלים. אשכחנא למצוה, לעכב מנא לן? אמר רב הונא בריה דרב יהושע: חטאת חטאתו. ולגירסא זו לא צרכינן תו לקרא דלעיל בזריקה. וניחא נמי הא דגרסינן לעיל: כדאמר רב הונא בריה דרב יהושע חטאת חטאתו, דמשמע דעיקר מילתא לא אתמר אההיא, והיינו משום דלבסוף לא קיימא. **מנחתם** ונסכיהם בלילה מנחתם ונסכיהם **אפי'** למחר. **הילכך** מצוה משלמים והנך קראי לעכב. וא"ת: למה לי למכתב בכולהו? לכתוב כח] *בהך, ואיך כולהו אתו מדכתיב: "זאת תורת החטאת" — תורה אחת לכל החטאות, כדלקמן בשמעתא דמבוג! ויש לומר: דבמסקנא לא

*) מהרש"ק מ"ז ויש למחוק ב' תיבות בשמיעת קול וכל"ל ולא מיירי בחטאת כו' ועיין חלופי גרסאות

שיטה מקובצת

א] (שנאמר) [דאמר קרא] וכפר עליו הכהן. גבי חטאת דשמיעת הקול כתיב (בויקרא ה') תימה אמאי שביק קרא דוכפר עליו הכהן על חטאתו אשר חטא דכתיב גבי חטאת חלב או מוכפר עליו הכהן מחטאתו דכתיב גבי שעיר נשיא וי"ל דההוא בחטאת קא מיירי ולא בקרבן חטאת [דוכפר] על חטאתו אשר חטא [לא מיירי] בקרבן א): ב] תיבות בכל עבודות ל"ש ונמחק: ג] ולשאר עבודות אות ב' נמחק: ד] ה"ג רש"י ועשה כו' שיהו כל עשיותיו לשם חטאת ואם אינו ענין למצוה לשינוי קודש [דהא] נפקא מהתם תנהו ענין לעכב בשינוי קודש אשכחן שינוי קודש בין למצוה בין לעכב שינוי בעלים בין למצוה בין לעכב מנלן אמר רב הונא אתיא חטאת חטאתו [דמשמע שינוי בעלים למצוה] וכיון דגלי גלי ומשתמע בין למצוה ובין לעכב. וקשה דמיד דשמעינן שינוי קודש למצוה הוי לן לאהדורי שינוי בעלים למצוה ולאהדורי [אח"כ] אשינוי קודש לעכב כי כך שיטת התלמוד בכל הסוגיא לאוקמי מצוה בשינוי בעלים קודם שנדע עיכובא בשינוי קודש לכך נראה [דגרסי' אם] אינו ענין בשינוי קודש דנפקא לן מהתם תנהו ענין בשינוי בעלים אשכחן למצוה בין בשינוי קודש בין בשינוי בעלים לעכב מנלן בין בשינוי קודש בין בשינוי בעלים אמר רב הונא אתיא חטאת חטאתו דמשמע לעכב בשינוי בעלים ונפקא לעכב בשינוי קודש ב) הכי דחטאת חטאתו לא משמע אלא בשינוי בעלים דוקא הואיל ופשטא דקרא משתמע שינוי קודש הוי מוקמינן ליה בשינוי בעלים ואם אינו ענין קרא דחטאת קאי אשינוי בעלים וכ"ש בשינוי קודש [דחטאת] חטאתו משמע לעכב וקאי אתרווייהו: ה] חטאת ואשכחן: ו] תיבות אם אינו ענין כו' לעכב מנלן נמחק: ז] רב הונא בריה דרב יהושע: ח] עיין בהשמטות בסוף המסכת: ט] אלא אמר רבא אתיא וכו' אשכחן שינוי קודש בין למצוה בין לעכב שינוי בעלים מנלן בשאר עבודות בין למצוה בין לעכב כך פי' רש"י ולא נהירא דחדא דקודם היה לנו להעמיד הפסוק בשינוי בעלים למצוה משינוי קודש לעכב כמו שהקשיתי לעיל ועוד דמה הרויח רבא למימר (חטאת) [אתיא מחטאת] מצורע הלא חטאת נזיר לא סלקינן מינה אלא מכח הני פירכא מה לחטאת נזיר שכן יש עמהם דמים אחרים והוא חושש ומביא עמו חטאת מצורע דשייך למיפרך הכי לכן נראה לפרש דאינו חוזר מקרא דנזיר רק מחטאתו משום קושיא דרבינא אבל לא חשש לאידך קושיא (דאי) [דמי] גמרי מהדדי וה"ק אלא אמר רבא מקראי דלעיל ידעינן שינוי קודש ושינוי בעלים למצוה ולעכב נפקא לן בשינוי קודש מועשה את החטאת והילכך פריך שפיר אשכחן שינוי קודש לעכב שינוי בעלים מנלן ומשני דכתיב וכפר על המטהר ולא על המטהר חבירו וקאי אכל עשיותיו כדכתיב ברישא דקרא ועשה כדפי' בקונטרס: י] כרת. חדא מחדא: יא] קבלה רבינן ליה תיבות היא מתרביא נמחק: יב] תיבת נמי נמחק: יג] מתיבות הרי למצוה כו' עד סוף הדבר נמחק: יד] ונסכיהם הכתובים בקרבנות החג מנחתם ונסכיהם: טו] תיבות לבא למחר נמחק: טז] בלילה ולבא למחר: יז] מנחתו דכתיב גבי נזיר: יח] הוא על המטהר ואכולהו עשיות: יט] שאין חטאתם: כ] כולהו אות ל' נמחק: כא] תיבת אם נמחק: כב] חלב ג) אבל אות ב' נמחק: כג] מחטאתו (וגבי) [וגלי] תיבת וקאי ל"ש ותיבת גם נמחק: כד] מתיבת ולא כו' עד תיבת קרבנו נמחק: כה] ולא בשעיר נשיא דהא כתיב מחטאתו: כו] לא כתיב לא זה: כז] קרא דוכיפר: כח] לכתוב בחד ואינך תיבת בהך ל"ש ונמחק:

א) והא דלא מייתי מקרא דשעיר נשיאה (ויקרא ד') עי' בתוס' בסוד"ה זריקה בשם י"מ. ב) נראה דל"ל ואף דחטאת חטאתו לא משמע וכו' משתמע שינוי קודש רק דמוקמינן ליה בשינוי בעלים בואם אינו ענין וכו' וקרא דחטאת וכו'. ג) אולי צ"ל חלב כו' חטאת תיבת אבל נמחק.

[לעיל ג: ד: ז. פסחים סב.]

רש"ק

רש"ק מ"ז

לקמן פד. תמורה יד. מנחות מד: [גב. תענית ב:]

נ"א ונסכיהם גבי קרבנות החג אפי' בלילה כו'

הגהות הב"ח

(א) גמ' שינוי בעלים מנלן (אם אינו ענין וכו' מנלן) תא"מ ונ"ב רש"י לא גרס ליה אלא ה"ג אשכחן שינוי קדש שינוי בעלים מנלן אמר רב הונא כו': (ב) שם עולתו מאי דרשת ביה ותו: (ג) רש"י ד"ה ההוא וכו' למחר לא בלילה: (ד) ד"ה אשכחן וכו' כתיב ואם נפש אחת תחטא:

[נ"ל חטאות חלב ונזיר]

נ"ל בחד נ"ק

מא מיי' פט"ו מהל' פה"מ הלכה יב:
מא ב מיי' שם הל' ח':

גמרא

חַטָּאת דַּעֲבוֹדָה זָרָה, (א) א] דִּשְׁמִיעַת הַקּוֹל וּבִטּוּי שְׂפָתַיִם, וְטוּמְאַת מִקְדָּשׁ וְקָדָשָׁיו, דְּלָא כְּתִיב בְּהוּ, מְנָלַן? חַטָּאת דַּעֲבוֹדָה זָרָה אָתְיָא מֵחַטַּאת חֵלֶב, שֶׁכֵּן כָּרֵת כְּמוֹתָהּ. וְהָנָךְ כּוּלְּהִי אָתְיָין בְּמָה הַצַּד.§ תָּנוּ רַבָּנַן: פֶּסַח בִּזְמַנּוֹ, לִשְׁמוֹ — כָּשֵׁר, שֶׁלֹּא לִשְׁמוֹ — פָּסוּל; ב] אוּבִשְׁאָר יְמוֹת הַשָּׁנָה, לִשְׁמוֹ — פָּסוּל, בשֶׁלֹּא לִשְׁמוֹ — כָּשֵׁר. (של"ו קבאיצ"ן ממה"ר בצ"א ב"א, סִימָן) מְנָא הָנֵי מִילֵּי? אָמַר אֲבוּהּ דִּשְׁמוּאֵל: אָמַר קְרָא ג] °"וְאִם מִן הַצֹּאן קָרְבָּנוֹ לְזֶבַח שְׁלָמִים לַה'", דָּבָר הַבָּא מִן הַצֹּאן — יְהֵא לְזֶבַח שְׁלָמִים. (ב) אֵימָא: שְׁלָמִים — אִין, מִידֵּי אַחֲרִינָא — לָא! אָמַר רַבִּי אִילָא א"ר יוֹחָנָן: "לְזֶבַח" — לְרַבּוֹת כָּל זֶבַח. אֵימָא: (ג) כָּל דְּשָׁחֵיט ד] לֶהֱוֵי כְּמוֹתָהּ! אִי הֲוָה כְּתִיב "לִשְׁלָמִים וָזֶבַח" — כִּדְקָאָמְרַתְּ, הָשְׁתָּא דִּכְתִיב "לְזֶבַח שְׁלָמִים" — לְכָל דְּשָׁחֵיט לֵיהּ שְׁלָמִים לֶהֱוֵי. אֵימָא: "לְזֶבַח" — כְּלָל, "שְׁלָמִים" — פְּרָט, כְּלָל וּפְרָט — אֵין בַּכְּלָל אֶלָּא מַה שֶּׁבַּפְּרָט: שְׁלָמִים — אִין, מִידֵּי אַחֲרִינָא — לָא! "לַה'" הֲדַר וְכָלַל. מַתְקִיף לָהּ ר' יַעֲקֹב מִנְּהַר פְּקוֹד: הָא לָא דָּמֵי (ד) כְּלָלָא בַּתְרָא לִכְלָלָא קַמָּא, כְּלָלָא קַמָּא מְרַבֵּי זְבָחִים וְתוּ לָא, כְּלָלָא בַּתְרָא "לַה'" — כָּל דְּלַה', וַאֲפִי' ה] לְעוֹפוֹת וַאֲפִי' לִמְנָחוֹת! הָא *תָּנָא דְּבֵי רַבִּי יִשְׁמָעֵאל ו] בִּכְלָלֵי וּפְרָטֵי (ה) דָּרֵישׁ כִּי הַאי גַּוְונָא: כְּלָל וּפְרָט וּכְלָל — אִי אַתָּה דָּן אֶלָּא כְּעֵין הַפְּרָט, מַה הַפְּרָט מְפוֹרָשׁ שֶׁהוּא שֶׁלֹּא לִשְׁמוֹ וְכָשֵׁר — אַף כָּל שֶׁהוּא שֶׁלֹּא לִשְׁמוֹ וְכָשֵׁר. אִי מַה הַפְּרָט מְפוֹרָשׁ, דָּבָר הַבָּא בְּנֶדֶר וּבִנְדָבָה — אַף כָּל הַבָּא בְּנֶדֶר וּבִנְדָבָה; עוֹלָה וּשְׁלָמִים — אִין, חַטָּאת וְאָשָׁם — לָא! ז] אֶלָּא: "לְזֶבַח" רִבּוּיָא הוּא. אֵימָא: לְכָל דְּשָׁחֵיט לֵיהּ לֶהֱוֵי כְּוָותֵיהּ! א"ר אָבִין:

דּוֹחִין

תורה אור: ויקרא ג

רש"י

חַטָּאת דַּעֲבוֹדָה זָרָה. דִּכְתִיב בְּפָ' "שְׁלַח לְךָ" וְלָא כְּתִיב בְּהַאי עִנְיָינָא, וְכֵן חַטָּאת דִּשְׁמִיעַת הַקּוֹל לָא כְּתִיב בְּהַהוּא עִנְיָינָא, דְּהַהוּא עִנְיָינָא בְּחַטָּאת דִּשְׁגְגַת כָּרֵת קַיְימָא, כְּדִילְפִינַן בְּהוֹרָיוֹת (דף ג.). שְׁמִיעַת הַקּוֹל. שְׁבוּעַת הָעֵדוּת "וְשָׁמְעָה קוֹל אָלָה" (שְׁמִיעַת ח] הַקּוֹל), וּשְׁבוּעַת בִּיטּוּי, וְטוּמְאַת מִקְדָּשׁ וְקָדָשָׁיו — בְּחַד עִנְיָינָא כְּתִיבִי, בְּקָרְבָּן עוֹלֶה וְיוֹרֵד: ט] "וְשָׁמְעָה קוֹל אָלָה", "אוֹ נֶפֶשׁ כִּי תִשָּׁבַע לְבַטֵּא", "אוֹ נֶפֶשׁ אֲשֶׁר תִּגַּע" וגו' וּמוֹקְמָא לַהּ בְּמַסֶּכֶת שְׁבוּעוֹת בְּטוּמְאַת מִקְדָּשׁ וְקָדָשָׁיו. אָתְיָין בְּמָה הַצַּד. מֵחַטַּאת חֵלֶב וְחַטַּאת נָזִיר וּמְצוֹרָע. דְּכִי פָּרְכַתְּ: מַה לְּחַטַּאת חֵלֶב שֶׁכֵּן כָּרֵת — חַטַּאת נָזִיר וּמְצוֹרָע יוֹכִיחוּ. מַה לְּחַטַּאת נָזִיר וּמְצוֹרָע שֶׁכֵּן יֵשׁ עִמָּהֶן דָּמִים אֲחֵרִים — חַטַּאת חֵלֶב תּוֹכִיחַ. הַצַּד הַשָּׁוֶה שֶׁבָּהֶן י] כו', אַף אֲנִי אָבִיא חַטַּאת דִּשְׁמִיעַת הַקּוֹל. וּמֵחַטַּאת חֵלֶב וַחֲדָא מֵהָנֵי לָא אָתְיָא, דְּאִי מֵחַטַּאת חֵלֶב וְחַטַּאת נָזִיר — אִיכָּא לְמִיפְרַךְ: מַה לְּהַצַּד הַשָּׁוֶה שֶׁבָּהֶן שֶׁכֵּן אֵינָן בָּאִין בְּדַלּוּת, תֹּאמַר בִּשְׁבוּעַת בִּיטּוּי שֶׁהִיא בְּעוֹלֶה וְיוֹרֵד. אִי מֵחַטַּאת חֵלֶב וְחַטַּאת מְצוֹרָע — אִיכָּא לְמִיפְרַךְ: מַה לְּהַצַּד הַשָּׁוֶה שֶׁבָּהֶן שֶׁכֵּן אֵינָן בִּשְׁאֵלָה, תֹּאמַר בִּשְׁבוּעָה שֶׁיֶּשְׁנָהּ בִּשְׁאֵלָה. שֶׁלֹּא לִשְׁמוֹ פָּסוּל. כִּדְאָמְרִי' (לעיל דף ז:). בִּשְׁאָר יְמוֹת הַשָּׁנָה לִשְׁמוֹ פָּסוּל יא]. כִּדְאָמְרִי' בְּמַס' פְּסָחִים (דף סא.): שְׁחָטוֹ קוֹדֶם חֲצוֹת פָּסוּל, דִּכְתִיב: "בֵּין הָעַרְבַּיִם", וְכַמָּה פְּעָמִים שָׁנָה הַכָּתוּב בִּקְבִיעוּת זְמַנּוֹ בְּי"ד בֵּין הָעַרְבַּיִם. שֶׁלֹּא לִשְׁמוֹ כָּשֵׁר. כִּדְמְפָרֵשׁ וְאָזֵיל. מְנָהָנֵי מִילֵּי. דְּבִשְׁאָר יְמוֹת הַשָּׁנָה שֶׁלֹּא לִשְׁמוֹ כָּשֵׁר. וְאִם מִן הַצֹּאן קָרְבָּנוֹ כו'. (ו) לָאו קְרָא יְתֵירָא קָא דָּרֵישׁ, אֶלָּא מַשְׁמָעוּתָא דִּקְרָא מַשְׁמַע לֵיהּ הָכִי: וְאִם יג] דָּבָר הַבָּא מִן הַצֹּאן, (ז) דְּהַיְינוּ פֶּסַח שֶׁאֵינוֹ בָּא אֶלָּא מִן הַצֹּאן, הָיָה קָרְבָּנוֹ — הֲרֵי הוּא לְזֶבַח שְׁלָמִים. וְעַל כָּרְחָךְ שֶׁלֹּא בִּזְמַנּוֹ קָאָמַר, דְּאִי בִּזְמַנּוֹ — הָא יָלְפִינַן לֵיהּ לְעֵיל דְּפָסוּל. וְאֵימָא שְׁלָמִים אִין כו'. שְׁחָטוֹ לְשֵׁם שְׁלָמִים לִיתַּכְשַׁר, אֲבָל שְׁחָטוֹ לְשֵׁם עוֹלָה — לִיפְסִיל. וּבְרַיְיתָא קָתָנֵי שֶׁלֹּא לִשְׁמוֹ כָּשֵׁר, וַאֲפִילּוּ שְׁחָטוֹ לְשֵׁם עוֹלָה אוֹ לְשֵׁם חַטָּאת. לְזֶבַח. קְרָא יְתֵירָא הוּא, דְּמָצֵי לְמִכְתַּב "לִשְׁלָמִים". אֵימָא לְכָל דְּשָׁחֵיט לֶהֱוֵי כְּוָותֵיהּ. יד] שְׁחָטוֹ לְשֵׁם עוֹלָה — יְהֵא עוֹלָה, דְּהָא אִתְרַבֵּי לֵיהּ כָּל זֶבַח. ה"ג: אִי הֲוָה כְּתִיב לִשְׁלָמִים וָזֶבַח כִּדְקָא אָמְרַתְּ. דְּאִי כְּתַב הָכִי הֲוָה מַשְׁמַע: יְהֵא כִּשְׁלָמִים אוֹ כִּשְׁאָר זֶבַח. הָשְׁתָּא דִּכְתִיב לְזֶבַח שְׁלָמִים. הָכִי מַשְׁמַע: לְכָל זֶבַח שֶׁיִּזְבָּחֶנּוּ לִשְׁמוֹ — שְׁלָמִים יִהְיֶה. וְאֵימָא לְזֶבַח כְּלָל כו'. אַמַּאי דָּרֵישׁ לְהַאי "זֶבַח שְׁלָמִים" הָכִי? דְּרוֹשׁ הָכִי: דָּבָר הַבָּא מִן הַצֹּאן יְהֵא לְכָל הַזְּבָחִים — כְּלָל, שֶׁכָּשֵׁר שֶׁלֹּא לִשְׁמוֹ. כִּי הֲדַר כְּתַב "שְׁלָמִים" — פְּרָט, שֶׁלֹּא הִכְשַׁרְתִּיו בַּעֲקִירַת שְׁמוֹ אֶלָּא א"כ שְׁחָטוֹ לִשְׁלָמִים, אֲבָל שְׁחָטוֹ לְשֵׁם זֶבַח אַחֵר — פָּסוּל. וַאֲפִי' טו] לְעוֹפוֹת. שְׁחָטוֹ לְשֵׁם (ח) חַטַּאת עוֹף. אַף כָּל שֶׁהוּא שֶׁלֹּא לִשְׁמוֹ. יָצָא לִשְׁמוֹ. חַטָּאת וְאָשָׁם לָא. שְׁחָטוֹ לְשֵׁם חַטָּאת וְאָשָׁם יְהֵא פָּסוּל, אֲפִילּוּ לִשְׁלָמִים. אֶלָּא לְזֶבַח רִבּוּיָא הוּא. אֵינוֹ לְשׁוֹן כְּלָל, וְלָא דָּרְשִׁי' לֵיהּ בִּכְלָל וּפְרָט. שֶׁאֵין כְּלָלוֹת וּפְרָטוֹת בָּאִין מֵרִבּוּי לָשׁוֹן אֶלָּא מִמַּשְׁמָעוּת הַמִּקְרָאוֹת, וּכְגוֹן (ב"ק דף סג.): "בְּכֹל אֲשֶׁר תְּאַוֶּה נַפְשְׁךָ" — כְּלָל. (ט) וְכֵן "מִן הַבְּהֵמָה" — כְּלָל, "בָּקָר וָצֹאן" — פְּרָט. אֲבָל "לְזֶבַח שְׁלָמִים" — שְׁתֵּי תֵיבוֹת דְּבוּקוֹת הֵן, כְּאִילּוּ כְּתִיב "לְזֶבַח טז] הַשְּׁלָמִים", וּקְרָא יְתֵירָא בְּעָלְמָא הוּא, דַּהֲוָה מָצֵי לְמִכְתַּב יז] "לִשְׁלָמִים". וְכָל מִקְרָא שֶׁל לְשׁוֹן יִיתּוּר אֵינוֹ לִכְלָל וּפְרָט אֶלָּא לְרַבּוֹת, וּכְמַאן דִּכְתִיב "לִשְׁלָמִים וָזֶבַח" דָּמֵי, דְּאִיתְרַבּוּ לֵיהּ כָּל הַזְּבָחִים.

דּוֹחִין

תוספות

לא קאי. ואע"ג דבפרק "דם חטאת" (לקמן דף צב.) תנן: יח] תורה אחת לכל החטאות – היינו במילתא דכתיבא התם: "אשר יזה מדמה על הבגד". ומיהו, איכא דאית ליה הך סברא לר' שמעון בריש מסכת מנחות (דף ג:). וא"ת: למה לי למכתב בחטאת חלב עכובא בכל עבודות? לכתוב בחדא, ונימא: מה שלמים לא חלקת יט] למצוה – אף חטאת לא תחלוק, כדקאמר לעיל! וי"ל: דכי האי גוונא זמנין דטרח ליה קרא וכתב. א"נ: אתי לדרשא אחרינא. וא"ת: מנא לן בחטאת נזיר עכובא בשנוי בעלים? ויש לומר: מ"חטאת" "חטאתו". אע"ג דלעיל לא קאי, עיקר פירכא *סמיך אותו "מי גמירי מהדדי".

חטאת דעבודה זרה אתיא מחטאת חלב שכן כרת כמותה. יש ספרים שכתוב בהן: חטאת דעבודה זרה וטומאת מקדש וקדשיו. ואינו נראה, דאע"ג דכרת כמותה – מכל מקום איכא למיפרך: מה לחטאת חלב שכן אינה באה בדלות, כדפרכינן לעיל גבי חטאת מצורע.

שמיעת קול. *דלא כתיב "לחטאתו" גבי עבודה, מנלן עכובא? אבל כתיב "לחטאת" על דברים אחרים, ואין בכך כלום.

כ](*ה"ג) **הנך** כולהו אתיין במה הצד כא]. הקשה רבינו תם: מה להנך – שכן אין באין בדלי דלות, תאמר בהנך! ותירץ: כיון דדלי דלות גופיה פסולה שלא לשמה, כב] היינו מנחת חוטא דפסולה שלא לשמה, כדתנן בריש מנחות (דף ב.), ומפיק לן מדכתיב: "כי חטאת היא" – אין סברא שמה שבאין בדלי דלות יגרום להם בעשירות להיות כשירין שלא לשמן, כיון שהדלי דלות עצמן פסול. וקשה: א"כ לעיל, דפריך גבי מצורע: מה להנך שכן אינן באין בדלות, תאמר במצורע. מאי קושיא? והלא דלות כג] היינו חטאת העוף, וחטאת העוף פסולה שלא לשמה, כדתנן בפרק "קדשי קדשים" (לקמן דף סד:) ומפיק ליה בתורת כהנים מ"חטאת היא", וכיון דפסולה בדלות – היאך יש לה לגרום בעשירות הכשר שלא לשמה? כד] ואם תאמר: והא בחטאת חלב למדה משלמים בהיקש למצוה, והיכי ילפי' שאר חטאות במה הצד? הא בעיא היא לקמן פרק "איזהו מקומן" (דף נ.) אי דבר הלמד בהיקש חוזר ומלמד בבנין אב! לאו פירכא היא כלל, דכולהו חטאות נמי ילפי' למצוה משלמים, ולעכב הוא דילפינן בשאר חטאות מהנך דכתיב עכובא בגופייהו. ואם תאמר: וחטאות הצבור, כגון שעירי ראשי חדשים ומועדות, מנלן? הא לא אתו במה הצד, דמה להנך – שכן שנוי בעלים פוסל בהן, מה שאין כן בקרבן צבור, כדאמר לעיל (דף ד.) דשנוי בעלים ליתא בצבור כביחיד! אע"ג דלא שייך שנוי בעלים בצבור – מ"מ פירכא טובה היא, כדאשכחן בפ"ק דקדושין (דף ה:): מה לכסף שכן פודין בו הקדשות ומעשר שני, תאמר בחופה. וכן פרק "החובל" (ב"ק דף פח.): מה לאשה שאינה במילה. ועוד קשה: חטאות פנימיות, לרבי שמעון דאמר: כל שאינו על מזבח החיצון אין בו משום פיגול – איכא למיפרך: מה להנך שכן פיגול פוסל בהן, תאמר בחטאות הפנימיות! ויש לומר: דבפר העלם דבר של צבור כתיב: "חטאת הקהל היא", ודריש מינה בת"כ שפסול שלא לשמו, אם כן אשכחן צבור וגם פנימי לעכב, ולמצוה ילפינן משלמים.

הגה"ה בשאר ימות השנה לשמו פסול. היינו קודם הפסח, דבעי עקירה, או כגון דנדחו בעלים לפסח שני. אבל אח"כ לא, דפסח בשאר ימות השנה שלמים, ושלמים לשם פסח קשחיט, כה] כדאמר בפ' "תמיד נשחט" (פסחים דף סד.) ובפ' שני דחולין (דף ל.). ומיהו, איכא למ"ד בסוף "אלו דברים" (פסחים דף עג:) דבעי עקירה.

לשמו פסול (*כתוב) בקונטרס: דלא חזו כו] למילתייהו. ורבינו ש"י הגיה: כדאמר בפסחים (דף סא.): שחטו קודם חצות – פסול, שנאמר "בין הערבים", וכמה פעמים שנה הכתוב בקביעות זמנו בארבעה עשר בין הערבים. וסוגיא דהתלמוד נמי משמע לקמן בגמרא*) כז]הפסח ששחטו שחרית, דמ"בין הערבים" נפיק. ואין לומר דנפיק מדדרשינן הכא "לזבח שלמים" שצריך שיעקרנו לזבח שלמים, דדילמא הני מילי למצוה, אבל לעכב לא. **ואם** מן הצאן קרבנו. פי' בקונטרס: לאו קרא יתירא דריש, אלא ממשמעות דקרא משמע ליה הכי. וזהו תימה: דאי לא כח] מייתי קרא יתירא – מנא ליה לאוקומו בפסח? ונראה דמייתורא דריש, דלא הוה צריך למכתב "לזבח השלמים" דאשלמים קאי. [ועי"ל:] דבסמוך דריש "כשב" לרבות פסח לאליה, ופירש רבינו ש"י: דמיותר, דמדכתיב בתר הכי בשלמים "ואם מן העז קרבנו" מכלל דעד השתא איירי בכשב. וה"נ י"ל, מדכתיב לעיל "אם מן הבקר קרבנו" – מכלל דהכא בצאן מיירי, אם כן (י) "הצאן" מיותר הוא למותר פסח. ברוך. **אי** הוה כתב לזבח השלמים כדקאמרת. הוה ליה למימר: אי הוה כתב כט] "לזבח" כדקאמרת, ד"שלמים" לא צריך כלל. **אלא** לזבח רבויא הוא. משמע ליה לגמרא שהוא רבויא, כדאמר *(ב"ק דף סג.): "בכל" – כללא, "כל" – רבויא. דמשמע ליה לחלק בין "כל" ל"בכל", הילכך לא דרשינן ליה בכללא ופרטא אלא בריבה ומיעט. ובקונטרס האריך בפירושו.

הערות בגליון

גי' רש"ק סמיך אמי גמירי מהדדי וגי' נ"ק לא קאי לעיקר פירכה סמיך דמי גמירי כו'

גי' נ"ק דלא כתיב על חטאתו גבי עבודה מנלן עכובא אבל כתיב על חטאתו כו'

נ"א הגה"ה

לעיל ז: ב"ק סד. חולין סו. [כריתות כב.]

נ"ל פירש בקונטרס נ"ק ואינו כרש"י בכאן ועיין בפסחים ס: ד"ה פסח בשאר *) [דף יא:]

גי' נ"ק כדאמרי' בב"ק למחלק בין כל לבכל כללא ובכל רבויא ה"ג משמע ליה לחלק בין זבח ובין לזבח הלכך לא כו' וכ"ה כת"י

שיטה מקובצת

א] ושמיעת אות ד' נמחק: ב] ובשאר ימות השנה לשמו פסול. דלא חזי למידי והתם בפסח שני פריך (שלא) לשמו פסול שלמים לשם פסח קשחיט ומשני לא נצרכא אלא לקודם זמנו דבעי עקירה לב"ע והילכך קתני פסול כל כמה דלא עקירה ולפסח עצמו לא (הוי) [חזי] דהא שינה בין הערבים לעכב. תוס' טוך: [וא"ה בגמרא שלנו שבדפוס לא נמצא ועי' תוס' ד"ה טעמא שלא לשמו גירסת ר"ת עב"ה:] ג] ואם מן הצאן. זה לשון הר"פ ואם מן הצאן פי' בקונטרס לאו קרא יתירא כו' ולא נראה דהא כתיב באותה פרשה אם זכר או נקבה ופסח אינו בא אלא זכר ועוד דכולה פרשה לא איירי אלא בשלמים והילכך איצטריך קרא לפרושי דין שלמים כמו ואם מן הבקר ואם לאו קרא יתירא מנ"ל לאוקמי בפסח ולכך נראה דמייתורא דקרא דריש דהא בתר הכי כתיב אם כשב אם עז וא"כ למאי איצטריך ואם מן הצאן דכתיב ברישא דקרא הלא בכלל כשב ועז הוא אלא ש"מ מייתורא הוא לפסח לדרוש דבר הבא מן הצאן יהיה לזבח שלמים. תוס' טוך: ד] דשחיט ליה להוי: ה] ואפילו עופות ואפי' מנחות: ו] ישמעאל הוא דדריש בכללי: ז] עי' בהשמטות בסוף המסכת: ח] שמיעת קול אות ה' נמחק: ט] ויורד שמיעת קול ושמעה קול אלה שבועת ביטוי או כו': י] שבהן שהן חטאות וצריכין לשמה בין בשינוי קודש ובין בשינוי בעלים אף: יא] פסול. דלא חזי למלתיה: יב] אלא ממשמעותא: יג] ואם מדבר: יד] כוותיה. ואם שחטו: טו] ואפילו עופות: טז] לזבח של שלמים אות ה' נמחק:

הגהות הב"ח

(א) גמ' חטאת דע"ז ודשמיעת: (ב) שם ואימא שלמים: (ג) שם אימא לכל דשחיט: (ד) שם לא דמי כללא כו': (ה) שם בכללי ופרטי כי האי גוונא דריש כלל: (ו) רש"י ד"ה ואם מן וכו' לאו קרא יתירא. נ"ב כלומר הפסח דקסד"ד דדריש ליה מכלל ופרט לזבח לא מיתורא הוא עד דמסיק אלא לזבח ריבויא כו' וכמו שפירש בקונטרס גופיה לפסח אבל מודה הקונטרס דמן הצאן ייתורא הוא דאתי לפסח וכדכתבו התוס': (ז) בא"ד דהיינו פסח. נ"ב לשמו נפקא לן מדכתיב מן הצאן קרבנו כלומר שקרבנו הפסח לשם קרבנו שהוא מחויב להקריב כגון עולה כו' דהיינו שלא לשמו: (ח) ד"ה ואפי' וכו' לשם עולת עוף: (ט) ד"ה אלא לזבח וכו' נפסק כלל כו' וכו' מקרא של ייתור לכלל אינו: (י) תוס' ד"ה ואם וכו' א"כ מן הצאן:

יז] למכתב וכן לשלמים כל מקרא: יח] תנן בהדיא: יט] חלקת לעכב אף: כ] הג"ה ותיבות ה"ג נמחק: כא] הצד. משלשתן כך פרש"י והדין עמו דהרי מנזיר ומצורע לא אתיא דאיכא למיפרך שכן יש עמהם דמים אחרים ואי מחטאת חלב כו' עד בשאלה וא"ת והשתא נמי דאתיא משלשתן איכא למיפרך מה להנך כו' ותירץ ר"ת דמה שבאים בדלי דלות לא מהני להכשירם שלא לשמה דהכתיב עשירית האיפה היא דמשמע היא לשמה כשירה שלא לשמה פסולה וא"ת כו': כב] לשמה דהיינו: כג] דלות במצורע היינו: כד] לשמה וי"ל דהואיל ד... איכא עולת העוף משום הכי פריך שפיר. תו' ר"פ ותוס' טוך: כה] קשחיט. ס"א למאן דאית ליה לא בעי עקירה גליון: כו] דלא חזי למילתיה: כז] בגמרא דהפסח: כח] לא מייתורא דקרא מנא ליה לאוקומי בפסח כיון דבשלמים כתיב. גליון: כט] כתב לשלמים וזבח:

מב א מיי' פ"ד מהל' קרבן פסח הל' ז:
מג ב מיי' פ"א מהל' מעה"ק הל' ח:

גמרא

תורה אור

דּוֹחִין קָדָשִׁים הַנֶּאֱכָלִים אֵצֶל קָדָשִׁים הַנֶּאֱכָלִין, וְאֵין דּוֹחִין קָדָשִׁים הַנֶּאֱכָלִין אֵצֶל קָדָשִׁים שֶׁאֵינָן נֶאֱכָלִין. אַטּוּ חַטָּאת וְאָשָׁם מִי לָא מִיתְאַכְלִי? אֶלָּא, דּוֹחִין קָדָשִׁים הַנֶּאֱכָלִין לְכָל אָדָם אֵצֶל קָדָשִׁים הַנֶּאֱכָלִין לְכָל אָדָם, וְאֵין דּוֹחִין קָדָשִׁים הַנֶּאֱכָלִין לְכָל אָדָם אֵצֶל קָדָשִׁים שֶׁאֵין נֶאֱכָלִין לְכָל אָדָם. רַבִּי יוֹסֵי בְּרַבִּי אָבִין אָמַר: דּוֹחִין קָדָשִׁים קַלִּים אֵצֶל קָדָשִׁים קַלִּים, וְאֵין דּוֹחִין קָדָשִׁים קַלִּים אֵצֶל קָדְשֵׁי קָדָשִׁים. מַתְקִיף לָהּ רַב יִצְחָק בְּרַבִּי א] סַבְרִיו, אֵימָא: שַׁחֲטֵיהּ לְשֵׁם מַעֲשֵׂר – לֶיהֱוֵי מַעֲשֵׂר; לְמַאי הִילְכְתָא? דְּלָא לִיבָּעֵי נְסָכִים, ב] וּלְמִלְקָא עֲלֵיהּ ג] (בְּ"לֹא יִמָּכֵר") °בְּ"לֹא יִגָּאֵל"! אָמַר קְרָא: °"הָעֲשִׂירִי יִהְיֶה קֹּדֶשׁ" – זֶה מַעֲשֵׂר וְאֵין אַחֵר מַעֲשֵׂר. אֵימָא: שַׁחֲטֵיהּ לְשֵׁם בְּכוֹר – לֶיהֱוֵי כִּבְכוֹר; לְמַאי הִילְכְתָא? דְּלָא לִיבָּעֵי נְסָכִים. ד] אִי נַמִי, דְּלֵיתְבֵיהּ לְכֹהֲנִים! בְּכוֹר נַמִי, עֲבָרָה *מִמַּעֲשֵׂר גָּמַר. וְאֵימָא: שַׁחֲטֵיהּ לְשֵׁם תְּמוּרָה – לֶיהֱוֵי תְּמוּרָה; לְמַאי הִילְכְתָא – לְמִלְקָא עֲלֵיהּ. ה] אִי נַמִי, לְמֵיקַם עֲלֵיהּ °בְּ"לֹא יִמָּכֵר וְלֹא יִגָּאֵל"! אָמַר מָר זוּטְרָא בְּרֵיהּ דְּרַב נַחְמָן, אָמַר קְרָא: °"וְהָיָה הוּא וּתְמוּרָתוֹ" – זוֹ ו] תְּמוּרָה, וְאֵין אַחֵר תְּמוּרָה. וְאֵימָא: שַׁחֲטֵיהּ לְשֵׁם תּוֹדָה – לֶיהֱוֵי כִּי תּוֹדָה; לְמַאי הִילְכְתָא – לְהַטְעִינוֹ לֶחֶם! מִי אִיכָּא מִידֵּי דְּפֶסַח גּוּפֵיהּ לָא בָּעֵי לֶחֶם, וּמוֹתָרוֹ בָּעֵי לֶחֶם? אִי הָכִי, הָשְׁתָּא נַמִי מִי אִיכָּא מִידֵּי דְּפֶסַח גּוּפֵיהּ לָא בָּעֵי נְסָכִים, וּמוֹתָרוֹ בָּעֵי נְסָכִים? אֲנַן הָכִי קָאָמְרִינַן: מִי אִיכָּא מִידֵּי דְּמוֹתַר תּוֹדָה עַצְמָהּ לָא בָּעֵי לֶחֶם, וְאִילּוּ מוֹתָר דְּאָתְיָא ז] לְהוּ מֵעָלְמָא בָּעֲיָא לֶחֶם? מַתְקִיף לָהּ רַב ח] [יֵימָר] בְּרֵיהּ דְּרַב הִילֵּל: וּמִמַּאי דִּבְמוֹתַר פֶּסַח כְּתִיב? דִּילְמָא בְּמוֹתַר אָשָׁם כְּתִיב! אָמַר רָבָא, אָמַר קְרָא: °"וְאִם מִן הַצֹּאן קָרְבָּנוֹ לְזֶבַח שְׁלָמִים", דָּבָר הַשָּׁוֶה בְּכָל(א) הַצֹּאן. מַתְקִיף לָהּ ר' אָבִין בַּר חִיָּיא, וְאִיתֵימָא ר' אָבִין בַּר כָּהֲנָא: בְּכָל אֲתַר אַתְּ אָמְרַתְּ "מִן" לְהוֹצִיא, וְכָאן "מִן" לְרַבּוֹת! אָמַר ר' מָנִי: הָכָא נַמִי "מִן" – לְהוֹצִיא, דְּלָא אָתֵי בֶּן שְׁתֵּי שָׁנִים וְלָא אָתֵי (ב) בִּנְקֵיבָה. מַתְקִיף לָהּ רַב חָנָא בַּגְדָּתָאָה: וּמִי מָצֵית אָמְרַתְּ דְּכִי כְּתִיב הַאי בְּמוֹתַר פֶּסַח כְּתִיב? ט] וְהָא מִדִּכְתִיב: °"אִם כֶּשֶׂב" (ג) °"אִם עֵז" – מִכְּלָל דְּלָאו בְּמוֹתַר פֶּסַח כְּתִיב! הַהוּא מִיבָּעֵי לֵיהּ *לְכִדְתַנְיָא: (ד) "כֶּבֶשׂ" – לְרַבּוֹת אֶת הַפֶּסַח לְאַלְיָה, כְּשֶׁהוּא אוֹמֵר: "אִם כֶּבֶשׂ" – לְרַבּוֹת *פֶּסַח שֶׁעִבְּרָה י] שְׁנָתָהּ, וּשְׁלָמִים הַבָּאִים מֵחֲמַת פֶּסַח, לְכָל מִצְוֹת שְׁלָמִים, שֶׁיִּטְעֲנוּ סְמִיכָה וּנְסָכִים וּתְנוּפַת חָזֶה וָשׁוֹק. כְּשֶׁהוּא אוֹמֵר: (ה) "אִם עֵז" – הִפְסִיק הָעִנְיָן, לִימֵּד *עַל הָעֵז שֶׁאֵינָהּ טְעוּנָה אַלְיָה. וְהָא מֵהָכָא נָפְקָא? מִדַּאֲבוּהּ דִּשְׁמוּאֵל נָפְקָא! דְּאָמַר אֲבוּהּ דִּשְׁמוּאֵל: "וְאִם מִן הַצֹּאן קָרְבָּנוֹ לְזֶבַח שְׁלָמִים" – דָּבָר הַבָּא מִן הַצֹּאן יְהֵא לְזֶבַח שְׁלָמִים. *וְאַכַּתִּי, מִדְּרַב נַחְמָן אָמַר רַבָּה בַּר אֲבוּהּ נָפְקָא, *דְּאָמַר רַב נַחְמָן אָמַר רַבָּה בַּר אֲבוּהּ: מִנַּיִן לְמוֹתַר פֶּסַח שֶׁקָּרֵב שְׁלָמִים – שֶׁנֶּאֱמַר: °"וְזָבַחְתָּ פֶּסַח לַה' אֱלֹהֶיךָ צֹאן וּבָקָר", וַהֲלֹא אֵין פֶּסַח בָּא אֶלָּא מִן הַכְּבָשִׂים וּמִן הָעִזִּים! אֶלָּא, מִכָּאן לְמוֹתַר הַפֶּסַח שֶׁיְּהֵא לְדָבָר הַבָּא מִן הַצֹּאן וּמִן הַבָּקָר, וּמַאי נִיהוּ – שְׁלָמִים! יא] אֶלָּא, תְּלָתָא קְרָאֵי כְּתִיבִי;

חַד

רש"י

דוחין קדשים הנאכלין. פסח זה מתחלה הוקדש לשם קרבן הנאכל – הילכך דוחין אותו אצל שלמים שהן נאכלין, ולא אצל עולה (ו). שאין נאכלין לכל אדם. אלא לזכרי כהונה. ליהוי מעשר. דהא קדשים קלים הוא. בכור ומעשר אין טעונין נסכים, בפרק "שתי מדות" (מנחות דף צ:). במעשר בהמה כתיב: "יהיה קודש לא יגאל", ודרשינן בבכורות בפרק "כל פסולי המוקדשין" (דף לב:) דהאי "לא יגאל" – לא ימכר הוא. עברה עברה. בבכור כתיב (שמות יג): "והעברת כל פטר רחם", ובמעשר כתיב: "כל אשר יעבור תחת השבט" (ויקרא כז). למילקא עלה. משום "לא יחליפנו". זו תמורה. (ז) ממש. יב] שהעומדת כשהיא חולין אצל בהמת קדשים והמיר, יג] הוא דהויא תמורה. ואין אחר. זבח (ח) יד] ראשון ששחטו לשם תמורה. ומותרו בעי נסכים. דהא אמרת שלמים ליהוי טו]. דמותר תודה עצמה. כגון הפריש תודתו ואבדה, והפריש אחרת, ונמצאת הראשונה – אין השניה טעונה לחם, כדאמרי' בפ' "התודה" (מנחות דף עט:): טז] זבח התודה טעון לחם, ולא ולדה ולא תמורתה ולא חליפתה טעונין לחם. ומותר דאתי לה מעלמא. תודה שבאה ממותר פסח. דילמא במותר אשם כתיב. האי "ואם מן הצאן", דאשם נמי איל תמים מן הצאן הוא, ואינו בא מן הבקר! בכל צאן. בכבשים ועזים, כגון פסח. לאפוקי אשם דאינו בא מן העזים. בכל אתר את אמר. בכל מקום אתה אומר: "מן" להוציא הוא, כגון "מן הבהמה" – להוציא רובע ונרבע, "מן הבקר" – להוציא את הנעבד, "מן הצאן" – להוציא את המוקצה (ב"ק דף מ:). וכאן אתה אומר מן לרבות. דקאמרת: יז] ["מן הצאן"] פסח, משמע שבא מכל צאן. ה"נ. כי מוקמינן לה בפסח, "מן" להוציא הוא, דלא אתי בן שתי שנים ולא אתי נקיבה. ומיהו "הצאן" – מכל מין צאן משמע, בין כבשים בין עזים, ומיעוטא ד"מן" לנקיבות אתא. ה"ג: דלא אתי בן שתי שנים ולא אתי נקיבה. והא מדכתיב אם כבש (ט) אם עז מכלל דלאו במותר הפסח הוא דכתיב. אלא בשלמים גרידי. וה"ק: אם נדר להביא מן הצאן – יביא איזה שירצה, או כבש או עז. דאי במותר הפסח כתיב – למה לי "אם כבש אם עז"? פשיטא דמכבשים ומעזים הוא בא, דהא בגופיה כתיב: "מן הכבשים ומן העזים" (שמות יב). לכדתניא כו'. לחלק ביניהם ולפרש הילכותיהן, לומר (י) שהכבש טעון אליה למזבח, והעז אין אלייתו בכלל אימורים. כבש. קרא יתירא הוא, דכיון דכתיב יח] [מעיקרא "ואם מן הצאן", וכתיב] בתריה "ואם עז" – מכלל דעד השתא בכבש איירי, דאין לך מן הצאן אלא שני מינין. לאליה. שתהא יט] קריבה עם אימורין כנגד הכליות ולמטה, דכתיב: "לעומת העצה יסירנה" – מקום שהכליות יועצות. שלמים הבאין מחמת פסח. חגיגת ארבעה עשר, כדאמרי' בפסחים (דף סט:). והא מהכא נפקא. דפסח שעברה שנתו קרב שלמים? והלא זה הוא מותר הפסח, והא ילפת לה לעיל מדאבוה דשמואל! ומאי ניהו שלמים. דבאין מכל צאן ובקר, בין זכרים ובין נקיבות.

עיברה

תוספות

דוחין קדשים קלים. נראה דבין ר' יוסי בר' אבין ורבי אבין איכא בינייהו בכור, דלרבי אבין ליכא למיפרך מבכור, דאין נאכל לכל אדם. דלא ליבעי נסכים. הוה מצי למימר דלא ליבעי תנופת חזה ושוק. כ] למאי נפקא מינה למילקא עליה בלא יגאל. תימה: היכי לקי אחר שחיטה כא] א"לא יגאל"? הא אמרינן בבכורות בפרק "כל פסולי המוקדשין" (דף לב:) דלאחר שחיטה מדרבנן? העשירי זה מעשר. אכתי דרשינן מינה (ב"מ דף ז.): עשירי ודאי ולא עשירי ספק. אי נמי דליתביה לכהנים. הוה מצי למימר נמי דלא בעי סמיכה, כדדרשינן בת"כ: "וסמך ידו על ראש קרבנו" ולא בכור ומעשר ופסח (מנחות דף לב:). דילמא במותר אשם כתיב. תימה: הא כתיב הכא "לזבח השלמים", ואילו מותר אשם קרב עולה! כב] וי"ל: דהאי דכתיב "לזבח השלמים" – לאו שיהיה לזבח השלמים, אלא שיעקור שם אשם ממנו לשוחטו לשם שלמים או לשם זבח אחר, כדדרשינן ליה (לעיל דף ח:) בכלל ופרט, ולעולם קרב עולה, ואתא קרא למימר דבעי עקירה. ושלמים הבאין מחמת פסח לכל מצות שלמים. פי' בקונטרס: חגיגת ארבעה עשר. וכן לקמן סוף "כל הפסולים" (דף לו.) גבי תודה שנאכלת ליום ולילה: מנין לרבות שלמי נזיר ושלמי פסח – ת"ל "שלמיו". ופי' בקונטרס: שלמי פסח – חגיגת י"ד. וקשה: דבפסחים ב"אלו דברים" (דף עא:) דריש מקרא בהדיא דחגיגת י"ד נאכלת לשני ימים ולילה אחד. כג] [ובת"כ בפ' "בשר זבח תודת שלמיו" מרבי חגיגת י"ד לשני ימים ולילה אחד], ושלמים הבאין מחמתו ליום ולילה! ונראה, דודאי שלמי פסח ד"כל הפסולין" (שם) היינו מותר הפסח, כד] כי ההוא דת"כ, ובפסחים פ' "האשה" (דף פט.) גבי חמשה שנתערבו עורות פסחיהם, דקאמר: וניתי מותר הפסח דנאכל ליום ולילה. ובפ"ק דר"ה (דף ה.) קרי למותר הפסח שלמי פסח. דחשיב פסח ל"בל תאחר". ופריך: פסח זימנא קביעא ליה כו'! ומשני: מאי פסח – שלמי פסח, סד"א הואיל ומחמת פסח קאתו. ועל כרחיה לאו היינו חגיגת י"ד, דכיון דקתני פסח – לא שביק מותר הפסח דמיקרי פסח טפי, דהיינו פסח ממש, ומוקי לה בחגיגת י"ד. ושלמים הבאין מחמת הפסח דשמעתין נמי היינו מותר הפסח. אע"ג דכבר תנא פסח שעיברה שנתו – האי שלמי פסח הוי לא עיברה שנתו כה] ולא זמנו, *)או עיברה זמנו ולא שנתו. אע"ג דמקרא אחרינא נפקי – הכי רגילות התנא, כמו (ב"מ דף ל.): "והתעלמת" דדריש פעמים שמתעלם, כגון זקן ואינה לפי כבודו, וכהן והוא בבית הקברות, כו] [ושלו מרובה משל חבירו. אע"ג] דקרא לא אתי אלא לזקן ואינה לפי כבודו. ובפ' "מי שהיה טמא" (פסחים דף צו:) פי' בקונטרס דהיינו תמורת פסח עצמו. ואע"ג דדרשינן התם: הוא קרב ואין תמורתו קריבה – הא מוכח התם דכל היכא דפסח קרב גם תמורתו קריבה. ולקמן פרק "ב"ש" (דף לז.) כז] בתחלתו נדקדק. וכן משמע דפריך: מותר הפסח ליהוי תודה, למאי? כח] להטעינו לחם. מי איכא מידי כו'. ולימא להיות נאכל ליום ולילה כמו תודה! אלא ש"מ: מותר פסח נמי בלאו הכי נאכלים ליום ולילה, דהיינו שלמי פסח. נ"ל ברו"ך.

חד

*) גי' רש"ק או עיברה זמנו ושנתו אע"ג כו'

שיטה מקובצת

א] ברבי סברין: ב] נסכים ולמלקא. ס"א ולמיקם עליה בלא (ימכר) [יגאל] תימה דהא [בפ' כל פסולי המוקדשים] ילפינן לה מתמורה מה תמורה מחיים אף [מעשר] מחיים וכי [עביד] פסח לשם מעשר אחר שחיטה הוא [ואינו עובר] עליו משום לא יגאל ואומר ריב"א דמכי שחיט [ליה] אתעקר משום פסח [ועדיין] הוא חי ואית ביה בלא יגאל כדאמרי' [יבמות דף קכ וגיטין דף ע] שחט שנים או רוב שנים הרי הוא כחי לכל דבריו. תוס' טוך: ג] תיבות בלא ימכר נמחק: ד] נסכים א"נ למיקם עליה בלא ימכר ובלא יגאל אי נמי כו': ה] תיבות א"נ למיקם עליה בלא ימכר ולא יגאל נמחק: ו] זו בתמורה: ז] דאתיא לה: ח] רב יימר: ט] והא מדכתיב אם כשב. פ"ה דאי במותר הפסח כו' וקשה לפי' שני דפי' לעיל דמייתורא דקרא קא דריש שפיר איצטריך אם כבש אם עז לגופיה לריבה ומיעט וריבה דכתיב גבי שלמים דאין מקרא יוצא מידי פשוטו והילכך איצטריך משום שלמים שאם נדר מן הצאן יביא מה שירצה או כבש או עז [ועוד] דלעיל היה לו להקשות זאת הקושיא לכך פי' הר"מ דהא אתקפתא להא דאמר דבר הבא מן הצאן דבר השוה בכל צאן וה"ק אא"ב במותר אשם איירי קרא ומאי מן הצאן מקצת צאן ניחא דאיצטריך אם כבש אם עז לגופיה לשלמים לומר שבאים מן הצאן שהרי מן הצאן ליכא למילף דהא הצאן לא משמע כי אם מקצת צאן דשייך באשם אלא אי אמרת קרא מיירי במותר הפסח ור"ל דבר הבא מכל צאן יהיה לזבח שלמים הא שלמים אקרי פסח ופסח ידעינן שפיר מקרא אחרינא שבא מכבש ועז דכתיב מן הכבשים ומן העזים תקחו וא"כ או כבש או עז למה לי אלא ש"מ דלא במותר פסח כתיב: י] שעיברה שנתו: יא] אלא תלתא קראי כתיבי. (פי') חד לקודם זמנו ונראה לפרש דקרא דלעיל ואם מן הצאן מיירי בקודם זמנו ולהכי בעי עקירה כדפי' לעיל לשמו פסול מכעין הפרט או מריבה ומיעט אבל אינך קראי מיירי לאחר זמנו ולא משתמע מינייהו דבעי עקירה אלא משתמע מינייהו דלגמרי הוו שלמים בלא עקירה ולמאן דאמר דלאחר זמנו נמי בעי עקירה אע"ג דלא מוכח מקראי מ"מ יליף לה מקודם זמנו וא"ת מאי פריך והא מהכא נפקא מהתם נפקא מן הצאן דבר הבא בכל צאן דמיירי קודם זמנו לעברה שנתו דאיירי לאחר זמנו וי"ל דעיקר [קושיא] מההיא דמייתי דזובחת פסח צאן ובקר מההיא דעברה שנתו דמיירי לאחר זמנו אבל מההיא דמן הצאן דמיירי קודם זמנו לא פריך דשפיר היה יודע דמיירי התם בקודם זמנו מדבעי עקירה ואגב דמצריך להו מצריך נמי קרא דמן הצאן כך נראה למורי. טוך: יב] שהועמדה: יג] והמיר בה הוא: יד] זבח אחר תיבת ראשון נמחק ס"א תיבת זבח אינו: טו] ניהוי ושלמים בעי סמיכה ונסכים הס"ד: טז] תיבת זבח נמחק: יז] דקאמרת מן הצאן: יח] מעיקרא ואם מן הצאן וכתיב: יט] שתהא אליתו קריבה עם אימוריו כנגד: כ] מה"ד ולמלקא ותיבות למאי נפקא מינה נמחק: כא] שחיטה על לא אות א' נמחק: כב] עולה לפר"ת או רועה לפרש"י כדאמרי' כל שבחטאת מתה באשם רועה וי"ל דאתא קרא לפרושי הא דאמרי' באשם רועה היינו קודם עקירה ששחטו סתמא אבל אם עקר אותו אשם בשעת שחיטה אשמועינן קרא דהוי שלמים. תוס' טוך: כג] אחד ובת"כ בפרשת בשר זבח תודת שלמיו מרבי חגיגת י"ד לשני ימים ולילה אחד: כד] הפסח אמנם ריב"א מפרש כפרש"י דבמותר פסח לא איירי א"כ היינו עברה שנתו: כה] עיברה שנתו וזמנו תיבת ולא ל"ש ונמחק: כו] ואבידתו מרובה תיבות ושלו משל חבירו ואע"ג ל"ש ונמחק: כז] בתחלתו מדקדק כן וכן משמע עוד לעיל דפריך: כח] למאי הלכתא:

הגהות הב"ח

(א) גמ' השוה בכל צאן כצ"ל ואות ה' נמחק: (ב) שם ולא אתי נקבה כצ"ל ואות ב' נמחק: (ג) שם מדכתיב אם כשב ואם עז: (ד) שם לכדתניא כשב לרבות: (ה) שם כשהוא אומר ואם עז: (ו) רש"י ד"ה דוחין וכו' אצל עולה שאין נאכל הס"ד: (ז) ד"ה זו תמורה תמורה ממש: (ח) ד"ה ואין אחר זבח אחר ששחטו: (ט) ד"ה והא מדכתיב וכו' ואם עז וכו' במותר פסח הוא וכו' במותר פסח כתיב למה לי אם כשב אם: (י) ד"ה לכדתניא וכו' לומר שהכשב וכו':

[לקמן לז: מעילה יג. תמורה ה:]

פסחים נו: לז. מנחות פג.

כמו ולעטמיך

[לעיל ז: מנחות פג: פסחים ע:]

חד

עין משפט נר מצוה

מד א מיי' פט"ו מהל' פסה"מ הל"ט:
מה ב מיי' שם הל"ז:
מו ג ד מיי' שם הל"ו:
מז ה מיי' שם הל"י:

*חד א] לעיברה זמנו ועיברה שנתו, וחד לעיברה זמנו ולא שנתו, וחד ללא עיברה לא זמנו ולא שנתו. וצריכי, דאי כתב רחמנא חד, הוה אמינא (א) – היכא ב] דעיברה שנתו וזמנו, דאידחי מפסח לגמרי, אבל עיברה זמנו ולא שנתו דחזי לפסח שני – אימא לא; ואי כתב רחמנא הני תרתי – משום דאידחי להו ממילתייהו, אבל היכא דלא עבר לא זמנו ולא שנתו, דחזי לפסח – אימא לא, צריכי.§ אמר רב משמיה דמבוג: חטאת ששחטה לשום חטאת נחשון – כשירה, דאמר קרא: °"זאת תורת החטאת", *תורה אחת לכל החטאות. יתיב רבא וקאמר לה להא שמעתא. איתיביה רב משרשיא לרבא, רבי שמעון אומר: *כל המנחות שנקמצו שלא לשמן – כשירות ועלו לבעלים לשום חובה, לפי שאין המנחות דומות לזבחים, שהקומץ מחבת לשם מרחשת – מעשיה מוכיחין עליה שהיא מחבת, חריבה לשם בלולה – מעשיה מוכיחין שהיא חריבה. אבל בזבחים אינו כן, שחיטה אחת לכולן, קבלה אחת לכולן, ג] זריקה אחת לכולן; טעמא דמעשיה מוכיחין, הא אין מעשיה מוכיחין – לא, אמאי? לימא: °"זאת תורת המנחה", *תורה אחת לכל המנחות! אלא אי איתמר הכי איתמר, אמר רב משמיה דמבוג: חטאת ששחטה על מנת שיתכפר בה נחשון – כשירה, אאין כפרה למתים. ולימא מת בעלמא! הא קמ"ל: טעמא דמת, הא ד] דחי דומיא דנחשון – פסולה, ומאי ניהו? חטאת נזיר וחטאת מצורע. ה] הני עולות נינהו! אלא אי איתמר הכי איתמר, אמר רב משמיה דמבוג: חטאת ששחטה על ו] שמחוייב חטאת כנחשון (ב) – כשירה, חטאת נחשון עולה היא. ז] איכא דאמר, אמר רב משמיה דמבוג: חטאת ששחטה (ג) לשם חטאת נחשון – פסולה, חטאת נחשון ח] עולה היא. ולימא: חטאת נזיר וחטאת מצורע! עיקר חטאת נקט. *אמר ט] *רב: חטאת חלב ששחטה לשם חטאת דם, לשם חטאת עבודה זרה – כשירה; לשם חטאת נזיר, לשם חטאת מצורע – פסולה, הני עולות נינהו. בעי רבא: חטאת חלב ששחטה לשם חטאת דטומאת מקדש וקדשיו, מהו? מי אמרינן כרת כמותה, או דילמא אין קבוע כמותה? י] *רב אחא בריה דרבא מתני בכולהו לפסולא, מ"ט? °"ושחט אותה לחטאת" – לשם אותה חטאת. א"ל רב אשי לרב אחא בריה דרבא: יא] [בעיא דרבא] היכי מתניתו לה? אמר ליה: אנן בשינוי בעלים מתנינן לה, יב] [והכי מתנינן לה] אמר רבא: גחטאת חלב ששחטה על מי שמחוייב חטאת דם וחטאת עבודה זרה – פסולה, על מי שמחוייב חטאת נזיר וחטאת מצורע – כשירה. יג] ובעיין לה הכי, בעי רבא: חטאת חלב ששחטה על מי שמחוייב חטאת דטומאת מקדש וקדשיו, מהו? מי אמרי' כרת דכמותה, או יד] דילמא אין קבוע כמותה? תיקו.§ *איתמר: שחטה לשמה לזרוק דמה שלא לשמה – רבי יוחנן אמר:ה פסולה, וריש לקיש אמר: כשירה. ר' יוחנן אמר פסולה – מחשבין מעבודה לעבודה, וילפינן ממחשבת פיגול. ור"ל אמר כשירה – אין מחשבין מעבודה לעבודה, ולא ילפינן ממחשבת פיגול. ואזדו לטעמייהו, דאיתמר: השוחט

ויקרא ו | שם | [צ"ל דרבא] | [ד' ה.] | מנחות ג: | [שם ג:] | שם ד | חולין לב:

טו] עיברה זמנו. זמן שחיטת הפסח. לא זמנו ולא שנתו. טז] ואם שחטו קודם הפסח לשם שלמים – כשר, ואע"ג דחזי לפסח ראשון. ממילתייהו. מפסח ראשון. משמיה דמבוג. שם חכם. חטאת ששחטה לשם חטאת נחשון. שעיר יז] חטאת [דחנוכת] הנשיאים. כשרה. ולא הויא שינוי קדש. דלא אמרי': חטאת נחשון, כיון דלדורון אתי ולא לכפרה על חטא – הרי היא (ד) יח] כשחיטה לשם עולה. וכ"ש דשינוי בעלים לא הוי, דלא שחטה להתכפר בה נחשון. ועלו לבעלים. ר"ש פליג אמנחות ומודה בזבחים. מחבת ומרחשת. שני כלים שבהם מטגנים את המנחות, שכל המנחות היו יט] עשר עשר חלות. מחבת צפה ומעשיה קשים – (ה) כ] מתוך שהכלי צף מעשיה מתפשטין, והאור שורף את השמן. מרחשת עמוקה, ומעשיה רוחשין ורכין – שאין האור שורף את השמן, וכשמניח אדם אצבעו עליה נראה כמו כא] רוחשת. חריבה. מנחת חוטא שאין בה שמן, דכתיב (ויקרא ה): "לא ישים עליה שמן". מעשיה מוכיחין. דמחשבה הניכרת שהיא שקר, סבר ר"ש דלא מהניא. שחיטה אחת לכולן. וכי שחיט עולה לשם חטאת ליכא היכרא דמשקר, הילכך מהניא כב] מחשבה. כ"ך שמעתי' במנחו"ת. טעמא כו'. אלמא אפי' לרבי שמעון דמהדר (ו) להיכשירא לא יליף מ"זאת תורת" וכ"ש דמדרבנן קשיא לך, דאמרי: אף במנחות לא עלו – אלמא לא דרשי כג] "תורה" להכי. ולרבא דאמר לעיל (דף ז.): חטאת חלב ששחטה לשם חטאת דם כשירה – ליכא למיפרך מינה, דהתם כיון דכי הדדי נינהו, דתרוייהו חטאת סתמא שמייהו, וכפרת שתיהן שוה על הכרת – אין שם שינוי קודש, והרי חטאת לשם חטאת נשחטה. ואילו מנחת מחבת ומנחת מרחשת – אין שמותיהן שוין, זו שמה לבדה וזו שמה לבדה. אלא לרב קשיא, דהא לשם חטאת נחשון שינוי גמור הוא, שהרי היא כעולה, וקאמר: כשרה, משום "תורת כד] חטאת". אלא אי איתמר. דרב, הכי איתמר, ובשינוי בעלים איתמר. שיתכפר בה (ז). היינו שינוי בעלים. שאין כפרה למתים. הילכך לא קרינא ביה במחוייב כפרה כמותו. הא חי. אם שחטה בשינוי בעלים לשם אדם חי. דומיא דנחשון. שמחוייב חטאת שאינה על חטא, הדומה לשעיר נחשון, כגון חטאת נזיר ומצורע הבאות להכשיר פסולה. ופרכינן הני עולות נינהו. ותנן כה] קיס לן לעיל (דף ז.): חטאת ששחטה על מי שמחוייב עולה – כשירה, והני כעולה דמו! כו]. פשיטא ל"ג. עיקר חטאת נקט. שורש החטאת, שהיא היתה חטאת יחיד ראשונה כז]. לשם חטאת עבודה זרה. רבותא נקט, אע"ג דלא דמיא לשאר חטאות, שהן בכבשה או שעירה, והיא אינה כשירה בכבשה אלא בשעירה כח]. בעיא דרבא היכי מתניתו לה. (ח) וכיון דאמרת דרבא בכולהו פסיל, ואפילו חטאת חלב לשם חטאת דם – כ"ש לשם חטאת דטומאת מקדש וקדשיו! מי אמרינן כרת כמותה. והוה ליה מחוייב כפרה כמותו, וקרינן ביה: "עליו" ולא על חבירו, וחבירו דומיא דידיה. או דילמא (ט) כו', דאין קבוע כמותו, שבא בעולה ויורד. שחטה לשמה. שלא חישב על השחיטה, אלא על הזריקה חישב בשעת שחיטה, דהיינו מעבודה לעבודה. מחשבין מעבודה לעבודה. כלומר: מחשבה מועלת מעבודה לעבודה, במחשבת שלא לשמו. כט] דילפינן ממחשבת פיגול. דמהניא ביה *הכי, דתנן בפרק שני (לקמן דף כז:): השוחט את הזבח על מנת לזרוק דמו למחר – פיגול. אין מחשבין מעבודה לעבודה. בשלא לשמו, דלא ילפינן לה מפיגול. דהתם עיקר מחשבתו המביאה לידי פיגול זו היא – ל] שיחשוב בעבודה זו לעשות עבודה אחרת מן אחת העבודות, להאכיל לאדם או למזבח חוץ לזמנו. וזריקה אכילת מזבח היא, והוא הדין לא] אם חישב על הקטרת החלב שאינה מן לב] עבודות. הילכך לא דמיא לשלא לשמו. השוחט

חד לעיברה שנתו וזמנו. ה"ה שנתו בלא זמנו, ואע"פ שבשעה שהקדישו לא היה ראוי לפסח, דכשיגיע זמנו – תעבור שנתו. דאפי' לג] מפריש נקיבה לפסחו או זכר בין שתי שנים – תורת שלמים עליו, כדתנן ב"מי שהיה טמא" (פסחים דף צז:): ירעה עד שיסתאב, וימכר ויביא בדמיו שלמים. איתיביה רב משרשיא לרבא כו'. לד] תימה: מאי קושיא? הא רבא הוא דמפרש טעמא דר"ש בריש מנחות (דף ג.): מ"זאת תורת"! ואומר ר"ת: דהכא גרסי' "רבה". ורבה לטעמיה, דמשני התם: כאן בשינוי קודש, כאן בשינוי בעלים. ועוד י"ל: דאפי' גרסינן "רבא" – רוצה ליישב דברי רב לכולהו אמוראי דהתם. ולפי' ר"ת קשה, דנראה דרב משרשיא תלמידו של רבא היה, ולא של רבה. ועוד י"ל: שרוצה רבא ליישב דברי רב משמיה דמבוג אפי' כרבנן דפליגי עליה דר"ש, דלית להו "זאת תורת". ורב משרשיא כשהקשה לו מר"ש היה יכול להקשות ממתני' דמנחות, אלא ניחא ליה למיפרך מברייתא, דאפי' לר"ש דמכשיר – לא מ"זאת תורת" מכשיר. וכן משמע מפי' הקונטרס. ואע"ג דבפ' "דם חטאת" (לקמן דף צג.) דרשינן: תורה אחת לכל החטאות, וליכא מאן דפליג – היינו במידי דכתיבא בהדיא בחטאת גופה דרשינן ליה לכ"ע, כגון לה] הני דפרק "דם חטאת". אבל שינוי קודש – לא כתב בחטאת. ובריש "איזהו מקומן" (לקמן דף מח.) דדריש: תורה אחת לכל האשמות. וקאמר: הניחא למאן דאית ליה "תורת", אלא למאן דלית ליה תורת – היינו לר"ש, ולרבנן לו] בריש מנחות (דף ג:) לרבא. לשם חטאת נזיר לשם חטאת מצורע. לעיל (דף ז.) איכא שמעתא אחריתי לז] *דרב, דמחלק בין שוחט [לשם חטאת] לשוחט לשם עולה. ושם פירשתי תרתי דרבא למה לי. [צ"ל דרבא] ושחט אותה לחטאת. לעיל בפירקין *דרשינן ליה [ד' ה.] למילתא אחריתי. ושמא הכא דריש מדלא כתיב "ושחט לחטאת אותה". על מי שמחוייב חטאת דטומאת מקדש וקדשיו מהו. *מיהו גרע ממי שאינו מחוייב כלום. מחשבין מעבודה לעבודה. כדאמר: כגון משחיטה לזריקה לח] (כמו שינוי בעלים). אבל משחיטה לקבלה – לא, דהא מפיגול יליף לה. וק"ו לט] דרב אשי דיליף משינוי בעלים *) לא הוי אלא משחיטה לזריקה, כמו שינוי בעלי'.

*) נ"א נמי לא הוי כו' נ"ק ותימה

שיטה מקובצת

א] חד לעברה זמנו ועברה שנתו וחד לעברה זמנו כו' ללא עברה: ב] היכא דעברה כו' אבל עברה: ג] זריקה אחת לכולן כו'. ולא אמר הולכה אחת לכולן משום דר"ש היא דמכשיר בהילוך משום דהוי עבודה דאפשר לבטלה והא דקאמר זריקה אחת לכולן ואע"ג דיש ניתנין במתן ד' ויש ניתנין במתן אחת הוא אין מעשיה מוכיחין דהא קיי"ל כל הניתנין במתן ד' שנתנן במתן אחת כיפר. תום' טוך: ד] הא חי דומיא: ה] הני עולות נינהו. ואין זו שינוי בעלים דלא פסלינן שינוי בעלים אלא א"כ שינה למחוייב כפרה כמותו וכיון דעולה לאו לכפרה אתא א"כ אין מחוייב כפרה כמותו. טוך: ו] על מי שמחוייב: ז] עולה היא ס"א ולאו בר מינה ואינו שינוי בעלים: ח] נחשון כעולה הוא אות י' נמחק: ט] אמר רבא: י] כמותה תיקו: יא] דרבא בעיא דרבא: יב] לה והכי מתנינן לה אמר רבא: יג] כשירה דהני עולות נינהו (והוי) [ולא הוי] שינוי בעלים דלאו מינה ובעיין: יד] דילמא אין קבוע כמותה. הקשה הר"ר יחיאל מפאריז תיפשוט ליה מדידיה דלא בעי קבוע כמותה דאי בעי (לעיל) אמאי איצטריך [לעיל לומר] הני עולות נינהו תיפוק ליה דחטאת מצורע אינו קבוע כמותה וי"ל דאיצטריך להאי טעמא דעולות נינהו משום חטאת דשמיעות הקול וביטוי שפתים פי' דשוחט חטאת דשמיעת קול על מי שמחוייב חטאת נזיר או חטאת מצורע דעתה אין קבוע יותר מזה. תום' טוך: טו] עברה: טז] אם: יז] שעיר חנוכת הנשיאים: יח] (כשחיטה) כשחוטה (ס"א כשירה): יט] היו באות עשר: כ] קשים שמתוך שהכלי: כא] כמו שרוחש הס"ד: כב] מהניא מחשבתו הס"ד והשאר נמחק: כג] דרשי זאת תורת: כד] תורת החטא': כה] ואנן קיימא לן: כו] דמו וי"מ הני עולה נינהו ושינוי קודש הוא ופשיט' דפסולה. גליון: כז] ראשונה וי"מ חטאת ראשונה (שמצינו שלא בא) [שלא מצינו שבא] על חטאת נקט: כח] בשעירה והוי כשינוי קודש אפ"ה כיון דכרת כמותו מין חטאת חד הוי. גליון: כט] מה"ד וילפינן ממחשבת כו' ביה כה"ג דתנן תיבת הכי נמחק: ל] היא שיחשב אות ו' נמחק ס"א שיחשב בשעת מאחת העבודות להאכיל כו': לא] הדין נמי: לב] העבודות: לג] דאפי' הפריש נקבה: לד] כו' טעמא דמעשיה מוכיחי' כו' ולא אמר תורה אחת והדר ביה רבא מכח קושיא זו וטעמא משום דמעשיה מוכיחים וקשה מידי הוא טעמא אלא לרבא ורבא קאמר התם דלאו משום מעשיה מוכיחים אלא משום זאת תורת כו'. תום' טוך: לה] כגון האי דפרק דם חטאת. ול"ל כולה להכי הוא דאתא דא"כ לכתוב ושחט לאותה חטאת ח"א גליון: לו] ולרבנן דריש מנחות: לז] אחריתי דרבא דמחלק בין שוחט לשם חטאת לשוחט: לח] תיבות כמו שינוי בעלים נמחק: לט] וק"ו נמי דרב אשי:

מסורת הש"ס

מנחות פג:
[מנחות ג:]
תוספתא דמנחות רפ"ק מנחות ב: מט.
[מנחות ג.]
[נ"ל רבא וכן משמע בתוס' דף ז. ד"ה אמר רבא ע"ש]
דמהניא ביה דתנן כו'

הגהות הב"ח

(א) גמ' הוה אמינא ה"מ היכא דעיברה: (ב) שם כנחשון כשרה חטאת. נ"ב פי' דהכי הוי דינא בשינוי בעלים: (ג) שם לשם חטאת נחשון פסולה. נ"ב פי' דהכי הוי דינא בשינוי קדש: (ד) רש"י ד"ה כשרה וכו' הרי היא כנשחטה לשם: (ה) ד"ה מחבת וכו' דמתוך: (ו) ד"ה טעמא וכו' להכשירה לא יליף מזאת התורה: (ז) ד"ה שיתכפר בה נחשון היינו שינוי בעלים הס"ד ואח"כ מ"ה אין וכו' במחוייב כפרה. נ"ב ע"ל תחילת דף ד' ודף ז' סוף ע"א: (ח) ד"ה בעיא וכו' דכיון: (ט) ד"ה מי אמרי' וכו' או דילמא אין כצ"ל ותיבת כו' נמחק:

מח א מיי' פ"ב מהל' שחיטה הלכה טו סמג עשין סג טוש"ע יו"ד סימן ז סעיף א:
מט ב מיי' שם הלכה טז:

גמרא

*הַשּׁוֹחֵט אֶת הַבְּהֵמָה ע"מ לִזְרוֹק דָּמָהּ לַעֲבוֹדָה זָרָה, וּלְהַקְטִיר חֶלְבָּהּ לַעֲבוֹדָה זָרָה — ר' יוֹחָנָן אָמַר: אאֲסוּרָה; מְחַשְּׁבִין מֵעֲבוֹדָה לַעֲבוֹדָה, בוְיָלְפִינַן חוּץ מִפְּנִים. א] רֵישׁ לָקִישׁ אָמַר: מוּתֶּרֶת; אֵין מְחַשְּׁבִין מֵעֲבוֹדָה לַעֲבוֹדָה, וְלָא יָלְפִינַן חוּץ מִפְּנִים. ב] *וְאִי אַשְׁמְעִינַן בְּהָא — בְּהָא אָמַר רֵישׁ לָקִישׁ, ג] אֲבָל פְּנִים מִפְּנִים אֵימָא מוֹדֵי לֵיהּ לְרַבִּי יוֹחָנָן; וְאִי אַשְׁמְעִינַן הָא — בְּהָא קָאָמַר רַבִּי יוֹחָנָן, אֲבָל בְּהַהִיא אֵימָא מוֹדֵי לֵיהּ לְרֵישׁ לָקִישׁ, צְרִיכִי. כִּי אֲתָא רַב דִּימִי אֲמַר: מְתִיב רַב יִרְמְיָה לְסִיּוּעֵיהּ לְרַבִּי יוֹחָנָן, וְרַבִּי אִילְעָא לְסִיּוּעֵיהּ לְרֵישׁ לָקִישׁ. רַב יִרְמְיָה לְסִיּוּעֵיהּ לְרַבִּי יוֹחָנָן: וּמַה בְּמָקוֹם שֶׁאִם אָמַר "הֲרֵינִי שׁוֹחֵט חוּץ לִזְמַנּוֹ" שֶׁהוּא כָּשֵׁר, שְׁחָטוֹ עַל מְנָת לִזְרוֹק דָּמוֹ חוּץ לִזְמַנּוֹ — פָּסוּל, מָקוֹם שֶׁאִם אָמַר "הֲרֵינִי שׁוֹחֵט שֶׁלֹּא לִשְׁמוֹ" פָּסוּל, שְׁחָטוֹ עַל מְנָת ד] לִזְרוֹק דָּמוֹ שֶׁלֹּא לִשְׁמוֹ — אֵינוֹ דִּין שֶׁיְּהֵא פָּסוּל? מַתְקִיף לָהּ רָבָא בַּר אֲהִילַאי: מַה לְּחוּץ לִזְמַנּוֹ (א) *שֶׁכֵּן כָּרֵת! אֶלָּא אָמַר רָבָא בַּר אֲהִילַאי, הָכִי קָאָמַר: וּמַה מָּקוֹם שֶׁאִם אָמַר "הֲרֵינִי שׁוֹחֵט חוּץ לִמְקוֹמוֹ" שֶׁהוּא כָּשֵׁר, שְׁחָטוֹ עַל מְנָת לִזְרוֹק דָּמוֹ חוּץ לִמְקוֹמוֹ — פָּסוּל, מָקוֹם שֶׁאִם אָמַר "הֲרֵינִי שׁוֹחֵט שֶׁלֹּא לִשְׁמוֹ" שֶׁהוּא פָּסוּל, ה] [שְׁחָטוֹ ע"מ] לִזְרוֹק דָּמוֹ שֶׁלֹּא לִשְׁמוֹ — אֵינוֹ דִּין שֶׁיְּהֵא פָּסוּל? מַתְקִיף לָהּ רַב אַשִׁי: מַה לְּחוּץ לִמְקוֹמוֹ — שֶׁכֵּן נוֹהֵג בְּכָל הַזְּבָחִים, תֹּאמַר בְּשֶׁלֹּא לִשְׁמוֹ — שֶׁאֵינוֹ נוֹהֵג אֶלָּא בְּפֶסַח וְחַטָּאת! אֶלָּא אָמַר רַב אַשִׁי, הָכִי קָאָמַר: וּמַה בְּמָקוֹם שֶׁאִם אָמַר "הֲרֵינִי שׁוֹחֵט לְשֵׁם פְּלוֹנִי" שֶׁהוּא כָּשֵׁר, לִזְרוֹק דָּמוֹ ו] (שֶׁלֹּא לִשְׁמוֹ) לְשֵׁם פְּלוֹנִי — פָּסוּל, מָקוֹם שֶׁאִם אָמַר "הֲרֵינִי שׁוֹחֵט שֶׁלֹּא ז] (ג) לִשְׁמָן" שֶׁהוּא פָּסוּל, [שְׁחָטוֹ ע"מ] לִזְרוֹק דָּמָן שֶׁלֹּא לִשְׁמָן — אֵינוֹ דִּין שֶׁיְּהֵא פָּסוּל? רַבִּי אִילְעָא לְסִיּוּעֵיהּ לְרֵישׁ לָקִישׁ: לֹא תֹּאמַר בִּזְרִיקָה, וְתֵיתֵי מִק"ו מִבֵּינַיְיא, מִשְּׁחִיטָה וְקַבָּלָה, לְמַאי הִלְכְתָא כְּתַב רַחֲמָנָא? לוֹמַר, דְּאֵין מְחַשְּׁבִין מֵעֲבוֹדָה לַעֲבוֹדָה. מַתְקִיף לָהּ רַב פַּפָּא: וְדִלְמָא דִּמְחַשְּׁבִין מֵעֲבוֹדָה לַעֲבוֹדָה! אִם כֵּן, לִשְׁתּוֹק קְרָא מִינֵּיהּ, וְתֵיתֵי מִקַּל וָחוֹמֶר דְּרַב אַשִׁי. וְאִידָךְ, פָּרֵיךְ הָכִי: מַה לְּהָנָךְ, שֶׁכֵּן טְעוּנוֹת צָפוֹן וְיֶשְׁנָן בְּחַטָּאוֹת הַפְּנִימִיּוֹת. וְאִידָךְ: ח] הָשְׁתָּא מִיהָא בִּשְׁלָמִים קַיְימִין. אִיתְּמַר: שְׁחָטָהּ לִשְׁמָהּ לִזְרוֹק דָּמָהּ שֶׁלֹּא לִשְׁמָהּ — רַב נַחְמָן אָמַר: פְּסוּלָה, ט] רַבָּה אָמַר: כְּשֵׁרָה. וַהֲדַר בֵּיהּ רַבָּה לְגַבֵּי רַב נַחְמָן מִק"ו דְּרַב אַשִׁי.§ "רַבִּי אֱלִיעֶזֶר אוֹמֵר: אַף (אֶת) הָאָשָׁם".§ תַּנְיָא, *אָמַר ר' אֱלִיעֶזֶר: חַטָּאת בָּאָה עַל חֵטְא וְאָשָׁם בָּא עַל חֵטְא, מַה חַטָּאת שֶׁלֹּא לִשְׁמָהּ — פְּסוּלָה, אַף אָשָׁם שֶׁלֹּא לִשְׁמוֹ — פָּסוּל. אָמַר לוֹ רַבִּי יְהוֹשֻׁעַ: לֹא, אִם אָמַרְתָּ בְּחַטָּאת שֶׁכֵּן דָּמָהּ לְמַעְלָה! אָמַר לוֹ רַבִּי אֱלִיעֶזֶר: פֶּסַח יוֹכִיחַ, שֶׁדָּמוֹ לְמַטָּה וּשְׁחָטוֹ שֶׁלֹּא לִשְׁמוֹ — פָּסוּל. אָמַר לוֹ רַבִּי יְהוֹשֻׁעַ: מַה לְּפֶסַח שֶׁכֵּן זְמַנּוֹ קָבוּעַ! אָמַר לוֹ רַבִּי אֱלִיעֶזֶר: חַטָּאת תּוֹכִיחַ. אָמַר לוֹ רַבִּי יְהוֹשֻׁעַ:

חוֹזְרַנִי

רש"י

הַשּׁוֹחֵט אֶת הַבְּהֵמָה. שֶׁל חוּלִּין (ג) לַעֲבוֹדָה זָרָה – אֲסוּרָה בַּהֲנָאָה כְּדִין זִבְחֵי מֵתִים, וְזִבְחֵי מֵתִים יָלְפִינַן (ע"ז דף כט:) "שָׁם" "שָׁם" מֵעֶגְלָה עֲרוּפָה. לִזְרוֹק דָּמָהּ לַעֲבוֹדָה זָרָה. (וַעֲבוֹדַת) הַשְּׁחִיטָה לֹא נַעֲשֵׂית לְשֵׁם עֲבוֹדָה זָרָה, אֶלָּא בִּשְׁעַת שְׁחִיטָה חִישֵּׁב י] *לַעֲבוֹד הַזְּרִיקָה לְשֵׁם עֲבוֹדָה זָרָה, וְלֹא זָרַק. מְחַשְּׁבִין מֵעֲבוֹדָה לַעֲבוֹדָה. מַחֲשָׁבָה הִיא לְעִנְיַן זִבְחֵי מֵתִים, יא] לֵיאָסֵר בַּהֲנָאָה. דְּיָלְפִינַן. עֲבוֹדָה זָרָה שֶׁהִיא חוּץ, מִמַּחֲשֶׁבֶת פִּיגּוּל שֶׁהוּא פְּנִים. מוּתֶּרֶת. לַאֲכִילָה. אֵין מְחַשְּׁבִין מֵעֲבוֹדָה לַעֲבוֹדָה. וְאֵינָהּ אֲסוּרָה אֶלָּא אִם כֵּן שָׁחַט לַעֲבוֹדָה זָרָה, שֶׁבִּשְׁחִיטָתָהּ עָבַד עֲבוֹדָה זָרָה, אוֹ זָרַק יב] לַעֲבוֹדָה זָרָה. פְּנִים מִפְּנִים. מַחֲשֶׁבֶת שֶׁלֹּא לִשְׁמוֹ מִפִּיגּוּל. הֲרֵינִי שׁוֹחֵט חוּץ לִזְמַנּוֹ. וְלֹא חִישֵּׁב עַל מְנָת לֶאֱכוֹל, וְלֹא עַל מְנָת לִזְרוֹק אוֹ לְהַקְטִיר, אֶלָּא עַל הַשְּׁחִיטָה חִישֵּׁב סְתָם חוּץ לִזְמַנָּהּ – כָּשֵׁר. דְּלָאו מַחֲשָׁבָה הִיא, יג] *דְּאֵין זְמַן אֶלָּא בַּאֲכִילַת אָדָם (ד) וּמִזְבֵּחַ יד] (דְּזֶהוּ) פִּיגּוּל. שֶׁכֵּן כָּרֵת. הָאוֹכֵל פִּיגּוּל אֲפִי' לְאַלְתַּר חַיָּיב כָּרֵת, הוֹאִיל וְחָמוּר – מְהַנְּיָא בֵּיהּ מֵעֲבוֹדָה לַעֲבוֹדָה. הֲרֵינִי שׁוֹחֲטוֹ חוּץ לִמְקוֹמוֹ. שֶׁלֹּא חִישֵּׁב לֹא עַל אֲכִילָה וְלֹא עַל זְרִיקָה, אֶלָּא (ה) טו] אָמַר: הֲרֵינִי שׁוֹחֵט חוּץ לִמְקוֹמוֹ – כָּשֵׁר, דְּהָא חָזֵינַן דִּבִמְקוֹמוֹ הוּא שׁוֹחֲטוֹ. וְעוֹד, דַּבַּאֲכִילַת אָדָם אוֹ מִזְבֵּחַ תָּלָה רַחֲמָנָא לְחוּץ לִמְקוֹמוֹ וְחוּץ לִזְמַנּוֹ, דִּכְתִיב: "וְאִם הֵאָכֹל יֵאָכֵל" וגו' וְיָלְפִינַן חוּץ לִמְקוֹמוֹ וְחוּץ לִזְמַנּוֹ מֵהַאי קְרָא לְקַמָּן (דף יג.). עַל מְנָת לִזְרוֹק דָּמוֹ חוּץ לִמְקוֹמוֹ (ו) טז] כו' פָּסוּל. (בְּפֶרֶק שֵׁנִי). וְהָשְׁתָּא לֵיכָּא לְמִפְרַךְ שֶׁכֵּן כָּרֵת – שֶׁאֵין חַיָּיבִין כָּרֵת עַל אֲכִילָתָן, כִּדְתַנְיָא לְקַמָּן [בְּפֶרֶק שֵׁנִי] (דף כח.). שָׁחַט לְשֵׁם פְּלוֹנִי כָּשֵׁר. דְּאֵין שִׁינּוּי בְּעָלִים חָל עַל הַשְּׁחִיטָה, דְּלֹא שַׁיָּיךְ שֵׁם בְּעָלִים אֶלָּא עַל הַכַּפָּרָה. וְהַיְינוּ דַּאֲמָרַן לְעֵיל (דף ד.) דְּשִׁינּוּי בְּעָלִים אֵינוֹ בְּד' עֲבוֹדוֹת. לֹא תֹּאמַר בִּזְרִיקָה. מְחַשְּׁבִין שֶׁלֹּא לִשְׁמוֹ, דְּרַבִּינַן לֵיהּ (ז) לְעֵיל יז] בְּכוּלְּהוּ עֲבוֹדוֹת. מִשְּׁחִיטָה וְקַבָּלָה. וּמַה שְּׁחִיטָה שֶׁכְּשֵׁרָה בְּזָר פְּסוּלָה בְּשֶׁלֹּא לִשְׁמָהּ, זְרִיקָה לֹא כָּל שֶׁכֵּן? יח] כִּי פָּרְכַתְּ: מַה לִּשְׁחִיטָה שֶׁכֵּן פּוֹסֶלֶת שֶׁלֹּא לְשֵׁם אוֹכְלִין בְּפֶסַח – קַבָּלָה תּוֹכִיחַ. דְּאֵין מְחַשְּׁבִין מֵעֲבוֹדָה לַעֲבוֹדָה. אֶלָּא בִּשְׁעַת זְרִיקָה גּוּפָהּ בָּעֵי מִיחְשַׁב. וְדִלְמָא. לְהָכִי כְּתָבֵיהּ, לְאַשְׁמוּעִינַן רְבוּתָא דִּמְחַשְּׁבִין מֵעֲבוֹדָה לַעֲבוֹדָה, יט] [שֶׁלֹּא] בִּשְׁעַת זְרִיקָה גּוּפָהּ בָּעֵי מְחַשֵּׁב. דַּאֲפִי' לֹא חִישֵּׁב עַל הַזְּרִיקָה בִּשְׁעָתָהּ, אֶלָּא בִּשְׁעַת שְׁחִיטָה – הָוְיָא מַחֲשָׁבָה. אִם כֵּן. דִּמְחַשְּׁבִין אָתָא לְאַשְׁמוּעִינַן, לִשְׁתּוֹק קְרָא מִינֵּיהּ, וְתֵיתֵי דִּמְחַשְּׁבִין מִקַּל וָחוֹמֶר דְּרַב אַשִׁי, כִּדְאָמְרַן: וּמָה אִם בְּמָקוֹם שֶׁאִם אָמַר הֲרֵינִי שׁוֹחֵט לְשֵׁם פְּלוֹנִי כו'. וְאִידָךְ. רַבִּי יוֹחָנָן, פָּרֵיךְ הָכִי: דְּלָא נָפְקָא לָן זְרִיקָה מִקַּל וָחוֹמֶר דְּקַבָּלָה וּשְׁחִיטָה. מַה לְּהָנָךְ כו'. הִלְכָּךְ לָאו קְרָא יְתֵירָא הוּא, דְּנֵילִיף מִינֵּיהּ דְּאֵין מְחַשְּׁבִין. הָשְׁתָּא מִיהַת בִּשְׁלָמִים קַיְימִינַן. דְּבִשְׁלָמִים כְּתִיבָא מַחֲשָׁבָה שֶׁלֹּא לִשְׁמוֹ, כ] הִלְכָּךְ מָלֵי לְמֵילַף זְרִיקָה מִשְּׁחִיטָה וְקַבָּלָה. וְלֵיכָּא לְמִיפְרַךְ צָפוֹן – דִּשְׁלָמִים לָא בָּעֵי צָפוֹן, וְלֵיתְנְהוּ פְּנִימִיּוֹת. שֶׁכֵּן דָּמָהּ לְמַעְלָה. מִחוּט הַסִּיקְרָא. דִּתְנַן בְּמַסֶּ' מִדּוֹת (פ"ג מ"א): חוּט הַסִּיקְרָא חוֹגֶרֶת בָּאֶמְצַע לְהַבְדִּיל בֵּין דָּמִים עֶלְיוֹנִים לְדָמִים הַתַּחְתּוֹנִים. וְיָלֵיף לְקַמָּן (דף נג.) מִן "וְהָיְתָה הָרֶשֶׁת עַד חֲצִי הַמִּזְבֵּחַ" – הַתּוֹרָה נָתְנָה מְחִיצָּה לְהַבְדִּיל. וְחַטַּאת בְּהֵמָה כא] נַעֲשֵׂית לְמַעְלָה, דִּכְתִיב בָּהּ (ויקרא ד): "עַל קַרְנוֹת", וְכֵן עוֹלַת הָעוֹף כִּדְלְקַמָּן (דף סד:). וּשְׁאָר זְבָחִים – שֶׁלֹּא פֵּירֵשׁ בָּהֶן – נַעֲשִׂין לְמַטָּה, דִּכְתִיב בְּהוּ "מִזְבֵּחַ" וְלָא כְּתִיב בְּהוּ קְרָנוֹת. וְכוּלֵּיהּ מִזְבֵּחַ לֵיכָּא לְמֵימַר כב] דַּהֲוֵה מְקוֹמָן, שֶׁהֲרֵי תּוֹרָה נָתְנָה מְחִיצָּה.

חוֹזְרַנִי

תוספות

ותימה: דלקמן (דף יג.) דפריך: וקבלה מי פסלה כו', ומשני: כאן במחשבת שלא לשמן, כאן במחשבת פיגול. אמאי לא משני: אידי ואידי במחשבת שלא לשמן, וקבלה כג] לא עשה בה מחשבה כמעשה, כגון בשוחט על מנת לקבל שלא לשמן, וזריקה כד] (לא) עשה בה מחשבה כמעשה? ונראה לי: דלקמן מיירי שחישב בעבודה עצמה, אם קבל [לגמור הקבלה] שלא לשמן – פסול, ואם קבל [לגמור] חוץ לזמנו – כשר. ואם זרק לגמור הזריקה חוץ לזמנו – פסול. וכן מקטיר לגמור ההקטרה למחר, דהוה פסול, אי לאו דמעטיה קרא לקמן משום דאין מעכבת כפרה. אבל ליכא לפרושי לקמן מחשבת פיגול דלא פסלה בקבלה – כגון שוחט על מנת לקבל כה] דמן חוץ לזמנו. דבשלא לשמן נמי לא פסלה, דמעבודה לעבודה ילפינן מפיגול *(ואי) במקבל על מנת לזרוק חוץ לזמנו הוה פיגול אלא כדפרשינן, בחישב בעבודה עצמה. ברו"ך. *ובלאו הכי תימה: דהוי מלי למימר קבלה לא עשה בה מחשבה כמעשה לענין שינוי בעלים.

ריש לקיש אמר מותרת. מודה ר"ל דחייב מיתה, כדאמרינן בפרק "ארבע מיתות" (סנהדרין סא.) מידי דהוה אמשתחוה להר, דהר מותר כו] ועובדו בסייף. ושחיטת מומר לא חשיב, כדפי' בפ"ק דחולין (דף יד.) גבי שוחט בשבת. ואין לתמוה: והיאך נהרג? דילמא מימלך ולא זריק לעבודה זרה, כדאמר בפרק "ד' מיתות" (סנהדרין סא.) כז] דניסת שאמר "אלך אעבוד" – פטור, דמימלך ולא עביד! דהכא ודאי לא מימלך, כיון דעבד מעשה, ששחט על מנת לזרוק. ועוד, הכא אפילו ידוע ודאי שלא יזרוק – חשיב עובד עבודה זרה בשחיטה [זו], כששוחט ע"מ לזרוק.

מקום שאם אמר הריני שוחט שלא לשמן כו'. וא"ת: שוחט שלא לשם אוכלין בפסח יוכיח, דשוחט שלא לשם אוכלין פסול, ושוחט ע"מ לזרוק שלא לשם אוכלין – כשר! ויש לומר: דלא דמי כח] התם, דזורק עצמו שלא לשם אוכלין – כשר.

לא תאמר בזריקה ותיתי בק"ו משחיטה וקבלה. תימה: כט] אמאי לא פריך: שכן טעונות לפון, וישנן בחטאות הפנימיות! וכ"ת: משום דבשלמים ל] קיימא – אם כן מאי לריך למילף מבינייא? ניליף בק"ו לא] מקבלה, שאין חייבין עליה בחוץ, ואפילו הכי פסלה בה מחשבה? ועוד: למה לי קרא בזריקה לשינוי בעלים, דדרשי' "לכפר עליו"? תיתי מבינייא משחיטה וקבלה! ועוד קשה: אמאי אין מחשבת אוכלין בפסח בזריקה? תיתי בק"ו משחיטה שכשירה בזר, כיון דלא פרכינן מלפון וחטאות הפנימיות! ומיהו, דילמא לב] (תכוסו) מיעוטא הוא. ואע"ג לג] דשלא למנויין דהיינו שינוי בעלים כתיב נמי לד] [א] ("תכוסו"), ולא ממעטי זריקה – לא דמי (עיין פסחים דף סא.). **והדר** ביה לה] רבה לגבי דרב נחמן מקל וחומר דרב אשי. לו] [היינו] [ב] לרבנן. דאליבא דר' שמעון ליכא קל וחומר, דאיכא למיפרך: מה לשינוי בעלים – שכן נוהג במנחות, תאמר בשינוי קודש שאינו נוהג במנחות לרבי שמעון (מנחות דף ג:).

חטאת

נ"א לעשות

ע"ז לד: סנהדרין סא: חולין לט.

נ"א וצריכי דאי

נ"א משום שלא עשה כלום דהא בזמנו שחט וגו'

[תוספתא ריש פ"א]

עי' בחלופי גרסאות

עיין צ"ק

[עי' תוס' ב"ק כה. ד"ה אני לא]

נ"ק

נ"ג

כ"א זאת

הגהות הב"ח

(א) גמ' שכן כרת. נ"ב עיין פרק כולל הרגל דף כה בתד"ה אני לא: (ב) שם שלא לשמן שהוא פסול לזרוק דמו שלא לשמו אינו דין: (ג) רש"י ד"ה השוחט את הבהמה וכו' ולהקטיר חלבה לעבודה זרה ועבודת השחיטה וכו' ולא זרק הס"ד ואח"כ מ"ה מחשבין: (ד) ד"ה הריני וכו' ומזבח הס"ד ותיבת פיגול נמחק: (ה) ד"ה הריני שוחטו חוץ למקומו וכו' אלא כך אמר וכו' דרחמנא חוץ למקומו: (ו) ד"ה על מנת וכו' למקומו פסול כצ"ל ותיבת כו' נמחק: (ז) ד"ה לא תאמר וכו' לעיל. נ"ב דף ד ע"א וע"ש:

שיטה מקובצת

א] ריש לקיש אמר מותרת. ונראה לפרש דמ"מ חייב סקילה ואע"פ שהבהמה מותרת דכה"ג אמרי' [בפרק ארבע מיתות בית דין] וא"ת היאך הבהמה מותרת הרי שחיטת מומר היא וי"ל דמשום פעם אחת לא מיקרי מומר [הואיל ולא הורגל בכך] דכה"ג אמרינן בחולין גבי השוחט בשבת דאסורה לאותו יום הא למחר מותר וצריך לומר [דלא מתסר משום דעבר באקראי] בעלמא הואיל ולא הורגל בכך וא"ת אמאי יהרג כו' א) וי"ל דהתם שאני דאינו עושה שום מעשה. לשון תוס' טוך: ב] מפנים וצריכי דאי: ג] ריש לקיש ובספר ישן כתוב אבל חוץ מפנים אימא מודי ליה לר' יוחנן [ופי'] דאי אשמועינן בהא בהשוחט לשמו בהא אמר ריש לקיש דכשירה דלא ילפינן לשמו מפיגול אבל חוץ מפנים אימא מודי לר"י דאסורה מחמת חומרא דעבודה זרה: ד] לזרוק דמו שלא לשמו אינו דין שיהא פסול [וא"ת שוחט שלא לשם] אוכליו דפסח יוכיח דבשחיטה שלא לאוכליו פסול וכו' ה"נ בשלא לשמו וי"ל דאיכא למימר בשוחט ע"מ לזרוק דמו שלא לשמו דין שיהא פסול כדין אם חישב בזריקה עצמה שלא לשמה דהשתא ליכא למימר שלא לשם אוכליו יוכיח שכשר בשוחט ע"מ לזרוק דשאני שלא לאוכליו דפסח כיון דבזריקה עצמה אינה נפסלת כשזורק שלא לאוכליו כדפי' בריש פירקין. תוס' טוך: ה] פסול שחטו על מנת לזרוק: ו] תיבות שלא לשמו נמחק: ז] שלא לשמו פסול שחטו ע"מ לזרוק דמו שלא לשמו: ח] השתא מיהא בשלמים קיימינן. וקש' דמשחיטה לחודיה ניליף זריקה וליכא למיפרך מה לשחיטה שכן נפסלת שלא לאוכליו בפסח דהשתא מיהא בשלמים [קיימינן] ואמר מורי דמ"מ פרכינן שפיר שלא לאוכליו וה"ק השתא מיהא בשלמים קיימינן ולא פרכינן פירכא דצפון דהוי בקדשי קדשים לשלמים דהם קדשים קלים אבל מדבר שהוא כפסח שהן קדשים קלים כשלמים פרכינן שפיר לגבי שלמים. תוס' מהר"פ: ט] פסולה רבא אמר כשרה והדר ביה רבא לגבי ר"נ: י] חישב לעשות הזריקה: יא] ליאסור: יב] זרק דמה: יג] היא ס"א משום דלא עשה כלום דהא בזמנה שחיט: יד] ומזבח הס"ד ומה"ד פסול פיגול ותיבת דזהו ל"ש ונמחק: טו] אלא כך אמר הריני שוחט לחוץ למקומו: טז] תיבת כו' נמחק: יז] לעיל לכולהו אות ב' נמחק: יח] שכן וכי: יט] מעבודה לעבודה דאפילו לא חישב והשאר נמחק: כ] לשמו דכתיב הזורק את דם השלמים שתהא זריקה לשם שלמים: כא] בהמה ניתנת תיבת נעשית נמחק: כב] למימר דהוי אות ה' נמחק : כג] וקבלה דלא: כד] תיבת לא נמחק: כה] לקבל דמו: כו] והעובדו: כז] מיתות דמסית שאמר: כח] דמי דשאני התם: כט] מאן דלא פריך ס"א מאי דס"ד השתא דלא כו': ל] דבשלמים קיימינן תיבות א"כ ל"ש ונמחק: לא] מקבלה ומה קבלה שאם אמר הריני שוחט ע"מ לקבל חוץ לזמנו כשר כדאמרינן לקמן דבעינן שיחשב באכילת אדם [או] באכילת מזבח קבל שלא לשמו פסול זריקה לא כ"ש וי"ל דאה"נ אלא דלא סגיא ליה דלא כתיב שחיטה דשחיטה גופיה לא אתי מינייהו משום דשחיטה כשרה בזר. תוס' טוך: לב] דלמא תכוסו: לג] ואע"ג דגבי שלא אות ד' נמחק: לד] נמי תכוסו: לה] ביה רבא אות ה' נמחק: לו] לרבה אליבא דר"ש ותיבת היינו ל"ש ונמחק:

הגהות צ"ק

[א] במכסת ולא ממעטי זריקה דלא דמי: [ב] לרבה אליבא דר"ש ליכא ק"ו כצ"ל ור"ל לרבה דמתרץ התם בפ"ק דמנחות דברי ר"ש דלא סתרי אהדדי דבש"ק ס"ל דעלו ובש"ב ס"ל דלא עלו לפ"ז איכא למיפרך מה לש"ב כו':

א) כוונתם לדברי התוספות בד"ה ר"ל שכתבו ואין לתמוה וכו'.

חוזרני חלילה. חזר רבי אליעזר ודנו דין אחר: חטאת נאמר בה "היא" א] בשחיטה — היא לשמה כשירה, שלא לשמה פסולה; ופסח נאמר בו "הוא" ב] בזביחה — הוא לשמו כשר, שלא לשמו פסול; אף אשם נאמר בו "הוא", הוא לשמו — כשר, שלא לשמו — פסול. אמר לו רבי יהושע: חטאת נאמר בה "היא" בשחיטה — היא לשמה כשרה, שלא לשמה פסולה; פסח נאמר בו "הוא" בזביחה — הוא לשמו כשר, שלא לשמו פסול. אבל *אשם לא נאמר בו "הוא" אלא לאחר הקטרת אימורין, והוא עצמו שלא הוקטרו אימורין — כשר! אמר לו *ר' אליעזר, הרי ג] אומר: °"כחטאת כאשם", ד] מה חטאת שלא לשמו — פסול, אף אשם שלא לשמו — פסול. אמר מר: אמר לו ר' יהושע: חוזרני חלילה. ה] ולמיהדר דינא וליתי ב"מה הצד"! משום דאיכא למיפרך: מה להצד השוה שבהן שכן יש בהן (א) צד כרת. "אמר ו] לו ר' יהושע: לא, אם אמרת בחטאת שכן דמה למעלה". ולימא ליה: לא, אם אמרת בחטאת שכן נכנס דמה לפני ולפנים! בחטאות החיצונות קאמרינן. שאם נכנס דמה ז] [לפני] ולפנים — פסולה! אית ליה לרבי אליעזר אף האשם. (ב) שכן מכפרת על חייבי כריתות! מחטאת דשמיעת הקול. ח] שכן טעונה ארבע מתנות! *כרבי ישמעאל, דאמר: כל הדמים טעונה ארבע מתנות. (שכן טעונה) על ארבע קרנות! וליטעמיך, האיכא אצבע, ט] *האיכא קרן, האיכא חודה! אלא, *חד מתרי תלת טעמי נקט. אמר מר: אמר לו ר' יהושע: לא, אם אמרת. י] לימא ליה רבי אליעזר: אשם נמי דמו למעלה! אמר אביי: יא] אאשם דמו למעלה לא מצית אמרת, ק"ו יב] מעולה: ומה עולה שהיא כליל — בדמה למטה, אשם שאינו כליל לא כל שכן? מה לעולה שכן אינה מכפרת! חטאת העוף תוכיח. מה לחטאת העוף שכן אינה מין זבח! עולה תוכיח. לא ראי זה כראי זה ולא ראי זה כראי זה, הצד השוה שבהן — שהן קדשי קדשים יג] ודמן למטה, אף אני אביא אשם שהוא קודש קדשים ודמו למטה. א"ל רבא מפרזקיא לרב אשי, ולפרוך: מה להצד השוה שבהן שכן אין להן קצבה, תאמר באשם שיש לו קצבה! אלא היינו טעמא דרבי אליעזר, דאמר קרא: °"הכהן המחטא אותה" — אותה דמה למעלה, ואין דמו של אחר למעלה. אי הכי, *חטאת נמי נימא: "אותה" — לשמה כשרה, שלא לשמה פסולה; הא שאר זבחים, בין לשמן בין שלא לשמן — כשרין! ההוא "אותה" לאו דוקא, דהא שייר פסח. הכא נמי לאו דוקא, דהא שייר עולת העוף! בזביחה מיהא לא שייר מידי. ואי בעית אימא: הא מני? רבי אלעזר ברבי שמעון היא, דאמר: האי מקום לחוד והאי מקום לחוד, *דתניא: דמים התחתונים ניתנין מחוט הסיקרא ולמטה, והעליונים — מחוט הסיקרא ולמעלה. אמר רבי אלעזר ברבי שמעון: במה דברים אמורין — בעולת העוף, אבל בחטאת בהמה — היא עצמה אין נעשה אלא על גופה של קרן.§ *תנן התם, שהיה רבי עקיבא אומר: כל דמים שנכנסו יד] להיכל לכפר — פסולים. וחכמים אומרים: חטאת בלבד. רבי אליעזר אומר: אף האשם, שנאמר: "כחטאת כאשם". בשלמא רבי אליעזר כדקאמר טעמא, אלא רבנן מאי (ג) טעמא? אמר רבא: אשם נכנס דמו לפנים פסול לא מצית אאמרת, קל וחומר מעולה: מה עולה

תוספות

חטאת נאמר בה היא. בכמה מקומות משמע דמדכתיב "היא" נפקא לן עכובא. ותימה: דלעיל נפקא לן מקראי אחרינא. ולעיל (דף ה*:) פירשתי. הרי הוא אומר כחטאת כאשם. באשם *מצורע כתיב והוה מצי למילף אשם מחטאת *)בגזירה שוה לג]* ד"עון" "עון" מחטאת דשמיעת קול, דהא למותרת נדבה גמירי, לד] ואין ג"ש למחצה, כדאמר בריש מנחות (דף ד.). אלא אי לאו היקשא – לה] הוה ממעט אשם מ"אותה". מה להצד השוה שבהן שכן צד כרת. ואע"ג דאשם תלוי נמי בא על כרת – אינו בא לכפר אלא להגן, ולכי מתיידע מייתי חטאת. וה"נ הוה מצי למימר: שכן באין בצבור. מחטאת דשמיעת הקול. וליכא למיפרך: מה לאשם חטאת שכן כרת, דהדא מהדא לא פרכינן כל דהו. ומה עולה שהיא כליל כו'. תימה: כיון דאתי האי ק"ו ומפיק מהיקשא, אם כן תהא עולה פסולה שלא לשמה, ק"ו מחטאת שאינה כליל. וכי תימא: מה לחטאת שכן מכפרת – פסח יוכיח! ומיהו, כיון דכתיב "אותה" בחטאת לא קשה. ותימה: (ח) לסברתו דעביד קל וחומר מעולה שהיא כליל, שלא לשמו נמי ליכשר באשם, לו] ותו לימא חטאת יוכיח!. הג"ה: כל דמים שנכנסו להיכל לכפר פסולים. לא דמי להא דאמר לז] (לקמן דף סג. ומנחות דף ח. ושם): לח] *[שלמים ששחטן] בהיכל כשירות, לא יהא טפל חמור מן העיקר. דהני מילי היכא דכתיב "אל פתח אהל מועד", שתלה לט] הכשירו בהיכל.

אשם

רש"י

חוזרני חלילה. ולא יקום הדין. ולקמן פריך: וניהדר דינא וניתי ב"מה הצד". נאמר בה היא טו] בשחיטה. שעיר נשיא. הרי הוא אומר כו'. ואין משיבין על ההיקש. ולקמן בסוף שמעתא מפרש טעמייהו טז] *דרבנן, דסמכי אהיקשא אחרינא, והך היקשא דרשינן למילתא אחריתי. יז] תיתי במה הצד. דפסח וחטאת נאכלין (ליום ולילה), אף אני אביא אשם. צד כרת. חטאת באה על שגגת כרת, ופסח חייבים עליו כרת, טהור שלא היה בדרך רחוקה. שכן נכנס דמה לפני ולפנים. כגון ביום הכפורים. בחטאות החיצונות קאמרינן. במתני' יח] דפסולה, ואע"ג דלא עיילי לפנים, ומינייהו יליף ר' אליעזר. שאם נכנס דמה לפנים פסול. פירכא היא. וה"ק, ולימא ליה: מה לחטאת החיצונה שכן אם נכנס דמה לפנים פסולה, דכתיב (ויקרא ו): "וכל חטאת אשר יובא מדמה" כו', תאמר באשם דלא מיפסיל בהכי. אית ליה לרבי אליעזר אף יט] באשם. שנכנס דמו לפנים פסול, לקמן בשמעתין. ולימא ליה ר' יהושע מה לחטאה שכן מכפרת על חייבי כריתות. מחטאת דשמיעת קול. יליף רבי אליעזר, דאינה באה על כרת. ולימא ליה שכן טעונה ארבע מתנות. תאמר באשם כ] שאינו טעון אלא שני מתנות שהן ד'. כר' ישמעאל כו'. ב"איזהו מקומן" (לקמן נג:): נאמר כאן "סביב" בעולה ואשם, ונאמר להלן "סביב" בחטאת [המילואים], מה להלן פיסוק ארבע מתנות, דהא ד' (ד) מתנות כתיבי בה, ואי אפשר לשתי קרנות בבת אחת, אף כאן פיסוק ד' מתנות – כא] באותה מתנה שנותן לקרן שהוא כשתים, צריך לפסוק לצפונה של קרן ולמזרחה של קרן. ולימא ליה שכן טעונין ד' מתנות על ד' קרנות. מה שאין כן באשם, דר' ישמעאל גופיה לא בעי בשאר זבחים אלא ד' מתנות בשתי קרנות. דקתני כב] כדר' ישמעאל: אי מה להלן ארבע מתנות כג] [על ארבע קרנות] אף כאן כו'! אמרת: עולה טעונה יסוד, וקרן מזרחית דרומית לא היה לה יסוד. וליטעמיך. טובא הוה ליה לרבי יהושע למיפרך, דהא איכא קרן, ואצבע, וחודה. שחטאת טעונה ליתן מתנותיה באצבע כנגד חודה של (ה) קרן, כד] אבן של אמה על אמה ברום אמה בד' מקצעות המזבח. מה שאין כן בשאר הדמים, דאפילו עולת העוף שהיא למעלה מחוט הסיקרא כדלקמן, אינה צריכה להגביה כ"כ ולתת על הקרן ממש, אלא שתהא למעלה מן החוט כל שהוא, כדתניא לקמן (דף נג.): עשאה למטה מרגליו אפי' אמה – כשרה. ואין שום זבח טעון כה] מתנות אצבע, אלא זורק מן הכלי אל קיר *המזבח למקצעותיו השנים, והדם מתפשט לצפון ולמערב. ואין מתנתו כנגד חודה במשך מלמעלה למטה, כחטאת שצריכה כנגד חודה, לקמן ב"איזהו מקומן" (דף נג.). ולימא ליה רבי אליעזר אשם נמי דמו למעלה. דהא רבי אליעזר מקיש אשם לחטאת. חטאת העוף. דמה למטה, לקמן בפרק "קדשי קדשים" (דף סג.). אינה מין זבח. אלא מין מליקה. אין להן קצבה. לדמיהן. ואשם יש לו קצבה לדמיו, בכסף שקלים. המחטא אותה. הזורק דמה. ובחטאת כתיב, ומיעט "אותה" בחטאת, למעוטי שאר קדשים ממקום מתן דמו של חטאת. אי הכי. בשחיטת חטאת נמי כתיב (ו) "אותה לחטאת", ומיעוטא הוא, כו] ולידרשה ר' אליעזר למעוטי אשם מפסול שלא לשמו! שייר עולת העוף. שהיא למעלה, דילפינן לקמן (דף סה.) מ"ומלק והקטיר": מה הקטרה בראשו של מזבח – אף מליקה בראשו של מזבח. בזביחה כז] לא שייר מידי. (ז) אדבר שהוא זבח לא שייר כלום, שכל הזבחים נתמעטו שלא יהא כח] דמו למעלה. ועולת העוף לאו שיורא הוא, דאינו זבח כמותו. הא מני. דלא חשיב עולת העוף שיור? רבי אלעזר בר' שמעון היא. דאמר האי מקום. דחטאת בהמה לחוד ודעולת העוף לחוד. אע"פ ששניהם למעלה אין מקומן שוה, הלכך במיעוטא דגבי זריקת כט] חטאת ליכא שיור. במה דברים אמורים. דעליונים לא קביע להו מקום, אלא ל] שיהא מן החוט ולמעלה. בעולת העוף אבל חטאת בהמה אינה נעשית אלא בגופה של קרן. האבן של אמה על אמה שבראש לא] מזבח. שכל למטה מן הקרנות פסולה, ואף על פי שהיא למעלה מן החוט ארבע אמות. כל דמים. החיצונים שנכנסו להיכל לכפר – פסולין. ואף על גב דלא כתיב אלא "וכל חטאת אשר יובא מדמה" וגו', מרבה רבי עקיבא קדשי קדשים וקדשים קלים מריבויא ד"כל" "וכל", לב] לקמן ב"כל הזבחים שנתערבו" (דף פב.). אלא לרבנן מאי טעמייהו. הא ודאי איתקש אשם לחטאת!

עולה

נ"ב ואין להקשות דליכא למיפרך מה [לעולה שכן] אינה מכפרת דליכא למימר חטאת העוף תוכיח כיון דגם חטאת העוף שלא לשמו פסול כדאיתא פרק קדשי קדשים דף סג ע"ב בפרש"י ע"ש ותו ליכא קוס יוכיח:

כדאית ליה וקרן לא הוי בכלל פירכא דלעיל דקאמר שכן דמה למעלה דהא עולת העוף דמה למעלה מחוט הסיקרא ולא בעי קרן כדפי' בקונטרס. תוס' טוך: י] אמרת בחטאת כו': יא] עיין בהשמטות (ב] מעולה וא"ת שלא לשמה נמי ליתכשר לר"א באשם מק"ו דעולה ומה עולה שהיא כליל לאישים כשר בשלא לשמו אשם דאינו כליל כו' דאיכא למיפרך (הכא) [הכי] מה לעולה שאינה מכפרת וליכא העוף [תוכיח] דחטאת העוף פסול שלא לשמו. תוס' טוך: יג] קדשי קדשים ודמו למטה: יד] שנכנסו לכפר להיכל: טו] היא בשחיטת אות ה' נמחק: טז] דרבנן ס"א טעמיה דר' יהושע דסמיך כו': מה הצד מפסח וחטאת דנאכלין: יח] במתניתין דפסולות: יט] אף האשם אות ב' נמחק: כ] באשם ארבע מתנות אינו טעון: כא] מתנות דאותה מתנה אות ב' נמחק: כב] דקתני התם: כג] מתנות על ארבע קרנות: כד] קרן ומלמטה והקרן היה אבן: כה] תיבת מתנות נמחק: כו] הוא ולידרשיה: כז] בזביחה מיהא: כח] יהא דמן אות ו' נמחק: כט] זריקת דם: ל] אלא שיהו: לא] שבראש כדלקמן: לג] שוה דעונו ותיבות עון עון ל"ש: לד] גמירי בריש מנחות ואין ג"ש וכו' תיבות כדאמר בריש מנחות נמחק: לה] עיין בהשמטות בסוף המסכת: לו] באשם וי"ל דתו ליכא למימר חטאת העוף יוכיח: לז] דאמר בפ"ק דמנחות שלמים עיין תוספות ד"ה מנחה שנקמצה: לח] שלמים ששחטו: לט] שתלה דכתיב באהל מועד הס"ד:

עוֹלָה שֶׁהִיא כָּלִיל, נִכְנַס דָּמָהּ לִפְנִים — כְּשֵׁרָה, אָשָׁם שֶׁאֵינוֹ כָּלִיל — לֹא כ"ש? מַה לְּעוֹלָה, שֶׁכֵּן אֵינָהּ מְכַפֶּרֶת. מִנְחַת חוֹטֵא תּוֹכִיחַ. וְלֵימָא: חַטַּאת הָעוֹף תּוֹכִיחַ! חַטַּאת הָעוֹף *בָּעֲיָא דְּרַבִּי אָבִין הִיא. (א) וְלִפְרוֹךְ: מַה לְּמִנְחַת חוֹטֵא, שֶׁכֵּן אֵינָהּ מִין זֶבַח! עוֹלָה תּוֹכִיחַ. *וְחָזַר הַדִּין, לֹא רְאִי זֶה כִּרְאִי זֶה, וְלֹא רְאִי זֶה כִּרְאִי זֶה, הַצַּד הַשָּׁוֶה שֶׁבָּהֶן — שֶׁהֵן קָדְשֵׁי קָדָשִׁים א] וְנִכְנַס (*דָּמָן) לִפְנִים כְּשֵׁרִין, אַף אֲנִי אָבִיא אָשָׁם שֶׁהוּא קוֹדֶשׁ קָדָשִׁים, וְנִכְנַס דָּמוֹ לִפְנִים כָּשֵׁר. אֲמַר לֵיהּ רָבָא מִבַּרְנִישׁ לְרַב אָשֵׁי, וְלִפְרוֹךְ: מַה לְּהַצַּד הַשָּׁוֶה שֶׁבָּהֶן — שֶׁכֵּן אֵין לָהֶן קִצְבָּה, תֹּאמַר בְּאָשָׁם שֶׁיֵּשׁ לוֹ קִצְבָּה! אֶלָּא הַיְינוּ טַעֲמַיְיהוּ דְּרַבָּנַן, דְּאָמַר קְרָא: "דָּמָהּ" — דָּמָהּ שֶׁל זוֹ, וְלֹא דָּמָהּ שֶׁל אַחֵר. וְאִידָךְ? "דָּמָהּ" — וְלֹא בְּשָׂרָהּ. וְאִידָךְ? "דָּם" "דָּמָהּ". וְאִידָךְ? "דָּם" "דָּמָהּ" לָא דָּרֵישׁ. בִּשְׁלָמָא לְרַבָּנַן, דְּאָמְרִי: אָשָׁם שֶׁשְּׁחָטוֹ שֶׁלֹּא לִשְׁמוֹ כָּשֵׁר — הַיְינוּ דְּאִיתְקַשׁ מִנְחָה לְחַטָּאת מִנְחָה לְאָשָׁם. *דְּתַנְיָא, רַבִּי שִׁמְעוֹן אוֹמֵר: °"קֹדֶשׁ קָדָשִׁים הִיא כַּחַטָּאת וְכָאָשָׁם", אמִנְחַת חוֹטֵא הֲרֵי הִיא כְּחַטָּאת — לְפִיכָךְ קְמָצָהּ שֶׁלֹּא לִשְׁמָהּ פְּסוּלָה, מִנְחַת נְדָבָה הֲרֵי הִיא כְּאָשָׁם — לְפִיכָךְ קְמָצָהּ שֶׁלֹּא לִשְׁמָהּ כְּשֵׁרָה; אֶלָּא לְרַבִּי אֱלִיעֶזֶר, לְמַאי הִלְכְתָא אִיתְקַשׁ מִנְחָה לְחַטָּאת וּמִנְחָה לְאָשָׁם? לְכִדְרַבִּי שִׁמְעוֹן, *דִּתְנַן: בשֶׁלֹּא בִּכְלִי שָׁרֵת — פְּסוּלָה, וְרַבִּי שִׁמְעוֹן מַכְשִׁיר; *וְאָמַר רַב יְהוּדָה בְּרֵיהּ דְּרַבִּי חִיָּיא: מ"ט דר"ש? אָמַר קְרָא: "קֹדֶשׁ קָדָשִׁים הִיא כַּחַטָּאת וְכָאָשָׁם", בָּא לְעוֹבְדָהּ בַּיָּד — עוֹבְדָהּ בְּיָמִין כְּחַטָּאת, (ב) בִּכְלִי — עוֹבְדָהּ בִּשְׂמֹאל כְּאָשָׁם. וְר"ש, הַאי קְרָא מַפֵּיק לֵיהּ לְהָכִי וּמַפֵּיק לֵיהּ לְהָכִי? עִיקַּר קְרָא לְכִדְרַב יְהוּדָה בְּרֵיהּ דְּרַבִּי חִיָּיא הוּא דְּאָתָא. וּמִנְחַת חוֹטֵא דִּפְסוּלָה שֶׁלֹּא (ג) לִשְׁמָהּ — ב] [טַעְמָא אַחֲרִינָא הוּא:] חַטָּאת טַעְמָא מַאי? דִּכְתִיב בָּהּ: "הִיא", מִנְחַת חוֹטֵא נַמִי כְּתִיב בָּהּ: "הִיא". ג] וּלְרַבָּנַן, לְמַאי הִלְכְתָא אִיתְקַשׁ אָשָׁם לְחַטָּאת? לוֹמַר לָךְ: מַה חַטָּאת טְעוּנָה סְמִיכָה, אַף אָשָׁם טָעוּן סְמִיכָה.§ "יוֹסֵף בֶּן חוֹנִי אוֹמֵר: הַנִּשְׁחָטִין" כו'.§ א"ר יוֹחָנָן: יוֹסֵף בֶּן חוֹנִי וְרַבִּי אֱלִיעֶזֶר אָמְרוּ דָּבָר אֶחָד. רַבָּה אָמַר: בַּאֲחֵרִים לְשֵׁם חַטָּאת פְּלִיגֵי. (ד) דְּתַנְיָא: *הַפֶּסַח שֶׁעָבְרָה שְׁנָתוֹ וּשְׁחָטוֹ בִּזְמַנּוֹ לִשְׁמוֹ, וְכֵן הַשּׁוֹחֵט אֲחֵרִים לְשֵׁם פֶּסַח בִּזְמַנּוֹ — רַבִּי אֱלִיעֶזֶר פּוֹסֵל, וְרַבִּי יְהוֹשֻׁעַ גמַכְשִׁיר. א"ר יְהוֹשֻׁעַ: אִם בִּשְׁאָר יְמוֹת הַשָּׁנָה שֶׁאֵינוֹ כָּשֵׁר לִשְׁמוֹ — אֲחֵרִים כְּשֵׁרִים לִשְׁמוֹ, בִּזְמַנּוֹ שֶׁהוּא כָּשֵׁר לִשְׁמוֹ — אֵינוֹ דִּין שֶׁיִּכְשְׁרוּ אֲחֵרִים לִשְׁמוֹ? אָמַר לוֹ רַבִּי אֱלִיעֶזֶר: אוֹ חִילּוּף הַדְּבָרִים, וּמָה אִם בִּשְׁאָר יְמוֹת הַשָּׁנָה שֶׁאֵינוֹ כָּשֵׁר לִשְׁמוֹ — כָּשֵׁר הוּא לְשֵׁם אֲחֵרִים, בִּזְמַנּוֹ שֶׁהוּא כָּשֵׁר לִשְׁמוֹ — אֵינוֹ דִּין שֶׁיּוּכְשַׁר לְשֵׁם אֲחֵרִים? וְיוּכְשַׁר פֶּסַח בְּאַרְבָּעָה עָשָׂר שֶׁלֹּא לִשְׁמוֹ! וְכָךְ אַתָּה אוֹמֵר? מַה לִּי הוּכְשְׁרוּ אֲחֵרִים בִּשְׁאָר יְמוֹת הַשָּׁנָה לִשְׁמוֹ — שֶׁכֵּן הוּא כָּשֵׁר לְשֵׁם אֲחֵרִים, וְיוּכְשְׁרוּ אֲחֵרִים בִּזְמַנּוֹ לִשְׁמוֹ? שֶׁכֵּן הוּא פָּסוּל לְשֵׁם אֲחֵרִים! אָמַר לוֹ רַבִּי יְהוֹשֻׁעַ: אִם כֵּן, ד] הוֹרַעְתָּה כֹּחַ פֶּסַח וְנָתַתָּ כֹּחַ בִּשְׁלָמִים! חָזַר רַבִּי אֱלִיעֶזֶר וְדָנוֹ דִּין אַחֵר: מָצִינוּ מוּתַר פֶּסַח בָּא שְׁלָמִים, וְאֵין מוּתַר שְׁלָמִים בָּא פֶּסַח. וּמַה פֶּסַח שֶׁמּוּתָרוֹ בָּא שְׁלָמִים, שְׁחָטוֹ בִּזְמַנּוֹ לְשׁוּם שְׁלָמִים — פָּסוּל, שְׁלָמִים שֶׁאֵין מוּתָרָן בָּא פֶּסַח, אִם שְׁחָטָם לְשֵׁם פֶּסַח בִּזְמַנּוֹ — אֵינוֹ דִּין שֶׁיִּהְיוּ פְּסוּלִין?

אָמַר

רש"י

עוֹלָה נִכְנַס דָּמָהּ לִפְנִים כְּשֵׁרָה. בֵּין לְרַבָּנַן בֵּין לְרַבִּי אֱלִיעֶזֶר. דְּלָא ה] דָּרְשִׁינַן "כָּל" "וְכָל", וְהֶיקֵּשָׁא נַמִי לֵיכָּא הָכָא. מִנְחַת חוֹטֵא. דְּקָרְבָּן עוֹלֶה וְיוֹרֵד דִּשְׁמִיעַת הַקּוֹל. תּוֹכִיחַ. שֶׁמְּכַפֶּרֶת, וְאִם נִכְנְסָה לִפְנִים — כְּשֵׁירָה, דְּלָא פָּסַל הַכָּתוּב אֶלָּא דָּם. וְנֵימָא חַטַּאת הָעוֹף תּוֹכִיחַ. וְהָכִי שַׁפִּיר טְפֵי, שֶׁהוּא מִמִּינֵי דָמִים וּרְאוּיָה לְהוֹכִיחַ עַל מִינֵי דָמִים. חַטַּאת הָעוֹף בָּעֲיָא דר' אָבִין הִיא. הֵיכָא דְּהִכְנִיס דָּמָהּ לִפְנִים בְּגוּלְגָּרְתָּהּ, שֶׁאֵין לְדָמָהּ קַבָּלָה. וּמִיבָּעֲיָא לֵיהּ בְּפֶ' "דַּם חַטָּאת" (לקמן לג:) אִם נִפְסְלָה בְּכָךְ אוֹ לֹא, וְלָא אִיפְשִׁיטָא לֵיהּ. דָּמָהּ. "אֲשֶׁר יוּבָא מִדָּמָהּ". וְלֹא בְּשָׂרָהּ. שֶׁאִם נִכְנַס בְּשָׂרָהּ לַהֵיכָל — אֵינָהּ נִפְסֶלֶת. דָּם דָּמָהּ לָא דָּרֵישׁ. דְּכֵיוָן דְּלָא סָגֵי לְמִיכְתַּב "וְכָל חַטָּאת אֲשֶׁר יוּבָא אֶל אֹהֶל מוֹעֵד", דְּאִיצְטְרִיךְ לְמִיכְתַּב "דָּם" לְמַעוּטֵי בָּשָׂר — אוֹרְחֵיהּ דִּקְרָא לְמִיכְתַּב "מִדָּמָהּ". קֹדֶשׁ קָדָשִׁים הִיא כַּחַטָּאת וְכָאָשָׁם ו]. בְּמִנְחָה הוּא דִּכְתִיב. וְקָא א"ר שִׁמְעוֹן: מִדְּקָא מַקִּישׁ מְנָחוֹת לְחַטָּאת וְאָשָׁם — לְהָכִי מַקִּישׁ ז] [לִשְׁנֵיהֶם, לוֹמַר לְךָ דְּיֵשׁ מֵהֶם כְּחַטָּאת וְיֵשׁ מֵהֶם כְּאָשָׁם], שֶׁתְּהֵא מִנְחַת חוֹטֵא כְּחַטָּאת — דְּלֹא לִשְׁמָהּ פְּסוּלָה, וּמִנְחַת נְדָבָה כְּאָשָׁם — דְּכָשֵׁר שֶׁלֹּא לִשְׁמוֹ. אֶלָּא לְרַבִּי אֱלִיעֶזֶר. כֵּיוָן דְּחַטָּאת וְאָשָׁם כִּי הֲדָדֵי נִינְהוּ, לְמַאי הִלְכְתָא אִיתְקַשׁ לְתַרְוַיְיהוּ? שֶׁלֹּא בִּכְלִי שָׁרֵת. שֶׁלֹּא קִדֵּשׁ הַקּוֹמֶץ בִּכְלִי שָׁרֵת — פְּסוּלָה. שֶׁהַמְּנָחוֹת הוּקְשׁוּ לִזְבָחִים לִיטְעוֹן אַרְבַּע עֲבוֹדוֹת: קְמִיצָה כְּנֶגֶד שְׁחִיטָה, מַתַּן קוֹמֶץ בִּכְלִי שָׁרֵת כְּנֶגֶד קַבָּלַת הַדָּם, הוֹלָכָה כְּנֶגֶד הוֹלָכָה, הַקְטָרָה כְּנֶגֶד זְרִיקָה. ור"ש מַכְשִׁיר. אִם הוֹלִיכוֹ בְּיָדוֹ בְּקוּמְצוֹ עַד הַמִּזְבֵּחַ וְהִקְטִירוֹ. כַּחַטָּאת וְכָאָשָׁם. לְהָכִי אִיתְקַשׁ מִנְחָה לְחַטָּאת וּלְאָשָׁם שֶׁאֵינָן שָׁוִין בְּהִלְכוֹתֵיהֶן, לוֹמַר לְךָ. בָּא לְעוֹבְדָהּ. ח] *בְּהִלְּכוֹת וְהַקְטָרוֹת בַּיָּד שֶׁלֹּא בִּכְלִי. עוֹבְדָהּ בְּיָמִין. שֶׁהַקּוֹמֶץ בָּהּ כִּזְרִיקַת דַּם חַטָּאת שֶׁהִיא בַּיָּד, בְּאֶצְבַּע וּבְיָמִין. דִּכְתִיב בְּחַטָּאת: "וְלָקַח הַכֹּהֵן מִדַּם הַחַטָּאת בְּאֶצְבָּעוֹ וְנָתַן" וגו', וְדָרְשִׁינַן לְקַמָּן בְּפ"ב (דף כד.): "בְּאֶצְבָּעוֹ וְנָתַן" — שֶׁלֹּא תְּהֵא נְתִינָה אֶלָּא בְּיָמִין, דְּכָל מָקוֹם שֶׁנֶּאֱמַר אֶצְבַּע וּכְהוּנָּה אֵינוֹ אֶלָּא יָמִין. בָּא לְעוֹבְדָהּ בִּכְלִי. רַשַּׁאי לְעוֹבְדָהּ בִּשְׂמֹאל — לְהוֹלִיךְ הַכְּלִי שֶׁקִּדְּשָׁהּ בְּתוֹכוֹ בִּשְׂמֹאלוֹ לַמִּזְבֵּחַ, וְלִיתֵּן בִּשְׂמֹאלוֹ מִן הַכְּלִי עַל הָאִשִּׁים. כִּזְרִיקַת דַּם אָשָׁם שֶׁהוּא מִן הַכְּלִי לַמִּזְבֵּחַ. שֶׁאֵינָהּ בִּנְתִינַת אֶצְבַּע, דְּלָא כְּתִיב אֶצְבַּע אֶלָּא בְּחַטָּאת. וּכְשֵׁרָה בִּשְׂמֹאל לְר"ש ט] בְּכָל הַזְּבָחִים חוּץ מֵחַטָּאת. י] דְּאָמְרִינַן לְקַמָּן בְּפֶרֶק שֵׁנִי (שם:): זָרַק בִּשְׂמֹאל פָּסוּל, ור"ש מַכְשִׁיר, חוּץ מֵחַטָּאת. מִשּׁוּם דְּרַבִּי שִׁמְעוֹן תַּרְתֵּי בָּעֵי, אֶצְבַּע וּכְהוּנָּה, דְּגָמְרִינַן מִמְּצוֹרָע דִּכְתִיב בֵּיהּ אֶצְבַּע וּכְהוּנָּה וְיָמִין — "וְטָבַל הַכֹּהֵן בְּאֶצְבָּעוֹ הַיְמָנִית". וּבִזְרִיקַת כָּל הַזְּבָחִים לָא כְּתִיב בּוֹ אֶצְבַּע אֶלָּא כְּהוּנָּה, חוּץ מֵחַטָּאת. מִנְחַת חוֹטֵא כְּתִיב בָּהּ (ה) כִּי חַטָּאת הִיא. גַּבֵּי שְׁמִיעַת הַקּוֹל בְּוַיִּקְרָא. וּלְרַבָּנַן. דִּפְלִיגִי עֲלֵיהּ דר' אֱלִיעֶזֶר בְּמַתְנִי', לְמַאי הִלְכְתָא כו'. חַטָּאת כְּתִיב בָּהּ (ויקרא ד): "וְסָמַךְ יָדוֹ עַל רֹאשׁ הַחַטָּאת". אָמְרוּ דָּבָר אֶחָד. דְּרַבִּי אֱלִיעֶזֶר נַמִי פָּסֵיל בַּאֲחֵרִים הַנִּשְׁחָטִים לְשֵׁם פֶּסַח בִּזְמַנּוֹ, וּלְשֵׁם חַטָּאת כָּל יְמוֹת הַשָּׁנָה. וּמִבָּרַיְיתָא דִּלְקַמָּן דָּיֵיק לָהּ רַבִּי יוֹחָנָן. וְרַבָּה אָמַר בַּאֲחֵרִים לְשֵׁם חַטָּאת פְּלִיגֵי. יוֹסֵף בֶּן חוֹנִי וְרַבִּי אֱלִיעֶזֶר. (ו) יא] וְלָא פָּסֵיל רַבִּי אֱלִיעֶזֶר אֶלָּא בַּאֲחֵרִים לְשֵׁם פֶּסַח, אֲבָל בַּאֲחֵרִים לְשֵׁם חַטָּאת — מַכְשִׁיר, כִּדְתַנְיָא כו'. וּבֵין רַבָּה וּבֵין ר' יוֹחָנָן דָּיְיקֵי מִילְּתַיְיהוּ מֵהָא מַתְנִי', וּבְמַסְקָנָא בָּעֵינָא לְפָרוּשֵׁי דִּיּוּקַיְיהוּ. הַפֶּסַח שֶׁעָבְרָה שְׁנָתוֹ. דְּתוּ לָא חֲזֵי לְפֶסַח. סְתָמֵיהּ שְׁלָמִים, כִּדְדָרְשִׁינַן לְעֵיל (דף ח:) מִקְּרָאֵי. וּשְׁחָטוֹ בִּזְמַנּוֹ לִשְׁמוֹ. דַּהֲוָה לֵיהּ שׁוֹחֵט שְׁלָמִים לְשֵׁם פֶּסַח. וְכֵן הַשּׁוֹחֵט. אֶחָד מִכָּל הַזְּבָחִים לְשֵׁם פֶּסַח בִּזְמַנּוֹ. אִם בִּשְׁאָר יְמוֹת הַשָּׁנָה שֶׁאֵינוֹ כָּשֵׁר לִשְׁמוֹ. כִּדְיָלְפִינַן לָהּ בְּמַסֶּכֶת פְּסָחִים (דף סא.): שְׁחָטוֹ קוֹדֶם חֲצוֹת — פָּסוּל, שֶׁנֶּאֱמַר: "בֵּין הָעַרְבָּיִם". וְכַמָּה פְּעָמִים שָׁנָה הַכָּתוּב לְעַכֵּב יב] קְבִיעוּת זְמַנּוֹ בי"ד בֵּין הָעַרְבַּיִם. אֲחֵרִים כְּשֵׁרִים לִשְׁמוֹ. דְּרַבִּי אֱלִיעֶזֶר מוֹדֶה בּוֹ. דְּלָא פָּלֵיג אֶלָּא בִּזְמַנּוֹ, כִּדְתָנַן בְּהֶדְיָא, אֲבָל כָּל יְמוֹת הַשָּׁנָה — אֵין שֵׁם שְׁחִיטַת פֶּסַח חָל עַל קָרְבָּן אַחֵר. אָמַר לוֹ רַבִּי אֱלִיעֶזֶר אוֹ חִילּוּף. יג] אִם ק"ו אַתָּה בָּא לִדְרוֹשׁ — יָכוֹל אֲנִי לְהַחֲלִיפוֹ בְּעִנְיָן אַחֵר, וְלוֹמַר דָּבָר שֶׁאֵינוֹ, וּלְהַכְשִׁיר פֶּסַח בִּזְמַנּוֹ שֶׁלֹּא לִשְׁמוֹ. וְיוּכְשַׁר פֶּסַח בי"ד שֶׁלֹּא לִשְׁמוֹ. וּבַדִּין הַזֶּה יד] אַתָּה יָכוֹל לְהַכְשִׁיר פֶּסַח בִּזְמַנּוֹ שֶׁלֹּא לִשְׁמוֹ. וְכֵן אַתָּה אוֹמֵר. בִּתְמִיָּה: הֲתִדְרוֹשׁ ק"ו טו] וְיִתַּכְּשְׁרוּ? טו] ק"ו שֶׁדָּרַשְׁתָּ יֵשׁ עָלָיו תְּשׁוּבָה. מַה לִּי הוּכְשְׁרוּ אֲחֵרִים כו' יוּכְשְׁרוּ אֲחֵרִים כו'. בִּתְמִיָּה. וּמֵהָכָא דָּיֵיק רַבִּי יוֹחָנָן לְמִילְּתֵיהּ, וְאָמַר דְּכִי הֵיכִי דְּפָסֵיל רַבִּי אֱלִיעֶזֶר בַּאֲחֵרִים לְשֵׁם פֶּסַח — פָּסֵיל יז] בַּאֲחֵרִים לְשֵׁם חַטָּאת, דְּהָא טַעְמוֹ דְּרַבִּי אֱלִיעֶזֶר — מִשּׁוּם דְּהוּא פָּסוּל לְשֵׁם אֲחֵרִים, יח] וְה"נ בְּחַטָּאת אִיתָא. וְרַבָּה דָּיֵיק מִסֵּיפָא, שֶׁחָזַר רַבִּי אֱלִיעֶזֶר מִדִּין זֶה וְדָנוֹ בְּדִין אַחֵר, וּמוֹדֶה דַּאֲחֵרִים לְשֵׁם חַטָּאת כְּשֵׁרִים. א"כ. אִם אַתָּה פּוֹסֵל אֲחֵרִים לִשְׁמוֹ בִּזְמַנּוֹ, יט] הוֹרַעְתָּ פֶּסַח וְנָתַתָּ כֹּחַ בִּשְׁלָמִים. שֶׁכָּל הַשָּׁנָה שֶׁהִיא זְמַן שְׁלָמִים — פֶּסַח הַנִּשְׁחָט (ז) לִשְׁמוֹ כָּשֵׁר, וְהַיּוֹם שֶׁהוּא זְמַן פֶּסַח — כָּל שְׁלָמִים הַנִּשְׁחָטִין לִשְׁמוֹ פְּסוּלִין. נִמְצֵאת מַחְשֶׁבֶת (ח) כ] שֶׁלּוֹ *גָּדוֹל כֹּחַ בִּשְׁלָמִים מִפֶּסַח. וּקְרָא הַשְׁתָּא דְּאַחְמוּר בְּפֶסַח מִבִּשְׁלָמִים, דִּכְתִיב בֵּיהּ "הוּא", וּבְכָל הַזְּבָחִים הִכְשִׁיר שֶׁלֹּא לִשְׁמָן.

אָמַר

תוספות

אשם שאינו כליל לא כל שכן. לא שייך למימר חטאת תוכיח. דאיכא למימר: מה לחטאת – שכן דמה למעלה, ושכן לד כרת, ושכן באה בנבור. **מנחת** חוטא הרי היא כחטאת. אין זה למד מלמד. דאע"ג דחטאת ילפינן למוה משלמים לעיל, מכל מקום עכובא *בגופיה כתיבי. ומנחת נדבה כאשם – לאו משום דנאשם ילפא כא] למנוה, דמנחה גופה איתקש לשלמים כאשם. אלא למימרא דלא הוי כחטאת. *בא לעובדה ביד עובדה בימין כחטאת. דכתיב בה "אצבע", דילפינן מגזירה שוה ממצורע דאצבע הוי ימין. וא"ת: הלא איבעיא לן פרק "איזהו מקומן" (לקמן דף נ.) אי ילפינן היקש מג"ש! ואי מצורע חולין כב] [הוא] – הוה אתי שפיר. כג] *[ולא] קשה למ"ד דבעי למד קדש ומלמד קודש פרק "איזהו מקומן" (גם זה שם). כד] **הכי** גרסינן: עיקר קרא לכדר' יהודה בריה דרבי חייא הוא כו'. תימה: דבריש מנחות (דף ג:) משמע לאידך דרשא עיקר. דפריך אביי: מכדי מחשבה דפסיל רחמנא היקישא הוא*. **הורעתה** כח פסח ונתת כח בשלמים. דבזמן שלמים – פסח לשם שלמים כשר, ואילו בזמן הפסח – שלמים לשם פסח פסולים. והלא יש פסוק בפסח לפסול שלא לשמו, ואילו בשלמים אין פסוק.

אמר

עין משפט נר מצוה

נא א מיי' פט"ו מהלכות פסה"מ הלכה ב:

נב ב מיי' פי"א שם הלכה ו:

נג ג מיי' פט"ו שם הלכה יב:

גי' ל"ק בגופיה כתיב הס"ד ואח"כ מה"ד מנחת נדבה כו'

עי' בחילופי גירסאות

גי' הל"ק ומ"מ קשה למ"ד דלא בעי כו'

[עיין במנחות ב: בד"ה מכדי מחשבה כו' לא קשיא מידי ע"ש]

מנחות י: כו. לקמן כה.

מסורת הש"ס

[לקמן לג:]

[קדושין כה. וש"נ]

[לקמן פב.]

מנחות ב:

שם כו.

נ"ל כהולכת הקטרה ל"ק

פסחים סב: תוספתא דפסחים פ"ד

נ"א גרוע

ויקרא ו

תורה אור

הגהות הב"ח

(א) גמ' בעיא דרבי אבין היא מה כנ"ל ותיבת ולפרוך נמחק: (ב) שם בימין כחטאת בא לעובדה בכלי עובדה: (ג) שם שלא לשמה ה"ט חטאת טעמא מאי: (ד) שם כדתניא הפסח: (ה) רש"י ד"ה מנחת חוטא כתיב בה חטאת כנ"ל ותיבת כי נמחק: (ו) ד"ה ורבה וכו' בן חוני ור' אליעזר ר"א לא פסיל אלא: (ז) ד"ה א"כ אם וכו' הנשחט לשמו נ"ב פי' לשם שלמים: (ח) בא"ד נמצאת מחשבת שלא לשמו גדול כחו בשלמים מבפסח:

שיטה מקובצת

א] קדשים ונכנסו לפנים תיבת דמן נמחק: ב] לשמה טעמא אחרינא הוא: ג] מנחת חוטא נמי כתיב בה היא. תימה לרבנן דר"ש דאמרי קדשה שלא בכלי שרת פסולה למאי הלכתא איתקש מנחת חוטא לחטאת ואשם אי משום פסול שלא לשמו במנחת חוטא תיפוק ליה מהיא כדאמרינן ואי משום כשרות דמנחת נדבה (לימא דאיתקש מנחת נדבה לאשם כדאמרי' לעיל) לשתוק מיני' ומזאת תורת העולה נפקא הואיל ותורת שלמים עליו כדפי' וכ"ת דאיצטריך היקשא לומר דמה חטאת טעון ימין (אני) [אף] קמיצה בעי ימין תיפוק ליה דבפ"ק דמנחות מייתי תרי קראי חד לקומץ וחד לקידוש קומץ ואי משום עבודת ימין לחוד (בא לעובדה בימין כחטאת עובדה בימין) הא אית להו לרבנן (קדשה שלא בכלי שרת פסולה) דכל מקום שנאמר אצבע או כהונה אינה אלא ימין וי"ל דאיצטריך הקישא כדדרשינן [בחולין דף כא ולקמן דף עח] מה חטאת אינה באה אלא מן החולין ובידו הימנית (אי מה חטאת פסולה שלא לשמה אף כל המנחות פסולות בשלא לשמה ת"ל כאשם) [אא"ה בחולין דף כ"א ולקמן דף צ"ה ע"א ובמנחות דף פ"ג ע"א ליתא להאי סיומא ואולי היה כך גירסתם או שהוא מדברי התוס' דרבנן בעי להאי כחטאת וכאשם להכי עכ"ה] ובידו הימנית דנקט לאו דוקא דהא עיקר דרשא כדנפקא לן במנחות דבעי ימין אלא אגב אינו בא אלא מן החולין נקט לה תוס' טוך: ד] ע' בהשמטות בסוף המסכת: ה] דרשי אות נ' נמחק: ו] וכאשם יש מהם שהוא כחטאת ויש מהם שהוא כאשם האי קרא במנחה: ז] מקיש לה שתהא מנחת חוטא והשאר ל"ש ונמחק: ח] עבודת הקטרה ביד: ט] לר"ש כדאמרי' בפ' שני [דף כד] בכל. ס"א מתיבת בכל עד תיבות משום דר"ש אינו: י] תיבות דאמרינן לקמן בפ' שני ל"ש ונמחק: יא] אליעזר דלא: יב] לעכב בקביעות: יג] חילוף כלומר אם: יד] הזה אני יכול תיבת אתה נמחק: טו] ויתכשרו ס"א ותכשירו שלא לשמו דלא תדרוש [ק"ו] זה כמו דלא תדרוש האחר שיש עליו כו': טז] אחרים כו' ועוד ק"ו: יז] פסח פסיל נמי באחרים: יח] אחרים והאי דין נמי בחטאת איתא ורבה דייק מסיפא דחזר ר"א: יט] הורעתה כח: כ] מחשבת שלא לשמו גדול כח בשלמים מבפסח: כא] ילפא דאשם גופיה לא ידעינן דכשר אלא מהיקשא וא"ת תיפוק [ליה] הכשר [מזאת תורת] דאיתקש [כל המנחות] כולהו לשלמים וי"ל דלכך בא זה הפסוק לאשמועינן דאין מנחת נדבה כחטאת אלא הרי הוא כאשם תוס' טוך: כב] חולין הוי תיבת הוא ל"ש: כג] שפיר [ומיהו עדיין] קשה למ"ד דלא בעי למד קודש ומלמד קודש כדפריך בפרק איזהו מקומן עכ"ה: כד] תיבות הכי גרסינן נמחק:

אָמַר לוֹ רַבִּי יְהוֹשֻׁעַ: מָצִינוּ מוֹתַר חַטָּאת בָּא עוֹלָה, וְאֵין מוֹתַר עוֹלָה בָּא חַטָּאת; וּמַה חַטָּאת שֶׁמּוֹתָרָהּ בָּא עוֹלָה, שְׁחָטָהּ לְשֵׁם עוֹלָה – פְּסוּלָה, עוֹלָה שֶׁאֵין מוֹתָרָהּ בָּא חַטָּאת, שְׁחָטָהּ לְשֵׁם חַטָּאת – אֵינוֹ דִּין שֶׁתְּהֵא פְּסוּלָה? אָמַר לוֹ רַבִּי אֱלִיעֶזֶר: לֹא, אִם אָמַרְתָּ בְּחַטָּאת – שֶׁכֵּן כְּשֵׁרָה לִשְׁמָהּ כָּל הַשָּׁנָה כּוּלָּהּ, תֹּאמַר בְּפֶסַח – שֶׁאֵינוֹ כָּשֵׁר לִשְׁמוֹ אֶלָּא בִּזְמַנּוֹ? הוֹאִיל וְהוּא פָּסוּל לִשְׁמוֹ, דִּין הוּא שֶׁיִּפָּסְלוּ אֲחֵרִים לִשְׁמוֹ.§ "שִׁמְעוֹן אֲחִי עֲזַרְיָה אוֹמֵר" כו'.§ רַב אָשֵׁי מַתְנֵי מִשְּׁמֵיהּ דְּרַבִּי יוֹחָנָן, וְרַב אַחָא בְּרֵיהּ דְּרָבָא מַתְנֵי מִשְּׁמֵיהּ דְּרַבִּי יַנַּאי: מַאי טַעְמָא דְּשִׁמְעוֹן אֲחִי עֲזַרְיָה? דְּאָמַר קְרָא: °"וְלֹא יְחַלְּלוּ אֶת קָדְשֵׁי בְּנֵי יִשְׂרָאֵל אֵת אֲשֶׁר יָרִימוּ לַה'" – בְּמוּרָם מֵהֶן אֵין מִתְחַלְּלִין, בְּנָמוּךְ מֵהֶם מִתְחַלְּלִין. וְהַאי לְהָכִי הוּא דְּאָתָא? וְהָא מִיבְּעֵי לֵיהּ לִכְדִשְׁמוּאֵל, *דְּאָמַר שְׁמוּאֵל: אמִנַּיִן לָאוֹכֵל אֶת הַטֶּבֶל שֶׁהוּא בְּמִיתָה? שֶׁנֶּאֱמַר: "וְלֹא יְחַלְּלוּ אֶת קָדְשֵׁי בְּנֵי יִשְׂרָאֵל אֵת אֲשֶׁר יָרִימוּ לַה'", בָּעֲתִידִים לִתְרוֹם הַכָּתוּב מְדַבֵּר! אִם כֵּן, לִכְתּוֹב קְרָא "אֲשֶׁר הוּרְמוּ", א] מַאי "אֲשֶׁר יָרִימוּ"? שְׁמַע מִינֵּיהּ תַּרְתֵּי.§ בָּעֵי רַבִּי זֵירָא: (א) כְּשֵׁרִין וְאֵין מְרַצִּין, וְכִי פָּלֵיג – בַּחֲדָא פָּלֵיג; אוֹ דִּלְמָא כְּשֵׁרִין וּמְרַצִּין, ב] וּבְתַרְתֵּי פְּלִיגֵי? אָמַר אַבַּיֵּי וְאִיתֵּימָא רַבִּי זְרִיקָא, תָּא שְׁמַע: הַבְּכוֹר וְהַמַּעֲשֵׂר שֶׁשְּׁחָטָן לְשֵׁם שְׁלָמִים – כְּשֵׁרִים, שְׁלָמִים שֶׁשְּׁחָטָן לְשֵׁם בְּכוֹר אוֹ לְשֵׁם מַעֲשֵׂר – פְּסוּלִין; וְאִי ס"ד כְּשֵׁרִין וּמְרַצִּין, בְּכוֹר בַּר רִיצּוּיֵי הוּא? אֶלָּא כְּשֵׁרִין וְאֵין מְרַצִּין; ג] וּמִדְּסֵיפָא כְּשֵׁרִין וְאֵין מְרַצִּין, רֵישָׁא נַמִי כְּשֵׁרִין וְאֵין מְרַצִּין. מִידֵּי אִירְיָא? הָא כִּדְאִיתָא וְהָא כִּדְאִיתָא. אֶלָּא מַאי קמ"ל? גָּבוֹהַּ וְנָמוּךְ קמ"ל? תָּנֵינָא: כֵּיצַד? קָדְשֵׁי קָדָשִׁים שֶׁשְּׁחָטָן לְשֵׁם קָדָשִׁים קַלִּים כו'! מַהוּ דְּתֵימָא: קָדְשֵׁי קָדָשִׁים וְקָדָשִׁים קַלִּים הוּא דְּאִיכָּא גָּבוֹהַּ וְנָמוּךְ, אֲבָל קַלִּים וְקַלִּים לָא. הָא נַמִי תָּנֵינָא: *שְׁלָמִים קוֹדְמִים אֶת הַבְּכוֹר, מִפְּנֵי שֶׁהֵן טְעוּנִין מַתַּן אַרְבַּע וּסְמִיכָה וּנְסָכִים וּתְנוּפַת חָזֶה וָשׁוֹק! הָא עִיקָּר, הַהִיא אַגְּרָרָא נְסִבָהּ.§ **מתני'** *הַפֶּסַח שֶׁשְּׁחָטוֹ (ב) שַׁחֲרִית בְּאַרְבָּעָה עָשָׂר שֶׁלֹּא לִשְׁמוֹ – רַבִּי יְהוֹשֻׁעַ מַכְשִׁיר, כְּאִילּוּ נִשְׁחַט בִּשְׁלֹשָׁה עָשָׂר; בֶּן בְּתֵירָא בפּוֹסֵל, כְּאִילּוּ נִשְׁחַט בֵּין הָעַרְבַּיִם. *)אָמַר שִׁמְעוֹן בֶּן עַזַּאי: מְקוּבָּל אֲנִי מִפִּי שִׁבְעִים וּשְׁנַיִם זָקֵן בַּיּוֹם שֶׁהוֹשִׁיבוּ אֶת **)רַבִּי אֱלִיעֶזֶר ד] בַּיְשִׁיבָה, שֶׁכָּל הַזְּבָחִים (ג) הַנֶּאֱכָלִין שֶׁנִּזְבְּחוּ שֶׁלֹּא לִשְׁמָן – כְּשֵׁרִין, אֶלָּא שֶׁלֹּא עָלוּ לַבְּעָלִים מִשּׁוּם חוֹבָה, חוּץ מִן הַפֶּסַח וּמִן הַחַטָּאת. וְלֹא הוֹסִיף בֶּן עַזַּאי אֶלָּא הָעוֹלָה, וְלֹא הוֹדוּ לוֹ חֲכָמִים.§ **גמ'** *אָמַר רַבִּי אֶלְעָזָר אָמַר רַבִּי אוֹשַׁעְיָא: מַכְשִׁיר הָיָה בֶּן בְּתֵירָא בְּפֶסַח שֶׁשְּׁחָטוֹ שַׁחֲרִית בְּאַרְבָּעָה עָשָׂר לִשְׁמוֹ, דְּכוּלֵּיהּ יוֹמָא זִימְנֵיהּ הוּא. וּמַאי "כְּאִילּוּ"? אַיְּדֵי דְּאָמַר רַבִּי יְהוֹשֻׁעַ "כְּאִילּוּ", אָמַר אִיהוּ נַמִי "כְּאִילּוּ". אִי הָכִי, אַדְּמִיפַּלְגֵי בְּשֶׁלֹּא לִשְׁמוֹ, לִיפַּלְגוּ בְּלִשְׁמוֹ! אִי אִיפַּלְגוּ בְּלִשְׁמוֹ, הֲוָה אָמֵינָא: אֲבָל בְּשֶׁלֹּא לִשְׁמוֹ מוֹדֵי רַבִּי יְהוֹשֻׁעַ לְבֶן בְּתֵירָא, הוֹאִיל וּמִקְצָתוֹ רָאוּי, קָא מַשְׁמַע לָן. וְהָכְתִיב: °"בֵּין הָעַרְבָּיִם"! אָמַר עוּלָּא בְּרֵיהּ דְּרַב עִילַּאי: בֵּין שְׁנֵי עַרְבַּיִם. תָּמִיד, דִּכְתִיב בֵּיהּ °"בֵּין הָעַרְבָּיִם", הָכִי נַמִי דְּכוּלֵּי יוֹמָא כָּשֵׁר? הָתָם, מִדִּכְתִיב: °"אֶת הַכֶּבֶשׂ ה] *אֶחָד תַּעֲשֶׂה בַבֹּקֶר", מִכְּלָל דְּבֵין הָעַרְבַּיִם – בֵּין הָעַרְבַּיִם מַמָּשׁ. (ד) אֵימָא: חַד בַּבֹּקֶר, אִידָךְ כּוּלֵּיהּ יוֹמָא! אֶחָד בַּבֹּקֶר, וְלֹא שְׁנַיִם בַּבֹּקֶר. נֵרוֹת, דִּכְתִיב °"בֵּין הָעַרְבַּיִם", הָכִי נַמִי דְּכוּלֵּי יוֹמָא כָּשֵׁר! שָׁאנֵי הָתָם, דִּכְתִיב: "מֵעֶרֶב וְעַד בֹּקֶר", *וְתַנְיָא: °"מֵעֶרֶב וְעַד בֹּקֶר" – גתֵּן לָהּ מִדָּתָהּ שֶׁתְּהֵא דּוֹלֶקֶת וְהוֹלֶכֶת מֵעֶרֶב וְעַד בֹּקֶר. דָּבָר אַחֵר: ו] אֵין לְךָ עֲבוֹדָה כְּשֵׁרָה מֵעֶרֶב וְעַד בֹּקֶר אֶלָּא זוֹ בִּלְבַד. קְטוֹרֶת דִּכְתִיב בָּהּ: °"בֵּין הָעַרְבַּיִם", הָכִי נַמִי דְּכוּלֵּי יוֹמָא כָּשֵׁר! שָׁאנֵי קְטֹרֶת, דְּאִיתְקַשׁ

*) ידים פ"ד מ"ב **) [נ"ל ר' אלעזר בן עזריה וכ"ה במשנה שבמשניות]

רש"י:

אמר לו רבי יהושע מצינו מותר חטאת בא עולה. כדתניא בתמורה (דף כג:): זה מדרש דרש יהוידע הכהן: כל דבר שבא ממותר חטאת וממותר אשם – ילקח בהן עולה לקיץ המזבח. והיכי דמי מותר חטאת – כגון הפריש מעות לחטאתו וניתותרו. אי נמי: מפריש שתי חטאות לאחריות, דקי"ל בתמורה (דף כד.) מתכפר באחת מהן, והשניה תרעה. ומה חטאת שמותרה כו'. ואם ק"ו כזה אתה דורש – יש לך לפסול עולה לשם חטאת. ומהכא דייק רבה מילתיה לעיל, מדלא אהדר ליה רבי אליעזר: אנא נמי פסילנא בנשחטין לשם חטאת. שכן כשרה לשמה כל השנה. לפיכך עולה הנשחטת לשם חטאת כשרה. ולא יחללו את קדשי. אין ז] (כאן) חילול כשירימו אותם לשם גבוה מהם. בעתידין לתרום. דהיינו טבל, דכתיב: "ירימו" דבר העתיד. ומסיים ח] בהא בסנהדרין פרק "אלו הן הנשרפין": גמר (ה) חילול מתרומה, דכתיב בה: "ומתו בו כי יחללוהו". *א"כ. דלכר"ש אחי עזריה לחודיה אתא, לכתוב "ולא יחללו אשר הורמו". מ"ש לשון עתיד דנקט? ש"מ למידרש ביה נמי הא. בעי רבי זירא. "לשום גבוה מהן כשרים" דקתני, כשרין ואין מרצין קאמר כת"ק. ולא פליג אלא בנמוך, דקאמר פסולים לגמרי. ובתרתי פליגי. לשם גבוה מכשיר לגמרי, ובנמוך פסיל לגמרי. ואילו רבנן בתרווייהו ט] מכשירים ואין מרצין קאמרי. ת"ש. מדקא מפרש מילתיה ונקיט בכור ומעשר, דלא לרצויי אתו – ש"מ: כשרין ואינן מרצין קאמר. ומדסיפא. הבכור והמעשר ששחטן לשם שלמים כשרים ואין מרצין, (ו) רישא – קדשים קלים ששחטן לשם קדשי קדשים – נמי כשרין ואין מרצין קאמר. הא כדאיתא כו'. "כשרין" דקתני גבי בכור – כשרין למילתייהו קאמר. י] [*ו"כשרים" נמי דקתני גבי קדשי קדשים – למילתייהו קאמר], ואפי' לרצות לשם חובה. אלא מאי קמשמע לן. האי דנקט הבכור והמעשר, אי לאו לגלויי עלה דרישא נקט לה, ולמימר דכשרין ואין מרצין קאמר? גבוה ונמוך קמשמע לן. בתמיה, וכי אתא לפרושי לן היכי דמי יא] נמוך לשם גבוה? תנינא. ברישא דמילתא. הא נמי תנינא. לקמן בפרק "כל התדיר" (דף פט.) דבכור נמוך משלמים. שלמים קודמין את הבכור. אם שניהם עומדים לישחט בעזרה ולהקריב. שהן טעונים מתן ארבע. שתי מתנות שהן ארבע. ובכור במתנה אחת, כדתנן ב"איזהו מקומן" (לקמן נו:). סמיכה ונסכים ליתנהו בבכור, כדילפינן במנחות בפרק "שתי מדות" (דף צ:). הא עיקר. שנשנית תחילה לצורך, לאשמועינן גבי פסול שלא לשמו, דאיכא בקדשים קלים גבוה ונמוך. ההיא. ד"כל התדיר", אגררא יב] נסבה, ששנה שם את הקודמים זה לזה, ונקט נמי האי בהדייהו אע"ג דכבר תנייה הכא. **מתני'** רבי יהושע מכשיר. דפסח בשאר ימות השנה חשיב ליה. בן בתירא פוסל. בגמרא מפרש להו. שבעים ושנים זקן. בגמרא מפרש אמאי לא תנא "זקנים". כל הזבחים הנאכלין. אבל עולה לא. לא הוסיף בן עזאי. על דברי חכמים לפסול חוץ מפסח ומחטאת, אלא העולה. **גמ'** מכשיר היה בן בתירא בפסח ששחטו שחרית לשמו. (ז) והוה ליה זמנו, לפיכך פסול שלא לשמו, כדאמר: פסח בזמנו שלא לשמו פסול. ומאי כאילו. נשחט בין הערבים? והאמרת דכולא יומא בין הערבים קרי ליה! מדקמכשרת ליה שחרית, וקרא כתיב "בין הערבים", אלמא סבירא ליה: בין ערב של אמש לערב של אחריו, יג] כדמפרשינן ליה לקמיה, דהיינו משעלה השחר, שפסק ליל של אמש, עד שתשקע החמה. ומאי "כאילו"? הא הוא גופיה בין הערבים! (ח). ליפלגו בלשמו. ולימא: יד] [פסח ששחטו בי"ד שחרית], ר' יהושע פוסל ובן בתירא מכשיר! אבל בשלא לשמו מודה רבי יהושע. דאע"ג דשחרית לאו זימניה הוא – פסול, הואיל ומקצתו של יום ראוי לשמו, קמ"ל. והא כתיב בין הערבים. לרבי אושעיא פריך: היכי מצי למימר פסח זמנו שחרית? בין שני ערבים. מעלות השחר עד שקיעת החמה, דהיינו בין סוף ערב דאתמול טו] ותחילת ערב דאורתא. ואימא חד בבקר. את הראשון לא ישהא יותר מחצות, והשני כל היום זמנו, דלא – שחרית, דלא – ערבית, כדכתיב "בין הערבים", טז] דמפרשת ליה כל יומא. ולא שנים בבקר. הלכך, על כרחך צריך להשהות השני עד הערב. מדתה. חצי לוג, לכל נר ונר. כך שיערו חכמים לילי תקופת טבת שלא תכבה כל הלילה, ובתמוז ובניסן ובתשרי אם תדליק שליש היום – לא איכפת לן יז]. אין לך עבודה. מעבודות שהן אמורות ביום, כגון עבודות הדם יח] *וקמצו וקטרת, שכשרין מהדלקת נרות ואילך. שזו מאוחרת לכולן. דאיתקש

תוספות:

אמר ר' אליעזר לא אם אמרת בחטאת. יט] *דין הוא שאחרים כשרים לשמו. [וקשה]: נהי דלא דמי לפסח, מ"מ ק"ו איכא. וא"כ כ] [תימא] יפסלו נמי מהאי דינא *מותר חטאת בא עולה, כמו דינא דמותר פסח בא שלמים! וי"ל: דאעיקר טעמו סמיך, כא] כדאיתא בפסחים (דף סב:*). וי"ל: דהא "לא אם אמרת" דקאמר רבי אליעזר – לדברי רבי יהושע קאמר, אליבא דרבי יוחנן. כב] ורבינו תם מצא בספר ישן ברישא דשמעתא כג] "רבה אמר: באחרים לשם חטאת", כד] ומלא "ובאחרים" בוי"ו. ורבה לא בא אלא לפרש דברי רבי יוחנן. ור' יוחנן עצמו מודה דבאחרים לשם חטאת פליגי, *ולא אמר "אמרו דבר אחד" אלא כה] באחרים לשם פסח. **הג"ה** אי איפלוג בלשמן כו'. ותימה: השתא נמי דפליגי בשלא לשמן אני יכול לטעות כו] כר"י לבן בתירא שיפסול י"ד לשמו שחרית, ולפרש טעמו משום דמקצתו ראוי! וי"ל: דמזה אינו חושש, משום דשום תנא לא מכשיר פסח שחרית אלא כז] זה. **הג"ה:** אחד בבקר ולא שנים בבקר. בעלמא

עין משפט נר מצוה:

נד א מיי' פ"י מהלכות מאכלות אסורות הלכה יט:
נה ב מיי' פט"ו מהל' פסה"מ הלכה יא:
נו ג מיי' פ"ג מהלכות תמידין הלכה יא:

נ"א כו' כלומר וא"כ
נ"א דמותר חטאת כו' כמו מדינא דמותר כו' נ"ק
[וד"ה שאני התם]
גי' נ"ק ולא אמרו דבר כו'

מסורת הש"ס:

תורה אור
ויקרא כב
רש"ק מ"ז
נ"א א"כ דלדרשת ר"ש כו' נ"ק כשם ס"י
סנהדרין פג. ע"ש
[לקמן פט.]
תוספתא דפסחים
גי' רש"ק ונ"א נ"ב וכו"ל קאמר ואף אלו
[פסחים כח. ושם איתא א"ר אושעיא א"ר אלעזר]
שמות יב
שם כט
שם
שם
שם כז
שם ל
[נ"ל האחד]
יומא טו. פסחים נט. מנחות פט.
נ"ל וקמצו של מנחה וקטרת וכו' ס"א

שיטה מקובצת

א] מאי אשר ירימו כו'. וא"ת ואימא כולה קרא לכדשמואל הוא דאתא כדמשמע מאשר ירימו וי"ל דא"כ לכתוב קרא ולא יחללו את אשר ירימו לה' את קדשי בני ישראל ל"ל ש"מ [דבא] לומר במורם מהם כו' וא"ת אכתי איצטריך לדרשא דלעיל ולא יחללו את קדשי בני ישראל קדשים מחללים קדשים ואין חולין מחללין קדשים וי"ל דא"כ לימא קרא ולא יחללו קודש מאי קדשים ש"מ דדרשינן נמי הא: תרתי. ס"א ואימא כולה להכי הוא דאתא א"כ לימא קרא הרימו מאי ירימו: ב] ובתרתי פליגי. [דלשם גבוה לת"ק] כשרים ולא עלו ולהאי תנא נמי עלו ופליג נמי (מסיפא) [בסיפא] דקתני פסולים דמשמע פסולים לגמרי ולת"ק כשרים ולא עלו וא"ת מי הזקיקו למימר [דפליג] (מסיפא) [בסיפא] ודלמא לא פליגי אלא (מרישא) [ברישא] דקתני כשרים דמשמע כשרים ומרצים אבל (מסיפא) [בסיפא] לא פליג כלל והא דקתני פסולים ר"ל דלא פסולים [לגמרי אלא] כמו פסולים דגבי תודה כדפרש"י לעיל [דף ז' ע"א] ונראה כיון דנפקא ליה מחילול משמע דפסולים לגמרי ע"ל דזה ליכא למימר דא"כ עלו [ולא עלו] מבעיא (כדהתם) לשנות וא"ת א"כ [ה"נ] ברישא דקאמר כשרים ור"ל דמרצין (כשרין ומרצין) ואמאי קאמר כשרין אלא עלו מבעיא ליה [למימר] וי"ל איידי דתני סיפא פסולים [דהוי] פסולים לגמרי קאמר ברישא כשרים: ג] ומדסיפא. פי' וכ"ת אדפשיט מסיפא דכשרין ואין מרצין [תפשוט] מרישא דכשרין ומרצין לכן אמר מדסיפא כשרין ואין מרצין כו' וק"ל: ד] אליעזר בן עזריה: ה] האחד תעשה: ו] אחד מערב עד בקר אין לך: ז] אין כאן: ח] ומסיים לה בסנהדרין תיבת בהא נמחק: ט] בתרווייהו כשרים אות מ' נמחק:

הגהות הב"ח

(א) גמ' בעי רבי זירא כשרין. נ"ב והא דפשיטא ליה בסמוך פסולין לגמרי היינו מכח דיוקא דקרא ולא יחללו את קדשי במורם מהן אין מתחללין הא בנמוך מהן מתחללין והיינו פסול לגמרי: (ב) שם במשנה בשחרית בי"ד: (ג) שם הנאכלים: (ד) שם ואימא חד: (ה) רש"י ד"ה בעתידין וכו' חילול חילול מתרומה: (ו) ד"ה ומדסיפא וכו' ואין מרצין קאמר רישא: (ז) ד"ה מכשיר וכו' דהוה ליה: (ח) ד"ה ומאי וכו' הערבים הוא הס"ד:

י] קאמר וכשרים דקתני גבי קדשים קלים כשרים למילתייהו קאמר ותיבת נמי ל"ש: יא] תיבות נמוך נמחק: יב] אגררא. אגב גררא נסבא: יג] אחריו כדמפרש לה לקמיה: יד] ולימא הפסח ששחט בשחרית לשמו ר' יהושע: טו] דאתמול לתחילת ערב: טז] הערבים כדמפרשת ליה כל יומא הס"ד ומה"ד האחד בבקר ולא שנים בבקר: יז] לן מיהו בירושלמי מפרש דביומי ניסן ותשרי היו עושין פתילות עבות לפי שיעור הלילות. תוס': יח] הדם ס"א היום וקמיצה וקטורת שכשרה מהדלקת: יט] בחטאת כו' ולפיכך דין הוא שאחרים כשרים לשמו וקשה: כ] וא"כ נימא תיבת תימא ל"ש ונמחק: כא] סמיך אקרא דכתיב זבח פסח הוא בהויתו יהא כדאיתא בפסחים בפ' תמיד נשחט: כב] ע' בהשמטות בסוף המסכת: כג] דשמעתא ורבה: כד] תיבות ומצא ובאחרים נמחק: כה] אלא מאחרים לשם פסח ע"כ: כו] לטעות בדברי בן בתירא ותיבת כר"י ואות ל' נמחק: כז] אלא הוא ולית הלכתא כוותיה הלכך ליכא למיחש דלמא אתי למטעי בדבריו הס"ד ותיבת זה נמחק:

דְּאִיתְקַשׁ לְנֵרוֹת. הָתָם נַמִּי כְּתִיב: °"שָׁם תִּזְבַּח אֶת הַפֶּסַח בָּעָרֶב"! הַהוּא לְ"יאוּחַר דָּבָר" הוּא דְּאָתָא, א] *דְּתַנְיָא: יְאוּחַר דָּבָר שֶׁנֶּאֱמַר בּוֹ "בָּעֶרֶב" וּ"בֵין הָעַרְבַּיִם", לְדָבָר שֶׁלֹּא נֶאֱמַר בּוֹ אֶלָּא "בֵּין הָעַרְבַּיִם" בִּלְבַד. וּמִי אִיכָּא מִידֵי, דְּאִילּוּ שָׁחֵיט לֵיהּ מִצַּפְרָא, אָמְרַתְּ: זִימְנֵיהּ הוּא, וְכִי מָטֵי בֵּין הָעַרְבַּיִם, אָמְרַתְּ: "יְאוּחַר דָּבָר"? אִין, *דְּהָא"ר יוֹחָנָן: ב] אהֲלָכָה, מִתְפַּלֵּל שֶׁל מִנְחָה וְאח"כ מִתְפַּלֵּל שֶׁל מוּסָפִין. וּ"בֵין הָעַרְבַּיִם" דִּכְתִיב גַּבֵּי קְטֹרֶת וְנֵרוֹת לָמָּה לִי? וְעוֹד, ג] *הֵשִׁיב רַבִּי תַּחַת בֶּן בְּתֵירָא לְדִבְרֵי רַבִּי יְהוֹשֻׁעַ: לֹא, אִם אָמַרְתָּ בִּשְׁלֹשָׁה עָשָׂר – שֶׁאֵין מִקְצָתוֹ רָאוּי, תֹּאמַר בְּאַרְבָּעָה עָשָׂר שֶׁמִּקְצָתוֹ רָאוּי; ד] וְאִם אִיתָא – כּוּלּוֹ רָאוּי הוּא! אֶלָּא א"ר יוֹחָנָן: בפּוֹסֵל הָיָה בֶּן בְּתֵירָא בְּפֶסַח שֶׁשְּׁחָטוֹ בְּאַרְבָּעָה עָשָׂר שַׁחֲרִית, בֵּין לִשְׁמוֹ בֵּין שֶׁלֹּא לִשְׁמוֹ, ה] הוֹאִיל וּמִקְצָתוֹ רָאוּי. מְגַדֵּף בָּהּ רַבִּי אַבָּהוּ: א"כ, פֶּסַח כָּשֵׁר לְבֶן בְּתֵירָא הֵיכִי מַשְׁכַּחַתְּ לָהּ? אִי דְּאַפְרְשֵׁיהּ הָאִידָּנָא – דָּחוּי מֵעִיקָּרוֹ הוּא, וְאִי ו] דְּאַפְרְשִׁינְהוּ מֵאֶתְמוֹל – נִרְאֶה וְנִדְחֶה הוּא! אֶלָּא אָמַר רַבִּי אַבָּהוּ: תְּהֵא לְאַחַר חֲצוֹת. אַבַּיֵּי אָמַר: אֲפִילּוּ תֵּימָא מִצַּפְרָא, *אֵין מְחוּסַּר זְמַן לְבוֹ בַּיּוֹם. רַב פַּפָּא אָמַר: אֲפִילּוּ תֵּימָא מֵאוּרְתָא,* לַיְלָה אֵין מְחוּסַּר זְמַן; דְּתָנֵי דְּבֵי ז] ר' יִשְׁמָעֵאל: גלֵיל שְׁמִינִי נִכְנָס לַדִּיר לְהִתְעַשֵּׂר. וְכִדְרַבִּי אַפְּטוֹרִיקִי, *דְּרַבִּי אַפְּטוֹרִיקִי רָמֵי, כְּתִיב: °"וְהָיָה שִׁבְעַת יָמִים תַּחַת אִמּוֹ" – הָא לַיְלָה חֲזֵי, וּכְתִיב: °"וּמִיּוֹם הַשְּׁמִינִי וָהָלְאָה יֵרָצֶה" – הָא לַיְלָה לָא חֲזֵי! הָא כֵּיצַד? ח] לַיְלָה לִקְדוּשָּׁה, וְיוֹם לְהַרְצָאָה. ט] א"ל רַבִּי זֵירָא לְרַבִּי אַבָּהוּ: לֵימָא קָסָבַר רַבִּי יוֹחָנָן: בַּעֲלֵי חַיִּים נִדְחִין? אֲמַר לֵיהּ: אִין. *דְּא"ר יוֹחָנָן: יבְּהֵמָה שֶׁל שְׁנֵי שׁוּתָּפִין, הִקְדִּישׁ חֶצְיָהּ, וְחָזַר וְלָקַח חֶצְיָהּ וְהִקְדִּישָׁהּ – קְדוֹשָׁה וְאֵינָהּ קְרֵיבָה, הוְעוֹשָׂה תְּמוּרָה, וּתְמוּרָתָהּ כַּיּוֹצֵא בָּהּ. *וּשְׁמַע מִינַּהּ תְּלָת; שְׁמַע מִינַּהּ: בַּעֲלֵי חַיִּים נִדְחִין, וש"מ: דָּחוּי מֵעִיקָּרָא הָוֵה דָּחוּי, י] וש"מ:

יֵשׁ

דברים טז | ויקרא כב | שם

תורה אור

דְּאִיתְקַשׁ לְנֵרוֹת. "וּבְהַעֲלוֹת אַהֲרֹן" וגו', וְהַיְינוּ בֵּין הָעַרְבַּיִם דִּקְטוֹרֶת. יְאוּחַר דָּבָר. יְאוּחַר פֶּסַח לְתָמִיד. דְּאַע"ג דְּכוּלֵּיהּ יוֹמָא זִמְנֵיהּ, אִי שָׁהְיֵיהּ עַד זְמַן שְׁחִיטַת הַתָּמִיד – תָּמִיד קוֹדֵם לוֹ. אִין דְּהָא"ר יוֹחָנָן. בְּמַסֶּכֶת בְּרָכוֹת. יא] הֲלָכָה. כְּדִבְרֵי הָאוֹמֵר: הָיוּ לְפָנָיו ב' תְּפִלּוֹת, אַחַת שֶׁל מִנְחָה וְאַחַת שֶׁל מוּסָפִין, שֶׁשָּׁהָא וְלֹא הִתְפַּלֵּל שֶׁל מוּסָפִין עַד יב] זְמַן חֲבֵירְתָּהּ – מַשְׁהִינַן לָהּ. וּבֵין הָעַרְבַּיִם דִּכְתִיב גַּבֵּי קְטוֹרֶת וְנֵרוֹת לָמָּה לִי. הוֹאִיל וּמִינֵּיהּ לָא הָוֵי מַשְׁמַע לָן בֵּין הָעַרְבַּיִם מַמָּשׁ, וּמִבָּעֵי לָן קְרָא יג] אַחֲרִינֵי לְפָרוּשֵׁי. וְעוֹד. תָּנֵי בַּתּוֹסֶפְתָּא תְּיוּבְתָּא לְר' אוֹשַׁעְיָא, דְּקָתָנֵי: הֵשִׁיב רַבִּי תַּחַת בֶּן בְּתֵירָא כו'. לְדִבְרֵי ר' יְהוֹשֻׁעַ. דְּאָמַר: כְּאִילּוּ נִשְׁחַט בי"ג. שֶׁאֵין מִקְצָתוֹ רָאוּי. לִשְׁמוֹ, הִלְכָּךְ לָא קָרֵינַן בֵּיהּ פֶּסַח בִּזְמַנּוֹ. אַלְמָא יד] דְּרַבִּי דְּס"ל כְּבֶן בְּתֵירָא, וּמִשּׁוּם דְּמִקְצָתוֹ רָאוּי לִשְׁמוֹ הוּא דְּקָאָמַר טַעְמֵיהּ. וְאִם אִיתָא. דְּבֶן בְּתֵירָא טו] שַׁחֲרִית מַכְשֵׁר לִשְׁמוֹ – כּוּלּוֹ רָאוּי לִשְׁמוֹ הוּא. מְגַדֵּף בָּהּ. בְּהָא דְּרַבִּי יוֹחָנָן. א"כ. דְּבֵין לִשְׁמוֹ וּבֵין שֶׁלֹּא לִשְׁמוֹ פָּסוּל. פֶּסַח כָּשֵׁר. בִּזְמַנּוֹ לִשְׁמוֹ, לְבֶן בְּתֵירָא. הֵיכִי מַשְׁכַּחַתְּ לָהּ אִי דְּאַפְרְשֵׁיהּ הָאִידָּנָא. בי"ד טז] בְּשַׁחֲרִית. דָּחוּי מֵעִיקָּרָא הוּא. דִּבְשַׁעַת הַפְרָשָׁה לָא חֲזֵי לְמִידֵי. וְשָׁמְעִינַן לֵיהּ לְר' יוֹחָנָן דְּאָמַר: יז] דָּחוּי מֵעִיקָּרָא הָוֵי דָּחוּי לְגַמְרֵי, שֶׁלֹּא יח] לְהֵירָצוֹת עוֹד. וְאִי דְּאַפְרְשֵׁיהּ מֵאֶתְמוֹל נִרְאֶה וְנִדְחֶה הוּא. דְּכִי אַפְרְשֵׁיהּ – חֲזֵי לְהַקְרִיבוֹ שֶׁלֹּא לִשְׁמוֹ, וְכִי מָטְיָא י"ד שַׁחֲרִית – לָא חֲזֵי לְמִידֵי, וְנִרְאֶה וְנִדְחֶה שׁוּב אֵינוֹ חוֹזֵר וְנִרְאֶה לְדִבְרֵי הַכֹּל! בִּשְׁלָמָא לְרַבָּנַן – פֶּסַח אֵינוֹ נִדְחֶה כְּלָל, אוֹ מִלִּשְׁמוֹ אוֹ מִשֶּׁלֹּא לִשְׁמוֹ, דְּעַד זְמַן שְׁחִיטָתוֹ חֲזֵי לִשְׁלָמִים, וּבִזְמַנּוֹ חֲזֵי לְפֶסַח. אֶלָּא לְבֶן בְּתֵירָא דָּחוּי הוּא! תְּהֵא לְאַחַר חֲצוֹת. מַשְׁכַּחַתְּ לָהּ פֶּסַח כָּשֵׁר לְבֶן בְּתֵירָא בְּמַפְרִישׁ לְאַחַר חֲצוֹת, דְּהַיְינוּ זְמַן שְׁחִיטָתוֹ, וַחֲזֵי לִשְׁמוֹ. אֲפִי' תֵּימָא מִצַּפְרָא. וְאֵין כָּאן דָּחוּי מֵעִיקָּרוֹ, הוֹאִיל וְרָאוּי הַיּוֹם אֵין כָּאן חִסָּרוֹן זְמַן רְאִיָּיתוֹ. לֵיל שְׁמִינִי נִכְנָס. הַוָּלָד יט] לְהִתְעַשֵּׂר. וְקַיְימָא לָן בִּבְכוֹרוֹת בְּפֶרֶק "מַעֲשַׂר בְּהֵמָה" (דף נז.): מְחוּסַּר זְמַן אֵינוֹ נִכְנָס לַדִּיר לְהִתְעַשֵּׂר כ]. הָא לַיְלָה. לֵיל שְׁמִינִי חֲזֵי, וְלָא הָוֵי מְחוּסַּר זְמַן. לִקְדוּשָּׁה. רָאוּי לְהַקְדִּישׁוֹ, וְאַע"ג דְּלָא חֲזֵי לַיְלָה לְהַקְרָבָה – קָאָמְרִינַן דְּמַקְדִּישׁ לֵיהּ. אַלְמָא לַיְלָה אֵין מְחוּסַּר זְמַן, הוֹאִיל וּמָחָר יִהְיֶה רָאוּי. לֵימָא קָסָבַר ר' יוֹחָנָן כו'. מִדְּאִיצְטְרִיךְ לָן לְשַׁנּוּיֵי אַלִּיבֵּיהּ בְּמַפְרִישׁ לְאַחַר חֲצוֹת, דְּאִי לָא שְׁמִיעַ לָךְ מִינֵּיהּ בַּעֲלֵי חַיִּים נִדְחִים – רָאוּי לְהַפְרִישׁוֹ לְעוֹלָם, דִּדְלְמָא אֵין דִּחוּי אֶלָּא בִּשְׁחוּטִין, כְּגוֹן: מֵת הַמִּשְׁתַּלֵּחַ כא] יִשָּׁפֵךְ הַדָּם, בְּמַסֶּ' יוֹמָא (דף סב.). הִקְדִּישׁ חֶצְיָהּ. אֶחָד מֵהֶם. וְעוֹשָׂה תְּמוּרָה. דְּהָא אֵינָהּ דְּשׁוּתָּפִין. (א) וְאֵינָהּ קְרֵיבָה. הוֹאִיל וּבִתְחִילַּת הַקְדָּשָׁה לֹא נִרְאֲתָה לְהַקְרִיב, דְּחֶלְיֵיהּ הָיְתָה חוּלִּין, וְדָחוּי מֵעִיקָּרוֹ הוּא – הִלְכָּךְ אֵינָהּ קְרֵיבָה עוֹד. וְתִרְעֶה, וְלוֹקְחִין בְּדָמֶיהָ אַחֶרֶת.

יֵשׁ

בעלמא דרשינן "אחד" – כב] מן המיוחד שבעדרו (מגילה דף כח.). **ובין** הערבים דכתיב בקטורת ונרות למה לי. בין הערבים דתמיד ניחא ליה, כג] לכדאמר בריש "תמיד נשחט" (פסחים דף נח.) דזימניה מכי ינטו צללי ערב. **ואם** איתא כוליה ראוי הוא. ולא מצי לתרץ דנקט מקצתו ראוי משום רבי יהושע. משום דהכי פריך: מנא ליה לר' אושעיא דבן בתירא מכשיר פסח שחרית? אי משום דפסול שלא לשמו – דלמא טעמא משום דמקצתו ראוי, דהא חזינן הכא דטעם טוב הוא. אבל לדברי ר' אושעיא דאינו תופסו לטעם טוב – א"כ מאי פריך רבי לרבי יהושע? הלא בכולו ראוי הוא תליא מילתא! כד]. **הג"ה:** אי דאפרשיה האידנא דחוי מעיקרא הוא. דלא דמי למחוסר כפורים, כה] דלא חשיב דחוי קודם הבאת קרבנו, דאין זמנו עד שיטהר ויטבול. אבל האי לא חזי לפסח ושלמים אע"פ שהיה זמן שלמים כו]. **רב** פפא אמר אפילו תימא מאורתא לילה אין מחוסר זמן. כז] בריש מנחות (דף ה.) משמע דרב פפא ס"ל יש מחוסר זמן לבו ביום. וצריך לחלק בין מחוסר זמן דהכא להתם כח]. **לילה** אין מחוסר זמן. וכן משמע בברייתא ובחגיגה (דף ט:) לרבי יוחנן, וכן במנחות פרק "שתי הלחם" (דף ק.), ובנזיר (יח:), וביומא פרק "אמר להם הממונה" (דף כט:). **לילה** לקדושה כט] יום להרצאה. א) הקשה ל] הרב רבי יוסף: דבתמורה (דף י.) משמע דתם במעי תמימה קדוש, דקדושה חלה אעובר במעי אמו. והיאך קדוש? בין לבר פדא בין לר' יוחנן? והא לילה לקדושה דוקא, אבל קודם לכן לא! לא]. **יום** להרצאה. תימה: תיפוק לי מ"ביום צוותו", ולמה לי דכתיב לב] "ביום השמיני"! וי"ל: דאי לא כתיב אלא "והיה שבעת ימים תחת אמו", הוה אמינא: אם שחט בלילה, אם עלו – לא ירדו. והשתא קמשמע לן דהוי מחוסר זמן, ותרד לג] [אפילו לר"ש], דאין פסולו בקודש. ובפ' בתרא (לקמן קיב:) נמי לד] תנן: מחוסר זמן ששחטו בחוץ – אינו בכרת, דאם עלו לא ירדו, מוכח התם דקרי מתקבל לפתח אהל מועד, וחייב כרת בחוץ. לה] ולר"י דאמר (לקמן דף פד.) בשחיטת לילה אם עלה לו] תרד – י"ל למ"ד בפרק בתרא (שם קכ.) אין לילה בבמה, השתא שהוא מחוסר זמן אם שחט לז] לילה אחר שביעי – פסול אף בבמה. וקשה למאן דאמר יש פסול לילה בבמה! יש לומר: דמודה אף ר"י דבבמה שחיטת לילה לא תרד לח]. **הג"ה:** קדושה ואינה קריבה. לא דמי ל"רגלה של זו עולה" דתמכר לצורכי עולה (תמורה דף יא:), דהתם אינה דחויה, כיון דבידו לקדשה. **ש"מ** בעלי חיים נדחין. וא"ת: מאי קמ"ל ר' יוחנן? מתני' היא בפ' "מי שהיה טמא" (פסחים לז:): המפריש נקבה לפסחו כו', ואמרי' עלה בגמ' (לח.): ש"מ תלת! וכי תימא: משום דאיכא פלוגתא דתנאי בבעלי חיים נדחין בפ' "שני שעירי" (יומא דף סד.), ואשמועינן ר' יוחנן דבעלי חיים נדחין – הא א"ר יוחנן חדא זימנא! וי"ל: דמפריש נקבה דחייה בידים, ואפי' לט] [רב] מודה התם דבעלי חיים נדחין. ומיהו, קשה מאכל חלב והמיר דתו, דהוי דחייה בידים. ועוד: דהוי נראה ונדחה, ולמה ליה לרבי יוחנן לאשמועינן? וצריך לדקדק בכל הנך מימרות דר' יוחנן, הנך תלת דבעלי חיים נדחים, ובשני מקומות דפליגי רב ור' יוחנן, בההיא דבפרק "שני שעירי", ובההיא דלקמן פ' "קדשי קדשים" (דף נט.) גבי מזבח שנפגם*. **ושמע** מינה יש דיחוי בדמים. פי' בקונט': בדבר שאין בו אלא קדושת דמים, מ] *לא תימא שאין דחוי מעיקרא (אין בו) אלא בקדושת הגוף. וא"ת: א"כ, דחוי מעיקרא ודחוי בדמים – הכל אחד, דכל דחוי מעיקרא אין בו אלא קדושת דמים! מא] וי"ל: דמשכחת לה בקבל דם בכלי שיש בו מים, דראשון ראשון דחוי, מב] וחזר ונהפך למראה דם. ובפ' "התערובת" (לקמן דף עח.) אמרי' דדם לתוך מים – ראשון ראשון בטל. ולענין כיסוי אינו כן, דאין דחוי אלא מצות. וה"ר חיים מפרש: יש דחוי בדמים – שדוחה תמורה שלא לקרב. מג] *ואמרי': כאן דאין קדושה אלא לדמים, לא אלימא להתפיס התמורה לדחותה מקדושתה לעשותה כיוצא בה. וכפי' זה משמע מתוך גירסת הספרים דכריתות, דגרסי' התם (דף כח.) כך: ש"מ בעלי חיים נדחין – דקתני: ואינה קריבה. וש"מ קדושת דמים מדחה – דקתני: ותמורתה כיוצא בה. וש"מ יש דחוי בדמים – דקתני: קדושה, למאי – לדמים. ודחוי מעיקרו לא קתני התם. ומיהו, ה"ר חיים גרים: דחוי מעיקרו, ולא גרים "יש דחוי בדמים". וכן יש כמה ספרים. ולפי' קשה מההיא דמפריש נקבה לפסחו, דלא קאמר התם: תמורתה כיוצא בה. ואמרי' עלה: יש דחוי בדמים. וכן מד] בפ' בתרא דכריתות (דף כח.) דקאמר ר' אלעזר אמר ר' אושעיא: מטמא מקדש עשיר שהפריש קן לכבשתו והעני כו', דקאמר: ש"מ תלת, ולא שייכא תמורה, מה] [דאין תמורה בעופות]. ורבינו ש"י פי' בתשובה כמו שפי'. מו] וכתב: דבר זה למדתי פירושו ממס' כריתות, דגרסי' התם בלשון זה: ש"מ קדושת דמים מדחה. כלומר, ש"מ אפי' מז] שלא קידשה מתחילה להקרבת גופו אלא מח] קדושת דמים, כגון הקדיש אליה ואליה שני חולין. מט] והכי נמי פרשינן ליה יש דיחוי בדמים – כגון נקבה לפסחו, לא חזיא גופא לפסח אלא לדמיה, וכי אקדשה – לדמים אקדשה. ואיידי דדחויה היא, דלא חזיא לאקרובי גופא לדבר שהוקדשה לה – אמרי' תדחה

מלקרב

א) עי' בתמורה י ע"ב שתירצו וז"ל וי"ל דקודש שנולד מאי מקדיש ליה ומייתי לה בבכורות מקרא עכ"ל רש"ק

נז א מיי' פ"ג מהלכות תפלה הלכה יא סמג עשין יט טוש"ע א"ח סי' רפו סעיף ד:
נח ב מיי' פט"ו מהל' פסה"מ הלכה יב:
נט ג עי' כ"מ פ"ו מהל' בכורות הלכה יד:
ס ד ה מיי' פט"ו מהל' מעה"ק הל' ד ופסק דקריבה ולא כר"י:

שיטה מקובצת

א] דאתא כדתניא: ב] עי' בהשמטות בסוף המסכת: ג] ועוד תניא: ד] עי' בהשמטות בסוף המסכת: ה] לשמו לשמו דבעי בין הערבים שלא לשמו הואיל: ו] דאפרשיה: ז] דתני דבי ר' ישמעאל נ"א דבי שמואל: ח] לילה לקדושה. אבל קודם ליל שמיני אינו קדוש ותימה דאמרינן בתמורה דעובר קדוש במעי אמו וי"ל דשאני התם דחלה קדושה [אגב אמו] אבל אם הקדישו קדושת הפה אינו ראוי לחול עד [ליל] שמיני. א"נ במעי אמו אינו ראוי להקרבה ורחמנא לא פסלי משום מחוסר זמן אלא כשנולד וראוי הוא להקריבו רחמנא פסליה משום מחוסר זמן (דקאמר) [דכתיב] אשר יולד אלמא בלידה תליא מילתא: ט] ויום להרצאה. וא"ת תיפוק ליה מביום צוותו להקריב ביום אתה מקריב ואי אתה מקריב בלילה ולמה [לי] ביום השמיני וי"ל דאיצטריך לר"ש דאמר [אם שחטום] בלילה אם עלו לא ירדו קמ"ל דהכא אם עלו ירדו דלא הוי פסולו בקודש. לשון תוס' טו"ך: י] וש"מ יש דחוי בדמים. י"ס גורסים וש"מ קדושת דמים נדחה והיא היא וי"מ דקדושת דמים מדחה התמורה לענין דאינה קריבה וליתא דבפרק בתרא (דתמורה) [דכריתות דף כח.] קאמר הני תלת גבי עוף וגבי עוף לא שייך תמורה ואע"ג דכולהו ש"מ דקאמר הכא משניות הן קאמר ש"מ כלומר דהלכה כך תוס' אחרות: יא] ברכות דהלכה והד"א: יב] עד זמן המנחה מתפלל של מנחה אע"ג דזמן המוספין קודם כיון דשהי עד זמן: יג] קרא אחרינא אות י' נמחק: יד] אלמא רבי אות ד' נמחק: טו] דבן בתירא מכשיר שחרית: טז] בי"ד שחרית הס"ד: יז] דאמר לקמן: יח] להירצות ס"א להראות: יט] הולד לדיר להתעשר: כ] להתעשר א"כ ש"מ דליל ח' לאו מחוסר זמן הוא הס"ד: כא] המשתלח ישפך ס"א ונשפך: כב] תיבת מן נמחק: כג] דאיצטריך לכדאמר: כד] מילתא ע"כ: כה] כפורים שהפרישו קרבנם קודם הבאתם דהוי דחוי באמצע דהתם לא חשיב: כו] שלמים ודאי כה"ג דיחוי מעיקרא הוא הס"ד: כז] זמן בבכורות ובריש: כח] להתם דהתם מיירי בעבודות שהקדים עבודת שחרית אבל הכא מיירי בהפריש הס"ד: כט] תיבות יום להרצאה נמחק: ל] הקשה. עי' בתוס' פרק בתרא (דף קיד): לא] לא וי"ל דלא שייך מחוסר זמן אלא כשנולד כדכתיב שור או כשב וגו' כדמשמע בפ' כיצד מערימין דיכול להקדיש בכור במעי אמו דלא ממעט ליה קרא אלא כשנולד הא במעי אמו קדיש ולא שייך ביה מחוסר זמן. תו"א: לב] ביום השמיני וי"ל דאי לא כתב אלא והיה (שמונת) [שבעת] ימים תחת אמו הוי אמינא (בהכא) [דהכא] גזירת הכתוב דהוי בלילה. גליון: לג] ותרד אפי' לר"ש משמע דאם עלה ירד דאין: לד] נמי דתנן מחוסר זמן כו' אינו בכרת ואי עלה לא ירד הא מוכח: לה] בחוץ ומיהו קשה לר"י דאמר: לו] עלה ירד קשה למה לי מיום השמיני תיפוק ליה דתרד משום לילה וי"ל: לז] שחט בלילה: לח] תרד ע"כ: לט] ואפי' רב: מ] קדושת דמים ולא תימא שאין דחוי מעיקרא פוסל תיבות ואין בו נמחק: מא] דמים דהיכן מצינו דחוי מעיקרא בקדושת הגוף וי"ל דמשכחת לה דחוי מעיקרא בקדוש קדושת הגוף בקבל: מב] דחוי ואפי' חזר ונהפך: מג] לקרב ולא אמרינן: מד] וכן התם פרק בתרא (דף כח): מה] תמורה בעופות ותיבות דאין תמורה (בעופות) ל"ש ונמחק: מו] שפי' כאן: מז] אפי' דבר שלא קדש: מח] אלא לקדושת: מט] חולין דחוי הוא מלהקריב גופו בתחילת הקדישו ואינו קרב לעולם הואיל ונדחה ידחה ולא נימא אין דחוי בקדשים אלא בדבר הקדוש לגופו ונדחה מהקריב אבל קדושת דמים לא לימא בו תורת דחוי ואי אתא לו שעת הכשר נקרבה כמו הכא דחזר ולקח חציה והכא נמי הכא פרישנא ליה:

אידחי

פסחים נט. | לקמן לג. ברכות כח. | [תוספתא פסחים פ"ד] | מנחות ה. [יומא סב:] | חגיגה ט: וש"נ | חולין פח. | קדושין ז. תמורה כו. [כריתות כז.] | פסחים לה. יומא סד. כריתות כז. כח. [תמורה כו: קדושין ז:] לקמן נט. עג:

הגהות הב"ח

(א) רש"י ד"ה ואינה נ"ל קודם ד"ה ועושה:

[ועי' תוספות יומא סד: ד"ה ברייתא] | ול"ל שאין דחוי אלא כו' נ"ק | ול"ל כיון דאין קדושה נ"ק

תורה אור

יֵשׁ דִּחוּי בְּדָמִים. *אָמַר עוּלָּא אָמַר רַבִּי יוֹחָנָן: אאָכַל חֵלֶב וְהִפְרִישׁ קָרְבָּן, וְנִשְׁתַּמֵּד וְחָזַר בּוֹ — הוֹאִיל וְנִדְחֶה — יִדָּחֶה. אִיתְּמַר נַמִי, אָמַר ר' יִרְמְיָה אָמַר רַבִּי אַבָּהוּ אָמַר רַבִּי יוֹחָנָן: *באָכַל חֵלֶב וְהִפְרִישׁ קָרְבָּן, וְנִשְׁתַּטָּה, וְחָזַר וְנִשְׁתַּפָּה, הוֹאִיל וְנִדְחֶה — יִדָּחֶה. וּצְרִיכִי: דְּאִי אַשְׁמְעִינַן קַמַּיְיתָא — מִשּׁוּם דְּהוּא דָּחֵי נַפְשֵׁיהּ בְּיָדַיִם, אֲבָל הָכָא דְּמִמֵּילָא אִידְּחֵי — א] כְּיָשֵׁן דָּמֵי. וְאִי אַשְׁמְעִינַן הָכָא — מִשּׁוּם דְּאֵין בְּיָדוֹ לַחֲזוֹר, אֲבָל הָכָא דְּיֵשׁ בְּיָדוֹ לַחֲזוֹר — אֵימָא לָא, צְרִיכָא. בָּעֵי רַבִּי יִרְמְיָה: אָכַל חֵלֶב וְהִפְרִישׁ קָרְבָּן, וְהוֹרוּ בֵּית דִּין שֶׁחֵלֶב מוּתָּר, וְחָזְרוּ בָּהֶן, מַהוּ? מִי הָוֵי דָּחוּי, אוֹ לָא הָוֵי דָּחוּי? אֲמַר לֵיהּ הַהוּא סָבָא: כִּי ב] פָּתַח רַבִּי יוֹחָנָן בִּדְחוּיִין — מֵהָא פָּתַח. מַאי טַעְמָא? הָתָם — גַּבְרָא אִידְּחֵי, קָרְבָּן לָא אִידְּחֵי. הָכָא — קָרְבָּן נַמִי אִידְּחֵי. "אָמַר שִׁמְעוֹן בֶּן עַזַּאי: מְקוּבְּלַנִי מִפִּי שִׁבְעִים וּשְׁנַיִם זָקֵן" כו'.§ לָמָּה לִי לְמִתְנָא "שִׁבְעִים וּשְׁנַיִם זָקֵן"? דְּכוּלְּהוּ בַּחֲדָא ג] שִׁיטְתָא הֲווּ קַיְימִי.§ "לֹא הוֹסִיף בֶּן עַזַּאי אֶלָּא הָעוֹלָה".§ אָמַר רַב הוּנָא: מַאי טַעְמָא דְּבֶן עַזַּאי? (ויקרא א) °"עוֹלָה הוּא אִשֵּׁה רֵיחַ נִיחוֹחַ לַה'", הִיא — לִשְׁמָהּ כְּשֵׁרָה, שֶׁלֹּא לִשְׁמָהּ פְּסוּלָה. אָשָׁם נַמִי כְּתִיב בֵּיהּ "הוּא"! הַהוּא לְאַחַר הַקְטָרַת אֵימוּרִים הוּא דִּכְתִיב. הַאי נַמִי לְאַחַר הַקְטָרַת אֵימוּרִים הוּא דִּכְתִיב! תְּרֵי "הוּא" כְּתִיבִי. גַּבֵּי אָשָׁם *נַמִי תְּרֵי "הוּא" כְּתִיבִי! אֶלָּא, ד] בֶּן עַזַּאי בְּקַל וָחוֹמֶר מַיְיתֵי לָהּ: וּמָה חַטָּאת שֶׁאֵינָהּ כָּלִיל, שְׁחָטָהּ שֶׁלֹּא לִשְׁמָהּ — פְּסוּלָה, עוֹלָה שֶׁהִיא כָּלִיל — לֹא כָּל שֶׁכֵּן? מָה לְחַטָּאת שֶׁכֵּן מְכַפֶּרֶת! פֶּסַח יוֹכִיחַ. מָה לְפֶסַח שֶׁכֵּן זְמַנּוֹ קָבוּעַ! חַטָּאת תּוֹכִיחַ. *וְחָזַר הַדִּין, לֹא רְאִי זֶה כִּרְאִי זֶה, וְלֹא רְאִי זֶה כִּרְאִי זֶה, הַצַּד הַשָּׁוֶה שֶׁבָּהֶן — שֶׁהֵן קָדָשִׁים וּשְׁחָטָן שֶׁלֹּא לִשְׁמָן פָּסוּל, אַף אֲנִי אָבִיא עוֹלָה שֶׁהִיא קָדָשִׁים, וּשְׁחָטָהּ שֶׁלֹּא לִשְׁמָהּ פְּסוּלָה. *מָה לְהַצַּד הַשָּׁוֶה שֶׁבָּהֶן, שֶׁיֵּשׁ בָּהֶן צַד כָּרֵת! בֶּן עַזַּאי צַד

יֵשׁ דִּחוּי בְּדָמִים. יֵשׁ תּוֹרַת דִּחוּי בִּקְדוּשַּׁת דָּמִים, אע"פ שֶׁאֵינָהּ קְדוּשַּׁת הַגּוּף. כְּגוֹן הָכָא, ה] שֶׁהִקְדִּישׁ חֶצְיָהּ — (א) לֹא קָדְשָׁה אֶלָּא לְדָמֶיהָ, שֶׁהֲרֵי אֵין לוֹ חֵלֶק ו] [אֶלָּא] בְּחֶצְיָהּ, וְאֵין קְדוּשָּׁה רְאוּיָה לִפְשׁוֹט בְּכוּלָּהּ עַל פִּיו, וַאֲפִי' הָכִי שַׁיָּיךְ בָּהּ דִּחוּי, וְתִדָּחֶה עוֹלָמִית. וְלָא אָמְרִי', לָא אַלִּימָא קְדוּשַּׁת דָּמִים לִיפָּסֵל מִשּׁוּם דִּחוּי. לִישָּׁנָא אַחֲרִינָא: יֵשׁ דִּחוּי בִּשְׁבִיל הַדָּמִים שֶׁלֹּא פָּרַע לִקְנוֹת חֶצְיָהּ שֶׁל חֲבֵירוֹ, שֶׁלֹּא הָיְתָה קְנוּיָה לוֹ כְּשֶׁהִקְדִּישָׁהּ, שֶׁעֲדַיִין לֹא קָנָה חֶצְיָהּ מִשֶּׁל חֲבֵירוֹ. וְאֵינ"ו נִרְאֶ"ה לְמוֹרִ"י. וְהֵמִיר דָּת. נִדְחָה מִקָּרְבָּן, ז] כְּ"הַכֹּל שׁוֹחֲטִין" (חולין דף ה:): מֵ"עַם הָאָרֶץ" — פְּרָט לְמוּמָר. וְנִשְׁתַּטָּה. נִדְחָה, דְּבָעֵינַן דַּעַת, בְּמַסֶּכֶת עֲרָכִין בְּפֶ' "הָאוֹמֵר מִשְׁקָלִי עָלַי" (דף כא.). נִשְׁתַּפָּה = שָׁקַט מִשִּׁעְמוּמוֹ, ח] כְּגוֹן עַל "הַר נִשְׁפֶּה" (ישעיה יג) דְּמִתַרְגֵּם: עַל טוּרָא שְׁלֵוְיָא. הוֹרוּ ב"ד שֶׁחֵלֶב מוּתָּר. נִדְחָה ט] לוֹ, דְּאִילּוּ עָבַר הַשְׁתָּא — לָאו בַּר קָרְבָּן הוּא, דְּאָמְרִינַן בְּהוֹרָיוֹת (דף ב:): יָחִיד שֶׁעָשָׂה בְּהוֹרָאַת ב"ד — פָּטוּר. מֵהָא פָּתַח. וְדוֹרֵשׁ בּוֹ שֶׁיִּדָּחֶה. הָתָם. גַּבֵּי מוּמָר וְשׁוֹטֶה, גַּבְרָא אִידַּחֵי מִקָּרְבָּן, קָרְבָּן לָא אִידַּחֵי תּוֹרַת חַטָּאת, זֹאת לֹא נִדְחֵת מִיִּשְׂרָאֵל, מִן הַכְּשֵׁרִין. אֲבָל הָכָא — תּוֹרַת קָרְבָּן זֶה נִדְחֵית מִן הַכֹּל. לָמָּה לִי לְמִיתְנֵי זָקֵן. לִיתְנֵי "זְקֵנִים". בַּחֲדָא י]. בִּישִׁיבָה אַחַת הָיוּ יוֹשְׁבִין, וְכוּלָּן הָיוּ כְּאִישׁ אֶחָד. לְאַחַר הַקְטָרַת אֵימוּרִין כְּתִיב. וְלֵיכָּא לְמִידְרְשֵׁיהּ לְעִיכּוּבָא, יא] *דְּעַצְמוֹ שֶׁלֹּא הוּקְטְרוּ אֵימוּרָיו כָּשֵׁר. וְהַאי "הוּא" דָּרְשִׁינַן *לְמִילְּתָא אַחֲרִיתִי. תְּרֵי הוּא כְּתִיבִי. וְאִם אֵין הַשֵּׁנִי עִנְיָן לְאַחַר הַקְטָרָה, דְּהָא כְּתִיב חַד — תְּנֵהוּ עִנְיָן לַעֲבוֹדַת דָּם, וְלִפְסוֹל בְּשֶׁלֹּא יב] לִשְׁמָן. חַד "הוּא" כְּתִיב בְּאֵיל עוֹלָה שֶׁל מִילּוּאִים בְּ"וְאַתָּה תְּצַוֶּה", וְחַד "הוּא" כְּתִיב בְּ"וַיִּקְרָא" גַּבֵּי עוֹלַת בֶּן צֹאן. אָשָׁם נַמִי תְּרֵי (אָשָׁם) הוּא יג] כְּתִיבִי. חַד בְּ"צַו אֶת אַהֲרֹן" אַחַר הַקְטָרָה, וְחַד בְּ"וַיִּקְרָא" — "אָשָׁם הוּא אָשֹׁם לַה'". וְאע"ג דְּלֵיכָּא חַד מִינַּיְיהוּ דִּכְתִיב גַּבֵּי עֲבוֹדַת דָּם, תֵּן הָאֶחָד בְּ"אִם אֵינוֹ עִנְיָן" לְכָךְ, כִּדְאָמְרַתְּ בְּעוֹלָה. צַד

מלקרב לעולם *אפילו לאחר פסח. דכל מותר הפסח הוי שלמים, ונקיבה לשלמים מיחזא חזיא, דקתני מתני': דמיה לשלמים, אבל איהי גופה לא, אלמא אלימא קדושת דמים לומר בה תורת דחוי, ולא אשכחינן תנאי דפליגי בהא מילתא, מיהו בהא מילתא טובא אתא לאשמועינן. יד] ורבינו חננאל מפרש: יש דיחוי בדמים — כלומר טו] דדמים דחוים, (והדיחוי בדמים) שלא יקריב מן הדמים קרבנו שהיה בדעתו להפריש. כמו יש דחוי בדמים ד"מי שהיה טמא" (פסחים דף צח.), דתנן התם גבי מפריש נקבה לפסחו: ירעה עד שיסתאב, וימכר ויביא בדמיו שלמים. ור"ש נמי פי' כן התם: יש דחוי בדמים — אפילו הדמים דחוין, שאין מביאין מהן פסח שהיה דעתו כן בשעת הפרשה. מיהו אינו כן, אלא טז] מביא מן הדמים פסח, כדתניא פ' בתרא דכריתות (דף כח.): המפריש נקבה לפסחו, ירעה עד שיסתאב ותימכר ויביא בדמיה פסח. ומתוך הך ברייתא רבינו שמואל מוחק בפרק "מי שהיה טמא" (פסחים דף צח.) שלמים, וגרים: יביא בדמיה פסח. אמנם אין גירסא זו נכונה, דאם כן היכי קאמר בגמרא: ש"מ יש דחוי מעיקרו, יז] [ויש] דחוי בדמים, [ובעלי] חיים נדחין? הלא כי נמי בעלמא אין דחוי — אין יכול להקדיש איהי גופה פסח, שהרי נקבה היא, ובפסח כתיב "זכר תמים בן שנה". א"כ על כרחך התם פ' "מי שהיה טמא" גרסי' שלמים. ור"ת אומר: דאין למחוק הספרים, דב"אלו קדשים" אמרי': המפריש נקבה לפסחו — תרעה ויביא בדמיה פסח, נשתיירה אחר הפסח — תרעה עד שתסתאב, וימכר ויביא בדמיה שלמים. ומתני' ד"מי שהיה טמא" בכה"ג מיירי, בנשתיירה אחר הפסח. ופירוש של יש דחוי בדמים הוי: יש דיחוי בדבר שאין בו רק קדושת דמים ולא קדושת הגוף. ול"ע בההיא דכריתות, יח] א"ר אלעזר א"ר אושעיא: מטמא מקדש עשיר כו', ומתיב רב עוקבא: המפריש נקבה לפסחו יט] תרעה, ילדה זכר — ירעה ויביא בדמיו פסח כו', ר"ש אומר: הוא עצמו יקרב פסח! ומשני: כ] כי אמרינן — לרבנן, ור"ש ס"ל דבע"ח אין נדחין, דתניא: מת אחד מהם — מביא חבירו שלא בהגרלה, דברי ר"ש. והשתא מאי ס"ד מעיקרא דפריך מר"ש? לסייעי' מרבנן! וי"ל: כא] דת"ק נמי מודה דבע"ח אין נדחין, והא דקאמר ירעה — טעמא כרבי אלעזר דתמורה פ' "אלו קדשים" (דף יח:), דתנן: המפריש נקבה לעולה וילדה זכר — ירעה, רבי אליעזר אומר: אף הוא עצמו יקרב עולה. ומפרש בגמרא דגבי מפריש נקבה לפסחו וילדה זכר — לא הוה א"ר אליעזר הוא עצמו יקרב פסח, דגמירי: למקום שהמותר הולך שם הולד הולך. ולפני הפסח, דאימיה קדשה לדמי פסח, שלא היה יכול להמתין עד שתלד הזכר ויקריבנו פסח — ולכך ולד נמי לדמי פסח, אע"ג דקסבר בע"ח אין נדחים. ומיהו קשה: אדפריך ליה מברייתא דכריתות — לסייעיה מת"ק דרבי אליעזר דתמורה דאית ליה בעלי חיים נדחין. דקאמרי במפריש נקבה לעולה וילדה זכר — ירעה. וממתניתין דפסחים כב] ופלוגתא דתנאי ביומא (דף סד:). ועוד קשה: היכי מייתי מההיא דמת אחד מהם, דאית ליה לר"ש כג] דאין נדחין? דלמא שאני התם דלא דחייה בידים! ועוד קשה: היכי מייתי מההיא דרבי אליעזר דפשיטא ליה כד] התם דבעלי חיים נידחים, ולעיל מבעיא ליה התם בכריתות (דף כז.)! ובתמורה פירשתי *לפני רבינו, דחידושא דרבי יוחנן הוי אע"ג דבידו לתקן וליקח חליה השני. וכן כה] רבי אלעזר אמר רבי אושעיא פ' בתרא דכריתות — בידו להפקיר נכסיו והוי עני, והוה ראוי הקן שהפריש. ומיהו, אין בידו כ"כ כמו נפגם המזבח כו] *בריש פ' "קדשי קדשים" (לקמן דף נט.) דחוי מעיקרו הוא וכשר. כז] [והכא] לכ"ע משמע דכשר דבידו לתקן, כדאיתא פרק "לולב הגזול" (סוכה דף לג.). ולכך נמי נקט רבי יוחנן אכל חלב והפריש קרבן והמיר דתו וחזר, שידחה, דהוה ליה נראה ונדחה. ולא נקט שהפריש קרבן לאחר שהמיר דתו — דההוא כשר, כיון דבידו לתקן בקל, כמו נפגם המזבח. וגם דחוי מעיקרו דכשר. ובכריתות פ' בתרא, דפריך לר' אושעיא מר' שמעון ולא מייתי ליה סייעתא מרבנן, משום דעד כאן לא פליגי רבנן ואמרי שנדחה, משום דאין בידו לתקן כלל בשעת הקדש, שהיא נקבה לפסחו. אבל היכא שבידו לתקן קצת, כגון מטמא מקדש עשיר שהפריש קן, דאי בעי מפקר נכסיה — מודה דלא הוי דיחוי. כל זה פי' רבינו הקדוש זצוק"ל. וקשה כח] לי על זה, מאי פריך לעיל: אי אפרשיה מאפרא דחוי מעיקרו הוא? הלא בידו להשהותו עד תלות כמו כט] הקדיש חובות בגלגל דכשירין, בשילהי פרק אחרון (לקמן קיח.), וכן ל] אותו ואת בנו! וש"מ דחוי מעיקרו הוי דחוי. תימה: דגבי לא] הדס אמרינן פ' "לולב הגזול" (סוכה דף לג:): היכא לב] (דאשכחן) דאשחור מערב יו"ט, דדחוי מעיקרא לא הוי דחוי! וי"ל: דשאני התם, דבידו לתקנו. תדע, דגבי לג] לולב שנקטם ראשו [מעי"ט] ועלתה בו תמרה [בי"ט] מיבעיא ליה אי יש דחוי אי לאו, לד] [ולא] פשטינן לה מהא, משום דנקטם אין בידו לתקנו. וא"ת: מ"ט דר' יוחנן דאמר דחוי מעיקרו הוי דחוי? לילף ממחוסר זמן דלא הוי דחוי, כדאמר בפ' "שני שעירי" (יומא דף סד.)! וי"ל: דשאני מחוסר זמן, דחוזר לה] [ונראה] ממילא. וא"ת: אמאי איצטריך לרבי יוחנן מיעוטא ד"מום בם" — הני הוא דכי עבר לו] מומס ירצו, *הא כל הדחויים אם עבר מומס לא ירצו, הואיל ונידחו אידחו? הא לז] מום עובר לא ילפינן [דלדחי], דלא הוי דחוי, דהתם ממילא הוי! וי"ל: דאיכא מום דאינו עובר אלא על ידי רפואה.

הכא קרבן אידחי. וגרע מדאידחי גברא. והא דמשמע איפכא בהוריות פ' בתרא (דף יא.) גבי נשיאות מהו שתפסיק — לא דמי, דהתם לא אידחי קרבן מן החלב שאכל, דעדיין הוא חייב קרבן. ור"ת פירש לח] איפכא, דגבי הורו ב"ד לא היה *דחוי, דגברא אידחי — שאינו יודע אם פטור אם לאו, קרבן לא אידחי — דאי לא דהתירו ב"ד היה קרב, ונמצא שלא היה דחוי אלא ע"י טעותו. אבל הכא — אפילו קרבן נמי אידחי, דכיון שהוא שוטה או מומר — פטור הוא לכולי עלמא. **בן** עזאי בק"ו מייתי לה. אף ע"ג דפסול שלא לט] לשמן מוליאו מידי פגול, דבעינן שיהיו כל מתירים בכשרות — לא דמיא להא דאמר בפ"ק *דפסחים (דף יח): כל דין שתחילתו להחמיר וסופו להקל אינו דין. תימה: ובן עזאי, אי דריש "אותה" לשמה כשרה שלא לשמה פסולה, הא שאר קדשים כו' — קל וחומר מאי אהני ליה? *ואי לא דריש — א"כ אשם ליעכב, מהיקישא ד"כחטאת וכאשם"! **מה** להצד השוה שבהן שכן יש בהן צד כרת. תימה: ולר"א דפסל חטאת ואשם — ליפסל נמי עולה, ותיתי מחטאת ואשם [ופסח]! וי"ל: דשייך קצת צד כרת באשם, משום דאיכא אשם תלוי. ומיהו לא שייך כמו בחטאת ופסח, כדמוכח לעיל.

צד כרת לא פריך. אשם נמי לייתי! אשם, פריך: מה להצד השוה שבהן – שכן ישנן בצבור כביחיד. ואיבעית אימא: צד כרת נמי פריך, ובן עזאי גמרא גמיר לה, והא דקאמר רב הונא קל וחומר – לא אמרה אלא *לחדד בה תלמידיו.§

מתני' *[א]הפסח והחטאת ששחטן שלא לשמן, קבל והלך וזרק שלא לשמן, או [ב]לשמן ושלא לשמן, או שלא לשמן ולשמן – פסולים. כיצד לשמן ושלא לשמן? לשם פסח ולשם שלמים. שלא לשמן ולשמן – לשם שלמים ולשם פסח. [ג]שהזבח נפסל בארבעה דברים: בשחיטה, ובקבול, [ד]ובהילוך, ובזריקה. רבי שמעון מכשיר בהילוך, *שהיה א] אומר: אי אפשר שלא בשחיטה ושלא בקבלה ושלא בזריקה, אבל אפשר בלא הילוך – שוחט בצד המזבח וזורק. רבי (א) *אליעזר אומר: המהלך במקום שהוא צריך להלך – מחשבה פוסלת, במקום שאינו צריך להלך – אין מחשבה פוסלת.§

גמ' וקבלה מי פסלה? ב] *והתניא: °"והקריבו" – זו קבלת הדם. ג] אתה אומר: קבלת הדם, או אינו אלא זריקה? כשהוא אומר: "וזרקו" – הרי זריקה אמור, הא מה אני מקיים "והקריבו" – זו קבלת הדם. "בני אהרן הכהנים" – [ה]שתהא בכהן כשר ובכלי שרת. *אמר רבי עקיבא: מנין לקבלה שלא תהא ד] [אלא] בכהן כשר ובכלי שרת? נאמר כאן: "בני אהרן", ונאמר להלן: °"אלה שמות בני אהרן הכהנים המשוחים", מה להלן בכהן כשר ובכלי שרת – אף כאן בכהן כשר ובכלי שרת. אמר רבי טרפון: *אקפח את בניי, אם לא שמעתי ה] להבחין הפרש בין קבלה לזריקה, ואין לי לפרש. אמר רבי עקיבא, אני אפרש: קבלה – לא עשה בה מחשבה כמעשה, זריקה – עשה בה מחשבה כמעשה; [ו]קבלו בחוץ – אינו חייב כרת, [ז]זרקו בחוץ – ענוש כרת; [ח]קבלוהו פסולין – אין חייבין עליו, [ט]זרקוהו פסולין – חייבין עליו. אמר לו רבי טרפון: העבודה, ו] *את הטית ימין ושמאל, אני שמעתי ואין לי לפרש, אתה דורש ומסכים לשמועה. בלשון הזה אמר לו: *עקיבא! כל הפורש ממך כפורש מחייו. אמר רבא: לא קשיא, ז] כאן – במחשבת פיגול, כאן – במחשבת שלא לשמה. דיקא נמי, דקתני: [י]"שהזבח נפסל", ולא קתני "מתפגל", ש"מ.§ ומחשבת פיגול לא פסלה בקבלה? והתניא: יכול לא תהא מחשבה מועלת אלא בזריקה בלבד, מנין לרבות שחיטה וקבלה? ת"ל: °"ואם האכל יאכל מבשר זבח שלמיו ח] *(פיגול הוא) לא ירצה" – בדברים המביאין לידי אכילה הכתוב מדבר. יכול שאני מרבה אף שפיכת שיריים *והקטרת אימורין? ת"ל: ט] °"ביום השלישי לא ירצה י] המקריב אותו לא יחשב", זריקה בכלל היתה, ולמה יצתה – להקיש אליה, לומר לך: מה זריקה מיוחדת שהיא עבודה יא] (ומכפרת) ומעכבת כפרה – אף כל יב] עבודה ומעכבת כפרה, [כ]יצאו שפיכת שיריים והקטרת אימורין, שאין מעכבין את הכפרה! אלא

צד כרת לא פריך. לפי שאינו שוה בשניהם. דחטאת אינו ענוש כרת על הבאתו, אלא שעל שגגת כרת הוא בא. ופסח ענוש כרת על הבאתו. אשם נמי לייתי. לפסול יג] בשלא לשמו מבנין אב, כדאמר רבי אליעזר לעיל (דף י:), דקא"ל רבי יהושע: חוזרני חלילה, ופרכינן: וליהדר דינא ולייתי במה הצד, וסליקנא להך אתקפתא משום דאיכא למיפרך: מה להצד השוה שבהן – שכן יש בהן צד כרת. ומשני: לבן עזאי אתם מפירכא אחריתא מסלק ליה, דלא לייתי בבנין אב. דפריך: מה להצד השוה שבהן – שישנו בצבור. פסח קרי ליה קרבן צבור, כדאמרן בסדר יומא בפ' "הוציאו לו" (דף נא.), משום דאתי בכינופיא. גמרא גמיר לה. מפי ע"ב זקנים, כדתנן. לחדד יד] תלמידיו. שיקשו לו תשובה עליו. א"נ, שיתנו לבם להיות חריפין לדרוש קלים וחמורים מאליהן, כבן עזאי טו]. **מתני'** וקבל והלך וזרק כו'. או או קתני, קבל או הלך או זרק (ב). או לשמו ושלא לשמו. שחישב בעבודה אחת לשמו ושלא לשמו. אבל אפשר בלא הילוך. הלכך לא חשיבא למיפסל. המהלך במקום שהוא צריך להוליך. הולכה זו מחשבה פוסלת בה, אם חישב בה שלא לשמה. ובגמ' מפרש למילתי' מאי צריך ומאי אין צריך. **גמ'** והקריבו. דכתיב בעולה: "ושחט את בן הבקר והקריבו בני אהרן טז] את הדם" – זו קבלת הדם, וללמד שצריך לקבלו בכלי. אתה אומר כו' או אינו אלא (ג) יז] לזריקה. דהא לשון הקרבה למזבח הוא, כדכתיב: "לכהן המקריב אותה" וגו'. והאי נמי בהקרבה למזבח משתעי, דהיינו זריקה. אבל קבלה *לא צריך [כלי] מאהל מועד ואילך. כשהוא אומר כו' זו קבלת הדם. כדאשכחן קבלה בעולת סיני (שמות כד): "ויקח משה חצי הדם וישם באגנות". ואע"ג דהקרבה לשון הולכה היא, כדאמרן לעיל (דף ד.): "והקריב הכהן את הכל" זו הולכת אברים לכבש, הכא כיון דזימנין יח] הולכה ליתיה כלל, כמו השוחט בצד המזבח – לא כתב לה קרא, ואקבלה הוא יט] דאכתביה. והיכא דאיצטריכא הולכה נפקא לן דהויא עבודה מדאפקא רחמנא לקבלה בלשון הולכה. בכהן כשר. לאפוקי חללים ובעלי מומין. ובכלי שרת. שיהו מלובשים בגדי כהונה, כ] דכהנים משמע (הכהנים) בכיהונם (לקמן דף יח:), והיינו בגדי כהונה. וכל היכא דקתני נמי "בכהן כשר ובכלי שרת" – בבגדי כהונה קאמר. אמר רבי עקיבא. ר' עקיבא לא משמע ליה מהכא, דאיכא למימר: "בני אהרן" – כל שהן. ו"הכהנים" בכיהונם – לא משמע ליה כא]. מה להלן בכהנים כשרין. הכתוב מדבר, דהא אלעזר ואיתמר כב] כתיבי. ובכלי שרת נמי הכתוב מדבר, דכתיב: "אשר מלא את ידם" – והיינו לשון רבוי בגדי כהונה דכתיב (ויקרא כא): "ומלא את ידו ללבוש את הבגדים", וכתיב נמי: "ובגדי הקדש אשר לאהרן יהיו לבניו אחריו למשחה בהם ולמלא בם את ידם" (שמות כט). כג] להבחין הפרש כו'. ואתה עושה את הקבלה כשאר עבודות. ואין לי לפרש. איני יודע לפרש מה הפרש שמעתי ביניהן. לא עשה בה מחשבה כמעשה. השתא סלקא כד] דעתך (ד) הא דקאמר אין מחשבה פוסלת בשבילה, אם חישב בה חוץ לזמנו או שלא לשמו. אלמא לא פסלה בקבלה כה]. קבלו בחוץ אינו חייב כרת. דשחיטה היא דכתיב כו] לחיובא ["ואל פתח אהל מועד"], וזריקה נפקא מ"דם (א) יחשב", לקמן בפרק "השוחט" (דף קז.). קבלו פסולין. זרים ושאר חייבי מיתות, כגון שתויי יין והדומין להם. אין חייבין עליו מיתה. דבעיא עבודה תמה שאין אחריה עבודה, בסדר יומא (דף כד.). ובפרק בתרא דהכא (דף קיב:) נמי תנן: אין בהם משום זרות, ולא משום טומאה, ולא משום מחוסר בגדים כו'. אתה דורש. מאליך ומסכים למה ששמעתי. מחשבת פיגול. דחוץ לזמנו לא פסלה בקבלה. דיקא נמי. [דתנא] דמתניתין לא איירי במחשבת פיגול. אלא בזריקה. במחשב בשעת זריקה ע"מ לאכול מזבחו ביום השלישי, כדכתיב בקרא דמחשבת פיגול "המקריב אותו לא יחשב", ילפינן מיניה בפ"ב (לקמן כט.) במחשב בשעת הקרבה לאכול מזבחו ביום השלישי הכתוב מדבר, כז] [והקרבה] היינו זריקה. בדברים המביאים. את הקרבן לידי היתר אכילה הכתוב מדבר. אף שפיכת שירים. אם שפך שירי הדם ליסוד על מנת לאכול בשר חוץ לזמנו, או אם הקטיר אימורין במחשבה זו. לא ירצה. היינו זריקה, שהיא מרצה כח]. בכלל היתה. בכלל הדברים המביאין לידי אכילה. שאין מעכבין. שירים אין מעכבין, כדתניא ב"איזהו מקומן" (לקמן דף נב.): יכול יעכבנו? תלמוד לומר: "ואת כל הדם ישפך", נתקו הכתוב ועשאו שירי מצוה כו'. הקטרת אימורין לא מעכבין כפרה, דכתיב: כט] "הדם הוא בנפש יכפר". *לא קשיא הא. *דקתני לעיל: מחשבת קבלה לא פסלה בפיגול – לא כשחישב בשעת קבלה על אכילת בשר, אלא במחשב בשעת שחיטה על מנת לקבל דם למחר. ל] דאילו זריקה כהאי גוונא – עשה בה מחשבה כמעשה, אם שחט על מנת לזרוק דם למחר – פיגול, דהיינו אכילת מזבח (ה) (ואי נמי) דאיתרבי בהדיא אפי' שפיכת שיריים, לקמן. הא דאמר כו'. לא] והאי דקתני: מנין לרבות שחיטה וקבלה – לב] (ו) מחשב בשעת קבלה על מנת לשפוך שירים או אחת משאר האכילות לג] קאמרי. ושפיכת שירים לא פסלה בהו מחשבה. דקתני לעיל: יכול שאני מרבה אף שפיכת שיריים. אלא באכילת בשר. כשחישב לאכול בשר חוץ לזמנו. מנין לרבות שפיכת שירים. וכל שכן תחלת זריקה. לא

א) [ע"ש כי הוא טעם ר"י אמנם טעמא דר"ע מאו זכח]

אתה אומר זו קבלת הדם כו'. לעיל (דף ד.) פי' בקונט' דמוקמינן "והקריבו" בקבלה ולא בהולכה, משום ד"והקריבו" נאמר מיד אחר שחיטה, וקבלה היא עבודה ראשונה שאחר שחיטה. ולפירושו קשה: היכי בעי למימר הכא "או אינו אלא זריקה"? אלא נראה דמוקמי' לה בקבלה או בזריקה לפי שהן עבודות חשובות שאי אפשר לבטלן, מה שאין כן בהולכה*.

בכהן כשר ובכלי שרת. פירש בקונטרס. כלי שרת – בגדי כהונה. וקשה: דהא נפקא לקמן בפרק שני (דף יז:) מקרא, דאין בגדיהם עליהן – אין כהונה עליהן, והוו להו זרים, ואפילו בעבודה דלא מעכבא כפרה! ויש לומר: דאי לאו גזרה שוה דהכא, הוה אמרינן: מה שהקפידה תורה אמחוסר בגדים היינו היכא דכתיבי בגדים, אבל היכא דלא כתיבי בגדים – לא. וגבי נתינת אש וסידור איברים לא הוה בעינא בגדים מכהן בכיהונו. אלא מדגלי רחמנא גבי קבלה גזרה שוה – ילפינן בכל דוכתא דהכהן הוי בכיהונו.

דיקא נמי דקתני שהזבח נפסל. במסקנא לא חיישינן להאי דיקא, דבקבלה נמי איכא פסול פיגול,

סב א מיי' פט"ו מהל' פסה"מ הל' א ז יא:
סג ב מיי' פי"ג שם הלכה א:
סד ג מיי' שם הלכה ד ופט"ו שם הלכה ג ופ"ד מהל' מעה"ק הל' י:
[ועי' תוס' יומא כז. ד"ה והקריבו]
סה ד מיי' פי"ג מהל' פסה"מ הלכה ט:
סו ה מיי' פ"ה מהלכות מעשה הקרבנות הל' א ופ"א מהל' פסולי המוקדשין הלכה כב:
סז ו מיי' פי"ט מהל' מעה"ק הלכה ו:
סח ז מיי' שם הלכה ג:
סט ח מיי' פ"ט מהלכות ביאת מקדש הל' א:
ע ט מיי' שם הל' ג:
עא י מיי' פי"ג מהל' פסה"מ הלכה ג:

תורה אור: ויקרא א; במדבר ג; ויקרא ז; שם

[ברכות לג:]
פסחים נט:
[נ"ל שהיה רבי שמעון אומר כ"ה במשנה שבמשניות]
נ"ל אלעזר
חגיגה יא. לעיל ד. [קדושין לו:]
[תוס' פ"א]
[שבת יז. קטז.]
עיין חלופי גרסאות [נ"ל שלא כך איתא בתוספתא]
[קדושין סו:]
נ"א ביום השלישי
[וכת"י הגי' והקטרת אימורין ת"ל המקריב אותו וכו']

הגהות הב"ח

(א) במשנה ר' אלעזר כצ"ל והמהלך: (ב) רש"י ד"ה וקבל וכו' או זרק בלא לשמו ולא לשמו כצ"ל והד"ה: (ג) ד"ה אתה וכו' אלא זריקה כצ"ל: (ד) ד"ה לא עשה וכו' סלקא דעתך דהכי קאמר: (ה) ד"ה לא קשיא וכו' אכילת מזבח ולאו נמי אפילו שיריים דאתרבו בהדיא לקמן: (ו) ד"ה הא דאמר וכו' כמחשב:

גליון הש"ס

גמ' יצאו שפיכת שיריים. לקמן דף לט ע"א:

שייך לע"ב יצ"א הא דקתני לעיל מחשבה לא פסלה בקבלה לא כשחושב כו'

שיטה מקובצת

א] שהיה ר' שמעון: ב] פסלה במחשבה: ג] (הדם אתה אומר קבלת הדם או): ד] אלא בכהן: ה] תיבת להבחין נמחק: ו] העבודה אם הטית: ז] לא קשיא הא דקתני לעיל דמחשבה לא פסיל בפיגול לא כשחישב בשעת קבלה על אכילת בשר אלא כשחישב בשעת שחיטה על מנת לקבל דמו למחר [לא] פסלה דבעינן מחשב בעבודה לאכילת אדם או אכילת מזבח ואילו זריקה כה"ג עשה מחשבה כמעשה אם שחט על מנת לזרוק דם למחר פיגול דהיינו אכילת מזבח כפ"ה ותימה למורי למה איצטריך לדחוק וליתן חילוק בין פיגול ושלא לשמו לוקמא כולה בשלא לשמו ובענין דשוחט ע"מ לקבל שלא לשמו כשר והיינו לא עשה בו מחשבה כמעשה ומתני' איירי במחשב בקבלה עצמה אבל בזורק עשה בו מחשבה כמעשה דשוחט ע"מ לזרוק דמו שלא לשמו פסול וי"ל דהא תינח לר"י אבל לר"ל מאי איכא למימר דקאמ' לעיל אף בשוחט ע"מ לזרוק דמו שלא לשמו כשר דאין מחשבין מעבודה לעבודה ומ"מ קשה לוקמא בשינוי בעלים דאף ר"ל מודה דשוחט ע"מ לזרוק בשינוי בעלים פסול ושוחט ע"מ לקבל בשינוי בעלים כשר [וי"ל] דלא מצי לאוקמא בשינוי בעלים דא"כ תקשה לך הלשון דקאמר לא עשה בו מחשבה כמעשה משמע הא אם עשה בה [מעשה] [שקבל הדם] בשינוי בעלים פסול וזה אינו דאפי' קבל בשינוי בעלים נמי כשר כדהוכחנו לעיל דלא שייך שינוי בעלים רק בזריקה אבל אי מיירי בפיגול ניחא דקתני לא עשה בה מחשבה כמעשה דאם היה מקבל חוץ לזמנו או חוץ למקומו פסול מיהא הוי תום' טוך: ח] תיבות פיגול הוא לא ירצה נמחק: ט] תיבות ביום השלישי א) לא ירצה ל"ש: י] המקריב אותו לא ירצה היינו זריקה שמרצה. תוס' הר"פ: יא] תיבת ומכפרת נמחק: יב] כל שהוא עבודה: יג] לפסול שלא אות ב' נמחק: יד] לחדד בה תלמידיו: טו] כבן עזאי. ס"א אינו: טז] אהרן הכהנים: יז] אלא זריקה אות ל' נמחק: יח] דזמנין דהולכה: יט] הוא דכתביה אות א' נמחק: כ] בגדי כהונה הכהנים משמע בביהונם: כא] ליה ומפקא ליה ממקום אחר הס"ד: כב] ואיתמר התם: כג] תיבת להבחין נמחק: כד] סלקא דעתי' דקאמר אין כו' בשבילה אדם שחישב בה: כה] בקבלה מחשבה שלא לשמו הס"ד: כו] דכתיב בחוץ לחיובא: כז] מדבר והקרבה היינו זריקה כדמסיים בדברים והד"א: כח] מרצה ס"א אינו וה"ג בת"כ ת"ל המקריב אותו ול"ג לא ירצה: כט] דכתיב כי הדם: ל] למחר ולכך לא פסלה דבעינן מחשב בעבודה לאכילת אדם או לאכילת מזבח ואילו זריקה נמי אתרבי אות ד' נמחק: לא] כו' והא אות י' נמחק: לב] וקבלה זהו במחשב: לג] האכילות למחר קאמר הס"ד:

א) נראה דצ"ל תיבות ביום השלישי ל"ש: י) לא ירצה המקריב אותו היינו זריקה שמרצה.

(וע' כ"מ מו: וע' מ"ש על גליון)

עב א מיי' פי"ג מהל' פסה"מ הל' ב ופי"ז שם הלכה ו:

עג ב מיי' פי"ג שם הלכה ז:

(וע"ע תוס' מעילה ז. ד"ה חישב)

עד ג מיי' פי"ז שם הלכה ג:

עה ד מיי' פי"ג שם הלכה ו:

אלא לא קשיא, הא – דאמר: "הריני א] [שוחט] ע"מ לקבל דמה למחר", הא – דאמר: "הריני מקבל דמה על מנת לשפוך שירים למחר". א"ל ההוא מרבנן לרבא: ושפיכת שירים והקטרת אימורין לא פסלה בהו מחשבה? ב] *והתנן: יכול לא תהא מחשבה מועלת אלא באכילת בשר, מנין לרבות שפיכת שירים והקטרת אימורים? ת"ל: °"ואם האכל יאכל" (ויקרא ז) – *בשתי אכילות הכתוב מדבר, אחת אכילת אדם, ואחת אכילת מזבח! לא קשיא: הא – דאמר: א"הריני זורק על מנת לשפוך שירים למחר", הא – דאמר: "הריני[ב] שופך שירים על מנת להקטיר אימורין למחר".§ א"ר יהודה בריה דרבי חייא: שמעתי, גשטבילת אצבע מפגלת בחטאת פנימית. ג] שמעה אילפא, אמרה קמיה ד] (א) דרב פדא. אמר: כלום למדנו פיגול אלא משלמים, מה שלמים אין טבילת אצבע מפגלת בהן – אף חטאת אין טבילת אצבע מפגלת בהן! וכי הכל משלמים ה] (ב) למדו? אי מה שלמים שלא לשמן אין מוציא מידי פיגול – אף חטאת שלא לשמה אין מוציא מידי פיגול! אלא מאי אית לך למימר – מרבויא דקראי קאתיא, ו] [ה"נ – מרבויא דקרא קאתי.] אמר ריב"ל: בעליה שמעתי, ז] שטבילת אצבע מפגלת. תהי בה רשב"ל: (ג) כלום למדו פיגול אלא משלמים, מה שלמים אין טבילת אצבע מפגלת ח] בהן – אף חטאת אין טבילת אצבע מפגלת בהן! וכי הכל משלמים למדו? אי מה שלמים שלא לשמן אין מוציא מידי פיגול – אף חטאת שלא לשמה אין מוציא מידי פיגול! אמר רבי יוסי ברבי חנינא: ט] אין, הכל משלמים למדו, הואיל וחוץ למקומו פוסל בשלמים, ושלא לשמו פוסל בחטאת; מה חוץ למקומו הפוסל בשלמים מוציא מידי פיגול, אף שלא לשמו הפוסל בחטאת מוציאה מידי פיגול. א"ר ירמיה: מצדה תברא; מה לחוץ למקומו הפוסל בשלמים – שכן נוהג בכל הזבחים, תאמר בשלא לשמו, שאינו נוהג אלא בפסח וחטאת בלבד! אלא מאי אית לך למימר? דבר הפוסל בהן – מוציאם מידי פיגול, דבר המעכב בהן – מביאן לידי פיגול; הכא נמי, דבר הפוסל בה – מוציא מידי פיגול, דבר המעכב בה – מביאה לידי פיגול. אמר רב מרי: אף אנן נמי תנינא: *זה הכלל, יכל הקומץ ונותן בכלי והמוליך והמקטיר; בשלמא קומץ – היינו שוחט, מוליך – היינו מוליך, מקטיר נמי – היינו זורק, אלא נותן בכלי מאי ניהו? אילימא דדמי לקבלה, מי דמי? התם – ממילא, הכא – איהו קא שקיל ורמי! י] אלא, כיון דלא סגי דלא יהיב – *על כרחיה עבודה חשובה היא; ה"נ, כיון דלא סגי דלא עביד לה – על כרחי' היינו הולכה. לא, לעולם דדמי לקבלה. ודקאמרת: הכא ממילא, התם איהו קא שקיל ויהיב; כיון דאידי ואידי מתן כלי הוא – מה לי ממילא, מה לי קא שקיל ויהיב. לימא כתנאי, דתני חדא: טבילת אצבע מפגלת בחטאת, ותניא אידך: לא מפגלת ולא מתפגלת; מאי לאו תנאי היא? יא] לא, הא – רבנן, הא – רבי שמעון. אי רבי שמעון – מאי איריא טבילת אצבע? האמר:

כל

לא קשיא הא. דקמרבי שפיכת שירים – כגון דאמר: הריני זורק, או אחת משאר עבודות, על מנת לשפוך שירים למחר. שהרי חישב להאכיל את המזבח חוץ לזמנו. **והא.** דמעטינהו לעיל – כגון דאמר: הריני שופך שירים כו'. כללא דמילתא: בעינן מחשבה בשעת עבודה על דבר יב] אכילת אדם או למזבח. הלכך, חישב בשעת שפיכת שיריים על אכילת בשר – לא כלום היא, דלא הואי מחשבה בשעת עבודה. **שמעתי** מרבותי שטבילת **אצבע.** האמור בחטאות הפנימיות: "וטבל הכהן אצבעו" וגו' (ויקרא ג), מפגלת בחטאת, אם טבל ע"מ להקטיר אימורים למחר. **כלום למדנו פיגול.** בחטאת אלא משלמים. דעיקר פיגול בשלמים כתיב "ואם האכל יאכל", ושלמים אין בהן טבילת אצבע, שכל הדמים בזריקה מן הכלי למזבח, חוץ מן החטאת שהיא במתנת אצבע. ופרכינן: יג] וכי הכל משלמים למדנו. (ד) דין פיגול בכל הזבחים יד] כדינו בשלמים? **אי מה שלמים** אין שלא לשמו מוציאו מידי פיגול. אם שחט במחשבת חוץ לזמנו, וקבל טו] והוליך שלא לשמן – לא יצאו מידי פיגולן, שהרי אין שלא לשמו פוסל בשלמים, והוה ליה קרב המתיר כמצותו בפיגול, בלא פסול מחשבה אחרת. **אף חטאת.** אע"פ שלא לשמו פסול בה – לא תוליאנה מידי פיגול. והאנן תנן בפ"ב (לקמן דף כט:): הפסח והחטאת ששחטן חוץ לזמנו וקבל והלך וזרק שלא לשמו – זהו שלא קרב המתיר כמצותו, ואינה פיגול ליענש כרת על אכילתו, כדילפינן בפ"ב (שם דף כח:) מקרא: כהרצאת כשר כך הרצאת פיגול, שיקרבו כל מתירין, דהיינו ארבע עבודות, בלא פסול מחשבה אחרת! **אלא מאי אית לך למימר מרבויא דקרא קאתי.** כל הזבחים לפיגול בת"כ, ולא משלמים למדו. הלכך, כל חד וחד מאי דפסיל טז] מוליאו מידי פיגול. וכן לענין הבאתו לידי פיגול, כל חד וחד מאי דכתיב ביה דהוי עבודה – מביאו לידי פיגול. הכי גרסינן: שטבילת **אצבע** מפגלת יז]. אין הכל משלמים למדנו. ודקשיא לך: בחטאת, היאך שלא לשמו מוליאה מידי פיגול? הואיל וחוץ יח] למקומה כו'. מחשבת ע"מ יט] לאוכלו חוץ למחיצת אכילתו דהיינו בכל העיר, וחוץ לעיר הוי חוץ למקומו – פוסל בשלמים. (ה) בהדיא מרבינן לה לפסולא בפ"ב, אלא שאין בו כרת. **מוציא** מידי פיגול. כדילפינן בפ"ב, שכל כ] מחשבת פסול מוליאתו מידי פיגול. **מצדה תברא.** תשובתה בלדה: אם מחוץ למקומו אתה לומד לשלא לשמו, ולהעמיד פיגול על עבודות הנוהגות בשלמים ותו לא, אלא שמוליאתה מידי פיגול תלמד בחטאת שלא לשמו מחוץ למקומו כא] דשלמים – יש להשיב: מה לחוץ למקומו – כב] דין הוא שיוליא מידי פיגול, שהרי כג] פסול וחמור לנהוג בכל הזבחים, תאמר כו'. **אלא מאי אית לך** למימר. אם באת לומר: הכל משלמים למדו, מה יש לך (ו) טעם כד] בשלא לשמו המוליא חטאת מידי פיגול? כך יש לך לומר: שלמים, דבר הפוסל בהו כגון חוץ למקומו, מוליאן מידי פיגול. **ודבר המעכב** בהו. כגון ד' עבודות הדם, כה] מביאין לידי פיגול. **הכא** נמי. אף חטאת, דבר הפוסל בה, כגון שלא לשמה – מוליאה. **ודבר המעכב בה** – כל הכתוב בעבודת דמה, וטבילת אצבע בכלל(ז). **אף אנן נמי תנינא.** דטבילת אצבע מפגלת. דתנן במנחות: "כל הקומץ", כו] בכל ד' עבודות [אם] חישב על מנת לאכול שיריים או להקטיר קומץ למחר – פיגול. **בשלמא** קומץ. מפגל, דהיינו כשוחט, שמוליא דם שהוא חלק גבוה *מן הבשר, כז] [והבשר] שיריים הם – אף זה הפריש קומץ מתוך שיריים. וכן שאר ב' **עבודות** כח] א) דמפגל מהיקישא דהוקש מנחה לזבח, דכתיב: "זאת התורה", ואמר לקמן (דף לא.) כט] דהך היקישא: מה שלמים מפגל ומתפגלין – אף כל מפגלין ומתפגלין. **התם ממילא.** נופל הדם בכלי, הכא קא שקיל בידיה ורמי. **אלא** כיון דלא סגי דלא יהיב. קומץ לכלי לקדשו בתוכו, כדאמרינן לעיל (דף יא.): שלא בכלי שרת – פסולה, ואמרינן טעמא במסכת סוטה בפרק שני (דף יד:): מידי דהוה אדם, ל] לאו אע"ג דקדישתיה סכין בצואר בהמה – הדר בעי לקבוליה וקדושיה בכלי זימנא אחריתי. קומץ נמי, אע"ג דקדשה מנחה כולה בכלי – בעי לקדושי קומץ זימנא אחריתי. הלכך עבודה חשובה היא, ומפגלה. הכי נמי בטבילת אצבע, כיון דלא סגי כו', היינו הולכה, שמוליך הדם באצבעו (ח) לקרבן למזבח. **לעולם** דדמי לקבלה. הלכך אתיא בהיקישא דאיתקוש מנחות לשלמים, דהא איתרבאי קבלה בשלמים לפגל כדאמרי' לעיל, ומתן כלי במנחה כקבלה בדם. אבל טבילת אצבע לא איתרבאי, ולא תיפשוט לא]. **לא מפגלת.** אם טבל על מנת להקטיר אימורין למחר. **ולא מתפגלת.** אם שחט [או קבל] ע"מ לטבול אצבע למחר. **מאי לאו תנאי היא.** דמר חשיב לה הולכה, ומר לא חשיב לה הולכה. **לא.** דכ"ע הולכה היא. והא דקתני אינה מפגלת – רבי שמעון היא, דאמר במתניתין: הולכה לא מפגלא, כדתנן: ורבי שמעון מכשיר בהילוך.

כל

א) נ"ל דהא נ"ק

ויש לפרש במסקנא דנקט לשון פסול דאיירי בשלא לשמן, דהוי בכל ד' עבודות. ומיהו אשכחן דיקא דלא קאי לבסוף, גבי כל הניסוך דמים באחר (קדושין דף כח.)*. **על** מנת לשפוך שיריים למחר. נ"ע בפרק קמא דמעילה (דף ז.) דמיבעיא לן: חישב לנשפכין, מהו? ופי' רבינו: דהתם מיירי שנשפך מן הכלי על הרצפה, ומיבעיא ליה אם מוליך אותו מקצת דם הנשאר בכלי על מנת לזרוק מאותן נשפכין חוץ לזמנו, שהרי ראויין לאוספן. או דלמא כיון דבכוס איתיה דם, וההוא דעל הרצפה הולך לאיבוד – לא פסלה בהו*. **הג"ה:** תהי בה ריש לקיש כלום למדנו אלא משלמים. תימה: הא ריש לקיש גופיה קאמר לקמן (יד.): מודה רבי שמעון בהולכת (אברים) חטאות הפנימיות. **אי** מה שלמים כו'. זה אין שייך לומר דמחשבת יום שני לא יפסול בחטאת כמו בשלמים, דפשיטא דבכל חד אזלינן בתר חוץ לזמנו דידיה.

אלא מאי אית לך למימר דבר הפוסל בהן כו'. השתא מסיק דמסברא יש לנו לומר כן, דדבר הפוסל מוציא מידי פיגול, ודבר המעכב בה מביא לידי פיגול כמו בשלמים. ואין שייך להקשות: שכן נוהג בכל הזבחים. **זה** הכלל כל הקומץ ונותן בכלי. בהגשה אין פיגול, דקמילה כנגד שחיטה, ואין לו פיגול קודם שחיטה.

מודה

תורה אור

[נ"ל והתניא]

[לקמן כח: מנחות יז. חולין פח:]

מנחות יב.

נ"א על ברחין היינו קבלה עבודה חשובה

נ"ק

נ"א מן הבשר שהם שירים אף זה כו' נ"ק

הגהות הב"ח

(א) גמ' קמיה דבר פדא: (ב) שם משלמים למדנו או מה: (ג) שם כלום למדנו פיגול וכן בכל הענין: (ד) רש"י ד"ה ופרכינן וכו' למדנו וכו' דין: (ה) ד"ה הואיל וכו' דבהדיא: (ו) ד"ה אלא וכו' מה יש לך לומר טעם: (ז) ד"ה הכא נמי וכו' בכלל מנוחה הס"ד: (ח) ד"ה אלא כיון וכו' לקרבו למזבח:

גליון הש"ס

גמ' הא דאמר. עיין לעיל דף ט ע"ב תוס' ד"ה מחשבין:

שיטה מקובצת

א] הריני שוחט ע"מ לקבל דמו למחר: ב] מחשבה והתניא יכול: ג] פנימית. ס"א אינו: ד] קמיה דבר פדא אמר ליה: ה] משלמים למדנו: ו] קאתיא ה"נ מרבוייא דקרא קאתיא: ז] שמעתי מרבי רש"י גרים שטבילת אצבע מפגלת ול"ג מפגלת אצבע פירוש ר"ל כך אם חשב בשעת זריקה ע"מ לטבול למחר [מפגלת] הטבילה וזה אינו דאין זה מחשב בעבודה לאכילת אדם או למזבח. מהר"פ: ח] מפגלת בה אות ן' נמחק: ט] אין הכל משלמים למדנו פרש"י ודקשיא לך כו' תימה אמאי לא אמרינן כמו כן הואיל וטבילת אצבע מעכבת בחטאת והולכה מעכבת בשלמים מה עבודה המעכבת בשלמים (המביאה) [מביאה] לידי פגול אף טבילה המעכבת בחטאת הפנימית (המביאה) [מביאה] לידי פגול [וי"ל] טבילת אצבע לא שייך כלל בשלמים אבל שלא לשמו דשייך קצת בשלמים לענין דאין מרצין שפיר ילפינן זה מזה. מהר"פ: י] אלא כיון דלא סגי. פ"ה כיון דלא סגי (איהו) כו' עד למזבח וא"ת א"כ מהאי טעמא בחטאות חיצונות נמי ליפסיל טבילת אצבע דלא סגי כו' ועוד קשה דבקומץ זוטא אמר ר' ינאי הולכה בזר פסולה משום דכיון דלא סגי דלא עביד עבודה חשובה היא והכי דחי האי טעמא במסקנא ואמר הר"ם (דמשני) [דמדשני] בדיבוריה קרא לכתוב בפנימית וטבל ובחיצוניות לא כתיב וטבל אלא ולקח ש"מ דלא אמרינן הך טעמא דכיון דלא סגי גבי חיצוניות וכן למסקנא לכך לא אמרינן הך סברא דלא סגי משום דא"כ אמאי כתיב בפנימית ולא כתיב בחיצוניות הא שייך האי טעמא אף בחיצוניות אלא ודאי האי סברא דלא סגי אע"ג דהוי בעלמא הכא ליתא ונראה הכל: יא] לא הא רבנן כו'. כלומר בין למר ובין למר הולכה היא אלא הא רבנן והא ר"ש כלומר הא ר"ש דהולכה לא פסלא במחשבה וה"ה טבילת אצבע נמי אע"ג דטעמא דר"ש בהולכה משום דאפשר לבטלה והכא בטבילת אצבע אי אפשר לבטלה מ"מ כיון דלא חשיבא טבילת אצבע עבודה רק מטעם הולכה לא יפסל בה טפי מחשבה מהולכה. כך נראה למורי מהר"פ ז"ל: יב] דבר שהוא אכילה: יג] וכי נמי: יד] הזבחים כדינן של שלמים הס"ד: טו] וקבל או הלך שלא לשמו לא יצאו: טז] דפסול ביה: יז] מפגלת ול"ג מפגלת אצבע: יח] וחוץ למקומו: יט] לאכול ממנו חוץ: כ] שכל מחשבה פסולה מוציאתו: כא] למקומו דבשלמים: כב] למקומו דשלמים: כג] שהרי פסולו: כד] טעם לומר בשלא: כה] הדם מביאו לידי: כו] הקומץ כו': כז] הבשר שהן שירים אף זה ותיבות והבשר הם ל"ש ונמחק: כח] עבודות מפגלים מהיקישא: כט] לקמן בהך היקישא: ל] אדם דם לאו: לא] תפשוט מנאי אי טבילת אצבע הוי כהולכה או לא הס"ד:

*כל שאינו על מזבח החיצון כשלמים אין בו משום פיגול! אלא, הא והא רבנן, ולא קשיא: כאן – בחטאות החיצונות, כאן – בחטאות הפנימיות. חטאות החיצונות פשיטא, (א) א] לא כתיב בהו "וטבל"! אצטריך, סלקא דעתך אמינא: הואיל וכתיב "ולקח", ואי אתי קוף רמי להו אידיה, בעי למישקל זימנא אחריתי (ב) – כמאן דכתיב "וטבל" דמי, [קמ"ל:] ב] להכי לא כתיב "וטבל", דמשמע הכי ומשמע הכי. § "רבי שמעון מכשיר בהילוך". § א"ר שמעון בן לקיש: ג] מודה רבי שמעון בהולכת חטאות הפנימיות שמחשבה פוסלת בהו, הואיל ועבודה ד] שאין יכול לבטלה. והאמר *רבי שמעון: כל שאינו על מזבח החיצון כשלמים אין חייבין עליו משום פיגול! ה] א"ר (ג) יוסי ברבי חנינא: מודה היה לפסול, מקל וחומר; ומה שלא לשמן שהוכשרו בשלמים – פסול בחטאת, חוץ לזמנו שפוסל בשלמים – אינו דין שיפסול בחטאות? (ד) ו] ואשכחן חוץ לזמנו, חוץ למקומו מנלן? אי מחוץ לזמנו – מה לחוץ לזמנו שכן כרת, אי משלא (ה) לשמה – שכן נוהג בבמה! ז] (חיוב) שלא לשמן במאי נוהג? בפסח וחטאת, פסח וחטאת בבמה לא ח] קרבו. ואיבעית אימא, הקישא הוא: "שלישי" – זה חוץ לזמנו, "פיגול" – ט] [זה] חוץ למקומו. אמר רבא: אם תימצי לומר ר' שמעון סבר לה כבריה, דאמר: *בין האולם ולמזבח צפון – אין מחשבה מועלת בהולכת חטאות הפנימיות אלא מפתח אולם ולפנים; ואם תמצי לומר סבר לה כרבי יהודה, דאמר: תוך עזרה מקדש – אין מחשבה מועלת בהולכת סילוק בזיכין אלא מפתח היכל ולחוץ; ואם תמצי לומר *סבר: קדושת היכל ואולם חדא היא – אין מחשבה מועלת אלא מפתח אולם ולחוץ; ואם תמצי לומר: תוך הפתח כלפנים – אין מחשבה מועלת אפילו פסיעה אחת אלא בכדי הושטת ידו; ואם תמצי לומר סבר: הולכה שלא ברגל לא שמה הולכה – אין מחשבה מועלת כלל. § *א"ל *אביי לאמוריה דרב חסדא, בעי י] מיניה מרב חסדא: הולכה בזר, מהו? א"ל: כשרה, ומקרא מסייעני: °"וישחטו את הפסח ויזרקו הכהנים יא] את הדם מידם והלוים מפשיטים". מתיב רב ששת: *איזר ב] ואונן

שיכור

תורה אור
דה"ב לה

רש"י

כל קרבן שאינו על מזבח החיצון כשלמים. שלמדנו מהם פיגול לכל הזבחים – אין בו משום פיגול. לקמן בפרק "בית שמאי" (דף מג.). בחטאות החיצונות. אינה מפגלת, דלא כתיב בהו "וטבל" אלא "ולקח הכהן מדם החטאת באצבעו", והיא לקיחה קבלה היא, ומינה ילפינן קבלה לקמן ב"איזהו מקומן" (דף מח.).

איצטריכא מהו דתימא הואיל וכתיב ולקח. דמשמע: הוא בעצמו יקח. ואי אתי קוף ורמי להו אידיה. על אצבעו, בעי מיהדר ומשקל. אלמא "ולקח" נמי יב] אאצבעו קאי, שיטבול אצבעו, אימא כמאן דכתיב "וטבל" דמי. להכי לא יג] כתביה טבילה. בהדיא, אלא כתב קבלה. יד] ומדסמכיה א"אצבעו ונתן" הוא דיליף לטבול אצבעו, שצריך ליקח בעצמו ולטבול. דמשמע הכי – דלא תהא טבילת אצבע טו] עבודה חשובה בהן לפגל, מדלא אחשבה קרא להצריכה בפירוש. ומשמע הכי – שצריכה היא לטבול טז] בחטאות (ו) החיצונה, ולא דלישקל קוף ולירמייה לדם על האצבע. דבעינן לקיחת אצבע מעליותא, ד"ולקח" נמי אאצבע קאי. שאי אפשר לבטלה. ◎דלאו אורח ארעא לשחוט בהיכל, ועל כרחו הוא שוחטו בעזרה ומוליכה בהיכל לקרנות מזבח פנימי ולהזאת פרוכת. כל שאינו. כל קרבן שאין מתן דמו על מזבח החיצון, לאפוקי חטאות הפנימיות. וקס"ד דה"ה לפסול יז] דשלא לשמו. מודה יח] הוא לפסול. נהי דאין בהן פיגול להתחייב כרת על אכילתו, אבל מודה הוא דמחשבה חוץ לזמנו פוסלתו מק"ו. והכי נמי הוה מצי לתרוצי ליה: אנן במחשבה שלא לשמו קיימינא, דפסלה בהו, אלא דבעי רבי יוסי בר' חנינא לאשמועינן דמחשבת חוץ לזמנו פסלה בהו לר"ש. חוץ לזמנו הפוסל בשלמים כו'. ומיהו כרת לא נפקא לן בו מינה, דהא ק"ו מכח שלא לשמו אתי, ודיו להבא מן הדין להיות כנדון. חוץ למקומו מנא לן. דהא חוץ למקומו נמי בשלמים כתיב, ומינייהו גמרינן לכל הזבחים. ולר' שמעון דלא גמר מינייהו אלא חיצונות כמותן – מנ"ל דפסלה בפנימיות? אי מחוץ לזמנו. ב"מה מלינו". אי משלא לשמו. ובק"ו, כדלעיל. שכן נוהג בבמה. יט] [בקרבן במת יחיד בשעת היתר הבמות, שהרי שנוי קדש הוא. תאמר בחוץ למקומו דלא, שאין מחיצה בבמה], וכל הבקעה מקומו עד סוף העולם. ומשני: שלא לשמו במאי נוהג. באיזה קרבן אתה מוצא פסולו – בפסח וחטאת. והני בבמה לא קרבי, דתנן לקמן (דף קיז.): כל הנידר ונידב – קרב בבמה, ושאינו נידר ונידב – אינו קרב בבמה. ואיבעית אימא. חוץ למקומו מחוץ לזמנו אתי. ולא פרכינן "שכן כרת", דהיקשא הוא, דאיתקש חוץ למקומו לחוץ לזמנו, בפ' שני (לקמן דף כח.) בקרא אחרינא, דאמרינן: "אם האכל יאכל ביום השלישי" – זה מחשבת חוץ לזמנו, "לא יחשב לו פיגול יהיה" – קרא יתירא הוא, לאתויי חוץ למקומו. וכיון דאיתקוש – גמרינן מהדדי, ואין משיבין על ההיקש. אמר רבא את"ל ר' שמעון סבר לה כבריה דאמר. לקמן בפ' שני (דף כ.). בין האולם למזבח צפון. חלק צפוני שבעזרה שבין האולם ולמזבח, אע"ג דלא קרינן ביה "על ירך המזבח צפונה", דהא במערבו של מזבח הוא – הוי צפון לענין שחיטת קדשים. אין מחשבה מועלת כ] בחטאות הפנימיות. אפילו לפסול. אלא מפתח האולם ולפנים. שאם חישב בהולכת הדם ממקום כא] שחיטתו עד האולם – אינה מחשבה, שהרי אפשר לבטל הולכה זו, לשחוט אצל פתח האולם. אבל אי סבר כרבי יוסי, דפליג אדרבי אלעזר בר' שמעון, ואומר: אין צפון אלא כנגד המזבח, מקיר כב] המזבח צפוני עד כותל העזרה צפונית – הויא לה עבודה שאין יכול לבטלה. דהא חטאת טעונה צפון לשחיטתה, דכתיב: "במקום אשר תשחט העולה" וגו', וצפון בעולה כתיב. ואת"ל. ר' שמעון סבר לה כר' יהודה, דאמר לקמן בפ' "קדשי קדשים" (דף נט.): תוך עזרה מקדש – כל רצפת העזרה בין האולם ולמזבח מקודשת להקטיר חלבים כמזבח עצמו, דכתיב: "ביום ההוא קדש המלך את תוך החצר", ותניא לקמן: דברים ככתבן, דברי ר' יהודה. אין מחשבה מועלת. לר' שמעון בהולכת בזיכי לחם הפנים, שהן מתירין את הלחם, כדם המתיר את הבשר וכקומץ המתיר את השיריים, והלחם מתפגל במחשבת עבודת הבזיכים הואיל והן מתירין. כג] *) רבי שמעון, אי כרבי יהודה סבר לה – אין מחשבת הולכה מועלת בה לפסול אלא מפתח היכל ולחוץ, משהגיע לפתח היכל עד שמגיע ליציאת אולם לרצפת העזרה שלפניו. דבכל ההיכל לא מהניא מחשבה, שהרי כל ההיכל כשר להושיב שם שלחן לסדר עליו עד הפתח. ואולם כי עזרה כד] סבירא לן. ומן האולם ולחוץ נמי לא מהניא מחשבה בהולכה, שהרי אפשר להקטירו על רצפת העזרה מיד אם ירצה. נמצאת הולכתו עד המזבח שלא לצורך. ה"ג: ואת"ל סבר רבי שמעון קדושת אולם והיכל חדא היא אין מחשבה מועלת אלא מפתח אולם ולחוץ. כלומר, ה' אמות של עובי כותל פתחו של אולם. דבכל חללו של אולם לא מהניא – דכפנים דמי, וחוץ לפתח לא מהניא – דאפשר להקטיר שם. ואת"ל סבר כה] לה תוך פתח האולם כלפנים אין מחשבה מועלת אפילו פסיעה שלימה אלא בכדי הושטת ידו. עומד בפתח האולם ומושיט ידו לרצפה היינו הולכה, ומהניא בה מחשבה. הכי גרסינן: ואם תמצי לומר הולכה שלא ברגל לא שמה הולכה אין מחשבה מועלת כלל. דהא הושטת ידו הולכה שלא ברגל היא. ויזרקו הכהנים את הדם מידם. [מידם] של שוחטין משמע, כו] ושוחטין זרים נינהו. ואשמועינן קרא שהזרים לוקחין אותו מיד המקבל, ומוליכין אותו כז] לזרוק.

*) נ"א ואי ר"ש כר' יהודה סבר כו' ל"ק

שיכור

תוספות

מודה היה לפסול מקל וחומר. מכאן מתרצים ההיא דפ' "הנזקין" (גיטין דף נד: ושם) דקאמר ר' יוסי: כהן גדול ביום הכפורים יוכיח, דכי אמר פיגול – מהימן, ור' יוסי סבירא ליה כר"ש בפ' "הקומץ זוטא" (מנחות דף יד.) דאין פיגול אלא בדבר הנעשה על מזבח החיצון. ולמאי דאמר הכא דמודה הוא לפסול – ניחא, דפיגול לאו דוקא. ועוד יש לפרש: היינו שלא לשמה, ולא נהירא. ומה שלא לשמן כו'. תימה: מה לשלא לשמן – שכן נוהג בד' עבודות, תאמר בחוץ לזמנו שאינו נוהג אלא בזריקה! וכי האי גוונא פריך לעיל (דף ד.) כח] *(מה לחוץ לזמנו שכן כרת). ויש לומר: דאי הוה פריך הכי הוה עביד ק"ו משנוי בעלים, כט] *דהוי כפיגל בזריקה. ומיהו, קשה: מה לשנוי בעלים – שכן פוסל בזביחה בפסח, ל] ◎או בזריקה לחודיה! וי"ל: דשלא לשמן יוכיח, וילפינן ב"מה הצד" משנוי קדש ושנוי בעלים לא]. הג"ה: תוך עזרה מקדש. טעמא דרבי יהודה לקמן בפרק "קדשי קדשים" (דף נט.) וצריך לדקדק: לר' יהודה, כיון דעזרה מקדש, ◎היכי משכחת לה בפסולין דאם ירדו לא יעלו? וי"ל: דמשכחת לה [באותם] דירדו בלשכה או באולם או על גבי דף. *ועדיף מאויר, דאמר בפ"ב (לקמן כו.): תלה ושחט פסול. א"נ, שחט על הרצפה ואח"כ נתן על הדף – דהשתא ירדו. *ול"ע: דלקמן (דף קכ.) מבעיא להו: ירדו מהו שיעלו! [וי"ל: דשחט על הרצפה ואח"כ נתן על הדף]. ועוד יש לומר: דמודה רבי יהודה בדמים לקמן דבעי מזבח, והדם לא עלה ברצפה. ותו: דלשון "אם עלו" דנקט – היינו לדינא דקודם דאתא דוד וקדיש רצפה, וקודם בנין שלמה. הג"ה לב].

שיכור

עין משפט נר מצוה

עו א מיי' פ"ט מהל' ביאת מקדש הל' א ב והלכה טו ופ"א מהלכות פסה"מ הלכה כו סמג לאוין שנו:

עו ב מיי' פ"ט מהל' ביאת מקדש הל' טו ופ"ג הלכה ז סמג לאוין שנ:

עיין בסוף המסכתא שנדפס בשם הרב הגאון המפורסם אב"ד דמדינת פפאלין שמיישב בטוב טעם שאין מהצורך למחוק הג"ה זו

*דלא הוי פיגול אלא בזריקה ל"ק

דלא עדיף מאויר ל"ק

ע' רש"ק ותוספי' גרסאות

רש"ק

מסורת הש"ס

[לקמן מג. מו: שבועות ז.]

[לקמן מג. מו: שבועות ז.]

ס"א ל"ג

[לקמן כח.]

רש"ק

[שם כ. יומא נו.]

[לקמן נח: נט. עירובין ב. יומא מד:]

יומא מט. נ"א רב ששת

שם

רש"ק

הגהות הב"ח

(א) גמ' פשיטא הא לא כתיב: (ב) שם זימנא אחריתי אימא כמאן: (ג) שם אמר רבי יוסף בר' חנינא מודה הוא לפסול וכו' שלא לשמה: (ד) שם אשכחן כל"ל ותיבת ו' נמחק: (ה) שם אי משלא לשמו וכו' בבמה: (ו) רש"י ד"ה להכי לא וכו' כחטאות הפנימיות ולא דלישקול:

גליון הש"ס

[illegible]

שיטה מקובצת

א] פשיטא דלא: ב] להכי לא כתיב וטבל כו'. וא"ת והיאך ס"ד לומר דלכתוב וטבל ולשתוק מולקח והא אצטריך לקמן לומר שתהא קבלה לשם חטאת וגם דקבלה טעונה צפון וי"ל דה"ק לכתוב תרתי וטבל עם ולקח: ג] מודה ר"ש כו'. פרש"י דלאו אורח כו' וקשה דאמרינן לקמן שלמים ששחטן בהיכל כשרים וכו' משום שלא יהא טפל חמור מן העיקר ולא פסלינן משום דלאו אורח ארעא ועוד דאמרינן התם עובד אדם עבודת רבו במקום רבו משמע דשפיר הוי אורח ארעא לכך נראה למורי דטעמא משום דחטאת טעונה צפון ובהיכל לא הוי צפון דאפילו למ"ד בין האולם ולמזבח קרוי צפון מודה דמבית החליפות ואילך לא הוי צפון וכ"ש בהיכל עצמו שמחיצות ההיכל מפסקת: ד] שאי אפשר לבטלה (ותיבות שאין יכול נמחק) והאמר ר' שמעון וכו'. וקס"ד דפסול שלא לשמו נמי ליתנהו בה וכ"ש פסול דחוץ לזמנו דלא יליף כלל משלמים ולכך פריך לריש לקיש ומשני דמודה לפסול אף חוץ לזמנו מק"ו ושלא לשמו אית ליה דמודה בה ר"ש וה"ה דהוי מצי למימר אנן בשלא לשמו קיימינן [ולא] בפיגול אלא דרוצה לתרץ לדבריו דאף בחוץ לזמנו דקפריך ליה מודה ר"ש דאף הוא פסול: ה] א"ר יוסי בר' חנינא. ע' תוס'

לקמן (דף קד ע"ב): ו] אשכחן אות ו' נמחק: ז] בבמה שלא לשמו: ח] לא קרבי ואבעית אימא היקשא הוא. עיין תוס' מנחות (דף עט ע"א): ט] פיגול זה חוץ למקומו: י] בעי מיניה. פי' שא"ל לאמורא שישאל מרב חסדא: יא] תיבות את הדם נמחק: יב] נמי אאצבע אות ו' נמחק: יג] לא כתב ביה טבילה: יד] ומדסמכי אצבעו אונתן הוא דיליף לטבילת אצבע: טו] אצבע חשובה עבודה: טז] לטבול בחטאות: יז] לפסול בשלא: יח] מודה היה לפסול נהי כו' כרת על אכילתן אבל מודה הוא דמחשבת חוץ: יט] בבמה בקרבן במת יחיד בשעת היתר במות שהרי שינוי קודש תאמר בחוץ למקומו דלא שאין מחיצות בבמה וכל הבקעה: כ] מועלת בהולכת חטאות הפנימיות: כא] ממקום שחיטה ועד האולם: כב] מקיר המזבח הצפוני: כג] מתירין ור"ש: כד] עזרה סבירא לן ס"א לא חשיב: כה] תיבת לה נמחק: כו] משמע השוחטין זרים: כז] המקבל ומוליכין אותו לזורק שהמקבלים את הדם היו כהנים והזרים היו מוליכין לזורק הס"ד ומה"ד אונן כל זמן שלא נקבר מתו הס"ד: כח] תיבות מה לחוץ לזמנו שכן כרת נמחק: כט] בעלים שאינו בד' עבודות כדין פיגול וא"ת מ"מ איכא למיפרך מה לשינוי בעלים שכן פוסל בזריקה עצמה תאמר בפיגול שאינו [אלא אם] מחשב מעבודה לעבודה ותירץ הר"ם דעבדינן ק"ו ממקום ומה מקום כגון שלמים דשלא לשמן לא פסל בהו חוץ לזמנו פסול בהו מקום כגון בחטאת דשלא לשמו פסל בהו אינו דין שיפסול בה חוץ לזמנו והשתא ליכא למיפרך מה לשלא לשמו כיון דמכח ק"ו מקום גמרינן. לשון תוס' הר"פ: ל] בפסח תאמר בחוץ לזמנו שאינו פוסל אלא בזריקה וי"ל דשלא לשמו יוכיח: לא] בעלים ע"כ: לב] הג"ה ע"כ:

אשיכור בובעל מום, בקבלה בהולכה בזריקה – פסול, גוכן יושב, דוכן שמאל! תיובתא. והא רב חסדא קרא קאמר. א] הדעביד מעשה אצטבא. רבה ורב יוסף דאמרי תרוייהו: הולכה בזר – מחלוקת ר' שמעון ורבנן; רבי שמעון דאמר: עבודה שאפשר לבטלה לאו עבודה היא – כשרה בזר, לרבנן – ופסולה. א"ל אביי: ב] והא שחיטה, דעבודה שא"א לבטלה, וכשרה בזר! א"ל: *שחיטה לאו עבודה היא. ולא? *והאמר ר' זירא אמר רב: ישחיטת פרה בזר – פסולה; ואמר רב (א) עלה: ג] אלעזר וחוקה כתיב בה! שאני פרה,* דקדשי בדק הבית היא? ולאו כל דכן הוא: קדשי בדק הבית – הויא עבודה, קדשי מזבח לאו עבודה היא? אמר רב ששא בריה דרב אידי: מידי דהוה אמראות נגעים, דלאו עבודה היא, ובעיא כהונה. והרי הולכת אברים לכבש, דעבודה שאפשר לבטלה היא, חופסולה בזר, דכתי': °"והקרי' הכהן את הכל [והקטיר] המזבחה", (ויקרא א) *ואמר מר: זו הולכת אברים לכבש! היכא *דגלי – גלי, והיכא דלא גלי – לא גלי. ולאו כל דכן הוא: ומה הולכת אברים לכבש, דלא מעכבא כפרה – בעיא כהונה, הולכת דם דמעכבא כפרה – [לא כ"ש]? (מיבעיא). *איתמר ד] [נמי,] אמר עולא א"ר אלעזר: הולכה בזר פסולה, אפילו לרבי שמעון. איבעיא להו: *הולכה שלא ברגל, שמה הולכה, או לא שמה הולכה? ת"ש: וכן יושב, וכן שמאל – פסול; הא עומד דומיא דיושב – כשר. דלמא יושב – דקשייף מישף, עומד – דומיא דיושב, ה] דנייד פורתא. ת"ש: *טשחט ישראל וקבל הכהן, נתנו לחבירו, וחבירו לחבירו. התם נמי, *דניידי פורתא. ומאי קמ"ל? °י"ברוב עם הדרת מלך". (משלי יד) ת"ש: *קבל הכשר ונתן לפסול – יחזיר לכשר. אימא: יחזור הכשר ויקבלה. איתמר, אמר עולא א"ר יוחנן: כהולכה שלא ברגל – לא שמה הולכה.
[פסחים סד.] [סה:]

אפשר

רש"י

שיכור. היינו שתוי יין ו]. מעשה איצטבא. עומדין במקומן הזר אצל הכהן המקבל. והכהן נותנו לו, ואוחזו, עד שבא הזורק ונוטלו מידו. ואין הזר ז] מקרבן לצד המזבח לא בהולכת רגל ולא בהושטת יד, אלא כאיצטבא זו שמניחין כלי עליה. והא שחיטה כו'. אלמא טעם לא בהא תלי. וליכא למיפסל לרבנן דמשום דסבירא להו דהולכה אי אפשר ח] *לבטל – א"כ בשחיטה דאי אפשר לבטל תיפסל בזר, והא שחיטה בזר כשרה! ומשני: שחיטה לאו עבודה היא. מדאתכשרו בה כל הפסולים. אבל מידי דהוי עבודה ואי אפשר לבטלה – פסול בזר. ואמר רב עלה. לפרושי ט] למילתיה: מאי טעם פסולה – דכתיב בשחיטתה: "ונתתם אותה אל אלעזר הכהן ושחט", וכתיב בה בפרה "חוקה", וכל היכא דכתיב "חוקה" – עכובא. שאני פרה. י] וחילוק טעם זה אינו מטעם עבודה, דהא אינה קדושת מזבח, אלא קדושת דמים בעלמא כקדשי בדק הבית. ועל כרחך טעם הפוסל בה לאו משום תורת עבודה, אלא גזירת הכתוב בעלמא היא. אבל בקדשי מזבח דשייכי בהן יא] עבודות – לא חשיבא להיות עבודה. הולכת אברים אפשר לבטלה. שאם רצה מפשיט ומנתח אצל המזבח. היכא דגלי גלי. הולכת אברים דגלי בהן כהן – בעינן כהן. אבל הולכת הדם, דלא גלי בהו כהן – לרבי שמעון יב] דאפשר לבטלה לא בעי כהן. אפילו לר' שמעון. דאע"ג דאמר ר' שמעון לא פסל בה מחשבה – משום דאין היתר הקרבן תלוי בה, ולא קרינא בה דברים המביאים לידי אכילה. אבל עבודה הוי ליפסל בזר. שמה הולכה. (ב) ופסלה בה מחשבה לרבנן. או אם עשאה זר – פסולה. או לא שמה הולכה. ולא פסלה מחשבה. וכן כהן יושב. קתני *דפסול בהולכה. יג] (ג) [הא עומד] דאינו מוליך אלא בהושטת יד, דומיא דיושב – כשר. אלמא שמה הולכה. דשייף מישף. שמגרר עצמו לצד המזבח. שייף = משפשף בקרקע. שייף = מגרר, כמו: שייף ליה מישחא (שבת דף י:), שף אחת ובועט שתים (מנחות דף עו.), *פדיי"ר. ודכוותה דוק מיניה בעומד דכשרה – דנייד פורתא בשפשוף רגלים. ת"ש דתנן בסדר הפסח: שחט ישראל כו'. כן היה דרכן לעשות. נתנו לחבירו. דקתני התם: הכהנים עומדים שורות שורות. יחזיר לכשר. שנתנו לו. ואשמעינן יד] תרתי בה: חדא – דלא מיפסל במאי דאפסקיה פסול. (ד) ואשמעינן טו] בה דהולכה זו שעשה הכשר שלא ברגל, שהושיט לפסול שהיה עומד בצד המזבח – לא נעשית בהכשר, ולא שמה הולכה. דקתני: יחזירנה למי שנתנה לו, טז] ואי הולכה שלא ברגל שמה הולכה – אמאי יחזירנה לאחור? יבא כשר ויטלנה מידו לצד המזבח, יז] וזה לא יושיטנה לו! אלא דמעשה אצטבא בעלמא עביד. אימא יחזור כשר. לצד המזבח, ויקבלנו – יטלנו מיד הפסול, דהולכת (ה) כשר קמא כשרה. לא שמה הולכה. ואינה כשרה להוליכה כן, ואין מחשבה מפגלת בה.

אפשר

תוספות

שיכור. פירש בקונטרס: שתוי יין ולא משמע כן בפרק "מומין אלו פסולין באדם" (בכורות דף מה:). אלא: שיכור – בשאר דברים המשכרים, יח] *ודלא כר' יהודה, דאמר מחלי עבודה. מיהו, שיכור דתנן התם – ודאי לא הוי שתוי יין, כדפרי' התם: בהדי מומין דמחלי עבודה בעי למיחשבה. אבל שיכור דהכא – פשטיה משמע שתוי יין. והא כדאיתא והא כדאיתא. ולכולי עלמא מחלל לעבודה, כדפריך התם בפשיטות: אחולי מיחל עבודה הוא*. והא שחיטה שאי אפשר לבטלה וכשרה. פרש"י: אלמא לאו באפשר לבטלה תלי, ואת אמרת לרבנן פסול. ותימה: דמאי פירכא? לרבנן ודאי לא בהא תלי, והא דפסלי בהולכה – משום דמקבלה ואילך מצות כהונה! אלא פריך דמכשיר לר' שמעון משום דאפשר לבטל – הא לא תלי בהא, מדמכשר זר בשחיטה אע"ג דאי אפשר לבטלה. ובסמוך דפריך מהולכת אברים – לרבי שמעון פריך, וכן יט] דמייתי אמר ר' אלעזר הולכה בזר פסולה כ] לרבי שמעון. **הג"ה:** שחיטה לאו עבודה היא. פירש בקונטרס: מדאתכשרו בה כל הפסולים. ואי אפשר לומר כן, כא] דאהכשר זר גופה מייתי לה כב] [הכא] ובפ"ק דמנחות (דף ו:). ומיהו יש ליישב פירושו: דכיון דבשום מקום לא בעי כהן בשחיטה – לאו עבודה היא. ולהכי פריך עלה מפרה. וה"ר יעקב דאורלינ"ש מפרש: לאו עבודה היא – לפי ששוה בחולין ובקדשים, א"כ לאו מטעם עבודה נוה המקום שחיטה. ולי נראה: לאו עבודה היא – מדמכשרינן לקמן בפ' שני (דף כו.) עומד בדרום והושיט ידו לצפון ושחט בקדשי קדשים, ובמקבל פסול, דדרשינן: אותו בצפון ולא שוחט בצפון, אבל מקבל בצפון. ובשלמים מכשירין עומד בחוץ והושיט ידו לפנים ושחט, ואם קבל – קבלתו פסולה, דדרשינן בפ' "כל הפסולין" (לקמן דף לב.): "בן הבקר לפני ה'" ולא שוחט לפני ה', אבל קבל – קבלתו פסולה, משום דכתיב: "לעמוד לפני ה' לשרתו", אלמא כל שירות לפני ה'. ש"מ כד] מדמכשיר רחמנא עומד בחוץ והושיט ידו לפנים ושחט – מכלל דשחיטה כה] לאו עבודה היא. ועוד: מדאמר בההיא שמעתא בפ"ב (דף כו.) כו] נתלה ושחט שחיטתו כשרה, דשחיטה על ירך אמר רחמנא ולא שוחט על ירך (אמר רחמנא) – אלמא דשחיטה לאו עבודה היא, דאי עבודה היא – לא הוה מכשר רחמנא בכי האי גוונא, דהא כז] נתלה וקבל אמרינן דקבלתו פסולה, משום דאין דרך שירות בכך. ומדפריך הכא ובפ' "חטאת העוף" (לקמן דף סח:) ובפ"ק דמנחות (דף ו:) מפרה, דאמר רב שחיטת פרה בזר פסולה – משמע קצת כפי' הקונטרס. מיהו, גם לפי מה שפירשתי יש ליישבו. אבל קשה לי לפירושו: דא"כ לשמעון התימני דבעי פרק "כל הפסולין" (לקמן דף לב:) שיהא כח] ידיו של שוחט לפנים מן הנשחט – הויא שחיטה עבודה א). **שאני** פרה דקדשי בדק הבית היא. בפ"ק דחולין (דף יא.) פירשתי ב). **והרי** הולכת אברים לכבש דאפשר לבטלה פסולה בזר דכתיב והקריב הכהן את הכל המזבחה ואמר מר כו' כט] שאני הכא דגלי קרא. הקשה ה"ר אליהו מאברוויקא הקדוש, דבפ"ב דיומא (דף כז.*) אמרינן: מדאצטריך למכתב כהן בהולכת אברים לכבש, פי' לגופיה לא אצטריך, אלא לגלות דהולכת עצים למזבח לא בעי כהן. ומדאצטריך מעוט להולכת עצים – א"כ סידור ב' גזרי עצים בעי כהונה ל] ג) (בלאו קרא מטעם). וא"כ רבי שמעון דבעי ב' כהנים התם (דף כו:) לשני גזרי עצים, מנא ליה? דהא כהן דכתב גבי הולכת אברים אצטריך לגופיה, משום דאפשר לבטלה! וי"ל: דרבי שמעון לטעמא, דאמר התם (דף מה.): הלכת אליתא לא צריך למכתב ביה כהן, ודכי תעלה על דעתך שזר קרב למזבח? ורבנן – אפשר דעביד במפוחא. וא"כ, רבי שמעון ע"כ שני גזרי עצים בעו כהונה בלא קרא, מטעמא דוכי תעלה על דעתך כו', דכמו דלית ליה במפוחא – לית ליה אפשר להו בזריקה. אבל לרבנן אית להו בזריקה כמו דאית להו במפוחא, וכהן דגבי הולכת אברים לגופיה לא אצטריך, דהא לית לא] טעמא דאפשר לבטלה, אלא לגלות על שני גזרי עצים דבעי כהונה. ובפ' "הקומץ רבה" (מנחות דף כ.) לב] אמר: לא מלח כהן אלא זר, פריך: וכי תעלה על דעתך שזר קרב? יש לומר: דאפילו לרבנן דאית להו במפוחא וזריקה פריך, שאין יכולין למלוח בטוב על ידי זריקה. לג] (כל זה בהג"ה דאיבעיא להו) ד) **איבעיא** להו הולכה שלא ברגל שמה הולכה או לא. פרש"י: לפסול בה מחשבה, וגם בזר. דאי שמה הולכה – מחשבה שלא לשמו או פיגול פוסלת בה, ואי לא שמה הולכה – לד] אינה קרויה עבודה, וצריך להחזיר המזרק אחריו ולעשות הולכה ברגל. וגם אם עשאה זר או יושב – אין בכך כלום, ויכול לתקנה לה] בכהן [בהולכת רגל] דכהן או אם זר מוליך [בהולכת רגל] – פסולה [ואינו] יכול לתקנה בכהן להחזירה ולהוליכה כהן. וקאמר, ת"ש: וכן יושב פסול, הא עומד דומיא דיושב, שאינו זז ממקומו – כשר. אלמא הויא הולכה ועשה עבודה כתקנה. ולכך נמי כי עשאה מיושב – פסול, דכתיב "לעמוד לשרת". אבל מיושב פסול לא מצי מוכח דהויא הולכה עבודה בלאו דיוקא, [משום] דדלמא לאו עבודה היא, ויושב פסול – היינו כי לא תקנה, ולא החזיר הדם לאחוריו לעשות הולכה אחרת.

הולכה

א) [ע' תוס' יומא מב. ד"ה שחיטה שכתבו ישוב על זה] ב) [ע"ע תוס' ע"ז כג: ד"ה אלא מעתה] ג) רש"ק מ"ז ד) ע' נ"ק שמהפך הגי' של תוס'

עין משפט נר מצוה

גי' הג"ק וכר"י דאמר ובס"י לרבי יהודה

עח א מיי' פ"א מהל' ביאת מקדש הל' א ופ"ט שם הלכה טו סמג לאוין ש:

[וע' היטב תוס' בכורות מה: ד"ה ובשאר]

עט ב מיי' שם פ"ו הל' ח ופ"ט הלכה טו:

פ ג מיי' פ"ה שם הלכה יז ופ"ט הל' טו:

[לקמן סח: יומא מב. מנחות ה. ו:]

פא ד מיי' פ"ה שם הל' יח ופ"ט הלכה טו ופ"ד מהל' עבודת יוה"כ הלכה ח:

פב ה ו מיי' פ"א מהל' פסה"מ הלכה כז:

פג ז מיי' פ"א מהלכות פרה הלכה יא ופ"ד הלכה יז:

[עי' לעיל ז: מנחות נב: מ"ק ז:]

פד ח מיי' פ"א מהל' פסה"מ הלכה כב:

נ"א קשיא

פה ט י מיי' פ"א מהל' קרבן פסח הל' יד:

פו כ מיי' פ"א מהלכות פסה"מ הלכה כג:

מסורת הש"ס

נ"א לבטל ותיפסל בזר א"כ כו' נ"ק

יומא מב. ע"ש מנחות ו: לקמן סח:

[יומא מב. וש"נ]

לעיל ד. לקמן כד: לה. פסחים סה: חגיגה יא. [יומא כז. מנחות י.]

[מנחות יג:]

גי' הג"ק דפסול הא אינו יושב ואינו מוליך אלא בהושטת יד כו' כצ"ל

[לקמן לב.]

[שם ד"ה הולכת]

הגהות הב"ח

(א) גמ' ואמר רב פפא עלה אלעזר וחוקה: (ב) רש"י ד"ה שמה וכו' פסלה בה מחשבה: (ג) ד"ה וכן וכו' דפסול בהולכה והא יושב אינו מוליך: (ד) ד"ה יחזיר וכו' פסול אידך אשמעינן וכו' דלאו הולכה: (ה) ד"ה אימא וכו' דכשר קמא:

שיטה מקובצת

א] קאמר דעבדי: ב] והא שחיטה. פ"ה נהי דרבנן עבדו אפשר כשאי אפשר מ"מ לא פסלה זר בהולכה שהרי יש עבודה שאי אפשר לבטלה (נמי) כגון שחיטה ומכשרה בזר אלמא טעמא דלאו הא בהא תליא ולא נהירא דשאני הכא דגלי קרא ועוד קשה דבסמוך פריך לר"ש מהולכת אברים והכא לא פריך לר"ש לכך נראה דה"פ איך יכשור ר"ש בהולכה משום דאפשר לבטלה הוא והא אין הדבר תלוי בזה דהא שחיטה שאי אפשר לבטלה וכשרה בזר א"כ היינו טעמא דגלי קרא דמקבלה ואילך מצות כהונה ופסלינן בזר בכל ענין בין אפשר ובין לא אפשר וקודם קבלה בכל ענין כשר והולכה בזר פסולה ואפילו לר"ש דלא [פסל בהולכה] בשלא לשמו (דלא דפסלה לר"ש) הואיל ואפשר לבטלה דשאני מחשבה דשלא לשמו דהוי כמחשבת פיגול דהתם כתיב ואם האכל יאכל דבעינן דברים המביאין לידי אכילה הלכך כיון דאפשר לבטלה ואין היתר הקרבן תלוי בהולכה (לזר) [לא] פסלה בה מחשבה אבל מ"מ עבודה היא ופסולה בזר: ג] עלה ס"א מאי טעמא: ד] אתמר נמי: ה] דנייד פורתא. [ותימה] אי אמרת בשלמא דלא נייד אשמועינן דהולכה שלא ברגל שמיה הולכה אלא אי אמרת דנייד מאי אשמועינן. הר"פ: ו] יין לקמן בפ"ב יליף מקראי דכל הפסולין מחללין העבודה חוץ מן השחיטה: ז] הזר מקרבו: ח] אפשר לבטלה דא"כ: ט] לפרושי טעמא למלתא מאי טעם פסולה דכתיב אלעזר בשחיטתה: י] פרה חילוק: יא] בהן עבודה לא אות ו' ת' נמחק: יב] שמעון דלא משוי אפשר לבטלה כאי אפשר: יג] בהולכה הא יושב אינו מוליך אלא בהושטת יד ולא פסול אלא משום יושב דבעינן לעמוד ולשרת הא עומד ומוליך ותיבות דאינו אלא ל"ש ונמחק: יד] ואשמועינן בה תרתי חדא: טו] תיבת בה נמחק: טז] לו ס"א צריך שיחזור לכשר שנתנה לו ואי: יז] המזבח וזר לא: יח] המשכרים לר"י תיבת ודלא נמחק: יט] וכן נראה: כ] פסולה אפילו: כא] כן והרי בהולכה נמי על זה אנו דנין דלתכשר [בזר] ויש לישב פי' הקונטרס לאו עבודה דלא מצינו בשום מקום דהקפידה תורה להצריך בה כהן הלכך אע"ג דאי אפשר לבטלה כשרה בזר ופריך והרי שחיטת פרה דבעינן כהונה אלמא עבודה היא ואפ"ה כשרה בזר בשאר קדשים.

שיטה מקובצת

מהר"פ: כב] הכא ובפ"ק: כג] אבל המקבל: כד] ש"מ מדאכשר: כה] דשחיטה. ס"א מכלל דשאר שחיטות לאו שירות היא: כו] דנתלה: כז] דהא דנתלה: כח] שיהא ידי השוחט לפנים: כט] כו' ומשני דשאני: ל] תיבות בלאו קרא מטעם נמחק: לא] לית להו: לב] רבה דאמר: לג] תיבות כל זה בהגה דאיבעיא להו נמחק: לד] הולכה אינה כו'. זה לשון תלמיד הר"פ הולכה שלא ברגל לענין דפסלה בה מחשבה לרבנן או אם עשה זר פסולה כך פי' הקונטרס ולא נהירא דמאי בעי אם פסל בה מחשבה ופשיט ליה מדקאמר הא עומד דומיא דיושב לפשוט ליה הא מפשיטות המשנה דפסלה יושב אלמא הולכה שלא ברגל הולכה וחשיבא עבודה היא דאי לאו עבודה היא אמאי מיפסלא ביושב לכ"נ דלענין דמפסל בה מחשבה פשיט ליה דפסולה דאי שמה הולכה א"כ איפסלא במחשבה ואי לא שמה הולכה אם כן הוי הולכה כמי שאינו וצריך לחזור ולעשותה אלא לענין לחזור ולעשות קא בעי והכי קאמר הולכה שלא ברגל שמה הולכה לענין שלא חסר עבודת הולכה ואינו צריך לחזור ולעשותה הלכך או לא שמה הולכה והוי ממש חיסר עבודת הולכה ואפילו אם עמד כהן צריך לחזור ולעשותה הלכך פשיט ליה מדיוקא דעומד דומיא דיושב כשר אלמא דשמה הולכה דאי לא שמה הולכה היאך עומד דומיא דיושב כשר הרי חסר עבודה ע"כ: לה] הכהן בהושטת יד דכהן ואי שמה עבודה אם זר מוליך בהושטת יד פסולה ואינו יכול כו' תיבות בהולכה רגל או בהולכת רגל נמחק:

אֶפְשָׁר לְתַקְּנָהּ, אוֹ לָא אֶפְשָׁר לְתַקּוּנָהּ? ת"ש: קִבֵּל הַכָּשֵׁר וְנָתַן לְפָסוּל — יַחֲזִיר לַכָּשֵׁר. א] וְנְהִי נַמִי דְּיַחֲזוֹר הַכָּשֵׁר וִיקַבְּלֶנּוּ, אִי סָלְקָא דַּעְתָּךְ לָא אֶפְשָׁר לְתַקּוּנָהּ, אִיפַּסְלָא לָהּ! מִי סָבְרַתְּ דְּקָאֵי זָר גַּוַּאי, לָא, דְּקָאֵי זָר בָּרַאי. אִיתְּמַר, אָמַר עוּלָּא אָמַר ר' יוֹחָנָן: הוֹלָכָה שֶׁלֹּא בָּרֶגֶל — פְּסוּלָה; ב] אַלְמָא ״לָא אֶפְשָׁר לְתַקּוּנָהּ. אֵיתִיבֵיהּ רַב נַחְמָן לְעוּלָּא: *נִשְׁפַּךְ מִן הַכְּלִי עַל הָרִצְפָּה וַאֲסָפוֹ — כָּשֵׁר! הָכָא בְּמַאי עָסְקִינַן — כְּשֶׁיָּצָא לַחוּץ. לְבָרַאי נָפֵיק, לְגַוַּאי לָא עָיֵיל? בִּמְקוֹם מִדְרוֹן. אִיבָּעֵית אֵימָא: בְּגוּמָא, וְאִיבָּעֵית אֵימָא: בִּסְמִיכָא. ״וְאִיכְפַּל תַּנָּא לְאַשְׁמוּעִינַן כָּל הָנֵי? וְעוֹד, אַדְּתָנֵי בְּאִידָךְ פִּירְקִין: *נִשְׁפַּךְ עַל הָרִצְפָּה וַאֲסָפוֹ פָּסוּל; לִיפְלוֹג בְּדִידֵיהּ: בַּמֶּה דְּבָרִים אֲמוּרִים — כְּשֶׁיָּצָא לַחוּץ, אֲבָל נִכְנַס לִפְנִים — פָּסוּל! תְּיוּבְתָּא. אִתְּמַר: הוֹלָכָה שֶׁלֹּא בָּרֶגֶל מַחֲלוֹקֶת ר"ש וְרַבָּנַן. ג] בְּהוֹלָכָה רַבָּתִי — דְּכוּלֵּי עָלְמָא לָא פְּלִיגִי דִּפְסוּלָה, כִּי פְּלִיגִי — בְּהוֹלָכָה זוּטַרְתִּי. מְחַכּוּ עֲלָהּ בְּמַעֲרָבָא: אֶלָּא חַטַּאת הָעוֹף ד] דִּפְסוּלָה בָּהּ מַחֲשָׁבָה, לְר"ש הֵיכִי מַשְׁכַּחַתְּ לָהּ? אִי דַּחֲשִׁיב עֲלָהּ מִקַּמֵּי דְּלֵיפּוּק דָּם — לָא כְּלוּם הִיא, וְאִי בָּתַר דִּנְפַק דָּם — ה] אִיתְעֲבִידָא לֵיהּ מִצְוָתוֹ! מַאי קוּשְׁיָא? דִּלְמָא מִדְּפָרֵישׁ (א) וְעַד דְּמָטָא לַמִּזְבֵּחַ. דְּהָא בְּעָא מִינֵּיהּ רַבִּי יִרְמְיָה מֵרַבִּי זֵירָא: הָיָה מַזֶּה, וְנִקְטְעָה יָדוֹ שֶׁל מַזֶּה עַד שֶׁלֹּא הִגִּיעַ דָּם לַאֲוִיר הַמִּזְבֵּחַ, מַהוּ? וְא"ל: ו] [״פְּסוּלָה, מ"ט?] ״וְהִזָּה וְנָתַן״ בָּעֵינַן! כִּי אָתוּ רַב פָּפָּא וְרַב הוּנָא בְּרֵיהּ דְּרַב יְהוֹשֻׁעַ מִבֵּי רַב, אָמְרִי: הַיְינוּ חוּכָא, וּבְהוֹלָכָה רַבָּתִי לָא פְּלִיגִי? ז] וְהָא כִּי פְּלִיגִי — בְּהוֹלָכָה רַבָּתִי פְּלִיגִי! *אֶלָּא, בְּהוֹלָכָה זוּטַרְתִּי — כּוּלֵּי עָלְמָא לָא פְּלִיגִי (ב) דְּלָא פָּסְלָה, ח] כִּי פְּלִיגִי — בְּהוֹלָכָה רַבָּתִי. הוֹלִיכוֹ זָר, וְהֶחֱזִירוֹ כֹּהֵן וְחָזַר וְהוֹלִיכוֹ — פְּלִיגִי בָּהּ בְּנֵי רַבִּי חִיָּיא וְר' יַנַּאי, חַד אָמַר: כָּשֵׁר, וְחַד אָמַר: ״פָּסוּל. מָר סָבַר: אֶפְשָׁר לְתַקּוּנָהּ, וּמָר סָבַר: לָא אֶפְשָׁר לְתַקּוּנָהּ. הוֹלִיכוֹ כֹּהֵן וְהֶחֱזִירוֹ, וְחָזַר וְהוֹלִיכוֹ זָר, אָמַר רַב שִׁימִי בַּר אַשִׁי: לְדִבְרֵי הַמַּכְשִׁיר — ט] פָּסוּל, לְדִבְרֵי הַפּוֹסֵל — מַכְשִׁיר. רָבָא אָמַר: אַף לְדִבְרֵי הַפּוֹסֵל ״פָּסוּל. מַאי טַעְמָא — דְּהָא צָרִיךְ לְאַמְטוּיֵיהּ

הדרן עלך כל הזבחים

רש"י

אֶפְשָׁר לְתַקְּנָהּ. בֵּין שֶׁעֲשָׂאָהּ זָר בֵּין שֶׁעֲשָׂאָהּ כֹּהֵן (ג) אָמְרִינַן י] דְּאֵין הוֹלָכָה, וּפְסוּלָה, דְּהָא נַעֲשֵׂית שֶׁלֹּא כְּהִלְכָתָהּ. מִיהוּ, יֵשׁ לָהּ תַּקָּנָה לַהֲחֲזִירָהּ לַאֲחוֹרֶיהָ וְלַחֲזוֹר לְהוֹלִיךְ בָּרֶגֶל, אוֹ אֵין לָהּ תַּקָּנָה? יַחֲזִיר לַכָּשֵׁר. אַלְמָא אֶפְשָׁר לְתַקְּנָהּ. וּנְהִי נַמִי כו'. כְּלוֹמַר, וְאִי נַמִי מְפָרַשְׁתְּ לָהּ (ד) *דִּבְכָשֵׁר יא] רִאשׁוֹן [שֶׁיּוֹלִיךְ] לְצַד הַמִּזְבֵּחַ קָאָמַר. וְכָל שֶׁכֵּן דִּשְׁמַעְתְּ יב] דְּהוֹלָכַת כָּשֵׁר קַמָּא, דַּהֲוַאי שֶׁלֹּא בָּרֶגֶל, כְּשֵׁרָה הִיא, יג] מִכָּל מָקוֹם ש"מ דִּכְשֵׁרָה ע"י תַּקָּנָה. אִיפַּסְלָא. בְּהוֹלָכַת כָּשֵׁר יד] רִאשׁוֹנָה. מִי סָבְרַתְּ דְּקָאֵי זָר גַּוַּאי. לְצַד הַמִּזְבֵּחַ, שֶׁהִקְרִיב הָרִאשׁוֹן טו] בְּהוֹשָׁטָתוֹ לְצַד הַמִּזְבֵּחַ. דְּקָאֵי זָר בָּרַאי. (ה) וְכָשֵׁר שֶׁהוֹשִׁיטָהּ לוֹ הִרְחִיקָהּ מִן הַמִּזְבֵּחַ, הִלְכָּךְ לָאו הוֹלָכָה הֲוַאי לִפְסוֹל, *וְכִי פָּשְׁטִינַן יַחֲזוֹר כָּשֵׁר וְיִטְלֶנּוּ. וְזָר מַעֲשֶׂה אִילְטָא הוּא דַּעֲבַד, דְּלֵיכָּא הוֹשָׁטַת יָד הַמְקָרַבְתּוֹ לַמִּזְבֵּחַ. טז] פְּסָלָהּ. וַאֲפִילּוּ עֲשָׂאָהּ כֹּהֵן פּוֹסֶלֶת הַדָּם. וְהַהִיא דִּפְסָחִים — כִּדְנָיְידִי, וְכִדְשָׁנִינַן. נִשְׁפַּךְ מִן הַכְּלִי עַל הָרִצְפָּה וַאֲסָפוֹ כָּשֵׁר. הוֹאִיל וְנִתְקַבֵּל בִּכְלִי. מִשְׁנָה הִיא בְּפֶ' שְׁלִישִׁי בְּ״כָל הַפְּסוּלִים״. קס"ד כְּשֶׁנִּשְׁפַּךְ (ו) וְנִתְפַּשֵּׁט בָּרִצְפָּה נִתְקָרֵב לְצַד הַמִּזְבֵּחַ, יז] וְקָתָנֵי כָּשֵׁר. וּנְהִי נַמִי דְּאָמְרַתְּ דְּצָרִיךְ לְהַחֲזִירוֹ לַאֲחוֹרָיו וְלַחֲזוֹר יח] וּלְהוֹלִיךְ בָּרֶגֶל, מ"מ בְּתַקַּנְתָּא סַגִּי לָהּ. כְּשֶׁיָּצָא לַחוּץ. כְּשֶׁנִּשְׁפַּךְ לֹא נִתְפַּשֵּׁט לְצַד הַמִּזְבֵּחַ, אֶלָּא נִתְפַּשֵּׁט לְהַלָּן מִן הַמִּזְבֵּחַ וְנִתְרַחֵק. וּפָרְכִינַן: לְבָרַאי נָפֵיק לְגַוַּאי לָא עָיֵיל. בִּתְמִיָּה, וְכִי אֶפְשָׁר לַדָּם נָזוּל שֶׁיִּשָּׁפֵךְ וְלֹא יִתְפַּשֵּׁט לְכָל לְדָדִין? בִּמְקוֹם מִדְרוֹן. יט] וּמְשׁוּפָּע חוּץ לַמִּזְבֵּחַ. בְּגוּמָא. שֶׁעוֹמֵד בִּמְקוֹמוֹ וְלֹא נִתְפַּשֵּׁט. אִי נַמִי בִּסְמִיכָא. דָּם עָבֶה, וְקָרוֹב לִקְרוֹשׁ. בְּאִידָךְ פִּירְקִין. בְּפֶ' שֵׁנִי. נִשְׁפַּךְ עַל הָרִצְפָּה. מִצַּוַּאר בְּהֵמָה, וְלֹא נִתְקַבֵּל (ז) בִּכְלִי. לִפְלוֹג בְּדִידֵיהּ. בְּהַהִיא דְּפֶרֶק שְׁלִישִׁי דְּאַיְּירֵי בְּקַבָּלַת כְּלִי, נִפְלוֹג בָּהּ חִילּוּק לִפְסוֹל, שֶׁפְּעָמִים שֶׁצָּף מִן הַכְּלִי לָרִצְפָּה פָּסוּל! כ] אֶלָּא מִדְּלָא אַשְׁכַּח פְּסוּל אֶלָּא מִצַּוַּאר בְּהֵמָה — ש"מ: נִשְׁפַּךְ מִן הַכְּלִי, לָא שְׁנָא נָפֵק לְבָרַאי וְל"ש עָיֵיל לְגַוַּאי — כָּשֵׁר. תְּיוּבְתָּא. דְּעוּלָּא. מַחֲלוֹקֶת ר' שִׁמְעוֹן וְרַבָּנַן. דְּמַתְנִי' הִיא, אִי הָוְיָא עֲבוֹדָה אִי לָא. לְרַבִּי שִׁמְעוֹן כא] לָא הָוְיָא עֲבוֹדָה, דְּהָא קָתָנֵי מַתְנִי': ר' שִׁמְעוֹן מַכְשִׁיר בְּהִילּוּךְ, דְּלָא פָּסַל בָּהּ מַחֲשָׁבָה בְּהוֹלָכָה שֶׁלֹּא בָּרֶגֶל, כב] וּמִשּׁוּם דְּלָאו הוֹלָכָה הִיא. בְּהוֹלָכָה רַבָּתִי כו'. מַסְקָנָא הִיא לְמִילְּתֵיהּ, דְּקָמְפָרֵשׁ וְאוֹמֵר: דְּכִי פְּלִיגִי ר"ש וְרַבָּנַן (בְּהוֹלָכָה זוּטַרְתָּא) כג] [בְּהוֹלָכָה זוּטַרְתָּא פְּלִיגִי], שֶׁשָּׁחַט בְּצַד הַמִּזְבֵּחַ וְזָרַק, דְּהַיְינוּ שֶׁלֹּא בָּרֶגֶל. אֲבָל בְּהוֹלָכָה רַבָּתִי, דְּהַיְינוּ בָּרֶגֶל — לָא פְּלִיגִי. וּלְקַמָּן מוֹתִיב לָהּ מִמַּתְנִיתִין, דְּשָׁמְעִינַן מִינָּהּ דִּבְשׁוֹחֵט נַמִי רָחוֹק מִן הַמִּזְבֵּחַ מַכְשִׁיר רַבִּי שִׁמְעוֹן, מִדְּקָתָנֵי: שֶׁאִם רָצָה שׁוֹחֵט בְּצַד הַמִּזְבֵּחַ וְזוֹרֵק. מְחַכּוּ עֲלָהּ בְּמַעֲרְבָא. [מְחַיְּיכוּ עֲלֵיהּ] דְּהַאי שְׁמַעְתָּא, דְּמוֹקֵי טַעְמָא דר"ש בְּהוֹלָכָה זוּטַרְתָּא, וּלְמֵימַר דְּלָאו הוֹלָכָה הִיא, וְאע"פ שֶׁאִי אֶפְשָׁר לְבַטְּלָהּ לָזוֹ — לָאו עֲבוֹדָה הִיא. אֶלָּא חַטַּאת הָעוֹף. דְּקַיְימָא לָן בְּפֶ' ״קָדְשֵׁי קָדָשִׁים״ (לקמן דף סה.) דְּפָסַל בָּהּ מַחֲשָׁבָה בְּהַזָּאַת דָּמָהּ כד] שֶׁהוּא עִיקַּר עֲבוֹדָתָהּ, דִּכְתִיב שָׁם: ״וְהִזָּה מִדַּם הַחַטָּאת עַל קִיר״ וגו' שֶׁאוֹחֲזָהּ בְּגוּפָהּ וּמַתִּיז דָּמָהּ לַקִּיר. וְהַךְ הַזָּאָה הוֹלָכָה זוּטַרְתִּי הִיא. וְכֵיוָן דְּטַעְמָא דר"ש מִשּׁוּם דְּהוֹלָכָה זוּטְרָא לָא פָּסַל בָּהּ כה] מַחֲשָׁבָה, הֵיכִי *פָּסַל בְּהַךְ? אִי דַּחֲשִׁיב עֲלֵיהּ מִקַּמֵּי דְּלֵיפּוּק דָּם. דְּהַיְינוּ בְּהַתָּזָתָהּ. הָא אָמְרַתְּ כו] לָא כְּלוּם הִיא. דְּהָא הוֹלָכָה זוּטַרְתִּי הִיא. וְאִי כז] בָּתַר שֶׁנֶּעֱקַר הַדָּם. וְנִיתַּז מִן הַצַּוָּאר חָשֵׁיב. הָא אִיתְעֲבִידָא מִצְוָתֵיהּ. דְּקס"ד מִכִּי נָפַק דָּם גְּמָרָהּ לָהּ עֲבוֹדַת הַזָּאָתָהּ, וְאע"ג דְּלָא מָטָא דָּם לַמִּזְבֵּחַ. אא"כ בְּהוֹלָכָה רַבָּתִי פְּלִיגִי, וְטַעְמָא דר"ש מִשּׁוּם דְּאֶפְשָׁר לְבַטְּלָהּ הוּא — הָא דְּחַטָּאת כח] אִי אֶפְשָׁר לְבַטְּלָהּ. אֶלָּא אִי אָמְרַתְּ (ח) מִשּׁוּם טַעַם דְּלָאו הוֹלָכָה הִיא, וּבְשֶׁלֹּא בָּרֶגֶל פְּלִיגִי, הֵיכִי פָּסְלָה בְּהַךְ? הֲלֹא אֵין כָּאן מַחֲשָׁבָה אֶלָּא בְּהוֹלָכָה שֶׁלֹּא בָּרֶגֶל! וּלְר' יוֹחָנָן דְּאָמַר לְעֵיל הוֹלָכָה שֶׁלֹּא בָּרֶגֶל לֹא שְׁמָהּ הוֹלָכָה, כט] [וְלָא פָּסֵיל בָּהּ מַחֲשָׁבָה] — לֵיכָּא לְמִיפְרַךְ מִידֵּי, דְּכִי אָמַר ר' יוֹחָנָן — ל] הוֹלָכָה רַבָּתִי קָאָמַר, שֶׁאֵין דַּרְכָּהּ בְּכָךְ. אֲבָל הַשּׁוֹחֵט בְּצַד הַמִּזְבֵּחַ — עִיקַּר הוֹלָכָתָהּ בְּכָךְ, וּמוֹדֶה בָּהּ רַבִּי יוֹחָנָן. לא] וּמַאי קוּשְׁיָא דִּלְמָא מִדְּפָרֵישׁ. דָּם דְּפָסֵק לָהּ הוֹלָכָה מִתְחִלַּת הַזָּאָה, וְיֶשְׁנָהּ לְהַזָּאָה עַד דְּמָטֵי לַמִּזְבֵּחַ, וְחַיְילָא עֲלָהּ הַמַּחֲשָׁבָה. דְּהָא בְּעָא מִינֵּיהּ כו' הָיָה מַזֶּה. בְּחַטַּאת הָעוֹף אוֹ בַּחַטָּאוֹת הַפְּנִימִיּוֹת. מַהוּ. מִי הָוְיָא עֲבוֹדָה בְּבַעַל מוּם וּפְסוּלָה, אוֹ לָא? דְּאִיכָּא לְמֵימַר מִכִּי פָּרֵישׁ דָּם גְּמָרָהּ לָהּ. וְא"ל פְּסוּלָה לב] מ"ט וְהִזָּה. דְּחַטַּאת הָעוֹף, אוֹ דְּחַטָּאוֹת הַפְּנִימִיּוֹת דִּכְתִיב בָּהֶן הַזָּאָה ״וְהִזָּה וְנָתַן״ — בָּעֵינַן הַזָּאָה דּוּמְיָא דְּנָתַן, דִּגְבֵי הַדְּדֵי כְּתִיבֵי: ״וְהִזָּה מִן הַדָּם וגו' וְנָתַן הַכֹּהֵן מִן הַדָּם עַל קַרְנוֹת״ וגו', אַלְמָא יֶשְׁנָהּ לְהַזָּאָה עַד שֶׁיַּגִּיעַ לַמִּזְבֵּחַ. הַיְינוּ חוּכָא. הָא דִּמְחַכּוּ בְּמַעֲרְבָא, מִשּׁוּם דְּקַשְׁיָא לְהוּ הָכִי. וּבְהוֹלָכָה רַבָּתִי לָא פְּלִיגִי וְהָא כִּי פְּלִיגִי כו'. דְּהָא לג] *דְּקָתָנֵי ״אֶפְשָׁר שֶׁלֹּא בְּהִילּוּךְ״ — ש"מ בִּדְהִילּוּךְ עָסְקִינַן, וְטַעַם מִשּׁוּם שֶׁאֶפְשָׁר לְבַטְּלָהּ הוּא, *וְהָא מִיהָא לֹא בִּיטֵּל. אֶלָּא בְּהוֹלָכָה זוּטַרְתִּי כ"ע לָא פְּלִיגֵי דִּפְסוּלָה. גָּרְסִינַן. וְטַעְמָא — מִשּׁוּם דְּא"א לְבַטֵּל. וּמַאן דְּגָרֵיס דְּלָא פָּסְלָה — טַעְמָא מִשּׁוּם דְּלָאו כְּלוּם הִיא וְאֵין שֵׁם הוֹלָכָה עָלֶיהָ, אֶלָּא כּוּלָּהּ צוֹרֶךְ זְרִיקָה הִיא, וְהָא לָא הֲוָה בְּדַעְתֵּיהּ לְמֵחְשַׁב אַזְּרִיקָה אֶלָּא אַהוֹלָכָה וְלָא חָשֵׁיב מִידֵּי. וּפְסוּל דְּחַטַּאת הָעוֹף כִּדְאוֹקֵי — מִדְּפָרֵישׁ וְעַד דְּמָטָא לַמִּזְבֵּחַ, וּמִשּׁוּם מַחֲשֶׁבֶת הַזָּאָה וְלֹא מִשּׁוּם מַחֲשֶׁבֶת הוֹלָכָה. הוֹלִיכוֹ זָר. בָּרֶגֶל, וְהֶחֱזִירוֹ כֹּהֵן שֶׁהָעֲבוֹדָה עָלָיו מוּטֶּלֶת, וְחָזַר *וְהוֹלִיכוֹ — כָּשֵׁר. וְהָא דְּתַנְיָא לְעֵיל: זָר וְאוֹנֵן בְּהוֹלָכָה פָּסוּל — כְּשֶׁלֹּא הוּחְזְרָה. אֶפְשָׁר לְתַקּוּנָהּ. לְהוֹלָכַת פְּסוּל. וְלָא דָּמְיָא לִשְׁאָר עֲבוֹדוֹת, דַּאֲפִילּוּ שְׁחִיטָה וְקַבָּלָה וּזְרִיקָה, מֵאַחַר שֶׁנַּעֲשׂוּ בִּפְסוּל — אִי אֶפְשָׁר לַחֲזוֹר וְלַעֲשׂוֹתָן בְּהֶכְשֵׁר. וְא"ת: קַבָּלָה נַמִי יֵשׁ לְתַקֵּן, כְּגוֹן שֶׁלֹּא קִבֵּל הַפָּסוּל כָּל הַדָּם, וְיָכוֹל כָּשֵׁר לַחֲזוֹר וּלְקַבֵּל! הַהִיא וַדַּאי כְּשֵׁרָה, לד] וּבְפֶ' שְׁלִישִׁי (לקמן דף לג.) תְּנַן לָהּ: אִם יֵשׁ דַּם הַנֶּפֶשׁ — יַחֲזוֹר הַכָּשֵׁר וִיקַבֵּל, וְכֵן בִּזְרִיקָה. הָכִי גָּרְסִינַן: הוֹלִיכוֹ כֹּהֵן וְהֶחֱזִירוֹ וְחָזַר וְהוֹלִיכוֹ זָר. אָמַר רַב שִׁימִי לְדִבְרֵי הַמַּכְשִׁיר. בְּהוֹלִיכוֹ זָר וְהֶחֱזִירוֹ כֹּהֵן, וְחָזַר וְהוֹלִיכוֹ. פּוֹסֵל. לה] *כֵּיוָן דְּהָתָם מ"ט מַכְשִׁיר — דְּאָזֵיל בָּתַר בַּתְרַיְיתָא, ה"נ זִיל בָּתַר בַּתְרַיְיתָא. לְדִבְרֵי הַפּוֹסֵל לו]. דְּאָזֵיל בָּתַר הוֹלָכָה קַמַּיְיתָא — מַכְשִׁיר, *כֵּיוָן דְּאָזֵיל בָּתַר קַמַּיְיתָא (ט). אַף לְדִבְרֵי הַפּוֹסֵל [שָׁם] פּוֹסֵל כָּאן דְּהָא צָרִיךְ לְאַמְטוּיֵיהּ לז] [מֵאַחַר שֶׁנִּתְרַחֵק צָרִיךְ לַחֲזוֹר וְלַהֲבִיאוֹ לְצַד מִזְבֵּחַ, נִמְצָא דְּהוֹלָכָה אַחֲרוֹנָה לְצוֹרֶךְ, כְּכָל הַהוֹלָכוֹת].

הָא

תוספות

הולכה שלא ברגל מחלוקת ר"ש ורבנן. יש מפרש פירוש אחר, אבל פירוש הקונטרס עיקר. **חטאת** העוף דפסלה [הזאה] היכי משכחת לה. כיון דמכשיר ר"ש בהולכה שלא ברגל. אלא ודאי אפכא מסתברא, ותלוי הדבר *באפשר לבטלה. דרחוק מן המזבח הולכה זו [אפשר לבטלה] — דאי בעי הוה שחיט בצד המזבח, ולא פסלה בה מחשב'. אבל שחט קרוב למזבח, דהולכה זו של הושטת יד לא אפשר לבטלה — פסלה בה מחשבה. ולהכי בחטאת העוף פסלה מחשבה בהזאה מכי נפיק עד דמטא למזבח, דלא אפשר לבטל דבר זה. אבל לאידך, דלא תליא באפשר ולא אפשר, אלא הולכה שלא ברגל לא חשיבא, והוי כאילו איתעביד — אם כן בחטאת העוף נמי כאילו אתעביד מצותו. ומשני: דרחמנא *מחשבה זו מחשבה שלימה. ברו"ך.

אלא חטאת העוף דפסלה בה מחשבה היכי משכחת לה. אי אמרת בשלמא בהולכה (*שלא ברגל) פליגי, אבל בזוטרתי דלא אפשר לבטלה פסלה מחשבה — משכחת לה מיקמי דתיפוק דם, משום דדם הנתון בצואר כנתון בכלי שרת. ולא דמי לבעיא דרבי אבין בריש ״דם חטאת״ (לקמן דף צג:) דאיבעיא ליה אי צואר ככלי שרת אי לא. אבל אי בזוטרתי לא פסלה לר' שמעון — היכי משכחת לה? אבל מכל זריקה דעלמא לא קשיא ליה, לא] אי מיקמי דליפוק דם מן הכלי — לאו כלום הוא, ואי בתר דנפק — הא איתעביד ליה מצותו, משום לט] [דמדמפריש] ליה עד דמטא לא איתעביד מצותו. מ] אבל בהזאה סד"א דלא צריך מזבח, מידי דהוה אהזאה דפרוכת ובין הבדים, דהויא הזאה אע"פ שלא נגע* מא]. הגה"ה.

פז א מיי' פ"א מהל' פסה"מ הלכה כז:

פח ב מיי' שם הלכה ז:

פט ג ד מיי' שם פ"א הלכה כז:

גי' הג"ה כאפשר לבטלה הולכה זו דרחוק מן המזבח דאי בעי הוי שחט בצד המזבח ולא פסלה בה כצ"ל

מחשבה להולכה זו עבודה שלימה הס"ד וכצ"ל נ"ק

נ"א רבתי

שיטה מקובצת

א] עי' בהשמטות בסוף המס': ב] עי' בהשמטות בסוף המסכת: ג] עי' בהשמטות בסוף המס': ד] העוף דפסיל: ה] הא איתעבידא מצותו. תימה תיקשי ליה אכל זריקה היכא פסלא בה מחשבה אי מקמי כו' ואומר השר מקוצי דהתם משעה שמנענע הדם בכלי לצאת הוי תחילת התחלת זריקה מקמי דליפוק דם מן הכלי וניכר לעינים שהדם מנענע ורוצה לצאת אבל הדם שבצואר העוף אינו נראה לעינים ועד שיצא לחוץ לא הוי התחלת הזאה ועוד תירץ ריב"א דבזריקות דמים בעלמא ידע שפיר דפסלה בה מחשבה מדפריש דם עד דמטי למזבח אבל הזאת חטאת העוף סד"א מדפריש גמרה לה עבודת הזאה מידי דהוה אהזאת פרוכת כו'. מהר"פ: ו] וא"ל פסולה מ"ט: ז] והא כי פליגי כו' וא"ת מאי פריך והלא כבר תירצנו לעיל זאת הקושיא דמיירי דאיכא הולכה מעט וי"ל דמ"מ פריך שפיר הכא דפשט המשנה משמע דמיירי בשוחט רחוק מן המזבח: אלא בהולכה זוטרתי כו'א) וטעמא משום דלא אפשר לבטלה וגם דרכה בכך והשתא ניחא דבחטאת העוף פסלה בה מחשבה משום דהוי כהולכה זוטרתי ולא הוצרכו לשנויא דלעיל. מהר"פ: ח] כי פליגי בהולכה רבתי. דלרבי שמעון לא פסלה כיון דאפשר [לבטלה] דשוחט בצד המזב' וזורק דאותה סברא דהשתא מיהא כיון ששחט ברחוק למזבח אי אפשר לבטלה לא ס"ל וקשה לריב"א דלעיל קאמר גבי טבילת אצבע דהוי כהולכה זוטרתי קאמר ר"ש דלא מפגלא אע"ג דלא אפשר לבטלה טבילת אצבע לכך נראה כגירסא אחרת אלא בהולכה זוטרתי כ"ע לא פליגי דלא פסלה משום דלאו כלום ואין שם הולכה עליה ופסולה דחטאת העוף מדפריש עד דמטא למזבח ומטעם מחשבת הזאה ולא מטעם מחשבת הולכה

וא"ת מ"מ תקשי מרבנן דקאמרי לעיל דטבילת אצבע מפגלא דהוי הולכה זוטרתי והיכי קאמר הכא דברי הכל לא פסלה וי"ל דלעיל היינו למאי דבעי למימר דהולכה (שדרכו) [שלא] ברגל (כבעיין דלעיל דמייתי מעומד דומיא דיושב) דשמה הולכה הלכך כ"ש הולכה זוטרתי דדרכה בכך דשמה הולכה ופסולה בה מחשבה אבל הכא דמסקינן דהולכה שלא ברגל לא שמיה הולכה ה"ה בהולכה זוטרתי. מהר"פ: ט] המכשיר פוסל: י] אמרינן דאינו הולכה: יא] דבכשר אחר שלצד המזבח תיבת שוליך ל"ש: יב] דשמעת מינה: יג] היא וא"כ מכל מקום: יד] כשר ראשון הס"ד: טו] הראשון את הדם בהושטתו: טז] פסולה: יז] המזבח קצת וקתני: יח] ולחזור ולהוליכו ברגל: יט] מדרון במשופע חוץ: כ] פסול וליתני הכי בד"א דאם נתן בכלי כשר כשיצא לחוץ אבל נכנס לפנים פסול: כא] שמעון לאו עבודה היא דהא תיבת הוי ל"ש ונמחק: כב] ברגל קאמר ומשום: כג] זוטרתי פליגי ששחט בצד המזבח וזורק דהיינו שלא ברגל אבל בהולכה רבתי ברגל לא פליג ולקמן מותיב ליה ממתניתין דשמעינן מינה דבשוחט רחוק מן המזבח נמי מכשיר ר"ש מדקתני שאם ירצה שוחט בצד המזבח וזורק הס"ד ומה"ד מחכו עליה דהא שמעתא דמוקי טעמא דר"ש בהולכה זוטרתי: כד] דמה שהיא עיקר: כה] פסל בה מחשבה היכי פסל בה כהן הס"ד ותיבת בהך ל"ש: כו] אמרת לאו כלום: כז] ואי לאחר שנעקר ותיבת בתר ל"ש: כח] דחטאת העוף אי אפשר כו' אי אמרת טעמא משום: כט] הולכה ולא פסיל בה מחשבה: ל] יוחנן בהולכה רבתי: לא] יוחנן הס"ד ומה"ד לאו כלום היא דהולכה זוטרתי היא ולא פסיל בה מחשבה הס"ד ומה"ד ומאי: לב] פסולה ומ"ט: לג] דהא קתני אבל אפשר: לד] כשרה דבפרק שלישי: לה] פיסל כאן דהתם מ"ט מכשיר משום דאזיל: לו] הפוסל שם דאזיל: לז] אמטוייה מאחר שנתרחק צריך לחזור ולהביאו למזבח נמצאת האחרונה הולכה לצורך ככל ההולכות: לח] ליה איך פסלה ביה מחשבה אי: לט] משום דפשיטא ליה תיבת מדמפריש ל"ש ונמחק: מ] מצותו דכתיב וזרקו בני אהרן על המזבח אבל בהזאה: מא] נגע. דאמרינן פעמים שלא היה נוגע בה:

א) סיום קו' זה נמצא בתוס' סוד"ה חטאת העוף.

גי' הג"ה כבכשר אחר של צד המזבח קאמר והולכת כשר קמא דהואי שלא ברגל כשרה היא מ"מ ש"מ דכשירה ע"י תקנה כצ"ל

לקמן לג.

הגהות הב"ח

(א) גמ' מדפריש דם ועד דמטא: (ב) שם לא פליגי (דלא פסלה) תא"מ ונ"ב ס"א דפסלה: (ג) רש"י ד"ה אפשר וכו' כהן לתקונה לאיזה הולכה: (ד) ד"ה ונהי וכו' ואי נמי מפרשת לה לכבשר אחר של צד המזבח דיחזור וכשר דשמעת מינה הולכת כשר: (ה) ד"ה דקאי וכו' וכשר וכו' נתפשט ברלפה ונתקרב: (ו) ד"ה נשפך וכו' בכלי פסול הס"ד: (ח) ד"ה הא איתעבידא וכו' אי אמרת טעמא דר"ש משום דלאו הולכה: (ט) ד"ה לדברי הפוסל וכו' כתר קמייתא הס"ד:

עי' משנה למלך פ"א מהל' פסה"מ ה' כב ופ' י"א הלכה א

גליון הש"ס

גמ' ואיכפל תנא עיין שבת ה ע"א.

הא צריך לאמטוייה. דקאמרת לחשובה עבודה מהאי יב] טעם, מחלוקת ר' אליעזר ורבנן (ד) במתני'. **בחוץ.** להלן מן המזבח, והכניסו בפנים יג] לצד המזבח. **והוציאו לחוץ.** כלומר, ריחקו מן המזבח הלך חוץ ופנים כולהו בעזרה. **הא צריך לאמטוייה.** יד] לכשיחזור ויקריבנו לצד המזבח, אם תהא אותה הולכה במחשבה פסולה טו]. **לאו כהילוך הצריך לעבודה דמי.** הואיל ושלא לצורך הוציאו, על כרחו הולך לחזור ולהכניסו. **אי תניא.** דמודה בזה ר' אליעזר, תניא. ואין מחלוקת בין ר"א לת"ק, אלא טז] אר"ש אבוה קאי ופליג.

הדרן עלך כל הזבחים

לאמטוייה. אמר ליה א] רב ירמיה לרב אשי: הכי אמר רב ירמיה מדיפתי, הא צריך לאמטוייה – מחלוקת רבי (א) אליעזר ורבנן. דתנן, ר"א אומר: המהלך במקום שצריך להלך – מחשבה פוסלת, מקום שאין צריך להלך – אין מחשבה פוסלת. ואמר רבא: הכל מודים, קבלו בחוץ והכניסו בפנים – זהו הילוך שצריך להלך. קבלו בפנים והוציאו לחוץ – זהו הילוך שאין צריך להלך. *לא נחלקו ב] אלא כשהכניסו וחזר והוציאו, *מר סבר: הא צריך לאמטוייה, ומ"ס: לאו כהילוך הצריך לעבודה דמי. איתיביה אביי, ר"א אומר: המהלך מקום שצריך להלך – מחשבה פוסלת, כיצד? קבלו ג] בחוץ והכניסו לפנים – זהו הילוך שצריך להלך, קבלו בפנים והוציאו לחוץ – זהו הילוך שאין צריך לילך; ד] והא חזר והכניסו, הילוך שצריך להלך הוא!

א"ל:* אי תניא – תניא ה]. §

הדרן עלך כל הזבחים

כל *הזבחים (ב) ו] שקבלו דמן אזר, באונן, גטבול יום, ז] *דומחוסר כפורים, הומחוסר בגדים, ושלא רחץ ידים ורגלים, *ערל, חטמא, טיושב, *עומד על גבי כלים, על גבי בהמה, *על גבי רגלי חברו – ח] פסל. *כקבל בשמאל – פסל, ר"ש מכשיר. § **גמ'** זר מנלן? דתני לוי: *"דבר אל אהרן ואל בניו לאמר ט] וינזרו מקדשי בני ישראל" וגו', י] בני ישראל למעוטי מאי? אילימא למעוטי נשים – קרבן נשים בטומאה קרב? אלא למעוטי גוים – השתא ציץ לא מרצה, דאמר מר: *ובגוים – בין בשוגג בין במזיד לא הורצה, בטומאה קרב? אלא הכי קאמר: וינזרו מקדשי בני ישראל ולא יחללו". *דבי רבי ישמעאל תנא: יא] אתיא בק"ו מבעל מום, (ג) מה בעל מום שאוכל, אם עבד – חילל,

זר

הגהות הב"ח

(א) גמ' מחלוקת רבי אלעזר כצ"ל וכן בסמוך וברש"י: (ד) רש"י ד"ה הא צריך וכו' במתני' הוא הס"ד:

שיטה מקובצת

א] אמר ליה רבינא תיבות רב ירמיה נמחק: ב] אלא כשהכניסו וחזר והוציאו וחזר והכניסו. ובאותו הולכה אחרינא פליגי לאו דוקא הכניסו דמשמע דקבל בחוץ דהא אפילו א) דקיבל בפנים נמי אלא לרבותא נקט דכבר עשה הולכה מ"מ הילוך אחרון חשיב. מהר"פ: ג] בחוץ. האי בחוץ ר"ל בעזרה ור"ל מן המזבח ולפנים והיינו קרוב למזבח. מהר"פ ז"ל: ד] תיבת והא נמחק: ה] אי תניא תניא והדרי בי. ופ"ה אי תניא דמודה ר"א תניא ואין מחלוקת בין ר"א ות"ק אלא אדאבוה קאי ופליג. ומעיקרא ס"ד דת"ק פסיל בהולכה ב) מדלא מפרש מידי ור"א בא לחלוק עליו וג' מחלוקת בדבר ולא ס"ד שבא לפרש דברי רבנן דפליגי עליה דר"ש. מהר"פ ז"ל: ו] הזבחים שקבל דמן: ז] ומחוסר כפורים. וא"ת מדקאמר מחוסר כפורים מחלל עבודה כ"ש טבול יום דבעי הערב שמש (נמי) ומחוסר כפרה [נמי] וי"ל דטבול יום מיירי בטבול יום דשרץ דאין צריך כפרה וא"ת אמאי נקט טמא מדקאמר טבול יום כ"ש טמא וי"ל הואיל ותני ערל תני טמא דבכל מקום דתני ערל תנא טמא כדאשכחן בפ' הערל ובהרבה מקומות וא"ת וטמא דקתני תיפוק שהוא מטמא את הכלי והכלי מטמא את הדם וי"ל דאיירי בטמא שרץ שהוא ראשון ואינו מטמא את הכלי ולא חשיב בעל מום ושתויי יין משום דכתיב בהו חילול בהדיא בבעל מום דכתיב לא יגש ולא יחלל ושתויי יין דכתיב ולהבדיל בין הקודש ובין החול אבל פרועי ראש דלא מחיל עבודה לא חשיב אלא הני דאי עביד חילל ואפילו למ"ד דמחיל עבודה י"ל דלא קתני להו משום דמוזהרים משעת ביאה ולא קתני אלא הני דאינן מוזהרין משעת ביאה וטמא דחשיב כשנטמא בעזרה. מהר"פ: ח] חברו. עי' בתוס' [ד"ה מין במינו] (לקמן דף קי ע"א): ט] וינזרו מקדשי בני ישראל. וה"ק וינזרו מקדשי בני ישראל ולא יחללו הא אם עבדו יחללו. מהר"פ: י] תיבת בני ישראל נמחק: יא] אתיא בק"ו מבעל מום. וא"ת טמא בקרבן צבור וכה"ג אונן יוכיח דאינן אוכלין ואפ"ה הן עובדין וי"ל דאיכא למיפרך מה להנך שכן אינן מוזהרין תאמר בזר שכן מוזהר דלעולם הוא יודע שיש אזהרה לזר ולא מבעיא ליה [אלא אם] מחלל וא"ת נילף מיושב דאוכל ואם עבד חילל וי"ל מה ליושב שכן פסול לעדות וממחוסר בגדים לא יליף דמחוסר בגדים לא פסול אלא משום זר ולא יליף משתויי יין ופרוע ראש דשתויי יין לא ידעינן אלא ממחוסר בגדים ושלא רחוץ ידיו ופרועי ראש משתויי יין א"נ איכא למיפרך שכן מוזהרין בשעת ביאה וא"ת ולפסול גזלן ק"ו מבעל מום מה בעל מום שכשר לעדות אם עבד חילל גזלן שפסול לעדות אינו דין שאם עבד חילל וי"ל משום דאיכא למיפרך מה לבעל מום שכן מוזהר תאמר בגזלן שאינו מוזהר. מהר"פ: יב] מהאי טעמא מחלוקת: יג] בפנים כלומר קרבו לצד המזבח. הס"ד ומה"ד קבלו בפנים והוציאו: יד] לאמטוייה לחזור ולהכניסה לצד המזבח ויקריבנו למזבח אם: טו] פסולה פסול הס"ד: טז] אלא בחזר והכניסו ואאבוה קאי ופליג ר"א אר"ש דר"ש קאמר דאין מחשבה פוסלת בהילוך כלל הס"ד: יז] ודמת ודשאר טומאות: יח] כח בקרבנן לדחות טומאה הס"ד: יט] עולתי לעזרה: כ] אף אצל תיבת אפילו ל"ש: כא] יתרחקו בטומאתם: כב] דכתיב כי מום בו. גליון תימה אמאי לא פירש הכא כדמפיק (בפרק אלמנה בסופו) [נקידושין דף סו] מברייתי שלום ולא כשהוא חסר ונ"ל דעיקר כדפי' הכא ושלם אצטריך לנודע שהוא בעל מום באמצע [העבודה] דבזה מיירי התם: כג] הא כי אות ד' נמחק: כד] היינו כוב אות ב' נמחק: כה] ואכילת קודש בטומאה כתיב אות ב' נמחק: כו] לאשמועינן דאית ביה ותיבת דכתיב נמחק: כז] יוחנן ורשב"ל לאשכוחי אזהרה: כח] מנא ליה אות ז' נמחק: כט] זרות כדאמרינן לקמן:

א) ר"ל דלאו דוקא הכניסו וחזר והוציאו דה"ה אם קבל בפנים והוציאו לחוץ ואח"כ חזר והכניסו ג"כ פליגי. ב) נראה דצ"ל פסיל בהולכה בהילוך שאין צריך להלך מדלא מפרש מידי: